RECORDS OF EARLY ENGLISH DRAMA

Records of Early English Drama

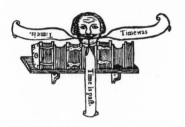

COVENTRY

EDITED BY R.W. INGRAM

UNIVERSITY OF TORONTO PRESS

TORONTO BUFFALO

© University of Toronto Press 1981
Toronto Buffalo London
Printed in Canada
Published in Great Britain by Manchester University Press

Canadian Cataloguing in Publication Data

Main entry under title:

Coventry: records of early English drama

(Records of early English drama)

Bibliography
Includes index.
ISBN 0-8020-5542-7
1. Performing arts – England – Coventry (West Midlands) – History
– Sources.   2. Theatre – England – Coventry (West Midlands) –
History – Sources.   3. Coventry plays.   I. Ingram, Reginald W.,
1930– II. Series.
PN2596.C68C68   790.2'09424'98   C81-094446-4

ISBN 0-8020-5542-7

The map of Coventry from John Speed's *Theatre of the Empire
of Great Britaine* was obtained from the Pollard and Redgrave
Short Title Catalogue, University Microfilms International, Ann
Arbor, Michigan.

The research and typesetting costs of
Records of Early English Drama
have been underwritten by the
Social Sciences and Humanities Research Council of Canada.

...

And for alsomyche as hit is right nesesarie & full nedefull to reduse maters into mynde that afore tyme ben don in eschueng stody & labur in suche cases that herafter arn lyke to falle ... hit apereth in writeng next after here foloueng.

Mayor Richard Boys, 6 May 1451
Leet Book I, f 155v

Contents

Records of Early English Drama

The aim of Records of Early English Drama (REED) is to find, transcribe, and publish external evidence of dramatic, ceremonial, and minstrel activity in Great Britain before 1642.

The general editor would be grateful for comments on and corrections to the present volume and for having any relevant additional material drawn to her attention.

Acknowledgments

As have the editors of each of the early volumes of Records of Early English Drama, I have relied on the assistance of colleagues in the REED office. I have asked a great deal of them, and never in vain. Cameron Louis and Sally-Beth MacLean have been particularly generous. Dr Louis checked all the transcriptions, never ruffled by even the least diplomatic of them, and provided the English glossary. Dr MacLean, REED's house editor, discovered and accepted my arduous and extensive definition of the verb 'to edit.' She took my text and endnotes (foul-papers, perhaps, to a less generous spirit) and with a discerning eye for detail and order pruned them of all manner of inconsistency and confusion. She is also largely responsible for the subject part of the index.

Any bibliography, no matter how brief, can benefit from items found by Ian Lancashire. Mine was also checked afresh by Mary Blackstone.

Abigail Young's translations relieved my small Latin; she also provided the Latin glossary. Anne Quick did palaeographical checks and the final check of the English glossary. Other details were provided by William Cooke, Theodore DeWelles, Pamela King, Willard McCarty, Michele Robinson, and Diana Wyatt. The initial indexing of names and places was done by Michael Bauer and Susan Peachey; Willard McCarty checked and grouped names for the final index. The photo-ready copy was set by Lyn Straka and Arlene Gold. Susan Peachey had the exacting task of preparing and proofreading the final text, with assistance from Anne Quick, Heather Phillips, and Andrew Rossman. Sheena Levitt's smooth running of the REED office enabled me to make the most valuable use of time during my visits there. Alexandra Johnston was the most valuable of general editors: her comments and queries on the text were always judicious and pertinent; as an arbiter on matters of debate she was sensible and firm. She also checked some of the transcriptions in England, collected data for the document descriptions, and contributed to the making of the index.

The production of this volume depended upon the free access to, and permission to publish from, documents resting in many archive offices and libraries. Among such places, my first thanks must go to the City Record Office at Coventry whose rich resources are the mainstay of this volume. From my first visit to the City Record Office during the last year of Miss D.A. Leech's tenure as city archivist in 1964, I, and those who have followed checking in my footsteps, have been handsomely treated there: first by Alan Dibben (and his assistant archivist, David Smith), and then by his successor, the current city archivist, David Rimmer and his archivist assistant M. Hinman. They have had books fetched — usually the same ones again and again — answered letters, dealt with queries at no little expense to their crowded time, and arranged for microfilms and photographs to be made. Other archive offices equally generous with any requests of this nature made of them were the Warwickshire County Record Office, Warwick; the Joint Record Office in Lichfield, Staffordshire; and the Shakespeare Centre at Stratford-upon-Avon. The director of the last, Dr Levi Fox (himself once city archivist at Coventry), has been especially helpful in aiding the production of this volume. The Cappers' Account Book and a quantity of Halliwell-Phillipps' papers are in his keeping at the Centre; as Honorary Secretary and General Editor of the Dugdale Society he gave ready permission to quote from *The Records of the Guild of the Holy Trinity, St. Mary, St. John the Baptist and St. Katherine of Coventry,* edited by Geoffrey Templeman as volume nineteen of the society's publications; finally, at very short notice, he checked some readings in the Cappers' Accounts for me. For the permission given and the help often rendered I am very grateful.

Two of the companies who performed plays in the Corpus Christi cycle still flourish in Coventry: the company of Cappers and Feltmakers and the Broadweavers and Clothiers' company; both possess records dating from the sixteenth century. I am most grateful to the masters of both companies for generously allowing me to publish whatever in their companies' rich records was germane to this book. I wish also to thank Mr Sidney Snape, secretary of the Broadweavers and Clothiers' company, for the pains he has taken on my behalf in this matter. Mr Julian Hoare, the secretary of the Cappers' company when I first asked if I might read and print extracts from the company's earliest account book, took an equal interest in my project and arranged, through the kind offices of Miss Jeanette Thompson, the administrative manager of *The Coventry Evening Telegraph* in whose building the account book was then kept, that I should read the book at my leisure in the comfort of the newspaper's boardroom. My thanks are also due to them.

I wish to thank the following libraries for permission to quote extracts from documents in their possession: the City of Birmingham Central Reference Library (reference department); the Trustees of the British Library; the Bodleian Library; the City of Coventry Libraries, Arts, and Museums Department (Coventry and Warwickshire Collection); the Public Record Office; and the Folger Library, Washington, D.C. Other libraries whose facilities were particularly useful in my researches were those of Edinburgh University, the University of British Columbia, the University of Toronto, the Pontifical Institute of Mediaeval Studies of Toronto, the Humanities Research Center of the University of Texas at Austin, and the city of Vancouver.

I am glad to thank people who helped me in particular but very different ways: Charles Phythian-Adams whose own work on Coventry sets an enviable standard; the

Right Honorable the Earl of Aylesford for allowing ready use of his copy of the earliest of the City Annals; the late Professor Arthur Brown for his unexpectedly prompt and encouraging reply to my suggestion that such dramatic records of Coventry as I was beginning to collect in 1964 could make a Malone Society volume; also to Richard Proudfoot who confirmed the agreement when he became editor of the Malone Society, and then equally gracefully allowed me to change my allegiance to REED when that project came into being; Richard Congdon, who, as editor at the University of Chicago Press gave me firm encouragement in 1963 to go ahead with a book on medieval dramatic entertainment in Coventry — the subject chosen because I wished to study Corpus Christi cycles as part of a city's annual entertainment. I chose Coventry not only because of its fame as a centre of civic religious drama, but also because I was born, raised, and educated there and its names and geography were mine to hand. In addition, I thought the available evidence had been published by Sharp and Halliwell-Phillipps and was, therefore, finite; my first visit to the City Record Office was to make this comfortable assurance doubly sure and the unexpected result is this volume. The line of Congdon's successors have, properly, long forgotten the once-expected book but I have always seen him and Chicago as the origin of this volume.

I wish also to acknowledge the help of the late Father Harold C. Gardiner who searched out notes made twenty years before and sent copies of them as a kind and valuable answer to a stranger's tentative and general question; Professor George Hibbard who twice let me explore some ideas raised by the material I was collecting in his Elizabethan Theatre Conferences at the University of Waterloo; Peter Meredith for allowing me to air an interpretive puzzle at the second Medieval Drama Conference at Leeds, and for going to Coventry to describe some documents more clearly than I had; the late A.N.L. Munby, Professor S. Schoenbaum, and Professor John Velz for their assorted aid in my efforts to track down some still missing notes and transcriptions that Halliwell-Phillipps took in his Coventry researches. Finally, my thanks go to Chaucer, Anthony Davis, Theodore de Welles, Richard Green, W.B. Guthrie, Alice Hamilton, Russell Jackson, Edward McGee, Betsy Taylor, Irene Whitehead, Robert Whitehead, and Patricia M. Wolfe.

Ultimately, after all the acknowlegments to so many who tried to make this book better than it is, I must affirm that the blemishes, omissions, and all the faults are mine.

The costs of my work have been aided by two summer travel grants (1964, 1968) and a senior fellowship (1967–8) awarded by the Canada Council, and two grants from the President's Research Fund (UBC) made in 1971–2 and 1972–3. Other research and publication costs of this volume have been supported through funds provided by the major editorial project grants of the Canada Council (now the Social Sciences and Humanities Research Council of Canada).

The preparation of this volume allowed my wife to discover that she had married not only a Coventrian but Coventry's dramatic records and history 1392–1642. The

Introduction was clarified by her insistence that it make sense to someone other than myself. She and my sons, Neil and John, were 'sent to Coventry' in an unlooked for way and for their release will give much thanks; but not so many as mine to them for being there with me.

RWI / University of British Columbia / 1980

Introduction

This collection records the dramatic, musical, and ceremonial activity in Coventry between 1392 and 1642 and the parts which citizens of every rank took in it. The purpose of the Introduction is to give a brief historical survey of this activity; to provide a guide to the kinds of documents used, both original (more extensive than usually thought) and antiquarian (more problematic than might be supposed); and to explain the manner of transcription and presentation of these documents. I have enjoyed access to many sources, both public and private: minutes of meetings, city and guild accounts and ordinances, legal contracts, wills, rental rolls, letters, and general memoranda. The material is presented in chronological order.

The aim of the Records of Early English Drama is to collect written evidence of drama, minstrelsy, and ceremonial activity, not to interpret it. The nature of the material gathered here invites interpretation; I hope that I have almost entirely succeeded in resisting that invitation. The minutes and accounts transcribed are not always 'complete' in our rigorous understanding of the term. The facts they offer can both clarify and mystify at the same time. Those who wrote the minutes or drew up the accounts did not feel bound by whatever rules of process they may have had. Then, as now, veils were drawn innocently or deliberately over events. The contents of this volume touch upon or illumine the history of drama, music, and ceremony in Coventry but do not, themselves, constitute that history. However, I hope that users of this volume will sense, as I have, something of the scope and richness of the 250 years of that history which ended with the coming of the civil war in 1642.

Drama, Music, and
Public Ceremonial

Drama

Coventry's Corpus Christi cycle came into existence in the last decades of the four-teenth century when the city was at its most flourishing and ranked among the half dozen most populous cities in England.[1] The woolsack, upon which the lord chan-cellor still sits, symbolized the source of England's wealth; Coventry's importance derived from its leading place in the cloth and wool trade. Its merchants carried on business throughout the land, free of toll, and upon the European mainland as well. Their scope might be marked in John Onley, 'the first English Man borne in Callis after it was taken by ye English His father was Standerd bearer to King Edward & his mother went over big with Child & was delivered there, he was twice Mayor of Callis and twice Mayor of Coventry' (City Annal, 1396, BRL: 273978). Inside Coventry, however, the struggle to unite all of the city's energies to the attainment of this mercantile prosperity had been won only after a long struggle with clerical ambitions for the city.

Coventry was important both as a market town and as a religious centre. The city centre was virtually a large churchyard, dominated on one side by the Benedictine Cathedral and Priory of St Mary with its three towers and spires. Other sides were bounded by the two parish churches of the city: Holy Trinity (still standing) and St Michael's (destroyed, save for its tower, spire, and walls, in the air-raid of 1940). The Cathedral of St Mary's was so rich that Robert de Limesey removed his episcopal seat thither from Chester in 1095, more or less to plunder the Cathedral.[2] The lord-ship of Coventry belonged to the earl of Chester, but between 1145 and 1154, the Priory, by means of forged charters, claimed half of the city as the supposed gift of Earl Leofric, who, with his wife Godiva, founded the orginal abbey in 1043. Thus, what was known as the 'prior's half' of the city came into being. This takeover was completed in 1250 when the earl of Chester's heir, Roger de Mohaut (Montalt), leased virtually all of what was known as the 'earl's half' of the city to the prior, who thus became the lord of the whole city.

The prior's rule was found increasingly irksome, especially in the fourteenth century when the increasing affluence of the leading merchants led to their seeking wider power in the city than the prior was willing to allow. Having failed to combat him by witchcraft in 1323, they found a surer ally in Queen Isabella when she inherited the diminished Chester legacy in 1330.[3] She took arms against the prior's lordship and used the citizens' dissatisfaction with his rule powerfully and successfully. In 1345, Coventry received a royal charter of incorporation. The prior struggled to maintain his large claims for another ten years, but in 1355 came to an agreement with the queen and the city, formalized in what is called 'the tripartite indenture.'[4]

The development of civic government in Coventry thus dates from 1345. A body of twenty-four leading citizens elected the mayor, coroner, and chamberlains on 25 January. All other civic positions, as they were created, were filled on this date except the bailiffs (also called sheriffs after Henry VI created the county of the city of Coventry in 1451). The bailiffs were the mayor's chief advisors; they were elected at Michaelmas, and by serving under two mayors, linked one mayoralty to the next.

The mayor used councils of various sizes and names, not nicely distinguishable, in the daily administration of the city. These may be seen as essentially two, however: 'first, the mayor's council, with a nucleus of the executive and a few permanent members ... and secondly, a larger body of varying numbers, representative of the ten wards summoned by the mayor to express the popular will concerning the common lands, or money matters, or to witness grants made under the common seal.... Of these the first council represented the governing body, the second the power of the community over the executive.' The distinction between the two is useful rather than absolute 'since the presence of officials and the summons of the mayor played a great part in the formation of both bodies.'[5]

The smaller body consisted of twelve men, ex-mayors and others who had held high office or were clearly destined to do so. These were the men who, to all intents and purposes, ruled the city, the group so often referred to as 'master mayor and his brethren.' This body was doubled in size to become the jurats who sat as the leet court and chose the officers of the city each year. The leet court sat at Easter and Michaelmas to act on petitions it had received and to perform as the legislative branch of the city's government.

It is from the Leet Book that much of the information about the council's regulation of the Corpus Christi cycle comes.[6] The Leet Book begins during John Goot's mayoralty in 1421, too late to tell us anything of the role of civic government in the genesis of the Corpus Christi cycle. The church, as guardian of religious observance, would have been the natural advisor about, and, where necessary, censor of the cycle's content. However, nothing is known of its part in the birth of the cycle, and there is very little evidence of any direct clerical intervention in Coventry's civic religious drama until the latter part of the sixteenth century. Nonetheless, the presence of the church permeated everyday life and inevitably affected the ceremonial and dramatic activities in the city. In surviving records, however, the emphasis is markedly upon the civic aspects of dramatic production.

The individual guilds could, if they chose, appoint a man to 'have þe Rewle of þe pajaunt,' as the Smiths did in 1453 (see p 27), but the authority of the council was needed to rule the cycle (and that authority was sometimes flouted). The rulers of the cycle were well aware that it was a national and not merely a local event, that it was a sacred entertainment which drew people from all over England. Casual reference proves the fame. In 1576, Mr Savage visited Coventry with his 'enterlude players.' He might have thought it an apt gesture to have his troupe play *The Nature of the .iiij. Elements,* by John Rastell, born and bred in Coventry of one of its old families.[7] He could also have put on, just as aptly, *The Playe Called the Foure* PP by Rastell's son-in-law, John Heywood, wherein the Pardoner is smilingly welcomed as an old acquaintance by the devil keeping hell-gate:

> For as goode happe wolde haue it chaunce
> Thys deuyll and I were of olde acqueyntaunce
> For oft in the play of corpus Cristi
> He hath played the deuyll at Couentry　　　　　(ll. 829-32)

A Coventry audience would have relished the allusion, as indeed audiences at other towns in the land must have, since Heywood had penned it some fifty years earlier. Preachers could safely end sermons on the Creed with the confident challenge: 'Yf you beleue not me, then for a more suerte & suffycyent auctoryte, go your way to Couentre, and there ye shall se them all played in Corpus Cristi playe.'[8] 'To be sent to Coventry' was not then to be shunned by society and condemned to lonely misery but to join festive thousands in a celebration that was reverential as well as holiday-making (and business-making) in a great market city.

Coventry's cycle is unique in that it consisted of ten plays only, each of which would have provided matter for three or four individual plays in York or Chester. Why this format was chosen is not known, nor whether the cycle was always so arranged.[9] The Drapers' pageant house is mentioned in a cartulary of St Mary's (now lost) of 1392; this is still the first reference to the Corpus Christi plays in Coventry (see p 3). The first reference in a surviving document is a civic quitclaim dated 1407 (see p 9). It is possible that the cycle was first played in 1392 and that the cartulary refers to a brand new pageant house; it is more likely, however, that the Drapers had owned the house for some years and that the cycle had been played at least as early as the 1380s.[10] It was to 'run' for some 200 years, and over so long a period it was inevitable, at times necessary, that individual plays of the cycle should be rewritten or revised. The one surviving manuscript play is that of the Weavers, which is a rewriting of an earlier version undertaken for that company in 1535 by Robert Crow. It is accompanied by two leaves from an earlier manuscript version of the play, presumably the one from which Crow worked and certainly one which he knew. Evidence of less wholesale revisions occurs in extant guild records.[11]

As episodes from the biblical story were grouped into a single play, so groups of companies were made chargeable for the production of these composite plays. The entries in the Leet Book testify to the accuracy of 'made chargeable.' Such wealthy companies as the Mercers and the Drapers always had the financial resources to make the production of a pageant no problem. The vicissitudes of the market, however, could reduce only slightly less substantial companies to financial weakness. This happened to the Cardmakers in 1531, for instance. At such times the authority of the leet court was required to transfer their pageant with all its 'pleyng geire accustumed belongyng & necessarie,' together with their chapel in St Michael's, to another company, in this case the prospering Cappers (see pp 131-3). Slighter changes of pageantry allegiance were also managed by order of leet: in connection with the Cardmakers/Cappers exchange, for instance, the contribution that the Cappers had traditionally made to the Girdlers' pageant was taken over by the Barbers, whose regular support of the Cardmakers' pageant was proudly dispensed with by the Cappers.

Neither all companies nor all craftsmen were willing to support the cycle voluntarily. In 1460, every company 'þat hath pagant to pley' was ordered to prepare and play it on pain of the masters being fined 100 shillings (see p 40). In April 1494, companies who did not support a pageant in any way were ordered to do so; this edict was sternly repeated at the Michaelmas leet because it had been ignored by 'dyuers self willed persones whech be theire willes wold obbeye no other rule ne ordre but after their owne willes grounded without reason' (see pp 79, 80). Clearly, after the 1494 performance of the cycle, complaints had been made to the mayor that looked-for assistance had not been offered. In 1533, the mayor had to step in and assign craftsmen and companies not officially contributory to a pageant to those companies already producing a pageant (see p 136). Three years later, every householder not a member of any company was told to 'associat & bere with some Craft before Whitsontyde next'; this would make every craftsman and trader in the city contributory to the Corpus Christi celebrations (see p 142). It is quite true that 'theire so doyng shall principally please god & contynue the goode name & fame þat þis Cite hath had in tymes past' (see p 80). However, such 'fame' cost money, and it was fair that all who profited by that 'fame' should bear the cost. It is well to remember that the only eyewitness account of the Coventry Corpus Christi celebrations ignored religion and aesthetics: 'the confluence of people from farr and neare to see that Shew was extraordinary great, and yielded noe small advantage to this Cittye.'[12]

This commercial aspect is usually stressed very little, if at all. Even those citizens who were whole-hearted in their support of the celebrations could find that they had to pay heavily for it. In 1539, Mayor Coton wrote to Cromwell to suggest a cessation of the cycle on the grounds that the debts incurred by many poorer tradesmen in maintaining the splendour of the occasion crippled them for the year to come (see pp 148-9). His brethren shared little of his sympathy for these oppressed citizens. Insulated by their wealth from such financial dangers, they were quite unwilling to give up a 'drinking' or feast for such a reason. Today such matters are remote from literary or religious considerations of the plays or of the feast of Corpus Christi itself, but not so for the Tudor Coventrians. In their eyes Coton was concerned with the costly and properly splendid prologue to, but yet what was only a part of, the most important fair of the year, the 'Great,' or 'Corpus Christi' Fair, eight days of celebration equally central to the religious well-being of the city and the economic livelihood of the city.

Coton's was the voice of economic reality: Coventry's prosperity declined greatly in the opening decades of the sixteenth century, as did that of the Midlands generally. Charles Phythian-Adams very fairly calls his detailed and convincing history of Coventry in these decades of hardship *Desolation of a City.* Nonetheless, despite the decay in the city's economy, the regular performance of the Corpus Christi plays and the rewriting of at least two of them in 1535 urge a consideration of the relationship between civic financial well-being and the economics of festive religious celebration.

Cromwell's reply has not survived, but Coton's appeal was refused. The cycle carried on, with only occasional interruptions, as, for instance, in 1564 and 1575 because of the plague.[13] Continuity of performance was expected in the city; the guild records give no inkling that 1579 would be the last year in which the cycle would be seen. Whatever the cost, Coventrians proved unwilling to give up their civic religious drama. In 1584, at extraordinary expense, the companies, with generous financial support from the civic treasury, produced the spectacular *Destruction of Jerusalem.* This did not herald another sequence of annual performances — possibly the expense was prohibitive. However, the taste for such entertainments remained, and on 19 May 1591, the council, at 'the request of the Comons of this Cittie,' allowed that one of 'the distrucion of Ierusalem the Conquest of the Danes or the historie of K E the 4 ... shalbe plaid on the pagens on Midsomer daye & St peters daye next' (see p 332). If the notice was short, so was the council's sympathy with the commons' request. If they had to bend to the latter, they took opportunity in the same order allowing the performances of a play to demand that all maypoles in the city should be taken down within three days.

The companies, heeding the cooler official attitude towards such plays, much reduced their financial support from the lavish levels of 1591. This parsimony would have saddened but in no way deterred Thomas Massey, upholsterer and member of the Mercers' company, who had 'þe rewle' of the 1591 play. He had no intention of letting this be the last civic play seen in the city. By his zeal he had become by this time Coventry's man for handling what civic entertainment there was, such as celebrations of the queen's holiday (see pp 338, 341, 346); however, his zeal for drama outran the council's tolerance in 1603 and he was briefly jailed. He struggled at law for ten years more at least. So determined, hot-tempered, and litigious a man left an unmistakeable trail through civic and guild records; an outline of his tangled career will be found in Appendix 6, pp 495-502.

Among other plays known to have been acted at Coventry is an interlude mentioned in one of the two surviving Priory pittancers' rolls: '... Item deliberaui domino priori die dominico post festum circumcisionis domini pro interludo xx s ...' (BRL: 168235, dated 1505–6). The play of St Katherine was performed in the Little Park in 1490 or 1491 (a guild of St Katherine was founded in 1343 and eventually became a part of the Trinity guild). In 1505, also in the Little Park, a play about St Christian was performed. Several city annals mention this play but none gives any details about it. That it was an especially memorable play is certain, because in 1528, two witnesses dated a baptism with reference to 'Magnus ludus vocatus seynt christeans pley (see pp 127-8).[14] Such reference delights and baffles at the same time. What made the play so memorable? Why, if it was so distinctive, was it seemingly not performed again? Was it a local production or a touring troupe's unusually exciting play? When Henry VIII and Queen Catherine came to Coventry in 1511, three 'Pageants' were set out to greet them. Two were of what would be called today tableaux vivants; the third, however, was 'a goodly Stage Play.' This may have been the regular Corpus Christi play of that company whose wagon it was played upon; possibly it was a revival of the play of St Katherine in suitable homage to the queen (see p 107 and endnote p 561). The mayor and his brethren were usually entertained by a performance of some kind when they paid their annual visit to the grammar school: in 1600 the scholars presented a tragedy, in 1617, a comedy.

The most mysterious dramatic entertainment, one performed annually, yet rarely mentioned in any records, is the Hock Tuesday play. Ostensibly, this celebrated a notable defeat of the Danes near Coventry, a victory in which the women were traditionally reckoned to have borne a great part.[15] It is first heard of in 1416 as a companion entertainment to the pageants (see p 7 and endnote p 542). The day is occasionally mentioned as a calendar mark unconnected with play-acting – in 1469 the Dyers hold a quarterage feast 'On hogh tuysday' (Dissertation, p 132; see also City Annals, p 114; Cappers' Records, p 171). Not until 1561 is the play mentioned again, as being 'put down' (see p 215). Nonetheless, the victory over the Danes is cited as one of the city's patriotic distinctions in the recorder's speech of welcome to Elizabeth in 1566, the remembrance of it being kept 'by certaine open shewes yearely' (see p 233); yet civic pride in the victory did not prevent the play's being put down again two years later. As with nearly everything to do with this entertainment, scarcely any mention of it is made until some seven years later when Captain Cox, a city aleconner and a mason by trade, took a group of his fellow-citizens to Kenilworth to perform this long-banned play before his queen.[16]

The queen so relished the lively show that Cox took his chance and asked that, as it was 'without ill exampl of mannerz, papistry, or ony superstition,' could it be allowed again in Coventry. Elizabeth's delight in the play was obviously translated into a request that the mayor could not ignore: in 1576 the Hock Tuesday play was being played again in Coventry (see pp 273, 276). Virtually everything known about the play comes from Robert Laneham's Letter describing the 1575 Kenilworth festivities. Who performed it in Coventry (before Cox and his men) is not known. Its popularity and history lie between the lines of surviving records, leaving one to wonder what other plays may lie there similarly unrecorded.

Many touring companies of actors and, as the Stuart period progressed, showmen of all kinds visited Coventry. Only twice was there trouble: in 1600, Lord Chandos' company was imprisoned for playing at the Angel in defiance of the mayor (see p 356); in 1615, a member of the Lady Elizabeth's company bandied words with one Thomas Barrowes, who at once complained to the mayor (see pp 393-4).[17] On the same day, the imposing wrath of the city recorder, Sir Edward Coke, was called upon 'Common players' who would act on Sundays (see pp 394-5). Between 1563 and 1590, there are scattered records of a troupe of travelling actors calling themselves 'The Players of Coventry' or 'Mr. Smythes Players of Coventrie' performing in the Midlands at Abingdon, Bristol, Leicester, Nottingham, and Coventry itself; their identity, as well as their connection with the city, remain obscure.[18]

Music

Music in Coventry was provided by the waits, who were maintained by the city to perform the duties of the Watch (see pp 483-4) and to act as musical entertainers. They are first noticed in an act of leet appointing them in 1423 (see p 83). The city found their livery, silver collars, and badges, and paid their wages, £1 a year each. Houses for them were provided by the Corpus Christi and Trinity guilds. They are frequent recipients of money for playing at feasts and celebrations, whether civic, guild, or religious. They were busy throughout Corpus Christi Day, for example: they played first in the procession, then as they were contracted for the plays (at different times as a group or as individuals), and finally for the official feasts that closed the day. Five of them, between 1495 and 1540, won sufficient financial standing to become members of the Corpus Christi guild.

The waits played outside Coventry (there are records of their playing at Abingdon and, more frequently, at Maxstoke Priory in Warwickshire).[19] This practice eventually became excessive, so that in 1467 they were forbidden to travel 'but to abbottes & priours within x mylees of þis Cite' (see p 45). One hundred and fifty years later (and again one is reminded of the large span of time these records cover and how deceptive it is to talk of the history of Coventry's waits or of its Corpus Christi cycle as though they form simple entities understood in the convenient terms of a generation), the city would have been glad to have them travel ten miles and more away. They had become such a contentious group that they were summarily disbanded (see p 437).

The disagreement was eventually settled, however, for in 1641 the city bought fine new liveries for its waits (see pp 446-7). Their names are not known, but it is to be hoped they did not include one whose surpassing fame as a musician turned out to have been bought by means of a pact with Satan, whose irresistible claiming of his own in 1640 was announced in *Fearefull Newes from Coventry*. [20]

There was a long tradition of teaching music in a more decent and devout way in the city. Once there was a 'songescoleslane' whose whereabouts has not been traced though it was possibly within the Priory precincts. Most unusual care was taken to ensure the presence of a music master, a man skilful and learned in music, to teach students willing to sing three times a week for an annual salary of fifty-two shillings.[21] The students who had 'tuneable voices and musicall inclinations' (as the twelfth order for the regulation of the school of 1628 phrased it), became, for the Carpenters, the equivalent of the young friars who sang for them at their annual feasts in the house of the White Friars 152 years earlier (see Carpenters' Accounts, pp 58 and 351; the general term 'musicians' probably covers the same entertainers before and after those dates).[22]

Ceremonial

Processions were the city's delight, common entertainment, and visible emblem of civic distinction. Their pageantry rested upon the splendour of the liveries worn by the clerics, the mayor and his attendants, and the masters and fellows of the guilds. The richness of the clerical dress can be surmised from the inventories of the Corpus Christi guild (see pp 98-9, 108-9) and from the sales of vestments forced upon Holy Trinity Church by the Reformation (see p 492). Scarlet and green were — and are yet — the civic colours, and the mayor and his brethren, accompanied by their symbols of office and their official bearers, paraded in them on a full calendar of occasions: at their own governmental meetings, riding the bounds, and viewing the common lands; to high services and, before the Reformation, to the Priory and friaries; on the especial ceremonial occasions of Corpus Christi Day, the Midsummer (St John's) and St Peter's Watches, and St George's Day procession. Annual payments to a variety of civic officers for livery supported this aspect of processional spectacle.[23] The guilds contributed by marching, each one in the distinctive livery of its own craft — the Drapers, for instance, in gowns of 'Sad pewke, tawne, otherells off browne blewe whych be nere of one color & an hode, the on halfe tawne or pewke & the other halfe skarlet' (Sharp, p 164, fn p). Company orders required attendance of members on processional occasions.[24]

The city's regular calendar of processions was frequently increased by visits of royalty; the holding of parliaments and councils of state (eg, 1404, 1457); and special religious events such as the triennial convocation of the general chapter of the Benedictine monks from 1498 until 1519 (see pp 88-9).

All processions demanded carefully organized pageantry. The pleasant vision of cheerful, attentive, if jostling, crowds and well-mannered procession had sometimes to give way to that of an unruly crowd thrusting in to see or to be a part of the show. In the processions themselves, inevitable arguments about precedence had to be settled. Praise of God and obeisance to the 'goode name & fame' of the city were combined by the guilds with a keen and understandable regard for their own honour.

More than once the leet court had to intervene and deal with such matters (see pp 16-17).[25]

In 1495, after the 'dyuers riottes & offences & gret discordes don & commytted vppon lammasse day caused be þat þat [dittography] many in nombre vndesired ryden with þe Chamberleyns,' the numbers who might ride were limited to thirty at most, chosen a week beforehand (see pp 83-4). This was an old tale: in 1421, for instance, the prior and others were troubled about the 'grett multytude of peopull' brought together on Midsummer and St Peter's Eves, for 'hit lyeth in no mannys power. thowȝe he ordeyn for hem as well as he can for to plese hem all And not onely for this cause but allso of grett debate and man slauȝghter and othure perels and synnes yat myght fall and late haue fallen' (see pp 7-8).[26] Fortunately, the control of such violent celebration apparently did lie in the power of man's authority at Coventry and, although problems arose over the years, the public processions were as orderly as might reasonably be expected.

Despite occasional discord, the processions are the best indicators of Coventry's sense of its dignity and power. None better exemplifies this than the Corpus Christi Day procession, the most splendid of them all. 'Following the train of companies of traders and artificers came the members or priests of the Trinity guild bearing the Host, the various religious bodies of the city probably walking behind the Sacrament. The Corpus Christi guild provided gorgeous vessels, wherein the consecrated elements were placed, and four burgesses hired by the fraternity carried a canopy of costly material over the same, while the effect of the religious ceremonial was heightened by banner and crucifix coming from the treasuries of the guilds. A pageant setting forth scenes in the life of the Virgin, the Annunciation, which, on account of its mystical meaning, was highly appropriate to the occasion, and the Assumption also figured in the train.'[27] With them came the mayor and the city's officers bearing the civic regalia. The whole represented Coventry — church, city, and trade, everyone from prior and mayor to journeyman — bedecked in its best pre-Reformation splendour.

In the latter half of the sixteenth century, the splendour faded. The occasions for ceremony were civic rather than religious and fell more into the latter half of the year, whereas the old religious processions had occurred in the first six months.[28] This shift emphasized the change in mood wrought by the Reformation in Coventry, a change which the Corpus Christi plays were nonetheless able to accommodate until 1579.

The single recurring item in the pages of this volume is for 'bearing harnes' on Fair Friday. At the opening of the Great Fair each guild provided men to parade with weaponry and banners in armour that was silvered or painted black; these men were mostly on foot, but a few rode on horseback. With the mayor and his brethren and city officials, they represented the secular power of the city. In a similar fashion but sometimes more joyously accompanied by wicker-work giants and giantesses and flaring torches, they kept the marching watches on Midsummer and St Peter's Eves (the latter was abolished in 1549, the former in 1564). These quasi-military parades remind us that the unchanging aspect of national history reflected in this volume is war, civil war as often as not. The destructive appetite of war for men, weaponry, and money was relentless. The city's own armoury was impressive and well-maintained. Occasionally it might be turned to unwarlike use, as in 1456 (see below, p liii, and p 29). In 1451, at the Easter leet, Mayor Boys had 'ordeyned that ther shulde be made iiij gonnes of brasse ij greter & ij smaller' by a Bristol artificer 'for strengthyng of the same [city] yif nede shulde hit requyre, (the whiche God forbede!)' (*LB*, p 260). Two hundred years later, civil war again seized the land. The city had been acquiring more and more arms and munitions, from the middle 1630s especially, until Alderman Banks was given 'by order of this House towardes the guarding and defending of this Citie the first day of october. 1642 two hundred poundes' (CRO: A 16, p 367). Coventry's silently harsh treatment of its Royalist prisoners was to bring a new and ineradicable meaning to the phrase 'sent to Coventry.' This volume contains enough, I trust, to show what the earlier and happier meaning of that phrase was.

Coventry Antiquarians

This volume places considerable reliance on the antiquarian transcriptions of Thomas Sharp (1770–1841), Thomas Daffern (c 1795–1869), J.O. Halliwell-Phillipps (1820–89), and, to a lesser extent, William Reader (1782–1852). Their qualities were as distinctive as their purposes were different. Their mode of transcription is so different from that followed by REED, yet their work so invaluable, that some prefatory consideration of the nature of this reliance must be made.

Any discussion of 'the ancient Books and Documents belonging to the Corporation [of Coventry], and the remaining Account Books and other writings of the Trading Companies' must begin, not with the books, but with a man. The presence of Thomas Sharp in any collection of records to do with 'the Pageants or Dramatic Mysteries anciently performed at Coventry' is not only due to his primacy as the historian of the city's drama and pageantry, but because his *Dissertation* (from whose second page and all-embracing title I have just quoted) has itself become, where it records material now lost, one of those 'remaining ... writings.' His book has also become, in ways he could hardly have foreseen, a foundation stone of the general study of medieval English drama. His illustrations of Coventry's practices tended to be taken as illustrations of England's practices. The frontispiece that he directed his 'young Artist of this City,' David Gee, to design of the 'Representation of a Pageant Vehicle at the time of Performance' gained the stature of documentary evidence and is still regularly reproduced in histories of English drama.

Sharp was neither the first nor the only man to attempt a local dramatic history, but such was the richness of his material, and such was the general quality and extent of his survey, that no comparable work was achieved for over a hundred years afterward.[29] Whatever critical comments are made below in the light of methods of modern scholarship quite outside Sharp's purpose, his own achievement still commands praise and admiration.

The disappearance and destruction of MSS over centuries are inevitable. In Coventry's case, the losses have been unduly severe. Many of the MSS which Sharp worked from, together with collections of his notes, went to the Staunton Collection at Longbridge House, near Stratford-upon-Avon, and from there to the Birmingham Central Reference Library, where, together with other irreplaceable Coventry material, they were burned in the fire of 1879. More such books and manuscripts in the Coventry Public Library were lost in the air-raid on the city in 1940.[30] The awareness of these losses has made Sharp's book seem even more valuable as not only a fine word but the final word on Coventry's dramatic history. It has also, however, shrouded the fact that a rich store of civic and guild documents still exists, nearly all of them in the Coventry City Record Office. 'The considerable body of information respecting the Pageants or Mysteries' that Sharp was able to draw upon can never be fully recovered, but it has not been entirely lost.

How much Sharp actually transcribed cannot be said; he gives the impression, and I suspect that it is not a false one, of having gone through everything. The foliation of some of the surviving documents is his, as are the lightly pencilled double crosses against entries; most of these marks were useful for the *Dissertation,* the others for memoranda towards the *Illustrative Papers on the History and Antiquities of the City of Coventry,* as his projected comprehensive history of his native city posthumously became. He compounded these scholarly felonies by commenting briefly on items here and there and translating occasional passages. He had so much material to hand when he came to write the *Dissertation* that he could use only a fraction of it. He had to choose among many items, but as he did so, he also allowed himself to choose only a part of an item. He omitted, quite deliberately, a word or words, a name or names. He felt free to edit — usually silently — what he chose to print.[31] This is less than graceful but yet not completely disgraceful, for if he marred what we would see as the fine and perfect weave of the carpet, he did not lose its design; more importantly, he did not edit or 'choose' in order to alter that design. So far as I can tell, he abbreviated no more than fifteen per cent of the items he printed. Nonetheless, every alteration, known or unknown, costs us information (and the majority of the transcriptions we have from the accounts of the Smiths', Dyers', and Trinity guilds are Sharp's alone without corroboration from any other source). Sharp's large stores of available but unused transcriptions are best revealed by some of his footnotes with their tantalizing supporting references, which are like flicks of a torch picking out single items from an otherwise dark but richly crammed storeroom.[32]

William Reader was his contemporary and friend. He probably searched even more widely in Coventry documents and had the benefit of access to his friend's manuscript collections, to which he was able to add. There was no rivalry between them; what rivalry Reader did encounter came from Birmingham, where a group of antiquarians, whose work came to nought, frustrated the original purpose of his research — to publish a revised and enlarged edition of Dugdale's *Antiquities of Warwickshire.*[33]

Whereas only an eager interest in drama would have led Sharp 'to collect a considerable body of information respecting the Pageants or Mysteries' once played in Coventry, and then to work upon it at the expense of the major work, Reader obviously felt no such attraction.[34] To the degree that drama was a part of Coventry's history, he recorded it, adding to Sharp's work where he was able to, but it did not deflect him from his purpose.

For Halliwell-Phillipps, on the contrary, local history mattered only in so far as it was connected with drama. He was the student of dramatic history who would have done for England what Sharp did for Coventry.[35] However, he narrowed (if that is the word) his sights to focus only on the matter likely to be useful to him in his Shakespearian projects. He was attentive to Coventry's dramatic history because it illuminated the traditions which Shakespeare inherited. Coventry was the home of the ancient cycle plays, other local drama, and touring plays which Shakespeare might have seen as a boy and young man.

The great amount that Halliwell-Phillipps transcribed is either published in *Illustrations of the Life of Shakespeare* and *Outlines of the Life of Shakespeare,* or cut up and pasted in his dozens of scrapbooks and boxes of loose manuscripts at the Folger Library.[36] He knew very accurately what was in the council's keeping at Coventry but carried out most of his Coventry research at Longbridge House, where the Staunton Collection was housed. His transcriptions are particularly valuable because they add greatly to Sharp's published transcriptions from the Smiths' Accounts (although, as will be seen below, this brings problems because his method of dating and Sharp's are often at loggerheads).

Thomas Daffern bent his quiet energy and perseverance to the transcription of complete guild records in Coventry, including those of the Carpenters, the Mercers, and, most valuable of all for REED, the Drapers.[37] Any kind of choice, editing, or interpretation was no part of his task. From the kinds of errors which he made, it seems that he had no particular knowledge of fifteenth and sixteenth century history. He was willing to admit defeat before a baffling word but was equally ready to hazard a shot at a word which wider knowledge would have told him was broad of the mark (eg, 'Blues' for 'elnes' in measurements of cloth, see p 241, l. 33). However, this small lack in basic knowledge is offset by the fact that he transcribed complete records.

The inherent qualities and skills of these men, and to some extent their different purposes, affected their transcriptions. Halliwell-Phillipps was first in rank as a scholar and Daffern clearly ranked fourth. I would also place Halliwell-Phillipps first as a transcriber, but in general there is no simple solution to the problem of choosing between transcriptions of the same item. Daffern tried his commendable best to transcribe all that was before him; so did Sharp, Reader, and Halliwell-Phillipps, but each of them in his own way felt free to translate as well as transcribe.

Broadly speaking, the antiquarian sources are of two kinds: entries which have a single transcription and those for which there are two or more. The ideal of the Records of Early English Drama is a modified diplomatic transcription of original manuscripts and ideals, by definition, are never quite attainable. Work on this, and the *York* and *Chester* volumes, proved again that the reading of some letters or words will never be settled. If it is not damage to the text that defies the reader, it is

xxviii   COVENTRY ANTIQUARIANS

the hand of the scribe. There will always be some letters and words that defy one 'correct' reading; two scholars read two different words and can argue their cases only to 'either/or.' This, of course, does not touch upon the 'simpler' questions of whether a certain letter is upper or lower case — questions which Professor A.S.C. Ross called 'improper, that is, there was no definite answer to them.'

Coventry's antiquarians sought to represent exactly what they saw before them, but interpreted that exactitude far less stringently than the diplomatic transcriber of today dares. Where two or more antiquarians copied the same item, the transcriptions are hardly ever identical. At its simplest, this is a matter of treatment of expansions, the introduction of 'modern' punctuation and spelling, the use of capitals, translating roman into arabic figures. In such plain cases each antiquarian transcribed according to his own rules (themselves flexible), but there is no doubt that it was the same item which each was transcribing. Here is an example from the Smiths' Accounts of 1567:

> 1568 pd for harnis men & poynts for hoge tuesday   20d
> (Reader, Bodl: MS Top. Warwickshire c.7, f 83)

> 1568 p'd for harnis men & pwynts for hoge twesday   xx d
> (Sharp, p 126)

> 1567 Paid for harnis men & pwyntes for hoge twesday   xx d
> (Halliwell-Phillipps, Folger Scrapbooks, Box 3)[38]

This is certainly the same item three times transcribed because Sharp said it was one of only two references to Hock Tuesday in the Smiths' Accounts (he quoted the other, and with nothing to gainsay him, one must accept that there are only two such references). There is no argument about its content. In other cases, there are clear verbal differences. An example from the Drapers' Accounts demonstrates this. Daffern has 'It to John bern for a lase & mending the bawling yn the toppe of the pageant viij d' (see p 468, l. 11). Sharp has 'Itm̃ for mendyng the bateling yn the toppe of the pagent viij d' (*Dissertation*, p 67). Sharp's 'bateling' makes the immediate sense that Daffern's 'bawling' does not and is further supported by '1470, It' p. xxv *lb.* yron war', to holde up the batellyng at seynt mary hall, p's iij s. j d. ob.' (*Illustrative Papers*, p 213).

Daffern's transcription, however, points to another feature, already mentioned, of Sharp's approach to his material: he silently edited entries. The 'bateling yn the toppe of the pagent' is an example of an entry concerning the appearance of the 'pageant vehicle.' Earlier on the same page, he had dealt with 'Machinery, &c.' In a list of illustrative items, he had merely mentioned 'A Windlass and three fathom of Cord,' which he clearly did not intend to be thought a transcription of a particular item. Thus, when he looked for an illustration of another topic, he took only that part of the entry relevant to his discussion. It is not clear from the original entry whether John Bern was responsible only for the lace or for the 'bateling' as well. In any case, Sharp often omitted proper names from his cited entries when his interest was in the work rather than the man who did the work. Sharp's concern was to illustrate and so he had the right to choose. One may agree or not about the choice, but only if it is known what kind of choice has been made. Without the original manuscript or the transcriptions of others to check him by, when can we be sure that seemingly complete entries have not been shortened?

Sharp presented the truth but not always the whole truth: there were occasions when he specifically claimed to present the whole truth but did not actually do so. For example, he included 'a literal copy of the entry of expences' incurred by the Smiths in the production of *The Destruction of Jerusalem*, headed 'Exspencys & paymentes for the pagente.' Halliwell-Phillipps reckoned the same entry 'sufficiently curious to be quoted at length' (*Illustrations*, pp 56-7; see also pp 307-9). Sharp (p 37) listed forty-two items, prefaced by a brief comment on the extraordinary number of rehearsals (six) and three items from 'the charges attending those rehearsals, in order to illustrate the subject of "musicians," and shew the zeal and care of the Company.' The reader assumes these were entered separately from the literal copy of the 'Exspencys & paymentes' list which Sharp then quoted. (Such a division of payments running contrary to the subheading is not unusual in guild accounts.) The additions in guild accounts can never be accepted without question, but the 'Som*m* is v li iij s vij d' which concludes this list is so far from the actual 'som*m*' of £4 13s 7d that one might ponder his accuracy as well as that of the accountant whose list he was copying. One does well to question Sharp in this instance, however, for Halliwell-Phillipps' list begins in the same way as Sharp's 'literal copy' but continues into the rehearsal and repair expenses as though all were originally a single account. He did not quote a sum total, suggesting that 'at length' does not mean 'in entirety.' If one compares his list with Sharp's down to the payment to Massey, one sees that he added three new items, restored names deleted in three others, and corrected (or changed) five of Sharp's costs. The extraordinarily low payment (considering the expensiveness of the production) of 'v d' to the musicians becomes 'v s.' Similarly, the 'dryvers of the pagente,' instead of a miserable 3d, receive 4s. Hewet's 'paynes,' on the other hand, turn out to be worth only 3d instead of 9d. Finally, a sixth cost is broken down into the two which it originally was: where Sharp has 'Itm̃ pd to Jhon Deane for hys Dyner sowper and Drynkynge xij d,' Halliwell-Phillipps offers two entries, neither of them in Sharp: 'item, paid to Jhon Deane and Fosson for theyre dyner on the playe daye, vj. d,' and 'item, paid to Jhon Deane for hys sowper and drynkynge, vj. d.'[39] These alterations bring the total expenses as far as the Massey item to £5 1s 3d, leaving the 'Som*m*' overcast by 2s 4d.

Halliwell-Phillipps' list does not end with Massey, however. Seventeen additional entries are transcribed. Two of these are among the three that Sharp quoted to show the 'zeal and care of the Company' before embarking on his 'literal copy.' The third entry is unique to Sharp. Interpret the transcribers' prefatory statements as one will, neither prints the full list of pageant expenses. Were there entries that both men left out? Are omissions of entries in accounts asserted to be complete more or less misleading than the silent conflation or editing of them?

Sharp is exposed because only he was writing a history of drama which enforced him to choose. Only four times did he say that a complete account was being printed; three of the four times, errors of one sort or another mar the attractiveness of the offer.[40] None is so error-strewn as the Smiths' 1584 transcription. On such occasions, however, Sharp's faults are revealed most openly, warning the reader to be wary in accepting what he transcribed. Frequently the reader's only choice is Sharp's transcription and, despite the dark case made against him, he is a trustworthy guide to Coventry's early dramatic history. His editorial manners do not, cannot indeed, rob his work of its essential value. When he omitted or edited, it was to suit the purposes of his discourse by illustration, not to suit an argument. In essence, he was guilty of sins of omission, not commission, and 'sins' often only in the court of present-day scholarship. Every transcriber will fall into error or argument over letters and words, and Sharp guarded himself against this. He corrected many errors, both his and his printers' thirteen, in the list of errata (p 226) and many more in his pencilled notes in his own copy of the *Dissertation* (BL: Add MS 43645). As did many of his contemporaries, he felt freer in handling his material than would a scholar today. It can be fairly said that this freedom was never allowed to become licence.

The Documents

Within each year, the text of this collection follows a standard order. That order is reflected in this section of discussion and description. Documents from antiquarian rather than original sources are identified in the left margin of the text by the symbols 'A' (for antiquarian compilation) and 'AC' (for antiquarian collection).

Civic Documents

The contents of the Coventry Record Office (CRO) have generally been known since 1896 by the class and number which J.C. Jeaffreson gave them in *A Calendar of the Books, Charters, Letters Patent, Deeds, Rolls, Writs, and Other Writings.* Later revisions and additions to this catalogue have been made (notably in 1931). A complete recataloguing of the holdings of the CRO, however, is now in progress. Wherever possible, the documents in this collection have been given their new 'accession numbers' according to the new definitive catalogue as well as their old references.

In 1451, a leet memorandum states: 'Also all the dedes, munimentes, Skrowes, Charters that longon to the lyuelode of the Chambur of this Cite of Couentre lyon in a Closette withe-in the forseyde Comen Cofur sauely ther to be kepte. To the whiche Cofur ther ben v lokkes & v keyes; of the whyche the Meyre hathe oon, the Mayster of the Trinite yeld anodur, the Mayster of Corpus Christi anodur, The Chamburlens anodur, & the wardens anodur, to thentent that they there shuld be the more sauely kepte' (LB, p 267). This fine archival ideal was not consistently maintained, but its spirit now rules the CRO (the quintuple barring of access to the records happily abandoned). As will be seen from the bibliographic descriptions of the documents, a carefully planned series of strengthening operations has been carried out by rebinding the older and frailer books while retaining as much of the original binding as possible. The available space in the reading room at the CRO allows only a small but choice library to assist the scholar, but in adjoining rooms the Coventry and Warwickshire Reference Library answers every need.

Leet Book I
Coventry, City Record Office, A 3(a); 1421–1555; Latin and English; paper; iv+457+iv; 380mm

x 265mm (written area variable); collation irregular (many insertions and excisions); modern foliation (first gathering foliated as -1 to -17 before regular numbering begins); no decoration; stained
African goat cover with old leather panels inlaid, original oak board binding extended by ¼″ during
1931 rebinding, front plates of clasps original; repaired and rebound 1931, original sewing holes
followed as closely as possible. Published by the EETS in four volumes (os 134, 135, 138, 146:
1907-13), transcribed and edited by Mary Dormer Harris (cited elsewhere as *LB*).

Leet Book II
Coventry, City Record Office, A 3(b); 1588-1834; English; paper; iv+623+iv; 340mm x 210mm
(written area variable); mainly gathered in 8's; contemporary pagination (to p 581) followed by
19th c foliation (ff 582-672) and 243 unnumbered leaves; some display capitals in later years;
early 20th c board binding covered in brown leather, embossed seal of elephant and castle centred
on front cover, paper title on spine: 'COURT LEET | 2 | LEET-BOOK | 1588-1834.'

The best and fullest account of the composition and content of the Leet Book (I)
is M.D. Harris' introduction to her edition (*LB*, pp ix-xvi), upon which these notes
rely. Originally there seems to have been a 'Mayor's Register,' many of whose entries
(and perhaps pages) were taken into the Leet Book in 1521 when the existing Leet
Book seems to have been 'newe made.' (The scribe's hand for the 1421-5 entries and
intermittently until 1445 is early sixteenth century.) From the 1460s on, the entries
appear to be contemporaneous with the events they record. Originally a judicial
body, the leet court became ever more a legislative assembly and the book comme-
morates the court's by-laws but includes much miscellaneous matter as well — letters,
roll calls of citizens subscribing to royal 'loans,' descriptions of visits — a kind of
superior annal, reliable in its dates.

Leet Book I is the single most valuable source of information about the day-to-
day life of Coventry from 1420 to 1555. It reveals how the mayor and his council
controlled the Corpus Christi cycle by arranging the changes of allegiance between
the different guilds which actually produced the individual plays and by dealing with
matters of every degree from rulings on individuals to orders for city-wide financial
support of the plays. In addition, the book notes selective details of some ceremonial
visits and deals with management problems associated with other ceremonial occasions — such as the riding of the bounds or the riding of the armed Watch on Midsummer and St Peter's Eves. As with very many of the documents in this collection,
the fullness of treatment accorded to (or demanded by) each mayor varies consi-
derably. For example, in 1526 and 1527 very little was thought to need doing or
very little was reported. Unfortunately, nothing was reported between 1555 when
the first Leet Book ends and 1588 when the second begins.

Chamberlains' Account Book I
Coventry, City Record Office, A 7(a); 1499-1573; English; paper; ii+191+i; 360mm x 268mm
(written area variable); collation irregular; modern pagination (first 140 folios), followed by 51

blanks; no decoration; rebound in dark brown leather in 1971 with old leather incorporated, paper title on spine: 'CORP. ACCOUNTS I WARDENS I 1a I 14 HENRY VII – 16 ELIZABETH I Book of the yearly accounts I of successive chamberlains I of the Corporation I of the City of Coventre I A7(a)'; early folios heavily damaged by damp in lower right hand edge and repaired.

Chamberlains' and Wardens' Account Book II
Coventry, City Record Office, A 7(b); 1574–1636; English with 14th c (?) Latin on front and back parchment strips; paper, with 6 parchment strips of variable size in front and back endpapers; v+457+iii; 425mm x 275mm (written area variable); collation impossible (stripped and sewn on to new bands 1969); modern pagination; no decoration; rebound in new boards in 1969, former skin incorporated in cover, illegible paper title on spine.

Chamberlains' and Wardens' Account Book III
Coventry, City Record Office, A 7(c); 1636–1710; English; paper; iii+637+iii; 310mm x 275mm (written area variable); collation impossible (stripped in 1969 rebinding and gatherings restitched on to five bands); modern pagination (to p 915); no decoration; brown leather binding, clasps lost but catches and 'W 2' on front cover, new skin on original boards to form spine 1969, illegible paper title on spine; scattered copies of legal documents and copies of letters to James I dated 1603 bound in upside down.

The accounts of the chamberlains and wardens may be distinguished, but the divisions between them were not rigidly adhered to. The chamberlains handled the murage, which extended past the walls, ditches, and gates to the roads and pavements within the city, as well as the finances of the lammas lands. They also provided livery payments for the sergeant and the beadles, and for the waits from 1549. From 1574, the payment to the waits is their only contribution to this volume.

The wardens dealt with the rentals of civic properties and paid for their maintenance. There are no surviving accounts collected formally together before 1574. Wardens also paid for mayoral feasts and entertainments, and rewarded travelling players. In doing this, they maintained the apparently unwritten agreement among civic officials in England that the names of the plays presented should not be mentioned. From 1574, the chamberlains' and wardens' accounts are entered in the same book.

Cheylesmore Manor Account Book
Coventry, City Record Office, A 9; 1542–1658; English; paper; ii+269+vii; 300mm x 205mm (written area variable); collation impossible (stripped in 1969 rebinding and gatherings stitched on to 4 new bands); contemporary foliation, modern pagination (pp 66-78, 430-90 blank); no decoration; new strip of leather glued on to original plain brown leather boards to form spine, 1969.

The Cheylesmore Manor Account Book justifies its name because it includes the rental of the manor and its properties in Coventry. (Cheylesmore was once a royal manor and most Plantagenet and Tudor monarchs stayed there.) It is a somewhat disorganized book that becomes more and more a mayor's expense book; it includes payments for the Cheylesmore leet dinners (these leets were held a week after Coventry's), musters, painting and decorating the city cross, musical instruments, etc.

Council Book
Coventry, City Record Office, A 14(a); 1555–1640; English; paper; 449 leaves; 310mm x 202mm (written area variable; many blanks); collation irregular (many insertions and excisions, order of ff 1–24 reconstructed during 1967 repair); modern pagination; no decoration; dark brown cover, original leather cover with elephant and castle stamp preserved and included in modern rebinding, 1967; considerable damage and repair throughout.

The Council Book looks, at first sight, as though it might fill the gap between the two Leet Books. However, it primarily deals with leases of city property, adjudications, caring for the city's armour, and, crossing into the wardens' area of responsibility, records of occasional payments to players and to those who manage civic celebrations.

Receipt Book
Coventry, City Record Office, A 17; 1561–1653; English; paper; iv+165+xviii; 302mm x 198mm (written area variable); mainly gathered in 12's; modern pagination (to p 331); no decoration; 20th c dark green tooled leather binding, green city crest of elephant and castle stamped on centre front cover, title on spine: 'CORP ACCOUNTS I TREASURER I 1a [on paper] I CITY I OF I COVENTRY I BOOK OF I RECEIPTS I 1561–1653 [gold stamped].'

Payments Out Book
Coventry, City Record Office, A 16; 1561–1653; English; paper; vi+232+xii; 302mm x 198mm (written area variable); mainly gathered in 12's; modern pagination (to p 464); no decoration; 20th c dark green tooled leather binding, worn on corners, elephant and castle stamped on centre front cover, title on spine: 'CORP ACCOUNTS I TREASURER I 1b [on paper] I CITY I OF I COVENTRY I BOOK OF I PAYMENTS I 1561–1653 [gold stamped].' Glosses in modern hand throughout.

The Receipt Book and the Payments Out Book are a pair of accounts begun at the same time, by the same scribe, using the same rubric. The Receipt Book begins: 'In this booke be Mencionede and Wrytten All & singuler sommes of Money growing & commyng to the Use of the Corporacion of the Citie of Couentree Aswell by reason of eny Accompt of eny Receivour Beillie or other Accompaunt of the same As otherwise Whiche haue been put into the Tresourie of the said Citie ...' (p 1). To this end, it includes freemen's fees, charity monies, and the handling of the leading bequests made to the city. However, it includes some payments one might expect to find elsewhere (see 1570, p 251).

The Payments Out Book defines itself: 'In this booke be Mencionede and Wrytten all & sing*u*ler so*m*mes of Money Whiche haue been taken out of the Tresourie of this Citie And payed either in the affaires & busynes of the Citie or otherwise' (p 1). This wide scope allows payments for practically anything and all the other account books' territories are infringed upon. Legal and parliamentary costs, payments to players, livery payments, pensions (to Philemon Holland among others), a musical instrument for the waits, house repairs, road upkeep, entertaining noblemen and other visitors, every kind of expense is met in these accounts. The book is a fine example of the Tudor refusal to be bound by petty restriction and red tape in bookkeeping.

Survey of Rentals
Coventry, City Record Office, A 24; 1581; English; paper; vi+96(leaves of Survey)+300 or more blanks+ii; 435mm x 275mm (written area variable); original collation obscured during 1968 rebinding; stripped and rebound in 1968; 16th c pagination (to p 170); display capitals; dark brown leather binding, original stamped title still visible centred on front cover: 'ANNO DM | 1581 | IOHN: MYLES | MAIOR'; original 14th c parchment endpapers preserved in back of new binding, Latin theological writing in 2 columns lined in red.

Rental Roll I
Coventry, City Record Office, no ascription; 1574; English; parchment; 1 membrane cut diagonally at bottom; 335mm (right side), 400mm (left side) x 157mm; contemporary title on dorse: 'Rental de [⟨...⟩] | Cheillsmore | 1574'; 320mm tear bottom right.

Rental Roll II
Coventry, City Record Office, E 13; 1639; English; parchment; 1 membrane; 715mm x 263mm; paper identification sticker on dorse: '1639 | Rental of the | Manor of Cheilesmore'; 130mm split centre bottom, split also beside ribbon-tie.

Quitclaim I
Coventry, City Record Office, 184; 6 February 1407; Latin; parchment; endorsed in several 16th c hands; originally folded in four, seal now partly attached, modern sticker identification: 'Seal of John Clerk, son and heir of Richard Clerk of Coventry merchant.'

Quitclaim II
Coventry, City Record Office, 100/37; 18 September 1609; English; parchment; 134mm x 320mm; orange seal; contemporary title on dorse: 'Release from | Wilks,' 19th c addition in pencil: 'Mill Lane | 7 James | 1610'; 150mm tear on lateral fold 40mm from top left.

These rolls and quitclaims mention the pageant houses of the Smiths in Mill Lane, the Whittawers in Hill Street, and the Girdlers in no specified place (actually in Mill Lane). The Girdlers paid a peppercorn rent for their pageant house to the Cheylesmore estate.

MISCELLANEOUS

Letter of Mayor Coton to Cromwell

London, Public Record Office, SP/1/142; 17 January 1539; English; paper; 1 leaf (f 66), originally separate, now bound with other papers in book form (ii+233+ii); f 66: 336mm x 212mm (255mm x 275mm), f 66v: 3 lines only; modern pencil foliation in bottom right corner, plus traces of previous (also modern) foliation, indicating perhaps different arrangement of sheets in earlier binding; no decoration; modern binding, title stamped on spine in gold: 'Letters and Papers | Henry VIII | XIV Pt. 1 | 2-210'; edges of first 2 lines gone, top right corner f 66.

Letter concerning Lady Elizabeth's Players from Mr Barrowes

Coventry, City Record Office, Misc 4 1946/9; 1615; English; paper; single sheet endorsed; 309mm x 200mm; repaired.

Letter of Sir Edward Coke to the Mayor

Coventry, City Record Office, A 79 p 113; 28 March 1615; English; paper; single sheet unendorsed; 155mm x 202mm (85mm x 150mm); writing one side only; once folded in 8; no longer incorporated in a book, separately wrapped in tissue, note naming Lady Elizabeth's Players pasted on bottom left.

Petition of Mary Marston

Coventry, City Record Office, W 83; no date; English; paper; single sheet unendorsed; 200mm x 307mm (90mm x 155mm); written continuously; no decoration; fold marks visible.

A Rental

'A rentall of certaine landes & tenements belongyinge to the Corporation of the cyety of Coventre,' 'Unpublished Documents Belonging to The County of Warwick,' *Warwickshire Antiquarian Magazine,* 1 (1859–77), 481-502 (full article pp 154-78, 240-80, 334-427, 467-502).

AC Thomas Massey Misdemeanour and Waits' Regulations

London, British Library, Add. MS 43645; 19th c, with one or two 17th c items; English; paper; iii+384+ii; 315mm x 235mm (written area variable, some printed sections); collation impossible (binding very tight); modern pagination; no decoration; 19th c dark green leather binding, gilt trim, title stamped on spine in gold: 'DISSERTATION | ON THE PAGEANTS | OR | DRAMATIC MYSTERIES | THOMAS SHARP | [and at bottom] COVENTRY 1825' (between SHARP and COVENTRY, 20th c BL designation). Sharp's own annotated copy of his *Dissertation.*

Will of William Pisford

London, Public Record Office, PROB 11/19; unavailable for MS examination (1979).

Of the four letters described above, Coton's touches on plays and ceremonial; Barrowes' and Coke's on the behaviour of actors; and the last is a neatly turned plea for the restitution of some property by Mary, widow (?) of the playwright John Marston who died in 1634.

The vigorous exposition of Thomas Massey's misdemeanour leaves repercussions noticed elsewhere (see Appendix 6). The provenance of the papers in this exchange is unknown. They are pasted into Sharp's copy of the *Dissertation* (BL: Add MS 43645), as is another early seventeenth century leaf concerning the waits' duties. Knowing the destruction that was to overtake his other papers, would that he had filed other things in this book. It is possible that the original of the 'rentall' was in Staunton's ill-fated collection (see pp xxv-xxvi).

The wills of many likely people were read, but barring a thorough search of the very large collection of Coventry wills in Lichfield and London, the long-known bequest by Pisford remains the only mention of the Coventry plays in a will.

City Annals

The annals are lists of the mayors of Coventry 'with Historical & memorable Events touching ye Antiquity of ye Auncient Citty & Corporation' (as the title page of Bodl: MS Top. Warwickshire d.4 puts it). Unlike many other documents in this volume, these are not records kept contemporaneously with the events they register. Coventry's first mayor, John Ward, was elected in 1346. All annalists agree on his primacy but only the Aylesford annal gives him that date. All differ to some extent on the order of his immediate successors and the dates of their service.[41] Aylesford's is the oldest annal, dating from early in the reign of Edward IV, whose claim to the thrones of England and France — both genealogical and by survey of historical event (especially in the last years of the reign of Henry VI) — it urges in great detail. Of the other annalists, two were Elizabethan, casting their eyes back over 230 years of civic history; the rest were seventeenth century writers, most of them post-Restoration, who ranged back 300 years and more. Their accuracy of detail can be impugned but their general grasp of Coventry's local history and the city's place in national history is reliable.

The annalists are far from agreement as to what constitute 'memorable Events'; hence, no annal duplicates another. Especially 'memorable Events' are commonly, but not always, recorded in all annals. In such cases, similarity of wording suggests common sources. Undoubtedly these existed, but as each annalist was free to use whatever sources he liked, the frequent similarities of entry are matched by equally frequent differences in items chosen and in details given. Personal inclination as well as material available also influences what each annal contains. Lack of documentation prevents setting out whatever nice explanation of the relationship between the annals there might have been. Thus BRL: 273978 is often an abbreviated version of Bodl: MS Top. Warwickshire d.4, but it omits events found in that annal and records others not found in it. The Bodleian annal's list of the twelve men who purchased the freedom of the city is followed by a second one, headed 'others say' (f 1). Those others must include the writers of the Elizabethan annal, CRO: A 28, and the late seventeenth century CRO: Acc 2/D, both of which agree with that second list but otherwise trace their own paths through Coventry's history. It is reasonable to suppose that the annalists were Coventry men; certainly the author of CRO: Acc 2/F was. His is the most domestic and gossipy of the annals: he thinks it worthy of notice that in 1613 'good wife Stark[i]es maide drowned in their Own Mill on St Stephens day.'

The most voluminous and insoluble clues to the authorship of the annals are given by Miles Flint, whose annal is scrupulous in its acknowledgments (BL: Harley 6388): 'This book was taken out of [five] Manuscripts. the one written by Mr Christofer Owen Mayor of this Citty, which contains the Charter of walter de Coventre, concerning ye Commons, &c. to Godfrey Leg, Mayor 1637. the other begining at the 36 Mayor of this Citty & Continued by several hands, & lately by Edmund Palmer, ˄ 'late' of this Citty, Counseller, till Mr Yardly late Mayor; & another Written by Mr Bedford, & collected out of divers others & continued to Mr Septimius Bott; and [...] ˄ 'two' other collected by Thomas Potter & continued to Mr Robert Beake & another written by Mr ffrancis Barnett to ye first year of Mr Jelliffs Majoralty & another written by Mr Abraham Astley, & continued to Mr Septimius Bott. & another written by Mr Abraham Boune, & to Humfrey Wightwilk 1607.'[42] Thus, Miles used eight annals, one of which was 'collected out of divers others' unnamed. It is likely that either Bedford's or Astley's annal is the one now in the Bodleian, and that Barnett's is the one now known as CRO: Acc 2/E. Essentially, Flint tells us that annals were being written between 1607 and 1690, with a flurry of interest — born of civic pride or competitiveness — in the 1680s.

Sharp's references to the annals he used are a mixture of enigmatic brevity and clarity. Most frequently he simply referred to 'MS Annals,' which may mean one or more annals. Nothing he quoted from it/them is found in quite the words he used among those surviving today, and most of what he quoted, both in the *Dissertation* and *Illustrative Papers,* was unique to his own 'MS Annals.'

Sharp named three annals: the 'Butler's Roll,' Codex Hales, and Codex Dugdale. His item dated 1519–20 is known only from the 'Butler's Roll,' an annal written in 1588 according to Sharp (p 132). The 1576 extract from the Codex Hales (see p 276) is likewise known from no other source (Sharp dates it 1575). Codex Hales was also used by William Thomas in his second edition of Dugdale's *Antiquities of Warwickshire* (1730). All Sharp's named annals are lost.

There are no 'good' or 'bad' annals, although there are detailed ones such as Bodl: MS Top. Warwickshire d.4, and others, such as BRL: 115915, with only occasional notes. Where events are mentioned in more than one annal, I have chosen the one that gives the most information. If another annal adds fresh information, this is entered as well.

As is frequently the case with the accounts and records used in this volume, matters one would like to see treated are either ignored or only referred to glancingly. Thus, little is told of happenings in the reigns of Edward III and Richard II; few of

the parliaments and councils held in Coventry (with their attendant ceremony and
entertainment) by Henry IV, Henry VI, Edward IV, and Henry VII are noticed and
then very briefly. Shakespeare has, perhaps, made the joust between Mowbray and
Bolingbroke just outside Gosford gate more memorable to us than it was to Tudor
Coventry. Of the surviving annals, only Aylesford's mentions it: '1398 Iohn Preston
Yat ȝere schulde have ben a battyll of gosford grene.' M.D. Harris quotes one other
reference from a lost annal: 'Two dukes should 'a fought on Gosford Green' (*Story
of Coventry*, p 11).

I have not collated the annals which I have used, as they are quite separate texts
rather than recensions of a single text. This avoids repetition of the same information
in slightly different ways. Endnotes, however, do record any substantive disagree-
ments over details of the same event.

London, British Library, Harley 6388; 17th c (annals from 14th c to 17th c); English; paper;
ii+58+iii; 195mm x 153mm (written area variable); collation difficult; pencil foliation contemporary with binding; no decoration; modern (19th c?) binding.

'A small Quarto, bought Dec. 17, 1690, by Mr. Humfrey Wanley' (1672–1726,
librarian to Harley, see *DNB*). This gives 'a List of the Mayors from the year 1348,
temp. Edw. III. till the Revolution.' It was once the property of Miles Flint (see
above p xxxviii).

Oxford, Bodleian Library, MS Top. Warwickshire d.4 (31431); 1344–1686; English; paper; 190mm
x 290mm; i+44 (1 insert); single booklet; ink foliation (1-37) centre bottom, and pencil foliation
(1-44) upper right corner (duplicate numbering p 16); no decoration; parchment binding, no title.

'A List of ye Mayors & Sheriffs &c of *Coventrey* with Historical & memorable
Events touching ye Antiquity of ye Auncient Citty & Corporation. from ye Year
1344, to ye year 1686.' The mayoral roll begins in 1348. This is the fullest of the
annals. It is written in one hand until 1629/30, after which the hand that has been
adding the names of the sheriffs since 1608/9 continues until 1675/6. The last ten
years are in a new hand. Some bailiffs are recorded intermittently, as part of an
effort to make this annal as full as possible.

Birmingham, Central Reference Library, 273978; early 18th c (annals 1344–1709, with 2 letters
dated 1888 inserted at end); English; paper; 34 leaves (plus 6 modern leaves added at rebinding);
197mm x 156mm (page and text area); one gathering of 34; unfoliated; no decoration; original
soft cover, decorated paper pasted over first and last leaves: newly rebound in red leather hard
covers with gilt design on edges, 'Coventry Mayors' on front cover; slight water damage on edges,
but otherwise excellent condition.

A fuller annal than most: generally, it follows the Bodleian annal of which it is often an abbreviation; however, it is not dependent upon that annal and includes entries of its own.

A Coventry, City Record Office, Acc 2/E (formerly A 43); 18th c antiquarian copy (annals 1348–1674); English; paper; 34 leaves; 192mm x 148mm (written area variable); single paper booklet; contemporary foliation, modern pagination; no decoration; parchment binding, 'E' stamped on front cover, 'General 6' and an illegible note pasted over spine.

A Coventry, City Record Office, Acc 2/F (formerly A 48); 18th c antiquarian (annals 1348–1703); English; paper; iii+84+iii; 185mm x 148mm (written area variable); collation difficult; contemporary foliation; no decoration; parchment binding, 'F' stamped on front cover, $\frac{'A'}{48}$ still visible on spine; last 18 ff bound upside down (last 4 blank).

AC William Dugdale, *The Antiquities of Warwickshire Illustrated; from Records, Leiger-Books, Manuscripts, Charters, Evidences, Tombes, and Armes: Beautified with Maps, Prospects and Portraictures.* 2nd ed. William Thomas (rev), vol 1 (London, 1730), 147-53.

The mayoral list runs from 1348–1723 (names only after 1686). Thomas revised Dugdale's original 'Catalogue of the Mayors' in the light of his careful comparison of it 'with another Manuscript Catalogue of them, which is in a wrought brown leather cover, *penes,* &c. and with that lately published by Mr. *Hearne* at the End of his Edition of *Fordun's Scotichronicon*' (p 147). Sharp quotes a unique entry from Codex Dugdale (*Dissertation*, pp 11-13) and Eld (see below) also refers to it; the annal was almost certainly burned in 1879. It is impossible to say whether the annal in the 'wrought brown leather cover' survives, with or without its cover.

AC Thomas Sharp, *A Dissertation on the Pageants or Dramatic Mysteries Anciently Performed at Coventry by the Trading Companies of that City, Chiefly with Reference to the Vehicle, Characters, and Dresses of the Actors. Compiled in a Great Degree, from Sources Hitherto Unexplored. To Which are Added, the Pageant of the Shearmen & Taylors' Company, and Other Municipal Entertainments of a Public Nature* (Coventry, 1825).

AC — *Illustrative Papers on the History and Antiquities of the City of Coventry; Comprising the Churches of St. Michael, Holy Trinity, St. Nicholas, and St. John; the Grey Friars' Monastery; St. John's Hospital and Free Grammar School; Jesus Hall, Bablake Hall, and St. Mary's Hall. From Original, and Mostly Unpublished Documents. Carefully Re-Printed from an Original Copy with Corrections, Additions, and a Brief Memoir of the Author, by William George Fretton* (Birmingham, 1871).

ANNALS CONSULTED

BL: Add MS 11364. Annals of the city of Coventry, comprising its history from the earliest period to the year 1703. Quarto. Presented by Joseph Gibbs.

BRL: 115915. 'A list of Coventry citizens entitled to wear swords,' 1352-1650. Pieces of parchment sewn into a roll; a mayoral list with very few events noted.

CRO: A 28. Elizabethan, ending with the visit of Queen Elizabeth in 1566, although other notes dated to 1588 appear.

CRO: Acc 2/D (formerly A 37). 1348-1684, continued to 1747. Very little commentary after 1550s; only mayors' names 1595-1642.

CRO: Catalogue of Private Accessions, 351 (Aylesford annal). Photocopy of original in collection of The Rt. Hon. the Earl of Aylesford, Packington Hall, Meriden, Warwickshire. Roll stating Edward IV's claim to the thrones of England and France. On the dorse is a list of Coventry's mayors covering national and local events from the city's incorporation in 1345; details of the last few years before the annal ceases in 1461 are very full.

CRO: Acc 17. George Eld (mayor 1834-5), was a friend of Sharp and a keen local historian. His 'Notes on the History of the City of Coventry' (1840) is a MS compilation covering 1345-1471.

Thomas Hearne (ed), *Johannis de Fordun Scotichronicon Genuinum, Una cum Ejusdem Supplemento ac Continuatione. E Codicibus MSS. Eruit Ediditque Tho. Hearnius, Qui & Appendicem Subjunxit, Totumque Opus (in Quinque Volumina Distinctum) Praefatione atque Indicibus Adornavit*, vol 5 (Oxford, 1722), 1438-78. A copy of an annal owned by Thomas Jesson of Christ Church, Oxford. The list of mayors runs from 1349; it is correct in order and date from 1392. It is not the fullest in detail of the annals but it does contain matter not found in any other.

Benjamin Poole, 'Notable Occurrences,' *Coventry: Its History & Antiquities....* (London, 1870), 402-14. A brief selection from the above sources, severely edited.

Cathedral Records

St Mary's Cathedral: Inventory
London, British Library, Egerton 2603 no. 17; 1494-1696; paper; English; 2 sheets (endorsement on 2nd) bound with other documents in book form (ii+70+ii); 275mm x 207mm; individual documents pasted on stubs 93mm wide; modern foliation; no decoration; red cloth binding, tooled in gold, spine stamped: 'EGERTON | 2603 | BRIT MUS | HISTORICAL | PAPERS | 1494-1696.'

St Mary's Priory: Pittancer's Roll
London, Public Record Office, E 164/21; 15th c; Latin; parchment; iii+262+ii; 343mm x 245mm (275mm x 190mm average text area); collation impossible (tight modern binding); 4 sets of foliation: contemporary roman numerals at foot of folios, later ink, modern pencil, and modern stamped

arabic foliation at top outer corners; no decoration; modern binding.

The inventory, with its sarcastic comment by Dr Loudon, and the pittancer's roll, mentioning the Drapers' pageant house, represent the once powerful church agencies in Coventry. An extract dated 1392 from a cartulary of St Mary's Priory, now lost, is also quoted from Sharp's *Dissertation*.

There are two more rolls from the Priory in the Birmingham Central Reference Library: a pittancer's roll of 1505–6 (BRL:168235) and a cellarer's roll of 1502–3 (BRL: 168239). Extracts from the BRL pittancer's roll will be found above on page xx, on page 492, and in the endnote to E 164/21 f 27 on page 542.

Guild Records: Original

The chronicle of surviving guild records in Coventry begins in 1434 with the Weavers' Deeds (pp 10-11). The kind of information, and the amount of it, varies very much between guilds.

The oldest surviving guild accounts in Coventry are the Carpenters', which begin in 1446. It is unfortunate, from REED's point of view, that, although they were always a numerous and stable guild, their connection with the Corpus Christi cycle lay in a commendably regular payment (for over a hundred years) toward the costs of the Tilers' pageant and in their equally regular work repairing pageant wagons and pageant houses. Coventry's fortune in possessing the Mercers' account books is undermined by their dating only from 1579; their pageant costs for that year tell us nothing except the not surprising fact that they spent about as much on their pageant as did the Drapers, their partners in wealth and city government.

The Mercers tantalize with too little, the Weavers by what 'ought' to be full details about their play and its production. There is the manuscript of the play itself in the hand of its 1535 reviser, Robert Crow, plus two leaves of the earlier play which he was revising; there are the ordinances of the company dated 31 Henry VI (1 September 1452 – 31 August 1453), account books beginning 1523, rentgatherers' accounts beginning 1521, a register of apprentices for 1550–1700, and six early fifteenth century deeds to do with the pageant house and the land it was built on. The pageant costs were entered in the main accounts, but incidental items are found in the rentgatherers' accounts. (There is no pattern to these latter items, no particular costs for which the rentgatherers were responsible.) This rich array of documents is all we can reasonably expect in order to show, in detail, how one company went about producing its play. However, what the scholar reasonably expects and what the Weavers thought reasonably necessary are quite different. Between 1523 and 1540, with the exception of 1525, only summary totals are given for what is generally called: 'Item spend on corp*us* crysty day xxviij s iiij d' (1530, f 12). In the 'full' accounts, several actors are never mentioned — the two Prophets who introduce the play, the three Doctors with whom Christ disputes in the temple, and the Archangel Gabriel. Stage directions always refer to Simeon's clerks in the plural, but in the list of actors' wages only one is ever paid.

The Cappers' company thrives yet and its great book of accounts runs from the reign of Henry VII to George V with one interruption: between 1556 and 1571 inclusive, the accounts were entered in a 'smale blacke boke' which was lost in the Birmingham fire of 1879. There are periods when the great book covers the company's affairs very cursorily, particularly in the first decades of the sixteenth century (see Appendix 1). Usually the production costs of their play are fully entered: the Cappers' guild is the only company to leave us with inventories of its playing gear (see pp 240-1 and endnote p 575) and a list of company members willing to act in the pageant (see pp 235-6). At the same time, it is not too proud to list members who fell upon hard times and received the city's charity, along with other daily affairs not found in other companies' accounts.[43]

The Corpus Christi guild was founded in 1348; the only account book remaining runs from 1488 until 1553. It is, with the Cappers', the handsomest of the surviving account books; both contain some fine examples of ornate penmanship and decorated initials. Membership of the Corpus Christi guild was drawn from the most prosperous of Coventry's society, but many wealthy merchants and noblemen from all parts of England were members also, as were kings, queens, and princes. Its rent roll was large; its visual opulence can be gauged from inventories of plate, jewels, and vestments (see pp 81, 97-8). What little we know of the Holy Trinity guild's possessions suggests that they could celebrate as splendidly.

A trade guild's capacity for opulent worship can be measured from the indenture conveying the Cardmakers' pageant, pageant house, and chapel 'with all & singler ther Appurtenances ornamentes vestymentes Iuelles & implementes' to the Cappers (see pp 145, 486-7). The variety of deeds also demonstrates the guilds' attitudes toward the pageant house. Indeed, the variety of guild documents presented here, taken as a body, shows well the different facets of the relationship of a guild to its pageant, admirably filling out the usually terse orders of leet about pageant responsibility. The fortunate survival of the original Cappers' and Weavers' Accounts (and the transcript of the full Drapers' Accounts) adds one more facet by allowing the reader to see what part the production of the play and the larger celebration of Corpus Christi Day as a whole played in the complete guild year. It is useful to remind ourselves that the Corpus Christi plays took their place with the celebrations on Midsummer and St Peter's Eves, and with the annual guild dinner (often called the choice dinner because it marked the choosing of the new masters for the coming year).[44]

Cappers' Records

Stratford-upon-Avon, Shakespeare Centre, Account Book I; 1485?–1925; English; paper; i+389+i; 392mm x 265mm (written area variable); collation irregular, composite volume made up of many booklets; modern pencil foliation (to f 350), ff 98-101 blank; black ink display letters in headings beginning 1573 (f 105 following), ink columns and borders beginning 1676 (f 205), red lining 1747 (f 287), decorated and illuminated letters after 1862 (f 347v); 20th c soft calf binding, no title; some damage through damp in early folios.

Cardmakers and Saddlers' Indentured Conveyance

Coventry, City Record Office, indentured conveyance Box I; 28 January 1537; English; parchment; 2 sheets, both indented; larger sheet (indented at top): 385mm x 562mm (240mm x 435mm), smaller sheet (indented at top): 205mm x 145mm (125mm x 365mm); written on one side; two seals attached; endorsed in late 16th c hand: 'A Composicion betwen the Citie & the Craft of Cappers' (left outer fold), and 'A Composicion between the Citie And the Craft of Cappers' (right outer fold).

Carpenters' Account Book I

Coventry, City Record Office, Acc 3/1; 1446–77; Latin and English; paper; ii+137+i; variable sizes: majority: 220mm x 145mm, ff 1-28, 53-60: 195mm x 145mm (written area variable); collation irregular; modern foliation; no decoration; rebound 1968 in brown leather incorporating some of the original skin binding, parchment fragments used to strengthen former binding and old labels pasted inside cover; heavily damaged and repaired.

Carpenters' Account Book II

Coventry, City Record Office, Acc 3/2; 1478–1652; English; paper; vi+349+iii; 282mm x 203mm (written area variable); collation irregular (bifolia and whole sections sewn haphazardly into original gatherings to double size of MS); modern foliation (2 unnumbered leaves after f 107; f 396 probably out of place although in numerical sequence); no decoration; plain brown calf board binding replacing original limp leather cover after 1969 repair, leaves sewn on to bands laced into binding boards; heavily damaged, MS stripped and repaired in 1969, many edges crumbled away.

Drapers' Indenture

Coventry, City Record Office, Acc 468/D 11/Box 5 no. 429; 20 September 1583; English; parchment; single sheet indented; 44.5mm x 50.5mm (44.3mm x 50.5mm), turn up at bottom 3.5mm; 8 seals remain of the 9 men named in the document: Thomas Nycolls, Richard Barkr, Raffe Ioynar, Robart Letherbaroe, Iohn Riley, Michael Ioynar, Thomas Hawkes, and Anthony Berye (Henry Sewall missing).

Mercers' Account Book

Coventry, City Record Office, Acc/15; 1579–1829; English; paper; 420mm x 280mm (written area variable); being repaired and rebound 1978-9.

Shearmen and Tailors' Deed of Conveyance

Coventry, City Record Office, 100/37; 1 September 1590; Latin; parchment; 241mm x 450mm; originally 13 seals (4 missing); title in faded 17th c hand on dorse: 'A dead ⟨...⟩ company I of Skynners & Dyers ⟨..⟩ I Couentrie ⟨....⟩ ther pagen housse I to Tho: Wilks.'

Weavers' Ordinances
Coventry, City Record Office 34/1; 15th–17th c; English; parchment; 13 leaves; 280mm x 215mm
(written area variable); 1[7], 2[6] (with 3 stubs); modern foliation; opening capital 'I' decorated in
blue and red ink, red ink initial letters and line fillers in early ordinances; heavy parchment covers
with leather spine, stitch marks on right margin of first gathering indicate original binding position;
16th c order bound upside down (f 13), ff 10-12 blank.

Weavers' Account Book
Coventry, City Record Office, Acc 100/17/1; 1523–1634; English; paper; i+152; 340mm x 238mm
(written area variable); mainly gathered in 8's; modern foliation; no decoration; dark brown leather
binding, hooks but no straps remain, paper title on spine: 'WEAVERS ACCOUNT I BOOK I 1523/4 to
1634 I No. 11.'

Weavers' Rentgatherers' Book I
Coventry, City Record Office, Acc 100/18/1; 1521–83; English; paper; iv+88+iv; 315mm x
205mm; stripped for rebinding 1969; modern foliation; no decoration; original soft calf binding
extended during 1969 rebinding, title on spine: 'WEAVERS, 8'; extensively damaged at edges.

Weavers' Rentgatherers' Book II
Coventry, City Record Office, Acc 100/18/2; 1584–1645; English; paper; ii+121+i; 285mm x
194mm (written area variable); gathered in 12's; modern foliation; no decoration; original parchment binding much scribbled on and torn, now kept in hard cardboard binder under a band, title
pasted on spine: 'Weavers 9'; pages badly dog-eared.

Weavers' Deeds
Coventry, City Record Office, 100/37/1-4; 1434–1441; Latin; parchment; single membranes;
100/37/1: 104mm x 350mm (90mm x 350mm), 100/37/2: 112mm x 285mm (95mm x 285mm),
100/37/3: 150mm x 312mm, 100/37/4: 129mm x 302mm (115mm x 302mm); written on one
side only; decorated initial 'S,' deeds 100/37/3-4.

Corpus Christi Guild Account Book
Coventry, City Record Office, A 6; 1488–1553; Latin and English; paper; i+352+i; 400mm x
266mm; bound in 32s (several insertions and deletions); modern foliation; no decoration; rebound
early 20th c in brown leather-covered boards, tooled, with title stamped in gold on spine: 'Corpus
Christi & St Nicholas Guild Accounts Henry VII AD 1488 To 1st Mary AD 1553'; some repair.

Guild Records: Antiquarian

This section extends the view of guild activities drawn from surviving original records.
It moves from the complete transcription of the Drapers' Accounts beginning in
1523 through extracts of varying richness from guilds which were of the first
importance in the dramatic history of Coventry — the Smiths — to slight extracts

from those who had next to nothing to do with the Corpus Christi plays — the Butchers. Guild ordinances confirm the importance of Corpus Christi Day celebrations and other ceremonial occasions in their calendars.

AC Butchers' Accounts
Oxford, Bodleian Library, MS Top. Warwickshire c.7 (28857); 1829; English; paper; 205mm x 335mm; 231 leaves; booklets of varying length bound together; 19th c pagination (duplicate numbering of pp 23, 41, 71, 112, 157, 220); no decoration; marbled board binding with soft calf spine, no title. Collection by Reader.

AC Cappers' Accounts
Oxford, Bodleian Library, MS Top Warwickshire c.4 (28854); 1829; English; paper; 210mm x 335mm; i+233; booklets of varying length bound together (many inserts and paste-ons); 19th c ink pagination (1-316, omitting inserts) and pencil foliation (1-233, including inserts), both in upper right corner; no decoration; marbled board binding with soft calf spine, no title. Collection by Reader.

Washington, D.C., Folger Library, Wb 137-200 (Halliwell-Phillipps, Literary Scraps); 19th c; English; paper; viii+84 (each scrapbook; some volumes have pages cut out); 310mm x 180mm (written area variable); pagination by stamping machine, pages divided on both sides into double columns; each volume bound in red or blue half calf with matching marbled boards, series and volume titles stamped in gold on spine. Title page [ii]: LITERARY SCRAPS: I CUTTINGS FROM NEWSPAPERS, EXTRACTS, I MISCELLANEA, ETC. I 'They are abstracts and brief chronicles of the time ++++ To I show virtue her own feature, scorn her own image, and the very age and I body of the time his form and pressure.' I SHAKESPEARE I LONDON: I JOHN CAMDEN HOTTEN, 74 & 75 PICCADILLY.

The above description applies to the series, with the exception of Wb 145 and Wb 157, which have a different format, but contain no dramatic records. The volume numbers do not correspond with Halliwell-Phillipps' order of compilation and may have been added after his death in 1889; he referred to the volumes by individual (and often misleading) titles.

J.O. Halliwell-Phillipps, *Illustrations of the Life of Shakespeare in a Discursive Series of Essays on a Variety of Subjects Connected with the Personal and Literary History of the Great Dramatist.* pt 1 (London, 1874).

— *Outlines of the Life of Shakespeare.* 9th ed. 2 vols (London, 1890).

Sharp, *Dissertation.*

AC Cardmakers, Ironmongers, and Saddlers' Accounts
Oxford, Bodleian Library, MS Top. Warwickshire c.7. See under Butchers' Accounts above.

Drapers' Accounts
Coventry, City Record Office, Acc 154; mid-19th c transcript of 1534–1623 accounts; English; blue-lined exercise paper; 192 leaves; 345mm x 215mm; 16 fascicles with 12 leaves each; 19th c foliation (to f 194; mistake in numbering ff 66-9, no ff 67, 68); no decoration; no binding, preserved in paper envelopes. Transcribed by Daffern.

Drapers' Ordinance
Coventry, City Record Office, Acc 99/6/1; 18th c; English; paper; 32 leaves; 205mm x 145mm (written area variable); collation impossible; modern foliation; no decoration; unbound paper booklet; paper deteriorating through dampness.

Dyers' Accounts
Oxford, Bodleian Library, MS Top. Warwickshire c.7. See under Butchers' Accounts, p xlvi.

Sharp, *Dissertation.*

Shearmen and Tailors' Accounts
Oxford, Bodleian Library, MS Top. Warwickshire c.7. See under Butchers' Accounts, p xlvi.

Smiths' Accounts
Oxford, Bodleian Library, MS Top. Warwickshire c.7. See under Butcher's Accounts, p xlvi.

Halliwell-Phillipps' Folger Scrapbooks, *Illustrations,* and *Outlines.* See under Cappers' Accounts, p xlvi.

Sharp, *Dissertation.*

Coventry, City Record Office, Acc 251 (Daffern); 1866; English; paper; 155 pages; 205mm x 335mm; pagination by Daffern; no decoration; no cover.

Daffern transcribed accounts for 1684–1822 in this book, with some old ordinances dating from our period (p 142 ff). Rule 5 from one of these ordinances is included in Appendix 3.

Charles Nowell, 'The Reader Manuscripts in the Gulson Library,' abstracted, edited, and published in *The Coventry Herald.* Full article series ran 8 January 1926 – 15 November 1929.

Nowell was city librarian. The Gulson Library was the name of the central lending and reference library in Coventry. This series of articles was intended 'to make the contents of this collection [Reader MSS] more widely known, and to conserve the manuscripts as much as possible, to abstract from these volumes those records which have not, as yet, so far as can be ascertained, appeared in book form' (Nowell: Reader

MSS 8 January 1926, p 1). The articles appeared under the titles of the buildings, guilds, or city institutions which they dealt with. Wherever they are used in this volume, the form of reference will be as follows: 'Nowell: Reader MSS 15 October 1926.' The articles are now the chief source of information about Reader (the first five are from Reader's survey of his family and life) and his collections. They also contain unique copies of Reader's transcriptions, such as the 1534 entry from the Smiths' Accounts (see p 140).

AC Tanners' Ordinances
Coventry, City Record Office, Acc 241; early 20th c transcript of 1605–1742 ordinances; English; typed transcript on onion skin; 40 leaves; 253mm x 184mm; modern pagination, original foliation noted; kept in purple cloth-covered board binder.

AC Tilers' Ordinances
London, British Library, Harley 6466; 18th c; English; paper; iv+94+iv; 200mm x 120mm; collation impossible; 18th c pen and 20th c pencil foliation; no decoration; brown speckled calf binding tooled and stamped in gold on spine and front cover, identification stamped on spine: '6466 | PLUT. XXXVIII G | MUS BRIT | BIBL. HARL. | H. WANLEY | COLLECTANEA | MISCELLANEA.'

AC Holy Trinity Guild Accounts
Halliwell-Phillipps, Folger Scrapbooks.

Sharp, *Dissertation, Illustrative Papers.*

A Geoffrey Templeman (ed), *The Records of the Guild of the Holy Trinity, St. Mary, St. John the Baptist and St. Katherine of Coventry.* Vol 2, Publications of the Dugdale Society, 19 (Oxford, 1944).

Miscellaneous

Two events of ceremonial splendour, two of individual and unlooked-for dramatic significance, and one visitor's description of a popular play seemingly taken for granted in Coventry make up the selections in this volume. Richard II contrived the joust between Bolingbroke and Mowbray to be theatrical, and its splendour is finely caught by Holinshed. James I included Coventry in his royal progress in 1617. Foxe tells the most moving story of any of Coventry's actors, that of John Careles, who was released for one day from jail to act on Corpus Christi Day before returning to die in the Fleet. Walter Smythe is memorable only because his baptism coincided with a memorable play. Robert Laneham (almost certainly Robert Langham, courtier and mercer of London) gives one of the rare eyewitness accounts of a Tudor play in performance, in this case a famous but otherwise mysterious annual Coventry play.

Bolingbroke and Mowbray Joust at Coventry
THE I Third volume of Chronicles, be- I *ginning at duke William the Norman,* I commonlie called the Conqueror; and I *descending by degrees of yeeres to all the* I kings and queenes of England in their I orderlie successions: I **First compiled by Raphaell Holinshed,** I **and by him extended to the** I **yeare 1577.** I **Now newlie recognised, augmented, and** I **continued (with occurrences and** I **accidents of fresh memorie)** I **to the yeare 1586.** I **Wherein also are conteined manie matters** I **of singular discourse and rare obser=** I **uation, fruitfull to such as be** I **studious in antiquities, or** I **take pleasure in the** I **grounds of anci=** I **ent histories.** I With a third table (peculiarlie seruing I this third volume) both of I names and matters I memorable. I *Historiæ placeant nostrates ac peregrinæ.* [London, 1587]. STC 13569.

Jailed Weaver Released to Act
THE I seconde Volume I OF THE ECCLE- I siasticall Historie, conteining the I ACTS AND MONVMENTS I of Martyrs, with a Generall discourse of these I latter Persecutions, horrible troubles and tumultes, stiered vp I by Romish Prelates in the Church, with diuers other things I incident, especially to this Realme of Englande and I Scotland, as partly also to all other forreine na- I tions appertaining, from the time of King I HENRY the VIII. to Queene I ELIZABETH our gra- I cious Ladie nowe I raigning. I *Newly recognised and inlarged by the Authour* I *IOHN FOXE.* 1583. I [rule] I AT LONDON I Printed by Iohn Day, dwelling ouer Aldersgate. STC 11225.

Proof of Age of Walter Smythe
London, Public Record Office, C 142/46/45; 11 January 1528; Latin; parchment; single sheet bound into book with other single documents; 326mm x 585mm (305mm x 550mm, indented along top); 3 folio numbers: contemporary in left margin (45), 19th c (?) ink on binding strip outer corner (55), modern blue pencil on inner binding strip (45); large flourished characters at text opening; good condition, 2 small vertical slits mended with parchment patches to back.

Robert Laneham's Letter
A LETTER: I whearin, part of the entertain= I ment vntoo the Queenz Maiesty, I at Killingworth Castl, in Warwik Sheer I in this Soomerz Progress 1575. iz I signified: from a freend officer I attendant in the Coourt, vnto I hiz freend a Citizen, I and Merchaunt I of London. I DE REGINA NOSTRA ILLVSTRISSIMA. I *Dum laniata ruant vicina ab Regna tumultu:* I *Lata suos inter genialibus ILLA diebus,* I *Gratia Dijs fruitur: Rumpantur & ilia Codro.* (np, [1575]). STC 15191. Facsimile, *Robert Laneham: A Letter [1575],* A Scolar Press Facsimile (Menston, England, 1969).

Visit of King James I
John Nichols, *The Progresses, Processions, and Magnificent Festivities of King James the First, His Royal Consort, Family, and Court, Collected from Original Manuscripts, Scarce Pamphlets, Corporation Records, Parochial Registers, &c. &c. Comprising Forty Masques and Entertainments; Ten Civic Pageants; Numerous Original Letters; and Annotated Lists of the Peers, Baronets, and Knights, Who Received Those Honours during the Reign of King James.* Vols 1, 3 (London, 1828). Facsimile, Burt Franklin: Research and Source Works Series, no 118 (New York, nd).

Most of the Coventry references in this volume come from the city's records. Some of the expenses to do with the visit of James I in 1617, however, were communicated to Nichols by Thomas Sharp from civic papers now lost. These have been drawn upon (see pp 403-5).

Editorial Procedures

Principles of Selection

In the record office one harvests widely, aware of the editorial winnowing to come and, it may be, sharing the feelings of the Victorian antiquary John Carter, if not his phraseology: 'Few, I believe, know how smoothly the moments fly over the head of an antiquary. Lost to the common occurrences of life, he immerges deep into the stream of remote ages; and every subject dating its origin from such sources, emits a charm that never fades. With rapture he beholds, he comments, or he copies by his pencil's aid. Insensible of private concerns, he hears no discordant sounds, feels no piercing cold, and sees no lowering skies.... Confessing a frame of mind open to a sense like this, I was tempted, when, on a Sunday afternoon, while engaged in examining St. Mary's Tapestry, the psalmody from the neighbouring St. Michael's Church wafted its long-drawn notes, to turn awhile my reflections from the scene before me, to own their more impressive power. And even as the melody died on the yielding air, the heavy toll from far-off Bablake's passing bell filled up the vacant hymn.'[45] The excitement is not gone, but the heavy toll is that of choosing among the common occurrences of life in Coventry between 1392 and 1642.

Some decisions were made in 1879 and 1940, but not the clerical ones. The Reformation left no more awesome sign of its power upon manuscripts than in the virtual obliteration of the ecclesiastical records of the churches and priories of Coventry. From St Mary's Cathedral there is only a list of its sacred relics; from the Priory, three account rolls and some random papers and transcriptions. From the parish churches of St Michael's and Holy Trinity, scarcely more remains. Zealous Coventrians destroyed the registers of St Michael's in 1569 because they saw signs of popery in them (see p 247); others were accidentally burned in 1697 (see *Illustrative Papers*, p 50); nearly everything else was lost in 1940. From Holy Trinity, some churchwardens' accounts beginning in 1561 survive and a collection of miscellaneous notes and extracts from assorted church documents (the earliest dated 1463). From these I have taken some items concerning the sale of vestments — which may possibly have ended as players' costumes — and church affairs in Appendix 5 (pp 491-4). From the various chapels and other religious houses of the city, no account books or registers survive — unless one allows some fragmentary records of the Trinity guild, whose chapel was St John's Church.

With the exception of the Leet Book, which begins in 1421, most of the documents in the city record office at Coventry date from the sixteenth century. One very large body of earlier material, however, has survived but is not truly accessible: there are several thousand pre-seventeenth century deeds in the CRO, nearly two thousand of them fourteenth century and earlier (the collection is still being added to). The immense task of cataloguing these can be but a small part of the office's daily business; nonetheless, it goes ahead. I decided not to attempt the task myself nor to wait upon its completion by others. However, certain of the Weavers' and Drapers' deeds have been separated long ago, among them those dealing with their pageant houses, and these have been newly transcribed and edited.

The CRO provides enough information to locate nine pageant houses. Those of the Weavers, Shearmen and Tailors, Pinners, Cappers, and Girdlers all stood on the west side of Mill Lane, the first three next door to each other; the Smiths' pageant house stood on the east side. It is known only that the Whittawers' pageant house was situated in Hill Street. Those of the Mercers and Drapers were in Gosford Street (the Drapers' first pageant house had been in Little Park Street). Of the probable ten, this leaves only the Barkers' (Tanners') unplaced. Accounts for repairs and maintenance of these houses, where guild records survive, are included in this volume.

The most important and voluminous accounts included are those for the production and performance of the pageants themselves. Second to these are the records of the Corpus Christi Day processions and celebrations, and of the other religious, civic, and guild festal days. I have omitted, in recording these occasions, accounts of the healthy (or unhealthy) eating and drinking that accompanied such events. However, as an illustration of stamina, diet, and prices, examples are given in Appendix 7 of payments for an annual guild feast and for a civic banquet prepared for Princess Elizabeth in 1604. Generally, where waits, musicians, or minstrels (however that word may be interpreted) were paid for their services on such occasions, that payment is entered but not the other costs of the dinner, 'sowper,' or 'drynkyng' of which it was a part.

The processions themselves were clearly dramatic when they included pageants, *tableaux,* or 'a goodly Stage Play'; without such accompaniment (or without records of such accompaniment), they were themselves pageants in which the procession was, as it were, one body of actors watched by an audience in the streets. If the procession was one of welcome to royalty or a distinguished guest, the guests were a pageant within a pageant. The attraction and power of a grand parade is one of the few present-day links with Tudor life in England that we have, whether it be the brash jollity of a holiday occasion or the moving dignity of a state funeral. Where such processions are described in the Coventry records, where special care has been taken to make a show, I have recorded it.

Every officer of the city had a livery which marked his status and the dignity of the city, as did the regalia which were carried in civic processions.[46] Records of livery, from the market beadle's coat to the mayor's great fur hat with the red 'taffaty' lining, have been omitted. Exceptions have been made for early references and especially grand refurbishing (as in preparation for the visit of James I in 1617, see pp 403-5).

The city's armour could be used for martial show — as when the mayor would not proclaim Queen Jane and the city walls were manned — or for peaceable pageantry — as when the splendid unused armour collected in 1455 was happily available to dress the welcome given Queen Margaret in the next year (see pp 29-34).[47] Details of the city armourer's job and an inventory of the city's armour have been copied from the Council Book for 1589 (see pp 324-5). The other accounts testifying to the city's care to purchase weaponry and keep it in good order are largely omitted.

The guilds also owned armour; this was to 'harnes' their men 'Pur le Ridyng on Corpus christi day and for Watche on Midsomer even' (see p 16). Such armed men also took part in the armed Watch on St Peter's Eve, marched with the pageant wagons of their company, and turned out on all festival days. When order for a muster came, a guild would sometimes go to great expense to dress its men and display patriotism and commercial pride at once. The amount of armour which a guild owned, the number of men it sent to parade — they ranged from two to eight — are useful indicators of guild status. Items concerned with the marching of these men are always included in this volume.

Church bells rang daily and continually through the day in Coventry — marking time, remembering the dead, greeting birth, sounding joy, warning of danger — nearly all these bell-pealings have been excluded, as have the costs for tending the bells.

Selection from abundance is always difficult. These records are not basic materials for a social history, or an economic history, or a religious history of Coventry, and yet they would form a part of any such history. In trying to gather records of drama, music, and ceremonial, I have chosen to err on the side of inclusion rather than exclusion.

Dating

All the dates in this volume conform to a year that begins on 1 January, whereas the documents date by a calendar year that began on 25 March. This change means that the Cappers' inventory, for instance, which they date 'iiijth of marche 1566,' appears in this collection dated 4 March 1567.

The civic and guild calendars sort well with this arrangement. Until 1556, mayors were elected on 25 January and assumed office on 2 February (the day on which the lammas lands were opened to the citizens and, hence, an important day in their year). From 1556 on, the mayor usually assumed office on 1 November. The other city officers were chosen at the same time as the mayor, with the exception of the sheriffs, who were elected on 29 September. The chamberlains delivered their accounts in the last week of October, the wardens theirs at the end of November or the beginning of December.

The mayoralty was closely connected with the two great religious guilds, for only a former master of the Holy Trinity guild was eligible to become mayor, and two years after holding that office, he usually became master of the Corpus Christi guild. These guilds, accordingly, elected their masters toward the end of the year: Holy Trinity on 18 October, Corpus Christi on 8 December.

The cloth trades elected in high summer and delivered their accounts at the end of the year. From 1521, the Cappers began to elect on 7 August; before that the masters were chosen on 26 July. They delivered their accounts in late December, usually St Stephen's Day; as with all guilds, the space between the end of the masters' year and the delivery of their accounts was needed to put those accounts into order. The Weavers elected on 25 July and usually delivered accounts on 23 January at their chief annual feast. The Fullers, like the Dyers, delivered accounts on 23 November and presumably elected in summer. In 1478, the Smiths rendered their accounts on 23 November but by the mid-sixteenth century changed to early January;[48] under Midsummer expenses for 1587 for the company, Sharp notes a payment of three-pence 'for bowes & flowers for our metynge house at þe day of the election of the new masters' (*Dissertation,* p 180). Those other guilds whose dates are known clustered their elections at the end of the year. In sequence they are: Tanners, Tuesday after Michaelmas; Cordwainers, 9 October; Butchers, 18 October (inaugural feast); Tilers, 26 December; Mercers, 27 December; Cardmakers, 29 December; and Drapers, 31 December (occasionally New Year's Day). The accounts of the Mercers were ordained to be handed in by Lady Day in Lent, those of the Drapers by 24 March. This pattern was likely followed by the other guilds in this group.

Such is the general framework into which the documents in this volume ask to be fitted. Legal papers such as leases, conveyances, deeds, court inquiries into attested age, and appointments usually are carefully dated. The orders in the Leet Book are clearly dated by the two annual leet courts, held at Easter and at Michaelmas. Miscellaneous notes, letters, and memoranda are dated with varying degrees of exactitude. The account books of the guilds present most of the dating problems in this volume.

The perspective offered by the chronological march of those complete accounts which we have, whether original or in antiquarian copy, is not easily won and is never totally or absolutely clear. Commercial man has always relished dates; money is lent for a fixed period, rents are due at given times, accounts are looked for at regular intervals. The Weavers and the Drapers were commercial men, and their accounts are firmly chronological. They are not, however, steady and continuous, and in some places they turn so awry as to defy absolute charting. The accounts abound with indications of *Anno Domini,* regnal years, mayoral years; days are fixed by a wide range of traditional holidays, religious festal days, and saints' days. Nonetheless, years are omitted, consecutive annual accounts are entered at widely separated places, some accounts are not dated, some are manifestly wrongly dated, and those that use most or all of the dating mechanisms available often offer only a choice of conflicting dates.

This is, unfairly, to look upon the darkest side first. The dates for many documents are clearly given or may be deduced with little difficulty. Where there is no date given but one can be deduced, that date is given and the evidence for it placed in an endnote. Where there is suspicion about the written date, the given date is accepted and the questions raised by it are also dealt with in an endnote. The commonest causes of dating problems may be briefly stated:

a) slip of memory on the accountant's part
b) slip of pen, confusing 'x' and 'v,' wrong number of minims
c) confusion of regnal year / mayoral year
d) omission of year(s) in account. Very occasionally this can be explained by the loss of leaves from a manuscript, as in the Weavers' accounts for 1525 and 1526, but generally there is no explanation. Presumably the accounts were entered elsewhere or in another way. Accountants were dependent upon bills, receipts, etc; the wardens' favourite device was 'as by a bill appeareth,' the bill apparently accompanying the account but not retained. In 1575, the Cheylesmore Manor Account Book mentions 'a booke of the partyculers therof & examyned vppon thys accompte' (p 80). Such evidence must lie also behind those accounts which consist simply of a receipts and expenses listing (and those which bring the pageant expenses together under a single figure, for example, 1524, Weavers, p 122; 1574, Drapers, p 269).
e) entering accounts at random rather than in a chronological sequence. Accountants liked to leave empty leaves and return to fill them later.

In the face of such puzzles, any certitude found is welcome. Only once have I come upon it in so welcome a form as in the Weavers' Rentgatherers' Book I: 'Thys ys the a covnpt of Iohan locoke and wyllyam dale Rentt gaderes of the wevers craft of covyntre of all there Resayts and payments for the spase of a yere that ys to saye frome the ffeyst of saynt Iames the apostell to the tyme that a holl yere be complyt & made s [sic] in saynt nycollas hall the xxiij day of Ienyvere in the xiiij yere of the Raynge of kyng henre the viij^th ' (f 4).

The Cappers' Accounts exhibit the most common problems of dating. The nature of this rich source of material I have touched upon earlier (see p xliii). The opening sequence of accounts is so resistant to orderly dating that it has been dealt with outside the main text as Appendix 1 (see pp 449-54). The constitutions and ordinances of the company were confirmed by the mayor at his leet held on 9 October 1520: masters were to be elected on 7 August and to render their account on 25 December (LB, p 670). The straightforwardness of ordinances is not often reflected in the company's adherence to them (see Drapers' Accounts in Appendix 2, pp 455-60). Only after the hiatus of 1556–71 are the annual accounts dated as being delivered as near the agreed date as possible — St Stephen's Day, 26 December. The last three entries before the great book was abandoned also carried dates: the account covering 1552–3 was delivered on 10 January 1554, that for 1553–4 on 13 January 1555, and that for 1554–5 on 12 January 1556. Halliwell-Phillipps' extracts from the other account book show that the movement toward a later January delivery continued; he noted that the accounts for 1563 were delivered on 24 January 1564, those for 1566 on 21 January 1567, and those for 1569 on 26 January 1570. The change to December probably came in 1571 because he noted that the accounts for that year were delivered in 1571.

This detailed introduction serves to illustrate what was generally the Cappers' mode of handling their annual accounts. The usual heading to an annual account — before 1554 — was the names of the masters, the regnal year, and the name of the mayor, with no indication whether this year was that of the election of the masters or of the presentation of their accounts. Only twice is this pattern broken, in the two years following the leet's confirmation of the company ordinance; additionally, both these entries have untypical headings — only the masters' names and the comment that they made their accounts on 14 January 1521 and on 3 February 1522 respectively.

Thus a pattern is set, but unfortunately one which does not solve the problem of the plague's effects on the performance of the Corpus Christi cycle in the mid-1540s. The Cappers did not act their play in 1545 and 1546. The only other original company records — the Weavers' — place the break in 1546 and 1547 (see endnote to Cappers' Records p 170 on p 568). If the dates on the Cappers' headings were taken as the years of election, not of delivery, the companies would agree on a break in 1546 and 1547.

The change of accounting patterns has been mentioned several times; the chief puzzle is, why the change? A lesser one is that while I date the hiatus in the Cappers' Accounts as between 1556 and 1571, this strictly bends the facts. In the great account book there are two brief notes, the one dated 20 February 1568 and the other ⟨..⟩ February 1570, before the regular accounts of the company are entered again in 1572. The note dated 20 February is the beginning of an account that stops after nine names have been entered on a quarterage (?) roll call. There are four empty leaves before the 1572 accounts commence.

The interrupted entry of accounts and their occasional omission are curious. The account dated 14 January 1521 follows one that was dated 12 Henry VIII. For some unknown reason the masters in that year had received the company's money and marks of office not from the masters serving in 11 Henry VIII but from those in office in 10 Henry VIII (as the account book specifically says, f 22). The account for 11 Henry VIII is only referred to in passing, as it were, the briefest fragment of its opening being given. This is not the only instance of oblique reference to a break in the run of accounts. At folio 51, after the presentation of the accounts dated 28 Henry VIII, folio 51v is left blank, and the next account is dated 32 Henry VIII. The sequence carries on until folio 85v, where, after the account for 1 Mary, those for 30 Henry VIII and 31 Henry VIII are written out. A note to the latter reads: 'Item Resseyvyd of Thomas Sanderes for hys a cont that he suold thawe brothe in to Rychard Wyghtman and Iohn Ston xv s' (f 89). Because Wyghtman and Ston were the masters in 30 Henry VIII, this comment presumably refers to the missing account for 29 Henry VIII. Whether Saunders (who was mayor in 1543) was paying a fine for bringing in his account late (it is nowhere written up in the extant book), or for neglecting to bring one in at all, is unclear.

These problems are exacerbated when the antiquarian transcriptions are considered. From the original accounts one may, in difficult cases, find clues to the solution of dating problems in the sequence of entries (though not a certainty, it is a guide), the occurrence of spaces showing where the accountant has left normal foliation, the scribe's hand, and all the incidental clues supplied by the whole account as against only the pageant and other festive/ceremonial expenses isolated from the rest of the annual account. With antiquarian copies, there is also the possibility that the transcriber has erred in his work. Where two or more have worked on the same text, a comparison may reveal a safe choice of readings or dates. This is often the case when Halliwell-Phillipps and Sharp can be compared.

Confusion of year of delivery with year of accountancy is the chief obstacle. The most obvious example of this occurs in Sharp's quotation of the Smiths' agreement with Colclow that he 'shull have þe Rewle of þe pajaunt.' It was, said Sharp, 'made in 1452'; he then quoted the agreement which was reached 'on munday next befor palme sonday Anno Henry (6th) xxxj. [1453]' (p 15). Henry's regnal years were 1 September – 31 August; Sharp took the start of the regnal year as the dating device, even when the document itself, as he noted, contradicted this. At other times, the contradiction lies between Sharp's dating of an event in the Smiths' Accounts and its appearance in another document which he was aware of: the costs of welcoming Prince Edward of York in 1461 he dated 1460 (*Dissertation*, p 152), although he referred to the Leet Book's notice of the same visit (LB, pp 312-20). Similarly, Sharp dated the costs of welcoming Queen Margaret in 1455 one year earlier than the visit (see pp 29-35).

Sharp's disagreeements with Halliwell-Phillipps are of a similar kind; he dated an account one year earlier than did the latter. Halliwell-Phillipps gave regnal dates for eleven of the extracts he made from the Smiths' Accounts between 1450 and 1499, delivered on 23 November (1450–1, 1471, 1477–9, 1488–9, 1493, 1495, 1499). Sharp gave dated items for eight of these years (he had none for 1479 or 1493). On three occasions he agreed with Halliwell-Phillipps — 1477, 1478, 1489. In 1451, there was some discrepancy (see endnote p 546), and for the other four, his dates were one year behind Halliwell-Phillipps. This is irritating 'proof' of dating; all one can certainly say is that Sharp sometimes dated by the year of accountability and sometimes he did not.

Sharp and Reader are especially confusing about dates when discussing the

Midsummer Watch. The original documents that survive agree that it was last kept in 1561. In his *Dissertation,* Sharp remarked the Smiths' use of 'waytts' on this occasion in 1545, 1559, and 1562, 'after which time the Watch ceased' (p 199). Two pages later, he recorded an expense incurred by the Dyers' celebrations of this Watch dated 1563, adding: 'In the following year only two Armed Men were set out on Midsummer Night, and this appears to have been the last time the Watch was kept on that evening' (p 201). Matters are not clarified by Reader. He dated the Butchers' entry 'pd for harnessyng vj men on Mydsom*er* evyn ij s' (see p 219) as 1562 (Sharp, p 194, dated the same item 1563). Nothing is straightforward.

Two general comments must be made. First, the companies, denied the traditional summer parades such as Corpus Christi, marched — on not quite so grand a scale — for the official opening of the Trinity Fair, 'feyr fryday.' According to Reader, the Butchers were doing this before any other company and while they were still marching in the Midsummer Watch (see pp 216, 219). Second, unlike the pageants which ended suddenly, catching the companies by surprise as it were, the Midsummer celebrations tended to fade away in the final years before they were done away with altogether. Nonetheless, surviving account books do not mention any Midsummer celebration after 1561; those of the antiquarians, however self-contradictory, do. Rather than weave a misleadingly chronological pattern, I have left the antiquarian entries to do with this matter unaltered.

Where only the dates of a single transcriber are available, they must be accepted; but there is an exception to this rule also. Sharp's items for 1498 are changed to 1499, and those of 1499 to 1500, to match Halliwell-Phillipps' items: this in turn has meant changing Sharp's items for 1500 to 1501, although his are the only ones given for that year, because they must belong to an account that follows the one he dated 1499. These I must assume were two separate accounts from which Sharp was working. This argument must lead one to alter his dates, of course; however, where a year's gap occurs, I revert to Sharp's dates because there is only surmise, no matter how strong, as a basis for change. And surmise must also face Sharp's own changing attitude toward dates. After 1500, on the few occasions where the two can be compared, Sharp's and Halliwell-Phillipps' dates match — with two inevitable exceptions in 1544 and 1553, where Sharp falls one year behind Halliwell-Phillipps again.

Unless a choice is made between 'rival' dates, items must be entered twice under consecutive years, and this only adds confusion to confusion. As an editor must choose, I have chosen to follow Halliwell-Phillipps' dates, because he was more often right than Sharp, took more care with dates, and explained why he used particular dates and how they derived sometimes from seemingly contradictory evidence. Inevitably, he was not always strict in following his own rules for dating; he dated an extract in his notes 1479 and printed it as 1480. He printed an item from the Smiths' Accounts dated 1440, an impossibility on the face of it, as their accounts date from 1449, but not necessarily wrong (see comments on the Drapers' Accounts which 'date' from 1534, pp 455-6); interestingly enough, he followed (or copied)

Sharp in offering this item (see endnote to *Dissertation* on p 546). How far these may have been typographical errors cannot be said. The choice lies between the almost certainly right and the very probably wrong; the last verdict must be 'not proven' but that cannot be so entered in this collection.

Layout

Each entry is preceded by a heading with year, MS or book identification, and folio or page number; antiquarian sources are noted in the margin as either Antiquarian Compilations (A) or Antiquarian Collections (AC). Italics indicate information supplied by the editor. Where documents from different MSS appear under the same year, they follow the sequence established in the Documents section of the Introduction.

I have attempted to preserve the general layout of the MS originals. Headings, marginalia, and account totals are printed in the approximate position in which they appear in the MSS. Totals are always included for complete accounts, but only occasionally with partial extracts, when the 'som*m*' appears below the excerpt in the MS and can give some idea of its cost relative to a year's expenses. In guild and civic accounts, however, it is not unusual for a 'som*m*' to be miscalculated by pennies, shillings, or even pounds; I have not corrected such errors where they occur. Right hand marginalia have had to be set in the left margin of the text, but this transposition is indicated by the symbol ® . The lineation of the original has not been retained in continuous prose passages.

Emendations and scribal errors are noted at the foot of the page. Also noted there are readings made by earlier editors or transcribers of words and phrases now obliterated. Peculiarities of MSS (such as decay or damage that affects the reading), scribal idiosyncrasies, and problems of dating are discussed more extensively in the endnotes.

Punctuation

The punctuation of the MSS has been retained. Virgules have been indicated as / and //. MS braces have not been reproduced unless they are a significant feature of the MS layout. Diacritics used to distinguish 'y' from 'þ' and 'u' from 'n' and line-fillers have been omitted.

Spelling, Capitalization, and Expansion

The spelling and capitalization of the original MSS have been preserved. 'ff' has been retained for 'F'; the standard and elongated forms of 'I' have been uniformly transcribed as 'I.' Ornamental or very large capitals in all MSS have been transcribed as regular capitals. Where it has been difficult to tell whether a letter is upper or lower case, I have opted for the lower case form.

Abbreviated words have been expanded according to scribal practice, with italics to indicate letters supplied. Where there is insufficient evidence in the MS to judge individual scribal spelling habits, abbreviations in Latin have been expanded to standard classical forms and in English to modern British forms. Abbreviations still in common use (eg, 'Mr,' 's,' 'd,' 'lb,' 'etc' or '&c,' and 'viz') and ones cumbersome to expand, such as those typical of weights and measures ('ob'), have been retained. Generally, a *punctus* is supplied where there is some sign of abbreviation in the MS. 'ꝯ,' 'Xp' have been expanded as 'chr*ist*' and 'Chr*ist*'; 'Ihs' as 'Ie*sus*.' The sign ℣ has been consistently expanded as 'es' in the English records. Otiose flourishes such as those found in ꝉꝉand ouꝊ have been ignored.

English words in Latin passages have not been declined. Place names, personal names, and surnames have only been expanded to normal spelling where that is ascertainable. All superlineated letters have been lowered to the line except when they are used with numerals (eg, x°, xxiijᵗⁱ).

Antiquarian Editing

The strict rules of conservative editing have not been applied to the antiquarian excerpts. This is because these men had particular idiosyncrasies that, at times, are such that following them would be adding their style to that of the original scribe. Thus, when Halliwell-Phillipps was concerned with a particular topic, the excerpts he chose to illustrate it were sometimes decorated with underlinings indicating which word or phrase he was interested in. For instance, in collecting items about the Devil as a character, he quoted the Smiths' account for 1561, 'Item, for pwynttes for the deman,' and underlined 'deman' seven times (see p 218, l. 9). His next illustration came from the 1488 accounts and was headed 'Devil' underlined, although of the four costs he listed, only the fourth had to do with his topic (see p 69, l. 25). It is a feature found in Sharp also (eg, pp 132, 179, etc). Such additions to the text have been removed. Halliwell-Phillipps also automatically adds periods and underlinings for italics in recording costs (ie, 'ij.s̲ iiij.d̲.'), where the customary scribal form in the surviving records would be 'ij s iiij d.' The costs have been printed in the simple form; again, this applies to Sharp's figures.

Brevigraphs have been expanded only where the manuscript transcript or the printed extract clearly indicates them. There is no system whereby the brevigraphs are printed in the *Dissertation,* and a variety of printed signs is used, whether at Sharp's whim or his printer's cannot be told. The end result is that 'Itm' is so printed in this volume whereas 'It'm' is expanded as 'It*em*.'

Where one antiquarian's transcriptions have been chosen over another's, substantive variants from the source omitted are given in the textual footnotes. For explanation of the methods of selecting antiquarian base texts, see the discussion in 'Coventry Antiquarians,' pp xxvii-xxx.

Notes

1 There is a brief demographic history of the city in the *Victoria History of the County of Warwick,* vol 8, pp 4-5 (hereafter cited as VCH *Warks,* vol 8). Charles Phythian-Adams' *Desolation of a City* (hereafter referred to only by its title) opens with 'An Urban Panorama' which discusses Coventry's population in relation to other leading towns and sets out Coventry's regional economic importance in firm detail (pp 7-30). See also 'Rankings of Provincial Towns, 1334–1861,' in W.G. Hoskins, *Local History in England* (London, 1959), 176-8. Hoskins treats the matter more fully in *Provincial England: Essays in Social and Economic History* (London, 1963), 68-85. Using the lay subsidy figures of 1523–7 as a base, he ranks Norwich, Bristol, Coventry, Exeter, and Salisbury in that order after London, whose population he computes at c 60,000. He thinks Norwich the only city that exceeded 10,000, possibly reaching 12,000/ 12,500. He suggests for Bristol 9,500/10,000; for Exeter and Salisbury 8,000. An actual but special figure of 6,601 is available for Coventry, deriving from a census taken during a dearth of 1520 (see Mary Dormer Harris, *The Coventry Leet Book* [hereafter cited as LB], pp 674-5). A little before this, on 21 December 1507, Princess Mary was betrothed to Charles, grandson of the Holy Roman Emperor Maximilian. The leading English noblemen and the most important cities and towns in the kingdom were made to stand security for the forfeit payable should the contract be broken. Coventry's stature is marked by its position in the list circulated by the court: London, York, Coventry, Norwich, Exeter, Chester, Worcester, Bristol, Hull, and Newcastle (see LB, pp 609-18). In the *Acts of Privy Council,* ns, vol 2 (1547–50) (London, 1890), 193-5, is a letter dated 6 May 1548, asking that the merchant lands be handed over to the city which otherwise would fall into utter decay; already, it is claimed, the population has fallen to between 11,000/12,000 (an exaggeration to add to the plea's urgency).

2 De Limesey's greed was notorious; he not only robbed the Priory estate for his own ends, but took from the Cathedral itself, scraping silver worth 500 marks from one beam alone (see M.D. Harris, *Life in an Old English Town,* pp 22-3, and Joan C. Lancaster, 'Coventry,' *The Atlas of Historic Towns,* vol 2, p 3).

3 See M.D. Harris, *Life in an Old English Town,* pp 66-8. In 1301, the bishop of Coventry was accused of worshipping the devil who appeared in the shape of a goat (see VCH *Warks,* vol 8, pp 208-10).

4 The charters around which the argument swirls are conveniently collected by A.A. Dibben in *Coventry City Charters*, The Coventry Papers, no 2 (Coventry, 1969). One further charter is recorded by R.H.C. Davis and Robert Bearman, 'An Unknown Coventry Charter,' *EHR*, 86 (1971), 533-47. Davis' is the most recent and cogent survey of the arguments (and the one followed here); it is found in 'The Early History of Coventry,' *Dugdale Society Occasional Papers*, no 24 (Oxford, 1976). Previous views can be found in M.D. Harris, *Life in an Old English Town*, the plainest statement of the traditional view in what is still the best overall history of the city; Joan C. Lancaster, 'The Coventry Forged Charters: a Reconsideration,' *BIHR*, 27 (1954), 113-40 and 'Coventry,' pp 1-7; 'The City of Coventry,' *VCH Warks*, vol 8, pp 1-3; P.R. Coss, 'Coventry before Incorporation; a Re-interpretation,' *Midland History*, 2 (1974), 137-51; and Diane K. Bolton, 'Social History to 1700,' *VCH Warks*, vol 8, pp 208-10. The 'tripartite indenture' was the final agreement reached between the mayor, the prior, and the queen and firmly recognized that authority in Coventry belonged essentially to the mayor and his brethren.

5 *LB*, p xxiv; see also *Desolation of a City*, pp 118-24.

6 See notes on the format of the Leet Book, pp xxxi-xxxii. Unfortunately no standard procedure is followed in decisions about or details of civic plays and pageantry. For example, the gathering of money for the visit of Edward IV in 1461 is mentioned but not the welcoming pageant(s) set out to greet him (see p 40).

7 Details of Rastell's career can be found in A.W. Reed, *Early Tudor Drama*, pp 1-8. His father-in-law was Sir Thomas More; the latter's adventure with a contentious friar at Coventry c 1508 is discussed on pages 224-9 of Reed's book. See also C.R. Baskervill, 'John Rastell's Dramatic Activities,' *MP*, 13 (1916), 557-60.

8 The complete story of the preacher's exhortation was published in a collection of *A. C Mery Talys* (1526), sigs Dii-Diiv by John Rastell. Although the story was a local Warwickshire one, its publication in a generally circulated book is one more indication of the national fame of Coventry's plays.

9 For a summary of the arguments that there were once more than ten plays in the cycle and the question of whether there were Old Testament plays in Coventry's cycle, see Hardin Craig, *English Religious Drama of the Middle Ages* (Oxford, 1955), 284-94. Craig's earlier and slightly different thoughts on this matter, together with a list of possible play topics, can be found in *Two Coventry Corpus Christi Plays*, pp xi-xix.

10 See endnotes to *Dissertation* pp 8, 11-12 on pages 542 and 583-4.

11 In the introduction to his EETS edition of the *Two Coventry Corpus Christi Plays* (pp xxvi-xxvii, xxxv-xxxviii), Hardin Craig deals at length and very severely with Crow's shortcomings as a poetic technician. Crow's abilities as a working playwright are proved by the naturalness of the play as a stage-piece. The question of revisions is looked at in my article ' "To find the players and all that longeth therto": Notes on the Production of Medieval Drama in Coventry,' *The Elizabethan Theatre V*, G.R. Hibbard (ed) (Toronto, 1975), 17-44.

2 Sharp, quoting from Dugdale's autograph *Antiquities*, inserted by him as the first of his 'Additional Illustrations' to his *Dissertation* (p 219). Although the rewards to actors scarcely change in any of the guilds from the first records to the last, it should be remembered that no such financial stability obtained in everyday living. The annal CRO: A 28, for instance, records under 1550: 'The first fall of money from a shillinge to nyne pence and from a grote to iij d. The second fall of money from nyne pence to sixe pence, And from three pence to twoo pence, & from ij d to a half peny ...' (f 35 col a). See *Desolation of a City, passim*, especially the table of harvest prices, page 56.

3 Other breaks in continuity cannot be definitely explained: in 1545 and 1546 the Cappers did not perform their pageant; in 1546 and 1547 the Weavers did not perform; in 1551 the Cappers and in 1552 the Weavers did not perform. The dates point to a lock-step that ought to be resolved but how I do not know. The Drapers' Accounts are of little help, as all these dates fall within their period of conflicting dates. It is known that there was a bad plague outbreak in the provinces in the middle to late 1540s (see Charles Creighton, *A History of Epidemics in Britain*, with additional material by D.E.C. Eversley, E. Ashworth Underwood, and Lynda Ovenall, vol 1 [New York, 1965], 302-3). There are two years when the Drapers do not present pageant expenses. One may be 1545; the other, for no very clear or convincing reason, is headed 1551 (possibly by the transcriber?). The Carpenters' records for 1544, 1545, and 1546 are missing. The whole seems contrived to mystify. See Cappers' Records p 170 and endnote p 568.

4 Walter Smythe, whose birth date was in question, was later murdered by his wife according to M.D. Harris (*Story of Coventry*, p 296). Hardin Craig remained firm in his belief that St Christian was an error for St Katherine (*Two Coventry Corpus Christi Plays*, p xxi, fn 5). Certainly she was a saint specially venerated in Coventry, but this is not sufficient proof to change a name.

5 Hock Tuesday celebrates either the great defeat of the Danes on 13 November 1002, or the death of Harthacnut on 8 June 1042, which removed a powerful and hated overlord. The latter suits the time of the celebration (Tuesday after Easter Sunday), although the women's legendary part in the battle of 1002 better suits their role in Coventry's Hock Tuesday play. Hocktide was, in any case, a nationally known festival, when first the men, on Hock Monday, had the rule and then the women, on Hock Tuesday, held sway. Sharp's discussion (pp 130-2) is still to the point. The general nature of Hocktide is discussed in A.R. Wright, *British Calendar Customs: England*, T.E. Lones (ed), Publications of the Folk-Lore Society, vol 97 (1936; rpt Kraus, 1968), 124-8. Warwickshire celebrations of the festival are treated in R. Palmer, *The Folklore of Warwickshire* (London, 1976), 102 and, more interestingly, 158-9. Some provocative suggestions about the relationship between Hocktide in Coventry and in Warwickshire and Shakespeare are made by F.V. Morley in 'The Impersonal Hamlet,' *University of Arizona Bulletin Series*, 30, no 5 (July, 1959), 7-22.

6 Cox appears in no surviving civic or guild records. The appointment of 'iiij ale Tastor*es*

in eu*ery* warde,' whose task it was at all times to 'gooe to the bruers howse and tast ther ale & se that it be abull' and to make sure that full measure was always given was agreed at the leet held on 8 October 1521 (*LB*, pp 677-8). For details of the performance see pp 272-5 and endnote p 581.

17 Probably the same man who was one of the signatories to the Shearmen and Tailors' Deed of Conveyance of 1590 (see pp 328-31).

18 See Murray, *English Dramatic Companies 1558–1642*, vol 2, pp 94-5.

19 In his edition of the *Liber Niger Scaccarii E Codice* (vol 2, p 595), Thomas Hearne prints extracts from 'a kind of Legger booke' in Christ's Hospital, Abingdon, written by Francis Little (an ex-mayor) in 1627. They concern a feast kept by the Fraternity of the Holy Cross in Abingdon during the reign of Henry VI, at which 'they had also Twelve Minstrells, some from Coventre, and some from Maydenhith, who had two shillinges three pence apeece, besides theyre dyet and horsemeat' (vol 2, p 598). This may possibly be dated 1445, the only year mentioned in the accounts of this feast. Whether Coventry's waits were among the minstrels cannot be known. The reward for performance is very high. There are other than dramatic and musical links between the two places, for the Coventry cross set up in 1541 was, by contract, to be modelled after that at Abingdon.

  J.R. Holliday prints extracts from a collection of miscellaneous computi, rentals, charters, etc, of Maxstoke Priory concerning minstrels and players from Coventry between 1431–58 in 'Maxstoke Priory,' *Transactions, Excursions and Reports of the Birmingham and Midland Institute, Archaeological Section*, 5 (1878), 91-3.

20 Lawrence Southerne, *Fearefull Newes from Coventry, or a True Relation and Lamentable Story of One Thomas Holt of Coventrey a Musitian: Who Through Covetousnesse and Immoderate Love of Money, Sold Himselfe to the Devill, with Whom He Had Made a Contract for Certaine Yeares. And Also of His Most Lamentable End and Death, on the 16. Day of February. 1641. To the Terror and Amazement of the Inhabitants Thereabouts* (London: John Thomas, 1642), *STC* 4753. Holt's 'fearefull newes' of music in Coventry might be balanced by that of 'Wm Vyott a mynstrall yn Coventre,' 'a mynstral both curtess and [kynd].' 'With a gud mynd' he gave a neighbouring canon what is now a MS poetry collection in the Bodleian (Douce 302, Summary Catalogue 21876). See *A Selection of English Carols*, Richard Leighton Greene (ed) (Oxford, 1962), pp 178-9.

21 Sharp, *Illustrative Papers*, p 164.

22 See VCH *Warks*, vol 8, p 32. For a detailed history of the grammar school, see VCH *Warks*, vol 2, pp 318-29; the matter of the singing school is dealt with on pages 324-5. Bablake College of St John's became city property after the dissolution, and in 1560 a 'Boys' Hospital' was added (VCH *Warks*, vol 2, p 329; vol 8, p 139). In the 1581 survey of rentals, the singing school that was part of St John's (ie, Bablake) is described: 'There ys in St Iohnes Singing schoole vij Panes of glasse and on Casement. And there ys Seat*es* & benches round a boute the same. There ys. also A Bell in the steeple' (CRO: A 24, p 71).

In 1534, the mayor and council decided that the too-regular payments during the year to the city's officers for livery were a feather-bedding of the latter's wages. However, their encroachment on this 'sacred' right at Easter was obviously so strenuously opposed that the Michaelmas leet restored the old ways (see pp 138-9).

For instance, the Dyers' rules of 1515, renewed in 1579, required that 'Every member shall be ready to give attendance on Midsummer night to fetch the Under-Master from his house, and from thence to go to the Head Master's house, there to take such things as shall be provided and afterwards attend upon both Masters before the Mayor and his brethren, to keep the King's watch; penalty, 13 s. 4 d.' (Nowell: Reader MSS 15 October 1926, p 33). Similar attendance and livery rules can be found — for the Weavers, pp 26-7; for the Drapers, p 460; for the Smiths, p 484; and for the Tilers, pp 484-5.

Companies took care to arrange matters of precedence within their own membership also: the 'ancient customs, precedents, and records' of the Cordwainers were renewed by the 'most ancient men of the said fellowship, together with the whole consent of the same' in 1577. One among them reads: 'Every member of the company residing in St. Michael's Parish, shall decently come every Sunday morning and evening to their seats in the same church, at or before the first lesson be read; the younger men to place themselves on the nethermost seat, every man according to his seniority' (Nowell: Reader MSS 7 January 1927, p 41).

The 'casual deaths' that such hot-blooded gatherings too easily provoked were no idle exaggeration on the prior's part. The Aylesford annal (CRO: Catalogue of Private Accessions, 351) records for 1448: 'vpon Corpus Christi evyn was a fray betwene syr vmfray Stafford and Syr Robert harecourt and sir vmfreys son Richarde and eyre was slayne with mony other on bothe partes.' In 1456, while Henry VI was holding parliament in the city, there was 'a gret affray ... bytwene þe Duke of Somerset men and þe wechemen of þe toun, and ij or iij men ʾof the tounʾ were kylled þere' (*Paston Letters and Papers*, N. Davis [ed], part 2 [Oxford, 1976], letter 567, 164-5). Mary Dormer Harris, *The Story of Coventry*, p 287.

See C. Phythian-Adams, 'Ceremony and the Citizen: the Communal Year at Coventry 1450–1550,' *Crisis and Order in English Towns 1500–1700: Essays in Urban History*, Peter Clark and Paul Slack (eds) (London, 1972), 57-85.

Sharp's method was followed and refined with excellent authority by F.M. Salter, *Mediaeval Drama in Chester* (Toronto, 1955). Further details of Sharp's life may be found in the *DNB* and the obituary in *The Gentleman's Magazine*, ns 16 (1841), 436-8. The Birmingham Central Reference Library catalogue for 1875–9 records large Coventry collections. Among 'Manuscripts Relating to Coventry' are listed:

> Antiquities, Mayors, Sheriffs, etc., of Coventry, fol., 1352, etc.
> Burton (H.) Miscellaneous Coventry Collections, fol., 1621, etc.
> Cappers' Company, Accounts of the, 5th to 14th Eliz., fol., N.D.
> ...

Coventry Sheremen and Taylors Pageants, Vellum, fol., 15th Cent.
Dyers' Company, Accounts of the, Rules, Orders, etc., 1432, 2
fol., 1785.

...

Laws of St. Mary's Gild, with List of Brethren, Possessions, etc.,
fol., 1279, etc. [The Register (1340? – c 1450) turned out not to
have been in the library and was purchased by Coventry Corporation in 1923. It was edited by M.D. Harris for the Dugdale Society,
Publications, 13 (Oxford, 1935).]

...

Registrum Chartarum Prior de Coventre, 2 4to, ?1446.
Sharp (T.) Transcripts of and Extracts from Original Documents,
fol.
Sharp (T.) Coventry Collections, 3, fol.
Smiths' Company, Accounts of the, 1449, etc., 2 fol., 1681.

...

Coventry Collections, MSS. and Printed, 4to.

...

Collectanea de Antiquit Coventriae, 4to.
History of St. Mary's, Coventry, fol.
Trinity Gild, Accounts of the, 2 fol., 1457–1548.

Among MSS destroyed in 1940 were:

Drapers' Company, Ordinances and Accounts, 1523–1764.
Tanners' Company, Orders and Minute Book, commencing 1605.
The Reader MSS, 30 volumes of transcripts, notes, etc, chiefly
concerned with Coventry.
Collection of Deeds, ranging from 14th to early 19th century.
Most of these had been transcribed by M.D. Harris, but this tran-
scription was also lost with the original deeds.

Virtually complete files of all Coventry newspapers beginning with the first, *Coventry
Mercury* (1743–1836), were lost. The file was more complete than the Colindale collection of the British Library.

31 For example, the first item in the sale of vestments in 1547 is entered as to 'Mr.
    Roghers, now mayre (and 4 other persons) ...' (*Illustrative Papers,* p 94; see also
    p 492). For other examples and discussion see below, pages xxviii-xxix and note 36,
    p lxviii.

32 Perhaps the clearest instance concerns the Smiths' appointment of a man to have 'þe
    Rewle of þe pajaunt' in 1453 (see p 27). Sharp has a footnote to the original quota-
    tion of this unique agreement: 'A similar Agreement was made in 1481 with Sewall

& Ryngald' (*Dissertation*, p 15, fn s). This was evidently similar enough to satisfy Sharp with merely a reference to it; but what were the differences? Why two men? Are there any clues as to who they were and why they were chosen? (See endnote to p 27 on p 548 for comments on this.) Is there any connection between this agreement and that made with the city waits at the same time? Nonetheless, whatever the questions, the reader might fairly suppose that Sharp had gathered here all the references to the making of such agreements that existed. This turns out to be a false assumption because a footnote in the *Dissertation* casually mentions, with reference to one John Yale, a hirer of cressets to the company in 1473 (see p 52), that he 'was at this period Manager of the Smiths' Pageant, by contract' (p 193, fn x). This suggests a certain continuity in this job, but, if so, are other 'managers' mentioned? How long was the position maintained? The account books probably do not answer these questions in anything approaching fullness, but there may well be more that suggests answers than the antiquarians' extracts produce.

A comprehensive guide to the Reader MSS was published by the city librarian, Charles Nowell, in a series of articles in the *Coventry Herald* during 1926–9 (see pp xlvii-xlviii). The following notes are taken from the seventh of Nowell's articles: 'Of his printed books may be mentioned his "History of Coventry," printed in 1810, with a later edition in 1830; pamphlets on St. Michael's and Holy Trinity (in 1815); the Charter of James I. (in 1816); a Guide to St. Mary's Hall (in 1827); a history of Leofric, etc. (1826, with later editions in 1830 and 1834); a larger work on St. Michael's in 1830; and the Domesday Book for Warwick (in 1835), with several other pamphlets on a variety of subjects' (Reader MSS 2 April 1926, p 11).

Reader has long been recognized as a painstaking, accurate, and industrious research worker and, in general, he was careful to give his authority for any statement outside his own experience which he included in records. An excellent example of this is shown in his *History of Coventry* (published in 1810) which has been used by every local historian since his time. In that volume he marked each paragraph, showing from which source he had obtained it. This *History* was subsequently published again, with additional information to date, in the year 1830, under the title of the 'New Coventry Guide.'

By profession, Reader was a printer and newspaper publisher, but by 1833 his business was ruined and he had to leave Coventry for Birmingham and then London, where he spent most of his declining years. For further details see the *DNB*.

Further proof of this interest is found in the large collection of letters at the end of Sharp's annotated copy of the *Dissertation* (BL: Add MS 43645). Of special interest are the exchanges between Sharp and Douce (to whom he dedicated the *Dissertation*), the latter persuading Sharp that the *Ludus Coventriae* are not the texts of the plays originally performed at Coventry.

The Edinburgh notebooks (vols 360-2) outline his prospectus — the examination of the civic records of over 150 towns. The list is no mere proposal: some places have nothing entered against them, others have a few notes; for Coventry, however, there is a very full list of the essential documents and MSS in the corporation's keeping, which would have done very well as a starting guide for this collection.

36 A very few extracts are copied into notebooks in the Shakespeare Centre, Stratford-upon-Avon, and in the Edinburgh University Library. I have been through all this material without finding any of the notes or original transcriptions used in his Shakespeare books, although some parts for a draft of *Outlines* exist at Edinburgh. That such a hoarder of notes and clippings should have destroyed this material seems most unlikely. There is now, available from the REED office, a microfiche edition of a computer-sorted index to the scrapbooks: *Halliwell-Phillipps Scrapbooks: an Index*, J.A.B. Somerset (comp), Records of Early English Drama (Toronto, 1979).

37 Thomas Daffern is the least known of the four antiquarians. He was a noted local historian but his fame did not spread beyond Coventry. He died there in January 1869, at the age of seventy-three, having spent nearly fifty years working first for the *Coventry Herald* and, from 1841 until his death, for the *Coventry Standard*. At the beginning of his transcription of the Carpenters' Accounts, he calls himself a book-keeper and shopman. He was a frequent contributor to the local press on matters concerned with Coventry and its history.

38 The discrepancy in dates will be discussed in the section on the dating of documents (see pp liii-lix).

39 The only other example of conflation I have found is of a rather different kind. On page 162, Sharp includes an account of the Corpus Christi guild for 'Corpus christi even & the day.' It follows two items dated 1539, but is actually the account for 1540 with certain entries replaced by their fuller equivalents from the accounts for 1541 and 1542: eg, 'James & Thomas of Inde' from the 1542 account replaces the plain 'James & Thomas' of 1540; 'iiij burgesses' is replaced by the 1542 entry, 'iiij burgesses for beryng the Canape over the Sacrament.' Sharp gives the fullest text possible, but not the fullest text that is actually given for any one year. Other of his devices may be seen by comparing his full list of the Smiths' accounts for 1490 with individual items he gives elsewhere in his general discussion of the Smiths' pageant.

40 Sharp's 'verbatim' pageant account for 1490 (*Dissertation*, pp 15-17) appears to be complete. Of the three accounts with missing items, that of 1584 has already been dealt with. The Cappers' account for 1565 (*Dissertation*, pp 49-50) is cut and pasted by Halliwell-Phillipps, who adds one item which makes sense of Sharp's total costs; he also corrects the transcription in thirteen places (slight errors, such as 'paide' to 'payd'). The 1584 Cappers' account can be compared with the original, revealing one omission, two readings of 'skaffolds' for 'skaffolde,' and four incorrect prices.

41 Each annal lists the twelve men who purchased the freedom of Coventry; normalized and in alphabetical order, these are Dodenhall, Freeborn, Hunt, Kersley, Mitchell, Norfolk, Rishall, Thimbler, Timber (or Thimber), Wallsall, Wellingborough, and Whiteweb. These appear in various orders and in spellings that quite alter the name (eg, Trimerlere for Timber, Barsley for Kersley, Willingbright for Wellingborough).

42 This extract from Flint's annal is given without his later cancellations and inserted

dates. Christopher Owen was mayor in 1662–3, Edward Owen (his father?) in 1635–6, and Godfrey Legg in 1637–8. The thirty-sixth mayor of Coventry was Richard Luff (1380–1), but the annalists' numbering of the mayors differs so widely that there can be no certainty that this annal began with his mayoralty; no extant annal begins with so late a mayor. Humphrey Wightwick was mayor in 1607–8, Robert Beake in 1655–6, Septimus Bott in 1686–7, and John Yardley in 1689–90. The first year of William Jelliff's mayoralty was 1674.

I have discussed aspects of 'fullness' in ' "Pleyng geire accustumed belongyng & necessarie": Guild Records and Pageant Production at Coventry.'

The Drapers gave notably extravagant feasts: that for 1560, whose cost is entered on pages 503–4, may be matched against the payments for what is possibly the same year expended on the pageant and Midsummer Night celebration (see pp 478-80). The pageant is much the least costly of the three.

These satisfying lines for the REED editor are quoted by Nowell, 'St. Mary's Hall and Guild,' (Reader MSS 20 August 1926, p 21). They conclude a passage quoted by Reader in one of his 'Guides to Coventry.' The Tudor tapestry still hangs in St Mary's Hall.

Coventry's sword of ceremony, the emblem of its civic authority carried before the mayor on all official occasions, merits a distinctive place in Sir Guy Francis Laking's discussion of 'Swords and Ceremony in England'; see *A Record of European Armour and Arms Through Seven Centuries*, vol 2 (London, 1920), 311-12, 319-22.

Hearne quotes a unique annal entry for 1553 showing another use of the city armour: 'This yeare the Duke of Northumberland sent to have the Lady Jane proclaimed. But the Maior, being ruled by the Recorder, would not proclaime her, but haveing order speedily proclaimed Queen Mary. There was taken in Coventry great store of Armour. There was a cry in Coventry, that the Cittie was fireing in foure parts, which caused the Common Bell to be rang, and the walls to be manned, and the gates to be made up, but there was noe hurt' (*Scotichronicon*, vol 5, p 1454).

Halliwell-Phillipps, Folger: Scrapbook, Wb 155, p 29.

Select Bibliography

This short bibliography includes books and articles with first-hand transcriptions of primary documents, together with a few essential reference works. No attempt has been made to list all works cited in the Introduction, textual footnotes, and Endnotes.

Bentley, Gerald Eades. *The Jacobean and Caroline Stage: Dramatic Companies and Players.* Vols 1, 2, 4 of 7 vols (Oxford, 1966, 1966, 1968).

Birmingham Free Library. *Catalogue of Birmingham Books in the Reference Department of the Free Library.* J.D. Mullins (comp) (Birmingham, 1874).

Burbidge, F. Bliss. *Old Coventry and Lady Godiva Being Some Flowers of Coventry History Gathered and Arranged* (Birmingham, [1952]).

Burgess, J. Tom. *Historic Warwickshire.* 2nd ed. Joseph Hill (ed and rev) (Birmingham, [1893]).

Chambers, E.K. *The Elizabethan Stage.* 4 vols (1923; rpt Oxford, 1974).

Craig, Hardin. *Two Coventry Corpus Christi Plays: 1. The Shearmen and Taylors' Pageant, Re-edited from the Edition of Thomas Sharp, 1825; and 2. The Weavers' Pageant, Re-edited from the Manuscript of Robert Croo, 1534; with a Plan of Coventry, and Appendixes Containing the Chief Records of the Coventry Plays.* 2nd ed. EETS, es 87 (1957; rpt London, 1967).

Dugdale, William. *The Antiquities of Warwickshire Illustrated; from Records, Leiger-Books, Manuscripts, Charters, Evidences, Tombes, and Armes: Beautified with Maps, Prospects and Portraictures.* 2nd ed. William Thomas (rev). Vol 1 of 2 vols (London, 1730), 134-200.

Fretton, W.G. 'Memorials of the Franciscans or Grey Friars, Coventry,' *Transactions, Excursions and Reports of the Birmingham and Midland Institute, Archaeological Section,* 9 (1882), 34-53.

— *Trading Gilds of the City of Coventry* (Hull, 1894).

Gooder, Eileen. *Coventry's Town Wall.* Coventry & North Warwickshire History Pamphlets, no 4. Rev ed (Coventry, 1971).

[Halliwell-Phillipps, James Orchard]. *Illustrations of the Life of Shakespeare in a Discursive Series of Essays on a Variety of Subjects Connected with the Personal and Literary History of the Great Dramatist.* Pt 1 (London, 1874).

– *Outlines of the Life of Shakespeare.* 9th ed. 2 vols (London, 1890).

Harris, Mary Dormer. *The Ancient Records of Coventry. A Paper Read before the Dugdale Society at St. Mary's Hall, Coventry on Saturday, October 25th, 1924.* Dugdale Society Occasional Papers, no 1 (Stratford-upon-Avon, 1924).

– *The Company and Fellowship of Cappers and Feltmakers at the City of Coventry* (London, [1921]).

–[ed]. *The Coventry Leet Book: or Mayor's Register, Containing the Records of the City Court Leet or View of Frank Pledge, AD 1420–1555, with Divers Other Matters.* 4 pts. EETS, os 134, 135, 138, 146 (London, 1907, 1908, 1909, 1913).

– *The History of the Drapers Company of Coventry* [Coventry, 1926].

– *Life in an Old English Town: a History of Coventry from the Earliest Times Compiled from Official Records.* Social England Series (London, 1899).

– 'The Manuscripts of Coventry,' *Transactions of the Bristol and Gloucestershire Archaeological Society,* 37 (1914), 187-93.

– (transcr and ed). *The Register of the Guild of the Holy Trinity, St. Mary, St. John the Baptist and St. Katherine of Coventry Transcribed and Edited from the Original MS. in the Possession of the Coventry Corporation.* [Vol 1]. Publications of the Dugdale Society, 13 (London, 1935). *See also* Templeman.

– *The Story of Coventry.* The Mediaeval Town Series (London, 1911).

The Historical Manuscripts Commission. John Cordy Jeaffreson. 'The Manuscripts of the Corporation of Coventry (Second Report),' in 'The Manuscripts of Shrewsbury and Coventry Corporations; the Earl of Radnor, Sir Walter Corbet, Bart., and Others,' *Historical Manuscripts Commission. Fifteenth Report,* Appendix, pt 10 (London, 1899), 101-58.

Ingram, R[eginald] W. '1579 and the Decline of Civic Religious Drama in Coventry,' *The Elizabethan Theatre VIII: Papers Given at the Eighth International Conference on Elizabethan Theatre Held at the University of Waterloo, Ontario, in July 1979.* G.R. Hibbard (ed) (Port Credit, Ont., forthcoming 1982).

– ' "Pleyng geire accustumed belongyng & necessarie": Guild Records and Pageant Production at Coventry,' *Records of Early English Drama: Proceedings of the First Colloquium at Erindale College, University of Toronto, 31 August – 3 September 1978.* JoAnna Dutka (ed) (Toronto, 1979), 60-92.

– ' "To find the players and all that longeth therto": Notes on the Production of Medieval Drama in Coventry,' *The Elizabethan Theatre V: Papers Given at the Fifth International Conference on Elizabethan Theatre Held at the University of Waterloo, Ontario, in July 1973.* G.R. Hibbard (ed) (Toronto, 1975), 17-44.

Jeaffreson, John Cordy. *A Calendar of the Books, Charters, Letters Patent, Deeds, Rolls, Writs, and Other Writings, in the Cases and Drawers of the New Muniment-Room of St. Mary's Hall, Made and Edited for the Corporation of the City of Coventry* (Coventry, 1896).

Lancaster Joan C. 'Coventry,' *The Atlas of Historic Towns.* Vol 2, [pt 3]. M.D. Lobel (gen ed) (Baltimore, 1975).

Murray, John Tucker. *English Dramatic Companies 1558–1642.* 2 vols (London, 1910).

Nichols, John. *The Progresses and Public Processions of Queen Elizabeth among Which Are Interspersed Other Solemnities, Public Expenditures, and Remarkable Events during the Reign of That Illustrious Princess Collected from Original Manuscripts, Scarce Pamphlets, Corporation Records, Parochial Registers.* 3 vols (London, 1823). [Facs Burt Franklin: Research and Source Works Series, no 117 (New York, nd).]

Nowell, Charles. 'The Reader Manuscripts in the Gulson Library,' articles published in *The Coventry Herald* (1926–9).

Phythian-Adams, Charles. 'Ceremony and the Citizen: The Communal Year at Coventry 1450–1550,' *Crisis and Order in English Towns 1500–1700: Essays in Urban History.* Peter Clark and Paul Slack (eds) (London, 1972), 57-85.

— *Desolation of a City: Coventry and the Urban Crisis of the Late Middle Ages* (Cambridge, 1979).

Poole, Benjamin. *Coventry: Its History & Antiquities. Compiled by Benjamin Poole, from Authentic Publications, Ancient Manuscripts and Charters, Corporation Records, Original Contributions, etc....* (London, 1870).

[Reader, William] . *The History and Antiquities of the City of Coventry, from the Earliest Authentic Period to the Present Time: Comprehending, a Description of the Antiquities, Public Buildings, Remarkable Occurrences, &c* (Coventry, 1810).

Reed, A.W. *Early Tudor Drama: Medwall, the Rastells, Heywood, and the More Circle* (London, 1926).

Robbins, Rossell Hope (ed). 'Welcome to Prince Edward at Coventry, AD 1474,' *Secular Lyrics of the XIVth and XVth Centuries* (Oxford, 1952), 115-17, 267.

Sharp, Thomas. *A Dissertation on the Pageants or Dramatic Mysteries Anciently Performed at Coventry, by the Trading Companies of That City; Chiefly with Reference to the Vehicle, Characters, and Dresses of the Actors. Compiled, in a Great Degree, from Sources Hitherto Unexplored. To Which Are Added, the Pageant of the Shearmen & Taylors' Company, and Other Municipal Entertainments of a Public Nature* (Coventry, 1825). [Facs with foreword by A.C. Cawley (Totowa, New Jersey, 1973).]

— *Illustrative Papers on the History and Antiquities of the City of Coventry; Comprising the Churches of St. Michael, Holy Trinity, St. Nicholas, and St. John; the Grey Friars' Monastery; St. John's Hospital and Free Grammar School; Jesus Hall, Bablake Hall, and St. Mary's Hall. From Original, and Mostly Unpublished Documents. Carefully Re-printed from an Original Copy with Corrections, Additions, and a Brief Memoir of the Author, by William George Fretton* (Birmingham, 1871). [For a set of the original pamphlets, some with title page and dated 1817–18, see BL 10358.h.19 (separately paginated).]

— *The Pageant of the Company of Sheremen and Taylors, in Coventry, as Performed by Them on the Festival of Corpus Christi; Together with Other Pageants, Exhibited on Occasion of Several Royal Visits to That City; and Two Specimens of Ancient Local Poetry* (Coventry, 1817).

— (ed)] . *The Presentation in the Temple, a Pageant, as Originally Represented by the Corporation of Weavers in Coventry. Now First Printed from the Books of the Company. With a Prefatory Notice.* [Presented to The Abbotsford Club by John Black Gracie] (Edinburgh, 1836).

Smith, [Sir] Frederick. *Coventry: Six Hundred Years of Municipal Life.* Rev ed (Coventry, 1946).

Templeman, Geoffrey (ed). *The Records of the Guild of the Holy Trinity, St. Mary, St. John the Baptist and St. Katherine of Coventry.* Vol 2. Publications of the Dugdale Society, 19 (Oxford, 1944).

Tyack, Geo. S. 'The Coventry "Mysteries",' *Bygone Warwickshire.* William Andrews (ed). The Bygone Series (Hull, 1893), 65-83.

The Victoria History of the Counties of England. *The Victoria History of the County of Warwick.* Vol 2. William Page (ed) (London, 1908). Vol 8. *The City of Coventry and Borough of Warwick.* W.B. Stephens (ed) (London, 1969).

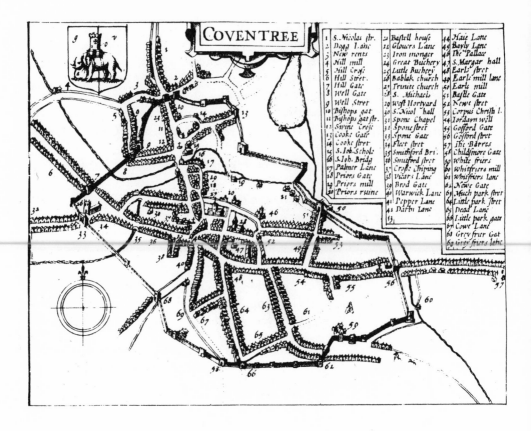

COVENTREE

1	S. Nicolas ftr.	22	Baftell houfe	44	Haie Lane	
2	Dogg Lane	23	Glowers Lane	45	Bayly Lane	
3	New rents	23	Iron monger	46	The Pallace	
4	Hill mill	24	Great Buchery	47	S. Margar hall	
5	Hill Crofs	25	Little Buchery	48	Earls ftret	
6	Hill Stret.	26	Bablak church	49	Earls mill lane	
7	Hill Gate	27	Trinute church	50	Earls mill	
8	Well Gate	28	S. Michaels	51	Baftle Gate	
9	Well Stret	29	Weft Hortyard	52	Newt ftret	
10	Bifhops gat	40	S. Nicol hall	53	Corpus Chrifti l.	
11	Bifhops gat ftr.	31	Spone Chapel	54	Iordayn well	
11	Swine Crofe	32	Spone ftret	55	Gofford Gate	
13	Cooks Gate	13	Spone Gate	56	Gofford ftret	
14	Cooke ftret	34	Fleet ftret	57	The Barres	
15	S. Ioh. Schol:	35	Smithford Bri.	58	Childsmore Gate	
16	S. Ioh. Bridg	36	Smitsford ftret	59	White friers	
17	Palmer Lane	37	Crofse Chiping	60	Whitfriers mill	
18	Priors Gate	38	Vicars Lane	61	Whitfriers lane	
19	Priors mill	39	Brod Gate	62	Newe Gate	
20	Priors ruine	40	Warwick Lane	63	Much park ftret	
		41	Pepper Lane	64	Little park ftret	
		41	Darbi Lane	65	Dead Lane	
		43		66	Little park gate	
				67	Cowe Lane	
				68	Grey frier Gat	
				69	Grey friers lane	

Map of Coventry from John Speed, *The Theatre of the Empire of Great Britaine,* vol 1

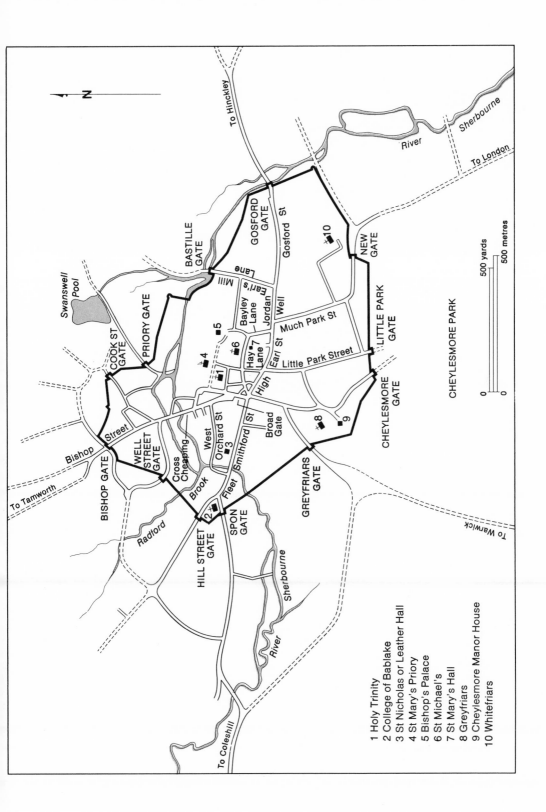

Map of Coventry c 1500, adapted from *The Victoria History of the County of Warwick,* vol 8, by permission of the general editor

Map labels:

To Hinckley

River Sherbourne

To London

Swanswell Pool

BASTILLE GATE

GOSFORD GATE

Gosford St

NEW GATE

PRIORY GATE

COOK ST GATE

Mill Lane

Earl's Lane

Bayley Lane

Jordan Well

■5

■4

†6

Hay Lane ■7

Much Park St

LITTLE PARK GATE

†10

Bishop Street

BISHOP GATE

WELL STREET GATE

Cross Cheaping

West Orchard St

Brook

Fleet

Smithford St

High St

Earl St

Little Park Street

Broad Gate

■8

■9

CHEYLESMORE GATE

GREYFRIARS GATE

CHEYLESMORE PARK

To Warwick

To Tamworth

Radford

HILL STREET GATE

SPON GATE

■2†

†1

■3

Sherbourne River

To Coleshill

N

500 yards

500 metres

0

0

1 Holy Trinity
2 College of Bablake
3 St Nicholas or Leather Hall
4 St Mary's Priory
5 Bishop's Palace
6 St Michael's
7 St Mary's Hall
8 Greyfriars
9 Cheylesmore Manor House
10 Whitefriars

RECORDS OF EARLY ENGLISH DRAMA

Symbols

A	Antiquarian Compilation
AC	Antiquarian Collection
BL	British Library
Bodl	Bodleian Library
BRL	Birmingham Reference Library
CRO	Coventry Record Office
H-P	Halliwell-Phillipps
LB	*The Coventry Leet Book*
PRO	Public Record Office
STC	*Short-Title Catalogue*
VCH *Warks*	*Victoria History of the County of Warwick*
*	(after folio, page, or membrane number) see endnote
®	right-hand marginalia
†	marginalia too long for the left-hand margin
...	ellipsis
⟨...⟩	damaged, lost, or obliterated letters
[ ]	cancellations, deletions, erasures
(blank)	blank spaces in the original where writing might be expected
° °	letters or words added by different or later hand
⌐ ¬	interlineations originally inserted above the line
∟ ⌐	interlineations originally inserted below the line
∧	MS caret
ǀ	change of folio, page, or membrane in passages of continuous prose

The Records

1392

AC   *St Mary's Priory: Cartulary*   Sharp: *Dissertation*
p 8   fn m*

... a tenement in Little Park street is in the Cartulary of St. Mary's,   5
fo. 85, b. described to be situated "int*er* ten*ementum* P*rioris* &
Con*ven*tus ex p*art*e una & dom*um pro* le pagent pannar*iorum*
Coventre ex alt*er*a."

1398

Bolingbroke and Mowbray Joust at Coventry

Holinshed: *Chronicles of England* vol 3
pp 494-5*

...

®Anno Reg.22   At the time appointed the king came to Couentrie, where the   15
two dukes were readie, according to the order prescribed therein,
comming thither in great arraie, accompanied with the lords and
gentlemen of their linages. The king caused a sumptuous scaffold
or theater, and roiall listes there to be erected and prepared. The
sundaie before they should fight, after dinner the duke of   20
Hereford came to the king (being lodged about a quarter of a mile
without the towne in a tower that belonged to sir William Bagot)
to take his leaue of him. The morow after, being the daie
appointed for the combat, about the spring of the daie, came the
duke of Norfolke to the court to take leaue likewise of the king.   25
The duke of Hereford armed him in his tent, that was set vp
neere to the lists, and the duke of Norfolke put on his armor,
betwixt the gate & the barrier of the towne, in a beautifull house,
hauing a faire perclois of wood towards the gate, that none might
see what was doone within the house.   30

®The order of the combat.   The duke of Aumarle that daie, being high constable of

England, and the duke of Surrie marshall, placed themselues
betwixt them, well armed and appointed; and when they saw
their time, they first entered into the listes with a great companie
of men apparelled in silke sendall, imbrodered with siluer, both
richlie and curiouslie, euerie man hauing a tipped staffe to keepe   5
the field in order. About the houre of prime came to the barriers
of the listes, the duke of Hereford, mounted on a white courser,
barded with greene & blew veluet imbrodered sumptuouslie with
swans and antelops of goldsmiths woorke, armed at all points.
The constable and marshall came to the barriers, demanding of   10
him what he was, he l answered; I am Henrie of Lancaster duke
of Hereford, which am come hither to doo mine indeuor against
Thomas Mowbraie duke of Norfolke, as a traitor vntrue to God,
the king, his realme, and me. Then incontinentlie he sware vpon
the holie euangelists, that his quarrell was true and iust, and vpon   15
that point he required to enter the lists. Then he put vp his sword,
which before he held naked in his hand, and putting downe his
visor, made a crosse on his horsse, and with speare in hand,
entered into the lists, and descended from his horsse, and set him
downe in a chaire of greene veluet, at the one end of the lists, and   20
there reposed himselfe, abiding the comming of his aduersarie.

Soone after him, entred into the field with great triumph,
king Richard accompanied with all the peeres of the realme, and
in his companie was the earle of saint Paule, which was come out
of France in post to see this challenge performed. The king had   25
there aboue ten thousand men in armour, least some fraie or
tumult might rise amongst his nobles, by quarelling or partaking.
When the king was set in his seat, which was richlie hanged and
adorned; a king at armes made open proclamation, prohibiting
all men in the name of the king, and of the high constable and   30
marshall, to enterprise or attempt to approch or touch any part
of the lists vpon paine of death, except such as were appointed
to order or marshall the field. The proclamation ended, an other
herald cried; Behold here Henrie of Lancaster duke of Hereford
appellant, which is entred into the lists roiall to doo his deuoir   35
against Thomas Mowbraie duke of Norfolke defendant, vpon
paine to be found false and recreant.

The duke of Norfolke houered on horssebacke at the entrie
of the lists, his horsse being barded with crimosen veluet,
imbrodered richlie with lions of siluer and mulberie trees; and   40
when he had made his oth before the constable and marshall that
his quarrell was iust and true, he entred the field manfullie,

saieng alowd: God aid him that hath the right, and then he
departed from his horsse, & sate him downe in his chaire which
was of crimosen veluet, courtined about with white and red
damaske. The lord marshall viewed their speares, to see that they
were of equall length, and deliuered the one speare himselfe to the   5
duke of Hereford, and sent the other vnto the duke of Norfolke
by a knight. Then the herald proclamed that the trauerses &
chaires of the champions should be remooued, commanding
them on the kings behalfe to mount on horssebacke, & addresse
themselues to the battell and combat.   10

The duke of Hereford was quicklie horssed, and closed his
bauier, and cast his speare into the rest, and when the trumpet
sounded set forward couragiouslie towards his enimie six or
seuen pases. The duke of Norfolke was not fullie set forward,
when the king cast downe his warder, and the heralds cried,   15
Ho, ho. Then the king caused their speares to be taken from
them, and commanded them to repaire againe to their chaires,
where they remained two long houres, while the king and his
councell deliberatlie consulted what order was best to be had in
so weightie a cause. Finallie, after they had deuised, and fullie   20
determined what should be doone therein, the heralds cried
silence; and sir Iohn Bushie the kings secretarie read the sentence
and determination of the king and his councell, in a long roll,
the effect wherof was, that Henrie duke of Hereford should within
fifteene daies depart out of the realme, and not to returne before   25
the terme of ten yeares were expired, except by the king he should
be repealed againe, and this vpon paine of death; and that Thomas
Mowbraie duke of Norfolke, bicause he had sowen sedition in the
relme by his words, should likewise auoid the realme, and neuer
to returne againe into England, nor approch the borders or   30
confines thereof vpon paine of death ...

1407
Quitclaim I CRO: 184*
(3 February)   35

Nouerint vniuersi per presentes quod ego Iohannes filius & heres
Ricardi Clerk de Couentre Mercatoris remisi relaxaui ac omnino
pro me & heredibus meis imperpetuum quietum clamaui Willelmo
Attilburgh Ricardo Southam seniori Iohanni Wymondeswold   40
Iohanni Onley Iohanni Preston & Iohanni Happesford totum ius
meum & clameum quod habui habeo seu quouis modo infuturo

habere potero post decessum predicti Ricardi patris mei in ˏ ʳillisˈ
omnibus Mesuagijs terris tenementis redditibus reuersionibus &
seruicijs cum omnibus pertinentijs suis que fuerunt Thome
Graunpe in vico parci Maioris in Couentre & Biggyng Remisi eciam
& quietum clamaui pro me & heredibus meis prefatis Willelmo   5
Ricardo Southam Iohanni Wymondeswold Iohanni Onley Iohanni
Preston & Iohanni Happesford totum ius meum & clameum quod
habui habeo seu quouismodo infuturo habere potero post
decessum predicti Ricardi patris mei in vna Grangia cum gardino
adiacente vno Cotagio duobus alijs Cotagijs vno Pagenthous in   10
hullestrete que Magistri de Whittawerescraft occupant & duobus
alijs Cotagijs in eadem strata de Hullestrete que Thomas Penkeston
occupat vno Curtilagio in eadem strata terre Ricardi Bykenhull
annexato vno magno Campo Vocato Muryholt vno alio Campo
vocato Chilternfeld vno alio Campo vocato Chilternhull & vno   15
alio Campo ˏ ʳvocatoˈ Wyndennilnfeld cum pertinentijs in
Couentre . habenda & tenenda omnia predicta Mesuagia terras
tenementa redditus reuersiones & seruicia cum omnibus
pertinentijs suis Aceciam predictam Grangiam cum gardino
adiacente Cotagia Curtilagium & Campos cum pertinentijs prefatis   20
Willelmo Ricardo Southam Iohanni Wymondeswold Iohanni
Onley Iohanni Preston & Iohanni happesford heredibus & eorum
assignatis libere quiete bene & in pace De Capitalibus dominis
feodi illius per seruicia inde debita & de iure consueta
imperpetuum Ita quod nec ego predictus Iohannes filius & heres   25
predicti Ricardi Clerk nec heredes mei nec aliquis alius pro me
nec nomine meo aut nostro aliquod ius vel clameum in predictis
omnibus Mesuagijs terris tenementis redditibus reuersionibus &
seruicijs cum omnibus pertinentijs suis Aceciam in predictis
Grangia cum gardino adiacente Cotagijs Curtilagio & Campis cum   30
pertinentijs nec in aliqua parcella eorundem decetero exigere seu
Vendicare potero aut poterimus quouis modo Set ab omni
accione iuris vel clamei inde simus exclusi imperpetuum per
presentes Et ego vero predictus Iohannes filius & heres predicti
Ricardi Clerk & heredes mei omnia predicta Mesuagia . terras   35
tenementa redditus reuersiones & seruicia cum omnibus
pertinentijs suis Aceciam predictam Grangiam cum gardino
adiacente Cotagia Curtilagium & Campos cum pertinentijs
prefatis Willelmo Ricardo Southam Iohanni Wymondeswold
Iohanni Onley Iohanni Preston & Iohanni happesford heredibus   40
& eorum assignatis contra omnes gentes Warantizabimus &
imperpetuum defendemus per presentes In cuius rei testimonium

hijs scriptis tripartitis sigillum meum apposui Hijs testibus
Iohanne Botone tunc Maiore Ciuitatis Couentre Roberto
Broddesworth & laurencio Waldegrane tunc Balliuis eiusdem
Ciuitatis Iohanne de Barwe Iohanne Scardeburgh Nicholao
Dudley & alijs Datum apud Couentre die Iouis proximo post   5
festum Purificacionis beate Marie Virginis Anno regni Regis
Henrici quarti post conquestum octauo

1410-11
St Mary's Priory: Pittancer's Roll PRO: E 164/21   10
f 27*

...

Vicus parci minoris in Couentria

Idem Iohannes Preston tenet per cartam ad terminum vite sue
vnum tenementum siue iiijᵒʳ cotagia ex dono Thome Marschall   15
Merceri in vico parci minoris ex parte orientali quorum reuersio
pertinet officio Pitanciarij post decessum dicti Iohannis ex
concessione predicti Thome que quidem cotagia valent per
annum xl s. vt patet per cartam dicti tenentis & mortificantur
licentia Regis per Willelmum Suwet & Ricardum Blaby pro   20
cantaria dicti Thome & situm est inter tenementum Prioris &
Conuentus quod Iohannes Goate tenet pertinentem cantarie
dominj Thome Poley ex parte vna & domum pro le Pagent
pannariorum Couentrie ex altera in latitudine & in longitudine
secundum metas &c.   xl s.   25

...

1416
City Annals Sharp: *Dissertation*
p 8*   30

...

The Pageants and Hox tuesday invented, wherein the King and
Nobles took great delight.

...

                                                                     35

1421
Leet Book I CRO: A 3(a)
f 9v *(2 April)*

...

To the reuerent And wurschipfull states that her byn And to all   40
wurthy men of this grett lete be this bill Schewid and Rad for as
moche as yerbe many good ordynancez maid by the maiour And

be hys good counsell god saue hem the wiche *with* the grace of
god schuld turne the town to grett worschip & psperite
We wold desiren a thyng the wiche was neu*er* ordenyd be no lete,
nor be counsell of the maiour and his peerys That hit myght by
your hye and good disc*r*ession be set in a nothur kynd. And that   5
is the grett multytude of peopull the wich is gatherid to gethur
on mydsomer evyn, and apon seynt peturs for we supposyn y*at*
hit lyeth in no mannys power. thow3e he ordeyn for hem as well
as he can for to plese hem all And not onely for this cause but
allso of grett debate and man slau3ghter and othur*e* perels and   10
synnes y*at* myght fall and late haue fallen And y*er*for 3if hit
lyke yow. we wold schew you how us thynkyuth best hit myght
be sett in bett*ur* Gou*er*nanse in Eschewyng of many peryls / If
hit lyke y*our* disc*r*ession vs thynkyth y*at* hit wer*e* good
Gou*er*nauns that [eschewyng] eu*er*y ward kept hem *with*in her   15
own ward in good and honest aray and eu*er*y ward *with*in hem
self chese hem ij wardens for to haue the gou*er*nance of the ij
nyght*es* beforseid and the maiour to walk *with* c*er*ten men the
wiche byn pleasyng vnto hym and the Baylyff*es* the same wyse
on the second nyght, for to walk thorow all the wardys of the   20
town and the maiour to gyve a subsydye of money to the
wardens of yche warde on the furst nyght and the Bayliffes to
doo the same on the second nyght [s⟨..⟩t⟨.. ..⟩ll⟨.⟩through] The
wich subsidye must be ordenyd be the maiour and his counsell
what hit schalbe in this mayres tyme and allso in tyme comyng   25
now 3e haue herd the entent of this bill wurche now by y*our*
disc*r*ession in the name of the Trinite

1423
Leet Book I CRO: A 3(a)   30
f 18* *(6 October) (Waits)*

...

Allso thei haue ret*ained* Mathew Ellerton Thom*a*s Sendell
Willi*a*m howton & Iohn Trumper*e* Mynstrells as for the Cite of
Couentr*e* and þat þei haue as oþ*er* haue had Afore them Allso   35
þat thai haue of eu*er*y hall place j d & of eu*er*y Cottage ob.
eu*er*y quart*er* & after þ*er* beryng bett*er* to be rewardyd And
also þai orden þat thei shall haue ij men of eu*er*y ward eu*er*y
quart*er* to help them gathur þ*er* Quarterage

...
                                                                           40

2 / psperite *for* prosperite, *brevigraph omitted*
15 / [eschewyng] *mistaken repetition from line above corrected by scribe*

1424
Leet Book I CRO: A 3(a)
f 21v* *(4 May)*
...

Allsoo þat the chamburlayns schall make a ryng at the Bullryng   5
to thend þat bullez may be baytyd as they haue byn hertofore
...

f 27 *(24 October)*
pro le weuers   10
...Item arbitrati sunt & ordinaruerunt quod dicti Iorneymen et
eorum quilibet soluet dictis magistris annuatim in futuro
quatuor denarios ad opus de le pagent eorundem & quod ipsi le
Iorneymen habeant cum magistris suis potacionem siue
collacionem sicut antea consueuerunt...   15

1428
Leet Book I CRO: A 3(a)
f 45v* *(4 October)*
                                                                        20

Hit is to haue in mynde that at a lete holden atte fest seynt
Michael the 3er of kyng Herri the sixt the vij the smythes of
Couentre put vp abille foloweng in thes wordes To you
fullwurshipfull Meir Recordour bayles & to all your discrete
counsell shewen to you the craft of Smythes. how thei were   25
discharged of the Cotelers pachand be alete in the tyme of Iohn
•Smiths pagent•   Gote then meire & quytances made be twene the forseid craftes
oder to oder lik as hit is well knowen & redy for to shewe And
now late Giles Allesley in his office of meyralte preyed the forseid
craft of smythes to take the gouernaunce of the seid pachand as   30
for his tyme & no forther And the seid craft did hit wilfully to
his plesaunce for the whiche cause the forseid pachand is yete
put to the forseid craft & thei han no maner of dute to tak hit
to hem Wyche thei beseche that ye of your grete goodnes
discharge the forseid craft of smythes of the pachand atte   35
reuerence of god & of Truthe and orden hit elles where ye ben
better avised be your good discression
     The Whiche bull be the avise of all the wurthy of the seid lete
and all oder apon the same lete beeng was onsuered & endosed in
this wise // hit is ordeyned that the smythes shull ocupie the seid   40
pachand forthe euery yere apon the payne of x li. to be payd at
euery defaute to the vse of the chambur
...

1429
Leet Book I CRO: A 3(a)
f 50 *(3 October)*

... also to iij Mynstrelles of the kynges xx s and to iij Trumpettes   5
of the kynges xx s Also to iij Mynstrelles of the quenes x s ...

1434
Leet Book I CRO: A 3(a)
f 73* *(12 June) (Visit of King Henry VI)*   10

Memorand*um* ... qu*o*d ho*mi*n*e*s de Couentre equitabunt
obuiand*o* Regi cum viri*dibus* Togis & Rubijs capicijs ...

Weavers' Deeds CRO: 100/37/1   15

Hec indentura fa*c*it testati*onem* qu*o*d Ri*c*ard*u*s Molle Ri*c*ard*u*s
Semer Thomas Darnewell de Couentr*e* Thom*as* Donton &
Thom*as* whitton de sheldon tradiderunt concesserun*t* & ad p⟨...⟩
plymmer Ioh*ann*i perkyn Rob*er*to Thomas Rob*t*o Styff Ioh*ann*i   20
Bordale Rob*er*to Glowcestre Nicho*la*o Gryve & Thom*e* Lerdyf
de Couentre vnam parcellam terre in le Millane in Couentre in*ter*
terram vocat*am* le Tailour paiont ex *p*arte vna & terr*am*
*p*redi*c*torum Ri*c*ar*d*i Ri*c*ar*d*i Thom*e* Thom*e* & Thom*e* ex *p*arte
alt*er*a in latitudine et longitudine a Regia via ib*ide*m vsq*ue* ad   25
terram eor*un*dem Ri*c*ar*d*i Ri*c*ar*d*i Thom*e* Thom*e* & Thom*e* et
continet *p*redi*c*ta *p*arcella t*er*re in latitudine *per* via*m* tresdece*m*
pedes & medietate*m* vni*us* pedis & in longitudine septemdecim
pedes & medietate*m* vni*us* pedis h*a*bend*am* & tenend*am* predicta*m*
*p*arcellam t*er*re *p*refatis Ioh*ann*i Ioh*ann*i Rob*er*to Roberto Ioh*ann*i   30
Rob*er*to Nicho*la*o & Thome & assign*at*is suis a festo *san*cti
Mi*c*h*ae*lis Archangel*i* anno regni Regis Henrici sexti post
conq*ue*stu*m* terciodecimo vsq*ue* ad fin*em* t*er*mi*n*i quater viginti
annor*um* de anno in annu*m* extun*c* pro*x*imor*um* sequ*entium* &
plenarie completor*um* Reddend*o* inde annuatim eisde*m* Ri*c*ard*o*   35
Ri*c*ard*o* Thom*e* Thom*e* & Thom*e* & assign*at*is suis tres solid*os*
octo denarios sterlingor*um* ad festum *san*cti Mi*c*h*ae*lis ar*c*hangel*i*
Et *p*redicti Ioh*ann*es Ioh*ann*es Robertus Robertus Ioh*ann*es
Robertus Nicho*la*us & Thom*as* vnam domu*m* vocat*am* a paiont
hows infra t*er*minu*m* *p*redict*um* de nouo edificabu*n*t bene &   40

20 / Robto *for* Roberto, *brevigraph omitted*

competent*er* & illam domu*m* cu*m* sic edificat*a* fu*er*it sustentab*unt*
rep*ar*abu*nt* & manutenebu*nt* sumptib*us* suis pro*pr*ijs & expensis
durante t*er*mi*no* p*re*di*c*to Et si contingat Reddit*um* p*re*dict*um*
aretro fore insolut*um* p*er* vna*m* mensem post aliquod festu*m* in
quo solui deb*et* extu*n*c bene licebit p*re*fatis Ric*ar*do Ric*ar*do   5
Thom*e* Thom*e* & Thom*e* h*er*edib*us* & assign*atis* suis in p*re*dict*am*
p*ar*cella*m* terre intrare & distringere & districti*ones* sic capt*as*
penes se retinere quousq*ue* de p*re*di*c*to Redditu eis plenarie fu*er*it
satisf*a*ctum Et si contingat Reddit*um* p*re*dictum in p*ar*te vel in
toto aretro fore insolut*um* p*er* vnu*m* annu*m* post aliquod festu*m*   10
in quo solui deb*et* extu*n*c bene licebit p*re*fatis Ric*ar*do Ric*ar*do
Thom*e* Thom*e* & Thom*e* in p*re*dict*am* p*ar*cellam terre intrare &
in pristino statu suo retinere ista dimissione non obstante Et
p*re*dictus Thomas Whitton p*re*dict*am* p*ar*cellam terre cum
p*er*tin*entijs* p*re*fatis Ioh*an*ni Ioh*an*ni Roberto Roberto Ioh*an*ni   15
Roberto Nich*o*lao & Thom*e* ac assign*atis* suis contra om*n*es
⟨...⟩tes warantisabit durante termino p*re*di*c*to p*er* p*re*sentes In
cuius rei testimoniu*m* p*re*sentib*us* tam p*re*dic*ti* Ric*ar*dus Ric*ar*dus
Thom*as* Thom*as* & Thom*as* q*uam* p*re*dicti Ioh*ann*es Ioh*ann*es
Robertus Robertus Ioh*ann*es Robertus Nich*o*laus & Thomas   20
p*re*sent*ibus* sigilla sua alt*er*natim apposueru*nt* hijs testib*us*
Ioh*ann*e Michell Maiore ciuitat*is* Couentr*e* Rob*er*to Southam vno
balli*u*oru*m* Ciuitat*is* p*re*di*c*te Ric*ar*do Sharp Ioh*an*n*e* Waraunt
Will*elm*o Swanne & multis alijs Datu*m* apud Couentre festo &
anno supradictis   25

1435
Leet Book I CRO: A 3(a)
f 88v *(23 April)*

...   30

The orden that the Sadelers and the peyntours off The Cite off
Couentre be fro this tyme fforward Contrebetory vnto þe paiont
off the Cardemakers and tha þey paye as the Cardemakers don
yerly vppon the peyne off C s. to be payd to þe vse off þe
Chamburlens   35

...

f 82v* *(3 October)*

...

Thei will þat the carpynt*er*s be associate vnto þe Tile*re*s &   40
pynn*er*s to maynten h*ur* pagent and h*ur* lyu*er*ey þat now is / &
that the maiou*r* call the substance of the Crafte of Carpynt*er*s

*•Carpenters
vnited in
fellowship
with tilers•*

and sett hem to geþer as one felawshipe

1439
Leet Book I CRO: A 3(a)
f 99* *(25 January) (Waits)*   5
...

hyt ys ordeyned that they Trumpet schall haue the rule off the
[waytes] whaytes And off hem be Cheffe.

Weavers' Deeds CRO: 100/37/2   10

Hec indentura testat*ur* qu*o*d Ric*ard*us Molle de Couentr*ia* weu*er*
Ric*ard*us Som*er* de eade*m* weu*er* Thomas Dernwell de eade*m*
wirdrawer & Tho*mas* Dunton de Sheldon husbondman
concesseru*nt* tradideru*nt* & dimiseru*nt* will*elm*o Gale & will*elm*o   15
fflowter custod*ibus* art*is* de Cardemakers Couentr*ie* Ric*ard*o Twig
custod*i* art*is* de Sadelers Ioh*ann*i warde custod*i* artis de peynto*urs*
Henrico Stevons & ⟨...⟩s Cl⟨.⟩rk custod*ibus* art*is* de ffremasons &
successorib*us* suis vnam vacuam placeam t*er*re iac*entem* in le
Millane in Couentr*ia* int*er* t*er*ram Thome wutton weu*er* quam   20
Magi*s*tri artis de weu*er*s tenent ex p*ar*te vna & t*er*ram gilde s*an*cte
Trinitat*is* Couentr*ie* ex p*ar*te altera in latitudi*ne* & in longitudi*ne*
a via Regia vsq*ue* ad t*er*ram ⟨...⟩ le de p*ar*ochia s*an*cti Michael*is*
Couentr*ie* se*cundu*m metas & diuis*as* ib*ide*m fact*as* ha*bendam* &
tenend*am* pre*di*ctam vacuam placeam t*er*re prefat*is* will*elm*o Gale   25
will*elm*o fflo⟨...⟩ Ioh*ann*i warde Henrico Stevons & henrico Clerk
& successorib*us* suis a festo Natiuitat*is* s*an*cti Ioh*ann*is Bapt*iste*
pr*o*ximo futuro post dat*am* pre*sentem* vsq*ue* ⟨...⟩ & vni*us*
annor*um* de anno in annu*m* extunc pr*o*ximorum sequ*entium* &
plenar*ie* completo*rum* Reddend*o* inde annuati*m* prefat*is* Ric*ard*o   30
Molle Ric*ard*o Som*er* Thome dernwell ⟨...⟩ vel assign*atis* suis
du⟨.⟩ante ⟨..⟩a vita Thome wutton weu*er* supr*a*dict*i* quatuor
solid*os* sterling*orum* ad quatuor anni t*er*mina vide*licet* ad festa
s*an*cti Michael*is* ⟨...⟩ annunc*iacionis* beat*e* Marie virg*inis* &
Natiuitatis s*an*cti Ioh*ann*is Bapt*iste* per equale*s* porc*iones* & post   35
decessum eiusd*em* Thom*e* wutton tunc reddend*o* inde annuati*m*
prefat*is* Ric*ard*o Molle Ric*ard*o Som*er* Thome Dernwell & Thom*e*
Dunton vel assign*atis* suis duos solid*os* sterling*orum* ad festa
supr*a*dict*a* Et insup*er* pre*di*cti will*elm*us will*elm*u*s* Ric*ard*us Twig
Ioh*ann*es Henricus & Henricus pre*di*ctam vacuam placeam t*er*re   40
post edifica*cio*nem inde fact*am* bene & competent*er* sustentabu*nt*
rep*ar*abu*nt* & manutenebu*nt* su*m*pt*ibus* eorum pr*o*prij ⟨...⟩g &

expens*is* durante toto *termino predicto* Et *predicti* Ri*card*us Molle
Ri*card*us Som*er* Thomas & Thomas hered*es* & assign*ati* sui
*predic*tam vacuam placeam t*erre* *prefatis* will*elmo* will*elmo*
Ri*card*o Twig Ioh*ann*i henrico & henrico & successorib*us* suis
vsq*ue* ad finem t*ermin*i supr*a*d*ic*ti modo & forma *premissis* contra   5
omn*es* gentes warantizabu*nt* & defend*ent* *per* *pre*sentes In cui*us*
rei testimoniu*m* *par*tes *predic*te hijs indentur*is* sua Sigilla
alternatim apposueru*nt* Datu*m* apud Couentri*am* duodecimo die
mens*is* Maij Anno regni Regis Henrici sexti post conquestum
decimo septimo   10

1441
Leet Book I CRO: A 3(a)
f 102v* *(22 April)*

...   15

Ordinatu*m* est q*uod* Robertus Eme et onnes alij qui ludunt in
festo Corporis chr*ist*i bene & suficient*er* ludant Ita q*uod* nulla
impedic*io* fiat in aliquo ioco sub p*en*a xx s cuiusl*ibet* deficient*is*
ad vsus muri levand*orum* *per* maiorem & Camerarios &c.
Item ordinant q*uod* Maior & Balliui *per* se ipsos & alios *probos*   20
homi*nes* ville de Couentre semel citra *fes*tum *Sancti* Michael*is*
arch*angel*i *pro*ximum futur*um* equitent ad videndu*m* metas &
bundas franch*ise* de Couentri*a* &c.

...

25

Weavers' Deeds CRO: 100/37/3

Sciant *pre*sentes & futuri q*uo*d nos Ri*card*us Molle Ri*card*us
Somer Thomas Dernwell de Couentri*a* & Thomas Donton de
Sheldon dedim*us* concessimus & hac *pre*senti carta *no*stra   30
confirmauim*us* Ri*card*o Cokkes Ioh*ann*i Tebbe will*elmo* Pace
Thome Dycons Ri*card*o Glover & Ioh*ann*i Egull de Couentri*a*
weuers vnam placeam t*erre* sup*er*edificat*am* vocat*am*
weuerspagenthowse in venella vocat*a* Mullelane in Couentri*a*
continent*em* in latitudi*ne* quatuordecim pedes & situat*am* int*er*   35
t*er*ram *pre*dic*t*orum Ri*card*i Molle Ri*card*i Somer Thome Dernwell
& Thom*e* Donton quam Mag*ist*ri artis Cissor*um* tenent ex *par*te
vna & t*er*ram quam Mag*ist*ri artis de Cardemakers tenent ex *par*te
alt*er*a in latitudi*ne* & in longitudi*ne* a via Regia ib*ide*m vsque ad
t*er*ram *per*tinent*em* altari b*eat*e Marie in ecclesia *san*cti Michael*is*   40

16 / onnes *for* omnes

Couentrie secundum metas & diuisas ibidem factas habendam &
tenendam predictam placeam terre superedificatam prefatis
Ricardo Cokkes Iohanni Tebbe willelmo pace Thome Dycons
Ricardo Glouer & Iohanni Egull heredibus & assignatis suis libere
quiete bene & in p⟨...⟩ imperpetuum Reddendo inde annuatim   5
Thome wutton de Couentria weuer durante tota vita sua vnum
denarium ad festum sancti Michaelis archangeli si petatur Et post
decessum ipsius Thome wutton tunc Reddendo inde annuatim
Magistro fratribus & sororibus hospitalis sancti Iohannis Baptiste
Couentrie & successoribus suis redditum predictum imperpetuum   10
pro omnibus alijs seruicijs secularibus & demandis Et nos vero
predicti Ricardus Molle Ricardus Somer Thomas Dernwell &
Thomas Donton & heredes nostri predictam placeam terre
superedificatam vocatam weuerspagenthowse prefatis Ricardo
Cokkes Iohanni Tebbe willelmo pace Thome Dycons Ricardo   15
Glouer & Iohanni Egull heredibus & assignatis suis in f⟨.⟩rma
predicta contra omnes gentes warantizabimus acquietabimus &
imperpetuum defendemus per presentes In cuius rei testimonium
huic presenti carte nostre Sigilla nostra apposuimus. Hijs testibus
Iohanne warant tunc Maiore Ciuitatis Couentrie Iohanne Lee &   20
Iohanne Lynne tunc Balliuis eiusdem Ciuitatis Ricardo Osbarn
Iohanne Grynder Iohanne Maydeford Thome Maydeford & alijs
Datum apud Couentriam sexto die Octobris Anno regni Regis
henrici sexti post conquestum vicesimo

25

Weavers' Deeds CRO: 100/37/4

Sciant presentes & futuri quod nos Ricardus Cokkes Iohannes
Tebbe willelmus pace Thomas Dycons Ricardus Glouer &
Iohannes Egull de Couentria weuers dedimus concessimus & hac   30
presenti carta nostra indentata confirmauimus Thome wutton de
Couentria weuer ad totam vitam suam vnum annualem redditum
quatuor solidorum annuatim percipiendum de vna placea terre
superedificata vocata weuerspagenthowse in venella vocata
Millelane in Couentria continenti in latitudine quatuordecim   35
pedes & situata inter terram Ricardi Molle Ricardi Somer Thome
Dernwell & Thome Donton quam Magistri artis Cissorum tenent
ex parte vna & terram quam Magistri artis de Cardemakers tenent
ex parte altera in latitudine & in longitudine a via Regia vsque ad
terram pertinentem altari beate Marie in ecclesia sancti Michaelis   40
Couentrie secundum metas & diuisas ibidem factas habendum &
percipiendum predictum annualem redditum prefato Thome

wutton & assign*atis* suis ad totam vitam suam annuat*im* soluend*um*
videl*icet* ad festa Natal*em* d*om*ini annu*n*ciac*i*onis beat*e* Marie
virg*inis* Natiuit*atis* *san*cti Ioh*ann*is Bapt*iste* & *san*cti Mich*ael*is
Arch*angel*i p*er* equal*es* porc*i*ones Et si contingat p*re*dict*um*
reddit*um* quatuor solid*orum* in p*ar*te vel in toto p*er* vnu*m* Mens*em*   5
post aliquem t*er*mi*num* t*er*mi*n*orum p*re*dictorum aretro fore
insolut*um* durante vita eiusd*em* Thom*e* wutton si petat*ur* tunc
b*en*e licebit p*re*fat*is* Thom*e* wutton & assign*atis* suis in p*re*dict*a*
plac*e*a t*er*re distring*er*e & districti*ones* sic capt*as* abduc*er*e
asportar*e* & penes se retin*er*e quousq*ue* de p*re*dicto reddit*u* cum   10
om*n*ib*us* inde arreragij*s* siq*ue* fuerint eis plen*ar*ie fu*er*it
satisfact*um* & p*er*solut*um* Et nos v*er*o p*re*dict*i* Ric*ard*us Cokkes
Ioh*ann*es Tebbe Will*el*m*us* Pace Thomas dycons Ric*ard*us Glouer
& Ioh*ann*es Egull & her*edes* n*ost*ri p*re*dict*um* annualem reddit*um*
quatuor solid*orum* p*re*fat*is* Thom*e* wutton & assign*atis* suis vsq*ue*   15
ad totam vitam suam vt sup*r*adict*um* est contra om*n*es gentes
warantizabim*us* acquietabim*us* & defendem*us* p*er* p*re*sentes In
cui*us* rei testi*m*oniu*m* huic p*re*senti carte n*ost*re indentat*e* sigilla
n*ost*ra apposuim*us* hijs testibus Ioh*ann*e warant tunc Maiore
Ciuit*atis* Couentrie Ioh*ann*e Lee & Ioh*ann*e lynne tunc Balli*u*is   20
eiusd*em* Ciuit*atis* Ric*ard*o Osbarn Ioh*ann*e Grynder Ioh*ann*e
Maydeford Thom*e* Maydeford & al*ijs* Dat*um* apud Couentr*iam*
decimo die Octob*r*is anno regni Regis henrici sexti post
conq*uestu*m vicesimo
                                                                          25

1442
Leet Book I CRO: A 3(a)
f 103v *(25 January) (Waits)*
...

Volunt quod h*ab*eant vesturas suas pro*ut* billa ista exigit & sub   30
Condic*ione* quod h*ab*eant vnu*m* Trumpet pro*ut* infra fit menc*i*o
&c. & lez skecons sub securitate inuent*a* h*ab*ebunt & v*idelicet*
h*ab*ebunt vnam xij panni p*ro* vestura & sibi debit*a* p*er* Gardianos
p*re*cij xx s & erga *fes*tu*m* corp*or*is chr*ist*i ...
                                                                          35

1444
Leet Book I CRO: A 3(a)
ff 109-9v
...

ffor alsomoche as the Crafte of Cardemakers Sadelers, Masons &   40
peyntors of the Cite of Couentr*e* be long tyme I past haue byn as
oone fellauship in bery*n*g Costys charg*es* and all o*þer* dueties of

Cardmakers
•Sadlers
Masons &
painters one
Company•
old tyme to ther pagent & to the said felauship longyng And now
late þat is to say in the tyme of Richard Braytoft maiour of the
said cite the said felauship for certen causes among hem movyd
wer lyke to departe and to breke þer felauship Wherfor certen
persons of of the said Craftez, shewyng to the maiour the causz   5
of ther grevance besought hym in this mattur to sett due
Remedye And so by goodly Leysur the maiour callyng a fore
hym & his counsell all the said hoole fellauship rehersid vnto
them the grevouse complayntes þat wern made to hym by certen
persons of the said felauship The for namyd felauship willyng to   10
be Ruled compromytted hem to abyde the Rule and ordynance of
þe meire and his councell and so by aduyse of the said meire and
his councell hit is ordenyd that the said iiij Craftes shalbe oone
felauship beryng Costes charges and all oþer Dueties to her pagent
& to þer felauship longyng ... And allso euery person of the said   15
Craftys shall pay yerely to the masturs xij d and all oþer Dueties
customes and 'laufull' charges þat Long to þe pagent & to the
said felauship ... Allso þat þer shall no man of the said iiij Craftes
play in no pagent on Corpus christi day saue onely in the pagent
of his own Crafte without he haue lycens of the maiour þat shalbe   20
for the yer ...

1445
Leet Book I CRO: A 3(a)
f 122v* *(3 April)*   25
...

Pur le Ridyng on Corpus christi day
and for Watche on Midsomer even

The furst craft ffysshers and Cokes
Baxsters and Milners   30
Bochers
Whittawers and Glouers
Pynners Tylers and Wryghtes
Skynners
Barkers   35
Coruisers
Smythes
Weuers
Wirdrawers
Cardemakers Sadelers Peyntours and Mason   40

5 / of of MS *dittography*

Gurdelers
Taylours Walkers and Sherman
Deysters
Drapers
Mercers 5

1447
Leet Book I CRO: A 3(a)
f 131v *(15 April)*

... 10

Et q*uo*d le Ruydyng in festo Corp*or*is chr*ist*i fiat p*ro*ut ex antiquo
te*mpore* consueuit &c.

...

1448 15
Leet Book I CRO: A 3(a)
f 133v* *(30 March)*

...

Volunt & ordinant ... q*uo*d nullus decet*ero* frangat pauimentu*m*
ad ponend*um* in eo ramos in vigil*iis* Natiuitat*is* *san*cti Ioh*ann*is 20
Bap*tist*e & *san*cti Petri ...

1449
Carpenters' Account Book I CRO: Acc 3/1
f 4* 25

...

It*em* sol. ad le pynnerus p*ro* le pagend x s.

...

It*em* sol. in festo Corp*or*is chr*ist*i p*ro*
torcheberers iiij d 30
It*em* sol. p*ro* fachynge de torches ob.

...

1450
Leet Book I CRO: A 3(a) 35
f 143* *(15 January)*

Hit is to haue in mynde that thes wurthy menne & also Comeners
here Vndur writon Ordeyneyned that for the welfare & also for
the p*re*seruacion of the pece withe in the Cite of Couentre [for 40
to be hadde] & also to strengethe the kynges lawes haue ordeynede
That eu*er*y manne that hathe ben Meyre withe in the Cite of

Couentre shall haue redy & dayly withe in his place that he
duellethe in iiij Iakkes or iiij haburions iiij Salettes iiij Sheff arowes
& [oder] iiij bowes & also oder wepons to the ˄ 'same' stuff
longeng And eu*ery* bayly that hathe ben withe in the same Cite
shall haue iij [sale] Iakkes or iij haburions iij Salettes iij Bowes iij   5
sheff arowes & oder wepons to the same stuff longeng and also
eu*ery* Chamburlen 'manne' & eu*ery* warden that hathe ben
warden or Chamburlen withe in the seyde Cite Cite shall haue ij
Iakkes or ij haburions ij Salettes ij Salettes ij Bowes ij sheff arowes
& oder wepons to the seyde stuff longeng And eu*ery* oder   10
Comener of the seyde Cite that may bere the coste shall haue a
Iakke or an haburion a salette a bowe & sheffe of arowes & also
oder wepon to the seyde stuff longeng Eu*ery* manne that hathe
ben Meyre apon the peyne to lose iiij li. eu*ery* [lo] manne that
hathe ben bayly to lose iij li. [& eu*ery* manne that 'hathe' bene   15
Chamburlen & 'Bayly' warden to lose iij li.] & eu*ery* manne that
hathe bene Chamburlen & warden to lose xl s. and eu*ery* oder
comener to lose xx s. and that eu*ery* manne make his stuff redy
betwene this day that is to sey the Thursday next after the feste
of sent hillary the xxviij yere of kyng herry the syxte & the fest   20
of Ester thenne next foloweng eu*ery* menne apon the payne as hit
is aboue rehersede Also hit is ordeynede be the seyde parsons that
eu*ery* manne whanne he hathe ordeynede hym his stuffe as hit is
aboue rehersede That he selle lene alen ne do awey non of the
seyde stuff ne wepons out of this Cite ne no p*ar*cell of hem but   25
that they kepe hem withe in this Cite/ ne that no manne of this
Cite were non of this seide stuff ne wepons withe in this Cite but
when he is comaundude be the meyre that shalbe for the tyme or
elles when the co*m*en belle is rongon or in p*re*seruacion of the
pece & kepeng the kynges lawes or for the goode rule of this Citie   30
or elles for some oder resonabull cause the kynges lawes ne his
pece therbie hurte ne empeyrede
Also that no taylour of this Cite make no Iakke but hit be abull
& of goode stuffe to kepe the mannes body that shall were hite
apon the peyne that who dothe the Contrary to lose xl s. at eu*ery*   35
defaute

(35 names)

---

8 / Cite Cite MS *dittography*   9 / ij Salettes ij Salettes MS *dittography*

f 149v   *(18 April)*

...

Qui ord*inaverunt* qu*o*d xl. hom*in*es Decentes bone & honeste
conu*er*saci*on*is ac fortes in corp*or*e ad laborand*um* & ad vigiland*um*
noctant*er* custodient & vigilabu*nt* villam a hora nouena vsq*ue* ad   5
pulsaci*on*em campane vocat*e* Daybell p*er* quod temp*us* s*e*cu*n*d*um*
Iuramentu*m* consuetu*m* bene & sufficient*er* custodient vill*am*
ist*am* &c. Qui hom*in*es quol*ibet* nocte eru*nt* bene & suficient*er*
apperalt*i* in Iakk*es* salet*tes* polaxes v*el* Gleyves & alijs cons*i*milibus
&c. Et q*uo*m*o*do ipsi xl hom*in*es vlt*er*ius temp*or*e vigilaci*on*is   10
eru*nt* gub*er*nati illud po*n*unt in discrescione Maior*is* & consilij si
&c.

...

Carpenters' Account Book I CRO: Acc 3/1   15
f 56*

...

Item payd to pynners pageand   x s.
Item paid to berers of torchez on corp*us*
christi day   iiij d   20
Item payd to j harp*er*   iij d
Item paied for A Iak to þe vse of þe Craft whe*n* þe [sold] me*n* of
Coue*ntr*e went to þe kyng   xiij s iiij d

...

25

f 56v

...

Item paid to Robert harp*er* for Midsom*er* ny3t & pet*er*
ny3t   xiiij d

...   30

AC   *Smiths' Accounts* Bodl: MS Top. Warwickshire c.7
f 83*

... Expens at Corpus christi tyde spend at conand makyng to   35
paynt ye paie*nt* 4d. It spend on ye players at last rehers 16d. It
spend on ye mynstrell at ye first cumyng 2d. It on old bredren
ye same day 6d. It payed for grese 1d. It resshis 1d. It*em* spend
at bryngyng downe of ye paie*nt* to Willi*am* Haddons 6d. It payed
ye torchberrers 8d. It spend in ale uppo*n* yem 1d. It payed for ale   40

8 / quol*ibet* *for* qual*ibet*

to ye players in ye pajent 12d. It for ij tre hopps to ye paient
whelles 4d. It spend on ye mynstrell diner & soper on Corpus
christi daye 20d. It payed Thomas Colclogh pro the playe 43/4 It
spend at havyng howe ye paiet 10d. It payed ye mynstrell for ys
hyyr 7/. summa 57/11.   5
... It payed for the crowne to ye wystyllyng 6/8 Payed for the
tyrrys yat war lost on Corpus christi day 12d. Payed John Mychall
pro Corpus christi hall hyyr 5/. ...

...

Expens on Missomore neȝt payed for wyne & ale 15d. It for ij   10
harnesse to John Mallor 3/4. It to John Bracy pro ij armor 12d.
It iij men for goyng in ye harnes 12d. It iiij sper berrers 4d. It ij
cresset berrers 2d. It ij dozen poyntts 4d. It ye harper 9d It
blakebuccram to ye spers ij d.
...   15

Exspense on seynt Petrs neȝt in brede 4d It in ale a cester 18d. It
ij dozen poyntts 3d It payd for armor 3/4 It ij men for goyng in
ye harnes 8d It ij sperberrers 2d It ij cresset berrers 2d It ye
mynstrell 7d. It payed for berryng ye cofor fro seynt michaelis to
ye trinite 2d It payed for ye buke to ye oft 2d ...   20

— Sharp: *Dissertation*
p 15 fn t* *(Corpus Christi)*
...

Item paid cloth to lap abowt pajent payntyng & all iij s vj d ob.   25
...

p 31
...
Item ij spers   iiij s iij d   30
...

p 192
...
Item paid for [hire of] ij armor   iij s iiij d   35

4 / howe ye paiet: *H-P, Illustrations, p 52, reads* home the pajent
7 / *Reader underlines* tyrrys *and glosses as* tires *in right margin*
10-11 / ij harnesse ... ij armor: *Sharp, p 193, merges the two items as* Item paid for ij
armor iij s iiij d
12 / *Sharp lists* iij men for goyng in ye harnes *as a St Peter's cost*
14 / ij d: *Sharp reads* vij d

p 197 *(Midsummer)*

... Item þe harper   ix d

...

5

1451
Leet Book I CRO: A 3(a)
ff 156-6v* *(21 September)*
°[1450]° °1451°

Receavinge the kinge   10

Memorandum that the xxjth day of Septembre the yere of our
soueren lorde afore rehersed The kyng our soueren lord cam from
leycesteur toward Couentre The Meyre beeng thenne that is to sey
Richard Boys & his wurthy bredurn arayed in Skarlet and all the
Cominalte cladde in grene gownes & rede hodes in haselwode be   15
yonde the brode Oke on horsbak attented the comeng of our
soueren lorde and also sone as they haddon syght of [hym] our
soueren lordes presens The Meyre & his peres lyghton on fote
mekely thries kneleng on ther knees dud vnto our soueren lorde
ther due obeysaunse ... the Meire be avyse of counsell hadde no   20
mase in his honde but his seriant attendeng apon the Meyre the
wordes afore rehersed sayde put the Mase in the Meyres honde &
the Meyre kysseng the mase offurd hit to the kyng The kyng
tarieng & herkeneng the Meyres speche // in fauerabull wyse seyde
thes wordes // Well seyde Sir // Meyre take your hors // The Meyre   25
then rode forthe afore the kyng bereng his mase in his honde withe
the knyght Constabull next afore the kynges Swerde The bayles
of this Cite rideng afore the Meyre withe ther mases in ther hondes
makeng wey & Rome for the kynges comeng And so they ridon
afore the kyng till the kyng come to the vttur yate of the priory //   30
The kyng then forthewithe sent for the Meyre & his bredurn be
aknyght to come to his presence & to speke withe hym in his
chambur and the Meyre & his peres acordeng to the kynges
comaundement come into his chambur & thries ther knelleng
dudde ther obeysaunse // ... The kyng then abydeng stille in the   35
seide priory apon Michaelmas Evon sende the Clerke of his Closet
to the Churche of sent Michell to make redy ther his Closette
seyeng that the kyng on Michaelmas day wolde go on procession
& also her there hygh masse // The Meyre & his Counsell
remembreng hem in this mater specially avysed hem to prey the   40
Bysshoppe of wynchester to sey high masse afore the kyng The
Bysshoppe so todo agreede withe all his herte // and agayne the

kynges comeng to sent Michell churche the Meyre & his peres
Cladde in Skarlet gownes withe ther clokes and all oder in ther
Skarlet gownes wenton vnto the kynges chambur durre ther
abydeng the kynges comeng // The Meyre then & his peres doeng
to the kyng due obeysaunse when he come fro his Chambur Toke   5
his mase & bere hit afore the kyng all his seyde bredurn goeng
afore the Meyre till he come to sent Michels & brought the kyng
to his Closette // Then the seyde Byssoppe in his pontificals
arayede withe all the prestes & ǀClerkes of the seyde Churche &
of Bablake withe Copes apareld wenton in procession abowte the   10
Churcheyarde The kyng devowtely withe many odur lordes
folowed the seyde procession bareheded cladde in agowne of gold
tussu furred withe a furre of marturn sabull // the Meyre bereng
the mase afore the kyng as he dudde afore tille he com ageyne to
his Closette // ... And when masse was don the Meyre & his peres   15
broughton the kyng to his Chaumbur in lykewyse as they fet hym
saue only that the Meyre withe his mase went afore the kyng till
he cam withe in his Chambur. his seide Bredurn abydeng at the
Chambur durre till the Meyre cam ageyne // And at Evesong tyme
the same day the kyng be ij for his body & ij yomen of the Crowne   20
sende the seyde Gowne & furre that he were when he went in
procession & gaf hit frely to god & to sent Michell Insomyche that
non of the that brought the gown wolde take no rewarde in no
wyse // And after all this don on the teusday next after the fest
of sent Michell then next sueng the kyng purposeng to remove   25
toke his hors & rode forthe toward kyllengworthe The Meire &
his peres & the Cominalte in lyke wyse as they ridon withe the
kyng into the Town So in the same wyse they ridon withe the
kyng towardes kyllengworthe till they comon to oplase be yonde
astill grove agayne abrode lane the ledethe to Canley And then   30
there the kyng willeng to speke withe the Meyre & his Bredurn

•the ffirst
sheriffs made
by the kinges
owne mouth•

seyde to hem thes wordes // Sires I thank you of your goode rule
& demene at this tyme & for goode rule among you afore hadde
and in speciall for your good rule of the yere last past / And where
as ye ben nowe Baylies we will that ye be herafter Sherefes and   35
this we graunt to you of our own fre wille & of no spesiall desire
// Moreour we charge you withe our pease Among you to be kepte
And that ye suffer no Ryottes Conuenticuls ne congregasions of
lewde pepull among you // and also that suffer no lordes lyuereyes
knyghtes ne Swyers tobe reseyued of no man withe in you for hit   40
is ageyne our statutes // And also that abey my comaundementes
and yif ye be thus ruled we wille be your goode lorde // And this

don the Meyre & his bredurn takeng ther leve of the kyng // so
they departed & ridon to Couentre agayne // Godde Saue the
kyng &c.//

...

                                                                              5

Carpenters' Account Book I CRO: Acc 3/1
f 12

...

Item paid to Thomas barbour for wax & makynge
of þe torchez aȝenst Corpus christi tyde   vj s. vijj d   10
Item paid to þe pynners & tylers to hur
paiaunt   x s

...

f 12v*   15

Item paid for bering of torchez   viij d
Item paid to j Mynstrall   xiiij d

...

Item paid for skowring of j salet   iij d   20
Item for ponttes   j d
Item spendyd in makyng of torchez   ij d
Item paid to þe armed mon   ij d

...

                                                                              25

                              Myȝhelmas quarter

...

Item paid to Mynstrell   iiij d

...

                                                                              30

AC   *Smiths' Accounts* Folger: Scrapbook Wb 137
      p 100*

...

Expens on Missomour daye & Corpus Christi daye & alle fallyng
this ȝer on o daye.   35
Spend to bryng the pagent into Gosford stret   v d
Item, a gyrdyll to the Cros   iij d
Item, armour   v s
Item, iij. men for goyng in the hernes   xij d
Item, iij. sperberrers   iij d   40

10 / vijj d *altered from* vij d

Item, ij. cressetberrers	ij d
Item, the torchber‿ 'r' ers	viij d
Item, payed for a pynt of wyne to Pilat	j d
Item, per ale to the players in the pagent	x d
Item, spend on the players at last rehersse	xxj d
Item, spend [on] at havyng home of the pagent	iij d
Item, payed for makyng of iiij. new torchis & stoff therto	x s
Item, Thomas Colclowght per the playe	xliij s iiij d

— Folger: Scrapbook Wb 150

p 17

Item, payed for glovys to the players	*(blank)*

...

p 31

...

Item payd for þe demons garment makyng & þ stof	v s iij d ob.
Item payd for collyryng of þe same garment	viij d

...

— Sharp: *Dissertation*

p 212

...

Item payd þe mynstrells for þer hyr	viij s
Item spend on þer bord on Corpus christi evyn & daye	ij s vj d

...

p 197 *(Midsummer and St Peter's Watches)*

...

Item ij harpers	xj d

1452
Carpenters' Account Book I CRO: Acc 3/1
f 13 *(St Mary quarterage)*

...

Item payd to þe pynars for þe paiant	x s

...

Item paid to þe mynstrellez	[iiij d] vj d

...

18 / þ stof: *H-P, Scrapbook Wb 191, p 108, corrects as* þe stof that went therto

AC   **Smiths' Accounts** Sharp: *Dissertation*
      p 26 *(Corpus Christi)*
      ...
      Item payed for vj skynnys of whitleder to godds garment   xviij d
      Item payed for makyng of the same garment   x d   5
      ...

      p 33
      ...
      Item payed for makyng of iiij gownnys and iiij hodds to   10
      þe tormentors and þe stof þat went þerto   xxiiij s x d ob.
      ...

      p 35
                                                                        15
      Item payed to þe mynstrells   viij s
      Item spend on mynstrells dinner & þer soper on corporis
      christi day   xx d
      ...
                                                                        20
      p 206*
      ...
      Exspens on missomer neȝt
      In ale & wyne   x d   Item in spices   viij d
      Item payed for iij doȝen poyntts vj d Item payed for iij harmor v s   25
      Item iij men for goyng in þe harnes xij d Item iiij speer berrers iiij d
      Item ij cresset berrs ij d Item þe panȝer berrer ij d Item the
      harper xij d
                                              Summa ix s viij d
                                                                        30
      p 198 *(St Peter's Watch)*

      Item þe mynstrell vj d ...

      1453   35
      Carpenters' Account Book I CRO: Acc 3/1
      ff 19-19v*
      ...
      Item for þe mynstrell at þe freres   ij d
      ...   40
      Item spendid At Corpus christi hall in wytsonweke when þey
      were to geder for þe lyvery   xj d

Item paid to Iohn Watfall for stremas & seynt Mary
day   xx d

...

Item delyuered to Iohn ffreman meyre for þe
pynners   x s   5
Item payd to þe Mynstrell on Corpus day
christi   xviij d l
Item payd to Robert harper ffor Midsomar ny3t & seynt Peter
ny3t   xij d

...   10

f 58

...

Robertus Crudworth harper & alicia vxor eius fecerunt finem pro
quatuor solidis & pro lumine   vj d   15
Resseued   vj d

...

Weavers' Ordinances CRO: 34/1
f 2v* *(23 January?)*   20

...

∘this is now∘

•pagant•

Allso hit is Ordenyd that what ∧⌈∘strange∘⌉ Iorneymann is
ffounde in worke with anny Maister of the occopacion at [the
goyng abowte the towne of the hede Maister for to gedder paggent   25
syluer:] And the [Iorney man do not pay for hym selfe iiij d: his
seyd Maister þe which he wyrkes with all at that tyme schall pay
hym In the payn of vj s viij d]

...

Allso hit is Ordeyned that what man of the Crafte which is warnyd   30
be the hede Maister for to exemble in congregacion &
communicacion for the welth and supportacion of the seyde
Crafte: or to weddyng or bereyng : [or vpon Corpus day christi]
that wyll not cum and weyt on the hede Maister at his
commaundement at an owre assignet be the somner . excepte A   35
resonable & lawfull exscuse he schall pay to the torchis [j li wax]
xij d

...

f 5*   40

[... And allso it is ordeynd that the Iorneymen of ye seyd Crafte

schall haue ȝerely vj s viij d And for that they schall haue owte the
paggent and on Corpus christi day to dryve it from place to place
ther as it schalbe pleyd And then for to brynge it geyn in to the
paggent house without ony hurte in ther defawte. And they for
to put the Maister to no more coste. And what Iorneyman that
wyll not agre to this ordenaunce what Maister that settyth hym
in worke or that he be a greyd schall forfett to the Crafte vj s viij d]
...

ff 5v-6*

...

°Also yt ys ordeynyd that when the padyent & the watche do not
go then schall the masters felow pay vnto the Body of the Crafte
v s [& so is be discharged for that yere °] °And also the masters
felow shall pay to the head master of ye crafte v s yf the pagentes
do goo [& so to be discharged for that yere °] |
And also the masters felow shall beare the charge of one of the
rehearsys
...

AC **Dyers' Accounts** Sharp: *Dissertation*
p 190*

... xij pencells for torches ...

AC **Smiths' Accounts** Sharp: *Dissertation*
p 15* *(19 March)*

...

These men above writen wer acordid & agreed on munday next
befor palme sonday Anno H. (6th) xxxj. That Thomas Colclow
skynner ffro this day forth shull have þe Rewle of þe pajaunt unto
þe end of xij yers next folowing he for to find þe pleyers and all
þat longeth þerto all þe seide terme save þe keper of the craft
shall let bring forth þe pajant & find Cloyes þat gon abowte þe
pajant and find Russhes þerto and every wytson-weke who þat be
kepers of þe crafte shall dyne with Colclow & every master ley
down iiij d and Colclow shall have ȝerely ffor his labor xlvj s viij d
& he to bring in to þe master on sonday next after corpus christi
day þe originall & ffech his vij nobulleȝ and Colclow must bring
in at þe later end of þe termeȝ all þe garments þat longen to þe
pajant as good as þey wer delyvered to hym. This was ordeyned
in þe time of William Melody Thomas Warner & William byngley

þen kepers of þe crafte.

...

— Sharp: *Dissertation*
p 196 *(Midsummer and St Peter's Watches)* 5

...

Expenses for þe baners ij ell cloþe xix d Item for ffrenge iiij s vj d
Item for steynyng of hem xiij s iiij d Item bokaryn ij d Item
j Crosse xvj d

... 10

— Bodl: MS Top. Warwickshire c.7
f 84* *(St Loy's Day annual dinner)*

...

Item paid to a luter viij d [1469] to ye waytez of Covetre xij d 15

...

1454
Carpenters' Account Book I CRO: Acc 3/1
f 21 20

...

Item for beryng of torches on corpus christi
day iiij d

...

Item paid to Mynstrels for Corpus christi day Midsomer 25
night & seint petir nyghs ij s viij d
Item paid to þe pynners & tylers x s.

...

f 24 30

... the receytes of fynes ...
Item receyvid of Robert Crudwurth harper for hys
fynes viij d

... 35

AC *Smiths' Accounts* Sharp: *Dissertation*
p 164

...

spendyd on þe mynstrell on corpus christi even & day xij d 40

...

1455
Leet Book I CRO: A 3(a)
f 165v *(22 May)*

...

Wherapon the seide Meire the tenour of this letter be hym well   5
considered Lat calle to come afore hym the counsell of this Cite
withe his bredurn afore whome this letter was redde & they haueng
tendurnes of the Well fare & also of the *pre*seruacion & saueegard
of our soueren lorde the kyng as every true legeman owethe thei
ordeyned that an hundred of goodemenne denfensabully with   10
bowes & arowes Iakked & saletted Arayed shuld be made redy in
all haste possibull to go to our souerenne lorde to sent albones &
to abide withe hym & to do hym seruice suche at hit shulde please
[his] his highnes to comaunde hem to do and the Meire & the afore
rehersede wurthy men They ordeyned that Will*ia*m Tybeandis   15
shulde be capeten to the fornamed C Menne

  And hereafter folouthe in Writeng the costes & the purveaunse

that wern made to the Capetayne & to the forseide C. menne
ffirst for to make anewe pensell in Tarturne xvj d In Ryband to
the same xiiij d & for makeng of the same pensell & a tassell of silke   20

xiiij d And for forbeng of the spere hede ij d It*em* for an garment to
the Capetenne first for a q*u*art*er* & di*midium* of grene clothe ix d
& for a q*u*art*er* & di*midium* vyolet ix d & for a q*u*art*er* & di*midium*
redeclothe ix d & for a q*u*art*er* & di*midium* of Musturdevylers
xij d & for the makeng of the same garment xvj d S*um*ma *(blank)*   25
  Also for xxv yerdes q*u*art*er* & half q*u*art*er* of grene & reede
clothe bought to make bendes to the forseide C Menne le yerde
xviij d S*um*ma xxxviij s. vij d ob & for the makeng of the same
bendes iiij s. ij d S*um*ma *(blank)* Ande foralsomyche as the forseide
Capeteyne ne the C menne at this tyme wenton not forthe for   30
certen tydenges that wern brought & also be cause the kyng was
remeued to london ageyne & his p*ur*pose helde not All the bendes
garment & pensell wern put & delyuerd into the wardens kepeng

1456   35
Leet Book I CRO: A 3(a)
ff 168v-70v* *(14 September)*

...

*Memo*ra*ndum* that the demene & rule that was made & shewed
vnto oure Sou*e*rayn lady the quene at Couentre was thus as it   40
foloweth yn Wrytyng that is for to sey furst at Bablake there was

made a Iesse ou*er* the yate right well and there were shewed too
speches, as foloweth

®ysay

Princes most excellent born of blode riall
Chosen quene of this region conforte to all hus   5
Wordes to y*our* magnificens woll I say thus
I ysay replete *with* þe spirite *pro*pheticall
like as mankynde was gladdid by the birght of Ih*es*us
So shall þis empyre ioy the birthe of y*our* bodye
The knyghtly curage of p*r*ince Edward all men shall ioy to se   10

vac*at* qu*od*
postea

Afturward with Inne the yate at the Est yende of the Chirche was
a pagent right well arayed & þerin was shewed a speche of seynt
Edward & an oþ*er* of seynt Iohn the Euang*e*list as foloweth
                                                                                                          15

®Ieremy

Emp*r*ice quene p*r*inces excellent in on p*er*son all iij
I Ieromy þe *pro*phete trew þeis wordes of you wyll say
this reme shall ioye þe blessyd tyme of y*our* natiuyte
the mellyflue mekenes of y*our* p*er*son shall put all wo away
vn to the rote of Iesse rote likkyn you well I may   20
the fragrante floure sprongon of you shall so encrece & sprede
that alle the world yn ich p*ar*ty shall cherisshe hym love & drede

Afturward with Inne the yate at the Est yende of the Chirche was
sette apagent right well arayed & þerin was shewed ij speeches on   25
of seynt Edward & the other of seynt Iohn Euang*e*list as foloweth |

®S Edward

Moder of mekenes dame m*ar*garete p*r*inces most excellent
I kyng Edward welcu*m* you *with* affeccion righ*t* cordiall
Certefying to y*our* highnes mekely myn entent   30
for the wele of the kyng & you hertely p*r*ay I shall
and for p*r*ince Edwarde my gostly chylde whom I love p*r*incipall
Prayng the Iohn euangelist my helpe þ*er*in to be
On that condicion right humbly I gif þis ryng to the
                                                                                                          35

®Iohn
Euang*e*list

Holy Edward crownyd kyng brothur in virginyte
My power playnly I wyll p*r*efer thi wyll to Amplifye
Most excellent p*r*inces of Wymen mortall y*our* bedeman wyll I be
I knowe y*our* lyf so vertuus þat God is plesyd therby
the birth of you vn to þis reme shall cause grete melody   40
The vertu*us* voyce of p*r*ince Edward shall dayly well encrese
Seynt Edward his godfader & I shall p*r*ay þerfore dowtelesse

Afturward [at] the Cundit yn the Smythfordestrete was right
well arayed & there was shewed iiij speches of iiij cardynall *vertues*
as foloweth

®Rightwesnes   I Rightwesnes that causeth treuth to be had   5
Mekely as a maydyn my langage wyll I make
and welcu*m* you *pr*inces right cherefull & glad
With you wyll I be dwellyng & neu*er* you forsake

®Temp*er*aunce   I temp*er*aunce to plece you warly wyll wake   10
And welcome you as most worthy to my power
besechyng youre highnes þis langage to take
I wyll feythfully defende you from all man*er* daunger

®Strengh   I Strengh þe iij^e vertewe wyll playnly appere   15
Clerely to conseyue you yn y*our* estate most riall
and welcu*m* yowe *pr*inces gladly wit*h* chere
for to do þat mowe plece you aray ws we shall

®Prudence   I *pr*udence of the iiij verteues highest in degre   20
Welcu*m* you dame m*ar*garete quene crowned of this lande
The blessyd babe þ*at* ye haue born Prynce Edward is he
Thurrowe whom pece & t*r*anquilite shall take þis reme on hand
We shall endowe both you & hym clerely to vnderstonde
We shall *pr*eser*u*e you *p*ersonally & neu*er* fro you disseu*er*   25
doute not *pr*inces most excellent we iiij shall do oure deu*er* |

Afturward at the Crosse yn the Croschepyng there were ordeyned
diu*er*se angels sensyng a high on the Crosse & there ranne out
wyne at mony places a long whyle   30

Afturward betwix the seyde Crosse & the Cundit be neþe that
were sette ix Pagentes right well arayed and yn eu*er*y Pagent was
shewed a speche of the ix Conqueroures / yn the furst was shewed
of hector as foloweth   35

®hector   Most pleasaunt *pr*inces recordid þ*at* may be
I hector of troy þ*at* am chefe conqueroure
lowly wyll obey yowe & knele on my kne
and welcum yowe tendurly to y*our* honoure   40
To this conabull Cite the *pr*incess chaumbur
Whome ye bare yn youre bosom Ioy to þis lande

Thro whome in prosperite þis empyre shall stand

In the secunde Pagent was shewed a speche of Alexander as
foloweth

5

®Alexander   I alexander þat for chyualry berith þe balle
Most curius in Conquest thro þe world am y named
Welcum yowe princes as quene principall
But I hayls you ryght hendly I wer worthy to be blamyd
The nobilest prince þat is born whome fortune hath famyd   10
Is your souerayn lorde herry emperour & kyng
Vnto whom mekely I wyll be obeying

In the thridde Pagent was shewed of Iosue as foloweth

15

®Iosue   I Iosue þat in hebrewe reyn principall
To whome þat all Egipte was fayn to inclyne
Wyll abey to your plesure princes most riall
as to the heghest lady þat I can ymagyne
To the plesure of your persone I wyll put me to pyne   20
as aknyght for his lady boldly to fight
yf any man of curage wold bid you vnright

In the fourthe Pagent was shewed of Dauid as followeth

25

®Dauid   I dauid þat in deyntez haue led all my dayes
That slowe þe lyon & goly thorowe goddys myght
Will obey to you lady youre persone prayse
and welcum you Curtesly as a kynd knyght
for the loue of your lege lorde Herry that hight   30
and your laudabull lyfe that vertuus euer hath be
Lady most lufly ye be welcum to þis Cite |

In the fyth Pagent was shewed a speche of Iudas as foloweth

35

®Iudas   I Iudas þat yn Iure am called the belle
In knyghthode & conquest haue I no pere
Wyll Obey to you princes elles did not I well
And tendurly welcum you yn my manere

7 / both M.D. Harris and Craig prefer to read curagious while noting the MS version
curius

Your own souerayn lorde & kynge is present here
Whome god for his godenes preserue yn good helthe
And ende you with Worship to this landys welthe

In the sixt Pagent was shewed a speche of arthur as foloweth   5

®Arthur

I arthur kynge crownyd & conqueroure
That yn this lande reyned right rially
With dedes of armes I slowe the Emperour
The tribute of this ryche reme I made downe to ly   10
Ihit vnto lady obey I mekely
as youre sure seruande plesure to your highnesse
for the most pleasaunt princes mortall þat es

In the vij Pagent was shewed a speche of Charles as foloweth   15

®Charles

I charles chefe cheftan of þe reme of fraunce
and emperour of grete rome made by elleccion
Which put mony paynym to pyne & penaunce
The holy relikes of criste I had in possession—   20
Ihit lady to your highnes to cause dieu refeccion
Worshipfully I welcum you aftur your magnificens
yf my seruice mowe plece you I wyll put to my diligence

In the viij Pagent was shewed a speche of Iulius as foloweth   25

®Iulius

I Iulius cesare souerayne of knyghthode
And emperour of mortall men most hegh & myghty
Welcum you princes most benynge & gode
Of quenes þat byn crowned so high non knowe I   30
the same blessyd blossom þat spronge of your body
Shall succede me yn worship I wyll it be so
all the landis olyue obey hym vn to

In the ix Pagent was shewed a speche of Godfride as foloweth   35

®Godfride

I godfride of bollayn kynge of Ierusalem
Weryng þe Thorny crowne yn Worship of Ihesu
Which yn batayle haue no pere vnder the sone beme
yhit lady right lowlely I loute vnto yowe   40

11 / vnto lady for vnto you lady

So excellent a princes stedefast & trewe
knowe I none cristened as you yn your estate
Ihesu for his merci incresse & not abate |

Afturward & last the Cundit yn the Crossechepyng was arayed   5
right well with as mony Virgyns as myght be þervppon and there
was made a grete dragon & seynt Marget Sleyng hym be myracull
& there was shewed full well this speche that foloweth

®*Saint*
Margaret

Most notabull princes of Wymen erthle   10
Dame margarete þe chefe myrth of þis empyre
~~ye be hertely welcum to þis cyte~~
To the plesure of your highnes I wyll sette my desyre
Bothe nature & gentilnes doth me require
Seth we be both of one name to shewe you kyndnes   15
Wherfore by my power ye shall ˄ ⌐haue¬ no distresse
I shall pray to the prince þat is endeles
To socour you with Solas of his high grace
he wyll here my peticion this is [endle] doutles
for I Wrought all my ⌐lyf¬ þat his wyll wace   20
Therfore lady when ye be yn any dredefull cace
Calle on me boldly þer of I pray you
and trist to me feythfully I woll do þat may pay you

Memorandum that the seyd Richard Braytoft Meyre resseyued of   25
Thomas Bradmedowe & Iohn Straunge late wardens of the fote
of her Acounte xxj li. xiij s ij d of the which the seyde Meyre payd
to Iohn Wedurby of leycetur for þe provicion & makyng of these
premisses of the welcomyng of oure Souerayn lady the quene &
for his labour Inne & out xxv s   30
...

Carpenters' Account Book I CRO: Acc 3/1
f 18v*

    35

Expenses on corpus christi tyde Midsomer ny3t ny3t Seynt
peter ny3t in bred Ale torche berers to þe Mynstrell   v s ⟨..⟩
& All oþer þinges   ob
Item paid to þe Pynners   x s
...   40

36 / ny3t ny3t *MS dittography*   37 / *Sharp, p 163, reads* v s v d *for* v s ⟨..⟩

f 26*

...

Item paid to the pynners & tilers   x s

...

                                                                          5

f 28*

...

[Item for beryng of torches on corpus christi day   iiij d]

...

                                                                         10

AC *Smiths' Accounts* Sharp: *Dissertation*
p 149 fn p*

...

Item to have owght the pagent at the comyng of the quene
that ys the parell to þe pagent and harneste men and þe harnes   15
to hem wyth and a cote armyr for arture & a crest with iij
grevyvyes xvij s xj d ob.

1457
Leet Book I CRO: A 3(a)   20
f 172v   *(14 March)*
(Royal council at Coventry 15 February - 14 March)

... and the seid xiiij day of Marche the kyng remeved from
Couentre to kelyngworth at which tyme the seide Meyre & his   25
brethern with a Godely feliship of the seid Cite that plesyd oure
seid souerayn lord right well attended vppon his hyghnes &
brought hym to the newe Crosse vppon the heth at the vtter
Syde of theyre fraunchice & there toke their leve of oure seid
souerayn lord havyng right grete thank   30

f 173* *(16 March)*
                       The Quene
The Wennesday the xvj day of Marche then next suyng remeved
the Quene from Couentre to Colshull and the Meyre & his brethern   35
with a feyre felyship of the Comens brought her on gate tyll that
•Queen   she was passed the fraunchice At which tyme the Meyre Rode next
Remoueth to   before her with a Mase yn his hande and the shirrefs with her
Colehill•   Whyte yardes next be[fo]fore the Meyre like as they be fore tyme
did be fore the kyng Savyng the kynges Swerd was next to hym   40

39 / [fo] *in* be[fo]fore *cancelled at line end*

and So they did neuer be fore the Quene tyll then for they bore
be fore that tyme Alwey theire seruauntes Mases be fore the Quene
at her comynges at which doyng her Officers groged [seyng]
seying the Quene owed to be met yn like fourme as the kyng
Shold Which yn dede as ys seide owe to be so except her   5
displeser wold be eschewed

(5 June)

                                                                           10
Memorandum that oon Whitsonday then next suyng oure seid
souerayn lord & oure souerayn lady the Quene went bothe a
procession at Couentre crowned And the Circuyte of the
procession was Thorowe be the Welyard yn to seynt Myghel
Chirche yarde & so vp be the belfrey & yn agayn at the Mynster   15
Durre that openeth yn to the Trynite chircheyarde at which tyme
ther Went of [s] the spiritualte a procession The Bysshop of
herford Which seid the high Masse The Priour of Couentre with
his Covent The Dene of the kynges Chapell with alle the hole
•procession on   Chapell and the Duke of Bukyngham folowed next to the kyng   20
whitsunday•   on his right hande and the lord Beaumont bere the kynges Treyne
The Erle of Stafford bere his Cap of astate & Sir Iohn Tunstall his
Swerde & there folowed mony lordes moo ordinatly aftur theyre
astates yn her Robes and the grete Officers. of housold yn theyre
aray Acustumed And then next folowed oure seid Souerayn lady   25
& the Duches of Bukyngham bere here Treyne & there folowed
then mony moo ladyes yn her Mantels Surcotes & other appareyll
to theyre astates acustumed afore which procession the Meyre &
his Brethern laburd to certeyn lordes of oure seid Souerayn lordes
Counsell be cause they were lerned that hit liked our Souerayn   30
lorde that he & oure Souerayn lady the quene that day wold goo
a procession them selff to knowe whedur ther shold be any other
procession then that as had byn that day afore tyme solemply
kept be the pepull of the Cite or elles they to wayte vppon his
highnes yn the tyme of that procession & to haue non other but   35
only that and then the kyng vnderstondyng the seid labour willed
that the Meyre & his brethern with the Cominalte shold keep
theyre owen procession that day as they had vsed be fore tyme
yn his absence & not to attende vppon his hyghnes but take
theyre vsuell disposicion acustumed yn the Cite to the worship of   40
god which was so don

f 173v* *(16 June)*

The Quene

On cor*por*is chr*ist*i yeven at nyght then next suyng came the quene
from kelyngworth to Couentre at which tyme She Wold not be
met but came *pr*euely to se the play there on the Morowe and She   5
sygh then alle the Pagentes pleyde saue domes day which myght
not be pleyde for lak of day and She was loged at Richard Wodes
the Groc*er* where Ric*hard* Sharp so*m*me tyme dwelled and there
all the pleys were furst pleyde at which tyme the Meyre & his
brethern send vnto her a *pr*esent which was sich as her suyth that   10
is to wit CCC paynemaynes a pipe of Rede wyne a dosyn Capons
of haut grece a Dosyn of grete fat Pykes a grete panyer full of
pescodes and another Panyer full of pipyns & Orynges & ij Cofyns
of Counfetys and a pot of grene Gynger and there were with her
then these lordes & ladyes that here folowen that is to sey the   15
duke of bukkyngham & my lady his Wyff & all their Childern the
lord Reu*er*s and my lady his Wyf the lady of Shrowesbery the
Elder and the lady of Shrowesbery the yonger with other mony
moo lordes & ladyes & the fryday then next suyng She remeved
to Colshull to her mete & so to Eculsale to the Prynce at which   20
tyme the seid Meire & his brethern with right a Good feliship of
the seid cite which plesid her highnes right well brought her to
the vtmast syde of theyre f*r*aunchice where hit plesyd her to gyff
them grete thank bothe for theyre *pr*esent & theyre gentyll
attendaunce   25

(16 August)

The kyng

The tuesday the xvj day of august then next suyng came the kyng
from kelyngworth to Couentre to Dyner at which tyme the Meyre   30
& his brethern with right a feyre feliship of the comens what on
hors bak & on fote met hym wherwith he was gretly plesyd & yaff
the Meyre & his brethern & alle the comens be his owen mouthe
rehersed grete thanke & the same day he rode agayn to
kelyngworth to his bed   35
...

Carpenters' Account Book I CRO: Acc 3/1
f 42v

...   40

Item spendid on Trinyte sonday at Robert Masons for to ged*er*

Marginal notes (left column):

Queen from kenellworth to Couentry

Remoueth to Colehill

King dined at Couentry

þe Crafte to geder aȝenst Corpus day christi At þe Meyres
Commaundement   viij d

...

Item paid to þe Minstrell on Midsomer nyȝt & peter nyȝt   xij d
Item paid to þe pynners   x s.   5

...

1458
Carpenters' Account Book I CRO: Acc 3/1
f 36   10

...

Item paide vn to þe pynners & tyllers pro corpus christi day   x s

...

(Midsummer and St Peter's Nights)   15
Item to owre Mynstrels on bothe nyghtys   xx d

...

AC *Holy Trinity Guild Accounts* Sharp: *Illustrative Papers*
p 134* *(Trinity Sunday)*   20

Item iiij Torcheberers, xij d. ... Item, histrionibus Civitatis vj s
viij d ...

                                                                       25

(St John Baptist's Day)
... Item histrionibus Civitatis, v s

...

— Templeman: *Records*   30
p 183 *(Assumption)*

... Also to the City Minstrels 5s. ...

1459   35
Leet Book I CRO: A 3(a)
f 179 *(2 October)*

...

hit was ordynid þat an honest man in euery [man] ward shuld be
assyned be þe Meir to go with þe waytes to gader thier wayes   40
quarterly & at the peticion of þe wates then beying

...

Carpenters' Account Book I CRO: Acc 3/1
f 35v *(Midsummer)*

...

It*em* for the dyghtyng of A Sallet & exspens*es* vppon [þe teylres
same nyght]   [xiij d] ⌈iiij d⌉   5
M*emorandum* in exspens*es* in Makyng of Thomas Grene ande
perys browne & oþer mo & payde to herre Merynton for the
torchys þ*at* cometh to   iij s vj d

...

                                                              10

f 45v

...

It*em* inexspens*es* vppon vppon Myssomer nyght & sent pet*er*
nyght Ande for the torchys Ande the Dyghtyng of A Sallet that
cometh to   ij s xj d   15

...

f 49v

...

[payde to the pyn*er*es & Ṭyllers p*ro* pagant   x s   20

...

It*em* payde to þe torcheberers p*ro* corpus chr*ist*i day   iiij d

...

It*em* payde for Torcheberres for corp*us* chr*ist*i day   iiij d]
It*em* payde to þe menstrell for s Myssomer ny3t & sen pet*er*   25
ny3t   ij s
It*em* payde to pynners & tylers   x s

...

AC   *Holy Trinity Guild Accounts* Sharp: *Dissertation*   30
      p 160

...

Exp*ensa* fact*a* in festo Corp*or*is chr*ist*i viz ad iiij*or* Torchberers ad
portend*um* iiij*or* Tortices p*er* tempus p*ro*cessional*is* circa le Cowpe
in quo continet*ur* corp*us* d*om*ini   xij d   35

...

13 / vppon vppon *MS dittography*
25 / *Sharp pencilled in St Crispin below the* s
34 / portend*um for* portand*um*
34 / *per: apparently consistent printer's abbreviation for* pro *used*

1460
Leet Book I CRO: A 3(a)
f 182 *(19 April)*

...

also hit is ordeyned þat eu*ery* Craft þat hath pagant to pley In /   5
that þe pagant be made redy & brought furth to play vppon þe
peyn of C s to be reased of iiij maistirs of the Craft*es* þat so offend

...

Carpenters' Account Book I CRO: Acc 3/1   10
f 38v*

...

It*em* payde for Torcheberres p*ro* corp*us* day chr*ist*i	ij d
It*em* to þe pynners pagante	x s

...   15

1461
Carpenters' Account Book I CRO: Acc 3/1
f 48v

...   20

In p*rimis* payde to þe pynners & tylers	x s
It*em* to þe torcheberrers for Corp*us* day chr*ist*i	iiij d

...

AC   *Smiths' Accounts* Bodl: MS Top. Warwickshire c.7   25
f 84*

... It*em* for the havyng [ought] owght of the pagent when the
Pryns came. [⟨...⟩] yn brede and ale, and to Samson wythe hys iij
knyghtys and to an harper 3/6 It*em* for golde for Samson's   30
garments and poyntys 4d It*em* for the ffeleschype when they went
to Kelyngworthe Castell vij d.

...

1462   35
Carpenters' Account Book I CRO: Acc 3/1
f 55*

p*ro* Tempore Thom*as* A Woode Nich*ol*us A Rededyche hys ffellow
on þe Wedynsdaye in Whyssonwoke As fore þe x s to þe pynners   40

32 / vij d: *Sharp, p 152, reads* iiij d

& tylers
[In *primis* harre Daulby   vj d
  Item Iohn haule   vj d
  Thomas A Woode   vj d
  Nicho*lus* A þe rededyche   vj d   5
  Thomas perys   vj d
  Iohn Davey   vj d
  Roberte Clarke   iiij d
  Thomas Walssche   iiij d
  Roberd dalton   vj d   10
  Iohn Brameley   iiij d
  Willia*m* Bannbrok   vj d
  Tho*m*as Iabet   vj d
  Tho*m*as Grene   vj d
  Roger Burrisley   iiij d   15
  Iohn Blake   iiij d vj d
  Iohn Tyresale   vj d]

f 61

...   20

In the tyme of Tho*m*as of wod & nycholas harison his felay
kepers of Carpenters Craft of Coue*n*tre haue payd to pynners &
tylers for the page*n*t   x s
...

Ite*m* payd to the mynstrell for corp*us* ch*ris*ti day mydsomer ny3t   25
& seynt pet*er*   xviij d
Ite*m* for torches bering on corp*us* ch*ris*ti day   ij d
...

f 61v *(White Friars' dinner)*   30
...

Ite*m* pay our mynstrelle   iiij d
...

AC *Smiths' Accounts* H·P: *Outlines* I   35
    p 338

... Item, expende at the fest of Corpus Christi yn reparacion of
the pagent, that ys to say, a peyre of new whelys, the pryce viij s;
item, for naylys and ij hokys for the sayd pagiente, iiij d; item,   40
for a cord and sope to the sayde pagent, ij d; item, for to have
the pagent ynto Gosford strete, xij d ...

— Bodl: MS Top. Warwickshire c.7
f 83* *(St Peter's Watch)*

...

Item for iiij chyldern to bere ye iiij sperys 4d ij *(blank)* for to
bere the ij torchys 2d ij stree hattys for ye chyldern 2d.   5

...

1463
Carpenters' Account Book I CRO: Acc 3/1
f 67   10

Item payd to the pynners & tylers for the pageant   x s
Item payd on Corpus christi day for torchis bering   ij d

...
          15

(Midsummer and St Peter's Nights)
Item payd to oure mynstrelles for both nygtes   viij d

...

f 68v *(14 August) (General dinner at the White Friars)*   20
...
Item to mynstrelles   xij d

...

f 82v*   25

Memorandum that y nycholas haryson has payd for my fynys
vj s viij d Item payd in the first ȝere of oure keping j d ∧ ⌐for
torches bering⌐ And seynt petur nyȝt xij d Item to oure mynstrelle
vj d Item payd to thomas of wood x s Item payd the secunde   30
ȝere on Corpus christi day j d Item on saynt petur nyȝt xij d & to
oure Clerk iiij d

...

AC   *Dyers' Accounts* Bodl: MS Top. Warwickshire c.7   35
f 115*
...
It in expense on mydsomer nygt & seynt peters nygt for ij whit
harnes hyryng & baryng of theme & of torches & speres & kakes,
spices, & wynes, & to mynstrells, & all odur costs & poynts &   40
gloves   xvij. s ix. d

...

AC **Smiths' Accounts** Sharp: *Dissertation*
p 212*

...

Item to the iiij mynstrells the same daye (Corp*us* chr*is*ti)   ix s

...   5

1464
Carpenters' Account Book I CRO: Acc 3/1
f 72v* *(27 May)*

...   10

At acolac*i*on made at westeley hows on the tr*i*nite sonday to
rec*eue* quarterages of foreners then payd to the pynners &
tylers   x s
        Su*m*ma Expens*es*   x s

...   15

f 73

...

It*em* payd on Corpus chr*is*ti day for torches beryng   ij d

...   20

It*em* payd to our mynstrell for corp*us* chr*is*ti day myssomer &
seynt pet*er* ny3t   xviij d

...

f 76   *(19 August)* *(Annual dinner)*   25

...

It*em* payd mynstrell*es*   viij d

...

f 76v   30

...

[It*em* to the mynstrell*es* þat day   viij d]

...

AC **Smiths' Accounts** Sharp: *Dissertation*   35
p 181 fn p *(St Peter's Watch)*

...

It*em* on þe Jorneymen the sayd nyght yn bred ale & wyn   xxiij d

...

32 / *MS cancellation of repetitive entry for l 16*

1465
Carpenters' Account Book I CRO: Acc 3/1
f 77v* *(17 February) (White Friars' dinner)*
...

Item to mynstrell*es* cook & turnebroche   v d   5
...
Item payd to tylers and pynners   x s
...

AC   *Smiths' Accounts* H-P: *Illustrations*   10
     p 52*

... Item, in expenses on Corpus Christi evyn to wasche the pageant,
and to have it in and out, and on the day in wyne, ale, rysches
and torches beryng and all odur thynges, and to hand in the   15
pageant, xiij d ...

1466
Leet Book I CRO: A 3(a)
f 201 *(25 January)*   20
...

Also they haue ordenyd that the wardens shall have the rewle of
makynge the meyr*es* [hatt*es*] cappus & the olde stuffe to be
®nota   kepyd to the town vse & when they make a newe furryd cappe al
this cost a boue xiijs iiij.d to be. payd on the meyrys cost   25
...

Carpenters' Account Book I CRO: Acc 3/1
f 85
...   30
Item payd to the tylers pageant   x s
Item payd for beyryng of torches on corpus chr*ist*i day   ij d
...

(Midsummer and St Peter's Watches)   35
Item for the mynstrill*es* both the ny3t*es*   xij d
...

AC   *Smiths' Accounts* Sharp: *Dissertation*
     p 21*   40
...
Item in expens*es* at the rehers in the p*ar*ke   iij d
...

— Bodl: MS Top. Warwickshire c.7
f 33

...

It to ij men *with* jakks *with* the Meyr iiij. d
...   5

1467
Leet Book I CRO: A 3(a)
f 207v* *(4 April)*
...   10
Also þat þe wayt*es* of þis Cite þat nowe be & her*eafter* to be shall
not passe þis Cite but to abbott*es* & pri*ours* wit*h*in x myle*es* of
þis Cite
...
                                                                       15
AC   *Smiths' Accounts* Sharp: *Dissertation*
     p 212
     ...
     It*em* payd to the weytes for Corpus chr*ist*i day & seynt loye day
     ther hyr & ther bord   viij s viij j   20
     ...

     — H-P: *Outlines* I
     p 338
                                                                       25
     ... Item, in met and drynk on mynstrelles and on men to drawe
     the pagent, xxij d ...

1468
Carpenters' Account Book I CRO: Acc 3/1   30
f 90v*
...
Payd to pynners & tylers   x s.
...
                                                                       35
(Midsummer and St Peter's Watches)
Item to mynstrell*es* for both ny3t*es*   xx d
...

AC   *Dyers' Accounts* Sharp: *Dissertation*   40
     p 190 *(Midsummer and St Peter's Watches)*
     ...
     payd for yernewerk to our torches   iij s iiij d

payd for iiij torches of xxxij li le li. v d   xiij s iiij d
peid for xij newe pencells & payntyng of hem   iij s vj d
peyd for iiij judasses for our torches   iiij s iiij d

...

5

p 194*

...

Expense to speke for speyres pencells & odur thyngus iiij s j d ob
payd for bukram for ij pencells   x d
peid for steynyng & payntyng of baners & spers   vij s iiij d   10
paid for frynge & bells to the baners & sperhedis   ij s iij d
peid for speyr chafts & bukrame   ij s iij d

...

— Bodl: MS Top. Warwickshire c.7   15
f 115

... to speke for speyres, pencells, & odur thyngus iiij. s j. d ob.

...

20

(Delivered by masters and keepers to their successors)
... these goodes longyng to the crafte, that is to sey - ij newe
speyres with newe pencells, & ij hedes of steel, & ij laton bells, &
xij newe pencells for the torches, & iiij newe torches, & iiij judasses,
& the bolles, and iiij surplis, & iiij stre hatts, & ij cote armurres.   25

...

AC   **Smiths' Accounts** Sharp: *Dissertation*
p 193 *(Midsummer and St Peter's Watches)*

...   30

Item for the hyr of iiij whyt harnys vj s viij d for beyryng of
them xvj d Item beyryng of iiij speyres iiij d iiij hatts for the
speyre beyrers j d
payd for payntyng of the speyre chafts freshe   xxiij d
payd for iiij newe pencells at london   viij s   35

...

p 198

...

(St Peter's Watch)   (Midsummer)   40
Item to þe mynstrell xx d   Item to þe mynstrell xl d

...

— Bodl: MS Top. Warwickshire c.7
f 33

...

It for ij jakkud men on the Meyre iiij. d   5

...

AC *Holy Trinity Guild Accounts* Sharp: *Dissertation*
pp 160-1

...

Item to iiij torcheberers in festo corporis christi	xij d 10
Item to Johanni Exale for peyntyng iiij judasys	iij s ⎮
Item eidem for xij pensells to þe same	xij d
Item soluti for clothe for the pensells	ij d ob.

...
15

1469
Carpenters' Account Book I CRO: Acc 3/1
f 95*

...

Item paid for beyryng torches on corpus christi day	vj d 20
Item to mynstrelles þat day	viij d
paid to pynners & tylers	x s

...

Item payd to metcalf ^ ˹& banbroke˺ for mynstrelles	ij s.

...
25

AC *Dyers' Accounts* Sharp: *Dissertation*
p 132

...

Expense for seynt marie quarter   30
On hogh tuysday at the hall, in bred xviij d ale, meat, &c. &c.

...

AC *Smiths' Accounts* H-P: *Illustrations*
p 51   35

Item, reparacion for the pagent and the pagent hows, for a gret
burd for the dur of the pagent howse, v d ...

---

31 / *Reader (Bodl: MS Top. Warwickshire c.7) glosses* hall *as St Nicholas and continues:*
bread, ale, spice, meat &c 14/5½

p 52

...

For x. pond yrne for the pagent and the weket, xv d; item, a
lachet on the pagent whele, j d ...

5

— Sharp: *Dissertation*
p 21*

...

Item for iiij Jaked men about the pagent   iiij d

...   10

1470
Leet Book I CRO: A 3(a)
f 209 *(12 April)*

...   15

Memorandum quod Ricardus Wode grocer deliberauit xij⁰ ⌈die⌉
Aprilis Anno regis Edwardi quarti x⁰ Ricardo braytoft iunior &
Ricardo alen guardianis vnum scochyn argenti cum colerio argenti
quod ordinatum erat pro vno de le waytes ville de Coventrie

20

Carpenters' Account Book I CRO: Acc 3/1
f 98v

...

paid for torches beyryng on corpus christi day   iiij d 25

...

paid to metcalf mynstrell   xij d
paid to tylers & pynners   x s

...

30

AC   *Dyers' Accounts* Bodl: MS Top. Warwickshire c.7
f 33 *(22 June)*

...

peid to iiij jakked men on far friday   vij. d 35

...

— Sharp: *Dissertation*
p 194 *(Midsummer and St Peter's Watches)*

...   40

Item for beyryng of speyrs & torches   vj d

...

AC   *Smiths' Accounts* H-P: *Outlines* I
p 338

...

Item, rysshes to the pagent, ij d; item, ij clampys of iron for the
pagent, viij d; item, ij legges to the pagent and the warkemanship   5
withall, vj d ...

— Sharp: *Dissertation*
p 181 fn p

...   10

Item on Corpus nyght spende upon the Jurneymen   v d

— Bodl: MS Top. Warwickshire c.7
f 33*

...   15

It on feyr fryday for men Schirreves xij. d - It on feyr fryday to
the meyr & men xiij. d ...

1471
Carpenters' Account Book I CRO: Acc 3/1   20
f 100

...

Item geven to Richard stendwysthe for fochyng the harn⟨..⟩ to
the maystur   v d
...   25

f 101v

...

Item payd for torches beyryng   iiij d
...   30

(St John's Night)
Item for mynstrelles that ny3t   v d
...
                                                                            35

(St Peter's Night)
Item payd for mynstrelles þat ny3t   x d
...
payd to tylers & pynners   x s.
...

23 / harn⟨..⟩ *originally* harnes; *top of 'e' visible through ink blot*

AC   *Smiths' Accounts* H-P: *Outlines* I
p 338 *(Corpus Christi)*

... Expenses to brynge up the pagent into the Gosford Strete
amonge the feliship, viij d; expenses for burneysshyng and   5
peyntyng of the fanes to the pagent, xx d; item, cloutnayle and
other nayle and talowe to the pagent, and for waysshyng of the
seid pagent and ruysshes, vj d ob.; item, at bryngyng the pagent
owt of the house, ij d; item, nayles and other iron gere to the
pagent, viij d ob.; expenses to a joyner for workemanshipp to the   10
pagent, vij d ...

— Sharp: *Dissertation*
p 20 *(Corpus Christi)*
...   15
Expens at mikelparke strete ende for ale to þe pleyers   x d
Item at Richard a woodes, dur for ale to þe pleyers   v d
...

p 35   20
...
Item paid to the waytes for mynstrelship   vj s
...

p 198 *(Midsummer Watch)*   25

... Item ij mynstrells ij s ij d ...
...

(St Peter's Watch)   30
Item ij mynstrelles xx d ...

1472
Carpenters' Account Book I CRO: Acc 3/1
f 103*   35

Item payd to þe tyllars & pynars   x s
...
Item ffor þe mynstrell   iiij d
...   40
Item ffor torch beryng on Corpusday christi   iiij d

A C   *Smiths' Accounts* Sharp: *Dissertation*
p 183 *(Ordinance at general annual meeting)*

... that any mayster for hens forward schalbe a lowed for midsomer
nyght for brede wyne & ale the seide nyght v s. & not a peny more.   5
Also itt is ordeyned by the felischipp that the maisters schallbe a
lowed for seint peters nyght iij s iiij d & nott a peny more
...

p 193   10

... assady & redde wax to mende the Crests at seynt peters
tyde   ij d ob.
Expens ayenest midsomer nyght Inprimis Assady to the Crests
vj d ij synnapers papuos ij Grene papuos & a golde papuos viij d   15
Red wax Rossen & white papuos ij d ob. makyng the Crests newe
xvj d.
...

— H-P: *Illustrations*   20
p 52 *(Corpus Christi)*

... Inprimis, sope to the pagent wheles and rysschys j d ob. ...

1473   25
Carpenters' Account Book I CRO: Acc 3/1
f 108 *(April 11 feast at White Friars)*
...
Item to þe mynstrell   iij d
...   30

f 108v

[Item on corpusday christi to þe pynars   x s.]
Item on corpusday christi ffor torch berars   vj d   35
Item payd at corpusday christi to þe pynars   x s
...

15 / *Sharp glosses* synnapers *as* cinnabar, red

(Midsummer Night)
Item a mynstrell   [viij d] x d
...

(St Peter's Night)   5
Item a mynstrell   iiij d
...

AC **Dyers' Accounts** Bodl: MS Top. Warwickshire c.7
     f 33   10
     ...
     paid to iij men for [bery] beyryng jakkus vj. d
     ...

     — Sharp: *Dissertation*   15
     p 214 *(Dinner at St Nicholas Hall)*
     ...
     paid to mynstrells   ij d
     ...
                                                                                     20
AC **Smiths' Accounts** Bodl: MS Top. Warwickshire c.7
     f 83*
     ...
     Nicholas Brome agrees to pay ij s. annually towards "waiges of
     the Smythes prest & pajent" ...   25
     An order same year that any man of the craft being summoned
     to the Master to ride to meet the King, the Queen, the Prince or
     any other business att ye Mayors commandment - on failing shall
     pay 3/4 without grace.
     ...   30

     — H-P: *Illustrations*
     p 53

     ... Item, a c cloutenayle to the pagent, iiij d; item, teynturhokes   35
     and spykynges, iij d; item, iron bondes and clyppis to the wheles,
     xiiij d; item, for waysschyng of the pagent, ij d; ...

     — Sharp: *Dissertation*
     p 193* *(Midsummer and St Peter's Watches)*   40
     ...
     for hyre of iiij Crestis to John Yale xvj d mendyng of crests iij d ...
     ...

1474
Leet Book I CRO: A 3(a)
ff 221-1v* *(28 April)*

◦Receavinge prince Edwarde◦

Memorand*um* that the xxviijth day of the Moneth of Aprill cam   5
oure lorde prince Edward out of Walys so by Warrewik to Couentre
and the Meire & his brethern *with* the diuers of Cominalte of the

◦prince Cometh
to Couentry◦

seide Citie clothed in Grene and Blewe metyng oure seid lorde
Prince vpon horsbake by yonde the Newe Crosse in a Chare beyng
of Age of iij yere *(blank)* there welcomyng hym to his Chaumb*er*   10
and yevyng hym there a C mark in a gilt coppe of xv ouncez *with*
a kerchyff of Plesaunce vpon the seid Coppe And then comyng in
to Citie And at Babulake yate ther*e* ordeyned a stacion therin
beyng kyng Richard *with* xiij other arrayed Lyke as Dukes
Mark*is*es Erles Vicouns and Barons & lordis *with* my*n*strallcy of   15
the Wayt*es* of the Cite and kyng Richard there havyng this
speche her*e* ffolowyng

Rex Ri*card*us

Welcom full high and nobull prince // to vs right speciall
To this yo*u*r chaumb*re* / so called of Antiquite   20
The p*re*sens of yo*u*r noble p*er*son / reioyseth yo*u*r hart*es* all
We all mowe blesse the tyme / of yo*u*r Natiuite
The right lyne of the Royall blode / ys now as itt schulde be
Wherfore god of his goodnes / p*rese*rue you in bodily helth
To vs and yo*u*r tenaunt*es* here p*er*petuall ioy / and to all the   25
londis welth

Also at the Condite afore Richard Braytoft the Elder a nother
stacion *with* iij P*at*riarkes there stondyng vpon the seid Condite
with Iacobus xij sonnes *with* mynstralcy of harpe and dowsemeris   30
& there Rennyng wyne in on place and there on of the seid
pat*r*iarkes havyng this speche vnder writtyn

[Nobull p*r*ince Edward my Cossyn and my knyght /
And v*er*y prynce of oure lyne / comen by dissent]   35

O god most glorious / [And] grounder and gyder of all g*r*ace
To vs iij P*at*riarkes thou p*ro*mysed / as scriptur*e* maketh rehersall
That of oure stok lynially / schuld p*ro*cede and passe
A prynce of most nobull blode and kyng*es* sonne Imp*er*iall   40

21 / your *for* our

The wich was full fylled in god / and nowe referre itt we schall
Vnto this nobull prynce / that is here present
Wich entreth to this his Chaumber / as prynce full reuerent

Also at the Brodeyate a Pagiont and seint edward beyng therin   5
with x a states with hym with mynstralcy of harpe & lute and
kyng Edward havyng this speche next foloyng

Nobull prynce Edward my cossyn & my knyght
And very prynce of oure Lyne comyn dissent | 10

I seint Edward haue pursued / for your faders Imperiall right
Wherof he was excluded / by full furius Intent
Vnto this your Chaumber / as prynce full excellent
ʒe be right Welcom / thanked be crist of his sonde   15
ffor þat that was oures / is nowe in your faders hande

Also at the Crosse in the Croschepyng were iij prophettes
standyng at the Crosse Seynsyng and vpon the Crosse a boven
were Childer of Issarell syngyng and castyng out Whete obles &   20
ffloures and iiij pypis rennyng wyne

Also in the Croschepyng a fore the Panyer a Pagent and iij kynges
of Colen therin with other diuers arraied and ij knyghtes armed
with mynstralsy of small pypis and on of the kynges havyng this   25
speche vnder writtyn

O splendent creator / in all oure speculacion
More bryghter then Phebus / excedent all lyʒt
We thre kynges beseche the / with meke mediacion   30
Specially to preserue / this nobull prynce þi knyght
wich by Influens of thy grace / procedeth a right
Of on of vs thre Lynnyally we fynde
his Nobull Moder quene Elizabeth ys comyn of þat kynde

        35

Also vpon the Condite in the Croschepyng was seint George
Armed and a kynges doughter knelyng a fore hym with a lambe
and the fader & the moder beyng in a toure a boven beholdyng
seint George savyng theire doughter from the dragon // and the

10 / verte folium *written at foot of page*

Condite rennyng wyne in iiij placez and mynstralcy of
Orgonpleyinge and seint George havyng this speche vnder writtyn

O myghty god oure all socoure celestiall
Wich þis Royme [d] hast geven to dowere   5
to thi moder and to me George proteccion perpetuall
hit to defende from enimies ffere & nere
And as this mayden defended was here
Bi thy grace from this Dragon devoure
So lorde preserue this noble prynce and euer be his socoure   10

f 219* *(6 October)*

...

Also for by Cause þat ouer grett nombre of peopull of this Cite
®Chamberlayns   yerely At openyng & ouerseyng of the Coiens of this Cite not   15
none to Ride   desyred nor appoynted by the Meire Shirreffes or Chaimbrleyns
or be at opening
Lamas but such   of this Cite by their own actorite taken on them to ryde with the
as are Apoynted   seid Chaimbrlens ofte tymes in excesse nounmbre & vnruly to
full Ill example & like to enduce ryott rather then good rule hit is
therffore ordeyned at this leete þat noy persone of this Cite othere   20
then shall hereaftur 3erely to be appoynted by the Meir shirrefes
et Chaummburlens of this Cite take on hem to Com or be at the
openyng of the fforseid Coiens vp the Peyne to fforfet At euery
defaute vj s viij d and to haue imprisonament of iij dayes and that
this ordenance be proclamed at euery lete day as other ordenances   25
ben

A   *City Annals* CRO: Acc 2/E
   f 13*

...   30

Richard Braytost ˄ ⌜or Braytoft⌝ Mayor 1473 ended 1474 this
yeare came Prince Edward to Coventry & had a hundred poundes
& a Cup given him. his ffather came at Easter after he kept St
Georges feast at Coventre. about this time was a great flood The
Prince was one of the Godfatheres of ye Maiors Child.   35

...

Carpenters' Account Book I CRO: Acc 3/1
f 115 *(White Friars' dinner)*

...   40
Item þe mynstrel   iiij d
...

f 115v

...

It*em* payd at corpusday chri*st*i to þe pynars	x s
It*em* ffor torch berars	vj d
It*em* þe my*n*strell	viij d 5

...

It*em* þe my*n*strell	xj d

...

It*em* þe my*n*strell	xj d

...   10

A C   ***Smiths' Accounts***   Sharp : *Dissertation*
p 154 *(28 April)*

...

Exp*en*ses for bryngyng furth the pagent a ȝenst the comyng of	15
the Quene & the prince	vij d

...

p 21 fn i *(Corpus Christi)*

...   20

Pd for swepyng the pagent & dressyng vij d.

...

p 164*

...   25

It*em* for horsbred to the horsses	iij d

...

p 198 *(Midsummer Watch)*

...   30

It*em* to ij mynstrelles for melody	iij s iiij d

...

1475
Leet Book I   CRO : A 3(a)   35
f 227v *(3 April)*

...

Hit is ordened at the p*re*sent leete that Eu*er*y Craft wit*h*in this
Cite com*e* wit*h* their Pageaunt*es* accordyng as hit haith byn of
olde tyme and to Com*e* wit*h* their p*ro*cessions & Ridyng*es* Also   40

16 / vij d: *Reader, MS Top. Warwickshire c.4, f 79 reads* 8d

when the byn required by the Mei*r*e for the worship of this Cite
peyne of x li. at eu*er*y defalt
...

Carpenters' Account Book I CRO: Acc 3/1   5
  f 118v*

...

⟨...⟩ payd at Corpus chr*is*ti day to þe tyllars & py*n*ars   x s
⟨...⟩o torchberars   iiij d
⟨...⟩ to mynstrelles   vj d   10
...

(Midsummer Night)
  Item þe mynstrell   xj d
...   15

(St Peter's Night)
  Item þe mynstrell   x d
...
                                                                          20

AC   *Holy Trinity Guild Accounts* Sharp: *Illustrative Papers*
     p 134 *(Trinity Sunday)*

     ... Item Waytes, vj s viij d ...
                                                                          25
(St John Baptist's Eve)
     ... Item le Waytes, v s Item p*aid* Torchberers, iiij d ...

1476   30
Carpenters' Account Book I CRO: Acc 3/1
f 123v
...

Ress*ey*vid In trenytie parychs ffor torch*es*   vj s ij d ob
Ress*ey*vid In seynt mykell parychs   x s. iii d   35
...

f 125
...

It*em* payd to þe pynars & tyllars   x s   40
...

It*em* mynstrells on corpusday Crysty   vj d In sp⟨..⟩

Item torch berars   iiij d
Item payde ffor ij torchys   xiij s. iiij d

...

Item ffor mynstrells on mydsomer ny3t & seynt petyr   ij ⟨.⟩

...   5

Carpenters' Account Book II CRO: Acc 3/2
f 7

... Item to Mynstralles ij s Item payd to ij torche beyras on   10
corpus day christi ij d ...

f 7v *(White Friars' dinner)*

... Item payd to þe ffrerys for syngyng iiij d ... Item payd ffor a   15
bolle for a torche ij d ...

AC   *Dyers' Accounts* Bodl: MS Top. Warwickshire c.7
       f 33   20
       ...
       payd for ij men on fayr friday with the meyr viij. d
       ...

       f 115   25
       ...
       It paid for a vestement iiij marcus.
       ...

                                                                   30
AC   *Smiths' Accounts* Sharp: *Dissertation*
       p 164   *(Corpus Christi)*
       ...
       Item ffor hors hyre to Herod   iiij d
       ...   35

       p 189 *(Midsummer and St Peter's Watches)*
       ...
       Item a new bolle to the Judas   ij d
       ...   40

1477
Carpenters' Account Book I CRO: Acc 3/1
f 129

...

It*em* ffor þe fforffet off þe torch*es* [xx d] xvj d 5

...

f 129v

It*em* payd to þe tyllars & pynars x s 10
...

It*em* ij to torchberars ij d
It*em* þe [þe] mynstrells xviij d
...

                                        15

AC   *Smiths' Accounts* Folger: Scrapbook Wb 155
    p 29
    ...

                Corpus Ch*ri*sti
            Soluciones ad le pleyers 20
Inprimis to Jhesus for gloves & all xxij d
Item, to Herode iij s viij d
Item, to Pylate iij s iiij d
Item, to Pilate wyffe ij s
Item, to Cayphas ij s vj d 25
Item, to Annas ij s ij d
Item, to the bedull iij s
Item, to ij Knyghtes iiij s
Item, to Petur iiij d
Item, to Pylates sonne iiij d 30
Item, to Malcus iiij d

  — H-P: *Outlines* II
  p 289
  ...   35

Item, to a peyntour for peyntyng the fauchon and Herodes face,
x d

...

---

12 / ij to *for* to ij   12 / ij *of* ij d *originally* ii

— Sharp: *Dissertation*
p 29*

...

Item for Assadyn, Silver papur & gold papur, gold foyle & grene
ffoyle   ij s j d   5
Item for Redd wax   ij d
Item payd to Thomas Suker for makyng the Crests   xxij d

...

p 30*   10

...

Item for sowyng of dame procula Wyff Shevys   iij d

...

p 31   15

...

Item for mendyng the demons Garment ...
Item for newe ledder to the same Garment   xxij d

...
                                                                          20

p 35

... Item xij peyr Gloveȝ to the pleyers xviij d ...
Item paid to the wayts for pypyng   v s

...   25

p 164

...

Item payd to iiij torchberers on corpus christi day   iiij d

...   30

p 212 *(St John's Night)*

...

Item payd to ij mynstrells   iij s
                                                                          35

1478
Carpenters' Account Book II CRO: Acc 3/2
f 11v

...

Item payde to þe tyllars   x s   40

...

Item payd to þe mynstrells at Corpus day christi   x d
Item payd torchberars   iiij d

...

Item þe mynstrells & Iohn & petyrs ny3t   ij s viij d
Item ffor mendyng off iiij torchis   iij s

...

                                                                          5

AC   *Dyers' Accounts* Bodl: MS Top. Warwickshire c.7
     f 115 *(Dinner after twelfth day)*

     ... It peid to pleiers. xvj d Paid to mynstrells. iij d.
     ...   10

AC   *Smiths' Accounts* Folger: Scrapbook Wb 155
     p 29*

     ...

     Corpus Christi   15
     Paid to Jhesu, xx d Paid to Herod, iiij s Item, paid to Pilat, iiij s
     Paid to Cayphas, ij s vij d Paid to Anne, ij s ij d Paid to the bedyll,
     iij s Paid to percula, ij s Item, paid to ij Knyght, iiij s Paid to
     Petur, iiij d Paid to Pilat son, iiij d Paid to Malcus, iiij d Payd to
     Demon, xvj d   20
     Expenses for quarterage & for yrne work for the pagent & wyn[e]
     for maystres Ysham   xv d

     ...

     — Sharp: *Dissertation*   25
     p 29
     ...
     Item for assaden for the harnes   x d
     ...
                                                                          30
     p 30
     ...
     Item for mendyng of dame procula garments   vij d
     ...
                                                                          35
     p 187 *(Midsummer and St Peter's Watches)*

     ... half a li. of betyng candills iiij d ...

     p 189   40
     ...
     Item payd for a torche of xiiij li & di.   iij s vj d
     ...

1479
Carpenters' Account Book II CRO: Acc 3/2
f 9v col b

... It*em* to pynners & tiller*es* at the fest of cor*pus* chri*ste* x s It*em*   5
for mette to þe torche berr*es* ij d ...

f 10 col a

It*em* þe toweysday be ffo*re* cor*pus* chri*ste* day when he went to   10
payd penur*es* & tiller*es* & gedd*er* ap q*u*ar*trage*s xij d for þer wag*es* ...

col b* *(White Friars' dinner)*

It*em* to the menstrell ij d ... It*em* payd to þe frer*es* for synggyn   15
iiij d ... It*em* to þe watt*es* xvj d
...

AC   *Smiths' Accounts*   Folger: Scrapbook Wb 148
       p 59   20
       ...
Expenses on Blak Monday to rehersse, in bred & ale vij d in eggus
& buttur, iiij d ob.
Expenses on the sonday xvj. day of May for to rehersse, in bred v d
Item, in ale x d In powdur beef, iiij d with mustard.   25
Expenses on Tuysday in Wytson weke to rehersse, in bred vj d
Item, ale xj d Item, in Kechyn, xj d Item, iij gees, xij d In spices
and sauce, ij d
Expenses on sonday aftur Holy Thursday at reherssyng   ix d
Paid for mendyng of pleyers garmentes xv d Item, for swepyng   30
pagent, ij d Item, for drynkyng at havyng doun the pagent, x d
...

1480
Carpenters' Account Book II CRO: Acc 3/2   35
f 14
...
Expens*es* for torches beyring on cor*pus* chri*sti* day   iiij d
...

11 / Item for *written above* wages *and not cancelled*

(Midsummer and St Peter's Nights)

Payd to mynstrel*les* for both nyght*es*   ij s.

...

It*em* paid to pynners & tylers   x s.   5

...

AC   **Dyers' Accounts**   Sharp: *Dissertation*
p 214*

...   10

It*em* geven to the Jurneymen mynstrells   iiij d

...

AC   **Smiths' Accounts**   Sharp: *Dissertation*
p 21 fn 1 *(Corpus Christi)*   15

...

pd for a quart red wyn for pilat ij d

...

p 28   20

...

Expen*ses* for a slop for herod
Pd for peynti*ng* & dressyng heruds stuf   ij d

...
                                                            25

p 30

... Expen*ses* for a jaket for þe bydull

p 32   30

... pd for mendyng of pilats hat   iiij d

...

— H-P: *Outlines* I   35
p 339* *(Corpus Christi)*

... Item, for havyng furth the pagent on the Wedonsday, iij d;
item, paid for ij peyre newe whelis, viij s; expenses at the settyng
on of hem, vij d; item, for byndyng of thame, viij d; paid to a   40
carpenter for the pagent rowf, vj d; ...

1481
Carpenters' Account Book II CRO: Acc 3/2
f 15 col b*

...

peid to pynners & tylers   x s.   5

...

peid to mynstrelles   ij s. vj d
peid to ij men with the meyr   viij d

...

10

AC   *Smiths' Accounts* Sharp: *Dissertation*
       p 213*

Thomas West mynstrell oon of the wayts & his wyf received   ij d   15
Adam West the wayt & his wyf brodur & sistur received   ij d
John Blewet the wayt made brodur & his wif   ij d
Brese the wayt & his wif brodur & sistur & paid finis   ij d
    And these iiij weyts were made brodur on this condicion
foloyng, to serve the crafte on corpus christi day for viij s & theyr   20
dener that is to say ilken of theme to take xij d & to set on xij d
of theyr finis un to all theyr finis be paid in this maner wis & this
yer they paid wax silver.

...

25

p 193 *(Midsummer and St Peter's Watches)*

...

Item paid for hyr of hewkus & crests   iiij d

...

30

1482
Leet Book I CRO: A 3(a)
f 249v* *(19 August) (Bond against William Bristowe)*

35

... Maior & Communitas ville de Couentria pro se & tenentibus
omnium & singulorum tenementorum ac inhabitancium in
Couentria predicta exigunt ... habere & exercere in eisdem parcellis
terre omnimoda ioca & lusos sua annuatim cotidie &
quandocunque eis placuerit videlicet ad sagittandum luctandum   40
currendum cum hominibus & equis & trepidiendum necnon
lurciatria ...

Carpenters' Account Book II CRO: Acc 3/2
f 16 col b *(Midsummer and St Peter's Nights)*

...
Item payd to mynstrell*es* for both nyght*es*   ij s.
Item payd to pynners & tylers   x s.   5
...

AC   *Dyers' Accounts* Sharp: *Dissertation*
      p 198
                                                                              10
      ...
      Item to þe ij mynstrells at mydsom*er*   viij d
      ...

AC   *Smiths' Accounts* Sharp: *Dissertation*
      p 193 *(Midsummer and St Peter's Watches)*   15

      ...
      Item p*ai*d for dyghtyng of speyrs & axis   iiij d
      ...

      1483   20
      Carpenters' Account Book II CRO: Acc 3/2
      f 17

      ...
      Item paid to pynners & tylers aftur custom   x s.
      ...   25

      (Midsummer and St Peter's)
      Item payd to mynstrelles   iiij d
      ...
                                                                              30
      (14 September) (Harvest dinner at White Friars)
      ... Item goven to ʒong freres iiij d
      ...

      (Other expenses)   35
      And xj s. iiij d was delyuerd for torches to Ric*h*ard Russell ⟨...⟩
      ...

AC   *Dyers' Accounts* Sharp: *Dissertation*
      p 196   40

      ...
      It for mendynge þe deyst*er*s ban*er*   x d.

p 199*

...

Item for Bukram to rolles iij d Item for steyning of þe rolles viij d

...

5

1484
Carpenters' Account Book II CRO: Acc 3/2
f 18v

...

Item payde to the pynerrus & tylerrus   x s   10

...

payd the mynstrallus at corpus chr*iste* tyde   iiij d
payde for torch beryng   ij d

...

15

1485
AC *City Annals* BRL: 273978*

...

In the year 1485 S*ir* Robert Only Marchant Mayor, attwhitsontide
K Rich*ard* 3d Came to Kenellworth, & att Corpus Christy Came   20
to Coven*try* to see their playes, the 22d of Au*gust* the Battle att
H 7th   Bosworth feild was fought between K Rich*ard* & the Earle of
Richmond, wherein the King with Divers others wàs Slain, K Rich
was shamefully Carryed to Leicester & Buryed their when he had
Reigned 2 years 2 Month & one day, the Earle being proclaimed   25
King in the feild Came to Coventry & the Citty gave him A
Hundred pounds & a Cup [of] ⟨..⟩d soe hee departed

1486
Carpenters' Account Book II CRO: Acc 3/2   30
f 22 col a

...

It*em* when the mast*er*s wente to gedre vp money for there
expense   v d
It*em* when þey payed pynn*er*s & tylars   vj d 35
Item to the pynn*er*s and the tylars   x s

...

It*em* to mast*er* Taberer   ij s

...

27 / *page corner torn away after* [of]

col b *(Harvest dinner)*

...

Item to þe ʒonge freres   iiij d

...

At Corpus christi tyde & mydsomur   5
ffurst to the mynstrell at Corpus Christi tyde for hys dyner   ij d
Item at mydsomer and seynte petur tyde for hys wayge   xviij d

...

A C   **Smiths' Accounts**   Sharp : *Dissertation*   10
p 20 *(Corpus Christi)*

...

Item for ale at þe newe ʒate   j d ob.

...
                                                                           15
p 27

...

Item for a tabarde & an hoode   iiij d

A   **Holy Trinity Guild Accounts**   Templeman : *Records*   20
p 78*

...

                              Fletestrete

...

De duobus tenementis ijᵒᵇᵘˢ waytes per annum xxvj s viij d   25
allocatum xxvj s viij d

...

1487

A C   **City Annals**   B R L : 2 7 3 9 7 8 *   30

...

In ye year 1487 Thomas Bayly Mayor, King Henry Came to
Coventry & with the ArchBishop of Canterbury & others of his
Councell Lords Spirituall & temporall Held a Councell & Raiseth
an Armye to Goe to Newarke vpon Trent, where Hee Slew ye Earle   35
of Lincolne, Martin Smart tooke the OrganMakers Son the
pretended duke of Clarances Son, & brought him to Coventry, the
Battaile was fought ye 16th June, the King Came to Coventry to

---

18 / *Sharp adds editorial* [the hire of] *after* hoode
25 / *Templeman inserts editorial* pro *before* ijobus

see there playes on St peters day, Hee Lodged att S*i*r Rob*e*rt
Onlyes in Smithford Street on wensday after St Peters day on
Tho*mas* Harrington was beheaded on ye Conduite by the Bull
and was buryed att the Grayfryers Hee Called himselfe the duke
of Clarences Son   5
...

Carpenters' Account Book II CRO: Acc 3/2
f 24v col a   10
...

•9s 4d•   It*em* to þe pynn*er*s   x s.
...
It*em* on corp*us* chr*ist*i day torcheberers and there
dyn*er*   iij d   15
It*em* to the mynstrell And his dyn*er*   ij s ij d
...

(Midsummer)   20
Item to the mynstrell   ij d
...

col b   25
...
It*em* to þe ȝonge freres   vj d
...

f 25 col a *(23 September dinner)*
...   30
It*em* to the mynstrell   ij s
...

1488   35
AC   *Dyers' Accounts* Bodl: MS Top. Warwickshire c.7
f 33
...
It*em* on fayre fryday harnessed men afore the meyre viij. d
...   40

AC   *Smiths' Accounts* Sharp : *Dissertation*
      p 28* *(Corpus Christi)*

Item paid ffor hyryng off a skarlet wood and a raygete ffor on
off the bisshoppis   v d   5
...

p 29

Item for mendyng of Arroddes Crast   xij d   10
...

p 30
...
Item to reward to Maisturres grymesby for lendyng off her geir   15
ffor pylatts wyfe   xij d
...

— Folger : Scrapbook Wb 191
p 110*   20
...
In exspences on the pleyar in Estur wyke & Wysson wyke.
Item, paid to Annas, ij s ij d
Item, paid to Pylattes son, iiij d
Item, paid to Judas & the diamond, xvj d   25
...

— Sharp : *Dissertation*
p 189 *(Midsummer and St Peter's Watches)*
...   30
Item for iiij new torchis to & peyntyng off the Judasses   v s ix d
...

p 196
...   35
Item paid ffor dyttyng off the pencells   xxij d
...

---

4 / *Sharp glosses* wood *as* hood   4 / *Sharp glosses* raygete *as* rochet
25 / *H-P glosses* diamond *as* demon

Corpus Christi Guild Account Book CRO: A 6
f 6v

...

Item I ten*emento* ibide*m* qu*o*d Ioh*an*nes Bluet te*net recepti* per
a*nnu*m   xxiiij s 5

...

f 8

...

Item pet*it* allocari p*ro* exp*ensis* fac*cis* ad gen*erales* dies sepultura 10
festu*m* corp*oris* christi S*anc*ti Nich*ol*ai Capit*alibus* d*o*minis
paup*eribus* et alijs soluc*io*nibus ac de lib*erat*a pannor*um* p*ro*ut
p*atet* p*er* libr*um* de expens*is* &c   xxx li. x s j d ob.

...

                    15

1489
Carpenters' Account Book II CRO: Acc 3/2
f 27 col a

...

Item to the tylars & pynn*ers*   x s 20

...

Item too mynstrels on corp*us* chr*ist*i day mydsom*ur* night and
seynte pet*ur* night   v s iiij d

...

                    25

f 27v *(Harvest dinner)*

...

Item to þe ʒonge ffreres   ij d

...

                    30

AC ***Dyers' Accounts*** Sharp: *Dissertation*
p 190

...

Item for peyntyng and v*ar*neshyng of the judasses for the
torches   viij d 35

...

p 199*

...

Item ffor renuing the chapeletts x d ...   40

10 / sepultura *for* sepulturas

— Bodl: MS Top. Warwickshire c.7
f 33

...

It ij jakked men on feyre fryday iiij. d

...   5

AC   *Smiths' Accounts* H-P: *Outlines* II
      p 290* *(November)*

                                                                            10

... Item, paid for a gowen to Arrode, vij s iiij d; item, paid for
peynttyng and stenyng theroff, vj s iiij d; item, paid for Arrodes
garment peynttyng that he went a prossassyon in, xx d; item,
paid for mendyng off Arrodes gauen to a taillour, viij d; item,
paid for mendyng off hattes, cappus and Arreddes creste, with   15
other smale geyr belongyng, iij s; ...

— Folger: Scrapbook Wb 155
p 29 *(Corpus Christi)*
...   20
               Costes of the plearres
Item, paid to God, ij s Item, to Arrod, iij s iiij d Item, to Pylate,
iiij s Item, to Keyfasse, iij s iiij d Item, paid to Annez, ij s ij d
Item, paid to Pylattes wyfe, ij s Item, paid to Dycar, the bedyll,
iiij s Item, paid to the ij. Knyghtes, iiij s Item, to Pylattes son,   25
iiij d Item, paid to the dyamond & to Judas, xvj d Item, paid to
Petur & Malkes, xvj d Item, paid for hyryng off our hale, v s

— Sharp: *Dissertation*
p 189 *(Midsummer and St Peter's Watches)*   30
...

It*em* for iiij chyldren þ*a*t bare Torches & spers   iiij d

...

p 194 fn b   35
...

paid for ij chyldren ffor beryng speris   ij d

p 196
...   40
Item paid ffor iij yardus Rede bokeram ffor our standarts
pr*ice*   ij s vj d

Item paid to the stener ffor workemanship ther off   x s viij d
Item paid for xij yards ffrenge xvij d Item settyng on of the
ffrenge iiij d
Item paid for shavyng of þe standarts   iiij d
...   5

Corpus Christi Guild Account Book CRO: A 6
f 17v

...

Item I tenemento ibidem quod Iohannes Bluet tenet recepti per   10
annum   xxiiij s

...

f 19

...   15

Item petit allocari pro solucionibus ad obitus capitalibus dominis
pauperibus mendyauntibus solucionibus diuersis & distribucione
pannorum   xxij li. xj s iij d

...
                                                                           20

1490

AC   ***Smiths' Accounts*** Sharp: *Dissertation*
       pp 15-17*

       ...

This is the expense of the furste reherse of our players in ester   25
weke.
Inprimis in Brede   iiij d
Item in Ale   viij d
Item in kechyn   xiij d
Item in Vynegre   j d   Summa   ij s ij d | 30
Item payd at the Second Reherse in Whyttsonweke in brede Ale
& kechyn ij s iiij d Inprimis for drynkynge at the pagent in havinge
forthe in Wyne & ale vij d ob. Item in the mornynge at diner and
at Sopper in Costs in Brede vij d ob.
Item for ix galons of Ale   xviij d   35
Item for a Rybbe of befe & j gose vj d
Item for kechyn to dener & sopper   ij s ij d
Item for a Rybbe of befe   iij d
Item for a quarte of wyne   ij d ob.
Item for an other quarte of heyrynge of procula is gowne ij d ob.   40

1 / *Sharp glosses* stener *as* painter

Item for gloves   ij s vj d
Item spend at the reparellynge of the pagantte and the expences
of havyng it in and furthe   xiiij d
Item in paper   ob.   Summa   xij s j d ob.
Memorandum payd to the players for corpus christi daye.   5
Inprimis to God   ij s
Item to Cayphas   iij s iiij d
Item to Heroude   iij s iiij d
Item to Pilatt is wyffe   ij s
Item to the Bedull   iiij d   10
Item to one of the Knights   ij s
Item to the devyll & to Judas   xviij d
Item to Petur & malkus   xvj d
Item to Anna   ij s ij d
Item to Pilatte   iiij s   15
Item to Pilatte is sonne   iiij d
Item to an other knighte   ij s   Summa   xxviij s
                                                 þe Mynstrell xiiij d
Memorandum that these bene the Garments that wer newe
reparellyd a gaynste corpus christi daye.   20
Inprimis iiij Jakketts of blake bokeram for þe tormentors with
nayles & dysse upon þem.
Item other iiij for tormentors of an other suett wythe damaske
fflowers.
Item ij of bokeram with hamers crowned.   25
Item ij party Jakketts of Rede and blake
Item a Cloke for pilatte |
Item a Gowne for pilattes sone
Item a Gowne for the bedull
Item a hode for the bedull   30
Item twoo Burlettis
Item a Creste for heroude.
Item a Fawchon for heroude
Item a hatt for pilatte.
Item a hatt for pilatts sone   35
Item ij myters for the bysschoppis
Item ij hatts for ij princes
Item iiij hatts for the tormentors
Item other ij hatts for the tormentors
Item a poll ax for pilatts sonne   40
Item a septur for heroude
Item a masse

Item a septur for pilatts sonne
Item iiij Scorges and a piller
Item ij Cheverels gyld for Jhe & petur
Item the devyls hede
    The somme of all the Costes and workemanschyp & colours   5
drawyth to xv s

p 213
...
Item payd to the wayts   v s viij d   10
...

Corpus Christi Guild Account Book CRO: A 6
f 22 *(Guild Fees)*   15
...
De Iohanne Bluet   iij s iiij d
...

f 24   20
...
De Iohanne Bluet   iij s iiij d
...

f 25v   25
...
                            Recepcio Cere ...
De Iohanne. Bluet de Couentre Mynstrell   xiiij d
...
                                                                           30

f 27v
...
Item petit allocari pro distribucionibus pannorum prout
patet   v li. iiij s ij d
...   35

1491
AC   *City Annals* BRL: 273978*
...   40
In ye year 1491 Iohn Wigston Mayor, the Queen was delivered of
A Son att Greenwich, A Play of St Katherine in the Little
Parke ...

Carpenters' Account Book II CRO: Acc 3/2
f 28v col a

...

Item to þe pynners and þe tylars   x s

...   5

col b *(Midsummer and St Peter's Nights)*

...

Item to þe mynstrels both nightes   v s iiij d

...   10

f 29v

...

           expenses ffor Wesontyde quarterage

...   15

Item for ij Torchebereres apon Corpis christi day   ij d
Item for their dener   iiij d
Item to the mynstrelles paid   iiij s
Item for ther denner   iiij d

...   20

Item paid to the penneeres and Tyleres for þe paidint   x s

...

AC   *Smiths' Accounts* Sharp: *Dissertation*
   p 36 fn e*   25

... þe new rygenale ...

p 196 *(Midsummer and St Peter's Watches)*

...   30

payd ffor beryng the standarts   ij d

...

Corpus Christi Guild Account Book CRO: A 6
f 28v *(Guild fees)*   35

...

De Iohanne Rastell filio Thome Rastell   vj s viij d

...

f 29   40

...

De Iohanne Bluet   iij s iiij d

...

f 31v

...

De Iohanne Bluet   iij s iiij d

...

f 34v *(Guild rentals)*

...

Item I tenemento ibidem quod Iohannes Bluet nuper tenuit
recepti per annum   xxiiij s

...

Item I tenemento ibidem quod Iohannes Bluet nunc tenet   xx s

...

f 36

...

Item petit allocari pro distribucione pannorum &c   v li. iiij s ij d

...

1492

AC   ***Smiths' Accounts***   Sharp: *Dissertation*
p 213* *(St Loy's dinner)*

...

peyd to þe weytts vj s to a mynstrele at þe halle iiij d ...

...

Corpus Christi Guild Account Book   CRO: A 6
f 37v *(Guild fees)*

...

De Iohanne Bluet   iij s iiij d

...

f 39

...

De Iohanne Rastell per manus Iohanne Seman   vj s viij d

...

f 39v

...

De Iohanne Bluet   iij s iiij d

...

f 43v *(Master's claims for expenses)*

...

Also he Asketh Allowans for lyue*r*eys of gounes & hod*es*
&c   v li iiij s

...   5

1493
Leet Book I CRO: A 3(a)
f 271* *(10 October)*

...   10

for Chaundlers   It*em* they ordeyned at þe lete that þe chaundelers shuld pay
3erely to þe smythes ij s. toward*es* their paient

AC   *City Annals* Bodl: MS Top. Warwickshire d.4
f 13v   15

The K*ing* &   Thomas Churchman Bucklemaker maior 1492 and ended in
Queene came   1493. In his yeare K*ing* Henry, and the Queene came to
to coventr*ey*   Killingworth at whitsontide from when ᴧ ⌐ce⌐ they came to
Coventrey to see our plaies at Corpus Chris*t*i tide & gaue y*em*   20
great com*m*endac*i*ons

...

— Dugdale: *Antiquities of Warwickshire*
p 149 col a*   25

...

Tho*mas* Chyrchman, or Churchman ...
In his Mayoralty K*ing* H*enry* 7. came to see the Plays acted by
the Grey Friers, and much commended them.

...   30

AC   *Smiths' Accounts* Folger: Scrapbook Wb 148
p 59

...

Item, spend at the reherse in Est[e] ⌐u⌐r weke bred ale &   35
wyteyle   xxj d
Item, spend at the reherse in Wytsone weke   xxiij d
Item, a reherse apone the sondey aftur   iiij d
Corpus Chris*t*i day.
Item, peyd for a spare & for neylles to m[i]⌐e⌐nd the pagent ij d ob.   40

Item, a clampe for the sam   ij d
...

Corpus Christi Guild Account Book CRO: A 6
f 45 *(Guild fees)*   5
...
De Iohanne Bluet   iij s iiij d
...

f 45v   10
...
De Iohanne Rastell filio Thome Rastell   iij s
...

f 46   15
...
De Iohanne Bluet   iij s iiij d
...

f 51v *(Rental roll)*   20
...
                                    Croschepyng
A tenement there yat Iohn Bluet holdeth payyng by yere   xx s
...
                                                                                                        25

f 52v *(Master's claims for expenses)*
...
Also he Asketh Alouaunce for lyuerez gounes & hodes v li iiij s ij d
...
                                                                                                        30

1494
Leet Book I CRO: A 3(a)
f 272v *(10 April)*
...
Also hit is ordeyned accordyng as hath be ordeyned & enacted be   35
The vnyon of   dyuers letes in tymes past þat þe Chaundelers & Cookes of þis
Chaundelers & Cite shall be contributory ⟨.⟩ to þe Smythes of þis Cite & to pay
Cookes to þe   ȝerely towardes þe Charge of theire priste & pagant euery
Smythes   Chaundeler & Cooke ij s. euery man faylyng of such payement to
lese at euery tyme xl s & to haue enprisonment till he paye þe seid   40
ij s. with þe arrerages in þat partie yf eny be And þe seid peyn ...

f 273

ffor asmoche as þe vnyte concorde & amyte of all citeez &
cominalteez is principally atteyned & contynued be due
Ministracion of Iustice & pollytyk guydyng of þe same forseyng   5
þat no persone be oppressed nor put to ferther charge then he
conuenyently may bere and þat euery persone withoute fauour
be contributory after his substance & faculteez þat he vseth to
euery charge had & growyng for the welth & worship of the hole
body and where so it is in þis Cite of Couentre that dyuers charges   10
haue be continued tyme oute of mynde for the worship of the
same as pagantes & such other whech haue be born be dyuers
Craftes whech craftes at þe begynnyng of such charges were more
welthy rich & moo in nombre then nowe be as openly appereth
for whech causez they nowe be not of powier to continue þe seid   15
Charges without relief & comfort be shewed to them in þat partie
/ And in asmoch as there be dyuers Craftes in þis Cite þat be not
charged with like charges as dyers skynners ffysshemongers
Cappers Coruisers Bochers & dyuers oþer Therfore hit is ordeyned
be þis present lete | that þe Mair & viij of his Counceill haue   20
auctorite to call all þe seid Craftes & other þat be not charged to
þe forseid Charges and them to adjoyn to such Craftes as be
ouercharged with þe forseid pagantes vppon peynes be hym & his
seid Counceill to be sette / And yf eny persone refuse such vnyon
& contribucion or such resonable measne to be taken be the   25
discrescion of þe seid Maire & his Counceill such person so
refusyng to forfet & paye such peyn in þat partie so to be sette
be þe seid Maire & his Counceill / And þat such resonable measne
in þe premissez so to be taken be þe seid Maire & his Counceill to
be of like force and effect as yf hit had be made at þis present   30
lete

...

f 273v* *(6 October)*

...   35

Also it is ordeyned at þe same lete at þe request of þe Inhabitauntes
dwellyng in Gosseford strete that þe pageantes ȝerely frohensfurth
be sette & stande at þe place there of olde tyme vsed ˄ ⸢lymyt⸣ &
appoynted vppon peyn of euery Craft þat doth to þe contrary to
lese at euery defalt vj s. viij d to þe vse of þis cite to be levyed & 40
paide

Contribution
to Craftes

þe standyng for
paiantes •in
Gosford
street•

Where hit was ordeyned at the laste lete that such [⟨.⟩] Craftes
that were not contributory to the Craftes as bere ȝerely charge in
þis Cite to þe worship of the same shuld be vnyed & adioyned to
the [c] Craftes so charged be þe discrescion of the Maire & his
Counceill which ordennance hath not be put in execucion caused   5

be dyuers self willed persones whech be theire willes wold obbeye
no other rule ne ordre but after their owne willes grounded without
reason whech may not be suffred yf þis cite shulde prospere &
contynue in welth hit is þerfor ordeyned at þis present lete that
all maner Craftes & persones occupying ony Crafte within þis   10
Cite not beying charged to eny yerely charge that is had & made
in this Cite for þe worship of the same ˄ ⌐as paiantes & such other⌐
that they betwixt þis & þe fest of seynt martyn next commyng
of their toward lovyng disposicion applye them self to Ioyn &
vnye themself ˄ ⌐or to be contributory⌐ to other Craft that is   15
charged as is aforeseid in relief of theire charge which theire so

•All freemen to
hold off Some
Company•

doyng shall principally please god & contynue the goode name &
fame þat þis Cite hath had in tymes past / And þat euery Craft &
persone that woll not of theire goode willes be þe seid fest applye
them to such vnyon as is afore rehersed that then such persone &   20
Crafte that refusyng obbeye stand & perfourme such ordre &
direccion of þe Maire & his Counceill in þat partie to be ordred &
made vppon þe peyn of euery person & Craft þat disobeieth to
lese at þe first refusell C s. at þe ijde x li & at þe iijde xx marc
...   25

AC   *Dyers' Accounts* Bodl: MS Top. Warwickshire c.7
f 33
...
Itm ij men in harnes to master meyer iiij. d   30
...

— Sharp: *Dissertation*
p 198 (*Midsummer and St Peter's Nights*)
...   35
Item paid to the menestrells on boeth nygts   xvj d
...

Corpus Christi Guild Account Book CRO: A 6
f 53   40

The Inuentori of All the Iuels & Plate that longeth to this yelde

which were in ye Inuentory of Iohn Pachet late Clerk of the same
yelde &c

...

A baner of veluet wrought with golde
A myter of veluet wrought with golde   5
A crosear copur & gilt
A girdull of blue silk harnest with siluer & gilt weyng cors &
all   iiij vnces & di
A girdull of rede sylk harnest with siluer & gilt weyng cors &
all   vj vnces iij quarters 10
A peir of bedes of syluer weyng vj vnces   vj vnces
A canope of silk brodurd with gold with ij sidez of the same for
ye procession on corpus christi day
ij copus of silk with R & A brodurd on the tepettes iij hodes
ij Iakkes A goune for A ship ...   15

f 54v *(Guild fees)*

...

De Iohanne Blewet   iij s iiij d
                                                                              20
...

f 55v

...

quietus est   De Iohanne Rasstell per manus Maystres semons   iij s iiij d 25

...

f 56

...

De Iohanne blewet   iij s iiij d 30

...

f 57v

...
                                                                              35
De Adam West mynstrell   iij s iiij d

...

f 58 *(Receipts for wax-money)*

...
                                                                              40
De Adam West mynstrell   xiiij d

...

f 60* *(Rental roll)*

...

Croschepyng

A ten*ement* there þat Iohn blewet holdeythe by yere   xx s

...   5

Iurden Well

A ten*ement* that Iohn Rengold holdeth by yere   xl s

f 61 *(Master's claims for expenses)*

...   10

Item he askethe allowa*u*nce for levery govns & hod*es* v li. iiij s ij d

...

1495

Leet Book I CRO: A 3(a)   15
f 273v *(12 January)*

...

*Me*m*orandum* þat the ffeliship & mysterye of Bocho*ur*s in
Couentr*e* remembryng þe ordenance lately made be Auctorite of
lete / for contribuc*i*on to be had & made be such craft*es* as be not   20
charged to such ordinary charg*es* and Cost*es* as be ꝫerely made &
boren for þe worship of þis Cite / callyng also to theyr*e* mynde

Contribuc*i*on
made be þe
bochers to þe
whittawers

the olde acqueyntaunce & amyte þat of long tyme hath be &
contynued be [wey] measne of ent*er*cours & of bying & sellyng
betwixt them & þe ffeliship of whittawers whech be ou*er*charged   25
to the charg*es* aboue rehersed & for their*e* relief in þe pr*e*missez
ᴧ 'at Couentry aforeseid' þe xijth day of Ianuar*y* the xth ꝫere of
þe reign of our sou*er*aign lord Kyng henr*e* þe vijth in þe pr*e*sence
of Rob*er*t Grene [of Rob*er*t Grene] then beyng Maire wer*e*
agreable & ther gr*a*unted to ber*e* & pay ꝫerely frohensfurth to þe   30
seid ffeliship of whittawers toward*es* þe ᴧ 'ꝫerely' charge of
their*e* paiant as long as they ther shalbe charged with þe seid
paiant xvj s. viij d be the hand*es* of þe kepr*s* ᴧ '& maisters' of þe
seid [Crafte] ᴧ 'ffelliship' of Bochers to be paide to þe kepers &
mastirs of þe seid feliship of Whittawers ꝫerely in þe vigill of þe   35
holy Trinite with*o*ute ferther delaye with*o*ut eny other or ferther
charge or besynesse be the*m* to be made or doon to þe seid
ffeliship of whittawers

ff 275-5v* *(29 April)*   40

...

Also hit is ordeyned at þe petic*i*on & desir*e* of þe Craft of

Cardmakers towardes theire charge þat they ȝerely ber in kepyng
theire pageant that the Craftes of Skynners & Barbours shall ȝerely
frohensfurth bere & pay to þe seid Craft of Cardmakers xiij s. iiij d
in þe forme suyng þat is to sey þe Maisters of þe Crafte of
Skynners & þe Maister of þe Barbours shall ȝerely in þe vigill of   5
þe holy Trinite pay vnto þe Maister of Cardmakers either of them
vj s. viij d And ˄ ꞌyfꞌ eyther of þe seid Craftes fayle of payement
at þat day they & euery singler persone of either of þe seid craftes
that payement denying to lese at euery defalt vj s viij d & in
defalt of payement theire bodies so forfetyng to be commytte to   10
prison theire to remayn vnto þe tyme they haue paide þat fyn &
ouer þat to fynde suerte þat eftsones he shall not defende in þat
partie |

Also hit is ordeyned &c. at þe peticion of þe Crafte of wryghtes
& Tylers & pynners that these persones whos names here folowen   15
shalbe ioyned & contributorye to þe Crafte of wrightes
frohensfurth for euer & to pay & bere ȝerely after theire porcion
as ther wrightes doo towardes þe charge of their pageant vppon
þe peyn of euery person doyng þe contrarie to lese at euery defalt
vj s. viij d & in defalt of payement of þat peyn theire bodies to   20
prison till they haue paide hit & ouer þat fynde suertee that he
eftesones offende not in þat partie These be þe names Iohn
Okley Kerver Richard percy wright Iohn cokkes wright Nicholas
slough Cartwright Iohn norton whelewright & Iohn knyght
whelewright   25

Also where hit was shewed at þis present lete be bill put in be þe
Girdelers that þe Crafte of Cappers ˄ ꞌ& fullersꞌ of theire goode
will were agreable to paye in þe fest of þe vigill of þe holy Trinite
to þe ˄ ꞌmaister of þeꞌ Crafte of Girdelers ȝerely xiij s. iiij d
towardes þe charge of theire priste & pageant &c. hit was ordeyned   30
& stablisshed be auctorite of þis present lete that þat agrement &
acorde shuld stande stable & to be perfourmed & kept [for]
frohensfurth for euer with more þat yf payement ȝerely be not
made in þe seid vigill then euery person þat denyeth such
payement to lese at euery defalt vj s. viij d with imprisonment as   35
˄ ꞌisꞌ aboue seid in þe Crafte of Carpenters
...

Also hit is ordeyned in asmoch as in tymes past þer hath ˄ ꞌbeꞌ
dyuers riottes & offences & gret discordes don & commytted
vppon lammasse day caused be þat þat many in nombre vndesired   40
ryden with þe Chamberleyns hit is þerfor ordeyned be þese
present lete that frohensfurth for euer ther shall but ij or iij at

Quot
equitabunt cum
Camerarijs in
festo quod
dicitur aduincula
sancti petri

most of awarde ruyde with þe seid Chamberleyns vppon lammasse
& they to be assigned & named be þe Meire & his Counceill v or
vj daies before lammasse and yf eny Chamberleyn hereafter
assigne eny oþer persone þen is assigned be þe Maire or eny   5
persone vnassigned take vppon hym to ruyde contrarie to þis
ordenance they to lese at euery defalt x s. & for defalt of payement
þerof his body to prison till he make payement & ouer þat to
fynde suerte þat eftsones he shall not offend &c
...   10

f 276 *(5 October)*

...

Okley & Cokkes

Also hit was ordeyned at þe request of þe Craftes of Carpenters
Tylers & pynners & vppon theire compleynt made be bill &c.   15
that Iohn Okley kerver & Iohn Cokkes shuld be contributory &
paye ȝerely vnto þe seid Craftes as other of þe seid craftes ȝere
doo & payn accordyng þe laudable customme & gude ordre of
þis Cite vppon þe peyn of either of þe seid Iohn Okley & Iohn
Cookes doyng the contrarie to lese at euery defalt xiij s. iiij d   20

...

A C   ***Smiths' Accounts*** Sharp : *Dissertation*
p 21 fn k   *(Corpus Christi)*

...   25

Item in expences on þe pleares for makyng them to drynke &
hete at every reste xij d

...

p 31   30

...

Item paid to Wattis for dressyng of the devells hede   viij d

...

p 32   35

...

Item paid for braband to pylatts hate v d & for canvas ij d ob.

...

p 35   40

...

Item paid for a strawen hate ob. a leffe of Roche clere j d

...

p 36

...

Item paid to John Harryes for beryng of þe Orygynall þat day   vj d

...

                                                                              5

p 29*

...

Item payd for iij platis to Heroddis Crest of Iron   vj d
Item payd for a paper of Aresdyke   xij d
Item payd to Hatfeld for dressyng of Herods Creste   xiiij d 10

...

— Folger: Scrapbook Wb 137
p 40

...   15

Item payd to the weytes, v s ...

Corpus Christi Guild Account Book CRO: A 6
f 62v *(Guild fees)*

...   20

De Iohn blewet Wayt   iij s iiij d

...

De Adam West Wayt   iij s iiij d

...

                                                                             25

f 65

...

De Adam West Wayt   iij s iiij d

...

De Iohn blewet Wayt   iij s iiij d 30

...

f 69v *(Master's claims for expenses)*

...

Item he askythe Allouaunce for leverey gownes &   35
hodus   v li iiij s ij d

...

1496
AC *Dyers' Accounts* Bodl: MS Top. Warwickshire c.7   40
    f 33

...

Item payd on feyre ffryday for weryng iij peyre bryggnyrns

watyng of Mast*er* meyr vj. d

...

ff 115-15v

...   5

It payd for skowryng of ij habyrgyns, and for iij skyrts of mayle,
& iij peyre of gassetts of mayle, & iij gorgetys of mayle, xij d.
It payd for beryng the ij stremers on Mydsomer nyght, and on
that day the Chapeter was here of blak monkys iiij d.
Memorandum thys byn they Costs of the makyng of the ij   10
~~newstreymers, ffirst iij ellen & *dimidium* of lynyn cloth iij s. j d.~~
It payd for halff ellen of blakbokrem for to put in the sper hedys
ij d. ob. |
It payd for xviij yards d*imidium* of ffryng, xviij. d
It payd to John Herll for the bryngyn of they dey*er*s Arms, of   15
London, that byn peyntyd in the same stremers, viij. d
It payd to Harre peynter for hys costs, of peyntyng, xxx. s
...

AC   *Smiths' Accounts* Sharp: *Dissertation*   20
     p 30 fn t
     ...
     Ryngolds man Thomas þat playtt pylatts wyff.
     ...

                                                                                    25

     p 36
     ...
     payd for copyying of the ij knyghts p*ar*tes & demons   *(blank)*
     ...

                                                                                    30

     p 196
     ...
     payd to the stondard beyrres & ffor poyntes   xj d
     ...

8 / ij stremers ... nyght: *Sharp (p 196) adds* ij d

Corpus Christi Guild Account Book CRO: A 6
f 70v *(Guild fees)*

...

D*e* Adam West Wayt   iij s iiij d

...   5

f 71

...

D*e* Iohn blewet Wayt   xxvj s viij d

...   10

f 76 *(Master's claims for expenses)*

...

Also he askythe alowance for leverey gowns & hod*es* v li iiij s ij d

...   15

Also they alow Iohn blewet more toward hys chemney   iij s iiij d

...

1497

AC   *Tanners' Ordinances* CRO: Acc 241   20
      pp 3-4* *(18 December)*

...

   Allso they haue made that all the whole company be redie with
the maisters to bringe forth the padiant and to be with the maisters
on Corpus xpi day and to follow the | procession in the worship   25
of the Cittie, vppon the payne of euerie default that day made to
pay to the company without any pardon xij d.

...

AC   *Smiths' Accounts* Sharp: *Dissertation*   30
      p 21 *(Master's oath)*

... kepe unto the uttermasse, all suche Laudable customs as Pagans,
Quartrage, Weddings, Burings and suche other like things as hathe
be in timis past usyd and customyd.   35

...

p 22 *(Rules for the journeymen)*

...

Also that they wate upon the hede mayst*er* upon Corpus chr*i*sti   40
daye to goo upon pr*o*ssession also to wate upon the mayst*er*s and
attende upon the pageaunt to the worsshipe of this cite, and the

crafte in like wyse to wate upon the maisters of the crafte and so
likewise to goo upon wache on myssomer ny3ght and santte peter
ny3ght.

...

p 20 fn f*

...

Item for the horssyng of the padgeant xij d ...

p 33 fn a

...

payntyng of the players harnys   xx s

Corpus Christi Guild Account Book CRO: A 6
f 77 *(Guild fees)*

...

De Iohanne Davy organpleyar   iij s iiij d

...

f 86v *(Master's claims for expenses)*

...

Item he askythe alowance for leverey gowns & hodes v li iiij s ij d

...

1498
Leet Book I CRO: A 3(a)
f 281 col b *(25 January)*

This 3ere the Chaptur of blak monkes was kept at Couentre
aboute þe visitacion of oure Lady and many of them cam on the
seturday at nyght & somme on þe Morowe & taried there vnto
wensday at which day they had a generall procession and they
came forth at þe south durre in þe Mynstere & toke theire wey
thurgh the newe bildyng downe þe Bailly lane And the Maire &
his Brethern in theire scarlet Clokes with all the Craftes in theire
best araye stode vnder þe Elme in seynt Mighelles Chirch3ard
And all þe pensels of þe Cite before them whech pensels there
went before the Crosse & ˰ ⌜þe⌝ maire with his Brethern & the
Craftes stode styll till þe presidentes cam whom the Maire th⟨.⟩r
toke [the] be þe handes & welcomed them to town & so folowed
þe procession which procession went down the bailly lane & so
forth as is vsuelly vsed oane seynt George day & so into þe priory

& ther*e* was a solempne s*er*mon seyde wher*e* the Mair*e* ther*e* satte
betwixt both p*re*sident*es* & aft*er* s*er*mon doon they dep*ar*ted
eu*er*y man to his loggyng & som with the Mair*e* to dyn*er* As dyu*er*s
of the*m* did before And so the dep*ar*ted furth of þe Cite
...   5

f 281v* *(17 October)*

M*emorandum* that this ʒer*e* the wensday the xvij day of Octobr*e*
a*n*no xiiij° R*egis* h*en*re vij prince Arthur the ffirst begoton son of   10
kyng henr*e* the vij^th then beyng of þe age of xij ʒer*es* & more cam
first to couentr*e* & there lay in þe priory fro Wensday vnto þe
Munday next suyng at which tyme he removed toward*es* london
/ Ayenst whos co*m*myng was þe Sponstrete ʒarte garnysshed with
the ix worthy and kyng Arthur then hauyng thus spech as foloweth   15

Hayle prynce roiall most amyable in sight
Whom the Court et*er*nall thurgh p*r*udent gou*er*naince
Hath chosen to be egall ons to me in myght
To sprede our*e* name Arthur & act*es* to aua*u*nce   20
And of meanys victorious to haue such habundaunce
That no fals treito*ur* ne cruell tirrant
Shall in eny wyse make profer to your lande
And rebelles all falce quarels shall eschewe
Thurgh þe fere of Pallas that fauoreth you*r* lynage   25
And all outward Enmyes laboreth to subdue
To make the*m* to do to yewe as to me dyd homage
Welcome therfor*e* the solace & comfort of my olde Age
Prince pereles Arthur Ico*m*me of noble p*ro*geny
To me & to your*e* Chambr*e* with all þis hole companye   30

And at the turnyng into þe croschepyng before Mr Thru*m*ptons
durr*e* stode þe barkers paiant well appareld in which was the
Quene of fortune with dyu*er*s other virgyns whech quene has þis
spech folowyng   35

I am dame fortune quene called full expedient
To Emprours & p*r*inc*es* prelat*es* with other moo
As Cesar. hecto*ur*. & sabius most excellent
Scipio exalted Nausica & Emilianus also   40

14 / ʒarte *for* ʒate   18 / gou*er*naince *for* gou*er*naunce

Valerius also marchus with sapient cicero
E and noble men breuely the truth to conclude all
My fauour verily had as storys maketh rehersall
With oute whom sithen non playnly can prospere
That in þis muitable lyfe as nowe procedyng   5
I am come thurgh love truste me intiere
To be with yewe & yours evirmore enduryng
Prynce most vnto my pleasure of all þat ar nowe reynyng
Wherfore my nowne hert & best beloued treasure
Welcome to þis youre Chaumbre of whom ye be inheriture   10

And the crosse in the Croschepyng was garnysshed & wyne there
rennyng And angels sensyng & syngyng with Orgayns and othere
melody &c.
And at þe Cundyt there was seynt George kyllyng the dragon and   15
seynt George had this speche folowyng

col a

O most soueraign lorde be dyne provision to be   20
the ruler of cruell Mars & kyng Insuperable
Ye reioyce my corage trustyng hit to se
That named am George your patron fauorable
To whom ye are & euer shalbe so acceptable
That in felde or Cite where so ever ye rayne   25
Shall I neuer fayle yewe thus is my purpose playn
To protect your magnyficence my self I shall endevour
In all thynges that your highnes shalt concerne
More tenderly then I ʒit did ever
Kyng duke yerle lorde or also berne   30
as ye be myn assistence in processe shall lerne
Which thurgh your vertue most amorous knygh
I owe to your presence be due & very right
like wyse as þis lady be grace I defended
That thurgh myschaunce chosen was to dye   35
fro this foule serpent whom I sore wonded
So ye in distresse preserve ever woll I
ffro all parell and wyked veleny
That shuld your noble persone in eny wyse distrayne
Which welcome is to þis your Chambre & to me right fa⟨..⟩   40

col b

And this balet was song at þe Crosse

                          Viuat le prynce arthur   5
Ryall prince Arthur
welcomme nowe tresure   to þis your Cite
with all oure hole Cure
Sithen in vertue dere
lorde ye haue no pere   as all we may see   10
Of your age tendre
Cunyng requyred
all hath contrived   your intelligence
and so receyued --
That yngland all playn   15
may nowe be right fayn   to theire extollence
Yewe long to remayn
Syng we þer foll all
Also let vs call   that he yewe defend
To god Immortall   20
In this breue beyng
Youre astate supporting   to your lyfes yend
And vertue ⌈ay⌉ spredyng

AC   *City Annals* CRO: Acc 2/E   25
    f 15

   ...

   Thomas Bond Draper ... In his year Prince Arthur came to
   Coventry & had 100 li. & a cup given him, & so he departed ...

                                                 30

AC   *Dyers' Accounts* Bodl: MS Top. Warwickshire c.7
    f 33* *(Fair Friday)*

   ...

   It for iiij men to the meyr viij. d

   ...   35

AC   *Smiths' Accounts* H-P: *Outlines* I
    p 339 *(Corpus Christi)*

   ... Item, for the horssyng of the padgeantt and the axyll tree to   40

the same, xvj d; item, for the hawyng of the padgeantt in and
out, and wasshyng it, viij d; ...

Corpus Christi Guild Account Book CRO: A 6
f 89v *(Guild fees)*
...
D*e* Iohn Davy organpleyar   iij s iiij d
...

f 90
...
D*e* Adam West Wayt   iij s iiij d
...

f 91v
...
D*e* Wyll blewet Wayt   iij s iiij d
...

f 93v *(Receipts for wax-money)*
...
D*e* Wyll blewet fili*o* Ioh*n* blewet   xiiij d
...

f 95v
...
It*e*m he askythe to be alowyd for leverey gowns &
hod*es*   v li iiij s ij d
...

1499
AC   *Smiths' Accounts* H-P: *Outlines* I
p 339

... Item, paid for ij cordes for the draught of the paygaunt, j d;
item, paid for shope and gresse to the whyles, j d; item, paid for
havyng oute of the paygant and swepyng therof and havyng in,
and for naylles and ij claspes of iron, and for mendyng of a claspe
that was brokon, and for coterellis and for a bordur to the
pagaunte, xix d ...

— H-P: *Illustrations*
p 51

... Item, payd for rente of the pagent hows iiij s vj d; item, payde
for the reperacion of the pagente hows, for a sylle and for sparrys   5
and lathe and nayle and warkmanschyp iiij s ij d ...

— Folger: Scrapbook Wb 155
p 31

...   10

Item, payd to Cayface for hys wages	iiij s
Item, payd to the bedell for his wages	iiij s
Item, payd to Anna for his wages	iij s
Item, payd to Dame Percula for his wages	ij s viij d
Item, payd to ij Knyghtys for ther wages	iiij s 15
Item, payd to Judas for [his] his wages	xij d
Item, payd to Pylate son for his wages	iiij d
Item, payde to Malkes for his wages	viij d
Item, payd to devyll for hys wages	xij d

                                                                        20

— Sharp: *Dissertation*
p 26 *(Corpus Christi)*
...

Item payd for mendyng a cheverel for god and for sowyng of gods
kote of leddur and for makyng of the hands to the same   25
kote   xij d

p 30 fn t
...

Item paid to pylatts wyffe for his wages   ij s 30
...

p 31

Item paid for peynttyng of the demones hede ...   35
...

p 35*

Item paid to the paynter ffor peyntyng of ther fasses   viij d 40
...

p 189 *(Midsummer and St Peter's Watches)*

...

Item paid ffor ix li wax for our Torches	iiij s vj d	
Item paid ffor a dossen rossen vj d Item ffor wyke & workmanshipe	ij s viij d	5

...

p 198   *(St Peter's Watch)*

...

Item paid to a mynstrell for þat nyght be sid our owen	vj d	10

...

Corpus Christi Guild Account Book CRO: A 6
f 98 *(Guild fees)*

...

		15
De Iohanne Davy organpleyr	vj s viij d	

...

f 101

...

		20
De Wyll blewet Wayt	iij s iiij d	

...

f 104v *(Master's claims for expenses)*

...

		25
Item he askythe alowaunce for leverey gowns & hodes	v li. iiij s ij d	

...

1500	30

Chamberlains' Account Book I CRO: A 7(a)
p 6

...

Item paid for Settyng of the postes in ye Croschepyng when ye Kyng was here in gret	ij s	35
Item for taking doune of ye same postes a geyn	x d	
Item for pavyng in ye Croschepyng there as ye postes stude of viij yardes	viij d	
Item for a lode of pebuls theder	ix d	
Item for a lode of pavyn sande	iij d	40
Summa iiij s vj d		

...

A C   *City Annals*   Bodl: MS Top. Warwickshire d.4
       f 14*

       ...

The King &
Queen came to
coventry

       Iohn Haddon drap*er* maior 1499 & ended in 1500. In his yeare
       K*ing* Henry 7th & ye Queene came to Coventry & were made   5
       brother & sister of corpus Christi, & Trinitie gild.
       °Iohn Whithead . Iohn Reinold*es* sherriff*es* °

       ...

A C   *Smiths' Accounts*   H-P: *Illustrations*   10
       p 53

       ... Item, for nayles to the pagente and hokes iiij d ob.; item, payd
       to John Gybbys for byndynge of the welys and clampys to the
       pagente xv d; item, spend on the jorneymen in bred and ale for   15
       havynge forthe pagente vj d ...

       — Sharp: *Dissertation*
       p 28
       ...   20
       It*em* payde for colours and gold foyle & sylv*er* foyle for ij myttyrs
       ...

       p 29
       ...   25
       It*em* payd to John Hatfelde for colours and gold foyle & sylv*er*
       foyle for þe crest and for þe fawchon
       ...

       p 35   30
       ... It*em* for colours and gold foyle & sylv*er* foyle for iiij Capps ...

       p 193   *(St Peter's Watch)*
       ...
       It*em* to Jorneymen þat ware the harness & for poynts   xj d   35
       ...

       Corpus Christi Guild Account Book   CRO: A 6
       f 111v   *(Master's claims for expenses)*
       ...   40
       Item he askythe alowa*un*ce for leverey gownus &
       hod*es*   v li iiij s ij d
       ...

1501

AC   *Smiths' Accounts* Sharp: *Dissertation*
p 196*

...

ffor berryng off the stremerus   ij d   5

...

Corpus Christi Guild Account Book CRO: A 6
f 116v *(Guild fees)*

...   10
De Wyllelmo blewet Wayt   xx d

f 120 *(Rentals)*

...

                              Croschepyng   15
A tenement ther þat Iohn blewet holdes payng yerly   xx s
ij Tenementes next in the hold of Wyll blewet & Wyll ostler per
annum   xxx s

...
                                                                            20

f 121 *(Master's claims for expenses)*

...

Item he askythe alowaunce for leverey gowns &
hodes   v li. iiij s ij d
... Item he payd for a crown of Syluer & gyld for the mare on   25
corpus christi day   xliiij s ix d ...

1502

AC   *Smiths' Accounts* H-P: *Outlines* II
p 290   30

... Item, paid for gloves to the pleyares, xix d; item, paid for
pyntyng off ther fasus, ij d ...

— Sharp: *Dissertation*   35
p 26

...

Item pd ffor a newe sudere for god   vij d

...

p 28

...

Item ffor vj ȝards satten iij quartrs	xvj s x d	
Item for v ȝardus off blowe bokeram	ij s xj d	
Item pd ffor makyng off herodus gone	xv d	5

...

p 33

...

Item ffor makyng off iiij Jaketes	ij s	10
Item ffor iiij ellne cloth ffor the jakkets & the hatts	xviij d	
Item pd to the pynnter ffor hys warkemonchipe	xxj s vij d	

...

p 35   15

| ... Item for borrowyng off a skerlet gone & a cloke | ij d |
| ... mendyng the massus | |

...

20

Corpus Christi Guild Account Book CRO: A 6
f 126v *(Master's claim for expenses)*

...

| Item he askythe Alowaunce for leverey govns & | | |
| hodes | v li. iiij s ij d | 25 |

...

f 127

The Inuentori of All the Iuels & Plate that longythe to thys yeld   30
The Wyche ys in the kepyng of Iohn Dudley Clarke of þe Same
yeld &c.

...

A Crucifyx with mary & Iohn of Syluer & parte gyld lakyng a
deadym weyng iiij ⌈xx⌉ vnces   35

...

---

3 / Item ffor: *Reader, MS Top. Warwickshire c.7, f 84 gives fuller reading* Item bought
off M William Pysforde ffor   12 / *Sharp glosses* pynnter *as* painter

A Crosstaffe of Syluer with mytter & Chalys gravyn in hyt weyng
xliiij vnces

...

A gyrdull of blew Sylke harnesyd with Syluer & gylt weyng cors
& all iiij vnces dimidium   5
A gyrdull of Red sylke harnest with syluer & gyld weyng cors &
all vj vnces iij quarters
A payr of bedus of Syluer weyng vj vnces
A baner of veluet wroght with gold
A mytter of veluet wroght with gold & a crosyar of coper & gyld   10

...

Also A nott with a couer All gyld gyffyn by Maister Iohn haddon
weyng xxxiiij vnces

...

                                                                   15

f 127v

Item iij hodes ij of theym furyd & on lynyd with gren Sarsnet
Item a canopy of Sylke brodoryd with gold with ij Sydes of the
same for the precession   20

...

Item a croun of Syluer & gyld brought in by Maister Rychard
Iakeson weyng ix vnces j quarter
Item A baner of blew Damaske bought by Mr chambers
Also a Twelly towell brought in by Maister Iohn padland   25
Item a canapy to bere ouer the the Sacrament of clothe of tyssew
browght in by Maister Thomas grove

...

A Sewt of Vestmentes payd fore by Maister Iohn humfereye &
Maister hanre Rogeres   30
In primis a vestment of blew clothe of gold
Item a cope of the Same clothe of gold
Item ij tynaculles of the same clothe of gold
Item iij awbus & iij amessus longyng to þe same
Item ij stolus & ij fanons longyng to the Same   35

...

26 / the the MS dittography

1503

A C   *Dyers' Accounts*   Sharp: *Dissertation*
p 194

...

Item for Cloth for the penselys iiij d Item peynteyng of þe   5
penselys ij s v d

...

— Bodl: MS Top. Warwickshire c.7
f 33   10

...

It for iiij men in brygerdyns to the meyr viij. d

...

A C   *Smiths' Accounts*   Sharp: *Dissertation*   15
p 193 *(Midsummer Watch)*

...

Item paid for castyng of our mayll   iiij d

...

    20

Corpus Christi Guild Account Book   C R O :   A 6
f 134 *(Master's claims for expenses)*

...

Also he askythe to be alowyd for leverey gowns &
hodes   v li. iiij s ij d 25

...

1504
Carpenters' Account Book II   C R O :   Acc 3/2
f 34v col a   30

Exspens pentocost quarter

...

To þe pynnars & tylars   x s

...

    35

To þe Mynstrell*es*   iiij s.

...

col b

...   5

To too torch berrers   iiij d

...

AC   *Dyers' Accounts*   Sharp: *Dissertation*
     p 181 fn p   10

...

It*em* to the Jernamen on me*d*somer nyght   xx d

...

Corpus Christi Guild Account Book   CRO: A 6   15
f 141 *(Master's claims for expenses)*

...

Also he askythe to be alowyd for leverey gowns &
hod*es*   v li. iiij s ij d

...   20

1505

AC   *City Annals*   CRO: Acc 2/F
     f 18*

...   25

Iohn Dadsbury In his year was the Play of St Christian played in
the Little Park ...

Carpenters' Account Book II   CRO: Acc 3/2
f 37v col b   30

...

Item p*ay*d to the pynners & tyllers   x s
Item p*ay*d to the Mynstrell   iij s.

...

                                                                        35

AC   *Smiths' Accounts*   Folger: Scrapbook Wb 150
     p 17

Expences on the playrs on Corpus Christi day.
Item, for a dosen of whyght gloves, xij d   40
Item, for ij pyre off reed gloves, viij d

...

— Sharp: *Dissertation*
p 164

...

Item payd for beryng off ij pencelis on prosacyon   ij d

...   5

Corpus Christi Guild Account Book CRO: A 6
f 148 *(Rental roll)*

...

          Croschepyng   10
A tenement ther that Iohn blewet holdes by yere   xx s

...

f 148v *(Master's claims for expenses)*

...   15

Also he askythe to be alowyd for [lerey] leverey gownus &
hodes   v li iiij s ij d

...

                    20

1506
Carpenters' Account Book II CRO: Acc 3/2
f 39 col b

...

[Item to þe pynners & Tylers   x s.] 25

...

f 40v col b

         spent vpon new brether

...   30

Item for . torcheberers for myssomer nyght seynt peters nyght &
corpus christi   v d

...

Item for iiij torches   vj s vj d
Item for a Mynstrell   iiij s   35
Item to the pynners & tylers   x s

...

A C   **Smiths' Accounts** Sharp: *Dissertation*
    p 15 fn v   40

... Resevyd amonge bredren and other good ffelowys toward the

Orygynall ij s ix d

...

Corpus Christi Guild Account Book CRO: A 6
f 153 *(Receipts for wax-money)*   5

...

De Iohn Gylbard organpleyar of seynt mycelles   xiiij d

...

f 154 *(Master's claims for expenses)*   10

...

Item he askythe to be alowyd for leverey gownus &
hodes   v li iiij s ij d

...
                                                                              15

1507
Leet Book I CRO: A 3(a)
f 297v *(20 April)*

Memorandum þat it is ordeyned at this Lete that the Craft &   20
ffeliship of Bakers shalbe contributories & charged from hensforth
with the Craft & feliship of smythes and to pay yerely to them

•bakers to
Contribute
13s 4d yearly
to the Smiths
pageant•

toward theyre pagent at corpus christi tyde xiij s iiij d and so to
contynewe from hensforth yerely &c.

...   25

Item it is ordened at this present lete that the ffelisship of
Corueseres shalbe contributory & chargeable with the crafte of

•Tanners
pageant•

Tanners yerly from hensforth and to pay xiij s iiij d and to begyn
theyre payment of the hole at corpus christi [day] ^ 'tyde' next
comyng and so forth yerly at euery corpus christi tyde to pay   30
xiij s iiij d &c.

bochers &
whittawers to
repaire A
pageant

Item it is ordened and agreed that [the] fromhensforth the feliship
& Crafte of Bochers shalbe yerly contributorye to the felyship of
whittawers toward ther pagent at corpus christi tyde xvj s. viij d
and so to continue yerly forth lyke as they dydde afore &c.   35

Carpenters' Account Book II CRO: Acc 3/2
f 43v

...

Item paid to the tyllers & pynners   X S.   40

...

1 / *Sharp adds* 'in sums of 1d. & 2d. each'

It*em* p*ai*d to the Mynstrell iiij s. & ij s of þ*at* to his fynes

...

It*em* p*ai*d to þe torch berrers for Corp*us* chr*ist*i daye & Sent Iohn
nyght & Sent pet*er* nyght   vj d

...   5

AC   *Tanners' Ordinances* CRO: Acc 241
      pp 4-5* *(20 April) (f 3)*
      ...

      Memorandum that att the Leet houlden att Couentry the | 10
Tewsday next afore the feast of St. Gorge the martyre afore
Robert Greene maior, Nicholas Haynes and William Muston
Sherieffes itt was agreed and graunted by the great inquest as it
appereth by a Bill put vp to theym by the fellowship and companye
of Tanners that the company of Corvisers should be contributors   15
and chargable with the said companye of Tanners and yearely
from thenceforth to pay to the said company of Tanners xiij s iiij d
and to Begin their payment on Corpus xpi day then next
followinge, and so much yearly euery corpus Christi day w*hi*ch
was allso confirmed and att the Leete houlden afore the said   20
Maior and Sherieffs the tewsday afore the feast of St. Denice last
past as apeareth by another Bill put then to the said inquest.
      ...

      Corpus Christi Guild Account Book CRO: A 6   25
      f 160 *(Master's claims for expenses)*
      ...
Also he askythe to be alowyd for leverey gowns &
hod*es*   v li iiij s ij d
      ...   30

      1508
AC   *City Annals* BL: Harley 6388
      f 27v*

                                                                         35

Richard Smith Merchant Mayor
he made the Bakers pay to the Smith 13s 4d towards Prest⟨.⟩
pageants

      Carpenters' Account Book II CRO: Acc 3/2   40
      f 45v col b
      ...
Item payd pynnar & tylars   x s

Item to the mynstrell*es*   iiij s

...

Item for beryng the torches myssom*er* nyght ⌐& corp*us* ch*ri*sti
day⌐   vj d

...   5

A C   *Smiths' Accounts* H-P: *Outlines* II
         p 290 *(Corpus Christi)*

... Item, paid for colour and coloryng of Arade, iiij d. ...   10

Corpus Christi Guild Account Book CRO: A 6
f 161v *(Guild fees)*

...

D*e* Iohn gylbard organpleyar   iij s iiij d   15

...

f 165v *(Master's claims for expenses)*

...

Also he askythe to be alovyd for leverey govns & hod*es* & M*aste*r   20
Rastell*es* fee   v li. viij s vj d

...

1509
Leet Book I CRO: A 3(a)   25
f 305v* *(25 January)*

...

ffirst it is ordeyned at this lete that the ffeliship and occupac*io*n
of Coruesers fromhensfurth shall pay & bere w*ith* the craft of
Tanners toward ther charg*es* xiij s. iiij d in lyke wise as M*aste*r   30
⌐Ric*hard*⌐ Smyth did com*m*aunde them when he was Meyre tyll
hit be better enquerid of &c.

...

Carpenters' Account Book II CRO: Acc 3/2   35
f 47v col b *(Michaelmas quarter)*

...

Item for the mynstrell*es*   iiij s

...

f 48 col a *(Harvest dinner)*

...

Item to pynears & tylars   x s

...

Item for torches   xx d   5

...

AC   *Dyers' Accounts* Sharp: *Dissertation*
      p 188   10

...

Item for iiij hats of strawe   vj d

...

p 199   15

... Item for the schapletes x d

...

Corpus Christi Guild Account Book CRO: A 6   20
f 171v* *(Masters claims for expenses)*

...

Item he askythe to be alowyd for leverey gowns &
hodes   v li. iiij s ij d

...   25

(Renovations to St Nicholas Hall)
... Also payed for the peyntyng & makyng grene of the ij bays of
þe hall next the Cupburd & for the clothe & the peyntyng of the
hyngyng that honges At the hy Deys next þe seyd cupburd as hyt   30
aperethe by the boke theroff xxxvj s iiij d ...

1510
Carpenters' Account Book II CRO: Acc 3/2   35
f 49v col a

...

Item to the pynnars & tylars   x s

...

col b

Item the mynstrell*es* st Iohns & st pet*er* nyght   iij s iiij d

...

Item to Mynstryll*es* on corp*us* ch*ri*sti day   v d   5

Item to torcheberars ⌜Missem*er* n*igh*t⌝   ij d

...

Item the torcheberars that nyght   ij d

...   10

AC   *Dyers' Accounts*   Bodl: MS Top. Warwickshire c.7
      f 115v

...

Resevyd of ye mastur of ye taylars, for ye hyre of wone of ye   15
crafts harnes ffor bowythe nyghtts of ye wache, v. s viij. d

...

Corpus Christi Guild Account Book   CRO: A 6
f 173 *(Guild fees)*   20

...

D*e* Iohn Gylbard organpleyr   iij s iiij d

...

f 175   25

...

D*e* Iohn Gylbard organpleyar   iij s iiij d

...

f 178v   30

...

Also he askythe alowa*u*nce for leverey gowns &
hod*es*   v li. iiij s ij d

...

                                                                             35

1511
Chamberlains' Account Book I   CRO: A 7(a)
p 38*

...

It*em* p*ai*d of ye Cokestrete yate at ye comyng of ye Kyng   v d   40

...

AC   *City Annals* CRO: Acc 2/E
       f 16*

       ...

       Iohn Stronge Mercer ... . In his year K*ing* Hen*ry* & the Queen
       came to Coventre & the Maj*o*r bare the sword before the King.   5
       Then were 3 Pageants set forth, one at Iordan well, with the 9
       orders of Angells. Another at Broadgate with divers beautifull
       Damsells. Another at the Cross Cheeping with a goodly Stage
       Play, & so passed forth & were rec*eue*d into the Priory. Then
       were certaine person peached of Heresy where of some bare   10
       ffaggotts before the Procession on the Markett day the Principall
       of them were one Mrs Rowley & Ioan Ward, who afterwards was
       burned for the truth.

       ...
                                                                                         15

       Carpenters' Account Book II CRO: Acc 3/2
       f 52 col b

       ...

       It*e*m payd to þe pynners & tylers   x s
       payd to the mynstrel*les* on sent Iohn ys nyght & sent petyrs   20
       nyght corp*us* chr*ist*i   iiij s

       ...

       payd to þe torchberers þe ⌈same⌉ tyme   vj d
       ...
                                                                                         25

       Corpus Christi Guild Account Book CRO: A 6
       f 179v *(Guild fees)*

       ...

       D*e* Iohn gylbarde organpleyar   iij s iiij d
       ...   30

       f 183* *(Receipts of wax-money)*

       ...

       D*e* Iohn Rastell fil*io* M*a*g*ist*ri Iohn Rastell p*er* man*us* M*ai*stress
       gang   xiiij d   35

       ...

       f 184 *(Master's claims for expenses)*

       ...

       Also   he   askythe   alowa*u*nce   for   leverey   gowns   &   40
       hodus   v li. iiij s ij d

... also ther ys payd for a ba*n*ner made new of blew Damaske for
the Damaske & for the fryng steynyng wi*th* the gold & all colorus
þ*at* long*es* therto & warkemanshype as hyt aperythe be the boke
theroff to the S*u*m of lix s vj d

5

1512
Carpenters' Account Book II CRO: Acc 3/2
f 54 col a

Expens at corp*us* chr*i*sti tyde mydsomer & sent petyrs tyde   10
Item i*n* prim*us* payde to the pynners & tylers S*u*m*ma*   x s
payde to the mynstrell*es* at mydsomer & sent pet*y*rs nygh*t*   iiij s
...
payd to the torchberers the same tyme & at corp*us* chr*i*sti
tyde   viij d   15
payd for vj pencels & the peyntyng of them   viij d
...

Corpus Christi Guild Account Book CRO: A 6
f 186v *(Guild fees)*   20
...
D*e* Iohn gylbard orgon playar   iij s iiij d
...

f 189   25

D*e* Iohn Rastell [deleud] ꞌfyl*io* M*agistri* Rastellꞌ p*er* Man*us*
Maistress gawyg   iij s iiij d
...
30
f 191 *(Master's claims for expenses)*
...
Allso he askythe alowa*u*nce for*e* leverey gown*es* &
howod*es*   v li. iiij s ij d
...   35
Also ther payd be the Seyd Maist*er* Th*omas* Grove for a new
Canapy for to bere ou*er* the Sacr*a*ment furst for vij yerd*es* &
d*imidium* of tessew vij li. x s Item for ix vnc*es* of Sylke for the
fryng ix s It*em* for v yerd*es* & d*imidium* of tewke to lyne hyt
wi*th* v s vj d It*em* payd for þe makyng the frynge xxij d It*em* payd   40
for makyng the canapy iij s iiij d It*em* payd for the careg of the
tessew fro london & for the cost & charge of the haloyng of the

Sewt of vestment*es* that maist Iohn humfer & M*aister* Hanr
Rogerus payd fore for þe seyd yeld v s iiij d ...

1513
Carpenters' Account Book II CRO: Acc 3/2   5
f 57 col a

...

Expens at corp*us* chr*is*ti tyde sent Iones nyght sent peters ˹nyght˺

...

Item p*ay*d to þc pynners & tylers   x s   10
It*em* p*ay*d to þe mynstrell*es* the same tyme   iiij s

...

Item p*ay*d to þe torch berers þe same tyme   viij d

...
                                                                      15

Corpus Christi Guild Account Book CRO: A 6
f 193v *(Guild fees)*

...

D*e* Iohn Rastell fil*io* M*agistri* Rastell p*er* Man*us* M*aistress*
gawge   iij s iiij d   20

...

f 198v *(Master's claims for expenses)*

...

Also he askythe alowa*u*nce for leverey gowns &   25
hod*es*   v li. iiij s ij d

...

Wherof the Seyd Maist*er* Iohn humfer payd for part of the new
Westment*es* that be of blewe clothe of gold   xiij li
                                                                      30
1514
Carpenters' Account Book II CRO: Acc 3/2
f 59v col b

...

Expens at corp*us* chr*is*ti tyde   35
It*em* p*ay*d to þe pynners & tilers   x s.
Item to þe mynstrell*es* þe sam tyme   iiij s.

...

It*em* to þe torchberers þe same tyme   viij d

...   40

---

1 / maist *for* maister, *brevigraph omitted*

Corpus Christi Guild Account Book CRO: A 6
f 201v *(Guild fees)*

...

De Wyll*elm*o forster organpleyr   iij s iiij d

...   5

f 205 *(Master's claims for expenses)*

...

Also he askythe alowa*u*nce for leverey gowns &
hod*es*   v li. iiij s ij d   10

... Maist*er* Roger*us* ys In [arega] arerage in bothe the acount*es*
cler   v li.
The Whyche v li. to the Seyd Maister hanr Roger*us* payd for a
part of The blew Suet of Vestment*es* bought when Maist*er*   15
Nych*ola*i burwey was meir of thes cety and So the Seyd Maist*er*
hanr Rogerus ayens thes yeld stond*es* Cler & Q*uietus* Est

1515
Carpenters' Account Book II CRO: Acc 3/2   20
f 62v col b

...

Expens of corp*us* ch*rist*i tyde mydsom*er* & sent peters nyght
Item pa*y*d to þe cowp*er*s & pynners & tylers   x s.
...   25
Item pa*y*d to the mynstrell*es* þe same tyme   iiij s
Item pa*y*d to the torchberers they same tyme   viij d

...

[Item pa*y*d for iij lb wax to dobbe the torchis þat was bowght of
hary patison at vj d þe lb]   [xviij d] ⸢xx d.⸣ 30
Item pa*y*d for rosyn & gom to þe same   viij d
Item pa*y*d to nycholas barbur for dobby*n*g of v torchis   xij d

...

Corpus Christi Guild Account Book CRO: A 6   35
f 212v *(Master's claims for expenses)*

...

Also he askythe alowa*u*nce for leverey gowns &
hod*es*   v li. iiij s ij d

...   40

It*em* he payed also therof for a vestement to corpus ch*rist*i
Chappell   iij li. vj s viij d

...

1516
Carpenters' Account Book II CRO: Acc 3/2
f 66v col a

   Exsspence*es* off Myssome*r* nyght & pett*eres* nyght 5
     & corposse chr*ist*i day
In p*rimis* payd ffor the brekeffast at morre*es* on ch*rist*i day
afforre the goyng to the pressyon   xij d [v⟨..⟩d]
It*em* payd the penne*res* wit*h* ther co*m*pany   x s.
...   10
It*em* payd the menstrell   iiij s.
...
It*em* payd ffor torche beryng In þe ȝere   viij d
...
                     15

AC *Smiths' Accounts* Sharp: *Dissertation*
  p 28 *(Corpus Christi)*
  ...
  It*em* payd to a peynter for peyntyng & mendyng of herodes 20
  heed   iiij d
  ...

  p 189 *(Midsummer and St Peter's Watches)*
  ...   25
  It*em* payd for iiij Judasses   iiij s
  ...

  Corpus Christi Guild Account Book CRO: A 6
  f 219v *(Master's claims for expenses)*   30
  ...
  Also he askythe alowa*u*nce for leverey gowns &
  hod*es*   v li. iiij s ij d
  ...
                 35

1517
Carpenters' Account Book II CRO: Acc 3/2
f 69* col b *(Midsummer and St Peter's Watches)*
...   40
It*em* to Mensterell*es*   iiij s.
It*em* payd ffor the berreyng off torche*es* bothe nyght*es* iiij d
...

AC   *Dyers' Accounts* Bodl: MS Top. Warwickshire c.7
     f 115v

...

6 Brigandines, 2 suits of white armour, on St. Peters Eve &c.

...   5

— Sharp: *Dissertation*
p 196 *(Midsummer and St Peter's Watches)*

...

Item payed to ij yongmen for beyryng þe streymers bothe   10
nyghts   iiij d

...

Corpus Christi Guild Account Book CRO: A 6
f 221v* *(Guild fees)*   15

...

De Iohn gylbard organpleyr   iij s iiij d

...

f 224v *(Master's claims for expenses)*   20

...

Also he askythe alowaunce for leverey govns &
hodes   v li. iiij s ij d

...
                                                                 25

1518
Chamberlains' Account Book I CRO: A 7(a)
p 53*

...

Item for his ij gounes   XX s   30
Item paid for a gowne of rede & grene for ye sergeant xiij s iiij d

...

Will of William Pisford PRO: PROB 11/19
f 67v* *(2 March)*   35

... And to the Crafte of Tanners vj s. viij d And vnto euery other
Crafte in Couentre that be either contributory to the fynding of
preest or pageond to the augmentacion of the diuine service of
god or to the contynuaunce of the laudable custumes of the Citie   40
iij s. iiij d ...

f 68v

... Also I bequeth to the paionde of the same Crafte I am of my
self my lyned scarlet gowne without ffurre and my Scarlet Cloke
to be kept to serve theym in their said paionde the tyme of the   5
playes And I bequeth to the Crafte of Tanners my lyned Crymsyn
gowne not furred to the same vse ...

Carpenters' Account Book II CRO: Acc 3/2
f 71 col a *(Harvest dinner)*   10
...
Item payd the menstrell   iiij d
...

col b   15
...
Item ffor berryng off torchees on christi day & myssomer nyght
& peteres nyght   viij d
Item payd the penneres   x s
...   20
Item payd the new Iodas torchees   ⌜vj s viij⌝ [iiij s.]
Item payd the menstrell   iiij s.
...

Corpus Christi Guild Account Book CRO: A 6   25
f 230 *(Receipts for wax-money)*
...
De Rychard Cokkes organpley   xiiij d
...

                                                                         30
f 231v *(Master's claims for expenses)*
...
Also he askythe alowaunce for leverey gowns &
hodes   v li. iiij s ij d
...   35

AC **Holy Trinity Guild Accounts** Sharp: *Dissertation*
    p 161
...
Item paid for beryng of the crosse on seynt Georges day,   40
Ascension, pentecost & corpus christi day   xvj d

Item to ij children for beryng þe candulstikks on þe same
dayes   iiij d
Item for beryng þe lantern on corporis christi day   ij d
...

                                                                              5

1518-(19)
AC   *City Annals* CRO: Acc 2/F
f 19v*
...   10
Henry Rogers Vintiner he kept open house the 12 days in
Christmas and one of his Seargants was Lord of Misrule
...

1519   15
Chamberlains' Account Book I CRO: A 7(a)
p 56 col b
...
Item paid for his Iaket for ridynge on lammes day   vj s viij d
...   20

AC   *City Annals* Sharp: *Dissertation*
p 11*

New Plays at Corpus christi tyde which were greatly commended.   25
...

p 132*
...
This year was a sodane ffloud on the whitsun weeke and it was   30
called the wett Sommer that men might not knowe the Sommer
from Wynter but by the greene leaves for it beganne on Hocks
Tuesday and contynued every day somewhat tyll Crystmas after.

Carpenters' Account Book II CRO: Acc 3/2   35
f 74v*
          Costis on saint Iohannes [i] . s peter nyght
...
Item paid for the cressettes   iiij s
Item paid for lyght to theym   viij d   40
Item paid for Berryng of theym   xij d
Item payed to the mynstrell   iiij s
...

f 75

...

Item payed to the pagyent   x s

...

                                                                 5

AC   *Dyers' Accounts* Bodl: MS Top. Warwickshire c.7
f 115v

...

It pd to the iiij torchberers for beryng of iiij Judaces byfor the
Sacrament, viij. d pd for ther brekfast, viij. d It payd for iiij new   10
Cressetts, v. s vj. d ...

    ⌐ Sharp: *Dissertation*
p 186

...   15

Item payd for iiij new Cressetts   v s vj d
Item payd for the bettyng to þe Cressetts   iij s
Item payd to a man for beryng the bettyngs both nyghts   iiij d

...

                                                                  20

Corpus Christi Guild Account Book CRO: A 6
f 238v *(Master's claims for expenses)*

...

Also he askythe alowaunce for leverey gowns &
hodus   v li. iiij s ij d   25

...

AC   *Holy Trinity Guild Accounts* Folger: Scrapbook Wb 173
p 2*

                                                                 30

Item, to the Kynges plears by the Maister, ij s viij d ...

1520
Cappers' Records SC: Account Book I
f 23v col a   35

...

Exspensys on myssomur ny3ht
Item paid for cressetes ly3ht   xvj d
Item paid for berryng cressetes & the wreyth   x d
Item paid for strawe hattes   ij d   40

...

Item paid for the gorddelors   vj s. viij d

...

f 24v col b

...

paid to the mynstrell þe the furst quarter   xij d

...
                                                                                      5

f 25v col b*

Exspensys on Sent peters ny3th
paid for the cressetes ly3th   xvj d
for berryng of the same   x d   10
paid to the mynstrell the last quarterage   xijj d

...

Robart Crow mayd breder
Iorge feget & he to pay for ys fyns

...   15

Carpenters' Account Book II CRO: Acc 3/2
ff 79-9v *(Midsummer and St Peter's Watches)*

...

Item payed for beryng the Cressettes   vj d   20
Item payed for lyght the Cressettes   x d
Item payed to the mynstrelles   iiij s |
            Exspences of the dynner daye

...

Item payed [for musterd] ˹to the mynstrell˺   iiij d   25

...

f 80

...

Item payed to the pynneres & tylers   x s   30

...

AC   *Dyers' Accounts* Sharp: *Dissertation*
     p 190

...   35

paid for iiij new Judaces   v s iiij d

...

3 / þe the MS *dittography*

Corpus Christi Guild Account Book CRO: A 6
f 246 *(Master's claims for expenses)*

...

Also he askythe alowaunce for leverey gowns &
hodus   v li. iiij s ij d   5

...

f 247 *(Rental rolls)*

Westorchard

...   10

A tenement with a cotage before the hall þat wyllelmo forster
late held per annum   xx s

...

Croschepyng

A tenement that Iohn blewet holdes by yere   xx s   15

...

1521

Cappers' Records SC: Account Book I
f 26v   20

paid for the ly3th at myssomur   iij s
paid for the berryng of the same   x d

...

paid to the gordelers   iij s iiij d   25

...

paid to the mynstrels at hys quarterage   xiiij d

...

f 27 col b   30

...

paid at hys quarterage to þe mynstrell   iiij d
paid to the gordelers   iij s. iiij d
paid for berryng of the ly3th   x d

...   35

Carpenters' Account Book II CRO: Acc 3/2
f 82v col b *(Midsummer and St Peter's Watches)*

...

Item payd for ij crochons   ix d   40
Item payd for beryng theym   ij d
Item for beryng of the cressettes   vj d

Item payd the Mynstrelles   iiij s
...

f 83v col a

Item payd to the pageant   x s
...

AC   *Dyers' Accounts* Bodl: MS Top. Warwickshire c.7
     f 115v
...
Item Reseived of the Barbors to the hernyse of the men vj. s viij. d
...

— Sharp: *Dissertation*
p 186
...
Item payd for viij li. of pyche for the bettyngs to the
Cressetts   viij d
Item payd for vj li of Ressyn to the same   vj d
Item payd for ij Stoon of bettings more for the
Cressetts   ix d
...

Corpus Christi Guild Account Book CRO: A 6
f 253v *(Master's claims for expenses)*
...
Also he askythe alowaunce for leverey gowns &
hodes   v li. iiij s ij d
...

1522
Leet Book I CRO: A 3(a)
f 334v *(6 May)*
...
Also hit is inacted that the Scheryffees of the Cytte nowe choson
& heraftur to be choson Schall were in ther gowndes nother
fforre of ffoynees nor marturnes nor no veluet in ther dwblettes
nor Ierkyns or partletees except he or thei be notyd and knowyn
in this Cytte to be of the substans of iij ⌈c⌉ li. & a bowe a pon
peyne of euere man so offendyng to fforfet xxti markes to be
leveyd by the Meyre to the vse of the Comen box

•apparell for
Shireffes•

Also that all Comeners with in this Cytte vndur the degre of a
Scheryffe schall Where in there gownees ffeore of ffox Schankees
or lambe & none other fforrees & in there Dublettes or Iakettees

bott chamlet Saten of Brygees or wolsted & none other Sylkes on
les he be [of] notyd & knowyn to be of the valure & Substauns   5
of a C li. & a bowe apon the peyne of euere man so offendyng
x li. to be leveyd by the Meire to the vse of the Comen box
Item that no seruant man or woman reteyneyd for wagees with
in this Citte where veluet in eny other aparell apon them apon

the peyne of ffarfatur of the same aparell to the vse of the Comen   10
box of the Cytte & vppon peyne of imprisoment

...

Cappers' Records SC: Account Book I
f 29v col a   15

...

paid to the Master of the gordlers   vj s viij d
paid for cressettes ly3th   xviij d
paid for the berryng of the ly3th & the stoffe   x d

...   20

paid to the mynstrell   ij d

...

f 31 col a

...   25

Item for cressettes ly3th   xviij d
Item for the berryng theof   x d

...

paid for makyng iiij torchys   vj s

...   30

Carpenters' Account Book II CRO: Acc 3/2
f 88v *(St John's and St Peter's Nights)*

...

Item payd to our mynstrell   ij s.   35
Item payd to the pageaunt'os'   x s

...

AC   *Dyers' Accounts* Sharp: *Dissertation*
p 186   40

...

Item paid for vj ston of bettyngs   ij s ij d

...

p 198

...

Midsummer. - p*ai*d ij mynstrells   ij s ...

Corpus Christi Guild Account Book CRO: A 6   5
f 257v* *(Master's claims for expenses)*

...

also he askythe alowa*u*nce for [leverey] gowns &
hod*es*   v li. iiij s ij d

...   10

1523
Cappers' Records SC: Account Book I
f 32v col a
                 Exspensys for the yere first offerd   15

...

Item p*ai*d to the mynstrell*es*   ij d

...

Item p*ai*d for Cresset lyght & the beryng   ij s iiij d

...   20

col b
                 Exspenc*es* for the ij^{de} quart*er*

...

Item p*ai*d to the Gyrdelers   vj s viij d   25
Item p*ai*d to fox when he played   vj d

...

Item p*ai*d for cresset light & beryng   ij s vj d
Item p*ai*d for two hattys   iiij d

...   30

Carpenters' Account Book II CRO: Acc 3/2
f 91 *(Pentecost dinner)*

...

Item p*ay*d for the mynstrell   ij d   35

...

f 92 *(Midsummer and St Peter's Watches)*

...

Item p*ay*d to the mynstrell*es*   iiij s   40

...

Item payd to the pageaunt   x s

...

Item payd for cressettes lyght   ix d
Item payd for beryng the same   ij d
Item payd for beryng of the cressettes   vj d   5

...

Weavers' Account Book CRO: Acc 100/17/1
f 3*
           Receytes of players   10
Resseyvyd of symons clarke   x d
Resseyvyd of Iochop   x d
Resseyvyd of our lady   x d
Resseyvyd of Ihesu   x d
Resseyvyd of Anne   x d   15
thomas williams mayd broder to þe Iurneymen   vj d
               Summa   iiij s viij d

...

          Exspesys & paymentes All the yere
...   20
spend on [christof] corpus christi day   xxvij s vij d ob.
spend on myssomer ny3th   xxiiij s v d

...

Corpus Christi Guild Account Book CRO: A 6   25
f 261v *(Master's claims for expenses)*
...
Also he askythe alowance for leverey gowns &
hodes   v li. iiij s ij d
...   30

1524
Cappers' Records SC: Account Book I
f 34 col a   35
...
Item paid to amynstrell   iiij d
...
Item paid to the Gyrdelers   vj s viij d
...   40
Item paid for Cressett lyght   ij s

Item p*ai*d the berers   iiij d

...

col b

...   5

Item p*ai*d for Cressett lyght   ij s
Item p*ai*d for beryng the same   iiij d
Item p*ai*d for beryng cresse*tes*   ix d

...

                                                                                        10

Carpenters' Account Book II CRO: Acc 3/2
f 95 *(Pentecost dinner)*

...

Item p*ay*d to the pynners & tylers   x s   15

...

Item p*ay*d for the cresset*tes* lyght   xviij d
Item p*ay*d for beryng the same   ij d
Item p*ay*d for beryng the cresset*tes*   iiij d
Item p*ay*d to the mynstrell   ij s   20

...

Weavers' Account Book CRO: Acc 100/17/1
f 3v*   25

...

                     Rece*ytes* of Wold fyne*es*

...

Ress*eyvyd* of the players Iahepth barsley   x *(blank)*
Ress*eyvyd* of ou*r* lady Rychard byrskow   x d   30
Ress*eyvyd* of Anne thomas sogdyn   x d

...

f 5

...   35

spend on corp*us* chr*ist*i day   xxx s viij d ob.
spend on myssom*er* ny3th   xx s vij d

...

Item for Wyne & bred to syng wi*th*all   xx d

Corpus Christi Guild Account Book CRO: A 6
f 264v *(Master's claims for expenses)*

...

Also he askythe alowaunce for leverey gowns &
hoddes   v li. iiij s ij d   5

...

1525
Cappers' Records SC: Account Book I
f 36 col a*   10

...

Item payed for the soteltys on Candelmase daye   vj s viij d
Item payd to Robert Crowe for the Goldenflecc   xx s
Item paid to Iohn Crowe and Wyllyam lynes for the
same   xiij s iiij d   15
Item paid for Cresset lyght   ij s vij d ob.
Item paid for beryng of the same   iiij d
Item paid for ij gallons wyne   ij s

...

Item paid for mend of the torches   xx d   20
Item paid to the Gudelers   vj s viij d

...

col b
                                                                       25
...

Item paid the syngers on candelmase daye   xx d
Item paid for sutteltes   ij s v d
Item paid to the players   iiij s iiij d
Item paid for payntyng the soteltes   xij d
...   30
Item paid for cressett lyght   ij s vij d
Item paid for beryng the same   iiij d

...

Carpenters' Account Book II CRO: Acc 3/2   35
f 98

...

Item payd the pynners & tylers   x s

...

f 98v col b *(Midsummer and St Peter's Watches)*

...

Item for cressett*es* lyght	xiiij d
It*em* for beryng the cresset*es*	viij d
Item for beryng matches	ij d
It*em* the mynstrell*es*	ij s

...

Weavers' Account Book CRO: Acc 100/17/1
f 5v*

...

Resseytes

Item Ress*eyvyd* of the masters for the pagynt money	xvj s iiij d

...

exspencys on corpus christi day

Item payd for met And drynk for the players	ij s x d
Item payd to symyon for hys wagys	ij s iiij d
Item payd to Ioph	xiiij d
Item payd to mare	x d
Item payd to sodden for Ane	x d
Item payd to symyon clark	x d
Item payd to Ih*e*su	xx d
Item payd to the Angles	viij d
Item payd for glovys	viij d
Item payd to þe synggers	xvj d
Item payd homon for dryvyng of þe pagent	v s iiij d

Corpus Christi Guild Account Book CRO: A 6
f 268 *(Master's claims for expenses)*

...

Also he askythe alowa*u*nce for leverey govns & hod*es*	v li. iiij s ij d

...

AC   *Holy Trinity Guild Accounts* Bodl: MS Top. Warwickshire c.4
f 57v*

... It pd for beryng the Crose at my Ladie Pr*in*ces comyng iiij d

...

1526
Leet Book I CRO: A 3(a)
f 344v* *(1 May)*

...

Item it is enacted that all Carvers with*in this Citie fromehensfurth   5
shalbe associat with the Craft of peyntoures and that eu*ery
Carver shall pay yeirelie to the peyntoures towardes the Charges
of ther pagiaunt xij d without contradiction vpon peyn for euery
defaut to forfett vj s viij d to the seid Craft of peyntoures and
that the seid Carvers fromehensfurth shalbe dismyssed &   10
discharged frome the Craft of Carpenters and that Richard
Tenwynter shall pay suche arrerages to the Carpenters as he
oweth theme for the xij d which he shuld haue payed theme
yeirelie in tymes past

...   15

arvers to be
sociat with
eynters

Chamberlains' Account Book I CRO: A 7(a)
p 85*

...

Item payed for takyng down the heedes & the quarters from the   20
yates   iiij d

...

p 86*
                                                                25
Expens for makyng of Pamentes & the Cariage of Mukk ageinst
my ladie princessis commyng &c

...

Summa xxxix s ij d ob

...   30

AC *City Annals* BRL: 273978*

...

In ye year 1526. Henry Wall Weaver Mayor, the Lady Mary Came
to Coventry & Lay att the Priory, the Mercers Pageant Gallantly   35
trimed stood in the Cross Cheaping, she stayed 2 dayes & att her
goeing away the Citty presented her with 100 ll. and A Kercheife

37 / ll. *for* li

Cappers' Records SC: Account Book I
f 38

... for almaner of paymentes and offrynges
Exspences of the Company mydsomer nyght Clarke and   5
Somner   lvj s x d
...

Weavers' Account Book CRO: Acc 100/17/1
f 6   10
...
Item spend on corpus christi day   xxviij s iiij d
Item spend on myssommor ny3ght   xviij s ij d
...
                                                                       15
Corpus Christi Guild Account Book CRO: A 6
f 271 *(Master's claims for expenses)*
...
Also he askythe alowaunce for leverey gowns &
hodes   v li. iiij s ij d 20
...

1527
Weavers' Account Book CRO: Acc 100/ 17/1   25
f 7
...
Resseyvyd of of Iohn borsley   xij d
Resseyvyd of Rychard brysco   x d
...   30

f 8
...
Item spend on corpus christi day   xxvij s ij d
Item spend on myssomer ny3ght   xvj s x d ob. 35
...
paid to the mynstrell for the yere   iij s
...

28 / of of MS *dittography*

Corpus Christi Guild Account Book CRO: A 6
f 274 *(Master's claims for expenses)*

...

Also he askythe alowaunce for leverey gowns &
hodus   v li. iiij s ij d   5

...

1528
Chamberlains' Account Book I CRO: A 7(a)
p 97*   10

...

Item payed for two Iakettes to the kepers of the beggars ayeinst
Corpus christi Tyde   x s

...

                                                                                  15

Carpenters' Account Book II CRO: Acc 3/2
f 100v *(Whitsontide)*

...

Item payd to the pynners   x s

...   20

f 101 *(Midsummer Watch)*

...

Item for the light of the Cressettes   ix d
Item for bering the cressett for both nyghttes   viij d   25
Item paid for bering of the bettinges   ij d
Item paid to the mynstrelles for myssomer nyght   xij d

...

Weavers' Account Book CRO: Acc 100/17/1   30
f 9

...

Item spend on corpus crysty day   xxvj s iiij d
Item spend on myssomer ny3ght   xviij s v d ob.
...   35
payd to the mynstrell All the yere   iij s

...

Proof of Majority of Walter Smythe PRO: C 142/46?45
(11 January)   40

... Et predictus Iohannes hyll etatis sexaginta annorum et vltra
solus examinatus de etate predicti walteri Smythe dicit super

sacramentum suum quod predictus walterus est etatis viginti vnius
annorum et vltra eo quod videbat quando dictus walterus Smythe
portatus fuit ad ecclesiam predictam Baptizandus & quando
revenit ab ecclesia predicta Baptizatus cum Magna societate modo
& forma prout predictus Thomas forman dixit Et vlterius dicit   5
quod bene recolit quod ad ffestum penticoste proximum
sequentem baptismatem predictam in anno vicesimo primo
supradicto Magnum ludum vocatum seynt christeans play
habitum et factum fuit in quodam Campo iuxta Ciuitatem
Couentrie predicte vocato lyttle parke in tempore Iohannis   10
Dudsburye tunc Maioris Ciuitatis predicte ... Willelmus Bredon
etatis quinquaginta annorum solus examinatus de etate predicti
walteri Smythe dicit super sacramentum suum quod predictus
walterus Smythe baptizatus fuit die anno & loco prout Iurati
predicti per veredictum suum predictum allegauerunt & dixerunt   15
vt bene recolit eo quod videbat predictum walterum portatum ad
ecclesiam predictam Baptizandum cum duobus funalibus que
numquam fuerunt illuminata et cum alijs circumstancijs predictis
Et eciam videbat eum reportatum ab ecclesia predicta baptizatum
cum funalibus predictis que ad tunc fuerunt luminata vnde   20
Robertus Store Capper portabat vnum funale Et ad ffestum
penticoste tunc proximum sequentem baptisma predictam
Magnus ludus vocatus seynt christeans pley habitus et factus fuit
in Campo iuxta Ciuitatem predictam vocato lyttle parke in
tempore Iohannis Dudsburye tunc Maioris Ciuitatis predicte qui   25
quidem ludus vt bene recolit factus fuit ad ffestum penticoste
predicte in anno vicesimo primo Regis henrici Septimi Supradicti
...

1529   30
Leet Book I CRO: A 3(a)
f 350v* *(8 April)*
...

The Cappers to
haue the weivers
pagiaunt

Item it is enacted at this lete that the Crafte of Cappers of this
Citie fromehensfurth shalbe owners of the weyvers pagiaunt with   35
all the implementes & apparell belongyng to the same pagiaunt
and that the seid Craft of weyvers shall yeirelie fromehensfurthe
pay vnto the Maister of the seid Crafte of Cappers vj s viij d and
so the seid Craft of weyvers fromehensfurth to be clerlie
discharged of ther seid pagiaunt & of ther name therof   40
...

22 / baptisma *for* baptismam

f 351v* *(12 October)*

...

Item it is enacted that the Craft of Cappers of this Citie shall pay
yeirelie fromehensfurth to the Craft of gurdelers xiij s iiij d And
that the Craft of Walkers shalbe fromehensfurth discharged of all   5
paymentes to the Craft & feliship of Girdelers & clerelie dismyssed
frome the seid Craft / and that the seid Craft of walkers shall pay
yeirelie a Sevennyght before Corpus christi day to the [Seid] Crafte
of weyvers tene shelynges in Consideracion of ther gret Charges
&c.   10

Carpenters' Account Book II CRO: Acc 3/2
f 110 col b
        Expencces of the Whissone tyde Quarterage
...   15
Item paid at that tyme to pynners Cowpers and tyllers   ⟨..⟩
...

f 111
         Expencces for mydsomer   20
Item paid to the mynstrell at mydsomer   xx d
...
Item paid for beryng the Cressettes and the podyng   vj d
Item paid for bettynges   [x d] [viij] ix d
...   25

Weavers' Account Book CRO: Acc 100/17/1
f 10
...
Item spend on corpus christi day   xxv s vij d   30
Item spend on myssomer ny3ght   xviij s vj d
...

f 10v
...   35
Item payd to the mynstrell for All the yere   iij s
...

AC   *Dyers' Accounts* Sharp: *Dissertation*
p 186*   40

...
Item paid for the clooth of a surplis for them þat bayre the
Cressetts   x d

Item paid for makyng of the surplys   j d

...

Corpus Christi Guild Account Book CRO: A 6
f 281   5

...

Thes byn the parselles foloyng of the dyscharg of þe seyd Rent
furst he askythe alowaunce for exspences made at
prinsypall festes and at generall days & at obetes &
to cheffe lordes & mendefaunces In money   xix li. vij s viij d   10
& for all alowaunce & Dyuers paymentes &
levereys as hyt shewythe in the boke theroff
by þe yere

...

                                                                            15

1530
Leet Book I CRO: A 3(a)
f 353v *(14 September)*

...

Item wher as the Craft of Cappers of this Citie haue vsed to pay   20

yeirlie vnto the Craft of Girdelers vj s viij d towardes ther pagiaunt
Itt is now enacted that the seid Craft of Cappers fromehensfurth
for certeyn consideracions alleged shall not pay the seid vj s viij d
in fourme aforseid

...   25

f 354

...

Item it is enacted that such persones as fromehensfurth woll
onelie vse & occupie the Craft of Carvers shalbe contributories to   30
the Craft to the Craft of peynters & not to the Craft of Carpenters

...

Weavers' Account Book CRO: Acc 100/17/1
f 11*   35

...

Resseyvyd of the masters of the Walkers   x s

...

30-1 / to the Craft to the Craft MS *dittography*

f 12

...

Item spend on corpus crysty day	xxviij s iiij d
Item spend on myssomer ny3ght	xvj s ix d
...	
Item payd to the mynstrell for þe yere	iij s

...

1531
Leet Book I CRO: A 3(a)
ff 357-8* *(10 October)*

...

Item wher as the Company feliship & Craft of Cardemakers &
Sadelers of this Citie meny yeires & of longe continuaunce haue
hadd & yet haue the cheif rule gouernaunce reparyng &
meyntenaunce as well of a Chappell within the parishe Churche
of seynt Michelles in the seid Citie named seynt Thomas Chappell
& of the ornamentes Iuelles & lightes of the same / As also of a
pagiaunt with the pagiaunt house & pleyng geire with other
appurtenaunces & apparelles belongyng to the same pagiaunt /
The Meyntenaunce & reparacion wherof haithe been & is yeirelie
to the greit charge cost & exspenses of the seid company & crafte
beyng now but a fewe persones in nomber & havyng but smale
eyde of eny other Craft for the same / So that ther seid Charge is
& like to be more ponderouse & chargeable to theme / then they
may convenyentlie bere or susteyn in shorte tyme to come oneles
prouision for a remedy may be spedilie hadd In considercion
wherof & for asmoch as the company feliship & craft of cappers
within this citie now beyng in nomber meny welthy & honest
persones & haue maid dyuers tymes Sute & request vnto the Meire
& his brethern the aldermen of this Citie to haue a certeyn place
to theme assigned & lymyted as dyuers other Craftes haue to sitt
to gether in ther seid parishe Churche to here ther dyuyne seruice
& bere suche charges for the same as by Maister Meire & his
brethern the Aldermen shalbe assigned It is therfor by the
Mediacion of Mr. Richard Rice now Meire of this Citie & of his
seid brethern the aldermen at this present lete assembled & by
auctoritie of the same with the agrement consent & assent of all
the seid parties Companyes & Craftes enacted ordeyned &
constituted that the seid company & Craft of Cappers frome

Cardemakers Sadelers & Cappers to be vnyte together (margin note)

hensforthe shalbe associat Ioyned & accompanyed with the seid
Craftes of Cardemakers & Sadelers in the gouernaunce reparying
& meynteynyng aswell of & in the seid Chappell named seynt
Thomas Chappell & of the ornamentes & lightes of the same As
of & in the seid pagyaunt | And pagiaunt House With the   5
Implementes Appurtenaunces pleaers reherces & pleyng geire
accustumed belongyng & necessarie to & for the same after suche
maner or better as it haithe been vsed & accustumed before tyme
And that euery housholder or Shop keper of euery of the seid
companyes & Craftes toward & for the charges & exspenses   10
aboueseid shall not onelie pay yeirelie to the Maisteres & kepers
of the seid Craftes at such tyme & day as the seid Craftes shall
appoynt xij d And vpon seynt Thomas day named the translacion
of seynt Thomas shall also offere yeirelie euery of theme j d at
the high Masse seid in the seid Chappell / But also the seid Maisters   15
company & Craftes fromehensfurthe shall applie & bestowe to &
vpon the seid reparacions & charges / All the reuenues rentes &
profittes of all soche landes houses & tenementes as they or eny
of theme now haue or herafter shall haue to the vse & behove of
the seid companyes & craftes And the viij s of yerelie pencion   20
which is yeirlie payed by the peynters & Caruers vnto the ʼseidʼ
charges shall yeirelie be payed & go to the same charges And that
the seid Maisters now electe & hereafter to be electe Maisters of
the seid Craftes shall yeirelie vpon suche a day as the seid Maisters
shall appoynt & agre accompeny theme selfes to gethers & bryng   25
in & make a true & a full accompt euery of theme to the other
of all ther seid receites revenues & profittes And the seid charges
& the charges of the kepyng of harnes belongyng to the seid
Craftes With the Weiryng of the same in the Watches & other
necessarie charges & busynes for the seid Craftes allowed payed   30
& performed the ouerpluse of the seid money of the seid revenues
profittes & money shalbe bestowed & put in a box With two
lockes & two Keyes the on key to remeyne With the Maisterz of
the Craft of Cardmakers & Sadelers / And the other Key to
remeyn with the Maisters of the Craft of Cappers sauelie to keip   35
the seid money in the seid box vntill they haue nede to bestow it
vpon the seid Charges or otherwise as they shall thynk convenyent
& the seid box to remeyn in the seid Chappell fastoned with a
cheyne
Also it is enacted by the auctoritie & consent aforseid that the   40

5 / verte ffolium written at foot of folio

Maisters & compeny of the Craft of Cappers shall fromehensfurthe
famyliarlie & louynglie accompeny & sitt togethers in the seid
Chappell With the seid compeny & craft of Cardemakers &[Saders]
Sadelers to here ther dyvyne seruice / and also shall go togethers
in ther processions & watches too & too togethers And that the   5
seid compeny & craft of cardmakers & sadelers shall haue the
preemynence & ouer hande in ther sittynges & goyng together
oon yeire / & the seid Craft & compeny of Cappers shall likewise
haue the preemynences & ouer hande in ther sittyng & goyng the
other yeir And so to continew frome yeire to yeire lovynglie   10
fromehensfurthe So that the seid Cardemakers & Sadelers shall
not lack ther rome nor sittyng in the seid Chappell |
Item it is enacted also that the Company & Craft of [Bakers]
 ˄ ꞌBarbarsꞌ of this Citie shall yeirelie fromehensfurthe pay vnto
the Company & Craft of Gurdelers of this Citie vj s viij d / toward   15
ther charges of the pagyant & processions at suche day & tyme as
they were wont to pay the seid some vnto the Craft of Cardmakers
vpon peyn euery of theme to forfeit for ther defaut xij d to be
levyed by distresse to the vse of the Citie
Item it is also enacted that the compeny & Craft of walkers of   20
this Citie shall yeirelie pay vnto the company & Craft of weyvers
vj s viij d towardes the charges of ther pagyant at such day &
tyme as it haithe be wont to be payed And that the Company &
Craft of Skynners shall likewise pay vnto the seid Craft of weyvers
yeirelie v s towardes ther seid charges   25
...

[the bakers]
The barbars to
pay yeirelie
vj s viij d to
the Girdelers

The Walkers to
pay yeirelie
vj s viij d to the
weyvers & the
skynners to
pay v s

Carpenters' Account Book II CRO: Acc 3/2
f 112 *(Pentecost dinner)*

...   30
Item payde to the plymars & tyllers   x s
...

       Exspensys for Medsommar nyght

...
Item payd for the lyght for bouth the nyghtes   ij s.   35
...
Item payd the Mynstrelles for Corpyscrysty day And Mydsomor
nyght & synt petters nyght   ij s. iiij d
...

31 / plymars *for* pinnars

Weavers' Account Book CRO: Acc 100/17/1
f 12v

...

Resseyvyd of the masters of the Walkers   x s

...

f 13

...

Item payd for mendyng of þe pagent howse wyndo   ij s

...

f 13v

...

Item spend on corpus crysty day   xxiiij s ij d
Item spend on myssomer nyȝght   xvj s viij d

...

Item payd to the mynstrell all þe yere   iij s

...

AC   *Dyers' Accounts* Bodl: MS Top. Warwickshire c.7
f 33*

...

It paid to iiij men for weryng almen revitts bifor Mr. Mayer on
ffayer ffriday viij. d

...

Corpus Christi Guild Account Book CRO: A 6
f 290v *(Master's claims for expenses)*

...

Also he askyth alowance for leueris and the stewardes
ffe   iiij li. xix s ij d

...

1532
Leet Book I CRO: A 3(a)
f 359v *(14 May)*

...

Peynters   Item it is enacted that the Craft of Peynters shald pay yeirelie
Gurdelers   fromeherforth iiij s of the viij s that they wer wont to pay to a
Cardemakers pagiaunt vnto the Craft of Gurdelers & the other iiij s of the seid
            viij s vnto the Craft of Cardemakers

...

Carpenters' Account Book II CRO: Acc 3/2
f 116 (Midsummer Watch)

...

Item payd for [the] barrynge the Cryssyt lyght	iiij d	
Item for the lyght	ij d	5
Item payd for the Cryssyt lyght	ix d	
Item payd to ij menstrys	x d	
Item payd to ij Mynstrelles for Corpyscryst Day	xij d	

...

10

f 116v *(St Peter's Watch)*

...

Item payd for Cryssyt lyght & bayryng of the sam	xiij d	
Item payd to hym þat bayr the Cryssyt lyght	ij d	
Item payd to ij Mynstrelles	xij d	15
Item payd for the Mynstrelles dynar & scoper	iiij d	

...

f 118v

paymentes for the yere		20
Item [paymen] payde to the plymars And tyllars	x s	

...

Weavers' Account Book CRO: Acc 100/17/1
f 14*   25

...

Reseyvyd of the Walkers	vj s viij d	
Reseyvyd of the skynners	v s	

...

Item spend on corpus crysty day	xxvj s vj d	30
Item spend on myssomer ny3ght	xviij s vj d	

...

payd to the mynstrell all the yere	iij s

f 14v   35

...

Item spend at the Reyseyvyng of the Walkers money And the skynners	vj d

...

21/ plymars *for* pinnars

AC   *Dyers' Accounts* Bodl: MS Top. Warwickshire c.7
      f 33*

      ...

      It paid to iiij men for weryng almen revitts bifor Mr. Mayer on
      ffayer ffriday viij. d   5

      ...

      Corpus Christi Guild Account Book CRO: A 6
      f 298v *(Master's claims for expenses)*

      ...   10

      Also he askyth a lowance for leverey Gowns & the stewardes
      ffee as apperithe bi the booke   iiij li. xix s ij d

      ...

      1533   15
      Leet Book I CRO: A 3(a)
      f 361 *(25 January)*

      ...

      Also it is enacted that such persones as be not associat & assistant
      to eny Craft which is charged with eny pagiant of this Citie as   20
      fishemongers bowyers flechers & suche other / shall now be
      associat & assisstaunt to such [the] craftes as Maister Meire shall
      assigne & apoynt theme

Craftes/ •All
men to
Associate to
some one
Craft as the
mayor shall
Apoynt•

      Cappers' Records SC: Account Book I   25
      f 45v col b*

      ...

      Exspences on the first quarter first payed for dyuers besynesse
      abowte the Cardmakers   iij s xj d
      ...   30
      Item payed for the Gyant   xxvij s viij d
      Item payed for Cressett lyght   ij s
      Item payed for beryng the same   x d
      Item payed for a presant to Mr mair   iij s viij d
      ...   35
      Item payed for iiij torchez   vj s viij d
      Item paid to the mynstrell on my quartreg daye   viij d

      ...

      f 46   40

      Exspences on the secound quarter first payed for besynesse

abowte the Cardmakers   viij d
Item payed to the mynstrell*es*   iij s
Item payed for cresset lyght   ij s
Item payed for beryng the same   x d
...   5

Carpenters' Account Book II CRO: Acc 3/2
f 120v

...

Item payed to the pynners & Tylers   x s   10

...

Weavers' Account Book CRO: Acc 100/17/1
f 14[a] *

...   15
                         Reyset*tes* In my yere
Reseyvyd of the Walkers   vj s viij d
Reseyvyd of the skyn*n*ers   v s
...
                                                                     20

f 14[a] v
                     Reyseyt*tes* of lowe brethern
...
Reseyvyd of owr mynstrell   wax
...   25
                      exspenc*es* In my yere
...
Item spend on corp*us* crysty day   xxvij s j d
Item spend on myssom*er* ny3ght   xv s
...   30

f 15
...
payd to the mynstrell   iij s
...   35

AC   *Dyers' Accounts* Bodl: MS Top. Warwickshire c.7
     f 33
     ...
     It pd for wering of hernis befor Mr. Meyr to iiij men on ffayer   40
     ffrydaye viij. d
     ...

Corpus Christi Guild Account Book CRO: A 6
f 305v *(Master's claims for expenses)*

...

Also he askytht allowauns for ... leverey gownys ...

5

A   *Holy Trinity Guild Accounts* Templeman: *Records*
p 156*

...

[f. 26b.] Expences on Trenete even and the day.

...   10

Payd to the Waytes of the cite   vj s viij d

...

p 157
[f. 27a.]   15
        Expences on Midsomereven and the day for the obett of
                Robart Schipley, Jone and Agnes his wifes.

...

Item to the Waites and poore pepull   xiij s iiij d
...   20
[f. 27b.]
                Expences on the Assumcion of our Ladye

...

Payd to the Waytes   vj s viij d
...   25

1534
Leet Book I CRO: A 3(a)
f 363 *(21 April)*

...   30

Also wher as the Shireffes of this Citie haue been Accustumed to
geve to euery seriaunt of this Citie dyuers lyvereys in the yeire
In consideracion of the ease of ther great charges It is now enacted
that the seid Shireffes fromehensfurth shalbe charged to geve vnto
euery of the seid seriauntes but onelie oon honest liuerey of iiij   35
seriauntes   yardes of brode cloith Ageynst Cristenmas And At corpus christi
tide suche Sleves Iackettes as they haue been wont to gyve vnto
the seid seriauntes And no moo liuereyes in the yeire And at
whitsontide next the seid Shireffes shall pay vnto [the] euery of
the seid seriauntes iij s iiij d in recompense of the lack of parte of   40
ther seid lyuereyes to theme yeven at Cristemmas last past

f 364 *(8 October)*

...

Seriauntes

It is enacted at this p*rese*nt leet that All & eu*er*y s*er*iaunt & officer
of this Citie shall fromehensfurth haue & enyoye all such liu*er*eyes
& fees yeirlie As thei in tymes past haue hadd & been Accustumed   5
to haue not w*ith*standyng An Acte maid At the last leet to the
cont*r*arie

...

Cappers' Records SC: Account Book I   10
f 47 col a

...

Rec*eiv*ed to paye the mynstrell*es*   iiij s iiij d

...
                                                                         15

ff 47v col b-48

Exspenc*es* for the yere
first payed to whyrrett for standyng of o*ur* pageant   iiij d
It*em* p*ai*d for vij ston of Cresset lyght   ij s iiij d   20
Item p*ai*d for beryng the same and Cressett*es*   x d
Item p*ai*d for Dryssyng the gyant   vj d
It*em* p*ai*d for beryng the gyant   xij d
It*em* p*ai*d for nayll*es* & Corde   ij d
Item p*ai*d for pont*es*   j d   25
Item p*ai*d two mynstrell*es*   iiij s
Spent at the kyng*es*hede on the Company   xij d

...

Rep*ar*acions made of the pageant and players Ger   xxxj s v d ob. |
ffirst payed for two Rehersys   ij s iiij d   30
Item p*ai*d to pylate   iij s viij d
Item p*ai*d to the Syngers   xvj d
Item payed to god   xvj d
Item payed to mother of deth   iiij d
Item payed to foure knyght*es*   iiij s   35
It*em* payed to the sprett of god   xvj d
Item payed to oure lady   xij d
Item payed to two bysshopp*es*   ij s
Item payed to two awngell*es*   viij d
Item payed to mare Magdeleyn   xij d   40
Item payed to two syde maryes   xij d

Item payed to the demon	xvj d
Item payed to the mynstrell	viij d
Item payed for the players supper	ij s
Item payed for drynke to the dryvers of the pageant	viij d
Item payed for foure harnesse	xvj d
Item payed for dressyng the pageant	viij d
Item payed for v dossan pontes	iiij d
Item payed for Rysshes	j d
Item payed to lewez for dryvyng the pageant	vj d
Item payed for mete and drynke to the players at the Swane	vj d
Spent at the dryvyng owte the pageant	vj d
Spent at the bryngyng yn the pageant	vj d
Item payed for glovez	xv d
Summa xxx s iiij d	

...

Carpenters' Account Book II CRO: Acc 3/2
f 121 *(Pentecost dinner)*

...

Item payd to the pynnars & tyllers	x s

...

(Midsummer)

Item the mynestrell	xvijj d
Item for Cressett ly3t	viij d
Item for makyng of A Crassett	iiij d
Item for the berar of the ly3t	iij d

...

AC *Smiths' Accounts* Nowell: Reader MSS 25-6 March 1927
p 47* *(Midsummer and St Peter's Watches)*

... four men in compleat armour, etc., also battle axes ...

1535
Chamberlains' Account Book I CRO: A 7(a)
p 142

...

Item for makyng cler the Streites when the Duk of Risemond & the Duk of Norfook come into the Citie	ij s vij d

...

Line numbers (right margin): 5, 10, 15, 20, 25, 30, 35, 40

A C *City Annals* Bodl: MS Top. Warwickshire d.4
     f 17v

Duke of
Norfolke &   ... Also this yeare the Duke of Richmond & Norfolke came to
Richmond   Coventrey & were honourably receaued of the maior & Citizens   5
receuied by ye in there liueries & had a banquett in ye streete one horsebacke,
Maior &c.   after which they went to Combe. /

     Cappers' Records SC: Account Book I
     f 49 col a   10
     ...
     Receyvid for the mynstrelles   iij s
     ...

     f 49v col b   15
     ...
     Exspences of the pageant for the same yere   xxxiiij s v d ob
     ...

     Carpenters' Account Book II CRO: Acc 3/2   20
     f 124 *(Pentecost dinner)*
     ...
     In primis payde to the pynners tyllores & Coupers   x s.
     ...
                                                                                    25
     f 125 *(Midsummer and St Peter's Watches)*
     ...
     Item A dosan spiced cakes   [torchis xij]   viij d
     ...
     Item payd ffor ij stone of light   x d ⟨.⟩ 30
     Item payd to the Mynsterll   [iij s. iiij d] ij s
     Item payd ffor berryng of þe cressett light   iij d
     ...

     Weavers' Account Book CRO: Acc 100/17/1   35
     f 15v*
     ...
                    Reyseyttes In my yere
     ...
     Item Resseyvyd of the Walkers   vj s viij d 40
     Item Resseyvyd of the skynners   v s
     ...

Reyseyttes of olde fynys

...

Ress<i>eyvyd</i> of wyllyam blakbowrn þe mynstrell   xij d

...   5

f 16*

...

Exspences In my yere

...

Item spend on corp<i>us</i> crysty day   xxvij s   10
Item spend on myssom<i>er</i> ny3ght   xvij s j d
Item payd for makyng of the play boke   v s

...

f 16v   15

...

Item p<i>ay</i>d for iiij Iodas torchys   v s
Item spend at þe Reyseyvyng of þe Walkers & sky<i>n</i>ners
money   viij d
Item p<i>ay</i>d for makyng of A whyt forde p<i>re</i>latt for Ih<i>esus</i>   viij d 20

...

Item payd to the mynstrell   iij s

...

1536   25
Leet Book I CRO: A 3(a)
f 367 *(9 May)*

...

Craftes
•Euery ffreeman   Item it is also enacted that eu<i>ery</i> householder of this Citie which
to hold of   is not associat to some Crafte shalbe associat & bere w<i>ith</i> some   30
some Company•   Craft before Whitsontyde next vpon peyne to be punyshed by
the discreci<i>o</i>n of the Meire &c.

Cappers' Records SC: Account Book I
f 50v col b   35

...

Rec<i>eived</i> of the Craft for mynstrell<i>es</i>   iiij s x d

...

f 51 col b   40
Item paid ffor the pageant and playing   xxxiij s ix d
Item paid for the Rep<i>ara</i>ci<i>o</i>ns of the same pageant   v s vij d

...

Carpenters' Account Book II CRO: Acc 3/2
f 128 *(Pentecost dinner)*

[In primis payd to the pynners tyllares & cowpers   x s]
...   5

f 129 *(Midsummer and St Peter's Watches)*
...
Item paid for cressete lygthe   x d
Item payd for beyrreng of the same   ij d   10
Item for berreng of the cresetes   iiij d
Item paid the mynstrellyes   xx d
...
In prymys payd pinnares tyllares & cowperys   x s
...   15

Weavers' Account Book CRO: Acc 100/17/1
f 17
...
Reysseyvyd of the Walkers   vj s viij d   20
Reysseyvyd of the skynners   v s
...

f 17v
...   25
Item spend on corpuscrysty day   xxvj s vij d
Item spend on myssomor ny3ght   xvj s
...

f 18   30
...
payd to the mynstrell for corpuscrysty day & myssomer
ny3ght   ij s
...
spend At the Reyseyvyng of the Walkers And skynners   35
money   vij d
...

1537
Leet Book I CRO: A 3(a)   40
f 368v *(24 April)*
...
Item wher as the meire [Aldermen] aldermen Beilleffes &

cappers

Cominaltie of this Citie by ther wrytyng indented & sealled with
ther comen Seall haue graunted given & dymysed vnto the
Maisterez kepers fraternitie & company of the Craft of Cappers
of this Citie The Chappell pagyaunt & pagyaunt house which was
latelie surrendered & given vpp by wrytyng to theme by the   5
ffraternitie & company of Cardemakers & Sadelers It is nowe
enacted by Auctoritie of this lete that the seid fraternitie &
company of Cappers shall enyoy the seid pagiaunt pagiaunt
house & Chappell Accordyng to the tenour of the seid wrytyng
indented   10

...

Chamberlains' Account Book I CRO: A 7(a)
p 156*   15

ffor pavyng in Gosforde Streit

...

Item bordes & neilles & setyyng vp the pale at the gild barne
ende   xiiij d   20

...

Cardmakers and Saddlers' Indentured Conveyance CRO: Box I
sheet 2* *(8 January)*   25

This Indenture Maid At the Citie of Couentre the Eight day of
Ianuarie in the xxviij^th yeire of the Reigne of our souereigne
lorde kyng Henrie the eight Betwene Iohn Iett nowe Meire of the
said Citie the Aldermen Beilleffes & Cominaltie of the same Citie   30
of the oon partie / And William Rogers & Thomas Castell of the
Citie aforsaid Cardemakers now Maisters & kepers of the Crafte
& facultie of Cardemakers of & in the said Citie / And Iohn
Sparkes & Roger Mott nowe Maisters & kepers of the Craft &
facultie of Sadelers of & in the same Citie / And all the hole   35
fraternitie felishipp & Company Aswell of the said Craft & facultie
of Cardemakers / as of the said Crafte & facultie of Sadelers of &
in the Citie aforseid oon the other partie Wittenesseth that at the
mediacion & request of the said Meire & Aldermen & for certayne
consideracions hereafter in these present Indentures expressed &   40
graunted The said Maisters feliships Companyes & fraternyties of
the said Craftes & faculties of Cardemakers & Sadelers by all ther
hole Assentes & consentes for theme & ther Successores of the

same Craftes within the said Citie Haue by these presentes
surrendred given graunted & dimised vnto the said Maire Aldermen
Aldermen Beilleffes & Cominaltie & to ther Successores for euer
Aswell ther Chappell within the parishe Churche of Seynt Michell
in the Citie aforsaid named seynt Thomas Chappell & the   5
Cardemakers & Sadelers Chappell / As also ther pagiaunt &
pagiaunt ∧ 'house' within the same Citie named the Cardemakers
& Sadelers pagiaunt & pagiaunt House with all & singler ther
Appurtenances ornamentes vestymentes Iuelles & implementes to
the said Chappell pagiaunt & pagiaunt House & to euery of theme   10
in eny wise belongyng & Apperteynyng conteyned & expressed
in a Cedule to these present Indentures Annexed Except & Alweies
saved & reserued to the said fraternitie & felishipp of Cardemakers
& Sadelers convenyent sittyng & rome in the said Chappell for
foure persones of the said Craftes of Cardemakers & Sadelers to   15
Here ther dyvyne seruice at all tymes hereafter The same Rome
& sittyng to be vnder the nether wyndowe on the south side of
the said Chappell betwene the Images of the Trinitie & seynt
Sebastiane / payng therfore yeirelie to the kepers or gouernores
of the said Chappell xvj d To Haue & to Holde the said Chappell   20
pagiaunt & pagiaunt House & other the premissez with all & singler
ther Appurtenances / Except before except vnto the said Meire
Aldermen Beilleffes & Cominaltie & to ther Successores for euer
to Assigne give & bestowe the same to eny other felishipp
fraternitie or Crafte of the said Citie at ther will & pleasure In   25
consideracion & recompense of which Aimeable surrender & gifte
And for that that the said fraternitie & felishipp of Cardemakers
& Sadelers & ther predicessores of Longe tyme hetherto haue kept
& meynteyned the said Chappell & pagiaunt in good order &
reparacion to the Honor of god & worshipp of the said Citie to   30
ther great costes & charges The said Meire Aldermen Beilleffes &
Cominaltie for theme & ther Successores Meires Aldermen
Beilleffes & Cominaltie of the said Citie do couenante graunte
Assure & fullie promyse & Affirme by these presentes vnto the
said felishipp company & fraternitie of Cardemakers & Sadelers   35
& to euery of theme & ther Successores of the said Craftes in the
same Citie that thei & euery of theme / ther said Successores &
euery particuler persone of theme shalbe at all tymes
fromehensfurth & for euer exonerated discharged releassed &
Aquyted of & for all offices paymentes exspenses costes pencions   40
contribucions & charges not onelie of for & consernyng the said

2-3 / Aldermen Aldermen MS dittography   27 / that that MS dittography

Chappell pagiaunt & pagiaunt House but also of for & concernyng
all other pagiauntes now yeirelie vsed Accustomed & kept by
other Craftes & fraternities within the same Citie And moreover
that no persone ne persones which now be or hereafter shalbe of
the said fraternitie & companye of Cardemakers & Sadelers or of   5
either of theme shalbe constreyned charged or compelled at eny
tyme hereafter to be at eny coste charge or exspenses for or
concernyng the said Chappell or eny of the said Craft concernyng
the meyntenance & keping of the said pagiauntes or pagiaunt
Housez or eny of theme / eny Acte caue ordinance or constitucion   10
maid or to be maid within this Citie to the contrarie not
Withstanding In wittenes wherof to the oon parte of these
Indentures remeanyng with the said fraternitie company &
felishipp of Cardemakers & Sadelers the said Meire Beilleffes &
Cominaltie haue put ther comen Seall And to the other parte of   15
the same Indentures remeanyng with the said Meire Aldermen
Beilleffes & cominaltie The said Maisters & kepers of the said
Craftes & faculties of Cardemakers & Sadelers for & in the name
of all the hole fraternitie & company of the said Craftes of
Cardemakers & Sadelers haue put ther sealles the day & yeire   20
aboue written

(Inventory)
... Item ij pagiont Clothes of the passion / ...
                                                                          25

Carpenters' Account Book II CRO: Acc 3/2
f 132
...
                    Exspence for penticost diner &c.
...   30

payd they pynnares tyllares & cowperys   x s.
...
they mynstele   xij d
ffor payd for they lyte   xiij d
...   35

Weavers' Account Book CRO: Acc 100/17/1
f 18v
...
Resseyvyd of the Walkers   vj s viij d   40
Resseyvyd of the skynners   v s
...

Res*seyvyd* of wyllyam blakbowrn mynstrell   xij d
...

ff 19v-20
...   5
p*ay*d for makyng of A hyng*es* to þe pagent howse
dore   viij d
p*ay*d for menddyng of the cresset*es*   ij d
spend At the Reys*seyvyng* of the Walkers money   viij d |
spend At þe Reys*seyvyng* of the sky*n*ners money   ix d   10
...
p*ay*d to the mynstrell   ij s
...
spend on corp*us* crysty day   xxx s j d
spend on myssom*er* nyght   xvj s ij d   15
...
Memorandum that I petor brown weyver hath payd All thyng*ges*
that longth vnto seynt petor nyght fryst the mynstrell xij d to
the harnys men viij d And for cresset lyght xv d And toe the
bayrers of stremers And cresse*tes* vj d   20
                    som ys iij s v d
...

1538
Cappers' Records SC: Account Book I   25
f 86 col b
...
Ite*m* Getheryd of the Craft for the mynstrel   iij s viij d
...

                                                                              30
f 87

Exspenc*es* for the same yere first payed for the
pageant   xxxix s viij d
...   35

Carpenters' Account Book II CRO: Acc 3/2
f 136 *(Midsummer Watch)*
...
Ite*m* payde ffor lyght   ix d   40
Ite*m* payde ffor beryng   vij d
...

col b

payde to the pynnar*ees* tylars & copars   x s

...

                                                                  5

Weavers' Account Book   CRO: Acc 100/17/1
f 20v

...

Ress*yvyd* of the Walkers   vj s viij d
Ress*yvyd* of the skyn*n*ers   v s   10

...

f 21
                       Ress*ettes* for bereall
                                                                  15
...

Ress*yvyd* At þe bereyng of owr menstrell*es* wyfe   x d
...

f 21v
                                                                  20
...

p*ay*d to the mynstrell   ij s

...

spend on corp*us* crysty day   xxvij s iiij d ob
spend on myssom*er* nyght   xvij s j d
                                                                  25
...

1539
Letter of Mayor Coton to Cromwell PRO: SP/1/142
ff 66-6v* *(17 January)*
                                                                  30

Right hono*u*rable in moost humble & faithfull wise c⟨..⟩maund
vnto y*our* lordeshipp*e* evenso thankynge yow for y*our* manyfolde
goode ⟨..⟩e shewed in sondre suytt*es* conc*er*nynge the p*re*ferment
of the com*en* welthe of this the kyng*es* Citie of Couentre / Wherby
I for my p*ar*te haue taken boldenes to manyfest & shewe vnto   35
y*our* lordedeshipp such thyng*es* as p*ar*tlie be thoccasion of the
decay & pou*er*tie of the said Citie / trustyng that by y*our* good
lordeships furtherunce to make therin some redresse / And
where as I & my bretherne haue wrytten vnto y*our* lordeshipp*e*
that the chargeable offices of meire & shireff*es* be a great occasion 40
of the decay of the said Citie / the trewithe is even so / And therin
it is thought by the com*en*ers here that many p*r*iuate charges now

accustumed in the said offices / myght be right well spared &
dymynysshed / ffor on Candelmasse day the newe meire is sworne
& taketh vpon hyme the office / which day he feasteth such
nomber of Citizens & Straungers that with thexpenses then [he
myght] more then convenyentlie nedeth he myght well keipp his   5
house half a yeire after / And likewise at Corpus christi tide / the
poore Comeners be at suche charges with ther playes &
pagyontes / that thei fare the worse all the yeire after / And on
Mydsomer even & on seynt peters even the maisters & kepers of
Craftes vse suche excesse in exspences in drynkyng / that some   10
suche as be not worthe v li. in goodes shalbe then at xl s charges
to ther vndoyng / and moche exclamacion is maid to me beyng
meire by the comeners for reformacion therin / and I without
thassent of my bretherne cannot help it / And meny of my seid
bretherne beyng past all suche offices & charges do litle regarde   15
theme that be to come / ner do not esteme the vndoyng of half a
dosen honest Comeners to be so ill a deid / as is the omyttyng &
lesyng of on accustumed drynkyng / Wherfore in the honour of
god lett it pleas your good lordeshipp to tender the premisses /
and to give further credence to this beirer therin / And also to   20
directe your lettres vnto vs for reformacion of the same excessive
charges / And then I dought not / but by reason therof / we shall
take suche order therin as shalbe boithe for the welthe &
worshippe of the Citie and duryng our lyves pray to god for your
lordeshippe longe to continew in honour / ffrome Couentre the   25
xvijth day of Ianuarie by your assured bedeman

                            (signed) wyllyam coton
                                    Mayre |

To the Right honourable
the lorde privey Seall   30
this deliuer

®the Meyer of
Coventre

Cappers' Records SC: Account Book I
f 89 col a   35

More Ressettes

...

Ressettes for the menstyrell   xij s x d
                                                             40

...

32-3 / marginalia written sideways along folio edge

f 89v col a

The expensses and paymentes for the pagant

Item paid to the mensterell	vj d	
Item paid for Rosches	j d	5
Item paid for sope	j d	
Item paid for brengyng owt the pagant	vj d	
Item paid for ponttes	v d	
Item paid for the playares sopar	ij s	
Item paid for dryweng of the pagant	xij d	10
Item paid for the playares drenkyng	xiij d ob.	
Item paid for brengyng in the pagant	vj d	
Item paid to pylatt	iij s viij d	
Item paid to God	xvj d	
Item paid to the sprit of god	xvj d	15
Item paid to yowr lade	xij d	
Item paid to mauwdlen	xij d	
Item paid to ij syd mares	xij d	
Item paid to ij bescheppes	ij s	
Item paid to iiij knyghtes	iiij s	20
Item paid to ij angelles	viij d	
Item paid to modor of dethe	iiij d	
Item paid to the deman	xvj d	
Item paid to the Sengyng men	xvj d	
Item paid to the menstyrlles on corpos christi day	vj d	25
Item paid for the hyre of iiij whit harnes	xvj d	
Item paid to leywes wryght for a day and [d] wark	ix d	
Item paid for tentorhokys	j d	
Item paid for gret nalles	j d	
Item paid to the clarke for bereng the boke	xij d	30
Item paid at the forst Rehers	xvj d	
Item paid at the Second Reheres	xx d	
Item paid for glowos	xviij d	
Item paid for a staf for a polax	ij d	
Item paid for kepyng of the wyend	j d	35

Summa xxxiij s ix d ob.

f 90 col b

...

Costes of myssymar nyght		40
Item paid for cressett lyght	ij s	
Item paid to the menstyrll	xiiij d	

Item paid to the cressett berares and to ij men that bare whyt
cottes   xiiij d
Item paid on sent petteres nyght to the mensterll   viij d
Item paid for mendeng of ij cresettes   ij d
                                    Summa v s ij d   5
...

Weavers' Account Book CRO: Acc 100/17/1
f 22
                                                                               10
...
Ressyvyd of the Walkers   vj s viij d
Ressyvyd of the skynners   v s
...

f 22v   15

...
Item spend At the Reyseyung of the Walkers money And the
skynners   viij d
                                                                               20

f 23

...
Item spend on corpus crysty day   xxvij s vj d
Item spend on myssomer nyght   xviij s
Item payd to the mynstrell   ij s   25
...

Corpus Christi Guild Account Book CRO: A 6
f 319v (*Rental of all guild properties*)
...   30
Croschepinge
...
allocaciones   Item William Androwes the weytt a tenement   (*blank*)
...
                                                                               35

f 322 (*Particular payments*)

Item payed for beryng the Crose & Candelstickes on seynt george
day the Assencion day & whitsonday   xij d
...   40
Item payed to the master for his liuerey   xxvj s viij d
...

Item for iiij li wax for the appostles light & the makyng
therof   iij s iiij d

Item a taper to burne in the Sacrament on corpus christi
day   iiij d

Item iiij new torches   iiij s vj d   5

...

f 322v

...

Corpus christi even & the day   10

generall dayes   Item in spice cakes ⌐viij d¬ / whit cakes ⌐ij s¬ / leoff bred ⌐xij d¬ /
bred for the appostelles ⌐vj d¬ / a Cester ale ⌐xviij d¬ / half a
Cester peny ale ⌐vj d¬ / Cheise ⌐vj d¬ / vj loynes of Mutton
⌐iij s ij d¬ / Chekynse ⌐xx d¬ / beiff for the appostles ⌐viij d¬ / to
the Marie for hir gloves & wages ⌐ij s¬ / for beryng the Crose &   15
candelstickes ⌐viij d¬ / to the Master to offer ⌐xij d¬ / the marie
to offer ⌐j d¬ / Kateryn & marget ⌐iiij d¬ / viij virgyns ⌐viij d¬ /
to gabriell ⌐iiij d¬ / to Iames & Thomas ⌐viij d¬ / to x apostelles
⌐xx d¬ / iiij burgeses ⌐xvj d¬ / vj Childrn for beryng torches ⌐ix d¬ /
iiij men to bere iiij torches ⌐viij d¬ / a woman to help in the   20
kechyn ij d. Summa xxij s vj d

...

1540
Leet Book I CRO: A 3(a)   25
f 380v *(12 October) (Smiths' Ordinances)*

...

•watch on   Item what person or persons of the seid Crafte that wylnot go in
midsomer   the watches on mydsomer nyght & seynte petur nyght or brekethe
night•   the watche withoute a lawfull cause to forfytt for Midsomer   30
nyght iij s iiij d in the name of a payn And for seynte peter nyght
xx d withowte eny grace

Cappers' Records SC: Account Book I
f 52v col b*   35

Ressetes for the menstrelles
                                Summa iij s ij d

...

f 53 col b

The Costes of the pagant

Item paid to pillat	iiij s
Item paid to God	xvj d
Item paid to the sprit of God	xvj d
Item paid to mare	xij d
Item paid to maodlen	xij d 5
Item paid to ij mares	xij d
Item paid to ij beschepos	ij s
Item paid to iiij knyghtes	iiij s
Item paid to ij angelles	viij d
Item paid to the Deman	xvj d 10
Item paid to the Sengares	xvj d
Item paid to the mensterell	viij d
Item paid to x drywares of the pagant	xx d
Item paid to iij men to kep the wynd	vj d
Item paid to a wryght	x d 15
Item paid for glowes	xvj d
Item paid for haweng in and owt of the pagant	xij d
Item paid for Rosches	j d
Item paid for Sope and gres	ij d
Item paid for kepeng of the boke to the clarke	xij d 20
Item paid for nallys for the pagant	j d ob
Item paid for ponttes	vj d
Item paid for wenkyll	j d
Item paid for hyrryng of iiij whit harnes	xvj d
Item paid for makeng of pylattes malle	xxij d 25
Item paid for mendeng of ij Senssares	vj d
...	
Item paid for the forst Reheres	xx d
Item paid for the pleares soppar	ij s
Item paid for the second Reheres	xx d 30
Item paid for drenkyng for the playares be twen the play tymes	xiiij d
Item paid for drenk to them that drowe the pagant	xij d

Summa xxxvijj s j d ob.

35

f 53v col a

Costes of corposchristi day and myssymor nyght

Item paid to the mensterlles of corposchristi day ˎand myssymor nyght and sent peteres nyght˒	xij d 40
Item paid to ij menstrelles of myssymor ewen	ij s viij d
Item paid for pentteng of the gyant	v s
Item paid for the candelsteke in hys hede and the lyght	ij d

Item paid for bereng of the ⌈gyant⌉ [Cressen]   xvj d
Item paid for vj ston of cresset lyght   xij d
Item paid for them that bar the cresset lyght   xij d
Item paid for ij cressettes that wer brokyn for the mendeng viij d
Item paid to Iohn crowe   viij d   5
Item paid toward the prest of my part   vij s vj d
Item paid at the tawarn when we went to se the lond   xvij d
...

Weavers' Account Book C R O : Acc 100/17/1   10
f 23v

Resseytes in the yere

...

Ressyvyd of the Walkers   vj s viij d
Ressyvyd of the skynners   v s   15
...

Ressyvyd of Wyllyam blakebowrn mynstrell   xij d
...

f 24   20

exspences In the yere

...

Item payd At the Reysseyvyng of the Walkers and skynners
money   iiij d
...   25
Item payd for skowryng of the whyt harnes   ij s
Item payd to the mynstrell   ij s
Item spend on corpus crysty day   xxvij s iiij d
spend In bred on myssomer nyght   iij s
In Ale   iij s   30
payd for cresset lyght   x d
payd to the ij Whyt harnys men   viij d
payd for beyryng of the stremers and cressetes   v d
...

                                                                                   35

Corpus Christi Guild Account Book C R O : A 6
f 325
...

Exspenses on Corpus christi even & the day

Item for berryng the Crose & candelstickes the even & the day   40
⌈viij d⌉ / ... peny bred for thappostles ⌈vj d⌉ ... beif for thappostles
⌈vj d⌉ / iiij li. & dimidium wax & makyng thappostles light

⸢ij s ix d⸣ / a taper to bryne [Summa xxij s iiij d] by the Sacrament
⸢iiij d⸣ / maries offoryng ⸢j d⸣ / the masteres offoryng ⸢xij d⸣ /
Maries wages & hir gloves ⸢ij s⸣ / to Kateryne & marget iiij d / vj
virgyns ⸢vj d⸣ / gabryell for beryng the lilly ⸢iiij d⸣ / to Iames &
Thomas ⸢viij d⸣ / to x other appostles ⸢xx d⸣ / to iiij burgeses   5
⸢xvj d⸣ / to vj Childerne for beryng vj torches by the Sacrament
⸢ix d⸣ / to iiij men for beryng the gret torches ⸢viij d⸣ / Russhes
for the Churche ⸢iij d⸣ / ... for makyng the lylly ⸢iij s iiij d⸣ / to
the weites ⸢iij s iiij d⸣ ...
                                                                          10

f 327

...
Item payd to the Master for his lyuerey   xxvj s viij d
Item payd to Robert leche for his ffee & lyuerey   xxxiij s iiij d
                                                                          15
...
Item iiij new torches weyng xviij li.   vj s
...

1541
Cappers' Records SC: Account Book I   20
f 55 col b

Ryseyttes [of] for ye mynstrell
Item gethered to ye mynstrell   iij s iiij d
                                 Som iij s iiij d   25
...
The costes of ye holle yere
...
Item paid for the pagant & playing   xxxiijj s iiij d
Item paid for repracions of ye pagant   xij d   30
...
Item paid at myssomer nyght for ye costes and saint
(*blank*)   xj s ob.
...
                                                                          35
Carpenters' Account Book II CRO: Acc 3/2
f 150

Item payde To pynars and tyllers   x s
                 Exspynsys apon Mydsomer nyght   40
...
Item for Cryssyt lyght   [x] x d

Item for berrynge of the leygth*es* for both the nygh*tes*   vj d
Item payde to the mynstrellys   xviij d
...

Weavers' Account Book CRO: Acc 100/17/1   5
f 24v

Reyss*ettes* In my yere
Reysseyvyd of the Walkers   vj s viij d
Reysse*yvyd* of the sky*n*ners   v s   10
...

ff 25-5v*

                              exspenc*es* In my yere
...   15
payd to the mynstrell   xx d
payd At the Reyseyvnyg of the walkers & sky*n*ners money   vj d
...

                        exspenc*es* on corp*us* crysty day
Item payd for ij Reyhersys   ij s   20
Item payd to symyon   iij s iiij d
Item payd to Ios*e*ph   ij s iiij d
Item payd to mare   xx d
Item payd to Ih*esus*   xx d
Item payd Ane   xx d   25
Item payd to symyons clarke   xx d
Item payd to the ij Angell*es*   viij d
payd for bred   vj d
and for Ale   xviij d
payd for bochere met   ij s   30
payd for A Amys for symyon   ij d
payd for Russys pynnys & frankynsence   ij d
payd to the synggers   xvj d
payd for glovys   x d
spend betwen the plays   vj d   35
payd to the Iorneymen for dryvyng þe pagent   iiij s ij d
payd to the wryght for mendyng þe pagent   xxj d
payd to Rychard Walker for A theyll   v d|
payd for smale pesys of tymber   v d
payd to the WhyllWryght for mendyng of the whyle   vij d   40
payd for Iron Worke to the pagent   x d
payd for gret naylys to the Whell*es*   iiij d

payd for v pene nayle And vj pane nayle   viij d
payd for bordys to the pagent   xij d
payd to thomas davson and thomas wyllyams for ij torchys   v d
payd to A Wryght for dravyng In owr pagent howse post &
naylys   xvij d   5

som ys xxxiiij s
exspences on myssomer nyght

Item In bred   iiij s
Item In Ale   iij s
payd for iiij li of comfettes   ij s   10
payd for ij li of blanchpowder   xviij d
payd for ij ston cresset lyght   x d
payd for bayryng of the whyt harnys   viij d
payd for bayryng of the cressetes   iij d
payd for bayryng of the straymers   ij d   15
to the boye that bere the cresset lyght   j d
and for poynttes   ij d
...

som ys xiiij s [vi d] viij d

20

Corpus Christi Guild Account Book CRO: A 6
f 329
...

Exspenses on Corpus christi even & the day
Item for beyryng the Crosse & Candelstickes ⌜viij d⌝ / ...   25
lovebred to the apostles ⌜xij d⌝ / ... Item for iiij new torches &
xij torches of wax for the apostles & vj for the sacrament
⌜xv s ij d⌝ / a taper to bryne by the sacrament ⌜iiij d⌝ / Maries
offeryng ⌜j d⌝ / the master offeryng ⌜xij d⌝ / Maries wages / &
hir gloves ij s / Kateryne & margarettes wages ⌜iiij d⌝ / viij virgynes   30
⌜viij d⌝ / to gabryell for beryng the light ⌜iiij d⌝ / to Iames &
Thomas ⌜viij d⌝ / x. apostles ⌜xx d⌝ / vj Childern to bere vj tapers
about the Sacrament ⌜ix d⌝ / Item iiij men that bare the great
torches ⌜viij d⌝ / for Russhes ⌜iij d⌝ / to the launder for wasshyng
⌜ij s⌝ / ...   35

f 329v

particuler
paymentes

...
Item to Mr Gardiner meir for his Cloke   xxv s
...   40

19 / xiiij s *corrected from* xij s

Item for the Masters liuerey   xxvj s viij d

Vakes of
tenementes

...

Item a tenement þat Androwes the weyt holdet in
Croschepyng   xiij s iiij d

... 5

AC   *Holy Trinity Guild Accounts*   Sharp: *Illustrative Papers*
p 134   *(Trinity Sunday)*

10

... to the weytes, vj s viij d ...

Exspenses on midsumer even & on the day
... the weytes vj s viij d ... to the Crosebeirers & torchebeyrers,
viij d ... 15

(St John Baptist's Day)
... The City Minstrells, 5s. ...

1542 20
Leet Book I CRO: A 3(a)
f 388v (25 April)

...

Craftes of
Tilers and
Cvipers•

Item it is also ordeyned that the feliship & Craft of Tilers shalbe
associat with the Craft of Cowpers & pynners and that the Craft 25
& company of Carpenters shalbe contributories to the said
Craftes of Cowpers & pynners after such porcion & rate as thei
haue been accustumed in tymes past

...

30

Cheylesmore Manor Account Book CRO: A 9
p 7 *(Muster)*

...

Item paid for iij Calf Skynnes for the Drummes lidd   ij s vj d
Item a Corde for the same   j d 35
Item ij whit Skynnes for the endes   ix d
Item ij long girdelles for the same   iiij d
Item for makyng the Case   xij d
Item to Coluan Cowper for his labor in the same   viij d

... 40

Cappers' Records SC: Account Book I
f 56 col a

...

Item recevyd for the mynstrell att mydsomer	iij s x d

...   5

f 57v col a

...

Paymentes att mydsomer	
Item paid for cresset lyght	ij s	10
Item paid to ye cresset berras	viij d
Item paid to ye stremers berers	iiij d
Item paid to ye mynstrell for hys wages	iij s iiij d
Item paid for makyng of a cresset	xviij d
Item paid for carryng of cresset lyght	ij d	15
Item paid at the hyryng of the mynstrell	ij d
Som viij s ij d	

col b

The costes of ye pagiant		20
Item paid to pylat	iij s viij d
Item paid to god	xvj d
Item paid to ye spret of god	xvj d
Item paid to mary	xij d
Item paid to maudlyn	xij d	25
Item paid to ij maries	xij d
Item paid to ij bysshopes	ij s
Item paid to iiij knyghttes	iiij s
Item paid to ij angelles	viij d
Item paid to the demon	xvj d	30
Item paid to ye syngers	xvj d
Item paid to ye mynstrell	viij d
Item paid to ye dryuers of ye pagiant	xx d
Item paid to the mother of dethe	iiij d
Item paid for thred to so the playng gere	ob.	35
Item paid for small corde	j d
Item to ij men for kepyng ye wynd	vj d
Item paid to a wryght	ix d
Item for gloues	xvj d
Item paid for grece	ob.	40

Item paid for russes	ij d
Item paid for naylles	iij d
Item paid for poynttes	vj d
Item paid for iiij whytt harnes	xvj d
Item paid for ye players sopper	ij s
Item paid havyng yn and out ⌈pagiant⌉	vj d
Item paid for ij reherses	ij s viij d
Item paid for drygkyng	xvj d
Item paid for mendyng the pagyant	x ⟨.⟩
som xxxiiij s ij d	

f 58 col a

pamentes for kepyng ye giant and and other paymenttes	v s ix d
...	
pamenttees for corpus chrysti day	xiij d
...	

Carpenters' Account Book II CRO: Acc 3/2
f 142v

Exspensys penticost quarter

...

Item payd to the Cowpers & tylers	x s.
...	

Myssomer ney3th

...

Item the mynstrell	ij s. ij d
Item for the Cressett ley3th	xv d
Item for the bayreryng ther of	iij d
...	

Weavers' Account Book CRO: Acc 100/17/1
f 26

...

Reysseytes In my yere

...

Reysseyvyd of the masters of the Walkers	vj s viij d
Reysseyvyd of the masters of the skynners	v s
...	

14 / and and MS *dittography*

f 26v

...

exspences In my yere

...

spend At the Reysseuyg of the Walkers And skynners   5
money   iiij d

...

payd to the smyth for mendyng of the cressetes   ij d

...
    10

f 27

exspences on corpus cryste day

Item payd for ij Reyhersys   ij s
Item payd to symyon   iij s iiij d
Item payd to Iosoph   ij s iiij d   15
Item payd to mare   xx d
Item payd to Ihesu   xx d
Item payd to symyons clarke   xx d
Item payd to Ane   xx d
payd to the ij Angelles   viij d   20
payd for dryveng the pagent   iiij s ij d
payd for bred And Ale that day   ij s
payd for bochere mett   iij s
payd for Russys pymmys And soape   iiij d
payd to the synggers   xviij d   25
payd for glovys   x d
spend be twen the plays   viij d
payd for iiij lood of ston with In the pagent howse   xiiij d
And for ij lood of pavyng ston   xviij d
payd for ij lode of sonde   viij d   30
payd to the paveor and hys mon   ij s
payd for Iron worke to the pagent   xij d
payd for makyng of Symyons mytor   viij d
payd for naylys to the pagent   iiij d
payd to the wryght for makyng þe [ij] ij lytyll whellys   iij d   35
som ys xxxv s j d

f 27v

exspences on myssomer nyght

...
    40

payd for ij whyt harnes men   viij d

24 / pymmys *probably for* pynnys; *extra minim MS*

payd for ij ston of cresset lyght   x d
payd to the ij boyes þat bere þe cressetes   iij d
payd to the stremmers bayrers   ij d.
payd to the boye that bere the lyght   j d
...   5

           som ys xv s

...

Corpus Christi Guild Account Book CRO: A 6
f 332   10

...

      Exspenses on Corpus christi even & the day

Generall   Item for beryng the Crose & candelstickes ⌐viij d¬ / ... bred for
dayes   the appostles ⌐vj d¬ / ... beiff for thappostles ⌐vj d¬ / Item for
            makyng the appostles & the sacrament light & new wax put to it   15
            ⌐iij s iiij d¬ / for makyng the lilly ⌐iij s iiij d¬ / Mr meires offeryng
            ⌐j d¬ / the Masters offeryng ⌐xij d¬ / to mary for hir wages &
            gloves ⌐ij s¬ / to Kateryne & margaret ⌐iiij d¬ / to vj virgynes
            ⌐vj d¬ / to Gabryell ⌐iiij d¬ / to Iames & Thomas of Inde ⌐viij d¬ /
            to x appostles ⌐xx d¬ / to iiij burgeses for beryng the Canape ouer   20
            the sacrament ⌐xvj d¬ [ix d] / Item vj Childern for beryng torches
            by the sacrament ⌐ix d¬ / iiij men that bere the great torches
            ⌐viij d¬ / Russhes to strewe the Church ⌐iij d¬ / ... wesshyng alles
            & amesses ⌐viij d.¬
            ...   25

f 332v

...

Item payd to Mr meire for his attendaunce   xxv s
...   30

1543
Cappers' Records SC: Account Book I
f 59 col b

        Expensys abowt ye pageant   35
paid for hauvyng forthe of ye pageant   vj d
paid to Repton ye smythe for Clyppes of Iorn to ye wheles of
they pageant and ye skaffolde   ij s. ij d
paid for wrethes to ye whele   ij d
paid for settyng vpp ye foreparte of ye pageant   v d   40

1 / n of ston *written over* w

paid for a whele to ye pageant   ij s. viij d

paid for ij pesys of tymber for ye for parte of they pageant   iiij d

paid for a peese drawen in n that berethe ye syde of ye
pageant   iiij d

paid for boordes abowt ye skaffolde & a bowt ye sepvlcer   5
syde   xij d

paid for naylles   vj d

paid to lewys & hys man for a day work   xij d

paid for a hok & mendyng ij hengys of ye wyndoes of ye pageant
house   xv d   10

paid for iiij haspes & iiij stapelles   iiij d

paid for a lace of ȝorne to Compas ye beame   xj d

paid for viij stapelles & iiij haspes   vj d

paid for great nayles   iiij d ob.

paid lewys ye carpenter for mendyng ye pageant howse & ye   15
wyndoes   v s. viij d

paid for havyng in of ye pageant   vj d

                  Svm ys xviij s viij d ob.

...

paid for ij Iornettes & viij penselles   ij s   20

...

f 59v col a

    expensys & paymentes abowt ye pageant & ye pleyares theroff

paid at ye furst Rehersse   xvj d   25

paid at ye second Rehersse   xvj d

paid for a li. of sope   j d ob.

paid for Rysches   ij d

paid for mendyng hellmowthe   ij d

paid for wasscheng ye angelles albes   ij d   30

paid for poyntes   iiij d

paid for a lok and a kaye   iiij d

paid for making ye demones head   xviij d

paid to Iohn sylver hande   j d

paid for gloves   xvj d   35

paid for balles for pylatt   iij d

paid for payntyng of hell mowght   iij d

paid for ye dryveres of ye pageant   xxj d

paid for ye keper of ye play bok   xij d

paid for drynk to they playeres   vij d   40

3 / n *probably missed cancellation*

paid for ye playeres svpper	ij s.
paid to iiij knythtes	iiij s.
paid for ye lone of ye knyghtes harnes	xvj d
paid to ye syngares in ye pageant	xvj d
paid to ye mynstrell in ye pageant	viij d 5
paid to ye sprett of god	xvj d
paid to pylatt	iij s viij d
paid to ye bysschoppes	ij s
paid to ye angelles	viij d
paid to mavdlen	xij d 10
paid to ye ladye	xij d
paid to ij maryes	xij d
paid to god	xvj d
paid to nycholys lewes for waytyng on ye pageant	x d
paid to ye demon	xvj d 15
paid to ye mynstrell for Corpus christi day & mydsomer nyght	ij s. viij d
paid for Cressett lyght	ij s. vj d

Svm ys xxxix s iiij d ob.

20

col b

more expensys on mydsomer nyght

paid for beryng ij lyght	x d
paid for makeng of a Cressyt and mendyng another	ij s. x d 25
paid for a henge to ye pageant wyndoe	x d

...

f 60 col b

...   30

expensys on seant peteres nyght

paid for Cressyt lyght	ij s. vj d
paid for beryng ye Cressytes	x d
paid for beryng ye stremares	iiij d
paid to ye mynstrell	ij s. 35

...

Carpenters' Account Book II CRO: Acc 3/2
f 153v *(Quarter Day)*

...   40

payd to the Cowpers & pynners	x s.
payd to the mynstrell on Corpusday & mydsomer ny3th	xvj d

...

Weavers' Account Book CRO: Acc 100/17/1
f 28

...

Reyseytes In my yere

...   5

Reysseyvyd of the Walkers   vj s viij d
Reysseyvyd of the skynners   v s

...

Reysseyvyd of [I] Iohn Covper owr menstrell   xij d
...   10

f 28v

...

exspences In my yere

...   15

Item paid for menddyng of A cressett   ij d
Item spend At the Reyseyvyng of the Walkers And skynners
money   viij d
Item payd to owr menstrell   ij s
...   20

ff 29-9v
exspences on corpus crysty day

Item payd for ij Reyhersys   ij s   25
Item payd to symyon   iij s iiij d
Item payd to Iosoph   ij s iiij d
Item payd to mare   xx d
Item payd to [Ioh] Ihesus   xx d
Item payd to Symyons clarke   xx d   30
Item payd to ane   xx d
Item payd to the Angelles   viij d
Item payd to the Iorneymen for dryvyng þe pagent   iiij s ij d
Item payd to the synggers   xvj d
Item payd for glovys   x d   35
Item payd for bred to the denner   viij d
Item payd for ale   xviij d
Item payd for bochere mett   iij s iiij d
Item payd for Russys pynnys And soope   iij d
Item spend be twen the plays   xj d   40
Item payd for hyre of the gray Ames   iiij d
Item payd for mendyng the pagent   vj d
som ys xxviij s iiij d |

Exspences on myssomer ny3ght

...

payd to the whyt harnys men	viij d
payd for cresset ly3ght	xviij d
payd beyryng of the stremmers	ij d
payd for beyryng of the cressettes	iiij d
payd to the boye þat bere the ly3ght	j d
payd for poynttes	ij d

...

som ys [x] xv s iiij d

...

Corpus Christi Guild Account Book CRO: A 6
f 337v *(Master's expenses)*

Corpus christi even & the day

... bred for thappostles ⌐vj d⌐ / ... beiff for thappostles ⌐ix d⌐ / ...
the meire to offer ⌐j d⌐ / the Maisters & Gentilwomen to offer
⌐xij d⌐ / to Marie for hir wages & gloves ⌐ij s iiij d⌐ / to vj vyrgyns
⌐vj d⌐ / to gabryele ⌐iiij d⌐ / to Iames & Thomas ⌐viij d⌐ / to the
other x appostles ⌐xx d⌐ / to vj Childern ⌐ix d⌐ / for beryng the
great torches ⌐viij d⌐ / to the launder for wasshyng ⌐xij d⌐ / for a
taper to bryne all nyght befor the sacrament ⌐iiij d⌐ / ij Childer
for beryng tapers ⌐ij d⌐ / for beryng the Crosse ⌐iiij d⌐

f 338v

...

particler
paymentes

Item to Thomas Enderby for makyng the apostles light	xx d
Item for more newe wax	xx d

...

1544
Cappers' Records SC: Account Book I
f 62 col a

Resettes for nwe brethern

...

Received of wyllyam wherret   iij s iiij d

...

col b

...

Received of the crafte for ye mynstrelles   iij s vj d

...

f 62v col b

Expensys of ye pagaynt

payd at the furst Reherse	xx d	
payd at the second Reherse	xx d	
payd to pylatt	iij s viij d	5
payd to god & ye mother of deth	xx d	
payd to ye spryt of god	xvj d	
payd to owr ladye	xij d	
payd to mavdlyn	xij d	
payd to ij maryes	xij d	10
payd to ij byschoppes	ij s	
payd to iiij knythtes	iiij s	
payd to ij angelles	viij d	
payd to ye devyll	xvj d	
payd to ye syngars	xx d	15
payd to ye mynstrell	viij d	
payd for dryvyng ye pagaynt	ij s	
payd for kepyng ye wynd	vj d	
payd for glovys	xviij d	
payd for havyng forthe & in of the pagaynt	xij d	20
payd for Rwssys	ij d	
payd for sope & gresse	iij d	
payd for poyntes	vj d	
payd for Incoll & wyar	ij d	
payd for harnys for iiij knythes	ij s	25
payd for drynke in ye pageant for ye pleares for bothe days	viij d	
payd to xij men for dryvyng the pageant	ij s	
payd for the plears svpper	ij s	
payd for drynke to ye plarars betwyne tyms	xviij d	30

f 63 col a*

payd for drynke for them that drove the pageant	xij d	
payd for makyng a whod for on of ye byschoppes	iiij d	35
payd for iij boordes for the skaffolde	xiiij d	
payd for naylles iij C	xij d	
payd to ij wryghtes	xij d	
payd to lowes for goyng with the pageant	x d	
payd to horsley for pentyng ye mall ye Rattell ye spade & ij crossys & hell mowthe	xvj d	40
payd for a yard of canvas for ye devylles mall & for makyng	viij d	

payd for makyng of xvj ball*es* & for ij skyns of lether   v d
payd for mendyng owr ladye crowne   ij d
payd for iij clamp*es* of Iorne for ye pageant   xij d
                    Svm xlvj s vj d

...   5

col b

Expensys on mydso*m*mer nyght
payd for cresset lyght   ij s xx d   10
payd to iij mynstrell*es*   vj s viij d
payd for beryng of iiij Cressytt*es*   viij d
payd for beryng ye pvdyng Ropp*es*   iiij d
payd for beryng ye stremars   iiij d
payd for beryng ye gyant   xiij d   15
payd to skynar ye smythe for makyng a cressyt & mendyng of
another   xviij d
payd for bottomyng of a cressyt   vj d
It*em* alowyd to knyght & showell when we Resevyd Rent   viij d
                    Svm xiiij s vj d   20

...

Weavers' Account Book   CRO: Acc 100/17/1
f 30*
...   25
                    Resse*yttes* for ye yeere

...

Resse*yvyd* of Iohan cowp*er* ye mynstrell   xij d
Resse*yvyd* of ye walkers   vj s viij d
Resse*yvyd* of ye skynners   v s   30
...
                    Resse*yttes* of brederne

...

Resse*yvyd* of rychard ye capp*er* borsleys man that playth
ane   wax   35
Resse*yvyd* of Iohan heynnys broder that playt Ih*e*su   wax
...

f 30v
...   40
                    exspynssis for ye yere
...

Item payd at the forst rehers   xij d

...

Item payd at the seconde rehers   xij d
Item spynt at ye resevyng of ye walkers monney & ye
skeners   xij d   5

...

ff 31-1v
         exspynssus on corpus cryste day
Item payd for bred   viij d   10
Item payd for ale   xij d
Item payd for boccherre meet   ij s
Item payd for nayllys and myndyng of ye paggant   viij d
Item payd to ye Iornneymen for dryuyng of ye
paggant   iiij s ij d   15
Item payd to symon for hys play   iij s iiij d
Item payd to Iosshef for hys play   ij s iiij d
Item payd to marrye   xx d
Item payd to ane   xx d
Item payd to symons clarke   xx d   20
Item payd to Ihesu   xx d
Item payd to ye to angells   viij d
Item payd to ye syngers yn ye paggant   xvj d
Item payd for rosshes pakethrd   ij d
Item payd for gloves   x d   25
Item spynt betwen ye plays at borssleys hows   viij d
               Summa xxiiij s vj d |
        exspynssus on medssomers nyght

...

Item payd to harnest men   viij d   30
Item payd for berryng of ye stremers & cressets   iiij d
Item payd for berryng of ye lyght   j d
Item payd for to stone of cryset lyght   x d
Item payd the mynstrell for hys wage   [ij d] ij s

...   35
             Summa xviij s vij d

...

14 / u of dryuyng *written over another letter*
30 / n of harnest *written over another letter*

AC   *Smiths' Accounts* Sharp: *Dissertation*
p 28*

...

payd for a bysschops taberd of scarlet that we bowght in the
trenete church   x s   5

...

p 185 *(Midsummer and St Peter's Watches)*

...

Item to robert morres for makyng of a cresset   xiiij d 10
payd for a peese of plat þat whent to the same   iij d ob

...

Corpus Christi Guild Account Book CRO: A 6
f 342v *(Particular Payments)*   15

... ij yardes briges satten for to mende vestymentes in owr ladyes
Chappell ꞌv sꞌ / a yard of bokern ꞌv dꞌ / j skene of silke ꞌvj d obꞌ /
for workemanshipp ꞌxij dꞌ / an elne of Cloth ꞌviij dꞌ / for
wasshyng albes ꞌiiij dꞌ / iij yardes of vestyment Rybyn ꞌvj dꞌ ... 20
On Corpus christi day

Generall   Item Russhes at seynt nicholas Church ꞌiij dꞌ / for berying the
days   Crose & Candellstickes ꞌviij dꞌ / for makyng the postell light
ꞌiij s iiij dꞌ / for makyng the lillie ꞌiij s iiij dꞌ / iiij newe torches
ꞌiiij sꞌ / for Mr Meir & the Masters offryng ꞌxij dꞌ / Maries offryng 25
ꞌj dꞌ / to Marie for hir wages & Gloves ꞌij sꞌ / to Kateryne &
marget ꞌiiij dꞌ / to vj virgyns ꞌvj dꞌ / to gabryell ꞌiiij dꞌ / to Iames
& Thomas ꞌviij dꞌ / to x appostelles ꞌxx dꞌ / to iiij brygeses for
beryng the [Canape] lightes ꞌix dꞌ / for beryng iiij great torches
ꞌviij dꞌ / Russhes & floures ꞌiiij dꞌ / for mendyng the torches   30
Cases ꞌiij dꞌ /

...

The brekefast
... bred for thappostelles ꞌvj dꞌ ... beiff for thappostelles ꞌvj dꞌ /
... for wasshyng the albes ꞌviij dꞌ / to prestes & Clerkes at seynt 35
Nicholas Church ꞌxij dꞌ

1545
Cappers' Records SC: Account Book I
f 64v col a*   40

...

Received of the crafte for mynstrelles money   iiij s ij d

...

col b

...

payd at chamber*es* howse ye monday befor hoktwsday   xiiij d

...

     5

f 65 col a

expensys on mydsomer nyght
payd to ye mynstrell*es*   x s
payd for peyntyng ye gyant   ij s iiij d   10
payd for beryng ye gyant   ij s
payd for Cressyt lyght   iij s vj d
payd for beryng ye cressytt*es*   vj d
payd for beryng ye stremars   iiij d

...

     15

payd to herrye thyrkyll for a cressytt   x d
payd for mendyng of a cressytt   vj d

...

f 65v col b *(St Peter's Watch)*   20

...

p*ai*d for Cressyt lyght   ij s.
p*ai*d for beryng of v cressyt*es*   x d
p*ai*d for beryng of ij stremar*es*   iiij d
p*ai*d for beryng lyght for ye cresset*es*   ij d   25

...

Weavers' Account Book CRO: Acc 100/17/1
f 32

...

     30

Reseytt*es* for beryals & od*er* thyng*es*

...

Ress*eyvyd* of the Walkers   vj s. viij d
Ress*eyvyd* of þe skynners   v s.

...

     35

f 32v

Exspensys for Corp*u*styd
payd for ij Reyherssys   ij s.
Item for bred   viij d   40
Item for Ale   xij d
Item for meytt   ij s.
It*em* for mendyng the pagont   vj d

Item to the Iurneymen for dryvyng the pagon iiij s.
Item spend be twene the plays viij d
Item for symeon iij s. iiij d
Item for Ioysef ij s. iiij d
Item for mary xx d 5
Item for ann xx d
Item for symeon clark xx d
Item for Ihesus xx d
Item for ij aungsels viij d
Item to the synggers xvj d 10
Item for glovys x d
Item for ryssys & pakthyrd j d ob.
...

Som xxvjjj s. [ii] j d ob.
Exspensys myssomer ny3th 15

...
Item for ij harnes men viij d
Item for pyntes ij d
Item for cressett ly3th x d
Item for beyryng the standerdes & the ly3th v [iiij] d 20
Item for the mynstrell xiiij d
Som xij s. xj d.
...

AC *Smiths' Accounts* H-P: *Illustrations* 25
p 51

... Item, payd for menddyng the look of the pagent howss dor
j d; item, payd for mendyng of the chest in the pagent howss
j d ... 30

— Sharp: *Dissertation*
p 198 *(Midsummer Watch)*
...
Item to the waytts xvj d ... 35

Corpus Christi Guild Account Book CRO: A 6
f 344v
Corpus christi day & the even

Generall
dayes
Item for beryng the Crosse & Candelstickes ⸢viij d⸣ / ... iiij newe 40
torches ⸢vij s⸣ / ... xij wax torches ⸢ij s vj d⸣ / for makyng wax
⸢xij d⸣ / a taper to burne before the Sacrament ⸢iiij d⸣ / to marie

to offer ⌈j d⌉ / the Master to offer ⌈xij d⌉ / for Maries wages &
hir gloves ⌈ij s⌉ / to Kateryne & marget ⌈iiij d⌉ / vj virgyns ⌈vj d⌉ /
for beryng the lillie ⌈iiij d⌉ / a new Coit & a peir of hoes for
gabriell ⌈iij s iiij d⌉ / to Iames & Thomas ⌈viij d⌉ / to x appostelles
⌈xx d⌉ / to iiij burgese ⌈xvj d⌉ / to vj Childers ⌈ix d⌉ / iiij men to   5
bere torches ⌈viij d⌉ / Russhes ⌈iij d⌉ / ... for makyng the lilly
⌈iij s iiij d⌉ / to the weyttes ⌈iij s iiij d⌉ /
...

1546   10
Cappers' Records SC: Account Book I
f 66v col b
...
expensys on they Crafte
...   15
paid to master saundors for ij swordes   iij s. iiij d
...

f 67 col a
...   20
paid to ye mynstrell   v s
...
paid at wyllyam westley at ye payeng for Reparacyons & to pay
for harnes   ij s vj d
...   25

col b
...
paid to ye mynstrell on Ihesus day at smytes tavern   xij d
...   30

Weavers' Account Book CRO: Acc 100/17/1
f 33
...
     Exspensys Mydsommor ny3th   35
...
Item payd to the mynstrell of corpus christi day And mydsomer
ny3th   xiiij d
...
Item payd to the harnysmen & the berers of the streymars & the   40
cressett ly3th   xij d
Item payd for ij ston of Creset ly3th   x d

Item for pyntes for the harneysmen   ij d

AC   *Smiths' Accounts* Sharp: *Dissertation*
      p 182*
      ...   5

    Also whatt person or persons off the seid Craftis that Wilnot
goo in the Watchis on midsomer night and seint petyrs night, or
breke the Watche without any lauffull cause to fforfet ffor
mydsomer night iij s iij d in the name of a paine and for seint
petyrs night xx d without any grace   10
      ...

Corpus Christi Guild Account Book CRO: A 6
f 347
                     Corpus christi day & the evene   15

Generall dayes
... Maries offeryng ⌈j d⌉ / the Masters offeryng ⌈xij d⌉ / to Marie
for hir wages & gloves ⌈ij s⌉ / to Catheryne & marget ⌈iiij d⌉ / to
iiij vyrgyns ⌈iiij d⌉ / to Gabriell ⌈iiij d⌉ / the xij apostles
⌈ij s iiij d⌉ / to iiij brugeses ⌈xvj d⌉ / to vj Childer for beryng the
light about the sacrament ⌈ix d⌉ / to iiij men yat bere the torches   20
⌈viij d⌉ / Russhes ⌈iij d⌉ / for makyng the lillie ⌈iij s iiij d⌉ / to the
weytes ⌈iij s iiij d⌉ / beiff for thappostles ⌈vj d⌉ / for wesshyng
albes amesses & surplesses ⌈xij d⌉ / ...

1547   25
Leet Book I CRO: A 3(a)
f 400 *(3 May)*

Cowpers
Item it is also enacted that the Cowpers of this Citie shall
fromehensfurthe be associat with the Tilers & pynners And bere   30
suche charges as thei haue doon in tymes past / And that the
Cowpers shalbe the hedd & cheffest of theim & stand charged
with the pagyaunt
      ...
                                                                                35

Cappers' Records SC: Account Book I
f 69 col a
              expensys on ye Crafte
spent at ye Crane   iiij s.
paid for iiij torches   iiij s.   40
      ...

paid for v yerd*es* & iij q*uarters* of bokram to lyne ye
palle   ij s. x d ob.
paid for a skene of sylke   j d ob.
paid to Ihon foster for lynyng of ye paule & for sowyng on of ye
velvet   xx d   5

...

col b
                  expensys on the pageant
paid for ye spret of god*es* cote   ij s.   10
paid for makeng of ye same cote   viij d
paid for ij starr*es*   xij d
paid for a dyadem   iiij d
paid for ij Rehersys   iij s
paid for hauvyng forth of ye pagiant   vj d   15
paid for hauvyng in of ye same   vj d
paid for dryvyng of ye pageant   ij s.
paid for kepyng of ye wynde   vj d
paid for ye plear*es* sopper   ij s.
paid for vj dessen of poynt*es*   vj d   20
paid for glovys   xv d
paid for drynke for ye plear*es*   vj d
paid for drynke in ye pageant   vj d
paid for Rysches   iij d
paid for nayles for ye pageant   iij d ob. 25
paid for a wyar & for Ryng*es*   j d
paid for sope   j d
paid for wrytyng ap*ar*te for herre p*ar*son   j d
paid to pylat   iij s. viij d
paid to god   xvj d   30
paid to ye spret of god   xvj d
paid to owr ladye   xij d
paid to mavdlyn   xij d
paid to ye syde maryese   xij d
paid to ij byschopp*es*   ij s   35
paid to ye iiij knytht*es*   iiij s
paid to ye ij angell*es*   viij d
paid to ye mother of deathe   iiij d
paid to ye demon   xvj d
paid to ye syngar*es*   xvj d   40
paid to ye mynstrell   viij d

paid for ye hyer of iiij harnes   xvj d

                 Svm ys xxxvij s.

f 69v col a

expensys on mydsomer nyght
paid for iiij ston of Cressyt lyght   ij s.
paid for beryng of ye Cressyt lyght   ij d
paid for beryng of ye Cressytes   x d
paid for iiij staffes for ye cressytes   j d
paid for beryng of ye stremeres   iiij d
paid for mendyng of ye Cressytes   xij d
paid for beryng of ye gyeant ij nyghtes   ij s.
paid for waxe Candell for ye gyant   j d
paid for Canvas to make ye gyeant a nwe skorte   ix d
paid for pentyng of ye gyant   iij s. viij d
paid to ye mynstrell for bothe nyghtes   iij s. iiij d

                 Svm ys xiiij s iij d

paymentes for Reparasyons
paid to Iohn Cowper for beryng of a dor & for ij bordes to mend
ye pagend hovse dor & for nalles   vj d
...

f 70 col a

expensys on sent peteres evon
paid for Cressyt lyght   ij s.
paid for beryng of v Cressytes   x d
paid for beryng of ij stremars   jj [x] jj d
paid for beryng lyght for ye Cressytes   ij d

Carpenters' Account Book II CRO: Acc 3/2
f 145 *(Pentecost dinner)*
...
Item payd to the Copers & peners   x s
...

f 145v *(Midsummer Watch)*
...
Item for Cresset ly3th   xiiij d
Item for berying of Cresset   ij d
Item for berying of þe ly3th   j d

Item to the menstrelles   xij d

...

Weavers' Account Book CRO: Acc 100/17/1
f 34v*   5

...

Item spent on ye compannye at ye makyng of Inuetory of ye
crafts 'gods'   vij d

...

                                                                               10

AC   *Smiths' Accounts* H-P: *Outlines* I
      p 339 *(Corpus Christi)*

      ... Paid for dryvyng of the pagent, iiij s iiij d; paid for russys and
      soop, ij d ...   15

      — H-P: *Outlines* II
      pp 289-90 *(Corpus Christi)*

      ... Paid to John Croo for menddyng of Herrode hed and a mytor   20
      and other thynges, ij s ...

1548
Cappers' Records SC: Account Book I
f 71v col a*   25

...

Resett for Rent

...

Reseived of ye Craft of ye whyttawers for ye hyer of our
pageande   iij s. iiij d 30

...

Reseived for one waxe torche   xx d

...

                  paymentes and expensys on they Crafte

...   35

paid for dressyng ye harnes   ij s ij d

...

gyven to harrye person at ye craftes desyer   xij d
paid for a wyndyng shete forhym   xij d
paid for shoynge our harnes before master mear   iiij d 40
paid for mendyng a splent & a arro case   iij d

...

f 72 col a

more expensys & paymentes

paid to ye mynstrell on Ihesus daye	xij d
paid to ye mynstrell at ye eatyng of hys venyson	ij s.
...	5
paid at ye sellyng of ij standers of brasse	viij d
...	
paid at ye Crane when they Crafte dyd see ye vestmentes	iij s ix d
paid at borsleys at ye fvrst Reherse	ix d 10
paid at ye sayed borsleys at ye second Rehers	xiiij d
...	

expensys on mydsomer nyght

paid for ye gyeande	xvj d
paid for beryng of v Cressyttes	x d 15
paid for beryng ye ij streamers	iiij d
paid for mendyng of ye gyeande	viij d
paid for mendyng of a Cressyt	ij d
paid to ye mynstrell	iij s. iiij d
	20

col b

paid for ye Cressyt lyght	xviij d

Svm ys viij s. ij d

expensys on ye pageant

	25
paid to ye plears at yer forst Rehers	xviij d
paid at ye second Rehers	xviij d
paid to pylat	iij s. viij d
paid to god	xvj d
paid to ye spryt of god	xvj d 30
paid to mavdlyn	xij d
paid to ye ij syed maryese	xij d
paid to ye ij byshshoppes	ij s.
paid to ye iiij knyghtes	iiij s.
paid to ye ij angelles	viij d 35
paid to ye mother of deathe	iiij d
paid to ye demon	xvj d
paid to ye syngars	xvj d
paid to ye mynstrell	viij d
paid for ye hyer of iiij harnes	xvj d 40
paid for dryvyng ye pageant	ij s
paid for drynk in ye pageant	vj d

p*ai*d for drynk for ye plears	vj d
p*ai*d for Rysches	iij d
p*ai*d for gloves	ij s. ij d
p*ai*d for poynt*es*	viij d
p*ai*d for kepyng ye wynde	vj d 5
p*ai*d for havyng ye pageant in & owt	xij d
p*ai*d for ye plears svpp*er*	ij s
p*ai*d for nayles for ye pageant	iiij d
p*ai*d for mendyng ye wyndo of ye pageant hovse & for a	
staple	iiij d 10
p*ai*d to skynar ye smythe for Clamp*es* & nayl*es* for ye whell*es* of	
ye pageant	xvj d
p*ai*d for sope	ij d
p*ai*d for mendyng ye pageant & for Iorn platt*es*	xx d
p*ai*d for lether for ball*es*	ij d 15
p*ai*d for mendyng ye pageant hovse	viij d
p*ai*d for ij standers for ye pageant	xij d

Svm ys xxxviij s. iij d

20

Carpenters' Account Book II CRO: Acc 3/2
f 147v col a *(Pentecost dinner)*

...

It*em* to the Copers & peners	x s

...   25

col b *(Midsummer)*

...

It*em* for Cresset lyght	xiiij d
It*em* for beryng lyght	ij d 30
It*em* for the berer of lyght	j d
It*em* for Menstrell*es*	xx d
It*em* for skoryng harnes	xij d
It*em* for A sord & a dager	iiij s vj d
It*em* for a belt	xij d 35
It*em* for a belt halfe	ij d
It*em* for settyng hyt þe halfe to mathu brothern	ij d
It*em* for ij Revitt*es* to sketton	ij d
It*em* for A dossyn pynt*es*	ij d
It*em* for beryng [harnes of fore] A harnes afore M*ai*ster	40
Mere	ij d
It*em* for ole	ob

Weavers' Account Book CRO: Acc 100/17/1
f 35

...

Item reseyvyd of the walkers	vj s ˹viij d˼
Item reseyvyd of the fareeres	v s 5

...

ff 35v-6

...

corpose cryste day   10

Item payd to symon	iij s iiij d
Item payd to Iossef	ij s iiij d
Item payd to marry	xx d
Item payd to Iehus	xx d
Item payd to ane	xx d 15
Item payd to symeons clarke	xx d
Item payd to the to anggells	viij d
Item payd to the synnggars	xvj d
Item payd for bred	vj d
Item payd for ale	xij d 20
Item payd for all manere of ⟨.⟩ meet	ij s
Item geven the Iornnymen be twene ye pleys	vj d
Item spynt at borssleys howse	vj d
Item payd for glovys	xij d
Item payd the mynstrell	iiij d 25
Item payd at the forst rehers	xvj d
Item payd at the seconde rehers	xvj d

som ys xxij s x d |
medsomer nyght

...   30

Item ye to whyt harnste men	viij d
Item the crysset lyght	xiij d
Item the crysset berrers	ij d
Item payd for ye mendyng of ye cryssetts	v d
Item to ye stremers berers	ij d 35
Item payd to the menstrell	viij d
Item to hem that bare the poddoyngs	j d

...

Item payd to the Iernneymen for drevyng of ye pagant	iiij s

som ys xx s and viij d   40

...

31 / ns *of* harnste *written over other letters*

AC   *Smiths' Accounts* H-P : *Outlines* II
       p 290   *(Corpus Christi)*

... Payd to the paynter for payntyng the players facys, iiij d ...

                                                                    5

— H-P : *Illustrations*
p 54

... Payd for makyng of the hooke to hang the curten on, iiij d ...

                                                                    10

1549
Leet Book I CRO : A 3(a)
f 408* *(14 May)*
...

Watche It*em* wher as in tymes past m*aiste*r meire for the tyme being   15
       haithe vsed to keipp a watche on midsomer nyght And the
       Shireff*es* another watche on seynt peters nyght It is now enacted
       at this p*rese*nt leet by auctoritie of the same that m*aiste*r meire &
       the Shireff*es* shall fromehensfurthe yoyntelie keipp onelie oon
       watche on Midsom*er* nyght at the indeferent cost*es* & charg*es* of   20
       m*aiste*r meire & the Shereff*es* That is the meire to pay the on half
       & the Shireff*es* the other half
       ...

Chamberlains' Account Book I CRO : A 7(a)   25
p 215*
...
It*em* to the weyt*es* for ther wag*es*   xxvj s viij d
...

                                                                    30

Cappers' Records SC : Account Book I
ff 74v-5 col a
...
p*ai*d for ij li. of Candell   v d
                                                                    35
col b
...
spent at borsley at ye furst Rehersse   ij s. iiij d
p*ai*d to ye plears at ye sayed Rehersse   xviij d
...   40
spent at ye Crane att ye pvttyng owt of pylat*es*
dooblitt   iij s. iiij d
...

paid for making of pylates doblet	xvj d
paid for Canvas for ye sayed dooblet	vj d

...

expensys vppon mydsomer nyght

paid for beryng ye Ioyand	xviij d	5
paid for mendyng of hys head & arme	xvj d	
paid for beryng of Cressettes	x d	
paid for beryng of ij stremares	iiij d	
paid for Carredge of ye lyght	iiij d	
paid for vj ston of Cressyt lyght	iij s	10
paid for mendyng of a Cressyt	j d	
paid to ye mynstrell	iij s. iiij d	
Spent at ye Crane on ye hed of ye Crafte on mydsomer daye	ij s. iiij d	
Svm ys xiij s. j d		15

expensys on the pageant

paid to ye plears at they second Rehers	xviij d	
Spent at ye sayed Rehersse	xj d	
paid to pylat	iij s. viij d	
paid to god	xvj d	20
paid to ye sprete of god	xvj d	
paid to mavdlyn	xij d	
paid to ye ij syde maryes	xij d	
paid to ye ij bysshoppes	ij s.	
paid to ye iiij knyghtes	iiij s.	25
paid to ye two angelles	viij d	
paid to ye mother of deathe	iiij d	
paid to ye demon	xvj d	
paid to ye mynstrell	viij d	
paid for ye hyar of iiij harnesse	ij s.	30
paid for dryvyng of ye pageant	ij s. iiij d	
paid for drynk	vj d	
paid for drynk for ye plears	vj d	
paid for Ryssches	iiij d	
paid for gloves	ij s. viij d	35
paid for poyntes	viij d	
paid for kepyng of ye wynde	vj d	
paid for havyng in & owt of ye pageande	xij d	
paid for ye plears svpper	ij s	
paid for nales & mendyng of ye pageande	iiij d	40
paid for a staple of Iorne	j d	
paid for mendyng of pylates malle & ye wynde Rope	iiij d	

p*ai*d for sope   ij d
p*ai*d for skowryng of maryes Crowns   j d
p*ai*d for ball*es* & ye makeng   iiij d
                              Svm ys xxxiij s. vj d
...   5

Carpenters' Account Book II CRO: Acc 3/2
f 140 col a *(Midsummer Watch)*
...

payd to Cowpars & pyners   x s   10
for cresset ly3t   xij d
for beryng of cresse*tes*   iij d
To the menstrell   viij d
...
                                                                          15

Weavers' Account Book CRO: Acc 100/17/1
ff 36v-7
...

It*em* res*eyvyd* of the skeners   v s
It*em* res*eyvyd* of ye masters of ye walkers   vj s viij d   20
It*em* res*eyvyd* of for Ih*e*sus viij d and for anne viij d
It*em* res*eyvyd* of symons clarke   x d
...
                              corp*us* cryste day
It*em* to symon   iij s [iij d] ⌐iiij d¬   25
It*em* payd to Iohssefe   ij s iiij d
It*em* payd to marye   xx d
It*em* payd to Ih*e*su   xx d
It*em* payd to ann   xx d
It*em* payd to symons clarke   xx d   30
It*em* the to angells   viij d
It*em* the lettell chyld   iiij d
It*em* payd the menstrell   viij d
It*em* payd for glovys   xij d
It*em* geven the Ierneymen for dreyvyng of ye   35
pagant   iiij s ij d
It*em* geven ye Ierneymen to dryke   vj d
It*em* geven the clarkes for syngyng yn ye pagant   xvj d
It*em* payd for brede   vj d
It*em* payd for ale   xviij d   40
It*em* payd for all manere of meyt   iiij s
                              som xxvij s viij d |

medsomer nyght

...

Item payd the whyt hernystmen	viij d
Item the stremere berres	ij d
Item payd for cresset lyght	x d
Item payd the cresset berres	ij d
Item the boye that bare the podyngs	j d
Item payd the mynstrel	ix d

som xij s vij d

...

Item spynt at the forst reherse	xvj d
Item spynt at the second rehers	xvj d

...

AC **Smiths' Accounts** Sharp: *Dissertation*
p 35

...

Item payd to the waytes for the pagent	ij s viij d

p 185

...

Item payd to þe boye þat bere þe podyngs	j d

...

1550
Chamberlains' Account Book I CRO: A 7(a)
p 219

wages &
ffes

...

Item payed to the weytes for ther wages	xxvj s viij d

...

Cappers' Records SC: Account Book I
f 77 col b

expensys on ye Craft

...

paid to ye plears for ye furst Rehers	xviij d
spent on ye Craft at ye sayed Rehers	xij d
spent at ye peakok on ye head of the Craft	v d
paid to ye plears for ye second Rehers	xviij d
spent at Borseleyes at ye sayd Rehers	ij s. v d
spent at smythes at ye byeng of ye taselles	viij d
paid to skonce for ye svrplyse	xij d

paid to Iohn loson for mendyng of ye demons Cot   iij s
paid to woolleys wyfe for wasscheng of ye allbes   iiij d
...

expensys on mydsomer nyght
paid for vj ston of Cressyt lyght   iiij s.   5
paid to ye berars of Cressyttes   viij d
paid for beryng of Cressyt lyght   iiij d
paid for Beryng ye ij stremares   iiij d
paid to ye mynstrelles   iij s iiij d
...   10

f 77v col a

expensys of the pageande
paid for havyng forthe ye pageande   vj d
paid for nales & for mendyng the tope of ye pageande   vij d   15
paid for balles & for mendyng of pylates Cloobe   iiij d
paid for poyntes   viij d
paid to pylat   iij s. viij d
paid to god & for mother of death   xx d
paid to ye iiij knygths   iiij s.   20
paid to ye ij byschoppes   ij s.
paid to ye demon   xvj d
paid to ye spryte of god   xvj d
paid to mavdlyn   xij d
paid to ye ij maryese   xij d   25
paid to ye ij angelles   viij d
paid for drynk in ye pageande & to ye plears   xij d
paid to ye plears svpper   ij s.
paid for dryvyng ye pageande   ij s. iiij d
paid for ye wynde   vj d   30
paid for havyng in of the pageande   vj d
paid to ye mynstrell   viij d
paid for gloves   ij s. viij d
paid for hyar of ye iiij harnes   ij s.
paid for making ye ij byschoppes gownse   xxj d   35
paid for furryng ye sayed gownse   ij s. iiij d
paid to ye syngares   xvj d
paid for Iames norres   iiij d
paid for cart nales for ye pageand   iij d
paid for sope   ij d   40
paid for Rysches for ye pageande   iiij d
paid for nales & boordes   iiij d

paid for settyng vp ye pageande   ij d
paid to master waryng for ye Rest of ye byschoppes gownse vij d
paid for hengys & nales for plasterars house   vij d
                              Svma xxxviij s. vij d
...   5

Weavers' Account Book CRO: Acc 100/17/1
ff 37v-8
...
Item reyseyvyd of the mastars of ye walkers   vj s viij d   10
Item reyseyvyd of the masters of the skynners   v s
...
Item reyseyvyd of hary bowator of hys fynnys beyng symeons
clarke   xx d
Item reyseyvyd of crystover dale playng Ihesu of hys fyns   x d   15
Item reyseyvyd of hew heyns pleyng anne for hys fyns   vj d
                         some xxxv s ij d
                       corpvs cryste day
Item payd to Iosshef   ij s iiij d
Item payd to symeon   iij s iiij d   20
Item payd to marry   xx d
Item payd to Ihesus   xx d
Item payd to anne   xx d
Item payd to symeons clarke   xx d
Item payd to ye angells and to ye lettel chyld   xij d   25
Item payd to ye syngars yn ye paggane   xvj d
Item payd to the menstrell   viij d
Item payd for glovys   xxij d
Item payd at the to reherssys   ij s
Item spent at borsley howse apone ye pleyers   iiij d | 30
Item payd to ye Iernneymen for dreyvyng of ye
pagant   iiij s ij d
Item payd for bred   iiij d.
Item payd for ale   xviij d
Item payd for all maner of bocherre meat   ij s   35
Item payd for veneger and spyc   iij d
                         some xxvij s ix d
                       medsomere nyght
...
Item payd the Whyt hernes berras   viij d   40

10-16 / reyseyvyd *represented by* s *only in MS*

Item payd to ye stremers berrers   iij d
Item payd to ye cresset berers   iij d
Item to a boye for berryng of ye podyngs   j d
Item payd for iij stone of cresset lyght   xviij d
...   5
Item payd the menstrel   viij d
...
Item payd for to dossen of poyntts   ij d
...
Item spent one the Walkers and skyners   xij d 10
...

1551
Chamberlains' Account Book I CRO: A 7(a)   15
p 221

Item paid to the iiij weytes for ther wages   xxvj s viij d
...
                                                                         20

Cappers' Records SC: Account Book I
f 79v col b
...
                Expensys on nwe payntyng for ye pageaunt   25
payd for lynnen Clothe to paynt   v s.
payed to horseley   xxxiij s. iiij d
payed for whyt incoll   x d
payed at androes   xiiij d
payed for makyng nwe of pylates malle   xx d 30
                        Svm xlij s.
...

f 80 col a
...   35
spent at ye showyng of the vestmentes   xvj d
...
payd to ye plears at ye fyrst Rehers   xviij d
spent at ye said rehers   xvj d
payed to ye plears at ye seconde Rehers   xviij d 40
spent at ye said ˄ ʿReʾhers   xx d
...

col b

Expensys on mydsomer nyght

payd for beryng ye gyand	xx d
payde to two mynstrelles	v s.
payde for beryng of ij stremers	iiij d
payd for beryng of v Cressyttes	x d
payed for beryng of ye Cressytes lyght	vj d
payd to Iohn lynes for Cressyt lyght	iiij s. viij d
payd for Candell for ye gyand	ij d
payd for dressyng & mendyng of gyeand	xviij d

Svm xiiij s. viij d

...

Mercers' Account Book CRO: Acc 15
f 2

This ys to Remember of certayne pwintes Which longen to our
crafte Ordened of olde tyme for mendyng of Dyuers fawtes
Which ar founden Within our said crafte Wherby our said crafte
ys noysed & slanderd a monge the commyn pepull as Well a
monge Strangers knowen & that to grett Dysworschipp to vs all
& no profett to the Said crafte

...

[Also hit ys ordend that euery man of the Same crafte shalbe
Redy to attend apon the iiij Masters of the Said crafte at euery
Wache When the Meyr commaundeth them to goo & also that
euery man to be Redy When the masters calleth or sendith his
bedull to come to Wedynges or beryinges euery man to come in
the payne of xij d at euery defaute & no peny pardoned]

*for to come to
ye kinges Wache
Wedinges or
beryinges*

Weavers' Account Book CRO: Acc 100/17/1
f 38v

...

Thy Reyseyttes in the yere

...

Reyseyvyd of mesteres of the walkers	vj s viij d
Reyseyvyd of the skynners	v s
...	
Reyseyvyd of herre bowater weyver	x d
Reyseyvyd of crystover dale weyver	x d
Reyseyvyd of hewe heynes capper	viij d

...

f 39

                paymentes for the pagent

Item payd for ij Reyhersys	ij s
Item payd to symyon	iij s iiij d
Item payd to symyons clarke	xx d 5
Item payd to mare	xx d
Item payd to ane	xx d
Item payd to Ioseyph	ij s iiij d
Item payd to Ihesu	xx d
Item payd to the Angelles & the womon for the chyld	xij d 10
Item payd to the Iornemen	iiij s ij d
Item payd for bred	viij d
Item payd for Ale	ij s
Item payd for All maner of mett	iij s vj d
Item payd for glowys	ij s 15
Item payd for pynnes And pacthryd	ij d
Item payd to the synggers for the pagent	xvj d
Item payd to the mynstrell	viij d
Item payd naylys And Russys	iiij d
...	20
Item payd for veneger and spyce	vj d
Item payd to Rafe houtt	iiij d
...	

                         the som ys xxxiij s iiij d

                costes on myssomer nyght   25

...

f 39v

...	30
Item payd for iij ston of cresset lyght	ij s
Item payd to the stremmer beyrers	ij d
Item payd to the cresset beyrers	iiij d
Item payd to the boye þat bere the lyght	j d
Item payd to the ij whyt harnys men	viij d 35
Item payd for poynttes	ij d
Item for candyll	ij d
Item [se] spend At the Reyseyvyng of þe walkers	
money	iiij d
spend At the Reysseyvyng of the skynners money	iiij d 40
Item payd for menddyng of A cressett	iiij d
...	

Weavers' Rentgatherers' Book I CRO: Acc 100/18/1
f 43

...

payd for A cressyt & settynge of the same   ij d

...   5

AC   *Smiths' Accounts* Sharp: *Dissertation*
p 198 *(Midsummer Watch)*

... to the menstrells iij s iiij d   10

...

1552
Leet Book I CRO: A 3(a)   15
f 418* *(4 October)*

...

Item yt ys allso enacted by aucthorytye aforesayd that the barbors
barbors   of thys Citie shalbe dyscharged of ther pencion of vj s viij d that
they were heretofore Charged yerelye to paye to the gyrdelers of   20
the same Cytye

...

Chamberlains' Account Book I CRO: A 7(a)
p 223   25

...

Item paid to iiij weytes for ther [lyuereyes] wages   xxvj s viij d

...

Cappers' Records SC: Account Book I   30
f 82v col a
paymentes for the pagyon
spent at ye fyrst Reherse of ye plears   xviij d
spent at borseley at ye Said Rehers   ij s.
paid to ye plears at ye Second Rehers   xviij d   35
spent at ye Said Rehers   xx d
for mendyng ye skaffold
paid for a quarter pesse   vj d
paid for a boord   vij d
paid for nailles   iij d   40
paid to ye wryghtes   vij d
paid for Clampes of Iorne   iiij d

paid for tenterhookes	j d	
paid for vj d nalles	j d	
paid for Sope	ij d	

The plears wages

paid to pylatt	iij s. viij d	5
paid to god	xvj d	
paid to ye mother of deathe	iiij d	
paid to ye spryt of god	xvj d	
paid to mawdlyn	xij d	
paid to ye ij maryse	xij d	10
paid to ye ij byschoppes	ij s.	
paid to ye iiij knyghtes	iiij s.	
paid to ye ij angelles	viij d	
paid to ye demon	xvj d	
paid to ye syngers	xvj d	15
paid to ye mynstrell	viij d	
paid for ye plears Svpper	ij s.	
paid for ye hyer of harnes	xx d	
paid for dryvyng ye pagen and for drynk to ye plears	xx d	
paid to viij men yat dryved ye pagyon	xvj d	20
paid to ye wryght for tendyng ye wynd	ix d	
paid for vj dessen of poyntes	xij d	
paid for gloves	ij s. iiij d	
paid for settyng in of ye pagen	iij d	
paid for drynk at ye settyng owt & Settyng in of ye		25
pagyon	xij d	
paid for Rvssches	iij d	
paid for ye matter of ye Castell of emavs	xiij d	
paid for makyng nwe of ye plea bok	v s	

Svm xlvj s. iiij d   30

col b

The charges on mydsomer nyght

paid to ye mynstrelles	iij s. iiij d	
paid for beryng v Cressyttes	x d	35
paid for beryng ye lyght	ij d	
paid for beryng ij stremars	iiij d	
paid for Cressyt lyght	iij s. vj d	
paid for Carryeng of ye gyeand	xvj d	
paid for waxe Candell	ij d	40

Svm ys ix s. viij d

...

Weavers' Account Book CRO: Acc 100/17/1
f 40v

payments for the yere

It*em* payd for to reherssys	ij s iiij d
It*em* payd for settyyng owt of the pagent and havyng yn	xx d
It*em* payd to the townwardens	iiij d
It*em* payd to rafe hout	iiij d

medssomere nyght

...

It*em* payd for ij stone of crysset lyght	ij s j d
It*em* payd to the crysset berres	ij d
It*em* payd to boys that bare the podyngs	ij d
It*em* payd to the ij whyt harrnyst men	viij d
It*em* payd for ij dosyn of poynts	iiij d
It*em* payd to the stremere berres	ij d
Item p'a'yd to the ij mynstrells	xvj d

...

AC *Smiths' Accounts* Sharp: *Dissertation*
p 22*

...

Reseyved of the Craft for pagent pencys   iij s iiij d

...

AC *Tanners' Ordinances* CRO: Acc 241
p 7 *(f 4)*

Allso that all men of the companye and occupacion be reddie in
their best apparrell at all tymes to wayte on the maisters, and to
keepe the watch on Midsomer night vppon payne of euerie man
iij d iiij d wit*h*out any pardon.

...

p 8 *(f 4v)*
...

  Allso it is ordayned by the Authorothie of the of the Leet that
for assmuch as the companie of Tanners be not of such substance
as they haue bin in tymes past to mentayne the padiant therfore
To their help and profitt the Corvisers w*hi*ch be not chardged
wit*h* the padiant therfore they shall pay yearlie vnto the said

---

31 / iij d *for* iij s   36 / of the of the *MS dittography*

company of Tanners towards the charge of the padiant xiij s iiij d
to be paid yerely from thence forth at the feast of holy Trinitye.

...

p 9 *(f 5)*   5

...

    Allso it is ordayned by Authorotie of the Leet that forassmuch
as the Tanners are not of Substance as they haue bin in tymes
past to mentayne the paiant, Therfore to ther help and proffitt
the Buchers which be not chardged shall pay yearly to the tanners   10
towards the charge of the padiant xiij s iiij d at the feast of the
holy Trinitye to be payd yearly from henceforth for euer.

...

1553   15
Chamberlains' Account Book I CRO: A 7(a)
p 230

...

  fees   Item paid to the weites for ther wages   xxvj s viij d
...   20

p 232* *(special allowances from Cheylesmore guild lands)*

...

And Allowed hyme also - x s paid for a vake house in baylie lane
ouer ageynst the procession way not allowed in his Accompt of   25
the Gild landes ...

Cappers' Records SC: Account Book I
f 84v col a
                 more paymentes for ye Craft   30

...

paid to ye plears at ye ffyrst Rehers   xviij d
spent at ye Said Rehers   iij s. iiij d
spent at borseleys   viij d
paid for tymber for makyng of a payre of tressylles   xx d   35
paid to ye plears at ye Second Rehers   xviij d
spent at ye Said rehers   ij s. viij d
paid to vavghen yat shwld have played in tompson sted   vj d
spent at Mr Smythes   ij s. iiij d
             Reparcyons of ye pageant   40
paid for a whele for byndyng & for nales   iiij s. viij d
spent at yat tym   xiiij d

p*ai*d for a peese of tymber	ix d
p*ai*d for nales & workmanshypp	x d
p*ai*d at settyng forth of ye pageant	vj d
spent at y*at* tyme	iiij d
p*ai*d for ij boord*es*	vj d 5
p*ai*d for nales & nalyng ye boord*es*	iiij d
p*ai*d for makyng nwe of pylat*es* malle	ij s. j d

Svm xj s. ij d

col b   10

payment*es* to ye plears

p*ai*d to pylat	iij s. viij d
p*ai*d to god	xvj d
p*ai*d to ye mother of death	iiij d
p*ai*d to ye spryt of god	xvj d 15
p*ai*d to mavdlyn	xij d
p*ai*d to ye ij maryes	xij d
p*ai*d to ye ij bischopp*es*	ij s.
p*ai*d to ye iiij knyght*es*	iiij s. viij d
p*ai*d to ye ij angell*es*	viij d 20
p*ai*d to ye demon	xvj d
p*ai*d to ye mynstrell	viij d
p*ai*d to ye Syngers	xvj d
p*ai*d for tentyng ye wynd	vj d
p*ai*d for drynk in ye pageant	vj d 25
p*ai*d for ye ye plears Svpp*er*	ij s.
p*ai*d to viij men y*at* drove ye pageant	xvj d
p*ai*d to ye Carpent*er* ffor tendyng on ye pageant	xij d
p*ai*d for drynk for ye dryvers betwext stagys	xviij d
p*ai*d for hyer of iiij harnes	xx d 30
p*ai*d for Rwsches for ye Chamber & for ye pageant	xiiij d
p*ai*d for vj doossen of poynt*es*	xij d
p*ai*d for xix payr of glovys	iij s. iiij d
p*ai*d for Sope & for a staple	iij d
p*ai*d for nales & nayling of boord*es*	vij d 35
p*ai*d for Settyng in of ye pageant	vj d
spent at y*at* tym	vj d
p*ai*d for a gallon of [Wy.] wyne when owr feast was	xij d

Svm xxxvj s, vij d

26 / ye ye MS *dittography*

expensys on mydsomer nyght

p*ai*d to ye mynstrell*es*	iiij s
p*ai*d for bearyng of ye Ioyand	xvj d
p*ai*d for beryng Cressyt lyght	vj d
p*ai*d for beryng ij stremars	iiij d
p*ai*d for beryng vij Cressy*tes*	xiiij d
p*ai*d for vij ston of lyght	iiij s. viij d
p*ai*d for a waxe candell	ij d
p*ai*d for rep*ar*acyons & mendyng of ye Ioyand	xxij d
Svm xiiij s.	

...

Carpenters' Account Book II CRO: Acc 3/2
f 157 *(Midsummer Watch)*

...

It*e*m ij ston of cresset Light	xiiij d
It*e*m for carying ye same	vj d
It*e*m for mending ye cresset	j d
It*e*m to ye mynstrell*es*	ij s.

...

f 157v

vppon the fellowship at Mr tomsons

It*e*m p*ay*d to ye mynstrell	ij d

...

(Other expenses)

...

It*e*m p*ay*d to the tylers	x s.

...

f 158

It*e*m the dressing the harnes to watson	

Item for skouring of the harnes Lynyng ye gorgett & reveyting &
Lethering   viij d
It*e*m p*ay*d to ye man for wearyng ye same harnes ij dayes & one
nyght   [xviij d] xij d
[It*e*m for poynt*tes*   j d]
                        Some [ij s iij d] xx d

Mercers' Account Book CRO: Acc 15
f 1v*

...

Me*morandum* Delyud to Newman the kuttler in the yere of o*wr*
lord god I Ml v C liij in seynt Mary hall be fore Mast*er* Rogers Mr   5
Myllar herry kyrven Willi*a*m pheny then beying masture*es* before
all the said felischipp the p*ar*sells foloing
Inp*r*imis vj salett*es* . vj peyr of Almayne Ryvett*es* vj peyr of
Splentt*es* vj gorgett*es* of Male [iiij byll*es*] & iiij salett*es* for
complet harnes & a ponard for ye iiij complet harness*es* It*em* iiij   10
byll*es* & [ij poll] & ꞌaꞌ pollax W*ith* iiij swordes & þe Sl⟨.⟩g⟨.⟩erd

Weavers' Account Book CRO: Acc 100/17/1
f 41

...   15
                          Reyseytt*es* In the yere

...
Reyseyvvyd of the walkers   vj s viij d
Reyseyvvyd of the sky*n*neres   v s
...   20

ff 41v-2
                          Paymen*tes* for the pagent
It*em* payd for ij Reyhersys   ij s
It*em* payd to symyon   iij s iiij d   25
It*em* payd to Ioseph   ij s iiij d
It*em* payd to mare   xx d
It*em* payd to symyon clarke   xx d
It*em* payd to Ih*e*su   xx d
It*em* payd to ane   xx d   30
It*em* payd to the Angell*es*   viij d
It*em* payd to the womon for hyr chyld   iiij d
It*em* payd for dryvyng of the pagant   iiij s iiij d
It*em* payd for glowys   xviij d
It*em* payd for synggers   xvj d   35
It*em* payd for bred   xij d
It*em* payd for Ale   ij s
It*em* payd for bochere mett   v s
...

                    som ys xxxij s vj d | 40

costes on myssomer nyght

...

Item payd to the ij whyt harnys men	[xvj] viij d
Item payd to the menstrell	xx d
Item payd for iiij ston of cresset lyght	ij s
Item payd to the stremmer beyrers	ij d
Item payd to the cresset beyrers	iiij d
Item payd to the boye that bere þe lyght	ij d
[Item payd for beyreyng of þe iiij Almon Reyvettes	viij d]
Item for poynttes	iiij d

...

1554

Chamberlains' Account Book I CRO: A 7(a)

p 233

...

fees &
wages

Item to the weyttes for ther wages	xxvj s viij d

...

Cappers' Records SC: Account Book I

f 92 col a

...

paid to ye plears at ye fyrst Rehers	xviij d
spent at ye said Rehers	ij s. viij d

...

paid to ye plears at ye seconde Reherse	xviij d
spent at ye said Rehers	ij s. viij d
spent on Corpus christi day	xij d

...

col b

expensys on the pageant

paid at settyng forthe of ye pageaunt	vj d
paid for sope	ij d
paid for poyntes	x d
paid for nales	v d ob.
paid for a boord	iiij d ob.
paid for Rvschys	iiij d
paid for drynk for ye dryvers of ye pageaunt	xviij d
paid for drynk for ye maisteres	xvj d

paid to ye mynstryll	viij d	
paid for settyng in of ye pageaunt	vj d	
spent at that tym	vj d	
paid for a quarter of Coles	viij d	

Svm vij s x d   5
paymentes to the pleares

paid to god	xvj d	
paid to ye mother of death	vj d	
paid to pylat	iij s. viij d	
paid to ye ij byschoppes	ij s.	10
paid to ye iiij knyghtes	iiij s. viij d	
paid to mavdlyn	xij d	
paid to the spryt of god	xvj d	
paid to the demon	xvj d	
paid to ye ij maryes	xij d	15
paid to the ij angelles	viij d	
paid to ye plears svpper	ij s.	
paid for tentyng of ye wynd & dressyng of the pageaunt	vj d	
paid to ye Carpenter for mendyng & tendyng of ye pagantes	xvj d	20
paid to x men yat drove ye pageaunt	xx d	
paid for hyer of iiij harnes	ij s.	
paid for xviij paire of gloves	iij s.	
paid to ye syngeres	xvj d	

Svm xxx s. iiij d   25
Expensys on mydsomer nyght

paid for vij ston of Cressytt lyght	iiij s.	
paid to ye mynstylles	vj s.	
paid for carridg of ij strameres	iiij d	
paid for Carridg of vj Cressyttes	xij d	30
paid for Carridge of ye Cressytt lyght	vj d	
paid for Carridg of ye Ioyand	xv d	
paid for mendyng & peantyng of ye Ioyand	ij s. vj d	

Svm xv s. vij d

...   35

Carpenters' Account Book II CRO: Acc 3/2
f 165

Paymentes at Midsomer   40

Item for ij stoon of cresset 'light'	xiiij d	
Item for the cresset berers	vj d	
Item for mending of the cresset	ij s.	

Item to the mynstrell*es*	ij s.
Item for beareng of the harnes	iiij d
...	

Moore paymentes

Item p*ay*d to the coupers	x s.	5
...		

Weavers' Account Book CRO: Acc 100/17/1
f 42v

10

Reyseytt*es* of the craft

Reyseyvyd of the sky*n*ners	v s
...	

Reyseyvyd of the walkers	vj s viij d	
...		15

f 43

Paymentes for the pagent

Item payd for ij Reyherssys	ij s	
Item payd to symyon	iij s iiij d	20
Item payd to Ioseph	ij s iiij d	
Item payd to mare	xx d	
Item payd Ih*esu*s	xx d	
Item payd to Ane	xx d	
Item payd to symyons clark	xx d	25
Item payd to the ij Angell*es*	viij d	
Item payd to the syngers	xvj d	
Item payd for dryvyng of the pagent	iiij s iiij d	
payd for the players de*n*ner And soopper	vij s	
payd to the womon for hyre chyld	iiij d	30
payd for glowys	xx d	
payd for Russes py*n*nes And pacthryd	ij d	
payd to Iames hewet for hys Reyggall*es*	viij d	
...		

som ys xxx s vj d

35

cost*es* on myssom*er* nyght

...		
payd to the ij whyt harnys men	viij d	
payd for ij ston And A halfe of cresset lyght	xviij d	
payd to the stre*m*mer beyrers And þe cresset beyrers	vj d	40
payd to the boye þat bere the lyght & poyntt*es*	iij d	
payd to the menstrell*es*	xvj d	

som ys xxj s j d

spend At the Reyseyvyng of the walkers money And the
sky*n*ners   x d

AC   *Dyers' Accounts*   Sharp : *Dissertation*
      p 186   5

...

p*ai*d to ij se*r*vers of the cressets   iiij d

...

p 200   10

...

Costes on Midsomer Nyght
p*ai*d for harnessyng ij men in complet harnesse   viij d
p*ai*d for harnessyng iiij men in Almayne Ryvetts   viij d
p*ai*d for ij stremer berers iiij d p*ai*d to iiij cressett berers viij d   15
to ij se*r*vers of the cressetts iiij d p*ai*d for ij dossen points iiij d
v stone of cressett lyght ij s xj d for mendyng the iiij cressetts x d
p*ai*d to John Swaneborn for the cloth that wentt to the hartts
cote & for payntyng þe same cloth ... p*ai*d to the company that
whent *with* the hartt & all that longith to hit   vj s viij d 20

...

AC   *Smiths' Accounts*   Sharp : *Dissertation*
      p 26 *(Corpus Christi)*

...   25

It*em* payd for v schepskens for gods coot & for
makyng   iij s

...

— H-P : *Outlines* I   30
   p 339

... Item, payd to payntter for payntyng of the pagent tope,
xxij d ...
                                                                              35

— H-P : *Outlines* II
   p 290

... Payd to John Hewet, payntter, for dressyng of Errod hed and
the faychon, ij s ...   40

1555
Leet Book I CRO: A 3(a)
ff 422-2v *(14 May)*
...

Skarlet gownes
[⟨...⟩]

It ys allso enacted that asewell the meyre & shyrry*fes* for the   5
tyme beinge as all other that haue bynne meyres & shyrry*fes* &
ther wifes shall were ther scarlet gownes vppon pr*in*cipall Dayes

•alderma*n* to
weare Tippets
vpon paine
x s•

& Dayes accustemed accordinge to the auncyent vse vppon peyne
of xx s |
Allso that eu*ery* alderma*n* shall were eu*ery* sondaye & other   10
pr*in*cipall dayes a velvet typpet vppon peyne of x s

•Shyrry*fes* /
serjaunts to
bear ther
maces before
them•

Allso that the shyrry*fes* for the tyme beinge shall at all tymes
when they be owte of ther howses [vse & ⟨..............⟩es] shall
haue ther *sergeantes with* ther mac*es* to goo before them & ther
yomen after them vppon peyne to forfeicte for eu*ery* defalte xx s 15

•mydsom*er*
night•

Allso that eu*ery* alderma*n* & shyrryf beinge able to Ride shall
acompanye m*aiste*r meyre & ryde w*ith* hym in the watche on
mydsomer nyght in ther scarlet & eu*ery* of them to haue a ma*n*
weytinge vppon hym w*ith* torche light vppon peyne of xx s

                                                                          20

Chamberlains' Account Book I CRO: A 7(a)
p 235
...

Ordinarie
payme*ntes*

It*em* p*ai*d to the weyt*es* for ther wag*es*   xxvj s viij d 25
...

Cappers' Records SC: Account Book I
f 94 col b   30
...

Expensys for mydsom*er* nyght	
p*ai*d for ix ston of Cressyt lyght	vj s.
p*ai*d to the mynstrell*es*	vj s.
p*ai*d for Carridg of ij stremars	iiij d
p*ai*d for Carridg of vij Cressytt*es*	xiiij d
p*ai*d for Carridg of ye Cressytt lyght	vj d
p*ai*d for Carridg of the Ioyand	xviij d
p*ai*d for mendyng & peantyng of ye Ioyand	ij s.
Svm xvij s. vj d	

f 94v col a

paymentes & expensys

paid to ye plears at ye ffyrst Reherse	xviij d
spent at ye said Reherse	iij s. ij d
paid for makyng of ij cressyttes	iiij s. 5
paid for mendyng of iij cressyttes	ix d
paid to ye plears at ye seconde Rehers	xviij d
spent at ye said Rehers	iiij s.
spent on Corpes Christi daye on the head of ye craft	iij s.
paid for mendyng of ye skaffold	viij d 10
paid for mendyng of ye whele	xiiij d
paid for mendyng of ye pageant house dore	vj d
paid for nales for ye pageant	vj d
paid for Rwschys for ye same	iiij d
paid for vj dossen of poyntes	xij d 15
paid for sope	ij d
paid for tenterhookes & for ij pesys of tymber	iiij d
paid to ye mynstrell	viij d
paid for ij lockers	iij d
paid for dryvyng of ye pageant & for settyng yt in & owt	iiij s 20
paid for drynk in ye pageaunt	xij d
paid to ye syngers	xvj d
paid for hyer of iiij harnes	ij s.
⟨.⟩aid for settyng in a pesse of ⟨.⟩ymber in ye pageaunt	iiij d
⟨.⟩aid for drynk at settyng fforth ⟨.⟩f ye pageaunt	vj d 25

col b

on the pageaunt

paid to god	xvj d
paid to ye mother of death	viij d 30
paid to pylat	iij s. viij d
paid to ye ij byschoppes	ij s.
paid to ye iiij knyghtes	v s.
paid to mavdlyn	xij d
paid to ye spryt of god	xvj d 35
paid to ye demon	xvj d
paid to ye ij maires	xij d
paid to ye ij angelles	viij d
paid to ye plears svpper	ij s.
paid for tentyng of ye wynde & dressyng of ye pageaunt	vj d 40
paid for xviij payr of glovys	iij s. ij d
paid for a skyn for balles for makyng & sowyng	v d

paid for a pesse of tymber   iij d
paid for waschyng ye shettes   ij d
                    Sum ys lvij s ij d ob.

...
                                                                    5

Carpenters' Account Book II CRO: Acc 3/2
f 168
                    Paymenttes at Mydsomer
...
Item for a new cresset   ij s iiij d   10
Item for mending the cressettes   ix d
Item for iiij ston of cresset light   ij s viij d
Item for bearing of þe thre Cressettes   vj d
Item for bearing of the light   ij d
Item for þe mynstrell   xij d   15
                    More paymentes
Item to the somner for bringing or cariing the cresset befor the
Mayre   j d
Item to the mynstrell vppon Corpus christi daye   vj d
...   20

f 168v

Item to the pynners & coupers   x s
...   25

Weavers' Account Book CRO: Acc 100/17/1
ff 43v-4
                    Resetes off the craff
...   30
Reseved off the master off the walkers   vj s viij d
Reseved off the master off the furreers   v s
...
        expenceses And paymentes ffor corposcryste Daye
Item payd ffor ij Rehersys   ij s   35
Item payd to semeon   iij s iiij d
Item payd to Ioseph   ij s iiij d
Item payd to Ihesu   xx d
Item payd to mary   xx d
Item payd to ane   xx d   40
Item payd to symons clarke   xx d
Item payd to the ij angells   viij d

Item payd to the letell chylde	iiij d
Item payd the syngers	xvj d
Item payd ffor dryvyng off ye pagant	iiij s
Item payd ffor glovys	xviij d |
Item the mynstrell	xij d 5
Item payd ffor Rossches sope & pakthryd	ij d
Item payd ffor bred	viij d
Item payd ffor alle	ij s
Item payd ffor bocchere mette	iiij s
the paymentts for corposcryste day ys xxx s	10

...

paymentes ffor medsomer nyght

...

Item payde the ij whyt harnes men	viij d
Item payde for ij stone & A halff off creset lyght	xix d 15

...

Item payde ffor beryng off the stremers	iiij d
Item payd ffor beryng off the cressettes	iiij d
Item payd to the menstrelles	xvj d
Item payd to the boye that bare podyngs	j d 20

...

Weavers' Rentgatherers' Book I CRO: Acc 100/18/1
f 48*

25

payd to the Wevers	v s

...

payd to the weveres on trynety sonday	viij s
Item payd to the weveres ffore hodes	xxxxii s
...	30
payd to the weveres att myhelmas quarter	xij d

...

AC   **Dyers' Accounts** Bodl: MS Top. Warwickshire c.7
f 116   35

...

Spend when ye crafte went in prosession for quene marye, vj. d
4 new Cressetts purchased.

...

— Sharp: *Dissertation*
p 186

...

p*ai*d to Skyner þe smyth for a new cressett & all þe olde cressetts
to bote xx d p*ai*d to coxe þe caryar for iij new cressetts vij s x d   5

...

p 201

Costes on Mydsom*er* nyght

p*ai*d for the hartts cote xx d p*ai*d for carying þe tree before þe   10
hartt   iiij d
p*ai*d to the dawnsers for daunsyng   xij d
p*ai*d for dressyng of the hartt & for mendyng the head   x d
p*ai*d to the heyrdman for blowyng before þe hart   iiij d
p*ai*d to John Stuards s*er*vand for leyding þe hart   iiij d   15

...

A C   *Smiths' Accounts* Sharp: *Dissertation*
p 164 *(Corpus Christi Day)*

...   20

p*ai*d to the mynstrells for prosesyon and pageants   ij s vj d

...

p 193 *(Midsummer Watch)*

...   25

p*ai*d for iiij complet harnes men   xvj d
p*ai*d for ij almayne Ryvets   iiij d

...

1556   30
Chamberlains' Account Book I C R O: A 7(a)
p 240 *(8 October)*

...

It*em* p*ai*d for the iiij weytes lyvereyes   xxvj s viij d

...   35

9 / *Sharp adds* inter alia

Carpenters' Account Book II CRO: Acc 3/2
f 173v

...

payd to the maisters of cowpers and tylars	x s	
payd to the mynstrell on corpuscrysty day	vj d	5
for mydsomer nyght		

...

payd for a mynstrell	viij d	
payd for cresset lyght	xxij d	
payd for bearyng ij cressetes and lyght	vj d	10

...

Weavers' Account Book I CRO: Acc 100/17/1
ff 44v-5

...		15

Ressett*es* in the yere

...

Ress*eyvyd* of the M*ayste*r of walker*es*	vj s viij d	
Ress*eyvyd* of the mayst*er* of skeners	v s	
...		20

Exspenc*es* & payment*es* in the yere
for Corpusscryste day

It*em* payd for ij rehersses	ij s	
Item payd to symeon	iij s iiij d	
Item payd to Iosephe	ij s iiij d	25
Item payd to Iesus	xx d	
Item payd to mary	xx d	
It*em* payd to ane	xx d	
Item payd to symeon*es* cla⸍r⸍ke	xx d	
Item payd to the ij Angells	viij d	30
It*em* payd to the chyld	iiij d	
Item payd to the synger*es*	xvj d	
It*em* payd for ye wast of ij tapar*es*	iij d⌐	
Item payd to Iames hewet for playing of hys Rygol*es* in the paygent	viij d	35
Item payd for gloves	xx d	
Item payd for dryvyng ye paygent	v s	
Item payd to ye mynstrell	xij d	
It*em* payd for Russhes sope & packe thryd	ij d	
It*em* payd for bred	xij d	40
Item payd for Ale	iij s	

Item payd for bochery mete   v s
          Som ys xxxiiij s v d
                    ᵒThis is the counteᵒ
     paymentes for mydsomer nyghte
...   5

Item payd for Karying ij whyt harnesses   viij d
Item payd for iiij stone of cressyt lyghte   ij s viij d
Item payd for berynge ij stremeres   iij d
Item payd for Karyng iiij cressytes   vj d
Item payd for Karying podynges   ij d   10
Item payd to the mynstrell   xvj d

...

Weavers' Rentgatherers' Book I CRO: Acc 100/18/1
f 49v   15

...

Item payd for clothe to make ye stremeres & payntynge of ye
same   xxvj s viij d

...
                                                                            20

AC   **Smiths' Accounts** Sharp: *Dissertation*
     p 185 *(Midsummer Watch)*

...

Item for ij new Cressets & mendyng of ij   vj s

...   25

Jailed Weaver Released to Act
Foxe: *Acts and Monuments of Martyrs*, vol 2
pp 1920 col b - 1921 col a*

...   30

It appeareth by the examination of the foresayd Iohn Careles,
that he endured prisoner the space of two whole yeares, hauing
wyfe and children. In the which his captiuity, first being in
Couentry Iayle, he was there in such credite with his keeper, yat
vpon his worde he was let out to play in the Pageant about the   35
City with other his companions. And that done, keeping touch
with his keeper, he returned agayne into prison at his houre
appointed.
    And after that being broughte vp to London he was indued
with such patience and constaunt fortitude, that he longed for   40
nothing more earnestly, then to come to yat promotion to dye in

Iohn Careles
dyed in prison,
and was buryed
in the fieldes.
the fyer for the profession of his fayth: & yet it so pleased the
Lorde to preuent him with death that he came not to it, but
dyed in prison, and after was buꞃyed in the fieldes in a dounghill.

Anno 1556,
Iuly.

...

5

p 1921 col b *(Letter to Philpot, fellow prisoner and martyr)*

...

I hope to be wyth you shortly, if all thinges happen aright: For
Careles accused
to the Councell
by certayne
backe friendes
in Couentrye
my olde frendes of Couentry haue put the Counsell in
remembraunce of me, not 6 dayes agoe, saying that I am more
worthy to be burned, then any that was burned yet. Gods
blessing on theyr harts for their good report. ...

10

1557
Chamberlains' Account Book I CRO: A 7(a)
p 244 *(15 October)*

15

...

ordynarie
paymentes
Item paid to the weyttes for ther iiij lyvereyes   xxvj s viij d

...

20

Weavers' Account Book CRO: Acc 100/17/1
ff 45v-6

...

Ressettes in the yere

...

25

Reseyvyd off the masters off walkers   vj s viij d
Reseyvyd off the masters off the skeners   v s

...

Exspences & paymentes in ye yere
for Corpus crystey day

30

Item payd for ij rehersses   ij s
Item payd to semeon   iij s iiij d
Item payd to Iossephe   ij s iiij d
Item payd to Ihesus   xx d
Item payd to marye   xx d   35
Item payd to Anne   xx d
Item payde to symeons clarke   xx d
Item payd to the ij Angels   viij d
Item payd to the chyld   iiij d
Item payd to ye syngers & to Iames hewyt for playinge of   40
Rygols   ij s.
Item payd for ye wast of ij tapars & frankynsence   iiij d

Item payd for gloves   xx d

Som ys [xxxviij s] |

paymentes

Item payd to the mynstryll   xij d
Item payd for dryvyng of þe paygent   v s   5
Item payd for russhess [ff] sope & pack thryd   iiij d
Item payd for bred   ij s
Item payd for ale   iiij s
Item payd for bocherye mett   vj s viij d

Svm ys xxxviij s iiij d   10

paymentes for mydsomer nyghte

...

Item payd for karying ij whyt harnesses   viij d
Item payd ij stone & halfe of cressett lyght   ij s ij d
Item payd for karying ij stremers   iiij d   15
Item payd for karying ij cressettes   iiij d
Item payd for karying podynges   ij d
Item payd to the menstryll   xvj d
...

                                                                           20

1558
Council Book CRO: A 14(a)
p 14* *(Receivers of White's alms money)*
...

To Rauff a man organpleyer   xl s   25
...

Carpenters' Account Book II CRO: Acc 3/2
f 177v col a *(Midsummer Watch)*
...   30

for ij stone of cresset lyght   xviij d
payd to the mynstrell   x d
payd for bearyng of our harnys ⟨......⟩ cressyttes and lyght   x d

col b   35

payd to the pynners and cowpers   x s
...

Weavers' Account Book CRO: Acc 100/17/1   40
f 47v
...

Resseyttes in the yere

...

Item Resseyvyd off the Masters of the Walkers	vj s viij d
Item Resseyvyd off the Masters off the skyners	v s

...

5

f 48

paymentes ffor corpus crystye day

Item payd at ij Rehersses	ij s
Item payd ffor dryvynge the paygent	v s
Item paid to symeon	iij s iiij d 10
Item paid to Ihossepthe	ij s iiij d
Item paid to Ihesus	xx d
Item paid to marye	xx d
Item paid to Anne	xx d
Item paid to symeons clark	xx d 15
Item paid to the ij Angels	viij d
Item to the chyld	iiij d
Item payd to the synggeres	xvj d
Item paid for the waste off ij tapares & insenc	ij d
Item paid for gloves	xxij d 20
Item paid for Russhes	ij d
Item paid ffor packe thrid & tenter hockes	j d
Item paid to the mynstrell	viij d
Item paid ffor bread & Ale	ij s viij d
Item payd ffor bochery mette	iiij s 25

som ys xxxj s iij d

paymentes ffor mydsomer nyght

...

Item payd to the mynstryll	viij d
Item paid ffor karying off ij whytt harnesses	[iij d] viij d 30
Item paid ffor berying ij stremeres	iij d
Item paid ffor beryng iij cressettes	vj d
Item paid ffor cressett lyght	iij s vj d
[Item paid to the mynstrell	viij d]

...

35

1559
Chamberlains' Account Book I CRO: A 7(a)
p 248 *(20 October)*

40

...

ordinarie paymentes	Item for the Weites Liuereyes	xxvj s viij d

...

Council Book CRO: A 14(a)
p 18 *(Receivers of White's alms money)*
...
ffurst to Iames Huwet organpleier   xl s
...   5

Carpenters' Account Book II CRO: Acc 3/2
f 180 *(Midsummer Watch)*
...
for ij stone and halfe of cressit lyghe   xxij d ob 10
for dressyng of the harnys   x d
for carryinge ij harnys ij cressittes & lyght   x d
to the ij mynstryls   xvj d
...
for a dossyn off poyntes   j d   15
...

col a
...
payd to the pynnars and cowpars   x s   20
...

Weavers' Account Book CRO: Acc 100/17/1
f 49
...   25
                    Recettees for [quter] in yere
...
Item Resseyvyd of the masters of the Walkeres   vj s viij d
Item Resseyvyd of the masteres of the skyners   v s
...   30

f 50

paymentes for Corpus Crystye day
Item payd for ij Reherssees   ij s   35
Item payd for dryvynge the paygentt   v s
Item payd to symyon   iij s iiij d
Item payd to Iossephe   ij s iiij d
Item payd to Ihasus   xx d
Item payd to mary   xx d   40
Item payd to anne   xx d
Item payd to symeones clarke   xx d
Item payd to the ij angeles   viij d

Item payd to ye chyld	iiij d
Item payd to the synngeres	xvj d
Item payd for glovees	xx d
Item payd for Russees packthred & nalees	iiij d
Item payd for the Rygoles	vj d 5
Item payd for bred and ale	iij s
Item payd for bochery mette	iiij s

       som ys xxxj s j d

            pamenttes for mydsomer nyght

...   10

Item payd to the mynstryll	xij d
Item payd for karying of ij wytte harnessees	viij d
Item payd for barynge of ij stremeres	iij d
Item payd for baryng iiij Cresettes	vj d
Item payd for Cresett lyght	iij s iiij d 15
Item payd for baryng the Cresett lyght	ij d

...

Weavers' Rentgatherers' Book I CRO: Acc 100/18/1

f 53*   20

...

Ressevyd of the talor & sharmen	iij s ⟨..⟩

...

AC ***Dyers' Accounts*** Sharp: *Dissertation*   25

p 198 (*Midsummer*)

... paid the mynstrell ij s

...

     30

AC ***Smiths' Accounts*** Sharp: *Dissertation*

p 193* (*Midsummer Watch*)

...

Item to two harnes men on fote iiij d to iiij harnes men that

Rode xvj d   35

...

— Bodl: MS Top. Warwickshire c.7

f 33

     40

... It pd for ij harnys men for master Mere on the feyre day & for

poynts vj. d ...

1560
Chamberlains' Account Book I CRO: A 7(a)
p 252 *(23 October)*

...

Item to the weites for ther Lyuereyes   xxvj s viij d   5

...

Carpenters' Account Book II CRO: Acc 3/2
f 182 col b *(Midsummer Watch)*

...   10

Item for iij stonne off cresset light   ij s vj d
Item for caryinge the harnys cresittes and lyght   xij d
[Item payde for a harnys   *(blank)*]
Item payde to the mynstrell   xij d

...   15

Weavers' Account Book CRO: Acc 100/17/1
f 50v

...

                    Recettees in the yere   20

...

Item Resseyvyd of ye masteres of ye walkeres   vj s viij d
Item Resseyvyd of ye masteres of ye skynnares   v s

...
                                                                         25

ff 51-1v

...

          Item pamynttes for oure pagent
Item payd for ij Reherssees   ij s
Item payd for dryveng ye paygentt   v s   30
Item payd to symyon   iij s iiij d
Item payd to Ihossepe   ij s iiij d
Item payd to Ihusos   xx d
Item payd to mary   xx d
Item payd to anne   xx d   35
Item payd to symeones clarke   xx d
Item payd to the ii angelles   viij d
Item payd to the chyld   iiij d
Item payd for gloves   xx d
Item payd for Russe & pacthred & nalees   iij d   40
Item payd for bred & ale   iij s
Item payd for bochery mette   iiij s

Item payd to the mynstrell   xij d

                som ys xxx s iij d |

pamenttes for mydsomer nyght

...

Item payd to the mynstrelles   ij s viij d   5
Item payd for berynge of ij wyte harnessees   viij d
Item payd for berynge of ii stremeres   iiij d
Item payd for of ij Cressettees   iiij d
Item payd for baryng of Cresett lyght   ij d
Item payd for Cressett lyght   ij s vj d   10

...

AC   *Dyers' Accounts*   Sharp: *Dissertation*
p 201 *(Midsummer Eve)*

...   15

paid for settyng forth þe hartt   vj s viij d

...

AC   *Smiths' Accounts*   Folger: Scrapbook Wb 191
p 112   20
              Payd for Corpus Christi day.
Item, for leying of stones yn the paggyn howse   vj d
Item, for a selldall for God   xij d
Item, to the carpyntars for mendyng the padgane   xvj d
Item, a ledge for the padgand   iiij d   25
Item, for yron worke   xx d
Item, for a loccar   j d
Item, for cordes   xij d
Item, to Pylate   iij s
Item, for hys glovys   iiij d   30
Item, for the rod   iij s
Item, for Petur & the Porter   xij d
Item, for pwyntes for the deman   j d

...

                                             35

— Sharp: *Dissertation*
p 193* *(Midsummer Watch)*

...

Item for a horse vj d Item horsebred for two horses iiij d

...   40

1561
Chamberlains' Account Book I CRO: A 7(a)
p 253 *(8 October)*

...

ordinary
paymentes

Item to the weytes for ther wages xxvj s viij d 5

...

AC *City Annals* Sharp: *Dissertation*
p 11*

... 10

This year was Hox tuesday put down

...

Carpenters' Account Book II CRO: Acc 3/2
f 183v col a *(Midsummer Watch)* 15

...

Item for iij stone off cresset light ij s.
Item for bearynge owre harnes cressittes and lyght xij d

...

Item to the mynstrell xij d 20
Item for a dossyn off poyntes j d

...

Item payde to the padgin x s

...

25

Weavers' Account Book CRO: Acc 100/17/1
f 52v

...

Item Resseyvyd on the Company toward ye pagentt [⟨...⟩] viij s
Item Resseyvyd on the Company toward mydsomer 30
nyght v s iiij d

...

Item Resseyvyd of the masteres of the waukeres vj s viij d
Item Resseyvyd of the masteres of the skynnares v s

... 35

f 53
pamenttees for owre pagentt
Item payd for ij Reherssesees ij s
Item payd for dryveeng the pagentt v s 40
Item payd to simeon iij s iiij d

Item payd to Ihoseppe   ij s iiij d

Item payd to Ihoseppe	ij s iiij d
Item payd to Ihesus	xx d
Item payd to mary	xx d
Item payd to anne	xx d
Item payd to symeones clarke	xx d 5
Item payd to the ij angeles	viij d
Item payd to the chelde	iiij d
Item payd for Russes pacthred & nayles	iiij d
Item payd Iames huytt for hys Rygoles & synggyn	ij s iiij d
Item payd for bred and alle	iij s vj d 10
Item payd for bochery mette	v s viij d

som ys xxxij s [x d] ij d

...

pamenttees for mydsomer nyght

... 15

Item payd to the mynstrell	ij s ij d
Item payd for baryng the ij whytte harnenes	viij d
Item payd for baryng the ij stremeres	iiij d
Item payd for baryng the ij Cressettees	iiij d
Item payd for baryng the Cressettees lyght	ij d 20
Item payd for Cressettees lygth	ij s vj d

...

AC   *Butchers' Accounts* Bodl: MS Top. Warwickshire c.7   25
f 100

...

Paid to the Whittawers towards theyr pagand	xiij s iiij d

...

pd for harnessing viij men on feyr fryday	ij s viij d 30

...

A   *Drapers' Accounts* CRO: Acc 154
f 51 *(Rentals)*   35

...

Itm Rec of myghell Roberts for the pagent house	ij s

...

Itm Rec of george bateman for the gardyn at the pagent house	xx d 40

...

7 / first e of chelde *written over* y

f 53

...

Exspencys and paymente

In primis payde for bearyng of harnys on feyre fradaye   viij d

...

f 54*

Charges of the watche

Itm payde for x Stonne of Cressyt lyght	viij s iiij d
Itm pd to iiij men for bearyng of harnysse	xvj d
Itm pd for iiij mens harnysse	viij d
Itm pd for beryng of iiij Stremers	viij d
Itm pd for Cressyt berers	viij d
Itm pd to ij berers of Cresyt lyght	iiij d
Itm pd for beryng of the gyantysse	xx d
It pd for Candylls	j d

Som xiij s ix d

The Charges of the pageant

Itm payde for iij Rehersys	vj s
Itm payde to the trompeter	iij s iiij d
Itm pd to the pleyers for to drynke	ij s
Itm pd for Ale for the drapers of the pageant	x d
Itm pd to god	iij s iiij d
Itm pd to ij dyvells	iij s iiij d
Itm pd for playing of the protestacyon	viij d
Itm pd to iij whyte Sowles and iij blank Sowles	x s
Itm pd to wormes of Conscyence	xvj d
Itm pd to iiij angells	ij s
Itm pd to the Syngyng men	ij s
Itm pd for kepyng of the wynde and of hell mowthe	xvj d
Itm pd to Robert Bro for iij worldes	iij s viij d
Itm pd to hym that kepte the fyer	iiij d
Itm pd for hanyng the pagent yn & owte & for openyng & shutyng	xvj d
Itm pd for dryuyng of the pagent and for dressyng of yt	ij s x d
Itm pd for blankyng of the Sowles facys	vj d
Itm pd to iij patrarckes	xviij d
Itm pd for the players Sowper & for playng of the Rygalls	v s

Som lj s iiij d

...

33 / hanyng *for* hauyng

AC   *Smiths' Accounts* Folger: Scrapbook Wb 191
p 110*

Recetes

Receved for paggan pens	iij s

Leyd owt for the pagande

Item, for wyare	ij d
Item, a spoke & a clype of yron	xij d
Item, the mynstrelles	ij s
Item, for pwynttes for the deman	i d

...

— Sharp: *Dissertation*
p 185 *(Midsummer Watch)*

...

Item for beryng of þe puddyngs iiij d ...

1562
Chamberlains' Account Book I CRO: A 7(a)
p 254* *(25 October) (Reparations)*

...

Item paid to Iames hewet for his parte of the weites	
Lyuereyes	viij s x d

...

Carpenters' Account Book II CRO: Acc 3/2
f 186 col b

Item paide to the pynnars and cowpars	x s

...

Weavers' Account Book CRO: Acc 100/17/1
f 53v

...

the receyttes

...

Item receyvyd of the walkeres	vj s viij d
Item receyvyd of the skynneres	v s

...

f 54

The paymentes for the pagente

In primis payd for ij reherssys	ij s

Line numbers: 5, 10, 15, 20, 25, 30, 35, 40

Item payd for dryvyng the pagent   v s
Item payd to symeon   iij s iiij d
Item payd to Iosephe   ij s iiij d
Item payd to Ihesus   xx d
Item payd to marye   xx d   5
Item payd to anne   xx d
Item payd to symeons clarcke   xx d
Item payd to the ij aungeles   viij d
Item payd to the chylde   iiij d
Item payd for russhes packthred & nayles   iiij d   10
Item payd to Iames hewet for hys rygoles   xx d
Item payd for syngyng   xvj d
Item payd for gloves   ij s vj d
Item payd for breade & ale   iij s vj d
Item payd for meate in the bocherye   v s viij d   15
...

Weavers' Rentgatherers' Book I CRO: Acc 100/18/1
f 59   *(Company feast)*
...   20
Item payd to the mynstrell   iiij d
...

f 59v

...   25
Item payd for baryng of harnysse   x d
Item for mendyng of the pagyon   viij d
...
Item for payntyng of the Vane   iiij d
...   30

AC   *Butchers' Accounts* Bodl: MS Top. Warwickshire c.7
     f 34*
     ...
     paid for harnessing viij men on feyr fryday ij s - viij. d   35
     ...

     f 100
     ...
     pd for harnessyng vj men on Mydsomer evyn   ij s   40
     pd to cresset berars the same nyght   iiij d
     ...

— Sharp: *Dissertation*
p 81, fn s*

... paid to the Whittawers towards theyr pagand   xiij s iiij d ...

5

AC   *Cappers' Accounts* H-P: *Outlines* I
     p 339*

... Item, spent on the craft when the overloked the pagyand, ij s;   10
item, payd for iiij harneses hyrynge, iij s; item, payd to the players
betwene the stages, viij d; item, payd for dressynge the pagyand,
vj d; item, payd for kepynge the wynd, vj d; item, payd for
dryvyng the pagyand, iiij s; item, payd to the dryvers in drynke,
viij d; item, payd for balls, vj d; item, payd to the mynstrell,   15
viij d ...

— Folger: Scrapbook Wb 191
p 111
...   20
Item, payd to Harrye Benett for mendynge the demonn cote and
makyng the head   v s
...

— Sharp: *Dissertation*   25
p 22, fn n

... Received of the ffellowship for pageant xxxij s iiij d ...

A   *Drapers' Accounts* CRO: Acc 154   30
     f 56
     ...

Receppts for Rentes

Item Receyvid of myghell Roberts for the pagent house   ij s
Item Receyvid of george batemen for the gardyn at the pagent   35
house   xx d

Charges for the pageant

Itm payde for iij Rehersys   vj s
Itm payde to the trumpeter   iiij s
Itm payde to the players for their drynkyng at the fyrste   40
stage   ij s

Itm payd for ale for the dryvers   xvj d
Itm payde for hauyng the pagent owte & in   xij d
Itm payde for dryuyng of the pageant   ij s vj d
Itm payde for dressyng of the pageant   vj d
Itm payde for openyng & shuttyng of the doores   vj d   5
Itm payde for kepyng of hell mowthe & the fyer   xij d
Itm payde for blackyng of the Sowles facys   vj d
Itm payd for kepyng of the wynde   viij d
Itm payde for the iij worldes   iij s viij d
Itm payd to Roberte Croo for goddes pte   iij s iiij d   10
Itm payde to ij demons   iij s iiij d
Itm payde for the prologe   viij d
Itm payde to iij whyte Sowles   v s
Itm payde to iij blauke Sowles   v s
Itm payde to ij wormes of Concyence   xvj d   15
Itm payde to iiij Angells   ij s
Itm payde to the Syngyng men   ij s
Itm payde to the players for there Sowper   iiij s
Itm payde for playeng of the Rygalles   xvj d
Itm payde to iij patryarkes   xviij d   20

f 57

Itm payde for Russhes and Sope   v d
Itm payde for nayles & pacckthrydd   iiij d   25
Itm payde for vj dossen of poyntes   xij d
Itm payde for Rossen and Candylls   iiij d
Itm payde to Roberte Croo for a hat for the pharysye   xij d
Itm payde more for ij dossen of poynts   iiij d
Itm payde for mendyng of ye trostyll   iiij d   30
Itm payde for a bynke   xij d
                                        Som lvij s xj d
Itm payde to newman for dressyng of our harnysse   viij s
Itm payde for beryng of harnysse on the feyre daye   xij d
...   35

AC   *Smiths' Accounts* Sharp : *Dissertation*
     p 20
     ...
     Item for settyng the padgande yn the first place   vj d   40
     ...

1563
Chamberlains' Account Book I C R O : A 7(a)
p 257 *(26 October)*
...

Item p*ai*d to the iiij weites for ther wa*ges*   xxvj s viij d   5
...

Weavers' Account Book C R O : A c c 100/17/1
f 54v
...   10

the receytes

...
Item rec*eyvyd* of the walker*es*   vj s viij d
Item rec*eyvyd* of the skynner*es*   v s
...   15

f 55
the payme*n*tes for the pagente
In p*ri*mis for ij rehersys   ij s
Item payd for the dryving of the pagente   v s   20
Item paid to symeon   iij s iiij d
Item paid to Iosephe   ij s iiij d
Item paid to Iesus   xx d
Item paid to mary   xx d
Item paid to anne   xx d   25
Item paid to symeons clarke   xx d
Item paid to the ij angell*es*   viij d
Item paid to the chylde   iiij d
Item paid for russhes packthryd & nayl*es*   iiij d
Item paid to Iamys hewete for his rygoles   xx d   30
Item paid for syngyng   xvj d
Item paid for gloves   ij s ij d
Item paid for meate in the bocherye   x s ix d
Item paid for bread & ale   vij s viij d
...   35

AC   *Cappers' Accounts* Folger: Scrapbook Wb 155
     p 31
     ...
Payments to the players.   40
Item, payd for the players sopper   ij s
Item, payd to God   xx d

Item, payd to the Spret of God   xvj d
Item, payd to the ij angells   viij d
Item, payd to the iij Maryes   ij s
Item, payd to Pylat   iiij s
Item, payd to the ij bysheopes   ij s   5
Item, to the iiij Knyghtes   iiij s viij d
Item, payd to the demon   xvj d
Item, payd to the syngers & makynge the songe   ij s iiij d
Item, payd to the mynstrell   viij d
Item, payd for our sopper at nyght   iij s   10
...

— Folger: Scrapbook Wb 177
p 3
...   15
                  Costes & charges of the pagyand
Item, payd for mendynge of the pagyand xx d
Item, payd for dressynge of the pagyand vj d
Item, payd for kepynge the wynde vj d
Item, payd for roshes ij d   20
Item, payd for ale in the pagyand xiiij d
Item, payd to the players betwene the stages viij d
Item, payd for ther drynkynge at the Swanne [do] dore ij s viij d
Item, payd for dryvynge the pagyand iiij s
Item, payd for gloves & poyntes iiij s ij d   25
Item, payd for balls viij d
Item, payd for hyrynge iiij harneses iij s

— Bodl: MS Top. Warwickshire c.7
f 159*   30
...
payd to Jhon a Grene, for the wryttynges, xvj d.
...

A   *Drapers' Accounts* CRO: Acc 154   35
    ff 58-9
    ...
                  Chargys of the pagent
In *pri*mis payde for iij Rehersys   vj s
Itm payde for hanyng the pagent owte and yn   xij d   40

23 / [do] *crossed out at end of line*   40 / hanyng *for* hauyng

Itm payde for dryuyng of the pagent	ij s vj d
Itm payde for kepyng of the wynde and hell mowthe	xij d
Itm payde for dressyng of the pagent & openyng & shuttyng the doores	viij d
Itm payde for kepyng of the fyers	iiij d
Itm payde for nayles and tentur hookes	viij d
Itm payde for Rossen and Candylls	ij d
Itm payde for Ale to the pagent and for the dryvers	xix d
Itm payde for leddgys and mendyng of the pagent	xviij d
Itm payde for Sope and pacck thrydde	iiij d
Itm payde for Russhes	ij d
Itm payde for mendyng the Sowles Coates	vj d
Itm payde for A lynke to Sette the worlds on fyer	vj d
Itm payde for A Cooate for god and for A peyre of gloues ffor hym	iij s
Itm payde to A Smythe for mendyng of the pagent	xx d
Itm payde for A Coarde to mende the gates of the pagent house	iiij d
Itm payde to Robert Croo for makyng of the iij worlds	iij s viij d
Itm payde for blacckyng of the Sowles facys	vj d
Itm payde to the players for there fyrst drynkyng	ij s
Itm payde to the trumpeter	iij s iiij d
Itm payde to god ffor his welke	iij s iiij d |
Itm payde to the ij dyvells	iij s iiij d
Itm payde to iij Savyd Sowles	v s
Itm payde to iij damnyd Sowles	v s
Itm payde for Speakyng of the prologe	viij d
Itm payde to ij wormes of Conscyence	xvj d
Itm payde to iiij Angells	ij s
Itm payde to the iij patryarkes	xviij d
Itm payde to the Syngyng men	ij s
Itm payde to James huyt for the Rygalls	xij d
Itm payde to the players for there Sowper	iiij s
Itm payde for poynts for the players & for the harnysyd men	xvij d
Itm payde for beryng of our harnyse on the feyre daye	viij d

Som iij l iiij s v d

...

AC   *Dyers' Accounts* Sharp: *Dissertation*
     p 201 *(Midsummer Eve)*

     ...

     p*ai*d to lynsey for the hartte   v s

     ...   5

AC   *Smiths' Accounts* Sharp: *Dissertation*
     p 36*

     ...

     It*em* to Robart Croo for ij leves of ore pley boke   viij d   10

     ...

     1564
     Chamberlains' Account Book I CRO: A 7(a)   15
     p 259 *(24 October)*

     ...

     It*em* p*ai*d to iiij weytt*es* for ther wag*es*   xxvj s viij d

     ...
                                                                                20

     Council Book CRO: A 14(a)
     p 50 *(Alphabetical list of receivers of White's alms money)*

     ...

     W*illia*m Androwes. the weit
     Rauf a ma*n* the weit   25

     ...

     p 54

     ...

     Thomas Clerke the weit   30
     Robe*rt* Clerke fideler

     ...

AC   *City Annals* CRO: Acc 2/F
     f 27*   35

     ...

     Tho*mas* Ryley Draper ... a Plague in this City and there died in St
     Michaells Parish of all Diseases 224

     ...

Weavers' Account Book   CRO: Acc 100/17/1
f 56 *(Payments)*

...

In primys for ij rehersys   ij s

...   5

Weavers' Rentgatherers' Book I   CRO: Acc 100/18/1
f 61

...

Item paid at losyns at ye settyng owt of ye pagente   vj d   10

...

Item paid for bearyng of ye harnysse ∧ 'ʔ poyntes' on fayer
frydaye   x d

...   15

f 61v

...

Item paid for nayles for the pagente   v d
Item paide for .3. Carte nayles for the whelles   iiij d
Item paid for settyng one of Ihesus sleues   ij d   20
Item paid for payntyng of Iesus heade   viij d
Item paid for solyng of Iesus hose   j d
Item paid [for] to Iohn dowley to make onle ye money for his
gowne   viij d

...   25

A   *Drapers' Accounts*   CRO: Acc 154
f 60

                              charges of the dyner   30

...

Itm paid for ij Rehersys   iiij s

...

Itm payde for berynge of our harnysse on the feyre daye & for
poynts   xij d   35

...

Itm payde for mendyng the pagent howse doore & undoyng of a
Coofer   iij d

...

AC   **Smiths' Accounts** Sharp: *Dissertation*
p 21* *(Corpus Christi)*

... 6d. pd for a chassyng stafhed ...

5

p 35
...
It*em* payd for iij cheverels and a berde   xij d
...

10

p 193 *(Midsummer Watch)*
...
Item payd to vij harnys men   ij s iiij d
...

15

1565
Chamberlains' Account Book I CRO: A 7(a)
p 260 *(29 October)*
...
rdinar*ie*   It*em* pa*i*d to the iiij weit*es* for ther wag*es*   xxvj s viij d   20
...

Weavers' Account Book CRO: Acc 100/17/1
f 56v
...   25
                              ffor the Receyt*es*
...
Item rec*eyvyd* of the walker*es*   vj s viij d
Item rec*eyvyd* of the skynner*es*   v s
...   30

f 57
                              The paymen*tes*
In p*r*imis ij rehersys   ij s
Item for the dryvyng of the pagente   v s   35
Item payd to symeon   iij s iiij d
Item payd to Iosephe   ij s iiij d
Item payd to Iesus   xx d
Item payd to marye   xx d

Item payd to Anne	xx d
Item payd to symeons clarcke	xx d
Item payd to the ij Angelles	viij d
Item payd to the chylde	iiij d
Item payd for russhes packthryde & naylles	viij d 5
Item payd to Iames hewet for his rygolles	xx d
Item payd for syngyng	xvj d
Item payd for gloves	ij s ij d
Item payd for meate In the bochery	viij s ix d
Item payd for bread & Ale	vj s viij d 10

Weavers' Rentgatherers' Book I CRO: Acc 100/18/1
f 63

...

Item paid for beryng of the harnys on ye fayre day	xj d 15

...

AC *Cappers' Records* Sharp: *Dissertation*
pp 49-50

...   20

Costes & charges of the pagyande

Item payd to pylate	iiij s
Item payd to the iiij knyghts	iiij s viij d
Item payd to the ij bysshopes	ij s
Item payd to god	xx d 25
Item paide to the sprytt of god	xvj d
Item payd to the ij angelles	viij d
Item payd to the iij maryes	ij s
Item payd to þe demon	xvj d
Item payd to the mynstrell	viij d 30
Item payd for vj dossyn of poyntes	xij d
Item payd for reprasyons of the pagyand, tymber nayles & iren	vij s viij d
Item payd for the hyer of iiij harnes & scorrynge of our harnes	iiij s 35
Item payd for dresynge & colorynge the bysshoppes hodes	ij s
Item payd for makynge the hoodes & mendynge maudlyn coate	xij d

Collation (Sharp: *Dissertation* pp 49-50, with Folger: Scrapbook Wb 177,
pp 12-13): *between* 30 *and* 31] Item payd for gloves iij s iiij d   33 viij]
x (?)

Item spent at taverne	xij d
Item payd for a hoke of Iren	xvj d
Item payd for one whelle	ij s ij d

Some xlj s x d.|

More charges of þe pagyand   5

Item spent at þe first rehearse at the brekefast of þe companye	v s viij d
Item spent at the second reherse	vj s ij d
Item payd to the players at þe ij reherse	iij s
Item payd at þe havynge out & settynge in of the pageand	xij d 10
Item payd for dressynge þe pagiand & kepynge the wynde	xij d
Item payde to the dryvers	iiij s
Item payde to the dryvers in drynke	viij d
Item payde to the players betwene the stages	viij d
Item payd for the players sopper	ij s viij d 15
Item payd for rosshes & small corde	iij d
Item payd for balles	x d
Item payd for iij gawnes of ale in the pagiand	xij d
Item payd to the syngers	xvj d
Item payd for a payre of gloves for pylate	iiij d 20
Item payd for grece	iij d
Item payd for our sopper at nyght	iij s
Item payd for furrynge of the hoodes	viij s

Some xxxix s x d.

...   25

A   *Drapers' Accounts* CRO: Acc 154
   ff 61-2

   ...

Chargys for the pagent   30

In pmis payde to the Players for iij Rehersys	vj s
Itm payde for iiij yards of boords to make pullpytts for the angells	viij d
Itm payde for a pece of wood to make feete for them & for bords to mend the pagent	xviij d 35
Itm payde for a Corde to open the wyndowes wall	x d
Itm payde for hauvyng the pagent owt and yn	xij d
Itm payde for dryvyng of the pagent	ij s x d

Collation continued: 8 reherse] reherse at the brekefast of þe companye
9 reherse] reherses

Itm payde for openyng and shuttyng of the pagent house wyndowes & dores	vj d
Itm payde for dressynge of the pagent	iiij d
Itm Settynge the worldes on fyre	iiij d
Itm payde for a C & halfe of vj nayle and for tenter hookes	xj d
Itm payde for Russhes Sope and pacck thrydde	vj d
Itm payde to the Carpenters for makyng ij pullpytts and for other worke done abowte the pagent	iiij s
Itm for Rosson and Candylls	iiij d
Itm payde for poynts for the harnysyd man and for the players	xvij d
Itm payde for wasshyng of the whyttawyers allbas	ij d
Itm payde to John huyt for payntyng of hell mowthe	xvj d
Itm payde to the trumpeter	v s
Itm payde to the players for there fyrst drynkyng	ij s
Itm payde for blacckyng of the Sowles facys	vj d
Itm payde for mendyng & makyng of the Sowles Coates	ij s iiij d
Itm payde for makyng of the worldes	iij s viij d
Itm payde to the players for there Sowper	iiij s
Itm payde to James huyt for the Rygalls	xij d
Itm payde to god for hys pte	iij s iiij d
Itm payde to the ij Demons	iij s iiij d
Itm payde to the iij Savyd Sowles	v s
Itm payde to the iij dampnyd Sowles	v s
Itm payde for playing of the prologe	viij d
Itm payde to the ij wormes of Conscyence	xvj d
Itm payde to the iiij Angells	ij s
Itm payde to the iij patryarches	xviij d
Itm payde to the Syngyng men	ij s
Itm payde for a peyre of gloves for god	ij d
Itm payde for iij yards of Redde Sendall for god	xx d
Itm pd to porter for keveryng the Earth quake	ij s
Itm payde for a lynke to Sette the worlds on fyre	vj d
Itm payde for ale to the pagent	ij s
Itm payde for vj fretts to the wheles	ij s
Itm payde for iiij Carte nayles to the wheles	vj d

...

Itm payde for nayles to Sett on the fretts wall	v d
Itm payde for ix yards and a halfe of bukram for the Sowles Coates	vij s

...

21 / pte *for* parte; *brevigraph omitted*

AC *Smiths' Accounts* Folger: Scrapbook Wb 177
    p 21*

...

Paid to Hewyt for payntyng & gylldyng the [faw] fawchyne, the
pyllar, the crose & Godes cote ij s vj d   5
Paid for ij hundreth of nayles for the padgand viij d
Paid for a spoke of yron for the padgand x d
Paid for fyve plates for the padgand x d
Paid for iiij new tr[u]ʹeʹlles for the skaffolde ij s iiij d
Paid for yron to the same trulles xviij d   10
Paid for a gyrdyll for God iij d
Paid for makyng a new crose ij s vj d

...

— Bodl: MS Top. Warwickshire c.7   15
f 33

... pd for iiij harnis men & poynts for master meyre xx. d ...

1566   20
Chamberlains' Account Book I CRO: A 7(a)
p 262* *(28 October)*

...

the weites   Item paid to Iames hewet for his fee   vj s viij d
             Item to Thomas Nicolas for his fee   vj s viij d   25
             Item to Richard Stiff for his ffee   vj s viij d
             Item to Richard Sadeler for his ffee   vj s viij d
                                   Summa xxvj s viij d

...

                                                                                 30

Receipt Book CRO: A 17
p 13* *(23 November)*

...

Item received the same day of Mr william hopkyns that remeaned
vpon his accompt for money by hyme received of the Craftes   35
ageynst the quenes comyng   xviij li. xix s /

...

4 / fawchyne *written in left margin*

Payments Out Book CRO: A 16
p 11

...

Item the said Tresourers then paid therof
the xxvj^th day of the said Nouembr to   5
Iohn Ryley & Richard Smyth lait Wardens
that was due to theme vpon ther aicompt
maid for ther office of Wardens by   iij^xx 1 li. x s
reason of the the quenes Maiestis beyng
here the xvij^th of August last   10

...

AC   *City Annals* Bodl: MS Top. Warwickshire d.4
ff 21v-2

...   15

Edmond Brownell Draper maior 1565 & ended in 1566 ... The

The receiving
of Queene
Elizabeth into
coventrey.

17th of August 1566 Queene Elizabeth came to Coventrey with a
great company of nobles, & was honorably receaued as in this
sorte. The sheriues in scarlett clokes with Twenty younge men of
honest reputation & well horsed, all in one Livery of fine puke,   20
mett her grace at the further side of the liberties towards
Woolluey, and euery ^ ʽoneʼ of them having a white rodd in there
hands which they deliuered to her grace, & she receaued them,
and deliuered the same to them againe, & so they rode before her
vntill they came neere to the Citty Where the Maior & all his   25
Brethren mett her grace, they being in skarlett gownes with foote
clothes, & the recorder being of the Throgmortons (a man both
for his gravety, wisdome, & Learning worthy of great
Commendacions as in his Oration following it may partly appeare
which for the same wanne him selfe noe small prayse &   30
commendacions & because it shall not be forgott I haue heere
written it in such order as he then spake it) he was in a gowne of
scarlett of the same manner that the Maior & his Brethren were,
& so the Maior & he kneeling downe the Maior having the | great
mase in his hand & being one the vpper hand of the recorder   35
vntill such time as he spake these wordes (In token whereof we
most humbly yeeld vp our selues vnto your maiesties most Regall
power & mercifull authority,) at which wordes, the Maior kissing
the mace deliuered it into her hands & so kneeled downe againe
one the other side of the Recorder, & when the Recorder   40

9 / the the *MS dittography*

A purse cost
20ty marks
with a c li in
it. /

deliuered the gift of the Citty which was a purse which cost 20ty
markes with one Hundred Pounds of Angells in it. When the
Queene Receaued it her guard sayd to the lords it was a good
gift she had but few such, for it was one hundred pounds in gold
to Whome the Maior answeared very boldly & it like your grace   5
there is a great deale more in it. What is that sayd the Queene. ⟨.⟩

Boldly spoken
of the Maior
with Wisdome.

the Maior answeared againe & sayd it is the faithfull hartes of all
your true Loving subiectes, I thanke you Master Maior sayd the
Queene it is a great deale more indeed. /

                                                                       10

The oration of mr Iohn Throgmorton to the Queene
at her graces comming to Coventrey he being
then Recorder of the Citty

...
                                                                       15

f 22v

... this auncient Citty which hath bin of longe time & times called
the Princes chamber the 3de Citty of your Realme ... remembred
of by Pollidorus Virgill ... & after the Arryvale of the Danes who   20
miserably afflicted the people of this Realme; the inhabitantes of
this Citty with there neighbours vtterly ouerthrew them in the
last conflict with the Saxons. A memoriall whereof is kept vnto
this day by certaine open shew'e's in this Citty yearely ...

                                                                       25

ff 24-4v*

... & so I end humbly craving of your Maiestie for my selfe
pardon for my rude barberousnes ffor the Citty tolleracion of
there poore estate which earnestly & most humbly desire yat   30
your highnes may so like with this there simple entertainement as
you may ofte to your graces contentacion & there great reioysing
v‸'i'sitt the same ...
This oration being ended ... Her grace ... deliuered the mace
againe to the Maior who rode before her grace next to the Earle   35
of Huntington who bare the sword & so came alonge from the
Bishopps gate to the white ffriers then being certaine Padgins as
in the Bisshopps streete at the Crosse at the Swann dore ... One
Munday her grace ridd forth at the Sponn streete gate & so to
Killingworth ... and so the Maior departing from her grace at the   40
vttermost part of the Liberties where the Queene deliuered the |
mace againe to the Maior with much commendacions ...

— BRL: 273978

... they Entered the Citty att BishopGate, & att the Cross & two
other places were Pageants Placed all which She passed by &
Came to the White Fryers where she Lodged Satterday & Sunday   5
Night, one Sunday all the Councell dined with the Mayor, & one
Monday Her Grace Rode forth ...

— Folger: Scrapbook Wb 177
p 11 *(Coventry Annals MS Longbridge)*   10

The Queen Mayor &c. "and so came alonge from the Bishoppes
gate to the White Fri[a]ʹeʹrs, there beinge ⟨..⟩ certen pagiantes as
in the Bishopes streat at the Crosse, at the Swane dore, & at the
White Friers gate."   15

— Sharp: *Dissertation*
p 158

... Att Saint John's Church stood the Tanners pageant, att the   20
Cross the Drapers pageant, at Littell parke street End the Smiths
pageant, in Much parke street End the Wavers pageant.

Carpenters' Account Book II CRO: Acc 3/2
f 188 col b*   25

Item paide to the pynars and cowpers   XX S
...

Weavers' Account Book CRO: Acc 100/17/1   30
f 57v
...

                         ffor the Receytes
...
Item receyvyd of ye walkers   vj s viij d   35
Item receyvyd of the skynners   v s
...

f 58
                         The paymentes   40
In primis ij rehersys   ij s
Item for dryvyng of the pagyent   v s

Item payd to symeon	iij s iiij d
Item payd to Iosephe	ij s iiij d
Item payd to Iesus	xx d
Item payd to marye	xx d
Item paid to Anne	xx d 5
Item payd to symons clarke	ij s
Item paid to the ij aungeles	viij d
Item payd to the chyld	iiij d
Item payd for Russhes packthred & nayles	viij d
Item payd to Iames hewet for the rygolles	xx d 10
Item payd for syngyng	xvj d
Item payd for gloues	ij s iiij d
Item payd for meate In the bocherye	ix s iiij d
Item paid for bread & ale	vj s
...	15

Weavers' Rentgatherers' Book I CRO: Acc 100/18/1
f 64

...

Item payd for bearyng the harnys vpon fayre daye	x d 20
...	
Item payd for awhele for the pagente	iiij s
Item payd for byndyng the whele & for carte nayles & other workemanshype that belongyng vnto hym	iij s iiij d
Item payd for astroke for ye whele	xij d 25
Item payd for naylles & sope & a clowte for ye axetre	xij d
Item payd to packwood & hys man	x d
...	
Item payd to newman for mendyng of ij poleaxes	viij d
	30

AC *Cappers' Accounts* BL: Add MS 43645
f 57*

...

The names of them that be agrayd to playe our pagyand & tobe
at commandement to that we shall be laydto atthe quenes   35
comynge

Item (sic)	Item thomas cowper
Item master robart wallden	Item jorge wynfeld
Item Jhon Jobber	Item hew hopkyns
Item Jhon heynes	Item roger pytmann 40
Item Jhon wallys	Item robart shawe
Item thomas pyewall	Item jorge hall

Item harrye heathe

Item nyclys harvye

Item martyn newnnam

Item wyllyam asheborne

Item thomas adlyngton

Item Jhon grene

Item wyllyam shene

Item thomas mussell

Item christopher torner

Item harrye godsonn

Item myghall tysoll

Item wyllyam kynge   5

Item harrye benett

— Folger: Scrapbook Wb 177

p 21   10

...

Item, payd to the demon	xvj d
Item, payd to the mynstrell	viij d
Item, payd to the syngers	xvj d
Item, payd for an ell bockram for one of the	15
byshoppes	xiiij d

p 31

...

Costes & charges of the pagiande.   20

Item, payd for prikynge the songes xvj d

Item, payd for wasshenge the abes ij d

Item, payd for sope iij d

Item, paid to the drivers in drinke viij d

Item, payd for balles x d   25

Item, payd for drivynge the pagiand iiij s

Item, payd for kepynge the wynde vj d

Item, payd for hiringe of iiij harneses & scow[ri]ringe of our owne

harnes iiij s

...   30

— Sharp: *Dissertation*

p 214

...

| Item payd att the gose etynge to the mynstrelles | xij d | 35 |
| Item payd to the mynstrelles on chusynge daye | xij d | |

...

28 / [ri] *crossed out at end of line*

A *Drapers' Accounts* CRO: Acc 154
ff 65-6

...

Payments ffor the pageantte

Inprymis for iij Rehersys	vj s	5
Itm for settyng fourthe the pageant	vj d	
Itm for settyng in the pageant	vj d	
Itm for dryvyng the pageant	ij s vj d	
Itm for kepyng of the wynde	vj d	
Itm for dressyng of the pageant & openyng and shuttyng the		10
dores	vj d	
Itm for kepyng hell mothe & the fyre	x d	
Itm pd to iiij Angells	ij s	
Itm pd to the two Demons	iij s iiij d	
Itm pd for ffetchyng and kepyng the ladder	ij d	15
Itm pd to the iij blacke Soules	v s	
Itm pd for blackyng ye Soules ffaces	vj d	
Itm pd to the wormes of Consyanc	xvj d	
Itm pd to the iij whyt Soules	v s	
Itm pd to Robert Crow for godds pte	iij s iiij d	20
Itm pd for playing the prologe	viij d	
Itm pd to the iij patryarks	xviij d	
Itm pd to Robert Crow for iij worldes	iij s viij d	
Itm pd to Jamys hewyt for Rigalls	xij d	
Itm pd to the Trompeter	ij s	25
Itm pd to the Syngyng men	ij s	
Itm pd to the pageant players for yer souper	iiij s	
Itm pd to Robert Crow for hys gloves	ij d	
Itm pd for poynts for ye souls & the demons	xiiij d	
Itm pd for Ryshes and Soupe	v d	30
Itm pd for Rosyn Candells & packe thryd	iiij d	
Itm pd to Thomas nycles for settyng a songe	xij d	
Itm pd to ij Carpentars for mendyng ye pageant	xiiij d	
Itm pd to mr pyxlye for xiij yards of ledgys	xiij d	
Itm pd for iij yards and ij fotte of bords	vij d	35
Itm pd for nayles and hooks for the pageant	xij d	
Itm pd to the players to dryncke	ij s	

20 / pte *for* parte; *brevigraph omitted*
27 / for yer souper: *Sharp (p 68) reads* for þer songs iiij d

Itm pd to mr brownes for battels of dryncke   xvj d
Itm for v yards of buckeram   iij s xj d

                    Som iij li xij d

...
                                                                        5

f 69

...
                    Paymets ffor the same yere

...

Itm pd to vij harnysed men at our fayre   xiiij d   10
Itm pd for ij dosyn of poynts for them   iiij d

...

Itm pd to the plears at oure dyner   v s

...
                                                                        15

AC   *Dyers' Accounts*   Bodl: MS Top. Warwickshire c.7
     f 116

...

It more that I leyd out at the agreement of the hole felischipp
ageynst the quenes magesty's comyng hyther to this citie,   20
xxiij. s iiij. d

...

AC   *Smiths' Accounts*   Folger: Scrapbook Wb 177
     p 31   25

...

Paid for iij. pwynttes of wyne yn the padgand   viij d
Paid for iij. gallance of ale yn the padgand   xviij d
Paid for a theale for the skaffold   iiij d
Paid for a stafe for the deman   iiij d   30

...

1567
Chamberlains' Account Book I CRO: A 7(a)   35
p 265 *(29 October)*

...
ordynare   It*em* p*ai*d to the iiij weytes for ther fee   xxvj s viij d

...

Carpenters' Account Book II CRO: Acc 3/2
f 190 col b

...

pade for the pagyn   x s

     5

Weavers' Account Book CRO: Acc 100/17/1
f 58v

...

          ffor the receytes

...   10

Item receyvyd of the walkeres   vj s viij d
Item receyvyd of the Skynneres   v s

...

f 59   15
          The paymentes
In primis ij rehersys   ij s
Item for dryuyng of the pagent   v s
Item payd to symeon   iij s iiij d
Item payd to Iosephe   ij s iiij d   20
Item payd to Iesus   xx d
Item payd to mary   xx d
Item payd to Anne   xx d
Item payd to Symeons cllarke   ij s
Item payd to the ij Aungells   viij d   25
Item payd to the chyld   iiij d
Item payd for russhes packthryd & nayles   vj d
Item payd to Iames hewet for ye rygolles   xx d
Item payd for syngyng   xvj d
Item payd for gloves   ij s ij d   30
Item for meate in the bochery   ix s vj d
Item for bread & ale   vj s

...

Weavers' Rentgatherers' Book I CRO: Acc 100/18/1   35
f 66

...

Item payd for Baryng the harnys on the fare day   xij d

...

AC   *Butchers' Accounts* Bodl: MS Top. Warwickshire c.7
f 100*

...

pd for watur ageynst ye comyng of the Quene   viij d

...   5

AC   *Cappers' Accounts* BL: Add MS 43645
f 57* *(4 March)*

Cappers Company

The inventary of all goodis late in the custody & Kepyng of   10
thomas lynycars late desesyde takein the iiijth of marche 1566
before nycolas harvy John howes & John Thinne & dellyveryde
to the handes of thomas hauy the day & yere a bove sene

for armerys

Item a corselete complete   15
Item apere of awmon Ryvets
Item iij Jackes & iij pere of splentts
Item iiij gorgyts iij Saletts iiij armyng swordes
Item ij bowes & too sheffs of arowes
Item ij velvete pawelles.   20

Pagaunte vestueres

Item ij stremars & pensells
Item mawdlen kertell. pylates dublyt
Item ij byshopes cottes with ther hoodes j pere of sleves
Item ij albes hedes pylatts hede   25
Item ij byshopes mytters
Item ij marryes hedes the spyryt of godes cote
Item godes hede & hys cotte & the spyryts hede
Item ij cortenns the dymons cote & his hed
Item iiij folles hedes   30
Item godes crose & the spyryts crose
Item pylates mawlle & his clobe
Item a dystaff & aspayde
Item vij cressets & viij *(blank)* to them
Item a baskete & a boxe   35
Item a wynles & a corde to the stevenn
Item iiij Cofferes

Collation *(with Folger: Scrapbook Wb 150, p 73):* 12 Thinne] Grenne
13 hauy] Harvy   13 a bove sene] aboveseid   14-20] *omitted*   25 hedes]
hodes   27 ij marryes hedes] iij. Maeryes hede   27 spyryt] Spyrytes
28 the] *illegible cancellation*   34 (blank)] coltes

Item ij marys coyffes
R more iiij lyly pennes for the whelles
R more ix ffannes
Item more iij maryes boxes
v small stremers   5
ix faynes with Iron steyles
Gods apparell of red say
paynted clothes for ye pagent

Delyuered ye 29 of Aprill 1573 all ye stuffe aforsayd unto   10
mychaell Tysall then Sumner
Delyvered to William Armes 1576 allthese Implements aforesayd.

— H-P: *Outlines* I
p 340   15

... costes and charges of the pagiand ... Item, payd for a cloutt to
the pagiand whelle, ij d; item, payd for a ponde of sope to the
pagiand, iij d; item, payd to the players at the second stage, viij d;
item, payd for balles, viij d; item, payd to the mynstrell, viij d;   20
item, payd to Pilat for his gloves, ij d; item, payd for assyden for
Pilat head, ij d; item, payd to Jorge Loe for spekyng the Prologue,
ij d ...

A   *Drapers' Accounts* CRO: Acc 154   25
ff 70-1*

      ...

                              Chargys for owre pagen
In prymis pd to ffossun for shottyng the pagen howsse wyndor
and a corde to ty hyt   ij d   30
Itm payd for the fyrst Reherse   ij s
Itm payd on trenyte Sondaye for ij Rehersys   iiij s
Itm payd for iij Blues of yelloo Canvas   ij s x d
Itm payd for Collering the soles cotts yelloo   xvj d l
Itm payd for the plears sopers   iiij s   35
Itm payd for iij Clypps of Iron & vj Cart nayle   ij s vj d
Itm payd for a C of vj peny nayle   vj d

Collation continued: 2, 3 R] Item   7 apparell] apparne   8 paynted]
payntes

33 / Blues *for* elnes (*cf Sharp, p 70*)

Itm for Carvyng bords and Crest ffor The boxxe of the padgen	iij s	
Itm pd to mr pyplye for bords & tymber	ij s vj d	
Itm pd to mr Colmen for iij Rent bords	xij d	
Itm pd pyecaring for bordes	xiij d	5
Itm pd to packewode for work at owr pagen	iiij s vj d	
Itm pd more for nayles	iiij d	
Itm pd to the saved & the daned sowles	x s	
Itm pd to the iiij Angells	ij s	
Itm pd to the plears at the fyrst stage	ij s	10
Itm pd for dryvng the pagen	ij s vj d	
Itm for settyng owt & settyng in the pagen	xij d	
Itm pd for dressyng the pagen & openyng and Suttyng the dowers of the pagen	vj d	
Itm pd for kepyng the wynd	vj d	15
[Settyng the worlds on ffyer]		
Itm pd for kepyng hell mowth and settyng the worlds on ffyer	x d	
Itm pd to the ij wormes of Concyans	xvj d	
Itm for makyng iij worlds	iij s viij d	20
Itm pd for the plears for Syngyng	ij s	
Itm pd to hewyt for hys Rygalls	xij d	
Itm pd for Cullern of apen that beryth The worlds and the black soles face	xij d	
Itm pd to the trompeter	ij s	25
Itm pd for drynck for the plears	xvj d	
Itm pd for poynts for the plears	xij d	
Itm pd for a lyncke	vj d	
Itm pd for Ryses teter hocks packthryd & sope	vj d	
Itm pd for makyng the Soles Cotts	ij s	30
Itm pd to Lowtts for playing godds part	iij s iiij d	
Itm pd for playing the prologe	viij d	
Itm pd iij patryarks	xviij d	
Itm pd the ij demans	iij s iiij d	
Itm for Rossin and Candels	iiij d	35
Itm for makyng hell mowth and Cloth for hyt	iiij s	
Itm payd for bearyng the harnes on fayre frydaye	xiiij d	
Itm payd for poynts ffor the Same	iiij d	

...

1 / boxxe *probably for* toppe *(cf Sharp, p 67)*

8 / daned *for* damed, *minim missing MS*   23 / apen *for* apec?

f 72

...

Payd thereof to John Rogerson for a solles Cotte   xij d

AC   *Smiths' Accounts* Folger: Safe E3 No 2*   5

Paid for harnis men & pwyntes for hoge twesday   xx d
Paid for dryvyng oure pagand & nayles at the qwens
commyng   vj s viij d
                        Charges for the padgand   10
Paid for borrowyng of Herodes gowne   viij d
...

— Sharp: *Dissertation*
p 31   15
...

Item payd for a stafe for the demon   iiij d
...

                                                                       20

1568
Chamberlains' Account Book I CRO: A 7(a)
p 267 *(26 October)*
...

Item paid to Iames hewet Thomas Nicoles Richard Stiff &   25
Richard Sadeler the waites for ther wages   xxvj s viij d
...

Payments Out Book CRO: A 16
p 15   30
...

Item delyuered ... to make prouision for the Duke of
Norffolk & other nobles the some of Thirtie poundes   xxx li.
...

                                                                       35
AC   *City Annals* Bodl: MS Top. Warwickshire d.4
f 24v*
...

Henry Kryvyn mercer maior 1567 & ended in 1568. ...
And in his yeare the Queene came to Killingworth vnlooked for.   40
Then were the padgins & hocke twesday plaied. /
...

Carpenters' Account Book II CRO: Acc 3/2
f 191v col a

...

paide to the pagyn   x s

...   5

Weavers' Account Book CRO: Acc 100/17/1
f 59v

...   10
                              ffor the receytes
<hr>
...

Item receyvyd of the walkers   vj s viij d
Item receyvyd of the skynners   v s

...   15

f 60

...

                              The paymentes   20
In primis ij rehersys   ij s
Item for dryuyng of the pagyente   v s
Item payd to symeon   iij s iiij d
Item payd to Iosephe   ij s iiij d
Item payd to Ihesus   xx d   25
Item paid to mary   xx d
Item paid to Anne   xx d
Item paid to symeons clarke   ij s
Item paid to the ij angelles   viij d
Item paid to the chyld   iiij d   30
Item paid for Russhes packthryd & naylles   vj d
Item paid to Iames hewet for the rygolles   xx d
Item paid for syngyng   xvj d
Item paid for gloues   ij s iiij d
Item payd for meate in the bochery   ix s vj d   35
Item paid for bread & ale   vj s

...

Item payd to ij men for theyr drynkyng & poyntes for waryng
owre harnys vpon hockestewysday   vj d

...   40

Weavers' Rentgatherers' Book I CRO: Acc 100/18/1
ff 67v-8

...

Item paid for iiij newe wheles for the pagent	xx s

...

Item paid for an exaltre for the pagent	xj d

...

Item paid for greate nayles for ye pagent wheles	ij s

...

Item paid for beryng of harnys on fayre fryday & for	
poynt*es*	x d

...

Item paid the mynstrel*es*	viij d	

...

Item paid to packwood for makyng of iij trestles & me*n*dyng ye	
page*n*t	xiiij d

...

f 68v

Item paid to mr pyxley for the tymbr that made the	
tresteles	ij s iiij d

...

AC   *Cappers' Accounts* H-P: *Outlines* I
p 339

... Item, paid for a ledge to the scafolde, vj d; item, paid for ij.
ledges to the pagiand, viij d; item, paid for grett naylles, vj d;
item, for makynge clene the pagiand house, ij d; item, paid for
washenge the pagiand clothes, ij d; item, for dryvinge the pagiand,
vj s vj d; item, paid to the players at the second stage, viij d ...

p 340

... Item, paid for balles, viij d; item, paid for Pylatt gloves, iiij d;
item, paid for the spekynge of the Prologe, ij d; item, paid for
prikynge the songes, xij d; item, paid for makynge and coloringe
the ij myters, ij s iiij d; item, paid for makynge of hellmothe new,
xxj d ...

— Sharp: *Dissertation*
p 126

...

Item payd for carryenge of ij harnesses & poynts uppon
hoc-tewsdaye   vj d   5

...

A   *Drapers' Accounts* CRO: Acc 154
ff 73-4*   10

...

Chargys ffor owre pagen	
Itm pd for Courd to tye ye pagen howse dore	j d
Itm pd for iij Rehersys	vj s
Itm for vij harnys men at the fayre	xiiij d 15
Itm pd for a cord for the wynde	ij s vj d
Itm pd for mendyng the wynde	ij d
Itm pd for [dryvng] dryvyng the pagyn owtt & in	xij d
Itm pd for cambes for one of the devells hose	xj d
Itm pd for Roos Candells	iiij d 20
Itm pd for dryvyng the pagen	ij s vj d|
Itm pd for Sope and Rossyn	vj d
Itm pd for kepyng hell mowth & settyng worldes one ffyre	x d
Itm pd to fosson for dressyng the pagen and openyng of and	25
Suttyng the dore & kepyng the wynde	xiiij d
Itm payd for makyng the devells hose	viij d
Itm pd to the trumpeter	xviij d
Itm pd for a yare of Read Saye	xviij d
Itm pd to the fower Sowlles & the damned	x s 30
Itm pd to the iiij angells	ij s
Itm pd to the plears at the fyrst stage	ij s
Itm pd to the ij wormes of consyans	xvj d
Itm pd for makyng the iij worldes	iij s viij d
Itm pd for the plears Supper	iiij s 35
Itm pd for Synggyng	ij s
Itm pd to hewytt for hys Rygalls	xij d
Itm pd for Collering ye blacke Solls faces	viij d
Itm pd for dryncke for the plears	xvj d
Itm pd for poynts for the plears	xij d 40
Itm pd for pleayng gods part	iij s iiij d

20 / Roos *for* Rossyn?

Itm pd for playng the prolog   viij d
Itm pd to the iij patryarks   xviij d
Itm pd to the ij devells   iij s iiij d
Itm pd for makyng the ij devells facys   x s
Itm pd for makyng a payre of hose with seare   xxij d   5
Itm pd for iij li of heasre   ij s vj d
Itm pd for poynts one the fayre daye   iiij d

...

Itm pd for drynck to the pagen   iiij d
Itm pd to ffrancys pynnyg for a playe   v s   10
                    Som iiij li vj s viij d

...

f 75
                    Reperacyons at wyes howse   15

...
Itm pd the tyler & hys man for viij dayes at wyes howse &
vnderwos & ye pagen howse   viij s
Itm pd for a strycke of lyme to ye page howse   vj d
...   20

1569
Chamberlains' Account Book I CRO: A 7(a)
p 270 *(25 October)*
...   25
Item paid to the iiij weites   xxvj s viij d
...

AC   *City Annals* Sharp: *Illustrative Papers*
     p 50*   30

John Harford   The Register of St. Michaels Parish was
destroyed by some who were so eager to burn Popish books, that
they burned the Registers, because they had some marks of
Popery in them.   35

Carpenters' Account Book II CRO: Acc 3/2
f 194
                    paymentes ffor the whole yere
Item paide to the pynners and cowpers   x s   40

...

5 / seare *for* heare *(cf Sharp, p 69)*

Item paide ffor a harnys to Mr pyxleye   ix s viij d
Item paide ffor carryinge off harnys on the ffair daye and ffor
poyntes   vj d
Item payde ffor a booe   iiij s
Item paide ffor a sheaffe off arrowes   iij s iiij d   5
Item paide for a sworde and a dagger   iiij s
...

Weavers' Account Book CRO: Acc 100/17/1
f 60v   10
...

ffor the Receytes

...
Item receyvyd of the walkers   vj s viij d
Item receyvyd of the skynners   v s   15
...

f 61
The paymentes

In primis ij rehersys   ij s   20
Item for dryvyng of the pagyent   v s
Item paid to symeon   iij s iiij d
Item paid to Iosephe   ij s iiij d
Item paid to Iesus   xx d
Item paid to mary   xx d   25
Item paid to Anne   xx d
Item paid to symeons cla'r'cke   ij s
Item paid to the ij angelles   viij d
Item paid to the chyld   iiij d
Item paid for Russhes packthryd & nayles   vj d   30
Item paid to Iames hewett for the rygoles   xx d
Item paid for syngyng   xvj d
Item paid for gloves   iij s
Item paid for meate in the bocherye   x s
Item paid for bread & ale   vj s   35
Item paid for beryng of the harnys on fayrer fryday & for
poyntes   x d
...
Item paid to owr Iorneymen for settyng owt owr pagyent   vj d
Item paid for smythy woorke belongyng to owr pagyente   xx d   40
Item paid for hangyng vp owr pagyent doore   vij d
...

Weavers' Rentgatherers' Book I CRO: Acc 100/18/1
f 69v

...

Item paid for baryng the harnys afayre fryday	viij d
Item paid for poinet*es*	iij d 5

...

AC   *Cappers' Accounts* Folger: Scrapbook Wb 177
p 51

...   10

Costes & charges of the pagiand.

Item, paid for bordes to mend the pagiand ⌃ ⌐ij s vj d⌐
Item, paid to the smythe for iij claspes of [iro] iron for the
pagiand xxij d
Item, paid to the smythe for iron claspes to the scaffolld xiiij d   15
Item, paid for sope to the pagiand whelles ⌃ ⌐iiij d⌐
Item, paid for a locker to the wind & for [rossh] rosshes iiij d
Item, paid for wasshenge the abes ij d
Item, paid for the balls viij d
Item, paid for small corde j d   20
Item, paid for mendynge of the bowe iij d

— Sharp: *Dissertation*
p 48

                                                                         25

... payd Thomas Nyclys for prikinge þe songes xij d.
...

A   *Drapers' Accounts* CRO: Acc 154
ff 77-8   30

...

Chargys of the pagen

Inprimus payd to gode	iij s iiij d
Itm payd for the prologe	viij d
Itm payd to the iij Saved Solles	v s 35
Itm pd to the iij damned Solles	v s
Itm pd to the ij wormes of Concyans	xviij d
Itm pd to the iiij Angells	ij s
Itm pd to the iij [patteryarks] pattryarks	xviij d
Itm pd to the Synging mene	ij s 40

---

13 / [iro] *crossed out at end of line*   17 / [rossh] *crossed out at end of line*

Itm pd to the ij demons	iij s iiij d
Itm pd ffor the Rygals	ij s
Itm pd for the iij worldes	iij s viij d
Itm for dryvyng the pagen	ij s ix d
Itm for havyng the pagen owt & in	xij d
Itm for openyng & Shuttyng the dore and dressyng ye pagen & the Wynde	xvj d
Itm for the plears Supper	iiij s
Itm for kepyng hell mowth and Settyng the worlds one fyre	x d
Itm pd to god for a payre of gloves	iij d
Itm pd for alle when the drese them	iiij d
Itm pd for alle for the pagen	xij d
Itm pd for blackyng there facys	vj d
Itm pd for Russhes	iiij d
Itm for Sope and Rosyn	v d
Itm for packthryd tenter hocks & candell	iij d
Itm a freat of Iron for one of the whells	viij d
Itm pd for poynts	viij d
Itm pd the plears for drynckyng	ij s
Itm for mendyng the pagen	ix d
Itm for borde and leadg	xij d
Itm for ij Corddes	ij s vj d
Itm pd for iij Rehersys	vj s
Itm pd the trumppeter	ij s vj d
Itm pd [the] Restyng the harnes	ij d
Itm for berreing a cott to Ruee	iiij d

Som lix s iij d

Payments

...

Itm pd for harnysshng men at the fayre	xiiij d
Itm pd for ij dosyn of poyntts	iiij d

...

Itm pd to John Rylye for a bowe	vj s
Itm pd mr nycolles for a Sheaf of arrowes & a case	iiij s viij d
Itm pd for fetheryng xxij Sheas arrowes	xx d
Itm pd more to hym for a bowe	iiij s iiij d
Itm pd for iij black bylles	iiij s iiij d
Itm pd to Thomas hacson for dycke	v s

...

36 / Sheas *for* Sheaf

AC   *Smiths' Accounts* Folger: Scrapbook Wb 177
     p 53
                         Charges for the padgand.
     Paid at the fyrst reherse to the plears & for ale ˄ ⸢ij s⸣
     Paid at the second reherse & for ale ij s   5
     Paid at the thryd reherse to here the plears xij d
     [Paid to the red]
     For ij spokes of yron xij d
     For nayles & pac[k]thryd j d
                                                                                  10

     — H-P: *Outlines* II
     p 289

     ... halfe a yard of Rede Sea ...
                                                                                  15

     — Sharp: *Dissertation*
     p 126
     ...
     paid for ij harnis men upon hocks twesday   viij d
     ...   20

     1570
     Chamberlains' Account Book I CRO: A 7(a)
     p 271 *(26 October)*
     ...   25
allowances   Item paid to Iames hewet for his fee of weit   vj s viij d
     Item to Richard Sadeler for the like fee   vj s viij d
     Item to William Stiff for the like   vj s viij d
     Item to Thomas Nicolles for the Like   vj s viij d
     ...   30

     Receipt Book CRO: A 17
     p 21* *(23 March)*
     ...
     [Item paid then to my lord of leisters seruantes at kenelworth vj s   35
     Item paid then to Mr Smythes pleyers   x s]
     ...

     Carpenters' Account Book II CRO: Acc 3/2
     f 196   40

     Item paide to the pynners and cowpers   x s
     ...

Item paide ffor the carriages off ij harnysses on the ffare
day   viij d
Item paide ffor poyntes   ij d
...

Weavers' Account Book CRO: Acc 100/17/1
f 61v
...

ffor the Receytes

...

Rec*eyvyd* of the walkers   vj s viij d
Rec*eyvyd* of the skynners   v s
...

f 62

The payme*nte*s

In *p*rimis ij rehersys   ij s
Item for dryvyng of the pagyente   v s
Item payd to symeon   iij s iiij d
Item payed to Iosephe   ij s iiij d
Item payd to Ihesus   xx d
Item payd to mary   xx d
Item payd to Anne   xx d
Item paid to symons clarke   ij s
Item paid to ye ij Aungells   viij d
Item paid to the chylde   iiij d
Item paid for Russhes packthryd & nayles   vj d
Item paid to Iames hewet for his rygoles   xx d
Item paid for syngyng   xvj d
Item paid for gloves   iij s
Item paid for meate in the bochery   x s
Item paid for bread & Ale   vj s
...

Item paid to *ow*r Iorneymen for settyng owt *ow*r pagent   vj d
Item paid for an extre for *ow*r pagyente   xviij d
Item paid for a new clowte & for nayles   vj d
Item paid for me*n*dyng of a pe*n*tyse broken *wit*h ye pagye*n*te x d
...

Item paid for ye hyer of ij beard*es* to harry benet   ij d
Item paid to Iohn hoppers for ij rehersys in ye halle   iiij d
...

Weavers' Rentgatherers' Book I CRO: Acc 100/18/1
f 72v

...

the receytes

...   5

Item rec<i>eyvyd</i> for apayre of pagent wheles   ij s ij d

f 74
Layed oute for expencys

...   10

Item paid for the carpe*n*ter for makyng an exaltre for ye
pagyante   xij d
Item paid for a trendell for ye scaffold & the makyng   iij d

...   15

A *Drapers' Accounts* CRO: Acc 154
f 80 *(Receipts)*

...

Rs of georg batman for a yers rent   iij s iiij d
...   20
Rs of mr myhell Robartts for a years Rent   iiij s

f 81*

...

Chargys of the pagyn   25
Payd for ij Rehersys   iiij s
pd for ij Cords for the pagen howse   viij d
pd for Settyng ye pagen in & owt   xij d
pd for Soupe for the wheles   iiij d
pd for gressyng the wheles   iij d   30
pd for A pere of new wheles   xj s
pd for poynts for the plears   x d
pd for Rossyn candell nayles & a lacke   viij d
pd for alle for the plears   iiij d
pd for alle at the Swanne dore   ij s   35
pd for the prologe   viij d
payd to god   iij s iiij d
pd iij Saved Sowles   v s
pd the ij wormes of Consyans   xviij d
pd the iiij Angels   ij s   40
pd iij pattryarkes   xviij d

pd to the Syngars	ij s
pd the ij demen	iij s iiij d
pd for the Rygalls	ij s
pd for iij worlds	iij s viij d
pd for dryvyng ye pagen	ij s ix d 5
pd for Sattyng ye dores & dresyng ye pagen	xvj d
pd for ye players Suppars	iiij s
pd for kepyng hell mouth & the worlds	x d
pd for a payre of gloves	iij d
pd for alle for ye pagen	xij d 10
pd for blackyng ye Solles facys	vj d
pd for Russhes	iiij d
pd for hyer of ye devells cott	iiij d
pd for mendyng the pagen dore	ij d

Som lvij s vij d 15
Payd for Rent and other Chargys

...

pd for harnest men at the fayre   xvj d

...

20

AC *Smiths' Accounts* H-P: *Outlines* I
p 339*

... Paid for laburrars for horssyng the padgang, xvj d; spent abowt
the same bessynes, xvj d; for takyng of the yron of the olde   25
whele, x d; paid for poyntes and paper, iij. d ...

1571
Chamberlains' Account Book I CRO: A 7(a)
p 274 *(23 October)*   30

...

Allocaciones   Item paid to the iiij weites   xxvj s viij d

...

Weavers' Account Book CRO: Acc 100/17/1   35
f 62v

...

The receytes

...

Receyvyd of the walkers   vj s viij d 40
Receyvyd of the skynners   v s

...

f 63

The paymentes

In primis ij rehearsys	ij s	
Item for dryuyng of the pagyente	v s	
Item payd to symeon	iij s iiij d	5
Item payd to Iosephe	ij s iiij d	
Item payd to Iesus	xx d	
Item payd to mary	xx d	
Item payd to Anne	xx d	
Item payd to symons clarke	ij s	10
Item payd to the ij aungeles	viij d	
Item payd to the chylde	iiij d	
Item payd for Russhes packthryd & tenterhookes & nayles	ix d ob.	
Item payd to Iames hewet for the rygoles	xx d	15
Item payd for syngyng	xvj d	
Item payd for gloves	ij s viij d	
Item payd for meate in the bocherye	ix s v d	
Item payd for breade & ale	vj s	
...		20
Item payd for settyng owt owr pagente	vj d	
Item payd for the hyer of ij beardes to harry benet	ij d	
[Item payd for a dowsyn of poyntes & bearyng owr harnys	ix d ob.	
Item payd owr quarter day for playing of the ape	viij d]	25
...		

Weavers' Rentgatherers' Book I CRO: Acc 100/18/1
f 75

...		30
Item payd for baryng the harnes on the fare day	x d ob.	
Item payd for Iern & workman fl shepp & nalles to the pagentt	xxij d	
...		
		35

AC *Cappers' Accounts* H-P: *Outlines* I
p 340

... Item, paid for mendynge the pagiand geyre, iij d; item, paid
for a yard of bokeram, xij d; item, paid for payntynge the   40

32 / fl *not cancelled*

demons mall and the Maris rolles, vj d; item, for makynge the
roles, ij d; item, paid to the players att the second stage, viij d ...

A   *Drapers' Accounts*   CRO: Acc 154
f 83 *(Receipts)*   5

...

Rs of georg batman   iij s iiij d

...

Itm pd for harnyshyng men & poyntts   xviij d

...   10

Itm payd to newman for the harnys   viij s

...

Repercyons

...

Itm pd for vj hunderyth of tylle for the pagen howse which   15
buloyd as yett   vj s

...

ff 84-5

...   20

Chargys of the Pagen

Itm payd for iij Rehersys	vj s
Itm pd for great nells for the pagyn howsse dores	x d
Itm pd for vj yards of buckeram to make the Solles Cotts & makyng them	vj s vj d 25
Itm pd for bord & ledgs for ye pagen dores	ij s vj d
Itm pd for ij hunderth vj peny nele	xij d
Itm pd ij carpenters A dayes work	xvj d
Itm for settyng the pagen outt & in	xij d
Itm for payntyng hell mouth & mendyng hyt	xvj d 30
Itm pd for Russhes candell & packthryd	viij d
Itm for Rosyn and tentr hocks & sope	vj d
Itm payd for poyntts for ye pagen	x d
Itm payd the trumpeter	xx d
Itm pd the plears for drynke	ij s 35
Itm payd for the prologe	viij d
Itm pd iij damned & iij Saved Solls	x s
Itm payd the ij wormes of Consyens	xviij d
Itm payd ij Demen	iij s iiij d
Itm payd Roo for hys cott	iiij d 40
Itm pd for iij worlds	iij s viij d
Itm payd the plears for ther suppr	iiij s
Itm for Rygalls and Synging	iiij s

Itm pd for dressyng the pagyn   ij s vj d
Itm pd for openyng and shuttyng the dores and kypyng the
wynd | xvj d
Itm pd for kepyng hell mouthe and settyng ye worlde on fyre &
blackyng ye facys   xvj d   5
Itm pd for iiij gallans of alle   xvj d
Itm pd the iiij Angells   ij s
Itm pd iij pattryarks   xviij d

                                        Som iij li. vij s

...   10

AC   *Smiths' Accounts*   H-P: *Outlines* I
      pp 337-8

      ... Paid for a lode of cley for the padgyn howse, vj d; paid for iiij   15
      sparis for the same howse, vj d; paid to the dawber and his man,
      xiiij d; paid to the | carpyntur for his worke, iiij d; paid for a
      bunche and halfe of lathe, ix d; paid for vj pennye naiylles, ij d ...

      1572   20
      Cappers' Records SC: Account Book I
      f 104

      ...
      Item payde ffor our dyner on the play Day   iij s iiij d
      ...   25

      f 104v

      The somme of ye paymentes for our pagent   iij li. xv s. j d
      ...   30

      Weavers' Account Book CRO: Acc 100/17/1
      f 63v
                              The receytes
      ...   35
      Item receyvyd of the walkers   vj s viij d
      Item receyvyd of the skynners   v s
      ...

      f 64   40
                              The paymentes
      In primis ij rehearsys   ij s
      Item for dryvyng of ye pagyente   v s

Item payd to symeon	iij s iiij d
Item payd to Iosephe	ij s iiij d
Item payd to Iesus	xx d
Item payd to mary	xx d
Item payd to Anne	xx d
Item payd to symons clarcke	ij s
Item payd to the ij angelles	viij d
Item payd to the chylde	iiij d
Item payd for packthryd & Russhes smalethryd & nayles	ix d ob.
Item payd Iames hewete for the rygoles	xx d
Item payd for syngyng	xvj d
Item payd for gloves	ij s viij d
Item payd for bochery meate	ix s v d
Item payd for bread & ale	vj s

...

Item payd for settyng owte owr pagyente	vj d

...

Item payd for ye hyer of ij beardes to harry benete	ij d

...

Weavers' Rentgatherers' Book I CRO: Acc 100/18/1
f 76

...

Item payd for baryng the harnys on the fareday	xij d

...

Item payd for a trendyll for the scaffoll	iiij d

...

A ***Drapers' Accounts*** CRO: Acc 154
f 85 *(Receipts)*

...

Rs of george batman	iij s iiij d

...

ff 86-7

...

pd for beryng harnes & poynts at ye fayre	xvj d

...

pd for tyllyng the pagen howse	iij s iiij d

...

pd to gulson for hys Sylver gownd	v s

...

pd for Carryge of iij polles to the pagen howse	iij d	
pd for the Same polles whon agayne	iiij d	

...

The chargys of the pagen

Payd for iij Rehersys	vj s	5
pd for A new whelle	vj s viij d	
pd for Cartt clowtt and neles	x d	
pd for a pounde of Sope	iiij d	
pd for ij clowtts & a streke for ye whele	iiij s x d	
pd for Settyng ye pagen owtt & in	xij d	10
pd for Rosyn Rysshes tenter hock & candell	viij d	
pd for Alle when the plears drese them	iiij d	
pd for poynts and lasys	ix d	
pd for the Prologe	viij d	
pd to god	iij s iiij d	15
pd the iij saved Solles	v s	
pd the iiij Angells	ij s	
pd the ij wormes of Consyens	xviij d	
pd the iij damned Solles	v s	
pd the iij pattryarks	xviij d	20
pd for [Syngyng] Synggyng	ij s	
Pd for the Rygalls	ij s	
pd the ij demen	iij s iiij d	
pd for the iij worldes	iij s viij d	
pd for dryvyng ye pagen	ij s vj d	25
pd for openyng and Shuttyng ye dores & dressyng ye pagen	ij s	
pd for cords for the dores	ij d	
pd to the Trumpeter	ij s	
pd for kepyng hell mouthe	x d|	
pd the plears for drynck	ij s	30
pd for alle	ix d	
pd the plears for ther Supper	iiij s	
pd for blackyng ther facys	vj d	
pd for payntyng hell mouth	xij d	
pd Robart Cotton for hys gloves	iij d	35
pd for mendyng ye demens cotts & hose & the farryshe hatt	xxij d	
pd for ij pound of heare for ye Same	xviij d	
pd John foxall for the demen hose	vj d	
Som iij li. x s iiij d		40

The Chargys of iiij new Gownes and iiij Surplesses

Payd to Wyllm walden for stufe	xliiij s j d	

Payd to John grene for canvas   lj s iiij d

pd to John gosnell for furryng the gowns   xx s

pd for makyng the gownes   x s

pd for makyng the Surplesse   xvj d

pd for wryttyng the buck   x s   5

                         Som vj li. xvj s ix d

...

AC   **Smiths' Accounts**   H-P: *Illustrations*

       p 55*   10

... charges for the padgand ... Paid for canvys for Jwdas coote, ij s; paid for the makyng of hit, x d; paid to too damsselles, xij d; paid for a poollye and an yron hoke and mendyng the padgand, xvj d; paid for cowntters and a lase and pwyntes for Jwdas, iij d ...   15

1573

Chamberlains' Account Book I   CRO: A 7(a)

p 277 *(26 October)*

...   20

The   Item payde to the iiij^{or} weites   xxvj s viij d.

allowances

...

Cappers' Records   SC: Account Book I

f 105v   25

...

paid to ye carpenter for mending the pagent howse dore   vj d

...

paid to ye players at ye first rehears   xx d

Spent ye same mornynge at mr waldens of certayne of ye   30

company which came to the rehearse   xviij d

...

Payed to ye players at ye second Rehearse   xviij d

...

paid for harnes, & to ye berers, & for poynt on ye fayre   35

day   xviij d

f 106* *(Choice Day)*

...

paid the same daye to ye mynstrells   xviij d   40

...

Paymentes and charges about the pagent.

paid to mr pyxley for tymber & bords for ye pagent
Scaffolde   ij s vij d

paid for a pece of tymber for an axeltrie wherof halfe is to spare
in mychael Tysals howse   ij s iiij d   5

paid for ij clowtes for ye axeltre, & for nayles for it, ye pagent, &
ye skaffolde   xv d

paid for sope for all ye wheeles   iiij d

paid to ij carpenters for ij day worke   iij s

paid for ij skaynes of sylke which mended the pall, and pylates   10
cloke   iiij d

paid for mendyng pylates cloke mawdlens cote, angels, surplis, &
ye maries Roles   xij d

paid for tenter hookes, and small nayles   iiij d

Spent of our selves & ye somner when we attended. ij dayes on   15
ye carpenters   viij d

for yron worke about ye axeltre & a clamp   ix d

Som xij s vij d
more charges in the pagent

paid to the mynstrell   viij d   20

paid for dressing ye pagent   vj d

paid to ye syngers   xvj d

paid for our supper on ye play day for our selves goodman
mawpas, ye mynstrell, ye dresser of ye pagent, & ye somner &
hys wyfe   iiij s   25

paid for balls   xij d

paid to pylate   iiij s iiij d

paid to ye iiij knyghtes   vj s viij d

paid to god   xx d

ij byshops   ij s   30

preface   iiij d

for harnes   xvj d

Spryte of god   xvj d

paid to ye demon   xvj d

Angels   viij d   35

iij maryes   ij s

paid for Russhes for ye pagent   iiij d

the players supper, & drynkyng   iij s iiij d

for drynkes in ye pagent   xj d

ffor dryvinge ye pagent, & setting it out & in, to ye   40
carpenter   vj s viij d

paid for glooves, & poyntes   iiij s vj d
paid for hyre, & mendynge of pylates clubbe   iiij d
                         Som xlv s. iij d

Carpenters' Account Book II CRO: Acc 3/2   5
f 198 col a
                    paymentes ffor the whole yere
Item paid to the pynners and cowpers ffor iij yeres   xxx s
...
paid ffor skowrynge off owre harnysses at ij tymes   iiij s vj d 10
paid ffor cariage off ij harnysses on the ffare ffryday and ffor
poyntes   vj d
                    chargis off owre ladye dynner
...
Item paid to a mynstrell   vj d 15
...

Weavers' Account Book CRO: Acc 100/17/1
f 64v
...   20
                         The Receytes
...
Item receyvyd of the walkers   vj s viij d
Item receyvyd of the skynners   v s
...   25

f 65
                         The paymentes
In primis ij rehearsys   ij s
Item for dryuyng of the pagyente   v s   30
Item payd to symeon   iij s iiij d
Item payd to Iosephe   ij s iiij d
Item payd to Iesus   xx d
Item payd to mary   xx d
Item payd to Anne   xx d   35
Item payd to symons clarke   ij s
Item payd to the ij angelles   viij d
Item payd to the chyld   iiij d
Item payd for packthryd Russhes smalethryd & nayles   ix d
Item payd Iames hewet for playng on the rygoles   iiij d 40
Item payd for syngyng   xvj d
Item payd for gloves   ij s viij d

Item payd for bocherye meate x s
Item payd for bread & ale vj s
...
Item payd for settyng out owr pagente vj d
... 5

Weavers' Rentgatherers' Book I CRO: Acc 100/18/1
f 77v
...
Item paide to the minstrels xvj d 10
...
Item paide for mendinge the pageand x d
Item paid for bearinge the harnes and poyntees on the feare
day x d
... 15

A *Drapers' Accounts* CRO: Acc 154
f 87 *(Receipts)*
...
Rs of georg batman iij s iiij d 20
...

ff 88-9 *(Payments)*
...
         Chargys of the pagyn howse 25
Payd to wyllyam Styfe carpenter l s iiij d
pd for ij lodes of Sande xij d
pd for ij lodes of cley xij d
pd for ij qr and A strycke of lyme x s iij d
pd for Stones to grondsyll wall xx d 30
pd for grondsyllyng xviij d
pd for lathe nayle & vj d nayle viij s vj d
pd for Sparrys xviij d
pd for bords and ledgys v s vj d
pd for A standard to beare the dore iiij d 35
pd for makyng the gutter & the dore xvj d
pd for v hundryth of tylles v s
pd to the tyler x s iiij d
pd for viij peny nayls vj d|
pd to Robynson for thatthng & dawbyng v s 40
pd to the plumer viij s vj d
pd to bevelye for Iron work viij s vj d
pd for Carryng the loade to & fro vj d

pd for A hyng & a hach	v d
pd for takyng downe the tyles	iij s iiij d
pd for studdyng pyples howse	iij d
pd for tylyng pyples howse	xiiij d
pd for viij hundryth hait lath	iiij s
pd for vj C Sappe lath	ij s vj d
pd for Settyng in & out ye pagen	xij d

som vj li. xiij s xj d

Chargys of the pagyn

payd to god	iij s iiij d
pd for the prolog	viij d
pd iij savyd Solles	v s
pd ij wormes of Consyans	xviij d
pd iiij Angels	ij s
pd ij patryarks	xviij d
pd the Syngers	ij s
pd the ij demons	iij s iiij d
pd for the Rygalls	ij s
pd for iij worlds	iij s viij d
pd for dryvng the pagyn	ij s ix d
pd for Shuttyng the dore dresyng the pagen & kepyng the wynde	xvj d
pd for the plears Suppar	iiij s
pd for kepyng hell mouth	x d
pd for alle & blackyng there facys	xvj d
pd iij damned Solles	v s
pd for alle at the Swane dore	ij s
pd for Settyng in & out ye pagyn	xij d
pd for a payre of gloves	iiij d
pd for poyntts	xviij d
pd for Rysshes Sope Rosyn tentr hocks & candell	xij d
pd for harnyssyng of men at ye fayre	xvj d
pd for iij Rehearsys	vj s
pd the trompeter	ij s
pd for alle at battmans	iiij d
pd for alle at the pagen	xij d

Som lvj s xj d

...

AC *Smiths' Accounts* Sharp: *Dissertation*
p 36*

...

pd for pleyng of petur	xvj d

pd for Judas p*arte*   ix d
pd for ij damsylls   xij d
pd to the deman   vj d
pd to iiij men that bryng yn herod   viij d
pd to Fawston for hangyng Judas   iiij d   5
pd to Fawsto*n* for Coc-croyng   iiij d
pd for Mr. Wygson's gowne   viij d
...

1574   10
Chamberlains' Account Book I CRO: A 7(a)
p 279 *(26 October)*
...

paymentes & Item to the Wayt*es* for theire Wagys   xxvj s viij d.
Allowances ...   15

Chamberlains' and Wardens' Account Book II CRO: A 7(b)
p 1 *(2 December) (Chamberlains)*
...
Item to the iiij°ʳ Waytes for their Lyue*ries* & theire   20
Wages   iiij li

p 2* *(Chamberlains)*
...
Item p*ai*d to ye lorde Munngye his plears   iij s iiij d   25
...
Item p*ai*d Mr Savage for his ent*er*lud playes   xl s

...
Item p*ai*d the last of Marche to mr Savage for an oracion made at
the Scoole before M*ai*ste*r* Maior & his bretherne   x s   30
Item p*ai*d to the Earle of Darbyes players   v s
Item p*ai*d to the lord Sanndos Bearewarde   iij s iiij d
...
Item p*ai*d to S*ir* ffoulke Grevile Bearewarde   xiij s iiij d
...   35
Item p*ai*d to the Earle of Leic*ester* Bearwarde   xiij s iiij d
...

p 3 *(Chamberlains)*
...   40
Item p*ai*d to the Eearle of Darbyes Bearward   v s
...
Item p*ai*d ye 29 of August to ye Earle of Essexe players   xx s

Item p*ai*d [ye] to the lorde Chamberlain players   xx s

...

Item p*ai*d to the Earle of Essex Musyssions   ij s vj d

...

Item paid to the Earle of leic*ester* musissions   ij s vj d   5

...

Rental Roll I CRO: unnumbered*

...

Item . the gyrdlers for ye pagend howse   iiij d   10

...

Cappers' Records SC: Account Book I
f 107v col a

...   15

Receaved off that money that was Receaued off the cardmakers
and sadlers   xiij s iiij d
Receaued off the walkers   vj s
Receaued off the skynners   iiij s
Receaued off the paynters and Ioyners   iij s iiij d   20

...

col b

...

spent vppon the heade off the company at christoffores bromlers   25
when we sewed ffor the money off the cardmakers and
sadlers   ij s vj d
spent at mr smythes vppon the heade off the company when we
sewed ffor the same money   xvj d
spent vppon the head off the company *with* the maisters off the   30
cardmakers and sadlers when we Receaued owre money   iij s
paide to Ihon hoppers ffor the hyre off iiij harnysses ffor the
ffaire ffryday   ij s
payde ffor wearynge off the same iiij harnisses and ffor
poyntes   x d   35

...

paide to iij mynstrels on the dynner day   xij d

...

paide to michell tysall ffor goinge to mr parffris and to the myll
at the Requeste off the company   x d   40

...

f 108

charges ffor the pagen

payd for the ij Reherses	iij s ij d	5
spent at mr waldyns at the ffirste Reherse	xij d	
paide to Ihon hoppors ffor hire off iiij harnises	xvj d	
paid at the settyng fforthe off pagyn	vj d	
payd ffor great nayles ffor the wheles	xviij d	
paide ffor one hundrethe off nayles	ix d	10
payd ffor one thele	viij d	
paide ffor one Iron clowte	ij d	
paide ffor iij claspes off Iron and ffor one Iron ffor the skafforde	ij s viij d	
paide to the carpenter ffor a day and halffe	xvj d	15
spent when we gave attendaunce at the Reparyng off the pagen	viij d	
paide ffor dryncke in the pagyn	xj d	
paide the players to drynck betwene the stages	ix d	
paide ffor balles	xij d	20
paide ffor small corde	j d	
paide ffor wyer howkes	j d	
paide ffor wasshyng the angells surplisses	j d	
paide ffor the players sopper	ij s viij d	
paide ffor ower owne supper	iiij s	25
payd ffor dressynge the pagyn	vj d	
paide ffor dryvyng the pagyn	vj s viij d	
paide ffor poyntes and gloves	iiij s	
paide to the mynstrell	viij d	
paide to pylate	iiij s iiij d	30
paide ij bisshoppes	ij s	
paide ffor the prologe	iiij d	
paide ffor god	xx d	
paide the spirite off god	xvj d	
paid iij maries	ij s	35
paid the iiij knyghtes	vj s viij d	
paide ij angells	viij d	
paide the devell	xvj d	
payde to the syngers	xx d	
lviij s x d		40

...

Carpenters' Account Book II CRO: Acc 3/2
f 200 col a
...

Item payde to the pynners and cowpers   x s
...   5

Weavers' Account Book CRO: Acc 100/17/1
f 66

         pamentees all the yere
Item paide for too rehersses   ij s   10
Item paide to simion   iij s iiij d
Item paid to Iosiff   ij s iiij d
Item paide to mary   xx d
Item paide to ane   xx d
Item paid to Iesus   xx d   15
Item paid to simiones clarke   ij s
Item paid to the ij angeles   [ij] viij d
Item paid to the Childe   iiij d
Item paid for russis pacthrid sope and nailes   jx d
Item paid for driving the pagand to the Iurnemen   v s   20
...
Item paid at the setting out of the pagand   vj d
Item paid for bred & alle   vj s
Item paid for bucherey meate   x s
...   25
Item paid for gloues   iij s
Item paid for singinge in the pagand   xvj d
Item paid for playing on the rigoldes   iiij d
         som ys xlvij s xj d
...   30

Weavers' Rentgatherers' Book I CRO: Acc 100/18/1
f 79
...
Item paid for bearing the harnes & poyntees on the fayer   35
daye   x d
...
Item paid for paving at the pagandhous   xiij d
...

A *Drapers' Accounts* CRO: Acc 154
f 90 *(Receipts)*

...

Rs of georg batman   iij s iiij d

...   5

f 91

...

The wholle Chargys of owre pagyn ys   iij li. ij s ij d

...   10

A C *Smiths' Accounts* H-P: *Outlines* I
p 340

... Paid for pleynge of Petur, xvj d; paid for Jwdas, ix d; paid for   15
ij damselles, xij d; paid to the deman, vj d; paid to iiij men to
bryng yn Herode, viij d; paid to Fawston for hangyng Jwdas and
coc-croyng, viij d; paid for Herodes gowne, viij d ...

1575   20
Chamberlains' and Wardens' Account Book II CRO: A 7(b)
p 9 *(25 October) (Chamberlains)*

...

Item payde to the iiij^{or} Waites   xxvj s viij d

...   25

p 6 *(28 November) (Wardens)*

...

Item paid to the iiij^{or} Weightes for theire Liueres &
Wagys   iiij li 30

...

p 7* *(Wardens)*

...

Item paid to Iohn Walland the lord Comptons Bearward   x s 35

...

Item paid to the Earle of Darbyes Bearward   x s
Item paid to the lord of hunsdonns Musissions   iiij s iiij d

...

Item paid to the Earle of Essex gesters   ij s

...

Item paid to two of the quenes Gard yat Came to survey for her
Graces progresse   vj s viij d

...   5

Item paid to the quenes Trumpeters   xl s

...

p 8 *(Wardens)*

                                                                                10

Also they do aske further allowaunce of money by theym payde
to the Earle of leicester [Musissions] Bearwarde   iij s iiij d
Item paid to the Earle of worcetters Mussissions   v s

...

Item paid to the lorde of hunsdons Musissions   xij d   15
Item paid to the Earle of leicesters players   xxvj s viij d

...

Item paid to the Earle of leicesters drumplayers & ij of hys fluet
players   v s

...   20

Item paid to the lord Chamberlayns players   x s
Item to the Earle of Warwickes players   vj s viij d
Item paid to the Earle of Essex players   vj s viij d

...

Item paid to the quenes Bearward   x s   25
Item paid for a base pyppe for the Waytes   vij s

...

Receipt Book CRO: A 17
p 29 *(7 June)*   30

...

Received of the Companyes ₍ 'the.. 7 . of Iune Anno predicto' 7
of money Which they shulde pay to the pagentes tobe imployed
to the poore   xj li. xviij s.

                                                                                35

Payments Out Book CRO: A 16
p 29 *(2 July)*

...

Item payde to Mr Iohn Saunders ... for a yooke of Oxen & xxti

32 / *second 7 not cancelled*

Sheppe yeven to my lorde of leic*ester*   xxj li. vj s viij d

...

A C *City Annals* Bodl: MS Top. Warwickshire d.4
     f 25v*

...

The Queene   Simon Cotton butcher maior 1574 & ended in 1575 ... In his
came to   yeare the Queene came to Killingworth castle againe & recreated
Killingworth herselfe there xij or 13 daies. Att w*hi*ch time Coventry men went
castle   to make her merry with there play of hockes Twesday & for
             there paines had a reward & venison also to make y*em* merry .
A plague in And this yeare there was a great plague in coventrey but especially
coventry.   in Bablacke for there died out of y*at* place xxty p*er*sons younge
             & old. /

...

Cappers' Records SC: Account Book I
f 109 col a *(Receipts)*

...

Receaued off the occupacion of walkers   vj s
Receaued off the occupacion off skynner   iiij s
Receaued off the Ioyners and paynters   iij s iiij d
                         the some is xiij s iiij d

...

col b *(Payments)*

...

paide to the players ffor one Reherse   xviij d
paide ffor breakffaste ffor the company at the same
Reherse   xviij d
paide ffor hyrynge off one harnys and skowrynge the
same   vj d
paide ffor caryage off ij harnysses and ffor poyntes   vj d
payde to m*aiste*r maiore   xxij s viij ⟨.⟩

...

Carpenters' Account Book II CRO: Acc 3/2
f 202
                    Receates off bretherne

...

Receauede off pynners and cowpers   xviij d

...

f 202v *(Payments)*

...

paide to the pynners and cowpers   x s

...

                                                                              5

Weavers' Account Book CRO: Acc 100/17/1
f 67*

The paymentes

In p*r*imis for one rehearse   xij d
Item payde vnto master mayor for the pagyauntes   xxij s   10

...

Item pay<i>d</i> for poyn<i>tes</i> to the harnes   j d ob.

...

A   *Drapers' Accounts* CRO: Acc 154   15
f 91* *(Receipts)*

...

Rs of georg batman   iij s iiij d

...

                                                                             20

f 92   *(Payments)*

...

payd for the pagen   xxvj s viij d

...

pd to Symon newman   viij s   25

...

pd for a Cord and medyng the pagen   vj d
pd for beryng harnys at the fayre   xv d

...

                                                                             30

Robert Laneham's Letter STC: 15191
pp 32-8*

...

Hok Tuisday   And heertoo folloed az good a sport (me thooght) prezented
by the   in an historicall ku, by certain good harted men of Couentree,   35
Couentree men. my Lordes neighboors thear: who understanding amoong them
ye thing that coold not bee hidden from ony: hoow carefull and
studious hiz honor waz, that by all pleazaunt recreasions her
highnes might best fynd her self wellcom, and bee made gladsum
and mery (the groundworke indeede and foundacion of hiz   40
Lordships myrth and gladnesse of vs all) made petition that
they moought renu noow their olld storiall sheaw: Of argument

Florileg.li
I.fol.300.

how the Danez whylom heere in a troubloous seazon wear for
quietnesse born withall & suffeard in peas, that anon by outrage
& importabl insolency, abuzing both Ethelred the king then and
all estates euerie whear byside: at the greuoous complaint &
coounsell of Huna the kings chieftain in warz, on Saint Brices   5
night. Ann. Dom. 1012.│(Az the book sayz) that falleth yeerely
on the thirteenth of Nouember wear all dispatcht and the Ream
rid. And for becauz the matter mencioneth how valiantly our
English women for looue of their cuntree behaued themseluez:
expressed in actionz & rymez after their maner, they thought it   10
moought mooue sum myrth to her Maiestie the rather.

The thing said they iz grounded on story, and for pastime
woont too bee plaid in oour Citee yeerely: without ill exampl of
mannerz, papistry, or ony superstition: and elz did so occupy the
heads of a number, that likely inoough woold haue had woorz   15
meditationz: had an aunoient beginning and a long continuauns:
tyll noow of late laid dooun, the knu no cauz why onless it wear
by the zeal of certain theyr Preacherz: men very commendabl for
their behauiour and learning, & sweet in their sermons, but
sumwhat too sour in preaching awey theyr pastime: wisht   20
therefore, that az they shoold continu their good doctrine in
pulpet, so, for matters of pollicy & gouernauns of the Citie, they
woold permit them to the Mair and Magistratez: and seyed by
my feyth, Master Martyn they │woold make theyr humbl peticion
untoo her highnes, that they might haue theyr playz vp agayn.   25

Captain
Cox.

But aware, keep bak, make room noow, heer they cum. And
fyrst captin Cox, an od man I promiz yoo: by profession a Mason,
and that right skilfull, very cunning in fens, and hardy az Gawin,
for hiz tonsword hangs at his tablz eend: great ouersight hath he
in matters of storie: For az for king Arthurz book, Huon of   30
Burdeaus, The foour suns of Aymon, Beuys of Hampton, The
squyre of lo degree, The knight of courtesy, and the Lady Faguell,
Frederik of Gene, Syr Eglamoour, Sir Tryamoour, Syr Lamwell,
Syr Isenbras, Syr Gawyn, Olyuer of the Castl, Lucres and
Eurialus, Virgils life, The castl of Ladiez. The wido Edyth, The   35
King & the Tanner. Frier Rous, Howleglas, Gargantua, Robinhood,
Adambel, Clim of the clough & William of cloudesley, The Churl
& the Burd, The seauen wise Masters, The wife lapt in a Morels
skin, The sak full of nuez. The seargeaunt that became a Fryar,
Skogan, Collyn cloout. The Fryar & the boy, Elynor Rumming,   40
and the Nutbrooun maid, with many moe │then I rehearz heere:
I beleeue hee haue them all at hiz fingers endz.

Then in Philosophy both morall & naturall, I think he be az
naturally ouerseen: beside poetrie and Astronomie, and oother
hid sciencez, as I may gesse by the omberty of hiz books: whearof
part az I remember, the Sheperdzkalender. The Ship of Foolz,
Danielz dreamz, the booke of Fortune, *Stans puer ad mensam*,   5
the hy wey to the Spitlhouse, Iulian of Brainsfords testament,
the castle of Loue, the booget of Demaunds, the hundred Mery
talez, the book of Riddels, the Seauen sororz of wemen, the
prooud wiues Pater noster, the Chapman of a peniwoorth of Wit:
Beside hiz auncient playz. Yooth & charitee, Hikskorner, Nugize,   10
Impacient pouerty, and heerwith doctor Boords breuiary of
health. What shoold I rehearz heer, what a bunch of ballets &
songs all auncient: Az Broom broom on hil. So wo iz me begon,
troly lo. Ouer a whinny Meg. Hey ding a ding. Bony lass vpon a
green. My bony on gaue me a bek. By a bank az I lay: and a   15
hundred more, he hath fair wrapt vp in Parchment and bound
with a whipcord.

And az for Allmanaks of antiquitee, (a | point for Ephemerides)
I weene hee can sheaw from Iasper Laet of Antwarp vnto
Nostradam of Frauns, and thens vnto oour Iohn Securiz of   20
Salsbury. To stay ye no longer heerin I dare say hee hath az fair a
library for theez sciencez, & az many goodly monuments both in
proze & poetry & at afternoonz can talk az much without book,
az ony Inholder betwixt Brainford and Bagshot, what degree
soeuer he be.   25

Beside thiz in the field a good Marshall at musters: of very
great credite & trust in the toun heer, for he haz been chozen
Alecunner many a yeere, when hiz betterz haue stond by: & euer
quited himself with such estimation, az yet too the tast of a cup
of Nippitate, hiz iudgement will be taken aboue the best in the   30
parish, be hiz noze near so read.

Captain Cox cam marching on valiantly before, cleen trust &
gartered aboue the knee, all fresh in a veluet cap (master
Goldingam lent it him) floorishing with hiz tonswoord, and
another fensmaster with him: thus in the foreward making room   35
for the rest. After them proudly prickt on formost, the danish
launsknights on horsbak, and then the English: each with their
®The Couentree   allder poll martially in their hand. Eeuen at the first entree the
play.   meeting waxt sumwhat warm: that by and by kindled with corage
abothsidez, gru from a hot skirmish vnto a blazing battail: first   40
by speare and shield, outragious in their racez az ramz at their rut,
with furious encoounterz that togyther they tumbl too the dust,
sumtime hors and man: and after fall too it with sworde & target,

good bangz a both sidez: the fight so ceassing, but the battail not
so ended, folloed the footmen, both the hostez ton after toother:
first marching in ranks: then warlik turning, the*n* fro*m* ranks into
squadrons, then in too trianglz fro*m* that intoo rings, & so winding
oout again: A valiant captain of great prowez az fiers az a fox   5
assauting a gooz, waz so hardy to giue the first stroke: then get
they grisly togyther: that great waz the actiuitee that day too be
seen thear a both sidez: ton very eager for purchaz of pray, toother
vtterly stoout for redemption of libertie: thus, quarrell enflamed
fury a both sidez. Twise the Danes had ye better, but at the last   10
conflict, beaten doun, ouercom and many led captiue for triumph
by our English weemen.

   This waz the effect of this sheaw, that I az it waz handled,
made mooch matter of good pastime: brought all indeed intoo
the great coourt, een vnder her highnes windo too haue been seen: 15
but (az vnhappy it waz for the bride) that cam thither too soon,
(and yet waz it a four a clok). For her highnes beholding in the
chamber delectabl dauncing indeed: and heerwith the great throng
and vnrulines of the people, waz cauz that this solemnitee of
Brideale, & dauncing had not the full muster waz hoped for: and   20
but a littl of the Couentree plea her highnes also saw: commaunded
thearfore on the Tuisday folloing to haue it ful oout: az
accordingly it waz prezented, whearat her Maiestie laught well:
they wear the iocunder, and so mooch the more becauz her highnes
had giuen them too buckes and fiue marke in mony to make   25
mery togyther: they prayed for her Maiesty, long, happily to
reign & oft to cum thither that oft they moought see heer: &
what, reioycing vpon their ampl reward, and what, triumphing
vpon the good acceptauns: they vaunted their play waz neuer so
dignified, nor euer any players afore so beatified.   30
...

1576
Chamberlains' and Wardens' Account Book II CRO: A 7(b)
p 11 *(25 October) (Chamberlains)*   35
...

Also for the wagys of the iiij^or waytes   xxvj s viij d
...

p 12 *(26 November) (Wardens)*   40
...

Item p*ai*d to the waytes theire wagys   iiij li
...

Item paid more to Newman for dressinge the harnes at the
ffayre   xxiij s iiij d

...

Item paid to the Earle of Worcester plears   vj s viij d
Item paid to Sir ffoulke Grevile Bearwarde   x s   5

...

Item paid to the Earle of Essex plears   x s

...

p 13   10

Item paid to the Earle of Essex Musicions   ij s vj d

...

Payments Out Book CRO: A 16   15
p 31* *(21 May)*

...

Item paid to Wyllyam Walden the xxjth day of
Marche Anno xviij° Elizabeth Regine towardes   vj li.
the reparacions of the Mercers padgyn ˄ ˈhowsesˈ   20

...

AC *City Annals* Sharp: *Dissertation*
pp 11-12*

...   25

Thomas Nicklyn Mayor. - This yeare the said maior caused hoc
twesday | wherby is mencioned a overthrowe of the Danes by the
inhabitants of this Citie to be againe set up and shewed forthe to
his great commendacion and the Cities great comoditie which
said hoc twesday was the yeare before plaide before the Quene at   30
Kenelworth in the tyme of her progresse by the commaundment
of the Quenes Counsell.

This year the Pageants or Hox tuesday that had been laid down 8
years were played again.   35

...

Cappers' Records SC: Account Book I
f 111 col a *(Receipts)*

...   40

Receaue off the skynners   iiij s
Receaued off the walkers   vj s

Receaued off the Ioyners   iij s iiij d

...

col b *(Payments)*

...   5

paid ffor skowringe ij harnises ffor the ffaire day   xiiij d
spent on the masters off skynners the walkers and Ioyners at
the Receate off their money   x d

...

                                                                   10

f 111v col a

...

paide ffor hyre off ij harnisses on oxe tewsday   viij d
payde ffor wearynge the same harnysses and ffor
poyntes   viij d   15
payde ffor wearynge ij harnysses on the ffare daye and ffor
poyntes   vj d

...

paide to the mynstrells and syngers   xx d

...   20

                    chargis off the pagyn

payde to the players at the ffirste Reherse   xviij d
spente at Mr waldyns at the same Reherse   ij s
paid to the players at the seconde Reherse   xx d
spente at wyllyam ashburnes at the same Reherse   ij s   25
spente at the setting ffowthe off the pagyn   vj d
paid to mr pyxley for bordes and ledgis   iij s
paid ffor carte nayles and other nayles   ij s vj d
paid ij carpenters ffor one dayes worke   xviij d
payd ffor ij yardes and halffe off bvckram to make the spirits   30
cote   ij s j d
paid ffor makynge the same cote   viij d
paid ffor mendynge the maries heare   viij d
paid [ffor] ffor a dore and hyngis and nayles behynd the
pagyn   xij d   35
payd ffor mendynge pylates clvbbe   iij d
paid ffor dressyng the pagyn   vj d
payde ffor poyntes ffor owre harnys   xij d
paid ffor gloves   iij s vj d
payd ffor sope ffor the wheles   iiij d   40
paid ffor dryvynge the pagyn   vj s viij d
paid ffor taynter howkes and laeth nayles   ij d ob.

paid ffor small corde   j d ob.

paide ffor iiij Iron clyppes ffor the wheles and shvttinge the
howkes ffor the ladder   ij s

payd ffor payntyng the bisshoppes myters and the devells
clvbbe   ij s   5

paid ffor mendynge the devells cote and makynge the devells
heade   iiij s vj d

paymentes

paide ffor Russhes   iiij d

paide ffor hyre off iiij harnisses and weppons   xx d   10

paid ffor packe thride   ob

paid ffor balls   xij d

paide ffor wasshinge ij svrplisses   j d ob

spente at Reparynge the pagyn   xij d

paide ffor a skeane off grene silke and mendinge pylates   15
gowne   vj d

paide ffor a skeane off sylke and mendinge the palles   vj d

the some xliiij s [x d] ˌiiij dˌ

paymentes to the players

paide ffor the prologe   iiij d   20

paid god and dede man   xx d

paide the ij bisshoppes   ij s

paide pylate   iiij s iiij d

paide the iiij knyghtes   vj s viij d

paide the spirite off god   xvj d   25

paide iij maries   ij s

paide ij angells   viij d

paide the devell   xvj d

paid the players ffor theire svpper   ij s viij d

paide pylate the bisshoppes and knyghtes to drynck betwene the   30
stagis   ix d

paide ffor dryncke in the pagyn   x d

paide the syngers   ij s

paide the mynstrell   x d

paide ffor owre supper   iiij s   35

the some is xxxj s v d

...

Carpenters' Account Book II C R O: Acc 3/2
f 204 col b   40

paymentes

paid to the pynners and cowpers   x s

...

paid ffor wearyng off ij harnyssis and ffor poyntes   vj d

...

Mercers' Account Book CRO: Acc 15
f 12v* *(6 December)*   5

...

Item the vjth day of the moneth of december Anno domini 1576
Thomas massy vpholstre is admyttd in to the ffeloeship &
company & hathe promysed [⟨.⟩] to the mastures & is consented
to gyve for his ffreedom ʿthereforeʾ the Somme of xxx s Lawful   10
moneys / In consyderacon of a yeres Service & more vnserved of
his aprentyship / as by his Indentures then showed dyd apeare /
& hathe promysed to paye xx s therof on St Ihons daye next
ffolloyng / & the other x s at mydsomer next comyng, promising
them to occupye his onlye Trade of vpholstrye   15

By me Thomas masse

Weavers' Account Book CRO: Acc 100/17/1   20
f 68
The paymentes

In primis . ij . rehersys	ij s
Item for dryvyng of ye pagyaunte	v s
Item payd to Symeon	iij s iiij d 25
Item payd to Iosephe	ij s iiij d
Item payd to Anne	xx d
Item payd to symeons clarcke	ij s
Item payd to mary	xx d
Item payd to Iesus	xx d 30
Item payd to the ij Angelles	viij d
Item payd to the chylde	iiij d
Item payd for syngynge	xvj d
Item payd for gloues	iij s
Item payd for playing on the Rygoles	iiij d 35
Item payd for brede & ale	vj s ix d
Item payd for Russhes packthryd soppe & nayles	ix d
Item payd for bochery meate	x s vj d
Item payd for ij beardes & a cappe	vj d

...   40

Item payd for poinctes & for beryng ye harnys vpon hockes
tewesday   x d

...

Item payd at ye settyng owt of ye pagyaunte to ye
Iorneymen   vj d
Item expencys at makenestes the same day   iiij d
...
                                                                              5

Weavers' Rentgatherers' Book I CRO: Acc 100/18/1
f 80 *(Choice Day)*
...
Item payd for bearyng harnys & for poynctes   x d
...   10
Item payd to the mynstreles   xvj d
...

A   *Drapers' Accounts* CRO: Acc 154
     f 93 *(Receipts)*   15
...
Rs of georg batman   iij s iiij d
...

     f 94 *(Payments)*   20
...
payd for beryng harnes apon hocks Tewysdaye   ij s
payd for poyntts for the Same   iiij d
...
payd for beryng of harnys one fayre frydaye   xij d   25
payd more for poyntts   iiij d
...
Payd for the Chargys of owre pagyn   iiij li. viij s vj d
...
                                                                              30
A   *Drapers' Ordinance* CRO: Acc 99/6/1
     f 1* *(9 November)*

A True Copy of a Survey & Terran made of all the Lands &
Tenements of & belonging to the Company and Fellowship of   35
Drapers of & in the City of Coventry the Ninth day of November
in the Eighteenth Year of the Reign of our Soveraign. Lady
Queen Elizabeth Queen of England and France & Ireland &c.
...
                                                                              40
     f 4v
...
A Pagent House in the Same Street upon the South Side of the

Sold to
Richard
Bancks

Same Street containing in breadth on the Street Side six yard. &
a half, Howsing 2 Bays with a Shoare & a Garden in breadth at
the over End 6 yards & a half, and at the ne⟨...⟩ End 3 yards in
breadth, in Leng⟨...⟩ bounding East upon the M⟨...⟩ upon Mr
Smallwood, butting South⟨...⟩ Whitefriar Lane   5

AC   *Smiths' Accounts* H-P: *Outlines* I
p 338

... Spent at Mr. Sewelles of the company about the pavynge of   10
the pajen house, vj d; payd for the pavynge of the pagen house,
xxij d; payd for a lode of pybeles, xij d; for a lode sande,
vj d ...

— Sharp: *Dissertation*   15
p 20 fn h
...
Spent on the companye after we had hard þe second
Reherse   ij d
                                                                                     20
p 21
...
pd for sent marye hall to reherse there   ij d
...
                                                                                     25
p 36
...
ffor the gybbyt of Jeȝie   xviij d
...
                                                                                     30
1577
Chamberlains' and Wardens' Account Book II CRO: A 7(b)
p 15 *(29 October)* *(Chamberlains)*
...
Also for the wagys of the iiij^{or} waytes   xxvj s viij d   35
...

p 17 *(23 November)* *(Wardens)*
...
paid to the Earle of Leicester Bearward   vj s viij d   40
...
Paid to my *Lord* Deleways plaiers   iij s iiij d
...

paid to the Queenes Bearward	iij s iiij d	
...		
paid to Sir foulk Gryvilles Bereward	xij s iiij d	
...		
Also paid to my Lord Staffordes players	v s	5
...		
paid for A present sent to Sir Iames Craffes controler of the Quenes maiesties house to the beare	xij s iiij d	
...		
paid to my Lord Chamberlyns players	x s	10
...		
Paid to the bearward of Pales Garden	x s	
...		

p 18 *(Wardens)*   15

...

paid to the Lord of Esseckes musitions	ij s vj d	
...		
paid to the Earle of Bathes players	vj s viij d	
paid to the Earle of Bathes Trompeters	iij s iiij d	20
...		
paid to the Lord Clintons players	x s	
paid more for paynting & gilding two poleaxes & staves	xij d	
paid to the Counties of Essex players	x s	
...		25
paid for A Drumer to the comissioners at the generall muster	xx s	
...		

p 19 *(Wardens)*   30

...

paid to the foure waites for their wages	iiij li	
...		

Cappers' Records SC: Account Book I   35
f 113 *(Receipts)*

...

Receaued of the masters off the walkers	vj s	
Receaued of the masters off the skynners	iiij s	
Receaued off the masters off the Ioyners	iij s iiij d	40
...		

f 113v *(Payments)*

...

paide to the mynstrells	xx d

...

spente on the masters off walkers, the skynners and Ioyners	vj d	5
paide ffor hyre off ij harnisses on the ffaire daye	xij d	
paide ffor wearynge off the same harnisses and poyntes	vj d	

...

chargis ffor the pagin

paid ffor the ffirste Reherse	xviij d	10
spent on the companye at the same	ij s	
paide at the seconde Reherse to the plaiers	xx d	
spente on the company	ij s	
spente at settinge fowthe off the pagyn	vj d	
spent on the good man malpas off avsley at the oversight off the		15
pagyn wheles	viij d	
spente at the Reparynge off the pagyn	xij d	
paid ffor mendinge the angells svrplisses and wasshinge	iij d	
paid to the carpenters ffor a dais worke	xviij d	
paid ffor vj newe clyppes and nayles	iij s	20
spente at the settinge in off the pagyn	vj d	
paide ffor hyre off ffowre harnyses ffor the pagyn	ij s	
paide ffor sope ffor the wheles	iiij d	

The some is [xvij s v d] xvj s xj d

...   25

paymentes to the players

paid ffor the prologe	iiij d	
paid god and dead man	xx d	
paid pylat	iiij s	
paid ij bysshoppes	ij s	30
paid iiij knyghtes	vj s viij d	
paide the spirite off god	xvj d	
paid iij maries	ij s	
paide the ij angels	viij d	
payde the devell	xvj d	35
paid the syngers	ij s	
paide to the mynstrell	viij d	
paid ffor dryvynge the pagin	vj s viij d	
paid ffor gloves	iij s vj d	
paid ffor poyntes	xij d	40
paid ffor wyer and howkes	iiij d	

paid ffor dressynge the pagin   vj d
to pylate and knyghtes to dryncke   ix d
ffor dryncke in the pagyn   ix d
ffor the players sopper   ij s viij d
ffor the masters and there company ffor svpper   iiij s   5
                              The some is xlij s x d

...

Carpenters' Account Book II CRO: Acc 3/2
f 206   10

...

paid for wearynge ij harnisses and ffor poynts on the ffaire
day   vj d

...

paide to the pynners and cowpers   x s 15

...

Weavers' Account Book CRO: Acc 100/17/1
f 69
                                                                         20
In primis ij rehearsys   ij s
Item for dryuyng of the pagyent   v s
Item payd to symeon   iij s iiij d
Item payd to Iosephe   ij s iiij d
Item payd to Anne   xx d   25
Item payd to symeons clarke   ij s
Item payd to mary   xx d
Item payd to Iesus   xx d
Item payd to the ij Aungeles   viij d
Item payd to the chyld   iiij d 30
Item payd for syngyng   xvj d
Item payd for gloves   iij s
Item payd for playng on the rygoles   iiij d
Item payd for breade & ale   vj s ix d
Item payd for Russhes packthryd sope & nayles   ix d   35
Item payd for bochery meate   x s vj d
Item payd for ij beardes & acappe   iiij d
Item payd at the settyng owt of owr pagyent to the
Iorneymen   vj d
                                                                         40
...
[Item payd to the Iorneymen at the swannedore   vj]

...

Weavers' Rentgatherers' Book I CRO: Acc 100/18/1
f 81v

...

Item payd for bearyng harnis & for poynct*es*	x d

...   5

Item payd for me*n*dyng of ye two angeles crownes	ij d
Item payd for a ledge for nayles & me*n*dyng of o*ur* pagent	iiij d

10

A   *Drapers' Accounts* CRO: Acc 154
f 95 *(Receipts)*

...

Rs of georg batman	iij s iiij d

...   15

f 96 *(Payments)*

pd for harnys beryng at the fayre	xv d
pd to newma*n* for kepyng ye harnys	viij s 20

...

payd for the Chargys of owre pagen	lvij s ob

...

25

AC   *Smiths' Accounts* H-P: *Outlines* I
p 341

... Paid to the plears at the fyrst reherse, ij s vj d; paid for ale,
iiij d; paid for Sent Marye Hall to reherse there, ij d; paid for   30
mendyng the padgand howse dore, xx d; paid for too postes for
the dore to stand upon, iiij d; paid to the carpyntur for his labur,
iiij d; paid to James Beseley for ij plattes on the post endes, vj d;
for great naylles to nayle on the hynge, ij d; paid to vj men to
helpe up with the dore, vj d ...   35

— Sharp: *Dissertation*
p 37 *(New play)*

ffor a lase for Judas & a corde	iij d 40

...

1578
Chamberlains' and Wardens' Account Book II CRO: A 7(b)
p 22 *(23 October)* *(Chamberlains)*

...

Paid to iiij Waytes at Lammas their fee 6s 8d a pece   xxvj s viij d   5

...

p 25 *(25 November)* *(Wardens)*

...

Item paid to the Waytes   iiij li   10

...

p 26* *(Wardens)*

...

   Laid out more at maister maiors appoyntement as followethe   15

...

Item paid to the Lord darbies playerz   vj s viij d
Item paid to Thomas Kyllingley in the Bushop streete for a
standing for maister maior & the maisters at the plays on the
quees hollyedaye   iiij s   20
Item gyven to the Erle of Essex players   iij s
Item gyven to the Erle of worseters playerz   v s

...

Item gyven to the quenes Beareward   xx s

...   25

Item gyven to the Lord vawse his beareward   iij s iiij d

...

Item gyven to the players at Mr Eglionbys   vij s

...

Item gyven to the keper of the quenes apes   ij s   30
Item gyven to the Lord dudleys misicions   v s
Item gyven to the Lord hunsdon his musicons   vj s viij d

...

p 27 *(Wardens)*   35

Item gyven to my Lord Montegles Bearward   v s
Item gyven to the Earle of darbies Playerz   x s
Item gyven to the Earle of darbies Bearward.   x s
Item gyven to the Lord Barckles playerz   v s   40

...

Item gyven to my Lord Comptons players   v s

...

Cappers' Records SC: Account Book I
f 114v *(Receipts)*

...

Receaued off the masters off the walkers	vj s	
Receaued off the masters off the skynners	iiij s	5
Receaued off the masters off the Ioyners	iij s iiij d	

...

col b *(Payments)*

...   10

paid ffor hyre off ij harnisses ffor the ffaire daye	x d
paid ffor wearynge the same harnisses and poyntes	vj d

...

f 115   15
                    chargis off the pagyn

paide the players at the ffirst Reherse	xviij d	
spente on the company at the same Reherse	ij s	
paide the players at the seconde Reherse	xx d	
spente on the company at the same Reherse	ij s	20
spente at the settinge ffowthe off the pagyn	vj d	
paide good man malpas ffor ij newe skaffolde wheles	vj s viij d	
spente at the Repayrynge off the pagyn	xij d	
paide ij carpenters ffor one dayes worke	xviij d	
paide ffor wasshinge the vestures	j d	25
paid Iames biesley ffor one newe clyppes and shewting off ij *(blank)*	viij d	
paide ffor sope ffor the wheles	iiij d	
paide ffor greate nayles smalle nayles and taynter howkes	ix d	
paide ffor hyre off iiij harnysses ffor the pagyn and weppons	ij s	30
spente at the settinge in off the pagyn	vj d	

                    the some is xxj s ij d
                    paymentes to the players

paide ffor the prologe	iiij d	35
paide god and the deade man	xx d	
paide pylate	iiij s	
paide the ij bysshoppes	ij s	
paide iiij knyghtes	vj s viij d	
paide the spirite off god	xvj d	40
paid ij maries	ij s	
paid ij angells	viij d	

paide the devell	xviij d
paide the syngers	ij s
paide the mynstrell	viij d
payde ffor balls	xij d
paid ffor gloves and poyntes	iiij s vj d 5
paide pylate and the iiij knyghtes to dryncke betwene the	
stages	ix d
paide ffor dryncke in the pagyn	xij d
paide ffor dressynge off the pagyn	vj d
paide ffor dryvynge off the pagyn	vj s viij d 10
paide the players ffor their svpper	ij s viij d
paide ffor mendinge pylates gowne and his clvbbes	vj d
paid ffor [ffor] the maisters svpper and his company	iiij s
paid ffor Russhes ffor the pagyn	iiij d
the some is ij li. iiij s ix d	15

...

Weavers' Account Book CRO: Acc 100/17/1

f 70   20

In primis ij rehersys	ij s
Item payd for dryvyng of the pagyent	v s
Item payd to Symeon	iij s iiij d
Item payd to Ioseph	ij s iiij d 25
Item payd to Anne	xx d
Item payd to symeons Clarcke	ij s
Item payd to mary	xx d
Item payd to Iesus	xx d
Item payd to the ij Aungeles	viij d 30
Item payd to the chylde	iiij d
Item payd for syngyng	xvj d
Item payd for gloves	iij s
Item payd for playing on the rygoles	iiij d
Item payd for bred & Ale	vj s ix d 35
Item payd for Russhes packthryd sope & nayles	ix d
Item payd for bochery meate	x s vj d
Item payd for .ij. beardes & a cappe	iiij d
Item payd at ye settyng out of owr pagent	vj d

...   40

A *Drapers' Accounts* CRO: Acc 154
  f 96 *(Receipts)*
  ...

Rs of georg battman   iij s iiij d
...   5

  f 97 *(Payments)*
  ...

pd for harnyssyng men at fere & poynts   xvj d
...   10
pd to the Syngers   ij s
...
Payd more for the Chargys of owre pagyn with the Reparyng of
hyt   lvij s vj d
...   15

AC *Smiths' Accounts* H-P: *Outlines* I
  p 341

... Paid for the cokcroing, iiij d; paid to Thomas Massy for a trwse   20
for Judas, ij s viij d; paid for a new hoke to hange Judas, vj d;
paid for ij new berars of yron for the new seyt in the padgand,
xij d ...

  — Folger: Scrapbook Wb 148   25
  p 57
  ...

       Chargys & exspences of owre padgange
Paid at the fyrst reherse & for ale   ij s iiij d
Paid at the second reherse & for ale   ij s iiij d   30
Paid at the howse to here the plears   vj d

1579
Chamberlains' and Wardens' Account Book II CRO: A 7(b)
  p 31 *(20 October) (Chamberlains)*   35
  ...

Item paid to the way*tes* for their wag*es* due at
lammas   xxvj s viij d
...

22 / the new seyt: *Sharp*, Dissertation, *p 18, omits* new

p 32 *(29 November) (Wardens)*

...

Item paid to the waytes for their ffee   iiij li

...

p 33 *(Wardens)*

...

Item gyven to the Countesse of Essex players   vj s viij d
Item gyven to the Earle huntington his Bearward   xiij s iiij d

...

Item gyven to the Earle of darby his beareward   x s

...

Item gyven to the Lord Barckeley his players   vj s viij d
Item gyven to the Lord Sheffeild his players   v s
Item gyven to the Lord Charles hawardes players   x s
Item gyven to the Lord Strange his players   x s

...

Item gyven to wallons the Beareward   xiij s iiij d
Item gyven to the queenes bearward   xiij s iiij d

...

Cappers' Records SC: Account Book I
f 116 col a *(Receipts)*

...

Receaued off the walkers   vj s
Receaued off the skynners   iiij s
Receaued off the Ioyners   iij s iiij d

...

ff 116v-17 *(Payments)*

payde to the mynstrells on the chewssynge daye   xx d

...

paide ffor skowrynge off owre harnys and hyre off one harnys
ffor the ffaire day   xij d
paide ffor wearynge ij harnysses and poyntes   vj d

...

expencis ffor the pagyn
paide at the dryvynge ffowthe off the pagyn and settinge in off
the same   xij d
paide ffor bordes to mende the pagyn dores   ij d
paide ij carpenters ffor a dayes worke   xviij d

paide the smythe ffor Iron worke	x d	
paide ffor one small hynge great nayles small nayles and teynter howkes	ix d	
spente at Reparynge off the pagyn	xij d	
paide ffor hyre off iiij harnysses	ij s	5
paid ffor balls	xij d	
paide Richard hall ffor makinge pylates clvbbe	xiiij d	
paid ffor ij pounde and halffe off woole ffor the same clvbbe	x d	
paid ffor ij great nayles ffor the wheles	iij d	10
paide ffor gloves and poyntes ffor the players	iiij s vj d	
paid ffor sope ffor the wheles	iiij d	
paid ffor wyer small corde and packthide	iij d	
paid ffor newe cordes to make ffaste owre pagyn dores	v d	
payd ffor mendynge pylates gowne	iij d	15
payde good man malpas ffor a newe pagyn whele	v s	
paide ffor Russhes ffor the pagyn	iiij d	

The some is xxj s vij d |

More chargis off the pagyn

paide to the players at the ffirst Reherse	xviij d	20
spente on the company at good man ashburnes at the same Reherse	iij s vj d	
paide to the players at the seconde Reherse	xx d	
spente on the company at mr waldyns at the same Reherse	v s iiij d	25
paide ffor the prologe	iiij d	
paide to god and the deade man	xx d	
paide vnto pylate	iiij s iiij d	
paide the ij bysshoppes	ij s	
paide the iij maryes	ij s	30
paid the iiij knyghtes	vj s viij d	
paide the ij angells	viij d	
paide the spirite off god	xvj d	
paide the devell	xviij d	
paide the syngers	ij s	35
paide the mynstrell	viij d	
paid ffor dryvynge the pagyn	vj s viij d	
paide ffor dressyng off the pagyn	vj d	
paide pylate and the knyghtes to drynck betwixt the stages	ix d	40
paide ffor drynck in the pagyn	x d	
paide the players ffor theire supper	ij s viij d	

paide ffor owre svpper and owre company iiij s

                    The some is l s vij d

...

Mercers' Account Book CRO: Acc 15

f 20v

                Paymentes ordnarye

...

paide ffor settinge out vj harnes men on the ffayre day   xij d

paide ffor ij dossen of poyntes to tye there harnes   iiij d

...

              Paymentes extreordinary

...

paide Bankes ffor hinges ffor the pagante housse wyndowes & to
norrisse to hange the windoes vp   ij s viij d

...

f 21

...

              Charges of the pagante.

Paide ffor ollde ordinarye chargees aboute the pagante ffor
plaieres wages, and all other thingees, the some of iij li. vij s viij d

Weavers' Account Book CRO: Acc 100/17/1

f 71

In primis for ij rehersys   ij s

Item for dryuyng of the pagyent   v s

Item payd to symeon   iij s iiij d

Item payd to Iosephe   ij s iiij d

Item payd to Anne   xx d

Item payd to symons Clarke   ij s

Item payd to mary   xx d

Item payd to Iesus   xx d

Item payd to the ij aungeles   viij d

Item payd to the chyld   iiij d

Item payd for syngyng   xvj d

Item payd for gloues   iij s

Item payd for playing on the rygales   iiij d

Item payd for bred & ale   vij s

Item payd for bochery meate   xj s

Item payd for russhes packthryd sope nayles ij berdes &
acape   xij d

Item payd for settyng out of owr pagyent vj d

...

A   *Drapers' Accounts* CRO: Acc 154
f 98 *(Receipts)* 5

...

Rs of george batman iij s iiij d

...

Payments for the Company

... 10

payd for harnys beryng at the fayre xvj d

f 99

...

Payd more for the Chargys of owre pagen liij s iiij d 15

...

AC   *Smiths' Accounts* Sharp: *Dissertation*
p 21

... 20

pd to the plears rehersyng in the palys xij d

...

p 37*

... 25

pd for a gowne to the tayllers & sheremen x d

...

1580
Chamberlains' and Wardens' Account Book II CRO: A 7(b) 30
p 37 *(25 October) (Chamberlains)*

...

Paid to the waytes for this yere past xxvj s viij d

...

35

p 41 *(Wardens)*

...

Item paid to the iiijor waytes dewe at Lammas iij li v s

...

40

p 45* *(22 November) (Wardens)*
          Laid out at maister maior his Comaundement
Item gyven to the Earle of worceter his players vj s viij d

<table>
<tr><td></td><td>Item gyven to the Lord Sandes bearward</td><td>xiij s iiij d</td></tr>
<tr><td></td><td>Item gyven to the Lord Barkley his players</td><td>vj s viij d</td></tr>
<tr><td>given to
Noble mens
servantes</td><td>Item gyven to the Lady Essex Muscicons</td><td>ij s</td></tr>
<tr><td></td><td>Item gyven to the Lord Barkley his Bearward</td><td>v s</td></tr>
<tr><td></td><td>Item gyven to the Lord of Darby his players</td><td>vj s viij d</td></tr>
<tr><td></td><td>Item gyven to the Earle of leicester his players</td><td>xxx s</td></tr>
<tr><td></td><td>Item gyven to the Earle of huntingtons Beareward</td><td>vj s viij d</td></tr>
</table>

Summa iij li xvij s

AC   *City Annals*   Bodl: MS Top. Warwickshire d.4
f 26*

...

A greate and
Suddaine
Earthquake.

Thomas Saunders butcher Maior 1579 & ended in 1580 ... In his
yeare was agreat Earthquake which was a suddaine Earthquake

Padgins Layd
downe. /

which hapned the vjth of Aprill 1580 almost generally throughout
England it caused such amazednes of the people as was wonderfull
for ye time & caused them to make there earnest prayers vnto

A disease called
speedy
repentance. /

Almighty god. And this yeare the padgins were layd downe &
then were both steeples poynted. And this yeare was a disease all
the land ouer called speedy repentance. /

...

— Sharp: *Dissertation*
p 39*

... this year the Pageants were again laid down ...

Cappers' Records   SC: Account Book I
f 118 col b

...

paide to the mvsicions at the gowse etinge   xij d

...

payde ffor mendynge the pagyn dores that boyes had opened
and ffor settinge in off the skaffolde   vj d

...

payd ffor wearynge the same harnysses on the ffaire day and ffor
poyntes   vj d

...

paid to the mynstrells on the dynner day   xx d

...

Mercers' Account Book CRO: Acc 15
f 23

...

p*aide* to vj Harnes men and ij dos*yn* pyntes or ffer
ffrydaye   xv d   5

...

A   *Drapers' Accounts* CRO: Acc 154
f 99 *(Receipts)*

...   10

Rs of georg batman   iij s iiij d

...

f 100 *(Payments)*

...   15

pd to Symo*n* newma   viij s

...

pd for beryng harnys at the fayre   xij d
pd for iij dosyn of poynts   iij d

...   20

pd for tying the wyndor of the pagen howse and for
Corde   iiij d

...

pd for Ryngyng at owre dyner   xij d

...   25

1581
Chamberlains' and Wardens' Account Book II CRO: A 7(a)
p 47 *(25 October) (Chamberlains)*

                            ordinary Charges   30

...

paid to the wayt*es* for this yere past   xxvj s viij d

...

p 49 *(15 November) (Wardens)*   35

...

fees & wag*es* paid

...

And to the wayt*es* for their wag*es* this yere past   iiij li.

...   40

p 50

...

Item gyven to the Lord Barkley his Bearward	v s
Item gyven to the Earle of Essex musicons	ij s
Item gyven to the Lord Montegle his players	vj s viij d 5

...

Item gyven to the Earle of Oxford his playerz	x s
Item gyven to A Synging man that brought ye Bishops lettere	ij s vj d
Item gyven to A Bearward here in december	xiij s iiij d 10
Item gyven to the Lord Barkeley his playerz	x s
Item gyven to A Beareward here in ffebruarij	xiij s iiij d
Item gyven by maister maior amongest my lord of leicester his officerz & servantes at Kyllingworthe	xxxiij s
Item gyven to A beareward here in october	xx s vj d 15

...

Survey of Rentals CRO: A 24

p 8*

...   20

Millane on the Est syde.

There is a peice of grounde whereon the Smythes Pagion howse
standeth conteininge by the streete in breadth iiij yardes & a
halfe and so is square of that measure And the said company of
Smythes have it in fee farme payinge to the Cittie v s rent by   25
yere And yt did some tyme belonge to the late Monasterie of
Rowley and yt boundeth vppon a garden belongeing to the
Corner howse at Millanston on the southe.

Cappers' Records SC: Account Book I   30
f 119 col b

...

payd ffor pavynge affore the pagyn howse dore	iiij d

...

payde to symon newman for ij plates off harnys	iij s 35

...

payd ffor carriage off harnis on the ffaire day and poyntes	vj d

...

Mercers' Account Book CRO: Acc 15   40
f 26 *(Ordinary payments)*

...

paide to harnest men on the fayre Daie	xv d

...

paide for A pece of corde to Ty vp the pagen house
wyndoes   vj d

...
                                                                                                    5

Weavers' Account Book CRO: Acc 100/17/1
f 73

...

Item payd to hewit & the minstrilles   xij d

...   10

A   *Drapers' Accounts* CRO: Acc 154
f 101 *(Receipts)*

...

Rs of georg battman   iij s iiij d   15

...

f 102 *(Payments)*

...

payd for cordes for the pagen howse dore   iij d   20

...

payd ffor v bylles   v s x d

...

payd to newman for iij hed pens   v s

...   25

payd for lether and nells for harnys   xv d
payd for Red Clothe and nells for bylles   v d
payd for halvyng v bylles   xx d

...

payd ffor harnys beryng and poynts   xvj d   30

...

1582
Chamberlains' and Wardens' Account Book II CRO: A 7(b)
p 64* *(25 October) (Chamberlains)*   35

...

Item paid to the waites for this yere past   xx s.

...

p 68* *(13 November) (Wardens)*   40

...

And to the iij waytes for their wages   iij li.

...

p 77 *(Chamberlains)*
    Charge*s* paid & laid out at m*aiste*r maiors Commandem*en*t

...

gyven to the earle of Essex men   ij s

...

p 78 *(Wardens)*

...

Item gyven to my Lord Shandos Bearward	xiij s iiij d
Item gyven to the Earle of worsters players	vj s viij d
Item gyven to the Lo*rd* Barkles players	x s
Item gyven to the Earle of lei*cesters* players	xx s
Item gyven to my lord Chamberlayns players	vj s viij d
Item gyven to my lo*rd* morleys players	v s
Item gyven to the Earle of oxfor*des* players	v s
Item gyven to the Earle of darbys Bearward	x s

                        Su*m*ma iij li. xvj s viij d

...

Cappers' Records SC: Account Book I
f 120 col b

...

payde ffor caryinge off harnys on the ffaire day and poyntes x d

...

f 120v

...

more to be added to the sayd byll in chargis for a weytt   v s ix d

...

Mercers' Account Book CRO: Acc 15
f 30

...

p*ay*de to vj hornist mene   ij s
p*ay*de for point*es*   iij d

...

Weavers' Account Book CRO: Acc 100/17/1
f 74v

...

It*e*m payd to ye mynstreles saynte osbornes nyght   ij s

...

Weavers' Rentgatherers' Book I CRO: Acc 100/18/1
f 84v

...

Item payd at mr chamberlaynes to the mynstreles   iiij d.

...

Item payd to the harnesmen   xviij d

...

Item payd more to the syngers   vj d

...

A   *Drapers' Accounts* CRO: Acc 154
f 103 *(Receipts)*

...

Rs of georg batman   iij s iiij d

...

f 104 *(Payments)*

...

pd for beryng harnys and for poyntts   ij s iiij d

...

1583
Chamberlains' and Wardens' Account Book II CRO: A 7(b)
p 82 *(24 October) (Chamberlains)*

...

ordinarie   Item paid to the waytes for their wages this yere past xxvj s viij d
paymentes
...

p 86 *(26 November) (Wardens)*

...

Ordinarie ffees   And to the foure waytes viz. Iohn Thomas Iames Hewyt Old
& wages paid   Styffe & anthonye Styff for their wages this yere Last past euerie
                  of them xx s   iiij li

...

p 89 *(Wardens)*

for repairing   Item paid for the repairing of the 2 swordes & for a great Chape
the Swordes   of Silver & gilt for them   xxvij s viij d
& hatt   And for tryming & repoyring the velvett hatt with gold Lace,
                 gold ffringe & buttons   xv s j d
                          Summa xlij s ix d

Item gyven to the Lord Shandoes Bayrwarde   vj s viij d
And to the Lord of Sussex players   x s
And to the Lord of Sheffeldes players   x s
And to the Lord Barkeles players & musicions   xiij s iiij d
And to the Lord Staffordes players   vj s viij d   5

And to the Lord Mungeys players   vj s viij d
And to the Lord dudles players & musicons   vj s viij d
And to the Erle of oxenfordes players   x s

p 89 *(26 November) (Wardens)*   10

And to the Earle of Essex players   x s
And to the Lord hunsdons musisions   vj s viij d
And to Sir Thomas Staunhopps musicons   ij s vj d
And to mr Nowells Musicons   iij s iiij d   15
And to the Erle of leicester his plommer   v s
And to the Lord vawses bearward   v s
And to the Erle of huntingtons beareward   vj s viij d
...

                                                                               20

Cappers' Records SC: Account Book I
f 121v col a

...

paid for bearynge harnes on the fayre day & for poyntes   x d
...   25

Drapers' Indenture CRO: Acc 468/D 11/Box 5 no. 429*

This Indenture made the Twentye daye of September In the fyve
and twentith yere of the raigne of our soveraigne lady Elyzabethe   30
by the grace of god of Englande ffraunce and Irelande Queene
defender of the faythe / & c. / Betwene Thomas Nycholis
Rycharde Barker Rauffe Ioyner Roberte Letherbarowe Iohn
Ryleye Mychaell Ioyner Thomas Hawks and Anthonye Berrye of
the cytie of Coventre Drapers on thone partie, And Henry Sewall   35
of the same cytie draper on the other partie Wytnessithe that the
sayde Thomas Nycholes Rycharde Barker Rauffe Ioyner Roberte
Letherbarowe Iohn Ryleye Mychaell Ioyner Thomas Hawkes and
Anthonye Berrye for the yerelie rente in these presentes specyfied
And for dyvers other good causes and consyderacions them   40
movynge haue deuysed graunted and to ferme lett And by these

*prese*ntes deuysen graunten and to ferme letten and setten vnto
the sayde Henry Sewall all those their Seventene Mesua*ges* or
Ten*eme*ntes and Cota*ges* and gardeynes to the same Mesua*ges*
and cota*ges* adioyning app*er*teyning & belonging And one close
or pasture with all and synguler their app*urtena*n*ces* scituate   5
lyenge and beynge in the saide cytie of Coventr*e* and the countie
of the same, as theye be by these *prese*ntes named and expressed,
that is to saye, ... And one Ten*eme*nte and a gardeyne at the
Iorden Well on the Northe syde the streete there in the tenure of
Rychard Greenell boundynge vpon the Lande of George Kevett   10
and the pagient Howses on the Easte p*ar*te, and vpon the lande of
mr Nycholes on the weste p*ar*te, and on the lande of m*is*tris
Brownell on the Northe p*ar*te, ... above named to these *prese*nte
Indentures enterchaungeably have put their handes and Seales
the daye and yere fyrst above Wrytten   15

thomas nycolls Richard barkr Raffe Ioy*n*ar Robart letherbaroe
Iohn Riley mychell Ioynar thomas hawkes Anthony Berye

                                                                                         20

Mercers' Account Book CRO: Acc 15
f 32
...

p*aide* for caringe of hornes on the faier daie	ij s iiij d
p*aide* for poynt*tes* & nayling the hornes	x d 25
p*aide* for mending the pageon howse	x d

...

A   *Drapers' Accounts* CRO: Acc 154
f 105 *(Receipts)*   30
...

Rs of georg battem	iij s iiij d

...

Payments

...   35

payd for iij cords & medyg the pagen howse	vj d
...	
pd at the ffayer for harnys bereg and for poyntts	ij s ij d
...	
pd for mendyng the pagen howse	xiiij d 40

...

AC   *Smiths' Accounts* Bodl: MS Top. Warwickshire c.7
      f 33

... pd for beryng harnes on the fere day before Mast*er* Maior &
poynts x. d ...   5

1584
Chamberlains' and Wardens' Account Book II CRO: A 7(b)
p 104 *(19 October) (Chamberlains)*

                                                                  10
ordynary   And to the wayt*es* for their wages this yere past   xxvj s viij d
payme*ntes*
                ...

p 108 *(24 November) (Wardens)*

                ...   15
ffees &   And to the iiij° wayt*es* viz. huytt two stiff*es* & Iohn Thomas for
wages paid   their wages this yere past   iiij li
                ...

p 112 *(Wardens)*   20

                Item given to the Earle of oxford*es* players   x s
                And to the Earle of Essex players   x s
                And to the Lo*rd* Mordent*es* beareward   vj s viij d
                And to the Lo*rd* mvnges musicions   iij s iiij d   25
                And to the Lo*rd* hunsdons beareward   vj s viij d
                And to the Lo*rd* Sheffelde*s* players   x s
                And to S*ir* Thomas Lucies players   x s
money given   And to the Earle of w*or*cesters players   xiij s iiij d
to noblemens   And to the Lo*rd* Bartley his players   x s   30
servant*es*   And to Sackerson the Earle of darby his bearward   xiij s iiij d
                And to the Earle of Essexe musicions   v s
                And to the Lo*rd* haward*es* musici*o*ns   v s
                And to the waytes of Cambridge   iij s iiij d
                And to the waytes of Chester   v s   35
                         Su*mm*a vj li. xj s viij d
                ...

Cheylesmore Manor Account Book CRO: A 9
p 127* *(17 December) (Bailiff's Expenses)*   40
...
And of x s gyven to Golston the musicion & his

leet dynn*er*s   men by the comaundem*en*t of mr maior & his   x s
               bretherne at the said dynn*er*

               ...

               Payments Out Book CRO: A 16   5
               p 51* *(15 April)*

               ...

               paid to mr Smythe of oxford the xv^(th) daye of
               Aprill 1584 for hys paynes for writing   xiij li. vj s viij d
               of the tragidye   10

               ...

A C   *City Annals* Bodl: MS Top. Warwickshire d.4
               f 26v*

The destruction   ...   15
of Ierusalem
first played. / Henry Breres drap*er* maior 1583 & ended in 1584 ... In his yeare
               the new play of the Destruction of Ierusalem was first plaied ...

               Cappers' Records SC: Account Book I
               ff 122v-3 col a *(Receipts)*   20

               ...

               Receaued off the walkers   vj s
               Receaued off the skynners   iiij s
               Receaued off the Ioyners and payntrs   iij s iiij d

               ...   25

                               Paymentes

               ...

               paide ffor wearynge ij harnysses on the ffaire day and
               poyntes   x d
               ...   30

               col b
               ...

                     paymentes ffor owre partes ffor the pagyn and acte
               payd ffor ffyve Reherses   v s 35
               spente at the same Reherses   xx d
               Spente at thomas Robynsons by tymes at the apponinge off
               thinges   x d
               paide ffor owr partes at the settinge and drivinge off the pagyn
               and skaffoldes   ij s vj d 40
               payd ffor dressynge the pagyn   vj d
               paide towarde the hyre off a drvm   xij d

payde ffor playinge off the same drvme	iij d
payde ffor mendynge off the skaffolde	vij d
payd ffor Russhes	iij d
payde ffor iij beardes	ij s vj d
paide sixe mvsicissions	ij s vj d
payde ffor the hyre off a trumpet	vj d
payd ffor mendynge off the players Reparrell	vj d
paide towardes the players breakffaste and drynck in the pagyn and anyght when the had playd	v s vj d
Paide more ffor ale that was dronck at the settinge in off the pagyn and skaffolde	iiij d
paide ffor makynge in off owre pagyn dores and small cordes	iiij d
paide ffor owre suppers and the iiij maisters off the sharmen and tayllers and the clarkes and summers	iiij s

The some is xxviij s ix d ∣

Paymentes to the Players

payde to owton	v s
payde to thomas Symcoxe	v s
paide to the barber	iiij s vj d
payde to bvtler	iiij s vj d
payde to hollande	iij s x d
paide christoffore tayller	ij s vj d
payde to hawkes	xvj d
payde to mathewe	ij s iiij d
payde to hawmon	xvj d
payde to mr myles sonne	xvj d
payde to holbage	xvj d
payde to Ihon Shewels man	viij d
payde to the captaynes lackies	xij d
payde xij souldyars to were Red cotes	ij s
paide ffor iij garlande made off bayes	vj d
payde ffor the temple	xij d
payde to Ihon Grene ffor makynge the booke	v s
payde ffor kepynge the boke	xij d

The some is xliiij s ij d

The some off owre parte xxij s j d

...

Carpenters' Account Book II CRO: Acc 3/2
f 208 col b*

...

Item payde the pynners and cowpers for iij yeres   xxx s

...   5

Mercers' Account Book CRO: Acc 15
f 34v

...

                            Recept*es* extraordinary.   10

...

Rec*eaved* of The Girdlers Toward*es* charges of the
playe   lij s ij d

...   15

f 35v   *(Payments)*

...

p*aide* ffor bearinge of Harnes on the faire daye   ij s iiij d

...

p*aide* ffor poynt*es* ffor the harnes   iiij d   20

...

ff 36-6v

Charge*es* of the pagante and the playe   25
p*aide* ffor hiering Apparell ffor the playeres & ffor
Carrig   xxxiij s
p*aide* ffor makinge ij Greene clok*es*   x s ij d
p*aide* Greene ffor the playe booke   v s
p*aide* The Girdlers that they paied ffor mendinge the   30
skaffolde   iiij s iiij d
p*aide* for bord*es* and Sparres 3s ffor nayles 14d   iiij s ij d
p*aide* Cookson the Carpenter   xij d|
p*aide* Ric*hard* ffereman ffor warninge the reherces   xx d
p*aide* The plaieres ffor Sundrye Rehearces   xj s x d   35
p*aide* ffor Drink when They plaied   vij s
p*aide* ffor the plaieres Supper   xj s vj d
p*aide* Diglyn ffor Dromminge   vij s
p*aide* Ric*hard* wootton v s. p*aide* Iohn Bande v s   x s

paide Iohn Greene iij s. paide wood iiij s   vij s
paide Simcoxe   vj s viij d
paide holande 12d. paide ffoster 4s. paide Longe 2s   vij s
paide yonge headley 18d. paide his ffather 12d   ij s vj d.
paide Buttler 4s. paide Hankes 16d.   v s iiij d   5
paide christofor Taylor   xvj d
paide holbadge   ij s vj d
paide Miles   xx d
paide Iohn hoppers   xx d
paide iij boyes that plaied   xvj d   10
paide ffor mvssike   v s iiij d
paide The Trumppeter   iij s iiij d
paide the painter   ij s
paide 12 Souldiours   iiij s iiij d
paide a Standerd bearer   xij d   15
paide Thomas massey   xvj d
paide Copestake   xij d
paide ffor Rushies & Sope   xiiij d
paide ffor Drivinge the pagant & skaffoldes   v s iiij d
paide ffor Settinge vp the pagant   viij d   20
paide ffor mendinge The pagant housse   iiij d
         Somma is viij li ix s vj d

Weavers' Account Book CRO: Acc 100/17/1
f 76v   25

Item paide for rehearses   ij s
Item paide at the settinge out of the pagion   vj d
Item paide on the pagion daye for bread and drincke   iij s viij d
Item paide for nayles and rushes   vj d   30
Item paide to Iohn Smythe   xvj s
Item paide for Drivinge of the pagion   v s
...
Item paide to Robert Baggerley for mending of ye pagion   vj d
...   35

Weavers' Rentgatherers' Book II CRO: Acc 100/18/2
ff 1-1v
...
payd for that whych belongeth to the pagyante   xij s   40
Also spent at pynnynges   xx d
...

payd for bearyng harnes the Last yere   ix d
payd for bearyng harnes thys yere   xviij d
...
payd for nayles & mendyng of the pagyent   iij d |
Item Charges spent at the Choyse daye   5
...
payd to ye syngers   xij d
...

AC   *Butchers' Accounts* Bodl: MS Top. Warwickshire c.7   10
     f 100v
...
Itm payde to the whyttawyers towards the pageant   xx s.
...
                                                                             15
A   *Drapers' Accounts* CRO: Acc 154
     f 106 *(Receipts)*
...
Rs of george batman   iij s iiij d
...   20

     f 107 *(Payments)*
...
pd for beryng harnys & ponytts at the fayre   ij s iiij d
...   25
payd for Chargys of the playes   vj li. iiij s
...

AC   *Smiths' Accounts* H-P: *Illustrations*
     pp 56-7* *(Destruction of Jerusalem)*   30

Imprimis, payd to the players for a reherse, ij s vj d; item, payde
to Jhon Grene for wrytynge of the playe-booke, v s; item, payde
to the trumpeter for soundynge in the pagent, v s; item, payde to
hym that playde on the flute, ij s vj d; item, payde to Jhon Foxall   35
for the hyer of Irysshe mantylles, viij d; item, gyvyn to the
dryvers of the pagent to drynke, iiij d; item, payde for sope for
the pagent wheles, iiij d; item, payde for a boorde for the pagente,
vj d; item, payde to Cookeson for makynge | of a whele to the

Collation (H-P: *Illustrations*, pp 56-7, with Sharp: *Dissertation*, pp 37-8):
32] *heading added* Exspencys & paymentes for the pagente

skaffolde, viij d; item, payde to the carpenter for mendynge the
pagente and for nayles, ij d; item, payde to William Barrat his
men for a berrage, iiij d; item, payde for a iron pynne and a cotter
for the skaffolde whele, iiij d; item, spent on the Companye at
Mr. Smythes on the pley even, ij s viij d; item, paid to Jhon Deane   5
and Fosson for theyre dyner on the playe daye, vj d; item, payde
to Williams for makynge of ij payre of galleyes, ij s; item, paid for
the masters breakfast on the playe daye, xx d; item, paid for the
players drynke to the pagente, ij s; item, paid for starche to make
the storme in the pagente, vj d; item, paid for carryenge of our   10
aperaill from pagent to pagent, vj d; item, paid for drynke at
Walkers for the muzizions, ij d; item, paid to Hewette for
fetchynge of the hoggesheaddes, vj d; item, paid to the souldyers
for waytynge on the captaynes, ij s vj d; item, paid for a pottell
of wyne to the pagente, x d; item, paid to the muzicions for   15
playenge on theyre instrumentes in the pagent, v s; item, paid for
the masteres and the players sowper, viij s vj d; item, paid to
Jhon Deane for hys sowper and drynkynge, vj d; item, paid to
William Longe for russhes, packthryd and tenterhookes, viij d;
item, paid to ij drumme-players, x d; item, paid to the dryvers of   20
the pagente, iiij s; item, paid to Hewet for hys paynes, iij d; item,
paid to Reignolde Headley for playenge of Symon and Phynea,
v s; item, paid to Gabryell Foster for playenge of Justus, Ananus,
Eliazar and the Chorus, vj s viij d; item, paid to Jhon Bonde for
playenge of the Capteyne, Jhoannes and the Chorus, vj s viij d;   25
item, paid to William Longe for playenge of Merstyars, Jacobus,
Hippenus and the Chorus, v s; item, paid to Jhon Hoppers for
playenge of Jesus and Zacharyas, iij s; item, paid to Henry
Chamberleyne for playenge of Pristus, a pece of Ananus and Zilla,
iij s iiij d; item, paid to Jhon Grene for playenge of Mathias and   30
Esron, ij s; item, paid to John Copestake for playeng of Esron
his parte, xx d; item, paid to Lewes Pryce for playenge of Niger
his parte, xvj d; item, paid to Frauncys Cocckes for playenge of
Solome, xij d; item, paid to Richard Fitzharbert and Edward
Platte for playeinge Chyldren to Solome, xij d; item, paid to   35
Christofer Dyglyne for hys ij drummes, vj s viij d; item, paid to
the awncyente berer, xij d; item, paid to Robert Lawton for

Collation continued: 14 ij s vj d] ij s   16 v s] v d   17 masteres ... vj d]
*Maste*r ... vj s   18 for hys sowper ... vj d] for hys Dyner sowper ... xij d
21 iiij s] iij d   21 iiij d] ix d   26 Merstyars] *Me*rsyars   27 v s] vj s viij d
36 Dyglyne for hys ij drummes] Dygbye for his ij drummers

kepynge of the booke, ij s; item, paid to Edmund Durrant for
payntynge, ij s; item, paid to Thomas Massye for the Temple and
for his beardes, iij s; item, payd to the players at the fyrst reherse,
vij d; item, payd moore to them at the second reherse, xx d; item,
paid unto the muzicyons the same tyme, vij d; item, payd unto   5
Cristopher Dyglyn the same tyme in earnest, iiij d; item, payd to
the players at the reherse on the Monday en Whytson wycck, ij s;
item, payd unto Cocckam in earnest for to playe on his bagpypes,
iiij d; item, payd to the players at the last reherse in Sent
Nycholas hall, iij s; item, payd for havynge the pageaunt owte,   10
viij d; item, spent at the Panyer at the fyrst reherse, ij s; item,
spent at Rychard Turners at the secund reherse, viij d; item, payd
to Henrye Chamberleyne for ij beardes, vj d; item, payd for a
clampe of iron weyng viij li for the pageant, xx d; item, payd for
nayles to fasten the said clampe, ij d; item, payd for a iron pynne   15
to the pageant, iiij d; item, payd for a iron to hold uppe the
stremer, iiij d; item, payd for the pageant howse rente, v s; item,
payd to Jhon Deane for takyng paynes abowte the pageant,
iij s vj d ...

                                                                         20
— Sharp: *Dissertation*
p 37

...

Item payd to a trumpeter in Earnest at Seynt nycholas
hall   iiij d   25

...

— Bodl: MS Top. Warwickshire c.7
f 83v

...   30

paid Master Shewell for the Pallys howse rent 13/4 ...

1585
Chamberlains' and Wardens' Account Book II CRO: A 7(b)
p 115 *(26 October) (Chamberlains)*   35

...

ordinary
paymentes Item paid to the waytes for their wages this yere
past   xxvj s viij d

...

Collation continued: 3 *after* iij s] Some is v li. iij s vj d   8 Cocckam]
Cockram   10 iij s] iij d   19 iij s vj d] ij s vj d

p 118* *(30 November) (Wardens)*

...

ffees & wages paid   And to the way*tes* for their whole yeres wages   iiij li.

...

And to old Styffe & his sone & Iohn Thòmas the eight of
december by m*aiste*r maior his appoyntm*en*t   xxx s

...

p 119* *(Wardens)*

Item given to the Lo*rd* Chamb*er*layns musicons   iij s iiij d
And to the Earle of leicesters players   xxx s
And to *our* way*tes* on the Leete dayde   iij s iiij d
And to *our* way*tes* at the old wardens accompt   ij s
And to the Lo*rd* Sheffeld*es* players   x s
And to Iohn wallans at a bearbayting   xiij s iiij d
And to S*i*r George hasting*es* players   x s
money given to noble mens servant*es*   And to Lo*rd* Staffforde*s* players   x s
And to A bearward that brought the queens beares   x s
And to S*i*r Thomas darbies music*i*on   ij s
And to the Earle of oxforde*s* players   xiij s iiij d
And to the Earle of Essex musicons   ij s vj d
And to the Lo*rd* vawse his Bearward   ij s vj d

...

p 122* *(30 November) (Wardens)*

The Charges of the eating of foure Buck*es* gyven by the Earle
of Leicester

...

gyven to Mr Goldston   ij s vj d

...

Cheylesmore Manor Account Book CRO: A 9
p 135 *(15 December) (Bailiff's expenses)*

⟨...⟩ to muscions   And of v s by hym paid by m*aster* maiors appoyntm*en*t to the
muscicons at the two Court*es* at Chellesmore   v s

...

Council Book CRO: A 14(a)
p 185* *(22 September)*

...

At this daye yt is agreed that mr Iohn marston shall have
iij li. vj s viij d yerelye ffee of this house to be of Counsell with   5
this Cittie to be paid hym from the feast of St michaell
tharchangell next during suche tyme as yt shalbe thought
Convenient to the maior & Counsell of this Cittie,

...
                                                                               10

p 187 *(15 December)*

...

At this daye yt is Agreed that william Styffe sometyme one of
the waytes shall have xx s [ye'r'ly] 'yerely' gyven hym by the
wardens of this Cittie during his Naturall Lyffe by v s A quarter   15

Cappers' Records SC: Account Book I
f 124 col a

payde for skowrynge off ij paire almayne Ryvittes and iij   20
sallyttes   xvj d
paide ffor Rubbynge off the same almayne Ryvettes after the
ffaire daye being wette   iiij d
payde to ij men ffor wearynge off off harnys on the ffaire day
and poyntes   x d   25
...

Carpenters' Account Book II CRO: Acc 3/2
f 210v*

...   30
Item payde ffor wearynge off ij harnisses and poyntes   x d
...
Item payd more Robbynge off harnys after the Rayne   vj d
...
paide the mynstrells and syngers at supper   ij s iiij d   35
...

24 / off off *MS dittography*

Mercers' Account Book CRO: Acc 15
f 38v

Charge*es* of the Dynner

...

paide to the waite*es*   ij s vj d   5

...

f 39

Payment*es* ordinary.

...   10

paide for Dressinge the Harnes   vij s

paide for mendinge the Harnes   v d

paide for Dressinge the harnes after the Raigne   vj d

paide for Bearinge the Harnes on the faire daye   ij s

...   15

Weavers' Rentgatherers' Book II CRO: Acc 100/18/2
f 3v
                                                                                 20

Payd at mr pexle*es* to the mynstryl*es* one saynt osborn*es*
nyght   iiij d

...

Peayd to fowr men for berryng of owre harness & for a dussen
of poynt*es*   xviij d   25

...

Peayd to the mynstryl*es* & singar*es* one the chossday at
dynner   xvj d

peayd more at super one the chosse day   vj d

...   30

A *Drapers' Accounts* CRO: Acc 154
   f 107 *(Receipts)*

...

Rs of georg batman   iij s iiij d   35

...

f 108 *(Payments)*

...

pd for harnys beryng & poyntts   ij s ij d   40

...

pd for pavying before the pagen howsse   iiij d

...

pd goldstone at owre dyner & at Mr Alderoyds   x s

...

pd newman for owre harnes   viij s

...

5

1586
Chamberlains' and Wardens' Account Book II CRO: A 7(b)
p 130 *(25 October) (Chamberlains)*

...

ordinary
paym*en*tes

Item paid to the wayt*es* of this Cittie for their wages this yere   10
past   xxvj s viij d

...

p 133 *(15 November) (Wardens)*

...   15

ffees &
wages paid

And to the waytes for their wages   iiij li.

...

And to mr marston for di a yeres ffee   xxxiij s iiij d

...

20

p 134 *(Wardens)*

...

Item given to the Queens ma*ie*sties players	xl s
And to S*ir* Thomas Stanopps musicons	xij d
And to the Lord Chamb*er*layns musicons	v s 25
And to the Earle of Sussex players	vj s viij d
And to the Lo*rd* dudley his musicons	xij d
And to Golston the 26 of october	ij s vj d
And to the Earle of Sussex players	x s
And to the Lo*rd* Sheffeild*es* men	v s 30
And to the Lo*rd* of Essex men	ij s vj d
And to the Lo*rd* Morden*tes* men	x s
And to Mr. Candishe men	xij d
And to the Lo*rd* Chamb*er*layns men	iij s iiij d
And to the Wayt*es* of Caimbridge	xij d 35
And to the Lo*rd* Admiralls players	xx s
And to Golston at the Chamb*er*layns accompt	ij s vj d

money gyven
to Noblemens
s*er*vant*es*

Su*m*ma vj li. xj s vj d

p 135 *(28 November) (Wardens)*   40

...

paym*en*tes at
Comaundem*en*t

Item given to the wayt*es* of westm*in*ster   vj d

...

p 138 *(Wardens)*

The Charges of the Eating of two Buck*es* gyven by the Earle of
Leicester
...   5
Item gyven to Mr Goldston   ij s vj d
...

Council Book CRO: A 14(a)
p 191 *(16 June)*   10
...

william Cotterell | At this daye yt is agreed that willi*a*m Cotterell Cutler shall have
for the kepe | the ou*e*rsight & keping of the Armorie, and that he shall have the
the armor | Charge of the same & to see the same kept Cleane & in good
repair w*i*th Buckles Lethers & all other thing*es* needfull for the   15
same, & also the sword*es* daggers girdles, gunnes flask*es* towch
boxes & all that belongeth vnto the same to be kept continualye
in good repaire, w*i*th the bowes arrowes bills speares, staves & all
other the armor artillerie & wepons belong to the Chamber of
this Cittie, And he shall have for the keping [of] & dressing the   20
same in forme aforesaid for his ffee xl s to be paid by the wardens
of this Cittie /
...

Payments Out Book CRO: A 16   25
p 57 *(31 August - 6 October)*
...
p*a*id for one of the pypes for the way*tes* w*i*th the Carriage of
yt   xxvij s
...   30

Cappers' Records SC: Account Book I
f 125 col b
...
It*e*m paide ffor wearynge off harnys and poyntes on the ffaire   35
daye   x d
...
It*e*m payde ffor ffetchinge downe off one ʿlockʾ hynge off the
pagyn   j d
...   40

Carpenters' Account Book II CRO: Acc 3/2
f 212v*

...

Item payd for wearynge off the same harnys on the ffaire day
and poyntes   x d   5

...

paide to the boyes of bablake on the choyse daye   iij d

...

Mercers' Account Book CRO: Acc 15   10
f 42
                         Paymentees ordinary

...

paide to the harnesbearrers on the faire daye   ij s
...   15
                         Paymentees extraordinary

...

paide for mendinge the pagant doare   vj d

...

paide more for mendinge the pagante doarees   iij d   20

...

Weavers' Account Book CRO: Acc 100/17/1
f 78v

...   25

spent at Iames ileges when we met a bovt the pagone   ij s vj d

...

Weavers' Rentgatherers' Book II CRO: Acc 100/18/2
f 5v   30

...

Payde to mr goldston at St osbornes nyght   ij s
...

Payd for bearinge of harnes and for ponytes   xviij d
Payd for nayles and to the carpenter for settinge vp Sertayne   35
boerdes at the padgen house   v d

...

Payd to mr goldston for mendinge our Instrumentes   xvj d
...

f 6

Payd when we went to se owr Land

...

Payde to the mynstry*es*   vj d

...   5

A   *Drapers' Accounts* CRO: Acc 154
     f 108 *(Receipts)*

...

Rs of georg batman   iij s iiij d   10

...

f 109 *(Payments)*

...

pd for mendyng the pagen howse   xij d   15
pd for nayles and corde   vj d

...

pd to the harnys me*n* at the fayre   ij s
pd for poynts for the Same   iiij d

...   20

AC   *Smiths' Accounts* H-P: *Illustrations*
     p 58

... Item, recievyd of Mr. Pyle for the pageant-howse, xx s; item,   25
recievyd of Henry Bankes for the pageant, xl s ...

     — H-P: *Outlines* I
     p 338

                                                                               30

... Item, paide to James Bradshawe for mendynge the pageant-
howse doores, iiij d; item, to Christofer Burne for a key and
settynge on the locke on the doore, v d; item, paide to Baylyffe
Emerson for halfe yeres rente of the pageant-howse, ij s vj d;
item, gyven to Bryan, a sharman, for his good wyll of the   35
pageante-howse, x d ...

1587
Chamberlains' and Wardens' Account Book II CRO: A 7(b)
p 143 *(25 October) (Chamberlains)*   40

...

ordinary   Item paid to the way*tes* for their wages this yere past   xxvj s viij d
paym*entes*
                 ...

p 149 *(14 November) (Wardens)*

...

ffees &
wages paid

And to the waytes for their wages this yere   iiij li.

...

5

p 150 *(Wardens)*

...

And of xxx s by them gyven by m*aiste*r maior his
Comaundem*en*t vnto the Earle of leicest*er* his players on Lamas
day Last   xxx s   10
And to the Erle of sussex pleyers in september   xiij s iiij d
And to the Queenes players in september   xl s
And to the L*ord* Admiralls players   xx s

money given
to noble mens
servant*es*

And to the l*ord* chamb*er*layns mucisions that came w*ith* the
Iudg*es* at the assisses   v s   15
And to the L*ord* Shandos players   x s
And to the L*ord* of Leicesters players in Iuly   xx s
And to the quenes players more in september   xx s
And to Mr goldston at the wardens Accompt   ij s vj d
And to the Wayt*es* of lecester   xij d   20
                  S*um*ma viij li j s x d.

...

p 152 *(Wardens)*

...   25

And gyve to A bearward of warwicke   xij d

...

p 153 *(Wardens)*

...   30

paid to dawson the paynter for paynting the followers
polaxes   xij d

p 154 *(Wardens)*

35

p*ai*d for gilding the strem*er* for the trumpet   x s

...

p*ai*d more to old Stiff for his ffee ʿallowedʾ   xx s

...

paym*en*tes at
Comandem*en*t
to the poore
people &
others.

p*ai*d to Mr goldston for Sounding the trumpet   ij s   40

...

p*ai*d ffor taffata sarcenet for the trumpett   viij s
p*ai*d for String*es* for yt   xij d

p*ai*d more for Silke & silk string*es*   xxj d

...

Cappers' Records SC: Account Book I
f 126 col b   5

...

It*e*m payde ffor wearynge off ij harnysses on the ffaire daye and
ffor poyntes   x d

...

It*e*m payde ffor takynge downe off tyle off the pagyne howse   10
and leade and carriage of the same   vij d

...

Carpenters' Account Book II CRO: Acc 3/2
f 214v   15

...

payde ffor wearynge off harnys and poyntes   x d

...

paide to the boyes off bablake on the choyse daye   iij d
payde to the syngers on the dynner daye   vj d   20

...

Mercers' Account Book CRO: Acc 15
f 44v

Payment*es* Ordinary.   25

...

p*ai*de for poynt*es* for the Harnes on the fayre daye   iiij d
p*ai*de to vj men for Bearinge the Harnes   ij s

...

30

Weavers' Rentgatherers' Book II CRO: Acc 100/18/2
f 7v*

Recetes ovte off the hous

...

Rec*etes* of Iohn Showell for the padgant   xl s   35
Rec*etes* for the Iourne of the padgant Howse   x s vj d

...

Paymente*es* for bulding of the
paggente House in the myllane
Item in prymvs payed at taking doune of the   40
House and the tilles for Hieryng of a rope   ij s x d
and carying of the Leade to the store House & for
drynke to the worke men that same daye

Item payd to the Carpeters for ther wages   iij li viij s iiij d
Item payd to the masones for ther wages   viij s iiij d
Item payd to the tilers for tiling and dawbing   xvij s viij d
Item payd for stone and for Carying of stone   xij s
Item payd for sand and Cleaye   v s ij d   5
Item payd for Lyme and for Heare to make moiter   ix s viij d
Item payd for tilles to good man Leache   ix s vj d
Item payd for tymber to Mr Showell mathow collenes and to
Thomas ffurnes   xxx s viij d
Item payd for Hinges Hokes and astaplee   xvj d   10
Item paye for spares for the show and stodes to the
wales   xj s viij d
Item payd for Caryage of timber   vj d
Item payd at the rearyng of the House at good
man Halles and Iockcons onthe nyght befor   x s xj d   15
& when the company met at the house
Item payd Iohn Showell for a hundred & halfe of
bryckes   ij s ij d
Item payd for lathe and nayles   xxiiij s vj d
Item payd to master pyxley for tymber   xxv s   20
Item payd to wylliam Clyston for adore   ij s
           Summe is xj li xvij s x d

f 8*

...   25
Item payd at Iames Ellidges when we sold our padgent   xiiij d
...
Item payd at pyninges when we solde the payntinge [of
the]   xvj d
...   30
Item payde to the Berers of the Harnes and for poyntes   xviij d
...

f 8v*

...   35
Item payd the day be fore we set the carpenters on worke   iiij s
...

A   *Drapers' Accounts* CRO: Acc 154
     f 110   40
...
Rs of george batman   iij s iiij d
...

Payd goldston at Rycc Aldersons for hys paynes   iiij s

...

payd for kepyng owre harnys to newman   viij s

...

payd for beryng harnys & poyntts at the fayre   ij s iiij d   5

...

1588
Chamberlains' and Wardens' Account Book II CRO: A 7(b)
p 160 *(23 October) (Chamberlains)*   10

...

<table>
<tr><td>Ordinary
paymentes</td><td>Item paid to the waytes for their wages for this yere
past</td><td>xxvj s viij d</td></tr>
</table>

...

   15

p 164 *(4 December) (Wardens)*

...

<table>
<tr><td>ffees &
wages paid</td><td>And of iiij li. by them paid to the waytes for their ffee this
yere</td><td>iiij li.</td></tr>
</table>

...

   20

p 166 *(4 December) (Wardens)*

...

paid to goodman Styffe   xx s

...

   25

p 172   *(Wardens)*

	To players Musicons & Bearwardes	
Item given to the Lord Staffordes players	vj s viij d	
to the Erle of huntingtons bearward	x s viij d	30
to the Bearward of this Cittie	v s	
to Another Bearward by maister maior	x s	
to Sir George hastinges players	v s	
to the Erle of Essex players	xx s	
to lake the Erle of Essex musicon	ij s	35
to Iohn wallance bearward	v s	
to A noble mans musicion	iij s iiij d	
to the Erle of Leicesters players	xl s	
to the Queenes players	xl s	
to the Erle of Sussex players	x s	40

(label at left for the above block: players &
musicions &
Bearwardes)

39 / l *in* xl s *written over* x

to the Lord Strange players   v s
to Mr Candishe musicons   iij s iiij d

                              Summa viij li. vj s. /

...

Council Book CRO: A 14(a)
p 199 *(13 April)*

...

Att this daye it is Agreed that mr Iohn marston shalbe Steward
of this Cittie & ys sworne   10

...

p 203 *(16 October)*

...

Leetes   It is agreed by this house at the mocion & request of mr Marston   15
                Stward of this Cittie that the Letes of this Cittie shalbe from
•of Coventry   henceforth kept on the twesdaye next after michaelmas & the
and   twesdaye [next] senight next after Easter. & Chellesmore the
Chilismore•   [thursday] 'wensday' after.

                                                                      20

Cappers' Records SC: Account Book I
f 127 col b

...

paid for poyntes and bearynge harnes   x d

...   25

Carpenters' Account Book II CRO: Acc 3/2
f 216 col b

...

paide ffor carriage off harnys on the faire day and   30
poyntes   x d

...

paide to the boyes off bablake   iiij d
paide to the mynstrells at Richard halls   xij d
spente at the Receauynge off owre armore   iiij d 35

...

Mercers' Account Book CRO: Acc 15
f 45v*

                              Receiptes for pagant stufe.   40
Received of Mr Henrye kirvin for certaine parsells   xij s
Received of Mr Diglyn for certaine parcelles   xvj s

Receaved of Iohn whit head for certaine parceles   xviij s
Receaved of Mr Roger kirvyn for certaine parcelles   vij s
Receaved of Edward wallker for certaine parcelles   iiij s iiij d
Receaved of Thomas Darlinge for a copper chayne   ij s iiij d
                        Somma is lix s viij d   5

f 46v

...

                    Paymentes ordinarye.

...   10

paid to the harnes bearrers on the faire daye   ij s
paid for poyntes for the harnes   iiij d

...

f 47   15
                  Paimentes extraordinarye

...

paid for Dressinge the mvskites   xviij d
paid for corne pouder & matches   vij s
...   20
paid for mendinge the paganthouse windowe   iiij d
...

Weavers' Account Book CRO: Acc 100/17/1
f 81   25
...

                  other peamentes
Item I gawe vnto nyclys wheller the same day for syngyng   viij d
...

    30

f 81v

...

Item peayd vnto the syngars at dynner   xij d
...

    35

Weavers' Rentgatherers Book II CRO: Acc 100/18/2
f 9v

...

payd for setting forth of the Harnest men   xviij d
...   40

A *Drapers' Accounts* CRO: Acc 154
f 111

...

Rs of georg batman   iij s iiij d

...   5

f 112

...

p*a*yd for beryng harnes at the fayre   ij s iiij d

...   10

p*a*yd mr goldeston by the masters Coma*n*dymet   iij s iiij d

...

p*a*yd mr maston half yers wagys   xiij s iiij d

...   15

1589
Chamberlains' and Wardens' Account Book II CRO: A 7(b)
p 176 *(22 October) (Chamberlains)*

...

ordinary   And to the wait*es* of this Cittie for their wages for this yere   20
payme*n*tes past   xxvj s viij d

...

p 180 *(26 November) (Wardens)*

...   25

And of xx s by them paid to old Stiffe w*hi*ch is allowed hym by
the house for A ffee   xx s

ffees &   ...
wages paid   And of iiij li. by them paid to the wayt*es* for their wag*es* this yere
past   iiij li   30

...

p 182* *(Wardens)*

payme*n*tes at   ...
Comaundem*en*t   given to Mr goldston there   iij s iiij d   35

...

And given to the Lord Strang*es* musicons   iij s iiij d
players   given to the Lord Chamberlens musicons   iiij s
muscicions And given to the Lord of Essex musicons   x s
Bearward*es* give to lake the Erle of Essex man   ij s   40

given to the Quenes players   xx s
given to Wallans the Berward & his Company   xiij s iiij d
gyven to the Quenes players   xx s
                                    Summa iij li. xij s viij d.
...   5

p 186 *(Wardens)*
...

        The Charges of Eating of ij Buck*es* gyven by   10
                    mr Seargiant Puckering

...
to mr goldston for his musick   ij s vj d
...
                                                                                            15

Council Book CRO: A 14(a)
p 67 col b* *(21 May)*

A trewe note Indented of all the Armor belonging to the Chamber   20
of this Cittie of Coventre And deliu*er*ed in Charge to Robe*r*t Pym
of the same Cittie Cutler the xxjth daye of maij 1589 to dresse &
kepe Cleane & saffe Mr Richard Smythe then being Maior.

1   Ten newe Corslett*es* with head peec*es* vambraces taces and
    Collors. /   25
2   Eight Almon [Ryvett*es*] Corslett*es* with head peec*es* Collers
    vambrac*es* & Taces . /
3   Three Corslett*es* with Collers vambrac*es* & taces without head
    peeces
4   One Almon corslet without Coller or head peece   30
5   One Almon corslet without Coller, headpeece, elbowe or
    forepart /
6   One backe & brest of an Almon Corslet
7   Two old Complet Armors
8   Eleven whit Comorrians with Crest*es*.   35
9   Twelve whit dutch morrions lyned with yellowe buckeram.
10 ffower black dutche morrians one of them lyned with yellow
    Buckera*m*
11 ffouretene flask*es* with flappes vnstrong /
12 Eleven tochboxes with str*ing*es   40
13 Three doson of newe flappes
14 ffoure Bandeliers.

p 68 col a

15 One broken flaske & the topp of a flaske
16 foure bundles of matche waying
17 ffoure horne flaskes without stringes 5
18 thirtene old Swordes without Scaberdes whereof iij be broken
19 fower old daggers & ij old dagger blades

In the gallorie

20 Seaventen black Comorions 10
21 two old white Sallettes
22 ffoure partizantes
23 two holbeardes
24 ffoure gleves
25 one speare poynt 15
26 Twentie two black bills
27 Twentie two bowes
28 Twentie foure sheiffe of Arrowes
29 Thirti one sculls
30 ffourtie one pykes headded 20
31 Ten light horsmens staves headded
32 Nyne Pykes without headdes
33 Twentie Light horsmens staves vnheadded

p 68 col b 25

34 Eleaven byll helver⟨.⟩
35 fourtene short staves
36 Eleven Curriors
37 Twentie three Callivers whereof two be broken 30
38 Twentie newe flaskes & tuchboxes stringed.

Richard Smythe maior
humfrey Smalewood
henry kervyn 35
Richard Barker

Cappers' Records SC: Account Book I
f 128 col b
... 40
payde towardes the Repaire off the pagyn howse v s
...

payde ffor carriage off ower leade to wayinge   iij d

...

payde ffor carriage off harnys on the ffaire day and ffor
poyntes   x d

...   5

Carpenters' Account Book II CRO: Acc 3/2
f 218v*

...

paide for dressynge off owre mvskit and ffor powdre   xvj d   10

...

paide ffor carriage off ij harnys on the ffaire daye and ffor
poyntes   x d

...

payde to Ihon launder and the boyes off bablake on the   15
chowsimge daye   iiij d

...

Mercers' Account Book I CRO: Acc 15
f 49v   20

...

p*aide* for j li. go*n*ne poulder   xvj d
p*aide* for skoweringe the mvske*tes* ˄ ⸢&⸣ for oyle   vj d

...   25

f 50

Paymente*es* Ordinarye /

...

p*aide* vj men for bearinge harnes the faire day   ij s
p*aide* for poynt*es* for the Harnes   iiij d   30

...

Weavers' Account Book CRO: Acc 100/17/1
f 82v

...   35

payd to the singers the same time   xij d

...

Weavers' Rentgatherers' Book II CRO: Acc 100/18/2
ff 11v-12   40

...

It*em* payd for Beryinge of the Harnes   xvj d

...

Item payd for a dosone of poyntes for the harnes   ij d

...

(At the master's)
Item geven to the singers the same nyghte   vj d | 5

...

Item geven to nycolas wheler at the masters Requeste   vj d

A   *Drapers' Accounts* CRO: Acc 154
    f 113 *(Receipts)*   10

...

Rs of georg batman   iij s iiij d

...

(Payments)   15
pd for beryng harnys & poyntts at the fayre   ij s iiij d

...

AC *Smiths' Accounts* Bodl: MS Top. Warwickshire c.7
    f 83v* *(Payments)*   20

...

Item paide for powder & matche on the Queen's holydaye 2/-

...

f 84* *(Receipts)*   25

...

Received in earneste for the iron at the pagent howse vj d ...

1590
Chamberlains' and Wardens' Account Book II CRO: A 7(b)   30
p 191 *(26 October)* *(Chamberlains)*

...

ordinary   And to the waytes for their wages this yere Last past xxvj s viij d
paymentes
...

      35

p 195 *(1 December)* *(Wardens)*

...

ffees &   And of iiij li. paid to mr Goldston for ye waites of this
wages paid Cittie   iiij li.
    And of xx s paid to old Stiffe Late one of the waites by consent 40
    of this house   xx s

...

p 198* *(Wardens)*

...

	Item given to the Erle of Essex musicons	ij s	
	given to the Iud*ges* musicons at the ij assises	vj s viij d	
To players	given to the earle of Essex players	x s	5
	given to the Queenes players ⌐& the turk⌐	xl s	
	given to the Lo*rd* admiralls players	xx s	
	given to the Erle of wirsters players	x s	
	given to Coventrie players	xl s	
	Svm*ma* vj li. viij s viij d		10

...

Cappers' Records SC: Account Book I
f 129 col b

...   15

payd ffor wearynge off harnys and poyntes on the ffaire
daye   x d

...

Carpenters' Account Book II CRO: Acc 3/2   20
f 220a col b

...

payd for wearynge off harnys and poyntes   x d

...

payde Ihon launder ffor his attendaunce   ij d   25

...

Mercers' Account Book CRO: Acc 15
f 52v

...   30

Charge*es* ordinarye & extreordinarye

...

p*aide* vj men for bearinge harnes & the faire daye. & ij doss*en* of
poynt*es*   ij s iiij d

...   35

Shearmen and Tailors' Deed of Conveyance CRO: 100/37*

Omnibus chr*ist*i ffidelibus ad Quos Hec p*rese*ns Carta peruenerit
Iohannes messem De Ciuitat*e* Couentr*ie* in Com*itatu* Eiusdem   40
Sharman Iohannes Rychardson de Eadem Sharman Ricardus
s⟨...⟩t De Eadem Sharman Thom*a*s tymson De Eadem Taylor

willelmus nebee De Eadem Sharman Ricardus yates De Eadem
Taylor Thomas Barrwes De Eadem Sharman Thomas Robynson
de Eadem Sharman ffraunciscus ffarmer De Eadem Taylor
Iohannes Robyns De Eadem Sharman Iohannes Rowley De Eadem
yoman Iohannes Barret De Eadem Taylor Et mauricum Reve De   5
Eadem Taylor Salutem in domino Sempiternam Sciatis Quod nos
prefatis Iohannes messem Iohannes Rychardson Ricardus Sharrat
Thomas tymson willelmus nebee Ricardus yates Thomas Barowes
Thomas Robynson ffraunciscus ffarmer Iohannes Robyns
Iohannes Rowley Iohannes Barrat Et mauricium Reve pro   10
Quadam Racionabile Et Competenti Summa bone Et legalis
monete Anglie nobis prefatis Iohanni messem Iohanni Rychardson
Thome tymson willelmo nebee Ricardo yates Thome Barrowes
Thome Robynson ffrauncisco ffarmer Iohanni Robyns Ihoni
Rowley Iohanni Barrat et mauricio Reve per Iohannem wylkes de   15
Ciuitate oxfford Clericum bene Et fideliter pre manibus Soluta
inde nos prefati Iohannes messem Iohannes Rychardson Ricardus
Sharrat Thomas Tymson willelmus nebee Ricardus yates Thomas
Barrowes Thomas Robynson ffraunciscus ffarmer Iohannes
Robyns Iohannes Rowley Iohannes Barrat Et mauricius Reve   20
fatemur nos plenarie fore persolutos Satisfactos et Contentatos
Deinde que Iohannem wylkes heredes Executores Et
administratores suos. Et Eorum Quemlibet inde Esse Acquietatos
Et Exoneratos Imperpetuum per presentes Alienauimus
feofauimus Barganizauimus vendimus nec non Dedimus   25
Concessimus Et hac presente Carta nostra Confirmauimus prefato
Iohanni wylkes vnum Tenementum Cum Eorum pertinencijs
vniuersis nuper vocatum Le taylors et Sharmens pagent house
Situatum Iacentem Et Existentem in Ciuitate Couentrie predicta
in Quodam vico vocato Le mylle Lane Ex parte occedentali   30
Eiusdem ⟨...⟩ nuper pertinentem. christofero waryn nuper De
Ciuitate Couintrie predicta Dyer modo Deffuncto vocatum Le
tylers et Coupers pagente house Ex Parte Australi Et terras
pertinentes Ad Artem Le Weavers nuper vocatas Le weavers
pagente house Ex parte boreali in Latitudine Et Extendit Se in 35
Longitudine A vico predicto vsque ad gardinum modo vel nuper
in tenura Siue occupatione Cuiusdam (blank) morgan de
Ciuitate De Couentria predicta Tailor vt per metas Et diuisiones
ibidem factas plenius Liquet Et Apparet Habendum Et tenendum
predictum Tenementum Cum Eorum pertinencijs vniuersis prefato 40

7 / prefatis *for* prefati   11 / Racionabile *for* Racionabili

Iohanni wylkes heredibus Et Assignatis Suis Ad Solum et proprium
opus Et vsum Eiusdem Iohannis wilkes heredum Et Assignatorum
Suorum Imperpetuum Tenendum De Cappitalibus Dominis feodi
illius per Seruicia inde prius Debita Et De Iure Consueta Et nos
vere prefati Iohannes messem Iohannes Rychardson Ricardus   5
Sharrat Thomas Tymson willelmus nebee Ricardus yates Thomas
Barrowes Thomas Robynson ffraunciscus ffarmer Iohannes
Robyns Iohannes Rowley Iohannes Barrat Et maurcus Reve Et
heredes nostri omnino predictum Tenementum Cum Eorum
pertinentijs uniuersis prefato Iohanni wylkes heredibus &   10
Assignatis Suis Ad opus Et vsum Supradictum Contra nos Et
heredes Et Successoribus nostris warrantazibimus Et Imperpetuum
Deffendemus per presentes Sciatis Insuper nos prefatos Iohannes
messem Iohannes Rychardson Ricardus Sharrat Thomas Tymson
willelmus nebee Ricardus yates Thomas Barowes Thomas   15
Robynson ffraunciscus ffarmer Iho[hs] Robyns Iohannes Rowley
Iohannes Barrett et mauricum Reve fecisse ordinasse Et in Loco
nostro per presentes posuisse Et Constituisse Dilectum nobis in
christo Robertum Lawton De Ciuitate Couentrie predicta Tanner
nostrum rerum Et legitimum Attornatum Ad intrandum pro nobis   20
vicibus nominibus nostris ⟨...⟩ Tenementum predictum cum Eorum
pertinencijs Et possessionem Ac Seisinam pro nobis vicibus Et
nominibus nostris Capiendam Et post huiusmodi possessionem Et
Seisinam Sic inde Captam Et habitu Ad inde plenam Et pacificam
possessionem prefato Iohanni wilkes Aut Suo in hac parte   25
Attornato pro nobis vicibus & nominibus nostris Deliberandam
Secundum tenorem vim formam Et Effectum huius presentis
Carte nostre Ratum Et gratum habent Et habiturum totum Et ⟨...⟩
Attornatus noster pro nobis vicibus Et nominibus nostris fecerit
in premissis per presentes In Cuius Rei Testimonium nos prefati 30
Iohannes messem Iohannes Rychardson Ricardus Sharrat Thomas
Tymson willelmus nebbe Ricardus Y⟨...⟩ Barrowe Thomas
Robynson ffransciscus ffarmer Iohannes Robyns Iohannes Rowley
& Iohannes Barret Et maurici Reve Signio presenti Carte nostre
Sigilla nostra Apposuimus Data prima die septembris Anno Regni   35
Domine nostre Elizabeth Dei gracia Anglie ffrauncie Et Hibernie

---

12 / Successoribus nostris for successores nostros
13, 14, 16, 17 / Iohannes for Iohannem   14, 15 / Ricardus for Ricardum
14, 15 / Thomas for Thomam   15 / willelmus for willelmum
16 / ffraunciscus for ffraunciscum

Regine ffidei Deffensore Et c. Tricesimo Secundo 1590

(signed with 6 other signatures done by personal marks)
IM Rychard Sharratt Thomas Robynson IR Iohn Rowlye IB
morricum Reue   5

Weavers' Account Book CRO: Acc 100/17/1
f 83v

...

payd to the singers on the Choyse daye   vj d   10

...

Weavers' Rentgatherers' Book II CRO: Acc 100/18/2
f 13v   *(Quarterage meeting)*

...   15

Item payd the same time ther to the wayt pleres   vj d

...

Item payd for a doson of poyntes   ij d
Item payd for beryinge of harnes   xvj d
...   20

A   *Drapers' Accounts* CRO: Acc 154
f 114 *(Receipts)*

...

Rs of george batman   iij s iiij d   25

...

f 115 *(Payments)*

pd Robart pyme for makyng Clene iiij mvskets iiij sords iiij   30
daggers iiij hed pesses   x s

...

pd for harnys & poyntts at the fayre   iij s iiij d

...

pd for nayles to hang the harnys   iij d   35

...

1591
Chamberlains' and Wardens' Account Book II CRO: A 7(b)
p 204   *(26 October) (Chamberlains)*   40

...

ordinary   And to the waytes for their wages this yere past   xxvj s viij d
paymentes
...

p 213* *(9 December)* *(Wardens)*

...

Item given to the Quenes players & the Erle of Sussex players 24
of marche   xv s

To the Erle of worcesters players 2 of Iune   x s   5

To players   To the lord dorcie his players 8 of Iune   x s

To the queenes players 24 of august   xxx s

to the quenes playeres 20 of october   xx s

To Thomas massie & his parteners   xx s

                                      Summa *(blank)*   10

...

                             ffees & wages

...

To mr Goldston   iiij li.

...   15

To old Stiffe   xx s

...

Council Book CRO: A 14(a)
p 216* *(19 May)*   20

pageons   It is also agreed by the whole consent of this house that the
distrucion of Ierusalem the Conquest of the Danes or the historie

•Destruction of   of K E the 4 at the request of the Comons of this Cittie shalbe
Ierusalem
Conquest of   plaid on the pagens on Midsomer daye & St peters daye next in   25
the Danes   this Cittie & non other playes. / And that all the mey poles that
History of King   nowe are standing in this Cittie shalbe taken downe before
Edward 4th.   whitsonday next, non hereafter to be sett vpp in this Cittie.

...

                                                      30

Cappers' Records SC: Account Book I
f 130 col a *(Receipts)*

Receaued off the masters off the walkers   vj s viij d
Receaued off the masters off the skynnars   iiij s   35
Receaued off the masters off the Ioynars and glaciars   iij s iiij d

...

col b *(Payments)*

...   40

payde ffor warynge off harnys and poynts on the ffaire
day   x d

payd to thomas massei towards the playes at mr maiors
appoyntmente   xx s

...

payd to Ihon grene ffor writing owre comyssion and our
svpplicacion   iij s iiij d   5
payd ffor settinge In off owre pagyn and making ffaste the
dores   xvj d
paide ffor one howke ffor the dore   ij d

...

10

Carpenters' Account Book II CRO: Acc 3/2
f 222v*

Item payde towarde the pagyns   vj s viij d

...   15

Item payde ffor wearynge off harnys and poyntes   x d

...

Mercers' Account Book CRO: Acc 15
f 55v   20

...

Chargees Ordinary.

...

paide vj men for bearinge harnes on the faire daye, 2s. & for ij
dossyn poyntes   ij s iiij d   25

...

f 56
Paymentees Extraordinarye.

...   30

paide Thomas Masseye towardes plainge the
pagantes   xxxiij s iiij d

...

paide for mendinge the pagant house windowes, & corde to
bynde them   xxj d   35

...

Weavers' Account Book CRO: Acc 100/17/1
f 84v

...   40

Item payd to singers on saynt osburnes nyghte   viij d

...

Item geven to the singers the said daye   vj d

...

Item payd to maister mayor for the padgantes   xx s

...

    5

Weavers' Rentgatherers' Book II CRO: Acc 100/18/2
f 17

...

Item payd to fore harnes men and for poyntes   xviij d

...   10

AC   *Butchers' Accounts* Bodl: MS Top. Warwickshire c.7
f 100v*

...

Itm paid to Whelar at Mr Mayor Comaundement towards the   15
pageants   xiij s iiij d

...

AC   *Cappers' Accounts* BL: Add MS 43645
f 57v* *(3 January)*   20

The Invitori of the Implments of the company of cappers being
taken the thirde daye of Januari 1590 in the xxxix^th yere of the
Raigne of oure soveraigne ladie elizabeth

   25

Itm one table one forme one carpet one paynted clothe one setlis
abowte the chaumber one coffer
Itm more one muskitte one headpese one girdle with the chargis
one sworde one dagger belonging to the same
Itm iij almayne Revettes iij headpeses vj paire of splentes one box   30
iij swordes ij daggers iij Jacks ij buckettes iij pesis of male
        In the under chaumber
Itm iij coffers one little cofer one boxe to put money in.
Itm ij pawles
Itm sixe cressites ij streamers and the poles ij bisshoppes myters   35
Itm pylates dublit ij curtaynes the spirate of godes cote godes
cotes and the hose pylates heade fyve maries heades one coyffe
mary maudlyns goune iij beardes gods head the spirites heade
sixe pensils iiij Rolles iij marye boxes one play boke.
The giandes head and clubbe pylates clubbe hell mowth iiij   40
standinge iij small stremars adams spade Ives distaffe ij angels

---

41 / Ives: *H-P:* Outlines *I, p 342, reads* Eves

awbes one dore for a seate.

...

A   *Drapers' Accounts*   CRO: Acc 154
    ff 116-17 *(Receipts)*   5

...

Res of georg batman   iij s iiij d

...

(Payments)   10
    pd Thomas massye for the pagen   xl s

...

pd John Syngler for meddyng the pagen howse   vj s viij d

...

pd for harnes & poyntts at the fayre   ij s iiij d | 15
pd Thomas Senye for nayle for the harnes   iij d
pd for nayles for the pagen howse   xiiij d
pd for Corde & horssyng the pagen   vj d

...

                                                                             20
AC *Smiths' Accounts*   Bodl: MS Top. Warwickshire c.7
    f 84

... It*e*m payd to Mr. Mayor towards the playes of the
pageaunts, xx s.   25

...

1592
Chamberlains' and Wardens' Account Book II   CRO: A 7(b)
p 217 *(24 October) (Chamberlains)*   30

...

ordinary   And to the wait*es* for their wages   xxvj s viij d
paymen*tes*

...

p 219 *(29 November) (Wardens)*   35
                                ffees & wag*es*

...

And of iiij li. paid to the wayt*es* this yere   iiij li.

...

and of x s p*ai*d to old Styff for di a yere   x s   40

...

p 221 *(Wardens)*

And of vj s viij d given to the Lord morles players	vj s viij d
And of x s given to the Erle of worcesters players	x s
And of x s given to the Lord Shandos players	x s
And of xij d given to the Erle of Essex musicons	xij d
And of v s given to mr duttons players	v s
And of vj s viij d given to the lord darcies players	vj s viij d
And of xiij s iiij d given to the Queens Bearward	xiij s iiij d
And of xx s given to the Lord Strange playerz	xx s
And of xl s given to the Queenes players	xl s

*To players &
bearwardes*

Summa vj li xij s viij d /

...

Cappers' Records SC: Account Book I
f 131 col b

...

payd ffor wearynge off harnys and poyntes on the ffaire day   x d

...

Carpenters' Account Book II CRO: Acc 3/2
f 224v

...

Item payd ffor wearynge off harnys and poynts   x d

...

payde Ihon launder and the boyes off bablake on the choyse
day   iiij d

...

Mercers' Account Book CRO: Acc 15
f 3v* *(11 October)*

...

Memorandum that this day being the xj[th] of october 1592 at
owr hall it is agred by the wholle company, that Richard
ffeareman owr Clarke shall have yerely xiij s iiij d to be paid him
quarterly. And shall also have for & during his life the Rent of
owr garden at the pagant howse / ...

f 59

Paymentes Ordanarie /

...

paide vj harneste men on coventre faire Daie & for 2 Dosen of

poyntes   ij s iiij d
...
paide for nayles & mendinge the pagene howse   vj d
...
5
Weavers' Account Book CRO: Acc 100/17/1
f 85v

...
Item payd to the singers at wylli*am* woralles [w] on saynt
osbornes nyghte   vj d 10
Item payd at good wyffe Rowleyes to the mvssiones when we
kepte our quarter day   ij s
...
Item payd to the mvsisiones the same day   ij s vj d
...   15

Weavers' Rentgatherers' Book II CRO: Acc 100/18/2
f 18v

...
Item payd to golston at the quarter day at nyghte   ij s 20
...
Item payd to the berers of Harnes at the fayre   xviij d
...

f 19   25
...
Item payd when we Reseued the moneys for the players
aparell   xij d
...

30
A *Drapers' Accounts* CRO: Acc 154
f 118 *(Receipts)*

Rsd of george battman for his Rent   iij s iiij d
...   35
          Payments for our Company thys yeere 1592
...
payd to James bradshawe for mendyng the paggon howse xviij d
payd for harnys beareng & poynts   ij s ij d
...   40

1593
Chamberlains' and Wardens' Account Book II CRO: A 7(b)
p 226 *(22 October) (Chamberlains)*
...

ordinary
paymentes

And to the waytes for their wages this yere past   xxvj s viij d   5

...

p 229 *(27 November) (Wardens)*
...

ffees &
wages paid

And of iiij li. paid to mr goldston in parte of his wages for the   10
waytes   iiij li.

...

p 231 *(Wardens)*

To players & Bearewardes   15

Item given to the Lord Admiralls players   xiij s iiij d
And to the Lord Shandos players   xiij s iiij d
And to the Queenes maiesties players   xl s
And to the Erle of pembrokes players   xxx s
And to the Tumbler that went on the Ropes   xx s   20
and to mr Burnabies Beareward   v s.
Summa vj li. j s viij d.

...

paymentes at
Comandment

paid for ij wynd Instrumentes called Curtalls that mr goldston
hathe for the Cittie   xxxiij s iiij d   25

Payments Out Book CRO: A 16
p 70 *(17 November)*
...

paid to Thomas massie & william Showell for their paynes on the   30
queenes hollidaye   xx s.

Cappers' Records SC: Account Book I
f 132 col a
...   35

Item geven to the mynstrels at the pecock   vj d

...

Item payde to christoffor turnar ffor mendynge the pagyn
dores   ij d

...   40

Item payde carriage off harnys and poyntes   x d
...

Carpenters' Account Book II CRO: Acc 3/2
f 226 col a   5
...

payd ffor wearynge off the harnys and poynts   x d
...
payde Iohn launder and the childerne off bablake   iiij d
...   10

Mercers' Account Book CRO: Acc 15
f 60*
...

Re*ceave*de more ffor 2 Littell Wheeles that were solde   xij d   15
...

f 62

Ordenarie paymend*es*   20
...
p*ai*d 6 [Ha] ʹmenʹ that Caried Harnes on the faire daie for owr
Companie, & for 2 dos*yn* poynt*es*   ij s iiij d
...

                        Extrordenarie Charg*es*   25
...
p*ai*d A workmane & for Corde, for mendinge the pagene
howse   vj d
...
p*ai*d for iij li of gunepowther & matche   iij s ix d   30
p*ai*d to 6 men that bare harnis on the Queens night   ij s
p*ai*de to 3 men that Caried & shot in owr muskett*es*   xviij d
...

Weavers' Account Book CRO: Acc 100/17/1   35
f 86v
...

It*em* geven to the singers the same daye at Iohn swetes   x d
...
It*em* geven to the mvssisiones the same daye   xviij d   40
...

Weavers' Rentgatherers' Book II CRO: Acc 100/18/2
f 20v

...

It*em* payd for berynge Harnes on the fayer day & for
poyntes   xviij d   5

...

(Choice Day)
It*em* geven to the singers the same daye   ix d
                                                                                        10
...

It*em* payd for scourynge the to gonies and for caryeng of them on
saynt Huese nyghte   xx d
It*em* payd to f*ore* men to bayer our harnes the same daye   xvj d
It*em* payd· for poyntes and maches   iiij d
                                                                                        15
...

A   *Drapers' Accounts* CRO: Acc 154
f 119 *(Receipts)*

...

Rsd of george batman for his yeares Rent   iij s iiij d   20

...

f 120 *(Payments)*

...

payde harnes berars at the feare   ij s ij d   25

...

payde for pavinge the strete of the pagen house   iij s

...

1594   30
Chamberlains' and Wardens' Account Book II CRO: A 7(b)
p 237 *(23 October)* *(Chamberlains)*

...

ordinary   And to the way*tes* for their wages this yere   xxvj s viij d
paym*en*tes   35
                 ...

p 240 *(20 November)* *(Wardens)*

...

ffees &   And of iiij li. paid to mr Goldston for his ffee for the waytes this
wag*es* paid   yere   iiij li.   40

...

p 245 *(Wardens)*
>   To players & bearward*es*
given to the L*or*d of darbyes players the 2 of decembr 93   xx s
given to mr Burnabies Beareward 22 of Ianuory   x s
given to the L*or*d mountegles players i of februory   xiij s iiij d   5
given to the Queenes players 4 of Iuly 94   xl s
>   Su*m*ma iiij li. iij s. iiij d

...

Payments Out Book C R O: A 16   10
p 70.* *(26 March)*

...

p*ai*d to Thomas massie & *willia*m Showell for their paynes on the
queenes hollidaye   xx s
>   15

Cappers' Records S C: Account Book I
f 132v col a *(Receipts)*

...

R*eceiv*ed of the Skynners toward*es* ye charge of the Musket on
St. hughes nyght   viij d   20

...

f 133 col a *(Payments)*

p*ai*d the same daye to the Syngers   iiij d   25

...

p*ai*d on St. hughes daye for bearinge of harnes, and for
poyntes   x d
p*ai*d for Gonnepowder   xviij d
p*ai*d to the bearer of ye muskett, & for matche   viij d   30
p*ai*d for nayles to the paginhowse dore   j d

...

col b

...   35

P*ai*d to Nicholas cowper for mendinge the pagent howse dore;
and for a ledge and a borde, and for nayles   xij d

...

Payed on the faire daye for caraienge of harnes, and for
poyntes   x d   40

...

3 / a *of* players *written over* y

Carpenters' Account Book II CRO: Acc 3/2
f 228

...

Item payde ffor werynge off harnys and poynts on the ffaire
daye   x d   5

...

Item paid Iohn powle ffor bringinge the harnis on the ffaire
day   ij d

...

Item payde to Iohn launder and the boyes off bablake   iiij d   10

...

Mercers' Account Book CRO: Acc 15
f 65v

...   15

Paymentes Extreordanarye

...

paide ffor corde & nayles & mendinge the pageone howse
dores   xx d

...   20

Ordenarie Paymentes

...

paide to vj men for Caringe Harnes on the ffaire daye   ij s iiij d

...   25

Weavers' Rentgatherers' Book II CRO: Acc 100/18/2
f 22v

...

Item payd to the mvssisiones and singers on saynt osburnes
nyght   ij s viij d   30

...

Item payd for adoson of poyntes   ij d
Item payd to the fore men that bare harnes on the fayre
day   xvj d

...   35

A   ### Drapers' Accounts CRO: Acc 154
f 121 (Receipts)

...

Reseved of george batmans wyfe her Rent   iij s iiij d   40

...

The payments ffor ye yeare 1594

...

pd to vj harnes berars & ffor poynts   ij s iiij d

...

(Company meeting)
pd to the musisions there   ij s

...

A C   *Dyers' Accounts*   Bodl: MS Top. Warwickshire c.7   10
     f 116

...

Sold ij harnysses wayinge in weighte lxxvj pound, at a penny a
pounde

...

1595
Chamberlains' and Wardens' Account Book II   CRO: A 7(b)
p 252 *(29 October) (Chamberlains)*

...

ordinary
paym*en*tes And to the wayt*es* for their wages this yere   xxvj s viij d

...

p 256 *(2 December) (Wardens)*

...

ffees &
wag*es* paid And of iiij li. paid to mr Goldston for his wag*es* for the wayt*es*
this yere   iiij li.

...

p 259 *(Wardens)*
Reward*es* to players & bearward*es*

To the Lo*rd* Stafford*es* musicions	xij d
To the Lo*rd* Ogles players	x s
To the Queenes Bearward	v s
To the Earle of Essex musicons	ij s
To the Lo*rd* Mountagues players	xiij s iiij d
To the Lo*rd* Morleys players	x s
To the Earle of Shresberies bearward	ij s vj d
To the Lo*rd* darsies players	x s
To the Lo*rd* Mountegles players	x s
To the Queenes Bearward 22 of maye	v s

To the Queenes Players 29 of august   xx s
To the Lord Shandoes players   x s
To the Lord Ogles players 28 of october   x s
                                    Summa v li. viij s x d
...   5

p 260

...

Paymentes at
Comaundement

paid to mr goldston for musick at the last wardens accompt by
maister maiors appoyntment   ij s   10
...

Cappers' Records SC: Account Book I
f 134
...   15
paid for carriage of harnys and poynts on the faire day   x⟨.⟩j d
...
paid for ij harnyste men and poynts on the qvenes holyday   x d
...   20

Carpenters' Account Book II CRO: Acc 3/2
f 230v
...
paid for wearynge of harnys and poynts   x d
...   25
paide Iohn launder and the boyes of bablake   iiij d
...

Mercers' Account Book CRO: Acc 15
f 68v   30
...
                    Paymentes Ordenarye
...
paide to vj^e Harnest men & for poyntes one the faire
daie   ij s iiij d   35
...

f 69
                    Paymentes Extreordenarie
...   40
paide to 3 men to carie & shute, in owr Muskettes Queens Holie

daye   xviij d
p*aide* for iij li gunepowther & matche   iiij s
p*aide* for the ffivetene for owre Pageone Howse   vj d
...

                                                                                5

Weavers' Rentgatherers' Book II CRO: Acc 100/18/2
f 25

...

It*em* payd for Baryinge of the Harnes and for poyntes   xviij d
...   10
It*em* geven to the mvsisiones the same Choyse daye   ij s
...

A   *Drapers' Accounts* CRO: Acc 154
    f 122 *(Receipts)*   15

...

It for the hyer of *oure* players Clothes w*ith* other suche
Stufe   iiij s
...

                                                                               20

f 123 *(Payments)*

...

payd for the harneshynge of vj men at *our* faire   ij s iiij d
...

payd for settynge furth of viij men for berenge of harnysh &   25
muskett of the corwnacyon day   vj s ij d
...

1596
Chamberlains' and Wardens' Account Book II CRO: A 7(b)   30
p 265 *(27 October) (Chamberlains)*

...

ordinary   And of xxvj s viij d paid to the wayt*es* for their wag*es* this
paym*en*tes   yere   xxvj s viij d
           ...   35

p 269 *(1 December) (Wardens)*

...

ffees &   And of iiij li. paid to mr Goldston for the wayt*es*   iiij li.
wages   ...   40

p 270 *(Wardens)*

...

Rewardes to Players & bearwardes

To the Earle of huntingtons beareward	vj s viij d	
To the Lord willoughbyes players	x s	5
To the Queenes players	x s	
To Sir ffoulk Grevylls bearward	x s	
To the morrisdauncers of Stonley	iij s iiij d	
To the Lord darsies players	vj s viij d	
To the Lord Ogles players	x s	10
To the Queenes Players	xl s	
To the Earle of darbies players	x s	
To the Lord Admiralls players	x s	
To the Queenes trumpeterz & the Earle of Essex musicions	iiij s vj d	15

Rewardes to
players &
bearewardes

Summa vj li. j s ij d

p 271 *(Wardens)*
Paymentes at Commaundement

...   20

paid to certen men that Carried armor on the quenes holidaye at night   ij s j d

...

paid to Thomas massie for hym selfe & the singers the same night   xx s   25

...

Cappers' Records   SC: Account Book I
f 134v col b *(Receipts)*

...   30

Receaued for fvrrs of the players gownes   xiiij d

...

Receaued of Richard Dabson for byshopps [w] hoddes   viij s

...   35

f 135 col a *(Payments)*

payde for wearyng of harnys on the quenes holyeday   x d

...

paid for wearyng of harnys and poynts on the faire daye   x d   40

...

Carpenters' Account Book II CRO: Acc 3/2
f 232v

...

paid for wearynge of harnys and poynts on the faire day   x d

...   5

paid Iohn lander and the boyes of bablake for the cownte
dynner   v d

...

Mercers' Account Book CRO: Acc 15   10
f 71v *(Extraordinary payments)*

...

paide for A fivtene ffor owr Pageone howse   vj d

...
                                                                                    15

f 72 *(Ordinary payments)*

...

paide to 6 men to weare Harnesse one the ffayre Daye & ffor 2
dossen poynt*es*   ij s iiij d

...   20

Weavers' Account Book CRO: Acc 100/17/1
f 89

...

It*em* payd on saynt Hueghes daye to them that bare   25
harnes   ij s j d

...

Weavers' Rentgatherers' Book II CRO: Acc 100/18/2
f 26v   30

...

It*em* payd on the Quenes daye for pouder and maches   ij s v d

...

(Quarter Day)   35
It*em* payd more the same time to the singers   viij d

...

---

6 / la *of* lander *altered from* sh *(for* Shingle, *another carpenter?)*

Item payd for barying of the harnes and for poyntes on the fayer
daye   xviij d

...

A   *Drapers' Accounts* CRO: Acc 154   5
      f 125

...

paid for the repaire of the pagin House by mr Tallanes
appointment   0 1 8

...   10

f 126

...

paid to Harnest men at the ffaire   0 2 4

...   15

1597
Chamberlains' and Wardens' Account Book II CRO: A 7(b)
p 281 *(26 October)* *(Chamberlains)*

...   20

ordinarye   And to the waytes of this Cittie towardes their wages this yere
paymentes   past   xxvj s viij d

...

p 287   *(7 December)* *(Wardens)*   25

...

ffees &   And of iiij li paid to mr Goldston for the waytes   iiij li.
wages paid
...

p 289 *(Wardens)*   30

...

To the Tumbler   iij s iiij d
To the Earle of harfordes players   xx s
To the Earle of darbies [players] bearward   x s
To the Lord mountegles players   x s   35
To the Earle of Essex musicions   v s
To the Lord Shandoes players   x s
Rewardes to   To mr Baggottes beareward   [v s] ij s vj d
players &   To the Queenes Players   xx s
bearwardes   To the Earle of [Essex] oxfordes beareward   v s   40

To the Earle of darbies beareward   v s
To the Earle of huntingtons players   x s
To the Earle of darbies plears   x s
To the Lord Ogles players   x s

                      Summa vj li. x d   5

...

Cheylesmore Manor Account Book CRO: A 9
p 190 *(29 September)*
The Rentall of the manor of Chellesmore   10

...

Cheiffe Rentes   The Comppany of girdlers for a Cheiff Rent out of their pagen
house   iiij d

...
                                                    15

Cappers' Records SC: Account Book I
f 136

...

Item paid for wearynge of harnys and poynts on the faire
day   x d   20

...

Item paide for mendynge of owre pawls   iiij d

...

Carpenters' Account Book II CRO: Acc 3/2   25
f 234

...

payd for wearynge of harnys on the faire day and for
poynts   x d
...   30
paide Iohn launder   iiij d

...

Mercers' Account Book CRO: Acc 15
f 74   35

...
                      Paymentes Extreordenarye

...
paid for the fifteens of pageone howse & Hall   xviij d
...   40

f 74v
                    Payment*es* Ordenarie
...
p*ai*d to 6 men ffor Caringe Harnis one the ffaire Daie. & ffor
poynt*es*   ij s iiij d   5
...

Weavers' Rentgatherers' Book II CRO: Acc 100/18/2
f 28v
...   10
It*em* payd for beryng harnes on the fare day and for
poyntes   xviij d
...

A   *Drapers' Accounts* CRO: Acc 154   15
     f 127
...
It pd for harnishinge vj men at our ffayre   ij s iiij d
...
                                                                        20
1598
Chamberlains' and Wardens' Account Book II CRO: A 7(b)
p 294 *(25 October) (Chamberlains)*
...
ordinary   And to the wayt*es* for their wages this yere   xxvj s viij d   25
paym*en*tes
...

p 301 *(5 December) (Wardens)*
...
ffees &   And of iiij li paid to mr Goldstons wiffe for the wayt*es*   30
wag*es* paid   wages   iiij li.
...

p 303 *(Wardens)*
...   35
                    Reward*es* to players & bearward*es*
To the Earle of huntingtons players   x s
To the Earle of Essex musicons   v s
To the musicons of london   v s
To the Lord stafford*es* players   vj s   40
To the Earle of darbies players   x s

To the Lord darsies players   v s
To the Lord morleys players   x s
To the Lord Barkles players   x s
To the Lord willowghbyes musicons   iij s iiij d
To the Earle of darbies players by a warrant from mr Clarke   5
maior   xx s.
                              Summa iiij li. iiij s iiij d

...

Cappers' Records SC: Account Book I   10
f 137

...

paid for wearynge of harnys and poyntes   x d
paide the mvssicions   xij d
paid Ihon pyckrynge for bordes for mending of owre pagyn   15
howse dore and for nayles and workmanshippe   ij s vj d

...

Carpenters' Account Book II CRO: Acc 3/2
f 236 col b   20

...

paid for wearynge of harnys and poyntes   x d

...

paide the boyes of bablake   ij d

...   25

Mercers' Account Book CRO: Acc 15
f 77

...

                        Paymentes Ordenarie   30

...

paid to 6 Harnis men & ffor poyntes one fayre daye   ij s iiij d

...

f 77v   35
                        Paymentes Extreordenarye

...

paid ffor mendinge pagen howse dore   iiij d

...

paid ffor A doobell 15 ffor ye pagene howse   xij d   40

...

Weavers' Account Book CRO: Acc 100/17/1
f 91

...

Reseyvyd for the Hier of the scarlet gowne of mores
Reeve   ij s vj d   5

...

Weavers' Rentgatherers' Book II CRO: Acc 100/18/2
f 30

...   10

Item payd at pyninges when we lent the players aparell to
cosselle   vj d

...

Item payd for berynge of the Harnes and for poyntes   xviij d

...   15

A   *Drapers' Accounts* CRO: Acc 154
f 129

...

It pd for harnessing vj men at our ffaire   ij s iiij d   20

...

f 130

...

It pd for ffiftine for the pagen howse   xij d   25

...

1599
Chamberlains' and Wardens' Account Book II CRO: A 7(b)
p 309 *(24 October) (Chamberlains)*   30

...

ordinary   And to the waytes for their wages this yere past   xxvj s viij d
paymentes

...

p 314 *(28 November) (Wardens)*   35

...

ffees &   And of iiij li paid to mr Goldstons wiffe for the waites
wages   wages   iiij li.

...

p 316 *(Wardens)*
        Rewardes to players & bearewardes by maister
            maiors Comaundement

To the Earle of penbrokes players the 12 of december	x s	
To the Lord willoughbyes players	x s	5
To the Earle of worcesters players	x s	
To the Lord morley his players	x s	
To hym that had the poppittes & Daniell	x s	
To the Earle of darbies beareward	x s	
To the Lord darsie his players	x s	10
To the Earle of penbrokes players the iiijth of Iuly	x s	
To the Lord Shandoos players the 4 of Iune	x s	

                         Summa iiij li. x s.

...

                                      15

p 317* *(Wardens)*

...

paid by maister maiors Comandement to Thomas		
Goldston at his going to Cambridge towardes his	xl s	
setling ther in Sir John harringtons Colledg		20

...

p 318* *(Wardens)*

...

given to the Earles trumpeters by the same note	x s	25

...

given to the Earles drummers	ij s vj d	

...

Cappers' Records SC: Account Book I   30
f 137v col a

...

Receavde of the skynnars towards the dressyng of		
svruitars	xiij d	

...   35

f 138 col a

...

paid at mr chaumberlaynes to the mvssicions	xij d	

...   40

paid for carriage of harnys and poynts   x d

...

Carpenters' Account Book II CRO: Acc 3/2
f 238v   5

...

paide for dressynge of owr furniture   iiij s iij d

...

paid more for dressynge of harnys for the faire day   xvj d
paide for wearynge of harnys and poynts   x d   10

...

Mercers' Account Book CRO: Acc 15
f 80v

...   15

Payment*es* Ordenarie

...

p*a*id 6 men to beare Armore one the ffaire daie ˈ& for
point*es*ˈ   ij s ij d

...   20

Payment*es* Extreordinarie

...

p*a*id mor A dobell ffifteene for the pageone howse   xij d
p*a*id for corde & nailes for pageone howse Wyndoes   viij d

...   25

Weavers' Account Book CRO: Acc 100/17/1
f 92

R*esetes* for for Sealing of Indenturs
R*eseyvyd* more for the Hiere of one scarlet goune   ij s vj d   30

...

Weavers' Rentgatherers' Book II CRO: Acc 100/18/2
f 31v

...   35

It*em* p*ayd* for barying of the Harnes   xviij d

...

29 / for for *MS dittography*

A   *Drapers' Accounts* CRO: Acc 154
    f 131

    ...

    It pd for 6 harnish men at ffayre   ij s iiij d

    ...   5

    It pd for ye ffiftine for ye padgon house   xij d

    ...

    It pd to Thomas Sency for ye padgon house windoes   viij d

    ...   10

    1600
    Chamberlains' and Wardens' Account Book II CRO: A 7(b)
    p 323 *(30 October) (Chamberlains)*

    ...

ordinary   And to the waytes for their wages this yere   xxvj s viij d   15
paymentes
              ...

              p 329 *(20 November) (Wardens)*

              ...

ffees &   And of iiij li. paid to the waites for yer wages   iiij li.   20
wages
              ...

              p 331* *(Wardens)*

              To the Earle of huntingtons players the 17 of December   x s   25
              To the Lord Staffordes players the 26 of December   x s
              To the Lord hawardes players 28 December 99   x s
              To the Earle of worcesters players 3 Ianuarij 99   x s
              To the Earle of lincolnes players 4 Ianuarij 99   x s
Rewardes to   To the Earle of Essex musicons 18 Ianuarij   v s   30
players &   To the Lord morles pleares 30 Ianuarij   x s
bearwardes   To the Lord darcies players 10 maj 1600   x s
              To the Lord dudles Bearward 3 Iulij   ij s vj d
              To the Earle of huntingtons players 7 Iulij   x s
              To the Lord Chandos players 19 Iulij 1600   x s   35
                          Summa iiij li. xvij s vj d
              be it had in mind that the lord Shandoes players were comitted
              to prisone for their contempt agaynst maister maior & ther
              Remayned vntill they made their submissione vnder ther hands as
              apeareth in the fyle of Record vnder their hands to be seene . / †   40

37-40 / *marginal note to the left of entry (l. 35) in MS*

p 332* *(Wardens)*

...

paid to mr Tovie, for his scolers playing A
tragidie Acted at m*aiste*r maiors house   xx s
the 22 of februarij 1599   5

...

Paid to mr Tovie & the Rest of the scole masters at
the walking of the Citties Land*es* in Lent by m*aister*
maurs appoyntm*en*t To mr Tovie 13s 4d to mr   xxvj s viij d
Arnold 6s 8d to mr Cawdrey & goldstone 6s 8d   10

...

p 333* *(Wardens)*

...

Paid to Thomas yong for iiij lynkes deliu*er*ed to   15
ffranc*es* nall that night that the L*ord* Shandos   xx d
players playd at the angell contrary to m*aiste*r
maiors pleasure

...
                                                                        20

Carpenters' Account Book II CRO: Acc 3/2
f 241 col a

...

paid for dressynge of harnys for the faire day   xvj d
paid for wearynge of harnys the faire day and for poynts   x d   25

...

col b *(Account Day)*

...

It*e*m paid to the mvssicons   vj d   30

...

Mercers' Account Book CRO: Acc 15
f 84

                    Paym*entes* Ordenarij   35

...

p*ai*d the ffifteene of the pagene howse   xij d

...

p*ai*d to 6 men for caringe harnis one the ffaire daye   ij s
p*ai*d ffor Poynt*es*   ij d   40

...

Weavers' Account Book CRO: Acc 100/17/1
f 93

              Resetes for [b] sealling of Indentures

...

Reyseyvyd for the Hier of our scarlet goune of Robart   5
batham   ij s vj d

...

f 93v* *(Payments)*

...   10
Item payd at walter barkleys when we hired our carlde gone to
tanvorthe   ij d

...

Weavers' Rentgatherers' Book II CRO: Acc 100/18/2   15
f 33v

...

Item payd for beryng of harnes on the fayre daye and for
poyntes   xviij d
...   20

f 34

Item payd to the sargant for geving Thomas massie somanes   ij d
...   25

A   *Drapers' Accounts* CRO: Acc 154
   f 133
...
Itm pd to vj harnesst men at the ffaire   ij s iiij d   30
...

1601
Chamberlains' and Wardens' Account Book II CRO: A 7(b)
p 337 *(27 October) (Chamberlains)*   35
...
ordinary   And to the waytes for their wages this yere past   xxvj s viij d
paymentes   ...

11 / r *of* carlde *written over* l

p 342 *(2 December)* *(Wardens)*

...

And of iiij li. paid to the waites for their wages   iiij li.

...

p 344 *(Wardens)*

...

Rewardes to Players & bearewardes by maister maiors Commandement

To Sir ffulke Grivells beareward	x s
To the Lord dudles Players	vj s viij d
To the Lord dudles players another tyme	iij s iiij d
To the Earle of huntingtons players	x s
To the Queenes Players	xxx s
To the Musicions of northampton	ij s vj d
To the Earle of Essex musicions	iij s iiij d
To the Earle of darbies [players] beareward	iij s iiij d
To the Earle of lincolnes players	x s
To the lord mountegles players	x s
To Mr Talbottes musicons	xviij d
To the Earle of worcesters players	x s
To the Lord Evers players	x s

Rewardes to players and Bearewardes

Summa v li. x s viij d

p 345* *(Wardens)*

Paymentes at Comaundement

...

paymentes at Comaundement

Paid to widdoe massam the virginall makers wiffe to bring her to basingstoke   iij s iiij d

...

p 346* *(Wardens)*

...

paymentes at Comaundement

given to Golston then   v s

...

Cappers' Records SC: Account Book I
f 140

...

paid for wearynge of harnys on the faire daye and byrynge of ij weapons and poynts   xij d

...

Carpenters' Account Book II CRO: Acc 3/2
f 243

...

paid for dressyng owr harny for the faire day   xvj d
paide for wearynge of harnys and poynts on the faire daye   x d   5

...

f 243v *(Account dinner)*

...

paid to the mvsicions   vj d   10

...

Mercers' Account Book CRO: Acc 15
f 87 *(Payments Ordinary and Extraordinary)*

...   15

pa*i*d 6 men ffor Caringe Harnis one the faire daie & for
point*es*   ij s iiij d

...

pa*i*d for viij li. of gune Powther spent Queens Hollie
Daie   ix s iiij d 20
pa*i*d for iij li. Matche ʼ& A skowerʼ   xv d 15d
pa*i*d to 6 mene to shute Queens Hollie Daie   iiij s

...

Weavers' Rentgatherers' Book II CRO: Acc 100/18/2   25
f 36

...

It*em* pa*y*d for berynge of harnes & for poynt*es*   xviij d

...

It*em* pa*y*d to the sargant for arestinge of Thomas   30
massie   xvj d

...

A   *Drapers' Accounts* CRO: Acc 154
    f 135   35

...

pd for Six Harnes men at the ffayer   ij s iiij d

...

pd on the Queens Holida ffor Six pound of powder & to Six men
to Showt in muskets at m*aiste*r maiors Appo*ynte*m*ent*   x s ij d   40

...

21 / v *of* xv *written over illegible letter;* 15d *is clarification.*

1602
Chamberlains' and Wardens' Account Book II CRO: A 7(b)
p 349·(27 *October*) (*Chamberlains*)

...

And to the waytes for their wages this yere past   xxvj s viij d   5

...

p 353 (20 *December*) (*Wardens*)

...

ffees &   And of iiij li. paid to the waytes for their wages   iiij li.   10
wages paid
...

p 354 (*Wardens*)

...

To the Lord morleys Players   x s   15
To the Earle of darbies players   xiij s iiij d
To the Earle of worcesters players   x s
Rewardes to   To the Earle of linckolnes players   xiij s iiij d
players   To the Lord Ogles players   vj s viij d
To the Earle of huntingtons players   x s   20
To the Lord dudles players   x s
To the Lord darsies players   vj s viij d
To the Lord Staffordes players   v s
                              Summa iiij li. v s

                                                                         25

p 356 (*Wardens*)

...

paymentes at   given to mr Arnold the vsher for his playe   xx s
Comaundement
...

                                                                         30

Cappers' Records SC: Account Book I
f 141

...

payde for werynge of harnys and poynts   x d
...   35
paid to the mvssicions   xij d

...

Carpenters' Account Book II CRO: Acc 3/2
f 245v   40

...

paid the mvssicyons   iiij d

...

payde for wearynge of harnys and poyntes   x d
...

f 246
...   5
paide to the mvssicions   xij d
...

Mercers' Account Book CRO: Acc 15
f 88*   10
...

               R*eseat*tes of owre Landes //
...

Re*seaved* of Ric*bard* Bank*es* for A howse in gosford Street, Late
the Pageone howse, sett p*er* Lease   xxvij s   15
...

f 90
           Paymen*tes* Ordenarie & Extreordenarie
...   20
p*ai*d to 6 bearers of harnis & poyn*tes* on ye faire daie   ij s iiij d
...
p*ai*d to Thomas Massie at comandment of the companie   xx s
...

                                                                                   25

Weavers' Rentgatherers' Book II CRO: Acc 100/18/2
f 38v
...

It*em* p*ayd* for setting forthe of our mvsketes on the quenes
nyghte   iiij s ij d   30
...

Item p*ayd* on the fayre daye to the harnes men   xvj d
...

A   *Drapers' Accounts* CRO: Acc 154   35
   f 137
...

pd to vj men ffor ye caringe of armor at ye ffayre   0 ij s iiij d
...

1603
Chamberlains' and Wardens' Account Book II CRO: A 7(b)
p 358 *(27 October) (Chamberlains)*

...

And to the wayt*es* for their wag*es* this yere past   xxvj s viij d   5

...

p 364 *(17 November) (Wardens)*

...

And of iiij li. paid to the wait*es* for their wages   iiij li.   10

...

p 366 *(Wardens)*

              Reward*es* to players & bearward*es*

To the Lord haywarde*s* Players	v s	15
To the Kyng*es* Players	xl s	
To the Earle of Worcesters players	xx s	
To the Lo*rd* dudleys beareward	v s	
To the lo*rd* mountegles players	v s	
To the Queenes players	x s	20
To the Lo*rd* darsies players	v s	
To the Lo*rd* darbies players	v s	
To the Earle of Sussex players	v s	
To the Earle of huntingtons players	v s	
To the Lo*rd* dudles players	v s	25
To the Earle of worcesters players	v s	
To the Earle of lyncolns players	v s	
To the Lo*rd* Shandoes players	v s	
To the Earle of nottinghams players	xx s	
Su*m*ma vij li. v s		30

Carpenters' Account Book II CRO: Acc 3/2
f 248v

...

paide for carriage of the harnys and poyntes   x d   35

...

payde to the mvssicions   xviiij d

...

Mercers' Account Book CRO: Acc 15
f 91

...

Res*eates* of Land*es*

...   5

Res*eaved* of Richard Bank*es* for A Howse in gosforde Street,
Late beinge the mercers Pageone howese p*er* Lease   xxvij s

f 92
                                                                      10
...

Payment*es* Ordenarie & Extreordinarie

...

p*ai*d Robe*r*t Pyme for Lendinge 6 Harnese one ye ffaire
daie   iiij s
p*ai*d 6 men for bearinge the Harnise & for poynt*es*   ij s iiij d   15

...

Weavers' Rentgatherers' Book II CRO: Acc 100/18/2
f 40v

...   20

It*em* p*ay*d to the mvsiciones at our qvarter day   vj d

...

[It*em* Geuen to the mvsisiones   vj d]

f 41   25

...

It*em* p*ay*d for carynge of the harnes on the fayre daye   xviij d

...

A   *Drapers' Accounts* CRO: Acc 154   30
     f 138

...

paide to Thomas Seney for harnessinge at ye faire   00 02 06

...

                                                                      35

1604
Chamberlains' and Wardens' Account Book II CRO: A 7(b)
p 370 *(20 October) (Chamberlains)*

...

ordinary   And of xxvj s viij d paid to the wayt*es* this yere   xxvj s viij d   40
payment*es*
...

p 375   *(22 November)* *(Wardens)*

...

And of iiij li paid to the way*tes* for their wages   iiij li.

...
                                                                                        5

p 377

Rewar*des* to players & bearward*es*

To the lo*rd* dudleys players the xth of Ianuary   v s
To the Earle of darbies players   v s
To the Lord Barkleys players   x s   10
To the Earle of huntingtons players   vj s viij d
To the Lord Ivers players   v s
To the Earle of linckolnes players   vj s viij d
To the Lord vawse his players   v s

Su*m*ma xliij s iiij d   15

p 379*

...

given to Iohn launder in the singing scole   v s

...
                                                                                        20

AC   *City Annals* Bodl: MS Top. Warwickshire d.4
        ff 30v-1*

...

Richard Page Drap*er* maior 1603 & ended in 1604 ... The 3de of   25
Aprill 1604 being twesday the Lady Elizabeth came to Coventry
w*i*th the lord Harrington & his Lady. w*i*th diuers other English &
scottish Ladies, the order was this, m*aiste*r Maior & his brethren
w*i*th all ye rest of the liuery ridd in scarlett gownes out of the
Church yard alonge the stree*tes* to Gibbet*tes* Ashe & there mett   30
her & the maior lited off his horse & kissed her graces hand & so
gott vp againe & ridd before her into the Citty w*i*th his brethren
& the rest of the Livery, two & two togeather, the lord Harrington
& all his men riding bare headed before the Cowch alonge the
stree*tes* from Gibbet*tes* Ashe to St Michaells church all the   35
companies of coventrey standing in there gownes & hoods from
Gosford gate alonge the streete to the Drapery dore. In St Michaells
church she hard a sermon sitting in m*aist*ris maioris seate her
selfe alone only her Ladies standing by & all the maiestrates
wiues in other seates, the preacher was one mr ⌐Iohn¬ Tovvey   40
who was co*m*manded to preach but halfe an howre, the sermon
being ended she came afoote from the Church to the St Mary hall

the Lord harrington ∧ 'went' bare headed before her, & all the
ladies attending vpon her Whereof one of them bare vp her traine,
& when she came into the Courte diuers gentlewomen kneeled
downe & kissed her graces hand & went vp into the hall where
there was a chaire of state sett at the vpper end of the hall for her   5

She dineth in
the St Mary
hall.

to dine att. Her attendances were the Lord Harrington standing
bare headed one her right hand & a Scottish Lady one her left
hand & when she gaue her a knife or a napkin she kneeled downe,
no body eating any thinge with her but her selfe, her graces carver
carving meate with a siluer forke & his knife, she was serued in   10
this manner all the maiestrates & the rest of the Livery did serve
vp the meate in scarlett gownes with the waites playing while
euery messe was served vpp to the table, when she had dined she
was convayed I vp into maistris maioris parler where there was
achaire of state prepaired for her & agreat fire of charcole to   15
make the roome warme ... (the city's gift was) apeece of plate

A peece of plate
giuen to her
grace which
Cost 29 li. 14s
2d more for
engraving the
⟨.....⟩ ∧ 'Citties'
armes and abox
2s vj d the gilt
cup & couer
waighed lxxxix
ounces & halfe
a quarter at vj s
8d anounce. /

Duble gilt which was 3 quarters of ayard hie the which the Lord
Harrington helped her grace to receaue because it was to heavy
for her to hold, it cost the Citty 29 li. 14s 2d ... After dinner shee
ridd from St Mary hall downe the crosse cheeping & round about   20
the Crosse in her Cowch the lord Harrington riding bare headed
before her, & the maior & maiestrates two & two togeather with
the rest of the liuery, all the companies standing in there gownes
& hoods from the crosse to the Bishopp gate, her grace lited &
went into the Liberary & gaue some money to it but what I   25
canot tell from thence her grace ridd alonge out at the Bishopp
gate to the Sponn end & so alonge downe the Sponnstreete, & so
through the Citty alonge to Gosford gate, all the Companies
standing alonge from the Drapery dore to Gosford gate in there

hoodes.

gownes & hoods, & so the maior with the maiestrates brought her   30
grace to Gibbettes Ashe & there kissed her hand & left her grace
with the lord Harrington & his traine to convay her grace to combe
from whence she came ... Many gifters of gold were giuen to them
that attended vpon her grace being her Chiefest attenders ...

35

Payments Out Book CRO: A 16
p 81 *(4 April)*
...
paid the 4 of aprill 1604 to mr hancockes that
he paid for the Cupp which was given to the   xxx li. 40
lady Elizabeth the kinges doughter

And to mr Collyns that was given by m*aiste*r maior to her graces
officers   v li.

...

Cappers' Records SC: Account Book I   5
f 142

...

p*ai*d for scowringe o*ur* harnes, for poynt*es* and men to weare
them   ij s iiij d

                                                                                 10

Carpenters' Account Book II CRO: Acc 3/2
f 250v

...

It*em* fo warninge the companie to meet the younge Princes   iij d

...   15

Mercers' Account Book CRO: Acc 15
f 94

                  Paymente*s* Ordenarie & Extreordenarie

...   20

p*ai*d R*o*be*r*t Pyme for hornese for fore. men. one the faire
daie   iiij s
p*ai*d 4 men for Bearinge the hornese. & for poynt*es*   xviij d

...

                                                                                 25

Weavers' Account Book CRO: Acc 100/17/1
f 97

...

                     R*esetes* for buryalles

...   30

R*eseyvyd* for the hier of ovr players Apparell   vj s

...

f 97v *(Payments)*

                                                                                 35

It*em* p*ayde* to fidlers and singers   xvj d

...

Weavers' Rentgatherers' Book II CRO: Acc 100/18/2
f 42v   40

...

It*em* p*ayd* for Carynge Harnes and for poyntes   ix d

...

A   *Drapers' Accounts* CRO: Acc 154
     f 140

     ...

     paid for harnish men & poyntes   xx d

     ...   5

     1605
     Chamberlains' and Wardens' Account Book II CRO: A 7(b)
     p 382 *(24 October) (Chamberlains)*

     ...   10

ordinary   And to the waytes for ther wages this yere paste   xxvj s viij d
paymen*tes*
     ...

     p 389 *(18 December) (Wardens)*

     ...   15

fees &   And of iiij li paid to the waytes for their wages   iiij li.
wages paid
     ...

     p 391 *(Wardens)*

     ...   20
                         Rewardes to players
     given to the Lord Comptons players the xix^th of Iuly 1605   x s
     given to the duke of Leonox players   xx s
     given to the Earle of herefor*des* players   vj s viij d
                         *Sum*ma xxxvj s viij d   25

     p 394 *(Wardens)*

     ...

     paid to Launder & Pole that teach in the singing schole   v s

     ...   30

     Council Book CRO: A 14(a)
     p 70 col a *(7 November)*

     deliu*er*ed forthe of the armory the 7 of november 1605 to the   35
     aldermen when the lady Elizabeth laye at mr hopkins

     To mr Breres iiij pykes & one *p*artizant ij black bills.
     To mr Showell ij Corslet*tes* iiij pikes & a *p*artizant ij bills
     To mr Richardson j Corslet j pike iiij black bills   40
     To mr howcot iiij pik*es* j Corslett iiij bills j *p*artizant
     To mr Walden ij pikes ij black bills j gleave
     To Mr Bedford ij horsemens staves A Corslet & ij bowes

To mr Gravenor j Corslet ij pikes .ij bills
To mr Rogerson iij bills ij pikes j Corslet
To mr letherbarowe iij bills

col b   5

To maister maior j partizant ij halberdes
...

Cappers' Records SC: Account Book I   10
f 143

...
paid for scowringe our harnes, & for wearinge it:
& for poyntes   ij s iiij d
paid for mendinge our pagent howse dore   iij d   15
...
paid for mendinge our Muskett   vj d
paid for scowringe it   vj d
...
paid for scowringe our sworde & dagger and for a chape for the   20
scabbarde   ij d
...
paid for scowringe of an other harnes that was almost
cankered   xij d
...   25

Carpenters' Account Book II CRO: Acc 3/2
f 252v

...
paid ij men for caryeinge the harnes   viij d   30
paid for j dossyn of poyntes   ij d
paid for powder on St Iames daye   xxj d
paid for match   j d
paid [for] a man that shott in the Muskett   ix d
...   35
paid the musysians   vj d
...

36 / *presumably at master's house at account feast*

Mercers' Account Book CRO: Acc 15
f 96

...

Paymentes Ordenary & Extreordenary

...   5

payd mr Pymm for hornes for 6 men one the faire day &
poyntes   vj s iiij d
payd 6 men for bering hornes one the faire day   ij s
...

10

Weavers' Account Book CRO: Acc 100/17/1
f 98v

...

Item payd for pouther and for caryng of oure peses   vj d
...   15

Weavers' Rentgatherers' Book II CRO: Acc 100/18/2
f 45

...

Item payd to them that bare Harnes and for poyntes   xviij d 20
...

A   *Drapers' Accounts* CRO: Acc 154
f 143

...   25

Pd to Harnes men at the ffayre   ij s iiij d
...

1606
Chamberlains' and Wardens' Account Book II CRO: A 7(b)   30
p 399 *(29 October) (Chamberlains)*

...

ordinarie   And of xxvj s viij d by theim paid to the waites for their wages
paymentes   this yere past   xxvj s viij d

35

p 403 *(3 November) (Wardens)*

...

ffees &   And of iiij li. paid to the waytes for ther wages   iiij li.
wages paid   ...   40

p 405 *(Wardens)*

...

Rewardes to players &c.

Given to the Lord Hunttingtons players	x s
Given to Lord of Herefordes players	xl s
Given to the Lord Mountioys players	vj s
Given to the Lord Shendoes players	x s
Given to the Queens players	xl s

*Sum*ma v li. vj s

...

p 407 *(Wardens)*

...

Given away to the scholem*aister*s the 2 of Iulie at the vew of the
schole to mr Tovie xx s to mr Arnold x s to mr Pole x s & to
Iohn Lauder v s   xl s

...

Cappers' Records SC: Account Book I
f 144 col a

p*ay*ed for scowringe o*ur* harnes, for poynt*es* & a man to beare it
to m*aster* maiors   xviij d

...

p*ay*ed for bordes nayles, & other thing*es* to mende the pagient
howse   xiiij d

...

Mercers' Account Book CRO: Acc 15
f 98

Paymentes. Ordenary and Extraordenary

...

P*ay*d Mr Pyme for Harnis for 6 men on the fayre day &
poynt*es*   vj s iiij d
Payd to. 6 men for bearinge the Armor   ij s

...

Weavers' Account Book CRO: Acc 100/17/1
f 99 *(Receipts)*

...

Rese*yv*yd of Thomas massie for the Hire of oure playres
aparell   ij s vj d

...

f 99v *(Payments)*

...

It*em* p*ayd* at pyniges when we Hired oure aparell to Thomas
masie   xvij d   5

...

Weavers' Rentgatherers' Book II CRO: Acc 100/18/2
f 47

...   10

It*em* p*ayd* for poyntes on the fayre daye   j d

...

A   *Drapers' Accounts* CRO: Acc 154
f 145   15

...

pd a Company of musissions   0 5 0

...

1607   20
Chamberlains' and Wardens' Account Book II CRO: A 7(b)
p 415 *(28 October) (Chamberlains)*

...

ordinary   And to the Way*tes* for ther Wag*es* this yere past   xxvj s viij d
paym*entes*   25
...

p 420 *(25 November) (Wardens)*

...

ffees &   And of iiij li paid to the Way*tes* for their Wag*es*   iiij li.
wag*es* paid   30
...

p 422 *(Wardens)*

...

Rewardes to players &c

Paid to the Queens players   xx s   35
Paid to the lord Shandies players   vj s viij d
Rewardes to   given to the lord Mountegles players   vj s viij d
players   given to the lord harford*es* players   x s
given to the Earle of Darbies players   x s
given to the lord Dudlies players   vj s viij d   40
given to the lord Barkeleys players   xx s

given to the lord Shandois players the j of Ianuary   x s

Su*m*ma iiij li x s

p 425 *(Wardens)*

...   5

Given to the schole*maiste*rs the 28 of marche

payme*ntes* at   to mr Arnold xx s to the vsher x s & to mr Pole v s & to lauder
Comandme*ntes*   v s & to the woman that Ringeth the bell xij d   xlj s

...

Paid to Trumpeters & Wayt*es*   iij s iiij d   10

...

Cappers' Records SC: Account Book I
f 145 col a

...   15

p*ay*ed for wearinge the harnes, at the fayre: and for poynt*es*   x d

...

Carpenters' Account Book II CRO: Acc 3/2
f 256v

...   20

p*a*id vnto the bearer of o*w*r harneys & poynt*es*   x d

...

Mercers' Account Book CRO: Acc 15
f 99v *(Payments ordinary and extraordinary)*   25

...

p*a*id mr Py*m*me for hornis for 6 men & for poynt*es*   vj s iiij d
p*a*id 6 men for bearing the hornes   ij s

...

                                                               30

Weavers' Account Book CRO: Acc 100/17/1
f 100v

...

I*tem* p*ay*d when we Lente our playeres Aparell   ij d

...   35

f 101

...

I*tem* p*ay*d when we toke in oure Harnes   ij d

...   40

Weavers' Rentgatherers' Book II CRO: Acc 100/18/2
f 48v

...

Item for bearinge the harnes and ponttes of the fayre day   xviij d

...   5

A   *Drapers' Accounts* CRO: Acc 154
f 147

...

it to them that did beayre the harnis at the ffayr   00 02 04   10

...

1608
Chamberlains' and Wardens' Account Book II CRO: A 7(b)
p 429 *(26 October) (Chamberlains)*   15

...

Ordynary   And to the waytes for their wages this yere   xxvj s viij d
paymentes.

...

p 435 *(30 November) (Wardens)*   20

...

ffees &   And of iiij li. paid to the waites for their wages   iiij li.
wages paid

...

p 438 *(Wardens)*   25
                    Rewardes to plaiers /
                    Paid to the Earle of Darbies players in december   x s
                    Paid to the Lord Barkleys players   xiij s iiij d
                    Paid to the Lord Mountegles players   vj s viij d
Rewardes to   Paid to the Duke of Lynnockes players   v s   30
players.   Paid to the Queens players   xx s
                    Paid to the lord dudlies players in marche   xx s
                    Paid to the Lord Candigis players in Iuly   iiij s
                    Paid to the Lord Shandigis players in August   vj s viij d
                    Paid to the Kinges Trumpeters the 10 of August   xxx s
                    Paid to the lord Vawseyes players the 30th of August   v s   35
                    Paid to the Kinges players the 29th of October   xx s
                              Summa vij li. viij d

p 440 *(Wardens)*   40

...

paymentes at   paid for Ringing for the lord Treasurer   v s
Comandement

...

p 441 *(Wardens)*

...

Given to the Schoolem*aiste*rs in m*a*rche ... To I*o*hn Launder v s

...

5

p 442* *(Wardens)*

...

paym*en*tes at Paid to the lorde Comptons men   xl s
Comandm*en*t

...

10

p 444* *(Wardens)*

Present*es* To the p*a*rlor for the lord Comptons men the 30 of September a
given qu*a*rte of white wyne & halfe a quarter of suggar & for breade
2d   xiiij d ob. 15

...

Cappers' Records SC: Account Book I
f 146 col a

...   20

p*a*id for scowringe, & bearinge harnes   ij s ij d

...

(Choice dinner)
Geven to the musitiens   ij s   25

...

Carpenters' Account Book II CRO: Acc 3/2
f 259v

...   30

Gyven the Musytians on Candlemas daye   xij d

...

p*a*yd for caryeinge o*w*r harnesse on the fayre daye   viij d
p*a*yd for poynt*es*   ij d

...   35

(21 September)
p*a*yd the Musytians the same daye   ix d
p*a*yd for mendinge o*w*r Muskett   viij d
p*a*yd for halfe a pound of powder   viij d 40

38 / the same daye *at guild dinner*

p*a*yd the man the caryed the Muskett   vj d

...

Mercers' Account Book CRO: Acc 15
f 101   5

...

              paym9ent*es* ordenary & extraordenary

...

payd p*ro* harnis p*ro* vj men one the faire day & p*ro*
poynt*es*   vj s iiij d   10
paid to vj men to Carri Harnis   ij s

...

Weavers' Rentgatherers' Book II CRO: Acc 100/18/2
f 50v   15

...

Itt*em* payde for caryinge of armer att the fayre daye   xviij d

...

A *Drapers' Accounts* CRO: Acc 154   20
f 149

...

It to them that bare the harnis at ye fayre   00 02 04

...

                                              25

1609
Chamberlains' and Wardens' Account Book II CRO: A 7(b)
p 448 *(25 October) (Chamberlains)*

...

And to the wayt*es* for theire wages this yeare past   xxvj s viij d   30

...

p 453 *(16 November) (Wardens)*

...

fees &   And of iiij li. paid to the wayt*es* for theire wag*es*   iiij li.   35
wages
...

p 455 *(Wardens)*

...

                    Reward*es* to Players. /   40
paid to the Lord dudleyes players on the leet daye   xx s.
paid to the Lord Mowntegles players the 4 of Iune   v s.

players	paid to the Lord Barckleyes players 13 Iune	x s.
	paid to the Lord Ivers players 17 Iune	x s.
	paid to the Lord Darbyes players the 24 Maij	x s.
	paid to the Queenes players to Thomas Swinerton	xl s
	paid to the lord Candishes men	v s. 5

Summa v li. / .

...

<table>
<tr><td>paymentes at
Comandment</td><td>paid william Townckes for gilding the sword and the greate mace
by note</td><td>XXXV S.</td></tr>
<tr><td></td><td>paid Thomas Smyth for mending the sword by note</td><td>xviij d   10</td></tr>
</table>

...

p 457 *(Wardens)*

...

paid the 23 of Maie to a man that would have Dawnced vppon   15
the rope   v s

...

Payments Out Book CRO: A 16
p 92 *(June)*   20

...

given to the princes players being 20 in nomber   iiij li.

Quitclaim II CRO: 100/37*
(18 September)   25

To all christian people to whome this present Wrytinge shall
come William Wilkes of the cittie of Coventre Skynner sendeth
greetinge in our lord god everlastinge / Knowe ye that I the said
William Wilkes for dyvers good causes & consideracions me   30
movinge Have remysed released and altogether for me my heires
& assignes for ever quitt claymed vnto Christpher Warren of the
Cittie of Coventre Dyer his heires & assignes in his full & peaceable
possession & seisin beinge, All my wholl right estate Tytle interest
& demaunde whatsoever of & in one garden scituate & beinge in   35
Mill lane in the said Cittie of Coventre on the west parte the
streate there / where a certayne howse called the Tailers &
shermans Pageant howse lately stoode / To have & to hold the
said garden with all & singuler the appurtenaunces vnto the said
Christopher Warren his heires & assignes for ever, So that nether   40
I the said William Wilkes nor my heires nor any of them any right
tytle interest or demaunde of in or to the premisses or any parte

or parcell thereof maye hereafter challeinge or have but from all
accion of right Tytle clayme & demaunde in the premisses be
vtterly barred & excluded for ever, And moreover I the said
William Wilkes the aforesaid garden and other the premisses vnto
the said Christopher Warren his heires & assignes agaynst me the   5
said William & my / heires or any other clayminge from by or
vnder vs any right tytle interest or demaunde in the premisses do
by / these presentes warrante & defend / In wytnes wytnes
whereof I have putte my hand & seale the eighteenth daye of
September in the seaventh yere of the raigne of our soveraigne   10
lord Iames by the grace of God kinge of England ffrance &
Ireland defender of the faith &c. And of Scotland the three &
fortith /
Sigillatum et deliberatum in pnntia

                                             15

(signed)
Gyles Gore   Sampson
                              Chambers   William Wilkes
Samuel Brownell

                                             20

Cappers' Records SC: Account Book I
f 147
...
paid for mendinge our pagent howse dores at sundry tymes xx d
...   25
paid for scowringe the harnes, against the fayre and for ij mennes
wages, & for poyntes   ij s vj d
...

(Choice dinner)   30
paid to the musitiens the same daye by consent of the
companye   ij s vj d
...

Carpenters' Account Book II CRO: Acc 3/2   35
f 262
...
paid for caryeinge owr harnes on the faire daye & for
poyntes   x d
...   40

8 / wytnes wytnes *MS dittography*   14 / pnntia *for* presentia

paid for caryeinge owr Muskett on St Iames daye   xij d

...

Mercers' Account Book CRO: Acc 15
f 103   5

...

Paymentes ordynarie & extraordinary

...

for ij dussen poyntes   iiij d

...   10

paide to vj men to Carry the Harnesse   ij s

...

for Gundpowder & Matche   xx d
for Carrienge the Muskettes to iij men   xviij d

...   15

Weavers' Account Book CRO: Acc 100/17/1
f 104v

...

Payd for pouther and matche vpon the Kinges day   0-2-8   20
Payd for tow mens wages for carringe the peaces   0-1-4

...

Weavers' Rentgatherers' Book II CRO: Acc 100/18/2
f 53   25

Payd on the fayr day for the carridge of our armour   xviij d

...

A *Drapers' Accounts* CRO: Acc 154   30
f 151

...

payd to them yat bare ye harnes at ye fayre   00 02 04

...

payd for mach & pouder for 3 men on Saint James day 00 02 04   35

1610
Leet Book II CRO: A 3(b)
p 55 *(9 October)*

                                                                                         40

It is further also ordered & enacted at this Leet, that everie person

Wayte-players

that hath been Maior of this Citie shall paie to the waite-players
of the same .iiij d. and everie one that hath beene Sherriff iij d
and everie one that hath been Chamberlayne or Warden ij d and
everie Comoner .1d. quarterly.

And that the said waite players shall plaie on theire waites, at   5
such times, and at & in such places, as shall best seeme good to
those who are the cheiff rulers of the Councell house of this Citie
in paine of everie one so refusing to paie to forfeite xij d to be
levied by waie of distresse.
                                                                               10
Chamberlains' and Wardens' Account Book II CRO: A 7(b)
p 464 *(24 October)* *(Chamberlains)*
...

ordinary   And to the way*tes* for theire wage this yere past   xxvj s viij d
pay*mentes*   ...   15

p 467 *(17 November)* *(Wardens)*
...

ffees   And of iiij li. paid to the way*tes* for theire wag*es*   iiij li.
                                                                               20
p 470 *(Wardens)*
                            Rewardes to players
                Given to the Lord Aburgavenyes players   x s
                Given to the Lord Evers players   xx s.
                Given to the Lord Mount Egles players   x s   25
                Given to the Lord Shandowes players   vj s viij d
                Given to a Company of Mussissions   ij s vj d
                            Su*m*ma xlix s ij d /

p 471 *(Wardens)*   30
                ...

pay*mentes* at paid for vj yard*es* of Clothe for iiij°r liveryes for the Cytties
Comande*ment*   way*tes*   iij li.
                ...

                paid to Iohn Launder in the singinge Schoole   v s. 35
                ...

p 473 *(Wardens)*

                [& v s w*hi*ch was p*ai*d to the Trumpeters   v s] 40
                ...

p 474 *(Wardens)*

...

And of v s w*hi*ch was paid to the Trumpeters   v s.

...

                                                                                              5

Payments Out Book CRO: A 16
p 100 *(8 August)*

...

paid to mr damport the same day that he laid out about the
highe wayes xx s & to the Citties musicions ⸢v s⸣   xxv s   10
paid to Ri*char*d Bullyn the same daye for iij Cognizance*s* for the
wait*es*   iij li.

...

paid to hym more that he gave away to pore Soldiers &
musicions   iiij li. vj s vj d   15

...

Cappers' Records SC: Account Book I
f 148   *(Account dinner)*

...   20

p*ay*ed to the musitiens   ij s

...

p*ay*ed for wyne at o*ur* Henne eatynge   iiij s viij d
Geven to the musitiens at the same tyme   ij s
p*ay*ed for dressinge o*ur* Armoure, & ij men to weare it   ij s ij d   25
p*ay*ed to the Gretian, at mr maiors request   iij s iiij d

...

(Choice dinner)
p*ay*ed to the musitiens, & to mr Spon   iij s vj d   30

...

Carpenters' Account Book II CRO: Acc 3/2
f 264v

...   35

P*ai*d for caryinge o*wr* harnes on the fayre daye & for
poynt*es*   x d

...

_____

14 / hym: *Mayor Sampson Hopkins*

Mercers' Account Book CRO: Acc 15
f 105

...

Paymentes Ordinary

...   5

To . Six men ffor bearinge Harnis on the ffayre daye   ij s
To . Iohn Scott ffor Dressinge the Armor & ⌐2 dozen
poynt*es*⌐   vj s iiij d
...

                                                                          10

A   *Drapers' Accounts* CRO: Acc 154
f 157

...

Paid to the harnessed men at the ffaire   £- 2 4

...   15

1611
Chamberlains' and Wardens' Account Book II CRO: A 7(b)
p 475 *(23 October) (Chamberlains)*

...   20

ordinary
paym*en*ts And to the Wayt*es* for theire Wag*es* this yeare past   xxvj s viij d
...

p 485 *(27 November) (Wardens)*

...   25

And of iiij li paid to the Wayt*es* for theire Wag*es* this yeare   iiij li.

...

p 487* *(Wardens)*

...   30

Rewardes to Players
Gyven to the Lord of Wist*es* players
Gyven to the Lord of Lyles players   ij s vj d
Gyven to the Lord Darsett*es* players
Gyven to the lord of Mungummeryes players   35
Gyven to the Lord Evers pr*esi*dent of wales his Musissions   ij s
Su*m*ma iiij s vj d

p 489 *(Wardens)*

...   40

paid the Swordbearer towardes his gowne xxvj s viij d and
towardes his Coate x s ...

paid the greate Mace bearer ... for his Coate vj s viij d and more
xxvj s viij d ...
paid the Towne serieante ... and for his Coate   vj s viij d
paid the Cryor for his wages . xl s . and for his Coate   xlvj s viij d
paid the Iailor and ij seriantes for theire Coates   xx s.   5
...
paid the Cloake berer for his wages by yere xl s and towardes his
gowne and Coate xx s ...
paid the Cooke towardes his Coate   x s.
...   10

p 490   *(Wardens)*
...
paid the 28th of Ianuary 1610 for 28. Constables
Staves painted with the Olyvaunte and ten   xiiij s.   15
oysteridge feathers

p 491
...
paid to Iohn Launder in the singinge Schoole   v s.   20
...

Cappers' Records   SC: Account Book I
f 149 *(Choice dinner)*
                                                                      25
paid to the musitiens. ij s. and geven to the
prisoners . iiij d.   ij s iiij d
...
paid to Mr. Bowyer for ij Gretians, the . 13. of October   ij s
...   30
paid for repayre of the pagent howse   xiij s xj d
...
paid for Scowringe the Harnes: for wearinge it on the fayre daye:
& for poyntes   ij s ij d
...   35

Carpenters' Account Book II CRO: Acc 3/2
f 267v
...
spent at the receipte of our harnes   vj d   40
...

paid for caryeinge owr harnes & for poyntes   x d

...

Mercers' Account Book CRO: Acc 15
f 107v   5
                              Paymentes ordynarie

...

to Six men for carrienge the armor on the faire daie   ij s

...
                                                                                                          10

Weavers' Rentgatherers' Book II CRO: Acc 100/18/2
f 56*

...

Payd for carriinge of the harneis on the fayre day   j s vj d

...   15

A   *Drapers' Accounts* CRO: Acc 154
f 160

...

pd at the ffayre for harnesse men and their paymosts   ij s 8d   20

...

1612
Chamberlains' and Wardens' Account Book II CRO: A 7(b)
p 497 *(28 October) (Chamberlains)*   25

...

And to the Waytes for theire Wages this yere past   xxvj s viij d.

...

p 505 *(25 November) (Wardens)*   30
                              ffees & wages

...

ffees & wages   And of iiij li. paid to the Waytes for theire Wages this
                      yeare   iiij li.

...   35

p 507 *(Wardens)*

...

                              Rewardes to Players
Gyven to the Lady Elizabeth her Players as appeareth by a bill   40
vnder Maister Maiors hand   iiij li.

Gyven to the Lord Dudley his Players as appeareth by the same
bill   vj s viij d.
Gyven to the Lord Mounteagles players as appeareth by a bill
vnder *Maiste*r Maiors hand   vj s viij d.
Gyven to the Earle of Darbey his players as appeareth by the   5
same bill   x s

           Su*m*ma v li iij s iiij d

...

p 509 *(Payments at Commandment) (Wardens)*   10

...

paid to the Lord Comptons bearward by *Maiste*r Maiors
Co*m*maundeme*n*t and by bill   x s.
paid to Willi*a*m Kelsey S*ir* George Boothes bearward as appeareth
by a bill Vnder *Maiste*r Maiors hand   v s. 15

...

p 512 *(25 November) (Wardens)*

...

Paid vnto the lord Barkeleys men xxij s when *Maiste*r Maior and   20
his Bretheren Did Dyne at Callowdon   xxij s

...

Payments Out Book CRO: A 16
p 105* *(12 February)*   25

...

Paid the same daie to the vauters   xx s

...

p 107 *(20 August)*   30

...

Given to the Princes highnes by the Cytie the 20th of August
1612 in gould   1 li.

...

                                                               35

AC   *City Annals* Bodl: MS Top. Warwickshire d.4
     f 32v

Prince Henry   ... Prince Henry came to Coventry with a great traine, & was
came to   worthily receaved by the Maior & his brethren with great ioy. He   40
coventrey.   & the rest of his people did supp in the St Mary hall y*a*t night. He
               Did ly at Mr Breres howse all night & went away the next
               morning ...

Cappers' Records SC: Account Book I
f 150 *(Account dinner)*

...

p*ai*d to the musitiens   xij d

...   5

p*ai*d for scowringe our Armour   xviij d
p*ai*d for wearynge of it, and for poyntes   vj d

...

Carpenters' Account Book II CRO: Acc 3/2   10
f 270v

...

p*ai*d for bearing o*w*r harnes on the faire daye & for poynt*es*   x d
...   15

f 271

...

to musitians   vj d

...   20

Mercers' Account Book CRO: Acc 15
f 110v
                    Paym*entes* ordinary and Extraordinary

...

p*ai*d for ij dozen of thridd point*es* for hornish   iiij d 25
p*ai*d Six Men for Carrienge the hornish   ij s

...

Weavers' Account Book CRO: Acc 100/17/1
f 108v   30

Giuen to Massye   0-vj d
Payd on the fayre day to the horenes men & for point*es*   j s viij d

...   35

Weavers' Rentgatherers' Book II CRO: Acc 100/18/2
f 60

...

Payd to the Musissions   iij s iiij d

...   40

39 / 3rd s *of* Musissions *written over* t

f 60v

...

Payd for bearinge the harnes on the fayre day and for
pointes   xviij d

...   5

A   *Drapers' Accounts* CRO: Acc 154
f 162 *(12 June)*

...

pd vj harnissde men at the ffayre   ij s ij d   10

...

1613
Chamberlains' and Wardens' Account Book II CRO: A 7(b)
p 522 *(27 October)* *(Chamberlains)*   15

...

And to the Waytes for this yeare past   xxvj s viij d.

...

p 526 *(23 November)* *(Wardens)*   20
                                   Fees & wages.

...

And of iiij li. paid to the Wayts for theire wages this
yeare   iiij li.

...   25

p 529 *(Wardens)*
                                   Rewardes to Players
Given to the Queenes players as appeareth by a bill vnder maister
Maiors hand   xl s.   30
Given vnto Two of the Company of the Children of Revells as
appeareth by an other bill   xx s
Given to the Queenes or the Lady Elizabethes players as
appeareth by another bill   iiij li.
Given to the Wayts of Worster and the Lord Willoughby his men   35
as appeareth by an other bill   iij s
Given to the Lord of Huntington his Musissions as appeareth by
an other bill vnder maister Maiors hand   v s.
                                   Summa vij li. viij s.

...   40

p 530 *(27 October) (Wardens)*

...

paid for pikes, plates and Hoopes to Thomas Hopkyns the
Smyth   xl s.
paid for xv. bills, as appeareth by a bill vnder M*aiste*r Maiors   5
hand   xx s.
paid for xvij. bills to Richard Heybeard as appeareth by a bill
vnder m*aiste*r Maiors hande   xxiij s viij d
paid for xviij. blacke bills to the same Man as appeareth by a bill
vnder m*aiste*r Maiors hande   xxiiij s   10
paid to Richard Heybeard for xviij. Crosse pikes
at ij s. a peece. xxxvj s. and for.ij. dozen of black
bill heads xxxij s and paid to Thomas Hopkyns   iij li. xiiij s viij d.
for fiue blacke bills at xvj d. a peece. vj s viij d.

                                                                        15

p 532 *(Wardens)*

...

paid giuen to the lord Compton his Beareward as appeareth by a
bill vnder m*aiste*r Maiors hande   v s.
...   20

p 535 *(Wardens)*

...

Given to younge Iohn Launder   v s.
...   25

Council Book CRO: A 14(a)
p 375 *(30 November)*

...

At this day it is agreed that Iohn Launder the yonger shall haue a   30
Lease of one Messuage or tenement wherein he now dwelleth for
School Rent   xxj yeres to beginn at Michaellmas [next] ˄ ˈlast pastˈ paying
Launder   xx s rent per Annu*m* at foure severall tymes in the yere, and
making sufficient reparac*i*ons
...   35

Payments Out Book CRO: A 16
p 109 *(3 April)*

...

paid for A drume the same daye   xx s   40
...

Cappers' Records SC: Account Book I
f 151 *(St Clement's Night)*

...

payed to the Musitiens the same tyme   ij s

...   5

Carpenters' Account Book II CRO: Acc 3/2
f 273

...

paid owr men that caryed harneys on the faier daye & for   10
poyntes   x d

...

Gyven the musitians   vj d

...   15

Mercers' Account Book CRO: Acc 15
f 112

...

　　　　　Paymentes ordenarie & extraordenary

...   20

paid to 6 men for carying the armor ⸢2s⸣ & for 2 dozen
poyntes 4d   ij s iiij d

...

Weavers' Rentgatherers' Book II CRO: Acc 100/18/2   25
f 63

...

Payd to maister Mayor for the Ladye Elizabeth   x s

...

payd to the harness men upon the fayre day   j s vj d   30

A *Drapers' Accounts* CRO: Acc 154
f 164

...

payde to sixe Armor bearers and for poynts   0 li ij s ij d   35

...

1614
Chamberlains' and Wardens' Account Book II CRO: A 7(b)
p 543 *(16 November) (Wardens)*   40
　　　　　　　Fees & wages.

...

And of .iiij li. paid to the Wayts for theire wages this

yeare   iiij li.

...

p 546 *(Wardens)*
                    Rewardes to Players.   5
Given to the king*es* players as appeareth by a bill vnder m*aiste*r
Maiors hand   xl s
Given to the Lord of Albignes players as appeareth by a bill
vnder m*aiste*r Maiors hand   x s
Given to the Princes players as appeareth by a bill vnder m*aiste*r   10
Maiors hand *with* theire names   xl s
Given to the Earle of Worcestors Musici*o*ns   ij s. vj d.
                    Su*m*ma iiij li. xij s vj d

p 549 *(Wardens)*   15

...

paid to the Wayt*es* for theire paynes at the Leete giuen by
m*aiste*r Maiors appoyntment   iij s vj d.

...

paid to the Lord Comptons Beareward as appeareth by a bill   20
vnder m*aiste*r Maiors hand   vj s viij d

p 554 *(Wardens)*

...

Given to younge Iohn Launder   v s.   25

...

Council Book CRO: A 14(a)
pp 382-3 *(2 July)*

...   30
At this day it is agreed that there shall be warned for the Watch
everie night fyfteen, of whom the Conestable shall be allowed
Watch • one man for warning them, and that eleven persons shall watch
besyds one of the officers, to whom shall be allowed the other
three men for his pains, and that they shall watch from the first   35
of Aprill vntill the first of September from nyne a clocke of the
night vntill three in the morning, And from the first of Septembre
to the first of Aprill from nyne to [three] fore and yf any of Mr
Maiors officers shall not duly obserue these howers, or some
other sufficient man for him, to see the watch truly kept, then   40
vppon iust proof | made by any of the Conestables of his
negligen⟨..⟩ herein, he shall loose his night*es* wages and the
conest⟨....⟩ that so fyndeth out his fault shall have the wage⟨.⟩ for;

that night in recompence of his pains therein

...

AC *City Annals* Bodl: MS Top. Warwickshire d.4

f 33*   5

...

Henry Dauenport clothier or drap*er* Maior 1613 & ended in
1614 ...

°This yeare there was an admirable Stratagem made by M*aster*
Maior [being] ⌃ˈconsisting ofˈ a Squadron in warlike manner &   10

Stratagem.   [ther] being very well ordered & completely furnished ˈcontayningˈ
[⟨...⟩sti⟨..⟩] [In ˈasˈ] Englissh Scottish Irish & Spanish . & divers
Captaines Liveteenaant*es* & Ensignes. Bills Bowes Speares &
gunnes, Pik*es* holberts & holbert diers being a very tough
Skermidg & acted at the Cross in the said Citie: In w*hi*ch Battell   15
death leech was fained to be slayne (being then one of the
liveteenaant*es* or Sergiant*es*) Barnaby Davenport was the cheif
Streamer or Standardbearer And in his displaying of the Color*es*
at the Crosse [he k⟨...... .⟩d⟨.....⟩yede / ⟨..⟩(⟨.⟩g⟨..⟩l⟨.........⟩) & ⟨...⟩i⟨..⟩)
⟨.....⟩ the ⟨..⟩g⟨.⟩ab⟨.⟩ soa⟨......⟩re⟨....⟩t⟨.⟩] he acted the same w*i*th   20
greate agilitie.°

...

Cappers' Records SC: Account Book I

f 152   25

p*ai*d for scowringe o*ur* harnes, & to ij men for wearinge it on the
fayre daye   ij s vj d

...

30

(Choice dinner)
p*ai*d to the musitiens   ij s
Allowed by consent which the musitien toke on me
vniustly   ij s vj d

35

Carpenters' Account Book II CRO: Acc 3/2

f 275v

...

p*ai*d for caryeinge o*w*r Armor on the fayer daye and for
poynt*es*   xiiij d   40

...

f 276

Paid for powther & match	xvj d	
paid for bearing owr muskett	vj d	
paid for powther & match [&] on St Iames daye	xxiij d	5
paid ij men that bare pikes that daye	xviij d	
paid for bearing owr muskett that daye	xij d	

...

Mercers' Account Book CRO: Acc 15   10
f 114

...

Paymentes Ordynary

paid Iohn Lax ffor Scoureinge the Armore and ffor poyntes	vj s iiij d	15
paid . To. Six men ffor Carryinge the Armor	ij s	

...

Paymentes. Extraordinary

...

paid to. neene men .vpon .St James Daye Apoynted by maister Major	iiij s vj d	20
paid pro vj li. Corne powder and Match	vij s iiij d	
paid To the Drummer ˹6d˺	vj d	
paid ffor the vse of.neene ffeathers	ij s iiij d	
paid and given the Men to Drinke	xij d	25

...

Weavers' Account Book CRO: Acc 100/17/1
f 112

...   30

Spent at the deliueringe of the harnes	iiij d	
payd to the harneis men and for pointes	ij s iiij d	

...

Weavers' Rentgatherers' Book II CRO: Acc 100/18/2   35
f 65

...

Payd for powder and Matche when the younge men traynd	0 ij s x d	
Payd more for pouder & matche vpon Sainte Iames day	0 iiij s x	40

...

40 / x *for* x d

A   *Drapers' Accounts* CRO: Acc 154
f 167

...

pd for ix harnesse men at the ffayre   0 5 0

...

1615
Chamberlains' and Wardens' Account Book II CRO: A 7(b)
pp 571-2 *(29 November) (Wardens)*

...

Rewardes to Players.

Gyven to the Queenes players as appeareth by a bill vnder
m*aiste*r Maiors hand the xvth of Aprill   xl s.
Gyven to the Lords of the Councell theire Trumpetors as
appeareth by a bill   v s.|
Gyven to the Lord Cheiffe Iustice his Trumpetors as appeareth
by the same bill   ij s.
Gyven to the Prince his players the vijth of November 1614 as
appeareth by a bill   vij s. iiij d.
Gyven to Prince Charles his players the same vijth of November
as appeareth by a bill   iiij li.
Gyven to one Pendleton who brought his M*aiesties*
letters patent*es* to shewe arte. and skill as   x s
appeareth by a bill vnder m*aiste*r Maiors hande
Gyven to the Queenes players called the Revells
the vijth of October 1615. as appeareth by a bill   xl s. iiij d.
vnder m*aiste*r Maiors hande
Su*m*ma ix li. iiij s viij d

p 575 *(Wardens)*

Paid to mr Henry Davenport for a drumm as appeareth by a bill
vnder M*aiste*r Maiors hande   xiij s. iiij d
...
Paid to the Wayt*es* att allholland dynner as appeareth by a bill
vnder M*aiste*r Maiors hand   vj s.
Paid the Wayt*es* att another tyme, by m*aiste*r Maiors
appoyntment as appeareth by a bill   v s.

...

p 580 *(Wardens)*

...

Gyven to younge Iohn launder   v s.

...

Council Book CRO: A 14(a)
p 394* *(14 August)*

...

At this day it is agreed that Edward Man, Roger Newland, Iohn
Ielfes, [&] Iohn Hill, & William Holsworth, shall goe to play with   10
the waytes about the Cytie according to the ancient Custom of
•Waits•   the said Cytie, for which they are to haue seven pounds by the
yere in money and quarteridg, ʹalsoʹ so that they play orderly as
thei should, out of which allowance they are to furnish them
selues with comely and sufficient Cloakes for the credit of the   15
place, they are also to play at all solom ffeastes, at Mr Maiors
commaund and not to goe forth of the Cytie with out licence
obtained therof the said Mr Maior.

...

Payments Out Book CRO: A 16
p 119*

...

Paid the fift day of Aprill 1615 to Mr Hancock
and Mr Harwell that they layd out at Warwick   xj s x d   25
Concerning the Players and other busines

...

p 121 *(12 August)*

...   30

Paid the same daie to the Waites for one yeres wages to come
beginning at Lammas last   vij li.

...

Letter concerning Lady Elizabeth's Players   35
CRO: Misc 4 1946/9*
                         28o die Marcij. 1615
One of the Company of the Lady Elizabethes players came to
this Cittie the 27th of March and said to Thomas Barrowes

Clothworker these wordes .videlicet.[Yf you were well served
you would be fatched vpp with pursivauntes, and that you would
haue [the] your throates cutt [such poor]] you are such people
in this Towne so peevishe that you would have your throates
cutt and that you were well served you would be fatched vpp   5
with pursevauntes /

Witnes hereof. *(signed)* Thomas Barowes

The names of the players names named in the patent the Lady   10
Elizabethes players bearinge date the xxxjth of May. Anno
Undecimo Jacobi.

Iohn Townesend	sworne officers. & non other
Iosephe Moore	named in the patent.
William Perry	
Robert ffintche	
George Bosgrove	
Thomas Suell	
Iames Iones	
Charles Martyn	Boyes
hughe haughton	
Iames Kneller	
Iohn Hunt	
Edward	
Raphe	
Walter Burrett	

.5. Horses in the Company

(reverse of sheet)
The misdemeanor of one of the Lady Elizibeths Players.   30

Letter of Sir Edward Coke to the Mayor CRO: A 79
p 113* *(28 March)*

fforasmuch as this time is by his maiestes lawes and Iniunctions   35
Consecrated to the service of Almightye God, and publique
notice was given on the last Sabaoth for preparacion to the
receyving of the holy Communion, Theis are to will and require
you to suffer no Common players whatsoever to play within
your Citie, for that it would lead to the hindrance of devotion,   40
and drawing of the artificers and Common people from their
labours. And this being signified vnto any such they will rest

therewith (as becometh them) satisfied, otherwise suffer you
them not, and this shalbe your sufficient warrant.
this 28th of March: 1615
                              (signed)   Edw Coke
•To the Maior and Iustices   5
within the citie of Coventre•
•The Lord Coke his lettere
concerning the Ladie Elizabeths Players.•

Cappers' Records SC: Account Book I   10
f 153   *(16 January)*

...

paid for scowryng our harnes, when my lord Cumpton was
here   xiiij d
...   15

paid for scowryng our harnes at Coventrie fayre and men to
weare them   ij s iiij d

...

Carpenters' Account Book II CRO: Acc 3/2   20
f 279

...

Paid for bearing owr harneys on the faire daye and for
poyntes   x d
Paid Echell for Car⟨.⟩ing owr Muskett to the Iustices and   25
attending on them   iiij d

...

Mercers' Account Book CRO: Acc 15
f 116   30
                    Paymenttes ordinary and extraordinary
...

paide to six men for carring the Armor ˈand for two dozen of
poynttesˈ   ij s iiij d
...   35

paide to Iohn Lax for two new muskettes with bandelers Restes
& Mouldes   xlvj s
paide to him more for lyneing varneshing and frindging two
hedpeeces   v s
paide him more for setting out of our muskettes when the Lord   40
Compton was heere   xij d

...

Weavers' Rentgatherers' Book II CRO: Acc 100/18/2
f 67

...

Payd for the bearyng of the armor att the fayre daye   ij s ij d

...   5

A   *Drapers' Accounts* CRO: Acc 154
f 169

...

pd to sixe men for wearing Harnesse at the ffaire   0 3 0   10

...

1616
Chamberlains' and Wardens' Account Book II CRO: A 7(b)
p 582 *(23 October) (Chamberlains)*   15

...

And to the Wayts for theire wages this yeare past   xxvj s viij d

...

p 591* *(27 November) (Wardens)*   20

...

                        Rewards to players

...

Gyven vnto one that had the King*es* Ma*i*esties warrant to shewe
Trick*es* with poppitt*es* as appeareth by a bill vnder m*a*ister   25
Maiors hand   iij s iiij d
Gyven to the Lord Willoughbeyes Men the xxiij^th of May
1616   ij s.
Gyven to the Lord Ivers Trumpeters the xxx^th of March
1616   ij s vj d   30
Gyven to the Wayt*es* of Leicester the same day   ij s
Gyven to the Wayts of Nottingham the same day   ij s
Gyven to the Wayts of Southam as appeareth by the same
bill   xij d
Gyven to the Wayts of Shrewsbury the same day   ij s   35
Gyven to the Prince his players 1 quarter of the pound of
refined Suger att the p*a*rlor & a quart of sacke   xvij d
Gyven to the Musici*o*ns the third of November 1616   xij d
Gyven to the Earle of Shrewsbury his players as appeareth by a
bill   v s.   40
Gyven to the Duk*es* and the Lord Treasurers Trumpeters   v s.

pp 591-2 *(27 November) (Wardens)*

Gyven to the Way*tes* of Shrewsbury   ij s vj d
Gyven to the Lord of Darbys beareward as appeareth by a
bill   iij s iiij d l   5
Gyven to the Lord Comptons Beareward as appeareth by a
bill   x s.
Gyven to the Wayts of Nottingham as appeareth by a bill   xij d
Gyven to an Italian that thrust himself through the side to make
experi*ment* of his oyle as appe*a*reth by a bill vnder m*aister*   10
Maiors hand   xx s
Gyven to the Prince his players as appeareth by a bill vnder
m*aiste*r Maiors hand   iij li.
Gyven to the Councells Trumpeters the xvjth of August
1616   x s.   15
Gyven to the Wayts of Lincolne as appeareth by a bill vnder
M*aiste*r Maiors hande   ij s.
Gyven to the Pallesgraves players as appeareth by a bill the xiijth
of Iuly 1616.   xl s.
Gyven to the Lady Elizabeth her players as appeareth by an   20
other bill   xl s.
Gyven to the Company of the Revells the xxjth of Iune 1616. as
appeareth by a bill vnder m*aiste*r Maiors hand   xx s.
Gyven to the Wayts of Hertford the vijth of Iune 1616.   ij s.
Gyven to the Lord of Derbyes players the xiiijth of May   25
1616.   x s.
Gyven to the Queenes players the xvijth of ffebruary
1615.   xx s.
Gyven to the Lord of Mounteagles players as appeareth by a
bill   x s.   30
Gyven to the Wayts of this City   ij s
Gyven to the Queenes M*aiesties* players the xiiijth of November
1615.   xl s.
Gyven to the ffencers the vth of November 1616   ij s.
                                    Su*m*ma xvj li. ij s ij d   35

p 593 *(Wardens)*
                    Payments att Commaundement . /
...
Paid to Iohn Launder and others w*hi*ch tooke paynes in settinge   40
downe and prickinge the notes for the Chymes in St Michaells
Church   ij s vj d
...

p 598 *(Wardens)*

...

Gyven to yonge Iohn Launder   v s.

...

    5

Payments Out Book CRO: A 16
p 130 *(9 October)*

...

Paid the same daie to the waites of the Citie for a whole yeres
wages   vij li   10

...

Cappers' Records SC: Account Book I
f 154

...   15

p*ay*ed for dressynge our harnes, and bearyng it   ij s x d

...

p*ay*ed for a bolt for *our* masters seate dore, in the Churche and
takynge downe *our* pageant seate dore   viij d

...   20

Carpenters' Account Book II CRO: Acc 3/2
f 281v

...

paid for shewing o*w*r newe Muskett afore M*aiste*r Maior the vth   25
of December   ij s vj d

...

(Candlemas at master's house)
Gyven the Musitians that daye   vj d   30

...

paid for Carryeing o*w*r harneys on the faire daye & for
poynt*es*   x d

...   35

Mercers' Account Book CRO: Acc 15
f 118

...

                       Payment*es* ordenarie, & extraordenary

...   40

paid to 6 men for carying it ⌐2s⌐ & for 2 dozen point*es*
⌐4d⌐   ij s iiij d

...

Weavers' Account Book CRO: Acc 100/17/1
f 115v

...

Given to the bearers of the harneys vpon the fayre day & for
point*es*   0-2-2   5

Weavers' Rentgatherers' Book II CRO: Acc 100/18/2
f 68v

...

Payd to Scot for the musketes   iiij s   10

...

Payd to Goodman Scot for tow new musketts the. 8th of
November   ij li-xij s
Payd more to Scot for tow sword scabbers and tow dagger
sheares   ij s   15

...

Spent when wee tooke in the harneis at wedgwodes   viij d

...

f 69   20

...

Payd to Goodman Scot for a pollax   ij s iiij d
Payd for a sword   j s viij d
Payd for the hire of tow blacke armors   j s viij d

...   25

1617
Chamberlains' and Wardens' Account Book II CRO: A 7(b)
p 600 *(29 October) (Chamberlains)*

...   30

And to the wayt*es* for theire wages this yeare past   xxvj s viij d

...

p 607 *(19 November) (Wardens)*
                    Reward*es* to Players.   35
Gyven to the Queenes Ma*jesties* players belonging to the
Chamber of Bristowe the xxiiij^th of ffebruary 1616. as appeareth
by a bill vnder M*aiste*r Maiors hand   xl s.
Gyven to Raph Shelmadyne the King*es* beareward the xxij^th of
May 1617, as apperth by a bill vnder M*aiste*r Maiors   40
hand   xxij s
Gyven vnto the Queenes players the xxij^th of October 1617 as
appeareth by a bill vnder M*aiste*r Maiors hand   xx s.

Gyven vnto the Princes players the xv^th of May, 1617. as
appeareth by a bill vnder *Maiste*r Maiors hand   xl s.
Gyven vnto the Trumpetors when *Maiste*r Maior and his
Bretheren walked the wall   v s.

Summa vj li. vij s.   5

p 611* *(Payments at Commandment) (Wardens)*

...

Paid vnto Mr Iames Cranford for acting a Co<i>m</i>medye the xxj^th of
December 1617 as appeareth by a bill vnder Maister Maiors   10
hand   xxxiij s

Payments Out Book CRO: A 16
p 138 *(23 August)*

...   15

Paid to Mr Butler and Mr Waryn the 23th day of August 1617 for
their expences in their iorney to the Court   v li. xiiij s

<table>
<tr><td>This money was
R Barkers fyne
for Radford
Medows</td><td>...
Paid to the Wardens the same day for to make prouission against
his Maiesties Coming   xl li. 20</td></tr>
</table>

p 139* *(29 August)*

Paid the Waight*es* the 29 of August 1617 for part of their yeres
wages begining at Lamas   iiij li. 25
Paid to Gilbert Tunkes the xth day of September 1617 for
Gilding the great Mace and the sword, and other wirke as
appeareth by his bill in the fyle   vj li. xiiij s
Paid the 17th day of September 1617 to Mrs Potts for mending
the swords scabbard   xx s 30
Paid the same day to Mr fflecher for Post Horses to Ashby when
his Ma<i>ie</i>stie was there   xviij s
Paid the same day to Burley the tayler for apparrell for the Kings
Iester   xxxvij s
...   35

pp 140-1 *(22 October)*

...

Paid more to Him the same day w*hi*ch he and his Brother Laid
out to the King*es* officers   xxx s 40

...

33 / Nichols, *Progresses of James I*, vol 3: Benley *for* Burley

(25 October)
Paid to Mr Hancok for money Laid out of at London for
prouision against the King*es* Coming to Coventry x li. |
Paid to Mr Potter w*hi*ch he had of Mr William Sewall w*hi*ch was
paid out at the King*es* beeing here xx li. | 5
Paid to Mr Hancock for a siluer cupp w*hi*ch was lost at his
M*ai*esties beeing here 49s
Paid to him more for that he laid out for Coppies from Leicester
of fees and rewards ij s
... 10

p 144 *(16 December)*
...
Paid the same day to Iohn Snell and Godfrey Legg w*hi*ch was the
foote of their accompt for the Kings dyet xlvij li. xvij s vij d 15
...

(29 December)
...
Paid more to Richard Bullen for altering the Cities Spoons the 20
same day xxxvij s iij d

AC **City Annals** Bodl: MS Top. Warwickshire d.4
ff 33v-4*
... 25
Samuell Myles drap*er* maior 1616 & ended in 1617. Rafe Walden
houses paynted & Michell Love sheri*ue*s. In the moneth of August 1617 sundry
people in Coventry caused there howses to be painted most of
the howses were painted w*i*th blacke & white painting against the
king*es* com*m*ing to Coventrey. the gates of the Citty were also 30
painted as the Newgate sponnstreete gate & Bishopps streete gate
& the Walke in the Crosse cheeping & the cunditt there also.
A great supper Likewise there was pro*u*ided agreat supp*er* in the St mary hall for
prouided for the king*es* maiestie & them y*a*t attended one him, w*hi*ch supp*er*
ye kinge. cost the Citty a great sum*me* of money. One the 2*de* of 35
Kinge Iames September 1617 being twesday our most noble & happy Kinge
came to Iames came to Coventry & many nobles w*i*th him who was mett
coventry by the Maior & his brethren in scarlett gownes with out the
bishoppe streete gate. & in meeting of his maiestie Doctor
Holland made an exellent oration vnto ... him for the w*hi*ch he 40
was much praised he was in a Suite of blacke sattin. The oration
being ended the Maior W*i*th all his brethren ridd bare headed
before his Maiestie & brought him into the Citty whoe came into

the Citty at the Bishoppe streete gate & so alonge the Crosse
cheeping & the hie streete and turned in at the hey lane & then
into ye Churchyard ... the next morning the king*es* ma*ies*tie came
riding from | the Whitefriers with the maior & his brethren in
scarlett gownes the Maior bearing the sword before the Kinge   5
who also ridd bare headed before him with all his brethren & so
ridd alonge the street*es* to the ffree schoole but came riding
backe againe *p*resently & so came riding backe againe alonge the
Crosse cheeping & ridd out att the Sponnstreete gate & at his
departing he gaue the Maior & the rest great thankes for all there   10
kindnes shewed to him & to his servan*tes*.

...

Cappers' Records SC: Account Book I
f 155   15

...

Laid out for a [Doore] Boord that was sett vpon the paggyn
house Doore   viij d.
Payd for the Harnest att the ffaier   xvj d
...   20

Carpenters' Account Book II CRO: Acc 3/2
ff 284v-5

...

Paid for skowring the harneys and the musket & borrowing   25
[the] ij bills   ij s iiij d |
Paid for Caryeing *ow*r harneys on the faier daye & for
poynt*es*   x d
...
Gyven Musitians on the dynner daye   viij d   30
...

Mercers' Account Book CRO: Acc 15
f 120 *(Payments ordinary and extraordinary)*
...   35
p*ai*d to vj men for Carrying the Armor   ij s
...

Weavers' Account Book CRO: Acc 100/17/1
f 117v   40

...

Payd to Iohn Lackes for tow blacke armors wee hired of him at
our fayre   0-2-0

Weavers' Rentgatherers' Book II CRO: Acc 100/18/2
f 70v

...

Payd to them that carried armor at the fayre   0-1-6

...   5

A *Drapers' Accounts* CRO: Acc 154
f 174

...

paid to vj men for the Carriage of Armor att Couentrey   10
fayre   ij s

...

AC *Visit of King James I* Nichols: *Progresses of James I* vol 3
pp 422-3   15

    Preparatory to the King's Visit to the City of Coventry, the
following Act of Leet was promulgated on the 6th of May:
    Whereas the King's most excellent Majestie intendeth to come
unto this Citie sometime this present yeare to view the same,   20
against whose coming it is verie fit and requisite, for the credit of
this Citie, that as well all and singular houses and buildings within
the same, and suburbs thereof, especially on the street side,
should be well and sufficiently repaired and amended, as also all
and singular bulks and paint-houses within the said Citie (on the   25
street side as aforesaid) should be in like repair, as also that all
streets in this Citie and suburbs thereof should be well and
sufficiently paved and amended where neede | is: And forasmuch
as there is expresse order and commaund given unto Mr. Maior of
this Citie by the right honourable the Lord High Chamberlaine of   30
England, that theise reparacons and pavements shall be made as
soone as conveniently maie be without any further delay; It is
therefore enacted, &c. that everie housholder of this Citie, and
suburbs of the same, shall, at or before the Feast-day of St.
James th' Appostle next ensuing, sufficiently repaire his or theire   35
house or building on the streete-side, and cullor and laie the same
with white and russet or other colours on the street-side, on pain
of xx s. And further, that everie house-holder of this Citie or
suburbs that hath any bulk or pain-house before his shopp on the
street-side, shall cause the same to be sufficiently repaired before   40
the said Feast, on pain of x s. And also that everie person

25 / *Nichols glosses* paint-houses *as* pent-houses

dwelling within this Citie and suburbs shall, before the next
Quarter Sessions, pave, or cause to be sufficiently paved, his or
their street, before his or their houses, on pains of xx s.

The particulars of his Majestie's reception are thus recorded in
the City Annals: 5

Samuel Miles, Mayor; In this year in the month of August
most of the houses were painted with black and white, and the
Gates, as New Gate, Spon Gate, and Bishop Gate, and also some
of the Conduits, against the King's coming; who, on September 2,
with many of his Nobles, came to Coventry, and was met by the   10
Mayor and Aldermen in scarlet gowns without Bishop Gate, and
Dr. Philemon Holland, drest in a suit of black satin, made an
Oration, for which he had much praise

...
                                                                              15

pp 430-1*

...

The following list of payments is also collected from original
documents in the City Treasury:

Expences of receiving the King at Coventry, September 2, 1617: 20
A Bill for black sattin 10 3/8 yds. at 13s. 6d. and

trimmings	11	1	11
Black velvet and black silk for foot-stools	2	10	3
One nail of crimson velvet and one Turkey purse		14	11
Charges of the Supper made for the King	147	17	7	25
Ringing at the three Churches	1	10	0
Fees to the King's servants and attendants	57	0	0
Total £.220	14	8	

The following is an "Account of Fees" paid at Coventry:

	£.	s.	d.	
				30
Sir Robert Osborne	5	10	0	
Mr. Gwyn with Lord Compton	2	4	0	
Fees of Stable Packe	7	0	0	
Yeomen Harbingers	1	0	0	
One of the Guard for keeping the door	1	0	0	35
Yeoman Usher	1	6	8	
Drummer	0	10	0	
Given Archee [the King's Jester]	5	0	0	
A Yeoman Usher keeping the door	0	10	0	
Yeoman Porters	2	0	0	40
Deputy Marshall and Trumpeter	1	0	0	
The Footmen	2	0	0	
Surveyors of the Ways	1	0	0	

	£.	s.	d.	
Coachmen	1	0	0	
Mrs. Stewart	0	10	0	
The Littermen	1	2	0	
Provost and Knight Marshall	0	13	4	5
Trumpeters	2	0	0	
Serjeant Trumpeter	1	0	0	
Pages and Grooms of Chamber	2	0	0	
Gentleman Shewers	2	0	0	
Gentleman Ushers	5	10	8	10
Quarter Waiters	2	0	0	
The Knight Harbinger	3	6	8	
Four Yeoman of the Mouth	2	0	0	
The Bottlemen for the field	0	10	0	
Messengers of the Chambers	0	10	0	15
Purveyor of the Skullery	0	6	8	
Gentlemen Harbingers	2	0	0	
Total £57		0	0	

...

20

1618
Chamberlains' and Wardens' Account Book II CRO: A 7(b)
p 616 *(28 October) (Chamberlains)*

...

And to the Waytes for theire wages this yeare past   xxvj s. viij d   25

...

pp 625-6 *(25 November) (Wardens)*

...

         Rewardes to players. /   30
Gyven to the Queenes Players the Third Day of December 1617
as appeareth by a bill vnder Maister Maiors hand   xx s.
Gyven to the Lady Elizabeths players the xij.th of December
1617 as appeareth by an other bill vnder Maister Maiors
hand   xl s.| 35
Gyven to the Earle of Shrewsbury players the xxth of December
1617 as appeareth by a bill vnder Maister Maiors hand   x. s.
Gyven to the Duke of Lenox his Trumpeter and the Marques of
Buckingham his Trumpeter the Marques of Winchester his
Trumpeter the Earle of Shrewesburys Trumpeter and the Earle of   40
leicesters Trumpeters the xij.th of September 1618 as appeareth
by a bill vnder Maister Maiors hand   l s
       Summa vj li.

p 628 *(Payments at Commandment)* *(Wardens)*

...

Paid to Iohn Launder the yonger   v s.

...

Payments Out Book CRO: A 16
p 145 *(20 January)*

...

This xx li. was for part of the xxvij li. ˹12d˺ laid out for the
Oxen to Mr Greene, by *Maiste*r Maior for this House†
Paid to Mr William Sewall Maior the xx^th day of Ianuarie 1617 in
part of a greater Sum*m* w*hi*ch this house oweth him   xx li.

...

Paid to *Maiste*r Maior w*hi*ch is the full sum*m* of the xxvij li. xij d
laid out for the oxen   vij li. xij d

...

p 149 *(14 June)*

...

Paid more the same daie to Iohn Wotton for making a freirs cote
when his M*ai*estie was here   ij s vj d.
Paid the 20th of Iune to the Kings Serieant at Arms, w*hi*ch was
left vnpaid at his M*ai*est*ie*s beeing here   iij li. vj s viij d.

...

p 151 *(31 October)*

...

Paid the same day to Mr Hopkins w*hi*ch he laid out for making of
Mr Doctor Hollands Shorte   xxiij s 23s

...

Paid more the same daie of the same money w*hi*ch was for a
shute of Satyn for doctor Holland & other thing*es*   xiiij li. vij s.

...

AC   *City Annals* Bodl: MS Top. Warwickshire d.4
      f 35v

William Sewall vintner maior 1617 & ended in 1618 ... In his
yeare was a Lottery in Coventrey w*hi*ch was kept at the St Mary
hall ... vnto w*hi*ch Lottery abundance of people resorted & some

29 / *first* x *written over* v; 23s *is clarification*

Did winne prizes, & others lost, the w*h*ich lottery was both for
gilt & siluer plate & also for spoones [⟨.. ....⟩ sp⟨.....⟩] gilded & for
siluer spoones & siluer canns to drinke in &c The owners thereof
gott abundance of money thereby for the people would neuer
leaue drawing till they had drawne all ... when any prize was   5
woone there was one that should blow a trumpett & should haue
some benefitt by eu*er*y prize that was woone if it were of any
valew & so should he y*a*t deliu*er*ed the lott*es* If it were a great
prize y*en* a ma*n* should Carry it in his hand alonge the stree*tes* to
ye parties howse y*a*t did winne it w*i*th a trumpett & a drumme   10
going before the party y*a*t bare the prize ...

Cappers' Records SC: Account Book I
f 156*

...   15
paid for hire of blacke armor on the faire day   xij d
paid for wearing the Companyes armour on the faire day   vj d
...

paid for a warrant for arresting of Henry Owyn for the Pageon
street   ij s   20
...

(Choice dinner)
paid for Musicke   ij s
...   25

Carpenters' Account Book II CRO: Acc 3/2
f 287

...
Paid for cariage of o*w*r Harneys & for poynt*es*   x d   30
...

gyven the Musitians   vj d
...

Mercers' Account Book CRO: Acc 15   35
f 123

...
Paid to vj Men for bearing of the Armor of the Companyes on
Coventrey fayre day   iij s.
...   40

2 / i *in* gilt *written over* o; t *written over* d

Weavers' Rentgatherers' Book II CRO: Acc 100/18/2
f 71v

...

payd for tow blacke armors to cot   0-ij s
Payd for point*es* and Charges to our harnes men   0-0-xxj d   5

...

Spent at tow times when wee met about our harnes   0-xij d

...

A   *Drapers' Accounts* CRO: Acc 154   10
f 177

...

Paid to the bearers of the Companyes armor on the fayre
day   ij s
...   15

1619
Chamberlains' and Wardens' Account Book II CRO: A 7(b)
p 644 *(10 November) (Wardens)*

...   20
                          Reward*es* to players.
Given to the Lady Elizabeth her players the ffowerth Day of
Ianuary 1618 as appereth by a Bill vnder M*aiste*r Maiors
hand   xxxiij s.
Given to the Lord of Worcesters Music*i*on the xiiij^th of Iune   25
1619 as appeareth by an other bill   ij s.
Given to the King*es* Seriant of the Trumpetors the xix^th of
August   xxij s.
Given to the Princ*es* players the xxv^th of October 1619   xx s.
                          Su*m*ma iij li. xvij s.   30

p 646 *(Payments at commandment) (Wardens)*

...

Paid for the Auncient and colours of this Citie
latly made for the Souldiers of the Artilery yard   35
and for making and mending of the same   vj li. xix d.
after it was burnt as appereth by a Bill of the
p*ar*ticulers thereof vnder M*aiste*r Maiors hand

Cappers' Records SC: Account Book I   40
f 157 col b

...

Paid for a Hornes to Iohn Scott for the ffaire   xvj d

Paid to ij Men for Cariing them and poynt*es*   x d
...

Carpenters' Account Book II CRO: Acc 3/2
f 290   5

...

p*ai*d for caryeing *ow*r Armor on the fayer daye & for
poynt*es*   x d
p*ai*d Iohn Lax for lending vs black armor   xij d
...   10

Mercers' Account Book CRO: Acc 15
f 125v
                          Pa yment*es* . Ordinary and Extraordinary
...   15
Payd to.vj men for wearinge it at the ffayre   iij s
Payd allowed Thomas Massy w*hic*h he leiyd out for the good of
the Company   v s
...
                                                                                  20

Weavers' Account Book CRO: Acc 100/17/1
f 121

...

payd Michaell Marson for weighting vpon the fayre day   vj d
...   25

Weavers' Rentgatherers' Book II CRO: Acc 100/18/2
f 73

...

Payd for tyringe of one blacke armor and carridge of it and   30
carridge of another on the fayre day   0-ij-*(blank)*
...

A   *Drapers' Accounts* CRO: Acc 154
    f 180   35

    ...

    Paid to the men w*hic*h bare harneys at the fayre   ij s iiij d
    ...

16 / it: *the armour*

1620
Chamberlains' and Wardens' Account Book II CRO: A 7(b)
p 662 *(29 November)* *(Wardens)*

...

Rewardes to Players. /   5
Given to Danieel Swynnerton & the Company of Players
belonging to the late Queene Ann the xxixth of March 1620   x s
Paid which was given to the Princes Players the xijth of August
1620   x [x] v s
Paid to the Kings Maiesties Players as appeareth by a Bill the xth   10
of Ianuary last   xxxiij s.
Paid to Starkey the Kinges Iester   v s.
Paid to the Musicions of Nottingham the xxijth of May   ij s.
Summa iij li. x s.
Payments at Commanndement . /   15

p 663 *(Wardens)*

...

Paid to Hamlett Bosworth Paynter for silvering the Polleaxes and
paynting the Trunchions which the followers vse at the ffaire as   20
appeareth by a Bill vnder Maister Maiors hand   xij d

...

Cappers' Records SC: Account Book I
f 158 *(Choice dinner)*   25

Paid for Musick   ij s
...
Paid for wearing of the armor at the fayer   xviij d
...   30
Paid for amending of the Pagent howse   iiij d
...

Carpenters' Account Book II CRO: Acc 3/2
f 293   35

...
Paid for Armor   vij s viij d
Paid for a gorgett   iij s
Paid for nayling, oyling, & workmanshipp   vj s
Paid for hyring, Armor at the faier   xij d   40
Paid ij men for caryeing Armor on the faier daye   ix d

...

Mercers' Account Book CRO: Acc 15
f 128v

            Paymentes Ordenary & extraordenarie

...

Paid to 6 men for bearing our Armour on the faire day   iij s   5

...

Weavers' Account Book CRO: Acc 100/17/1
f 122v

...   10

Giuen to Michaell Marson for Lokinge to our harneis on the fayre
day   0-vj d

...

Weavers' Rentgatherers' Book II CRO: Acc 100/18/2   15
f 74v

...

Layd out to Iohn Scot for tow blacke armors   0-ij s 0d.
for carridge of the harneis and for pointes   0-ij s-j d.

...   20

A   *Drapers' Accounts* CRO: Acc 154
    f 183

...

Paid to vj men that bared harnes at the ffayre day   iij s   25

...

1621
Chamberlains' and Wardens' Account Book II CRO: A 7(b)
pp 676-7 *(21 November) (Wardens)*   30

...

            Rewardes to Players.
Paid which was given to William Peadle & other players Dauncers
vpon Ropes the 29th of November last as appeareth by a Bill
vnder Maister Maiors hand   x s.   35
Paid which was given to Martyn Slathier one of the Players of the
late Queene Elizabeth the 23th of December 1620. as appeareth
be an other Bill vnder Maister Maiors hand   v s.
Paid which was given to the Players of the Lady Elizabeth the vth
Daie of Ianuary 1620. as appeareth by a Bill vnder Maister Maiors   40
Hand   xxij s.

Paid which was given to Henry Walker & Iohn Walker who
brought the Kinges warrant to shewe workes of Arte concerning
the Castell of Winsor.the xij^th of May 1621 as appeareth by a
Bill vnder Maister Maiors hand   ij s. vj d.|
Paid which was given to the Wayte Players of the Ladie Grace the   5
29th of Iuly 1621. as appeareth by a Bill vnder Maister Maiors
hand   iij s.
Paid which was given to the Wayte Players of Newarke the xj^th
of September last as appeareth by a Bill vnder Maister Maiors
hand   xviij d.   10
Paid which was given to Gilbert Reason one of the Princes
Players who brought a Commission wherein himself and others
were named the 24th of August last as appeareth by a Bill vnder
maister Maiors hand   xx s.
Paid which was given to the Kinges Seriant Trumpeter and to   15
Tenn more of the Kinges Trumpiters the 24th of August 1621. as
appeareth by a Bill vnder Maister Maiors hand   iij li. vj s.
Paid more which was given the same daie to the Wayte players of
Newarke as appeareth by the same Bill vnder Maister Maiors
hand   ij s.   20
                        Summa vj li xij s. /

...

p 680 (Wardens)
                    Presents given this yeare   25

...

To Sir Iohn Suckling knight one of the Maisters of the requests
to the Bull ...   iij. s iiij. d
...

                                                                      30

Cappers' Records SC: Account Book I
f 159

...

Paid to Iohn Scott for a Black Harnes a Man to carry it on the
fayer day   xviij d   35

...

Carpenters' Account Book II CRO: Acc 3/2
f 295

...   40

Gyven the Musitions   vj d
paid for a pyn for our Muskett   iij d
...

Paid for hyring Armor on the fayer day   xij d
Paid for caryeing *our* Armor that daye   x d
...

Mercers' Account Book CRO: Acc 15   5
f 129v

...

> Paiment*es* ordenary and extraordenary. /

...

Paid to six men for bearing Armour on the ffaire day in   10
Iune   iij s
...

p*a*id six men p*ro* bearing Armour 16th August 1621 & Iohn Lax
for pr*ou*iding them Armour   vij s
...   15

Weavers' Account Book CRO: Acc 100/17/1
f 123v

...

payde to Mvssiscione*es*   ij s vj d   20
...

Weavers' Rentgatherers' Book II CRO: Acc 100/18/2
f 75[a]

...   25

Payd to Iohn Scot for three blacke armors   0-iij-0
Payd to foure men that did weare those harnesses and one of our
owne   0-ij-0
...

Payd to Gilbert tonkes for varnishin Michaell marsons   30
cunisons   j s 6d

A   *Drapers' Accounts* CRO: Acc 154
f 185

...   35

Paid to Six Men that beare Harnes at the Two ffayres   vj s
...

AC *Shearmen and Tailors' Accounts* Bodl: MS Top. Warwickshire c.7
f 34   40

...

payed 4 men for beareing the armor at the Faier 2/6
...

f 74v

...

Given the Musitions att the Count Dinner 2s/- ...

f 80   5

...

Paide foure men, for bearing armour on the faire day xvj d ...

1622
Chamberlains' and Wardens' Account Book II CRO: A 7(b)   10
p 689 *(4 December) (Wardens)*
                        Rewardes to Players. /
Paid which was given to the Lord Stanhopps Trumpeters the
xviijth of Ianuary 1621. /   xij d.
Paid which was given to Sir Iohn dancing his wayte-players the   15
xxiiijth of November. 1621.   xij d.
Paid which was given to Two severall Company of Weight-players
the xxth of May 1621. as appeareth by a Bill vnder *Maister*
Maiors hand   iiij s.
Paid which was given to the Weightplayers of the Earle of   20
Northampton the Nynth of August as appeareth by a Bill vnder
Maister Maiores hand   ij s vj d.
Paid which was given to the Kinges Players for Bristow youthes
the same Nynth of August as appeareth be a Bill vnder *Maister*
Maiores hand   xv s.   25
Paid which was given to the Kings Trumpeters the Marquesse of
Buckingham and the Earle of Oxfordes the xiiijth of August
1621. as appeareth by a Bill vnder *Maister* Maiors hand   v s.
Paid which was given to the Weightes of Nottingham the vjth of
August 1621. as appeareth by a Bill vnder *Maister* Maiores   30
hand   ij s vj d.
Paid which was given to the Lord Burghley his musicions the last
of September 1621. as appeareth by a Bill vnder maister Maiores
hand   xij d
                        Summa xxxij s   35

...

Payments Out Book CRO: A 16
p 193* *(9 February)*
...   40
Paid more the same day to one William dannyell a player being
one of the Revells Company   v s.

...

p 198

...

Paid the 19th of Iune Anno domini 1622. to Iohn Rogerson and
Iohn Barker late Wardens which they paid to the Schoole Masters
of the ffree Schoole the last yere both at the visitacion xl. s   5
and at the Comedy xx s ...

Cappers' Records SC: Account Book I
f 160

...   10

Paid for [b⟨..⟩wing] ⸌ ˹borowing˺ of Two black Harnesse & for
Two Men to Weare them on the New ffayre daie in Easter
Weeke   iij s
Paid to William davys for borrowing of one black harnesse for
one Man on the ffaire daie the 21.th of Iune. and for   15
wages   xviij d

...

Paid to William davis for one Black harnis for one Man on the
ffaire daie the xvjth of August & for wages   xviij d

...   20

Carpenters' Account Book II CRO: Acc 3/2
f 299

...

paid the Musitions at Candlemas   vj d   25

...

for hiring harnes at the faire & for bearing it   ij s x d

...

paid for Armor & to them that caried it at the faire   xx d

                                                                         30

Mercers' Account Book CRO: Acc 15
f 132

...

             Paymentes ordenary and extraordenary. /

...   35

Paied Iohn Lax for Armor for vj men in April 1622   iiij s
Paied to vj men for bearinge the Armor   ij s

...

Paied to vj men for bearing Armor on the faire day in Iune   ij s

...   40

Paied Iohn Lax for Armor for vj men in August 1622   iiij s
Paied vj men for bearinge the Armor   ij s

...

Weavers' Rentgatherers' Book II CRO: Acc 100/18/2
f 77v

...

Item paide to Iohn Lax for too black armors which wee hiered of
him at the new faire at somar was twelue moneth and for three   5
men that wore those too armors and our one black armor   0-3-6
Item paide to Iohn Lax for three black armors which were hiered
of him at winter faire was twelue moneth not being in the last
account   0-3-0
Item paide too fore men that wore those three armors and our   10
one black armor   0-2-0

...

Item paid to Iohn Lax for three black armors the [fore] ˄ 'three'
faire daiees   0-9-0
Item and for men that carryed those and our one black armor at   15
all ffairees   0-6-[6d]

A   *Drapers' Accounts* CRO: Acc 154
f 188*

...   20

Paid for bearing of Armor 4 faire dayes   ix s
Paid to John Lax for his fee viij s and keeping Armor two new
ffaires viij s   xvj s

...

                                                                       25

1623
Chamberlains' and Wardens' Account Book II CRO: A 7(b)
pp 709-10 *(3 December) (Wardens)*

...

                    Rewards to players.   30
Paid which was given to Gilbert Reason and William Eaton
players to the Prince his highnes the xxiij^th of december. 1622.
as appeareth by a bill vnder Maister Maiors hand.   xx s.
Paid which was given vnto the Players of the Lady Elizabeth the
xxiiij^th of Ianuary 1622 as appeareth by a bill vnder Maister   35
Maiors hand   xiij s. iiij d.
Paid which was given to Martin Slathier and others players of the
late Queene Elizabeth as appeareth by a bill vnder Maister Maiors
hand   v s.
Paid which was given to Nottingham Trumpeters the xij^th of   40

december 1622. xviij d. and more given the same day to two
Companyes of Musicions of other places. xviij d. as appereth by
a bill vnder Maister Maiors hand.   iij s.
Paid which was given to the Weightes of Worcester the ix^th of
May 1623. xij d. and more the same Daie to the Weightes of   5
Pomfret xij d. as appeareth by a bill vnder Maister Maiors
hand.   ij s.
Paid to the Weightes of Gloucester as appeareth by a bill vnder
Maister Maiors hand.   xij d
Paid to the Weightes of Maxfeild the xxvij^th of May. 1623.   xij d   10
Paid to the Musicions of Lichfeild the xxviij^th of May
1623.   xij d.
Paid to the Weightes of Lincoln the xth of Iune 1623.   xij d.
Paid to the ffencers the xxv^th of Iuly 1623. whoe fenced on
St Iames his night   xij d. 15
Paid to the Kinges Trumpeters the vj^th of August 1623   v s./|
Paid which was given to William Wood a player of the Revells the
xxviij^th of August 1623 as appeareth by a bill vnder Maister
Maiors hand.   ij s vj d
Paid to the Trumpeters of the Earle of Oxford the xviij^th of   20
Aprill 1623. as appeareth by a bill vnder Maister Maiors
hand.   ij s
Paid to the Weightes of Derby and Newarke the xx^th of
September 1623. as appeareth by a bill vnder Maister Maiors
hand   ij s. 25
Paid which was given to the kinges players for bringing xx
Bristow youthes in Musick the xxvj^th of September 1623.   xv s.
Paid which was given to the Lord Staffordes Trumpeters the xv^th
of October 1623.   xij d
                              Summa iij li. xv s. x d.   30
...

p 715 *(3 December)* *(Wardens)*
...

Paid for wyne to the Parlour that night when the   35
Prince came to London forth of Spayne. ij s.
paid which was given to the ffencers . ij s vj d.
to the Sexton of St Michaells for ringing all   xiiij s. vj d.
night x s . as appeareth by a bill vnder Maister
Maiors hand   40
...

Cappers' Records SC: Account Book I
f 161 *(Account dinner)*

Paid for Musick the same daie   ij s
...
Paid for wearing of the Harnesse on the ffaire daie this yere   iiij s
...

Carpenters' Account Book II CRO: Acc 3/2
f 302v

...
for Carrying our harnes at the faire in Aprill   x d
for hyring that Armor   xij d
...

f 303

...
Payd Thomas Sherman for harnes & his wages   xij d
...
for bearing harnes on the faire daie   viij d

Mercers' Account Book CRO: Acc 15
f 134

...
                    Paymentes ordenary & extraordinary.
...
paid six men for bearing armor vpon 3 ffayer dayes   vj s
...

Weavers' Rentgatherers' Book II CRO: Acc 100/18/2
f 79

...
Item paid toe Iohn Scot for translating our Armor   1-4-0
...

f 79v

...
Item paid toe twoe men for carrying hornies   0-1-0
Item paid to Iohn Lax for scowaring and varnishing one armor
and repareing of the other three Armors and for exchanging of a
Muskit   1-4-6
...

It*em* paid toe fore men for beareing armor the 16th of
August   0-2-0
...

A   *Drapers' Accounts* CRO: Acc 154   5
    f 190

    ...
    Paid for bearing Armor at the faires   ix s
    ...

                                                                        10

    1624
    Chamberlains' and Wardens' Account Book II CRO: A 7(b)
    pp 730-1 *(24 November) (Wardens)*
                            Reward*es* to Players.
    Paid w*hi*ch was given to [the] xj. of the King*es* Trumpeters the   15
    xxj^th of August last as appeareth by a Bill vnder Maior*es*
    hand   iiij li.
    Paid w*hi*ch was given to fower of the Princ*es* Trumpeters in
    August last as appeareth by a Bill vnder M*ais*ter Maior*es*
    hand   xl s.| 20
    Paid w*hi*ch was given to the Lady Elizabethes Play*er*es in Iuly last
    as appeareth by an other Bill vnder M*ais*ter Maior*es* hand   xij s.
    Paid w*hi*ch was given to Bartholomew Cloys being allowed by the
    Maister of the Revells for shewing a Musicall Organ with divers
    strang and rare Motions in September last as appeareth by a Bill   25
    vnder M*ais*ter Maior*es* hand   v s.
    Paid to fower Trumpeters of the Revells as appeareth by a Bill
    vnder M*ais*ter Maior*es* hand   v s.
                            Sum*ma* vij li. xij s.
    ...   30

    Payments Out Book CRO: A 16
    p 217 *(31 January)*
    ...
    Paid to a Man that tossed a pike before Mr Maior & his bretheren.   35
    the same day.   ij. s vj. d
    ...

    Cappers' Records SC: Account Book I
    f 162   40

    ...
    Paid for wearing of Harnesse on the ffaire dayes   ij s
    ...

(Choice dinner)

Paid for Musick the same tyme   ij s

...

Paid for two ffysteenes for the the Pagent House   viij d

...   5

Carpenters' Account Book II CRO: Acc 3/2
f 305v

...

payd the Musitions   vj d   10

...

for Carrying harnes on the summer faire daie   viij d
and for poynt*es*   ij d

...   15

f 306

...

p*ai*d the Musitions at the Accompt   xij d

...

p*ai*d the Musitions at the Accompt sup*er*   iiij d   20

...

Mercers' Account Book CRO: Acc 15
f 135v

...   25

Payments ordynary and extra ordinary

...

p*ai*d men for wearing Armor at the 2 fayres   0-iiij s 0

...   30

Weavers' Account Book CRO: Acc 100/17/1
f 130

...

It*em* paid ffor bearing harnis at the ffaire   0-2-0

...   35

AC   ***Shearmen and Tailors' Accounts*** Bodl: MS Top. Warwickshire c.7
f 79v

...

Paid for ringing on *our* dinner daie 2. s/-   40

...

4 / the the MS *dittography*

1625
Chamberlains' and Wardens' Account Book II CRO: A 7(b)
p 747 *(29 November) (Wardens)*

      Rewardes to players .   5
Paid which was given to the Prince his players. as appeareth by a
bill vnder *Maister* Maiors hand the xxiiijth of December
1624   xx s.
paid which was given to the players of the late Queene Anne in
December aforesaid as appeareth by another bill vnder *Maister* 10
Maiors hand   xij s. vj d.
paid to Martyn Slatier, Robson, & Silvester late servantes to the
late queene Anne the xvj.th of October 1625.   v s.
          Summa xxvij. s vj. d
       Payments at commaundement   15
...

p 748* *(Wardens)*
...
paid for 12. staves being black for the Constables in severall 20
wards the 13.th of April as appeareth by a bill vnder *Maister*
Maiors hand.   iiij s.
...

Cappers' Records SC: Account Book I   25
f 163
...
payd for bearing our Armor at Summer faire   xij d
...
                    30
(Choice dinner)
payd for Musicke   ij s
...
payd for Boardes & Nayles for our Pagean howse ij s ij d
...   35

Carpenters' Account Book II CRO: Acc 3/2
f 308v

paid for Carriing harnes at the faire   x d 40
...

Mercers' Account Book CRO: Acc 15
f 139v

Paymenttes ordenary & extraordinarie

...

payd for men wering Armor at ye 3 faires   00. vj s. iiij d   5

...

Weavers' Account Book CRO: Acc 100/17/1
f 132

...   10

paid ffore men for beareing harnis at somar ffaire   0-2-0

1626
Chamberlains' and Wardens' Account Book II CRO: A 7(b)
p 758* *(Wardens)*   15

...

Rewards to players
Nothing

...
                                                                                       20

Cappers' Records SC: Account Book I
f 164

...

Paid two men for Carying our harnes att the ffaire   viij d
...   25

Carpenters' Account Book II CRO: Acc 3/2
ff 312-12v

...

paid for Carrieing our harnes att the faire   x d | 30
given the Musitions   vj d

...

Mercers' Account Book CRO: Acc 15
f 142   35
Payments ordinary and extraordinary

...

Paide for vj men bearinge armor at our fayre   0. ij s. 0

...

Paide the waytplayers for playinge at our feast on Saynt Iohns   40
daye   0. ij s. vj d

...

1627
Chamberlains' and Wardens' Account Book II CRO: A 7(b)
p 766 *(24 October) (Chamberlains)*
...

And of liij. s iiij d. payd to the way*tes* of this City for theire   5
wages for this yeare past, as appeareth by a bill vnder M*aiste*r
Maiors hand   liij s. iiij d.
...

p 774 *(28 November) (Wardens)*   10
...
                        Rewards to players
Paid [to] w*h*ich was given to the King*es* players the xvj^th of
November. 1626. as appeareth by a Bill vnder M*aiste*r Maiors
hand   ij s. vj d.   15
Paid to the Revells the xxj^th of December. 1626. as appeareth by
another bill   ij s.
                        Su*m*ma iiij s. vj d.

p 775 *(Wardens)*   20

                    Payments at Comaundement.

...
Paid to the said Gilbert Tonck*es* for dressing vp gilding and
enammelling of [th]foure of the Cityes Crest*es*, xiij s iiij d and for   25
8 yard*es* of 8d broad ribbin to hang the Crest*es* about the wayt
players neck*es*. v s. iiij d. the 24th of May. 1627. as appeareth by
a bill   xviij s. viij d.
...

                                                                        30

p 776* *(Wardens)*
...
Paid for 4. cloakes for the wayte players of the City v*idelice*t Mr.
Iaack Walden for 12. yard*es* of broad cloth at 8s. a yard —
4li. 16s. 0d., for 8. yard*es* of Greene Bayes, at 2s [2d] a yard —   35
17s. 4d. of Mr. Iohn Clark. for 20. yard*es* of silke, and silver lace
at 4.d½ - 7s. 6d., j q*uarte*r of j oz of silk. vij d. for Canvas to
stiffen the Capes viij d. for making [vp] the Cloakes at ij s. vj d. a
peece x s. the xth of March last as app*ea*reth by a bill vnder
m*aiste*r Maiors hand   vj li. xij s. j d   40
...

Council Book CRO: A 14(a)
p 553   *(29 August)*

...

Deliuerd forth a double Curtall & a tenor Cornet to the Waytes   5
videlicet Edward Man, & William Beddell.

...

p 554 *(17 October)*

...

Wayts.   At this daie it is agreed that the Wayts of this Citie shall have   10
foure Markes per annum Wages from this house and liverye
ˆ'Cloakes' [Clokes] once in three yeares : so long tyme as they
performe theire duties to the approbation of this house.

...
                                                                            15

Cappers' Records SC: Account Book I
f 165

...

paid to two men for Carrying harnes at the summer faier   viij d
...   20

Carpenters' Account Book II CRO: Acc 3/2
f 315

...

paid william Hood & Iohn dix for Carrying our armour at the   25
faire   viij d
...

f 315v
...   30
paid the Musitians   vj d
...
paid the musitions at the Count   iiij d
...
                                                                            35

Mercers' Account Book CRO: Acc 15
f 145

...

payd vj men for beareing armor the 25 of May 00-ij-00
...   40

Weavers' Account Book CRO: Acc 100/17/1
f 136v

...

paid 4 men for carrying harnis at the faire   0-2-0
...   5

AC   *Drapers' Accounts* Bodl: MS Top. Warwickshire c.7
f 34

...

pd for bearing the harnes af[ore]'ter' Mr. Maior iiij. s   10
...

1628
Chamberlains' and Wardens' Account Book II CRO: A 7(b)
p 787 *(29 October) (Chamberlains)*   15

...

And of liij s. iiij d. paid to the Way*tes* of this City for theire
wages for this yeare past, as appeareth by two bills thereof vnder
m*aiste*r Maiors hand   liij s. iiij d
...   20

p 795 *(26 November) (Wardens)*

...
                          Rewards to players
Paid w*hi*ch was given to the high Sherriff*es* Trumpeters. v s. and   25
to the Major Dru*m*mer of Ireland. ij s. vj d. as appeareth by a bill
vnder M*aiste*r Maiors hand in Aprill last   vij s.
Paid & given to the King*es* Revells, to Nicholas Hanson one of
that Company in Aprill last as appeareth by a bill vnder M*aiste*r
Maiors hand   v s.   30
Paid for wyne bread and beere for the ffensors on tewsday night
the xth of Iune last in reioycing for the good successe of the
Parliament. ix s, and also paid, w*hi*ch was given to the M*aste*r of
the dauncing horse. iij s. as appeareth by a bill   xij s
Paid w*hi*ch was given to the King*es* players, as app*e*areth by a bill   35
the first of September last   x s.
Paid which was given to the King*es* players, as appeareth by a bill
the ix^th of Ianuary last   v s
                          Sum*ma* xxxix s vj d

AC   *City Annals* Sharp: *Dissertation*
p 12*

...

On the 1st daye of August 1628 being Lamas daye, certaine of
our poore Com*m*oners rose, and pulled downe the hedges of a   5
peece of the Comon ground at whitley at the hether end next to
Barnes close w*h*ich in former tyme was inclosed and taken out of
the Comons their, to defraye some charges for the Pageants
playing here in this Cytty, and Midsummer watch, w*h*ich said
Pageants and watch have bine put downe many yeares since, and   10
yett the said peece of Com*m*on ground has remayned severall and
inclosed untill now.

Cappers' Records SC: Account Book I
f 166   15

...

Payd to 2 men for beareing *our* hornenes att Coventry
fayer   [x] viij d

...
                                                                                                    20

Carpenters' Account Book II CRO: Acc 3/2
f 317v

...

payd for Musique at Candlemas   vj d
...   25
given the musitians   vj d

...

Mercers' Account Book CRO: Acc 15
f 147v   30
                    Paymentt*es* Ordynarie and extraordynary

...

Payd to 6 men for Carriing Armour at the fayre   00-ij s 0
...
                                                                                                    35

Weavers' Account Book CRO: Acc 100/17/1
f 137v

...

It*em* paid for Carrying of harnis at the faire   0-2-0
...   40

7 / *Sharp writes* Barnes (Barons) close; Barons *probably Sharp's own gloss*

Weavers' Rentgatherers' Book II CRO: Acc 100/18/2
f 87
...

Item Given to the Musick on Choyce daie   0-3-0
...   5

1629
Chamberlains' and Wardens' Account Book II CRO: A 7(b)
p 806 *(28 October) (Chamberlains)*   10
...

And of Liij s. iiij d. paid to the Waytes of this Citie for theire
wages for this yeare past, as appeareth by two bills thereof vnder
Maister Maiors hand   liij s. iiij d.
...   15

p 812 *(2 December) (Wardens)*
...
               Rewardes to players.
Paid which was given to strange wayte players at severall   20
tymes .   vij s vj d.
Paid which was given to one Lacy who had a warrant to show
feates of Activity the 5th of Iune last   xj s.
             Summa xviij s. vj d.
         Paymentes at Commaundment /   25
...

p 813
...
Paid for Cloth & making vp of fower Cloakes for the Waite   30
players this yere 23 Iuly last as appeareth by a bill vnder *Maister*
Maiors hand of the particulars thereof   vij li. xij s. j d.
...

                                                                               35

Payments Out Book CRO: A 16
p 258   *(18 February)*
...

Paid to Mr Philemon Holland doctor which he formerly allowed
for Standerdes left in the Schoole house by mr Cranford l. s and   40
v. s to *Mistris* Cranford the 18. of february *Anno* 1628.   lv. s
...

Cappers' Records SC: Account Book I
f 167

...

Paid to two men for Carrying our harnisse at the Sumere
ffaire   viij d   5

...

Carpenters' Account Book II CRO: Acc 3/2
f 320

...   10

paid for cariage of our Armor   x d

...

Mercers' Account Book CRO: Acc 15
f 149v   15
                    Paymenttes ordynary and extraordynarie

...

paid for 6 men carriinge Armour at the ffayre   00 ij s 0

...
                                                                                              20

Weavers' Account Book CRO: Acc 100/17/1
f 138v

...

paid for Carrying of Armore   0-2-0

...   25

(Choice Day)
more to the waightes the same daie   0-3-4

...
                                                                                              30

1630
Chamberlains' and Wardens' Account Book II CRO: A 7(b)
p 820 *(27 October) (Chamberlains)*

...

And of liij s iiij d paid to the Waite playars of this Citie for theire   35
Wages this yeare last as appeareth by two bills thereof   liij s iiij d

...

p 827 *(8 December) (Wardens)*
                    Rewards to players   40
Paid given to fower Trumpetters who had been at Sea for the
Earle of Warwick who had losse by sea having speciall Certificat

from Divers noble men in Ireland in May last as app*eare*th by a
bill   x s
Paid given to William Vincent who came with Com*m*ission from
the Kings Ma*jes*tie to shew feats of Activitie & legerdemaine in
August last as app*eare*thc by a bill vnder M*aiste*r Maiors   5
hand   v s
Paid given to Ioseph More & others that was sworne servants to
the King that the should not play in Iune last as app*eare*th by a
bill   xx s
Paid given to one licenced to shew a rare peece of work of the   10
portraitures of the King of Bohemia his queene and
Children   x s
Paid given to the Waite players of Derby in October last as
app*eare*th by another bill vnder M*aiste*r Maiors hand   ij s
Paid given to Richard Tompson who had Com*m*ision to play the   15
Worlds Wonder   iij iiij d
Sum*ma* l s iiij d.
Payments at Comaundement

...
                                                                                        20

p 829 *(Wardens)*

Paid for half a yard of greene taffata v s iiij d
for half a yard of Crimson Taffata in greane. vj s
for sowing silke iiij d and for 3 yards of 4d ribbin   25
xvij d for 8 sheets of royall paper & thridd x d for   xxvj s iij d
4 yards & a q*uar*ter of deepe silke fring xj d for
making xij d & a box to keepe it xx d being for
a *(blank)* for the Trumpett

...
                                                                                        30

Council Book CRO: A 14(a)
p 579* *(10 March)*

...

Whereas there hath been a controversie between the Company of   35
Cappers and the p*ar*ish of S*ain*t Michaell in this Citie, w*hic*h is

•Cappers•   now ended, and to the end the Cappers might surrender vp theire
deed in w*hic*h the Pageaunt house in Mill lane is contayned. and
to have a deed back from this house. It is now agreed that there
shall be a deed made thereof accordingly.   40

16 / iij iiij d *for* iij s iiij d

Cappers' Records SC: Account Book I
f 168

...

Paid to 2 men for Carrying our harnesse att our su*m*mer
ffaire   viij d   5

...

Spent when wee toke Possession of the Padgeon house   iiij d
Spent at the Starre   iiij d
Spent when we gaue possession to Mr. Iesson   ij d

...   10

Carpenters' Account Book II CRO: Acc 3/2
f 322v

...

given the musitions the same time   vj d   15

...

p*a*id for Carrieing the Armor   viij d
spent at putting on the Armour   ij d
spent when we went to speake for dressing the Armor   ij d

...   20

given the Musitians   vj d

...

f 323

...   25

given the Musitians   vj d

...

Mercers' Account Book CRO: Acc 15
f 152   30

                    Paymentes Ordinary and extraordinary

...

paid six men for bearing Armoure at our faire   00 .ij s 00

...

                                                                                           35

Weavers' Account Book CRO: Acc 100/17/1
f 141

...

paid for beareing of harne*es*   0-2-0
giuen the musision*es* at the Choyce Daie   0-3-4   40

...

1631
Chamberlains' and Wardens' Account Book II CRO: A 7(b)
p 835 *(26 October)* *(Chamberlains)*

...

And of liij s iiij d paid to the Waite players of this Citie for there   5
Wages this yeare past as appeareth by two Bills vnder M*aiste*r
Maiors hand .   liij s iiij d

...

pp 842-3 *(23 November)* *(Wardens)*   10

...
                            Rewards to players
Paid given to the Musitions of the Earle of Essex the 14th of
ffebruary last   ij s vj d
Paid given to the Waits in Rippon in Yorkshire the 17th of May   15
last   ij s
Paid given to an other Companie of Waite plaiers called Worcester
Waite*s* the 24th of Maie last   ij s vj d
Paid given to another Companie of Musitions the 15th of Iune
last   xvj d| 20
Paid given to the Waite*s* of New Market the 14th of Iuly last   ij s
Paid given to the Waite*s* of Derby the first of August last   ij s vj d
Paid given to the Waite*s* of Nottingham the 30th of August
last   ij s
Paid given to the King*es* Trumpettors the 17th of October   25
last   iij s
Paid given to Robert Knipton & Iohn Carr*e* players of the Revells
the 23th of September last as appeareth by a bill   x s
Paid given to Ioseph More Iohn Townesend & other players to
the Ladie Elizabeth the 30th of March last by a Bill   xx s   30
Paid given to the Musitions of the Earle of Rutland . the 27th of
November 1630 by a bill vnder M*aiste*r Maiors hand   ij s
                         Summ*a* xlix s x d

...
                                                                             35

Payments Out Book CRO: A 16
p 280 *(17 December)*

Paid for 4. Cloak*es* for the Waite players and two
Coat*es* for the Beadles: for making & Clothe as   40
appeareth by a bill of the p*ar*ticulars the xvij^th   ix. li iiij. s iij. d
of december .1631. to m*aste*r Rogerson & m*aste*r Iohn Clark.

...

Cappers' Records SC: Account Book I
f 168v

...

Payd for beareing the Armor   viij d

...   5

Carpenters' Account Book II CRO: Acc 3/2
f 325v

...

Paid for Carrieing harnes at the faire   x d   10

...

given the musitians   iiij d

...

f 326   15

...

paid the musitians   vj d

...

Mercers' Account Book CRO: Acc 15   20
f 154v

...

                    Paymentes Ordinarij and Extraordinarj

...

paid for vj men Bearinge Armor   00 ij s-00   25

...

Weavers' Account Book CRO: Acc 100/17/1
f 143

...   30

paid foure men for beareing harnis at the faire   0-2-0

...

paid to the waightes   0-4-0

...
                                                                           35

1632
Chamberlains' and Wardens' Account Book II CRO: A 7(b)
p 851 *(24 October) (Chamberlains)*

...

And of liij s iiij d paid to the waite players of this City for theire   40
wages this yeare past as appeareth by two Bills thereof vnder
Maister Maiors hand   liij s iiij d

...

p 859* *(12 December) (Wardens)*

...

Rewards to players

Paid to the Players of *(blank)* by a Bill x s
Paid to William Costine Thomas Hunter Henry ffussell with 5
theire assistant*es* Licenced to set forth and shew an Italiann
motion with divers & sundry storyes in it the 25th of September
1632 as appeareth by a Bill x s
Paid to the players of the Revells the xxth of December last as
appeareth by a Bill vnder Maister Maiors Hand x s 10
Paid to straunge waite players at severall tymes this yeare x s
Summa xl s

...

Payments at Commaundement

... 15

p 861

...

Paid for mendeing the drumm of the Cityes ij s
... 20

Council Book CRO: A 14(a)
p 607 *(19 September)*

...

Wayts. It is agreed that the Waytes of this Citie shall have fower poundes 25
and ten shillinges per annum, allowed them by this Citie from
henceforth to be paid by the Wardens only during the pleasure
of this house payable at Christmas and Midsomer

...

30

Cappers' Records SC: Account Book I
f 169

...

Paid for bearing our Armor at the faire viij d
... 35

Carpenters' Account Book II CRO: Acc 3/2
f 328

...

paid for Carrieing our harnes ix d 40
...

Mercers' Account Book CRO: Acc 15
f 156

...

Payd 6 men for Carrying the armour   0. 2. 0.

...

Weavers' Rentgatherers' Book II CRO: Acc 100/18/2
f 95

...

paid for Carrying harni*es* at the fare to foure men   0-2-0

...

1633
Chamberlains' and Wardens' Account Book II CRO: A 7(b)
p 878 *(4 December) (Wardens)*

...

Rewards to players
Paid to the Cities waitplayers for theire wholl yeares wages
ending at Mich*ae*lm*a*s last as appeareth by two bills thereof vnder
M*ai*ste*r* Maiors hand   iiij li. x s
Paid given to Preston waits ij s vj d to Shrewsbury
wait*es* ij s vj d to Rippon waites ij s to Hallifax
wait*es* ij s to Mr. Perry one of the king*es* players
that came with a Comission x s to Newark waites
ij s to Kendall waites ij s to William Costin Thomas
Hunt and Henry ffussell licenced to set forth an   liiij s ij d
Italian motion x s to Nottingham waites ij s vj d to
Darby waites ij s to those that come with L*e*tt*e*r*e*s
patent*es* with the sight of the portraiture of
Antwerpe x s to theise that came with L*e*tt*e*r*e*s
patent*es* for roots — vj s viij d
Summ vij li. iiij s. ij d
Payments at commaundement

p 879 *(Wardens)*

...

P*ai*d to Gilbert Toncks Goldsmyth ... for the silver and gold of
the 4 Crests for the Cities waites and for the guilding and
colouring of them all a new xx s as appeareth by a bill vnder
Maiors hand   xxx s vj d

...

30 / Antwerpe *italicized in MS*

Council Book CRO: A 14(a)
p 616 *(19 June)*

...

It is also this daie further agreed that from henceforth on such
dayes and times as have been heretofore observed as Scarlet   5
dayes, everie one of this Citie that by place is to weare scarlet
shall duly weare scarlet notwithstanding anye cause of mourning
or otherwise to the contrary

...
                                                                           10

Cappers' Records SC: Account Book I
f 169v

...

paid for wearing one Armor att the fare & to Scott   0-2-4
...   15

Carpenters' Account Book II CRO: Acc 3/2
f 330

...

paid for Carrieing armour on the faire daie   ix d 20
...

Mercers' Account Book CRO: Acc 15
f 158v
                        Paymentes Ordnary and xterordnary   25
...
Paid Belly Banks for rent for the pagin house   vij s
...
Paid 6 men for Caring the Armor at Somer faire   ij s
...   30

Weavers' Account Book CRO: Acc 100/17/1
f 147v

...

Item paid fore men for carrying harnies   0-2-0 35
...

1634
Chamberlains' and Wardens' Account Book II CRO: A 7(b)
pp 894-5 *(3 December) (Wardens)*   40
...
                        Rewardes to players.
Paid to the Cities wayte-players for theire wholl yeares wages

ending at Michaelmas last, as appeareth by two Bill*es* thereof
vnder *Maister* Maiors hand   iiij li. x s. |
Paid given to Grynes & other players who came by warrant in
december last as appeareth by a bill vnder *maiste*r Maiors
hand   v s.   5
Paid given to the Princ*es* players in August last   xl s
paid given to the King*es* Trumpeters the same moneth   xl s
to the Wait*es* of Rippon. ij s. to the Wait*es* of Derbie [ij s] and
Lincolne. iij s as appereth by a bill vnder *maiste*r Maiors
hand   v s.   10

Summ*a* ix s.

...

Cappers' Records SC: Account Book I
f 170   15

...

p*ai*d two men for Carryinge our Armor att the faire   00-00-08
...

Carpenters' Account Book II CRO: Acc 3/2   20
f 331v

...

p*ai*d for Carryeing our armor at the faire   viij d
spent at setting firth the Armor   iij d
spent at putting on the Armor   ij d   25
...

Mercers' Account Book CRO: Acc 15
f 160v

...   30

Payements Ordinary & xtraordinary

...
Paid Mr Richard Bankes ffor Rent ffor the Paggen
houses   00 vij s 00
...   35
Paid to Six Men to Carry it at Sommer ffaire   00 ij s 00

...

Weavers' Account Book CRO: Acc 100/17/1
f 149v *(Receipts)*   40

...
Rec*eave*d of Robe*rt* Betsone for the old harnis   0-2-8
...

f 150 *(Payments)*

...

paide for carrying the armor   0-2-0

...

giuen the Musick at the feaste Daie   0-4-0   5

...

1635
Chamberlains' and Wardens' Account Book II CRO: A 7(b)
p 908 *(2 December) (Wardens)*   10

...

                          Reward*es* to Player*es*
Paid to the Cities waite-players.xlv s. the 10th of Aprill last in
full discharg of theire former wages they being from thenceforth
vtterly discharged   xlv s.   15
Paid to the king*es* players who brought a Co*m*mission from Sir
Henry Harbert 13. Aprill. last   ij li. x d.
Paid to Nottingham Wayt*es* at two times.   iij s. vj d.
Paid given to the Wait*es* of Darby.   ij s
Paid given to the Wait*es* of Rippon.   j s.   20
Paid given to William Daniell who brought a Co*m*mission for the
Revell*es*. vi*delice*t for himself & 16. more in Iune last   x s.
                    Su*mm*a v li. xj s. vj d.

...

                                                                   25

Council Book CRO: A 14(a)
p 634 *(4 March)*

...

It is also farther agreed that whereas often heretofore the Waite
players of this Citie being the Cities weight*es* haveing been verie   30
troublesome vnto this house as also at variance amongst them
Wayts.   selves by theire sundrie difference*s*: It is [there] ordered
therefore that they are & shall be discharged from this Cities
service, and from being any longer the Cities wait*es*, and that
from henceforth they shall have no more allowance from this   35
Citie: and farther that they shall bring in such instrument*es* of
musick as they have of this Cities.

...

Cappers' Records SC: Account Book I   40
f 170v

...

p*ai*d for a man for tending our armor iij tymes before Mr

Maior   xij d
paid ij men for Carrieing Armor at the faire   viij d
...

Carpenters' Account Book II CRO: Acc 3/2   5
f 333v

...
paid for Carryeing the Armor at the fayre and for holbert*es*   xij d
paid for a belt   ij s ij d
paid for nickle for the bandileres   iij s iiij d   10
...

Mercers' Account Book CRO: Acc 15
f 162v
...   15
               Paymentts Ordnarij & Extraordnary

...
paid Mr Gilbertt Adderley for 3 muskett*es* & 3 bandeleers bought
in London   iiij li. vj s 00
...   20
paid 6 men for for beareinge our Armor vpon the So*m*mer ffayer
Day   00 ij s 00
paid for 3 Beltts for our Comp*anyes* swordes   00 vj s 00
paid ffulke Waldern for a brande to marke our
Muskett*es*   00 j s vj d   25
...

Weavers' Account Book CRO: Acc 100/17/1
f 151v
...   30
paid for 4 men for Carrying harnes   0-2-0
...
paid for twoe new belt*es*   0-4-0
spent when we met and bought the sword*es* and a musket   0-1-0
paid to Peter baxter for the muskit   0-12-0   35
paid for a marking Iorn   0-1-0
paid to Tho*m*as Sher*m*an Cuttler for change of twoe new
sword*es*   0-10-0
more for twoe new rest   0-2-4

21 / for for *MS dittography*

more for 12 new boxes stinges and pursees   0-3-6

1636
Chamberlains' and Wardens' Account Book III CRO: A 7(c)
pp 8-9 *(29 November) (Wardens)*   5
...
                    Rewardes to playeres.
Paid given to the Queenes players at the parlor   xxv s.
paid given to Richard Erington & William Daniell players of the
Revelles the 22th of Aprill last   xxij s.   10
paid given to the kinges players of Blackfriers given at the
Councel house in August last   xx s.
paid given to the kinges players   v s.
paid given to the players dauncers on the rope   vj s. viij d
paid given to the players that would have shewed a sight about   15
witches   vj s.
paid given to a Company of players   ij s. vj d.
paid given to the Kinges Beareward   ij s. vj d.
paid given to a soldier that tossed a Pike at the Crosse before
*Maiste*r Maior and his Bretheren   j s. vj d.| 20
Paid given to the Waytes of Nottingham   ij s. vj d.
paid given to the Waytes of Lincolne the Second Daie of Augst
last   ij s. vj d.
paid given to the Waytes of Nottingham the 17th of August
last   ij s. vj d. 25
paid given to the Waites of Lincoln the 29th of August
last   ij s. vj d.
                    Summa v li. j s. ij d
...
                                                                        30

p 11 *(Wardens)*
...
paid given awaie at the ffree schoole at the visitacion thereof in
Aprill last ... Mr Launder v s ...
                                                                        35

Payments Out Book CRO: A 16
p 310 *(August)*
...
paid to seaven of the kinges Trumpeters in August last whereof
one was the Serjant Trumpeter   iij. li   40
...

Cappers' Records SC: Account Book I
f 171

...

p*ai*d for scowreing the Armor & bearing it att the fayer   ij s iiij d

...   5

Carpenters' Account Book II CRO: Acc 3/2
f 335v

...

p*ai*d for Carryeing our Armor at the faire   viij d   10

...

Mercers' Account Book CRO: Acc 15
f 165v

...   15

                Paiements Ordinary & Extraordinary

...

Paid for 6 men to Carry the Armor   00 03 00

...

                                                                            20

1637
Chamberlains' and Wardens' Account Book III CRO: A 7(c)
p 29 *(29 November) (Wardens)*
                    Reward*es* to player*es*.
Paid to the Players which came to the Councel house   x s.   25
paid to William Daniell and others of the Revell*es* the vth of
December last   x s.
paid given to ffeild the beareward .2s.6d. to the lord Deputies
waite players. 2s. 6d.   v s.
paid given to the Waites of Derby 2s.6d. to the Wait*es* of Rippon   30
.2s.6d.   v s.
paid given to the Wait*es* of Nottingham .3s. to them that had a
shew vnder the Maister of the Revell*es* seale the 21th of May,
6s.8d.   ix s. viij d.
paid given to Walter Neare that went about to shew a child borne   35
without Armes   ij s. vj d.
paid given to the Wait*es* of Nottingham the 14th of August xviij d.
                    Su*mm*a xliij s. viij d.

...

Payments Out Book CRO: A 16
p 326 *(Easter)*

...

p*ai*d given awaie at the visitac*i*on of the Schoole ... & to Iohn
Launder x s ...   5

p 321 *(9 August)*

...

paid given to the Company of the Artillery in this Citie at the last
shew. the same daie   XX S.   10

...

Cappers' Records SC: Account Book I
f 171v

...   15

p*ay*ed for bearing our Armor att the faire   viij d

...

Carpenters' Account Book II CRO: Acc 3/2
f 337   20

...

paid for carryeing the Armor at the faire   viij d

...

Mercers' Account Book CRO: Acc 15   25
f 168v

...

p*ay*d 6 men ffor Caryinge the Armor vpon the ffaire
day   00 03 00

...   30

1638
Chamberlains' and Wardens' Account Book III CRO: A 7(c)
p 46 *(27 November) (Wardens)*

...   35

Reward*es* to player*es*.

Paid given to the Beareward of the Earle of Peterboroughes the
. 26th : of ffebruary . last. 1637. by bill   ij s. vj d.
paid given to the Trumpeters of the Earle Northumberland*es*
the .12th : of december 1637. by bill   ij s vj d.   40

paid given to Robert Browne, Georg Hall & Richard Iones players
by warrant, who had a motion to shew expressing the world*es*
abuses the .12th: of Ianuary last by bill vnder m*aiste*r Maiors
hand   xij s.
Paid given to Mr. Gyn and his Company who came with a Patent   5
to shew Trick*es*. by bill   v s.
paid given to the King*es* Beareward the .13th: of Aprill last. by
bill   iij s. iiij d.
paid given to Robert Tayler and Ann Mossock, players who came
by warrant to shew the world*es* Creation the .12th. of Iuly 1638.   10
by bill   iij s iiij d.
paid given to the Players that had warrant to shew an Italian
motion, and shew, the .12th of Ianuary 1637. by bill .   x s
paid given to the King*es* players, and hocus pocus   xx s.
paid to the Way*tes* of Nottingham, and Derby .ij s. vj d. and to   15
the Way*tes* of Newark .ij s. vj d   v s.
paid to the Bearward of the lord Morden   ij s.
                          Su*mm*a iij li. v s. viij d.
...
                                                                         20

Cappers' Records SC: Account Book I
f 172
...
p*ai*d for Carryeing our Armour att the faier   viij d
...   25

Carpenters' Account Book II CRO: Acc 3/2
f 339
...
p*ai*d for Carryeing the Armor att the faire.   viij d   30
paid att setting out the Armour.   iiij d
...

Mercers' Account Book CRO: Acc 15
f 171v   35
...
                Paiementts ordnarij & Extraordnarij
...
p*ai*de vnto 6 men p*ro* beareinge the Armour vpon the Somm*er*
ffayre day   00 03 00 40
...

1639
Chamberlains' and Wardens' Account Book III CRO: A 7(c)
p 60 *(27 November) (Wardens)*
...

Rewardes to players		5
Paid given to the Wayts of Derby	ij s. vj d.	
Paid given to the Wayts of Nottingham	ij s vj d.	
Paid given to the Wayts of New Castle	ij s. vj d.	
Paid given to one Iohn Shepheard 15 febr*uary* last who came		
with Comission to shew a Sow with 6 Leggs	vj s viij d	10
Paid given to Christopher Tomson the 20th of february who		
came with Commission to shew the Creation of the		
world	xiij s. iiij d.	
Paid given to 3 Trumpeters the 19th of Ianuary	xviij d	
Paid given to the Wayts of Leeke	ij s. vj d.	15

...

Rental Roll II CRO: E 13
...

The Company of girdlers for their Pagen house   0-0-4   20
...

Cappers' Records SC: Account Book I
f 172v
...   25
paid for Carryeing the Armour on the faire daye   0-0-8
...

f 173
                                                                              30
paid for our parte of mending the Armour. with the
Skinners   0-5-0
...

Carpenters' Account Book II CRO: Acc 3/2   35
f 340v
...
payed for dressing our musket, for a new purse to the bandileres
and a new worme & skower & bullett moulde   xxiij d
payed to the Muster Master   xij d   40

f 341

...

p*a*yd for Carryeing the Armor att the fayer and dressing
it   xviij d

...

given the Musitions more than was gathered   iiij d

...

Weavers' Rentgatherers' Book II CRO: Acc 100/18/2
f 106

...

paid for beareing Armor at the faire   0-2-0

...

A C   *Cardmakers, Ironmongers, and Saddlers' Accounts*
Bodl: MS Top. Warwickshire c.7
f 34

...

pd for carryinge *o*u*r* Armo*u*r at the faire 1/6

...

1640
Chamberlains' and Wardens' Account Book III CRO: A 7(c)
p 73 *(25 November) (Wardens)*

...

Reward*es* to Player*es*
Paid given to Anthony Barker who brought Co*m*mission to shew
an Italian motion & vaulting the 9th of december 1639 as
appeareth by abill vnder M*ais*te*r* Maiors hand   vj s.
p*a*id given to Willi*a*m Peadle & Thomas Peadle
his sonn & fower children & Charles Sale & the
rest of his assistants that had authority by   xx s.
Co*m*mission for dauncing & vaulting & other
feats of activity the 24th of december 1639
as appeareth by a bill vnder M*a*iste*r* Maiors hand   35
p*a*id given to Georg Corden servaunt to the Earle
of Leic*es*te*r* Willi*a*m Iohnson servaunt to the lord
Clifford Georg Sanderson servaunt to the Lord   xlviij s. ij d.
Goring & 13 more assistants players who had
the Kings patent to play xlviij s. ij d. w*h*ich was
given them & w*h*ich was paid for theire Scaffolds
they had built the 9th of Ianuary last past as
appeareth by abill vnder M*ais*te*r* Maiors hand

p*ai*d given to the Earle of Arundells Trumpeters 19th Aprill last
by a bill vnder *Maiste*r Maiors hand   iij s iiij d
p*ai*d given to Ieremy Allin & leonard Smith togeather w*i*th the
rest of theire company being stage-players the 19th of August
1640 as appeareth by a bill vnder *Maiste*r Maiors hand   xx s.   5
p*ai*d given to the Lord Cavendish waytes .2s.6d.
to Mr. Starkeyes musitions .xviij d. to the wayts of
Leeke xviij d. to the wayts of Nottingham xviij d.   xv s.
to Captaine Sneads trumpeters ij s by abill p*ai*d given
to the wayts of New Castle xij d. to humfrey Ensall   10
and Phillip ffeild the kings Berward .v s. 20 Novemb*er*
1639 by a bill
                               Su*mm*a v li. xij s. vj d.
...
                                                                           15

p 99 *(Wardens)*
...
p*ai*d given at the visitation of the Schoole this yeare ... to mr
Launder & Richard Maddock x s. ...
                                                                           20

Cappers' Records SC: Account Book I
f 173v
...
p*ai*d for Carrieing Armour att the fayer   0-0-8
...   25

Carpenters' Account Book II CRO: Acc 3/2
f 342
...
p*ai*d for a new skaberd for the sword   xviij d   30
...
p*ai*d for Carryeing Armor at the faire   viij d
...

Mercers' Account Book CRO: Acc 15   35
f 177v
                    Payments ordinary & extraordinary
...
P*ai*d for carring the Armour Iune the 5th 1640   00 ij s 0
...   40

1641
Leet Book II CRO: A 3(b)
p 174 *(12 October)*

Skarlet
gownes

It is ordered and enacted at this Leet that the new Sherriffs now   5
elected & all others hereafter to be chosen Sherriffs shall (within
a monethes warning given by Mr Maior of this City and his
brethren of the Councelhouse of this City for the time being or
the most part of them) provide themselves of Scarlet gownes and
tippetts in paine of Tenn pounds.   10

•Hoodes•   And that the Maiors wifes shall weare hoods on the festivall
dayes.

°this act agreed on to be entred but not proclaimed°†
     15

Chamberlains' and Wardens' Account Book III CRO: A 7(c)
p 87 *(1 December) (Wardens)*
                    Rewardes to Playeres
Paid given to the waites of Leeke   ij s.
paid given to the Earle of Shrewsburryes waitees by a bill ij s vj d.   20
paid given to the Wayts of Nottingham in Iuly ij s. vj d . & in
October ij s   iiij s. vj d.
                    Summa ix s.
                Payments at Commaundement
...   25

p 88*
...

paid to Eliz*a*beth Toncks widow for altering of
the great Mace for silver of the pipes & ball &   30
the Barrs of the Crowne & the spindle weighing
9 oz & 9 d weight & for making of them lix s. vj d.
for guilding the newe work xxij s. vj d. for   ix li. viij s
guilding the rest of the Mace iij li. for silver &
making the ackorne & leaves for the sword xj s. &   35
for guilding of the sword xxxv s. as appeareth by a bill
...

paid for 12 yardes & half of scarlet cloth at xj s. vj d.
vij li. iij s. ix d. 3 more of the same viij s. vij d. & for 8
yards of green bayes at ij s. xvj s. for cloakes for this   40

40 / xvj s. *for* xvj d.

Cities waytes as appeareth by a bill vnder   ix li. xviij s. vij d.
Maister Maiors hand & for 5 neckloopes silk
Canvas & 2 oz half of silver lace xix s. iij d. &
to Iohn Gorton for making of these Cloakes xj s
...   5

Payments Out Book CRO: A 16
p 359 *(December)*
...
Paid to Michaell Iefford for 17 linckes and 8 torches as appereth   10
by a note on the file in december. 1641.   1. 0. 6.
...

Cappers' Records SC: Account Book I
f 174   15
...
paid for dressing the Armour xx d for Carryeing it att the faire
8d   0-2-4
...
                                                                           20
Mercers' Account Book CRO: Acc 15
f 179v
...
                    Payments ordinary & Extraordinary:
...   25
Paid to Six men for Carrying Armor at our ffayre tyme   00 03 00
...

1642
Chamberlains' and Wardens' Account Book III CRO: A 7(c)   30
p 98 *(7 December) (Wardens)*
...
                    Rewardes to players
Paid given to the Earle of Leicesters Trumpeters
ij s x d. the xixth of Ianuary 1641. given to mr   35
Piercy & his company who came by commission
to play . x s. paid. given to William Vincent who
had commission for him and his company to daunce
vpon the ropes & shew other trickes of legerdemeane
x s & to other musitians playing that night at   xxxviij s. vj d.   40
Maister Maiors dore the 3d. of December 1641.
ij s given to the lord Deputy of Irelandes Trumpeters

the xxiijth of february 1641. iij s. to the Waits of
New castle vnder lyne xviij d. given to the trumpeters
of the troopes w*h*ich came with the Lord Brooke
& the lord Gray x s. the xxviijth of August 1642

                                        Summ xxxviij s. vj d.   5

...

Payments Out Book CRO: A 16
p 366 *(June)*

...   10

p*a*id to Mr Hopkins for 80 escutcheons, for the Cities Musk*e*t*e*s
and 2 drummes   7. 2. 6
p*a*id to Mr Basnet for 30 paire of bandeleeres   3.10.0

...
                                                                                15

Cappers' Records SC: Account Book I
f 174v

...
p*a*id for Carryeing and dressing the Armour   0-2-4
...   20

APPENDIX 1

Undated Cappers' Accounts

At least one leaf seems to be missing from the Cappers' Account Book, for what is now folio 1 takes up in the middle of an account. That on folio 1v is dated 1495; thus, those on folio 1 probably end the 1494 account. From this uncertain start the accounts pursue a bewildering course until 1520, whereafter the accounting is straightforward. Assuming that folio 1 represents 1494, twenty-five accounts are needed to cover the years up to 1519, and there are just that number. Not all are complete and one of them is barely begun. Sixteen of them, however, are dated: unfortunately nearly half of these dates serve only to confuse. If one follows what regnal years are given, some of the mayors named are 'wrong': if one pins faith on the mayors, not all the regnal years match. Indeed, a record for quirkish accounting allows three consecutive, but quite different, accounts to claim the same mayor (who was only mayor for one term), and two of these use the same regnal year also. It is quite unsurprising, therefore, that an order of leet passed in October 1520, directing the Cappers to elect their masters on 7 August and those masters to present their accounts by 25 December of the year in which they relinquished office, should result in accounts for 1521 being dated 21 January (old style) and for 1522 being dated 2 February (old style). Thereafter, the Cappers ceased to name the actual day of presentation. Before 1520, only twice had a particular day been mentioned, St Anne's Day, 26 July (in 1502 and 1503 but not in accounts consecutively entered). Possibly this had been election and/or presentation day before the change to 7 August. Rather than attempt to choose one of the many patterns that match the twenty-five accounts to the available years, I have placed the accounts together in this appendix.

Fortunately, this confusion of dates has no effect upon the Cappers' contribution to Coventry's dramatic entertainments. In this period they contributed 6s 8d annually to the Girdlers' pageant (the seeming irregularity may be due to fragmentary accounts), and occasionally marked contributions to other Corpus Christi Day, Midsummer Day, and St Peter's Day activities.

The accounts for this quarter century are prefaced by a list showing their sequence and what evidence for dating they offer so that the reader may have an overview of the sequence. Pageant payment to the Girdlers is indicated by a 'G' in the right column. The mayoral term in Coventry ran from 2 February to the following 1 February at this time.

f   1   undated
f   1v   1495
f   3   undated
f   3v   undated (leet order 29 April 1495; Cappers to
           contribute to Girdlers)   G
f   4v   xv⟨...⟩ (ripped off)   G
f   5   Henry VII 17th regnal year (22 August 1501-21 August
           1502)   G
f   5v   1502 feast of St Anne (26 July)   G
f   6   undated   G
f   7v   1503   G
f   8   St Anne's Day 1504   G
f   9   undated   G
f 10   R. Smyth mayor (1508-9)   G
f 11v   J. Saunders mayor (1510-11) Henry VIII 2nd regnal
           year (22 April 1510-21 April 1511)   G
f 12v   J. Saunders mayor (1510-11) Henry VIII 2nd regnal
           year   G
f 13v   J. Saunders mayor (1510-11)   G
f 14v   T. Grove mayor (1514-15) (J. Saunders master)   G
f 15   J. Hardwyn mayor (1513-14) mvᶜxiiij   G
f 16v   J. Clarke mayor (1515-16)   G
f 17v   undated (no expenses)
f 18   undated
f 19   H. Rogers mayor (1517-18)   G
f 20   Henry VIII 9th regnal year (1517-18)   G
f 22   Henry VIII 10th regnal year (1518-19)
f 23   undated (no expenses)
f 23v   J. Bond mayor (1520-1) Henry VIII 12th regnal year
           (1520-1)   G

f 1v col a

...

Item payed to þe menestrell for his fee   iij s

...

Item delliuerid to William Bryge & Iohn Grene Maisteres of the   5
Craffte to the harnessyng of the ij men   xxxiij s
Expences in harnessyng of the men
Inprimis payed ffor a pyr of brygantyrones   x s
Item payed ffor a stondare of mayll gosetes & a ffalle   ij s viij d
Item payed ffor a pyr of splentes & a swrede   ij s x d   10
Item payed ffor a gordell to þe Swerde   iij d

Item payed ffor a bowe	ij s	
Item payed ffor a sheff of arreus	ij s	
Item payed ffor a gordell to them	ij d	
Item payed ffor canvas to lyne þe stondares & þe ffalle & þe makyg	vij d	5
Item payed ffor a boklar	ij s xvj d	
Item payed ffor a sallett	ij s iiij d	
Item payed ffor a Casse to the arrous	ix d	
Item payed ffor poyntes	j d	
Item payed ffor Cloth to þe Iaket	xv d	10
Item payed ffor the makyng	iiij d	
Item payed to þe men þat bere them at þe ffeer	ij d	
Item payed to the harnesmen in ernest	j d	
Item payed ffor mendyng of the brygantyrens to mak them met to the sodyars	iiij d	15

Summa totalis of þe harnes xxxj s [v] d ij d

f 3v

...

Memorandum david (blank) orgone pleyar in Sent Michelles &   20
vxor euius receptus est In ffraternitate predicta Soluendi pro
ffinibus vj s viij d

f 4

...   25

Item paid to the gordelares	vj s viij d

...

f 4v

...   30

Item paid to the gordelarus	vj s viij d

...

Item paid to þe menestrell	ij d

...

Item paid to þe menestrell at Corpus christi	xij d	35

...

f 5

...

Item paid to þe menestrell at Corpis christi day	xij d	40

...

21 / euius for eius

Item paid to the gordilares   vj s viij d
...

f 6
...   5
Item paid to the gordelarus   vj s viij d
...
Item paid to þe menestrell   vij d
...
                                                                      10
f 6v
...
Item paid to the gordellares   vj s viij d
Item paid ffor xxiiij lb off torchis   v s x d
Item paid to the menestrell   vij d   15
...

f 7v
...
Item payed to the gordelares   vj s viij d   20
...

f 8
...
Item paid to the gordelares   vj s viij d   25
...

f 9
...
Item payed to the gordelarus   vj s viij d   30
...

f 10v
...
Item payd to the Gurdelars   vj s viij d   35
...

f 11v

ffyns   40
Robert Croo   xx d
Robert Crow made brother ... payd wax sylver. /
...

Item to the gurdelars   vj s viij d
...

f 13
...   5
Item payd to the Gurdelars   vj s viij d
Item payd for Makyng torches   v s vj d
...
Item payd to mynstrelles more than was gatherd   xviij d
...   10

f 14
...
Item to the Gurdelars   vj s viij d
...   15
ffor harnes
Item for fatheryng the arrows   xiiij d
Item for medyng the Brekyn Irons   viij d
Item for fostyan   vj d
Item for mendyng the splentes   viij d   20
Item for poyntes   ij d
Summa (blank)
...

f 14v   25

... Item for the Gurdelres vj s viij d ...

f 15v
...   30
Item to the gurdelers   vj s viij d
...
Item for a mynstrell for the yere   iij s viij d
...
Item for beryng the cressytt and for stuffe to make   35
lyght   iiij d
Item yevyn to the Ioorneymen   xvj d
...
Item for ij Citacons for Robert Crow Iohn knyght Robert
Knyght Edward corbe Dave Heyns William Whytt   xij d   40
Item for cytyng   xij d
Item for encreyng the cawse   ij d
Item for makyng the proccur   iiij d

[ffr] for a mynstrell at last quarter   iiij d

...

f 17 col a

...   5

Item to The Gerdyllars   iij s iiij d

...

col b

                                                                          10

Expenses of The Second quarterayges
Item payd to The Gerdylars   iij s [iiij d]

...

f 18v col b   15

...

Item for the torchys   iij s

...

f 19 col b   20

...

Item payd to the gyrdelers   vj s viij d

...

f 20v   25

...

Item to the Gordleyrs   vj s viij d

...

f 22v   30

...

Item for makyng of iiij cressetes   v s. viij d
Item for the lyght to the cressetes   ij s. viij d
Item for the gordelers   iij s. iiij d
Item for bokram for the standars berers   xxj d   35
Item for iiij hattes for the berers   iiij d
Item for the berers of the cressetes   vj d
Item offord with Tomlynson   ij d
Item the torche berers   ij d
Item to Wodward for makyng of letter   iiij d   40

...

thomas Alyn schuld pay to the somner & to the torch berers vj d

...

APPENDIX 2
Undated Drapers' Accounts

'The oldest Book of Accounts of this Company now to be found, commences in 1534', writes Sharp (p 66). This book survives today only in a transcription by Daffern (CRO: Acc 154). The first fifty-five folios of the transcript contain the accounts from 1524-68 and various miscellaneous agreements. I believe that the *terminus ad quem* for this appendix should be 1561 because from that year the accounts follow in due order by foliation, regnal and mayoral year until the end of the transcript. Before that date there are duplications, confusions, and contradictions that are insoluble without the destroyed MS; and I suspect that even had it survived everything would not have been certainly ordered.

It is, however, quite possible to organize the accounts into a chronological pattern — into several patterns indeed. One must pick and choose amongst the dating evidence in order to do so and hope that one's reading of the evidence is reasonable. Sharp, who had the advantage of working from the original MS, took his usual way with regnal years, the time the account covered, and the time when it was delivered.

The dates which Sharp gives to items, when compared with those Daffern gives, are equally likely to be the same, one year earlier, or one year later. The uncertain chronology is especially aggravating because at some time in the 1550s (1556? 1557?) the Drapers almost certainly had their Doomsday play rewritten and thoroughly and expensively refurbished their pageant wagon and costumes. As a result, production costs rose abruptly by over one hundred per cent from what they had been and remained high until 1579.

Most of the annual accounts can be firmly dated; some, however, share the same date, others are contradictorily dated within themselves. There is a discrepancy of a decade at folios 32-8 when accounts for 1565-8 occur, while there are none for 1555-8 (that headed 1566 is dated 1556 internally). Puzzlement about dates is offered from the first entries in the account book, a book which dates from 1534 but contains accounts for 1524 and 1525.

The Drapers begin their new account book by reasserting (and possibly revising) their ordinances. One of these calls for the four masters to be elected on 31 December, while another states that these 'mastures aftur there yere ys Cumyn up shall bryng In there accowmpts before owr lladye daye nextt ffollowyng' (f 3). These ordinances were set down at the meeting held on 31 December, 1534 and are followed by the accounts of the masters who affirmed them. As these accounts are undated, it is reasonable to assume they were presented at, or shortly after, the first meeting and cover the expenses for 1534. It is possible, however, that they are for the year 1535, the named masters being those elected on 31 December 1534. As two later accounts are also offered for these two years, no unequivocal dating of the first accounts is possible. The second set is dated 1525, and rouses the query whether the original scribe or Daffern should not have dated it 1535. Possibly an old account, forgotten or mislaid for ten years, was entered in the new book? The third account is undated. The fourth, however, presents the receipts and expenses for 1524, being the account of the masters elected 'M^{ll} v^C & xxiij' (f 8). This awkwardness is, unfortunately, characteristic of the Drapers' accounts until 1561.

Some of the awkwardness, of course, may be due to Daffern's wrong transcriptions. Where he sees his error, he scores it out — as on folio [17] 15. Reliable though he usually is, it is inevitable that he does not see some errors for what they are. But he cannot have mistaken all those dates which would need altering in order to produce whatever chronologically tidy sequence is sought by a particular historian or critic. Nonetheless, those clues which an original MS provides are much wanted here where the dating is so unexpected and erratic. Surely Daffern added the explanatory bracketed dates for the regnal years of Henry VIII that stand at the head of the accounts on folios 12, 14, and 17? And the one beginning that sequence on folio 10: 'the xxviijth yeare (1537) of the reign of our Sou$e$raign Lorde kynge Henr the viijth'? They are correct, but why should he choose suddenly to insert them, if he did insert them? Sharp, as has been noticed, is unhelpful in resolving dating problems, as is Halliwell-Phillipps who seems not to have looked at these accounts; his rare references to them are by means of Sharp.

Thirty accounts are entered in the folios considered in this appendix. One, that of 'Edward pelle for the hallfe yeres Rent beynn dewe at our ladye daye 1562' (f 51), is a unique rental. It would appear that the Drapers, like the Weavers, kept their rental transactions separate from the other business of the company, probably recording it in a rentgatherers' book (as did the Weavers). That so powerful a company should have extensive property is not surprising; however, were it not for this rental, the only indication of their holdings would be the rental list with which their regular annual account opens. Why the Drapers entered certain rents in their company's accounts I do not know, nor why the full rental list should, for once, be entered by Edward Pelle. In the following list all the evidence for dating is gathered together. This includes all dated material found between the accounts — agreements, fines, forfeits, etc. The various forms of the rubric for the day when the masters were chosen are represented by 'NYE'. Thus, for account 6 on folio 12, 'NYE 29 H VIII' abbreviates: 'chose on Newe yeares Evyn the xxixth yeare of the Reign of our Sourign Lorde kynge Henry the viijth'. After the folio number I have put the year(s) covered by the account as far as I have been able to determine them: thus, on folio 19 the masters chosen on 'NYE 32 H VIII' would be reckoned to hand in the account for 1541; however, the rubric reads 'NYE 32 H VIII 1542' and, if '1542' is

correct, then the account covers 1543. 'NYE 32 H VIII' comes toward the end of a
regnal sequence, while 1542 starts an annual sequence that soon drops the regnal
indicator; the choice is entered as '1541:1543.' Other dating clues, such as when the
St Peter's and Midsummer Watches ceased to be kept, give little help.

1)	f 4	1534:1535	Undated; account of the masters who ratified the 1534 ordinances — 'maysturs of Draps Ao Dm 1534'
2)	f 5	1525	NYE 1525
3)	f 7	undated	Incomplete; receipts only with sum total for expenses
4)	f 8	1524	NYDay 1524 ('M^{ll} v^C & xxiij')
5)	f 10	1537	NYE 28 H VIII; '(1537)' between regnal year and Henry
6)	f 12	1538	NYE 29 H VIII; at head of account on a single line '(1538)'
7)	f 14	1539	NYE 30 H VIII; at head of account on a single line '(1539)'
8)	f 17	1540	NYE 31 H VIII; at head of account on a single line '(1540)'
	f 19		Agreement dated 5 March 1541
9)	f 19	1541:1543	NYE 32 H VIII 1542; if the sequence of regnal years is correct, the dates added to this account and those added to the next two are either errors or possibly indications that the accounts were handed in late. However, if they were late, there is no indication of the fine of 10s being levied in any of the three years. This is also 'The accownse of mastr Cottbort Joynor then beyng merre ...'; he was mayor 2 February 1541 until 1 February 1542.
10)	f 21	1542:1544	NYE 33 H VIII 1543
11)	f 22	1543:1545	NYE 34 H VIII 1544; pageant costs are part of this account but not of the next one. However, the uncertainty of their dates does not help solve the problem of when or how the cycle was played in 1545–7 (see footnote 13, p lxiii and endnote, p 568).
12)	f 24	1546	NYE 1545; the masters for this account were Cuthbert Joynour, Thomas Ryley, Richard Banwell, and Edmund Brownell. Account no. 11 ends with a note that it is brought in before Christopher Waren, Cuthbert Joynour, and Thomas Smith who were then masters of the Drapers. Waren is the first master for account no. 11, the other two have been masters earlier, and

Joynour is to be master with three others for account no. 12. This explains one of the missing accounts between 1543:1545 and 1546.

	f 25		Agreement crossed out of 9 November 1561
			Agreement of 10 May 1561
	f 26		Agreement of 13 August 1563

13) f 26 1535 NYE 1534; if account no. 1 is 1534, this and the next account fill two missing years.

14) f 27 1536 NYE 1535

15) f 28 1537:1550 NYE 1536; at head of account on single line: 'Ao do 1550'.

16) f 29 1551 NYE no date; at head of account on single line: 'Ao 1551'. Incomplete? No pageant costs except for rehearsal.

ff 30-1 Agreement of 1 September 1552; 9 sections, 51 signatories.

17) f 31 1554 NYE 1553; the masters are the same as those indicated in 1552 agreement above.

18) f 32 1565 NYE 1564; this account and that following do not duplicate the accounts for 1565 and 1566 that occur in the reliably dated sequence of accounts beginning in 1562. I believe that they should be dated 1555 and 1556. See note to account 20.

19) f 33 1566 NYE 1565; expenses for 31 January 1554 when the duke of Suffolk was prisoner in the city are added as an extra at the foot of this account. So also are charges incurred for Midsummer 'when master norton was mere'; William Norton is the first master for this account and was mayor for the year beginning 2 February 1554. He need not have been master and mayor at the same time (but see Sharp, p 193, n z).

20) f 35 1567 NYE 1566; the masters are Riley, Pelle the elder, Smith, and Day, and the expenses of their year on company business and festal occasions exceed their receipts by £4 17s 10½d. It is the masters' duty to make good this discrepancy out of their own pockets. Accordingly, on folio 37, a note records that the company 'resevyd of thys' sum the larger part — £4 8s — from Riley and Pelle the elder, Pelle the younger, and Brownell rather than Smith and Day. Money received to settle an account in April 1556 must relate to expenses incurred in 1555 at the latest,

and by masters elected NYE 1554. Neither the groups of masters for other years in these accounts, nor the requirement in any year of £4 8s explain these discrepancies. Scribal error may explain the monetary error; the scribe was Pelle the younger who seems to have been in charge of management of rentals for the Drapers (see note to folio 43).

21)	f 38	1568	NYE 1567
22)	f 40	1558	NYE 1557; this cryptic account, in full, reads: 'The connt of m bele Wyllyam smallwood hewe daye Thomas burdon masters of the felousshyp of the draps on newe yeres even ano domyno m ccccc l & vij — ye dessed & mayd newes no samie'. Hugh Day died this year, apparently so soon after election as to nullify it.
23)	f 40	1558	'masters of the felershep of the draps ano domyni 1558 [m ccccc l & ix]'.
	f 43		Agreement, headed by a single line containing '(1558)'; 21 December money received from Edward Pelle. More received 25 March 'before the day abewse written'. Received more of him 29 June 3 Eliz. I (1561).
24)	f 44	1560	1560
	f 47		Note that H. Homes owes money due at Christmas; the item and page headed 'the 29 of July'.'
			Another forfeit due 20 September 1562 and to be paid before 1 January
			Note of a fine, dated 15 September 1562 due by Christmas next, and received 'an domini 1563'
			Forfeit for quarrelling on 3 December
			Fine paid 25 September 1563
			Forfeit paid 27 February 1563
25)	f 47	1560	1560; the same rubric as the previous account
	f 51	1562	Special rental for the half year due on 25 March
	f 53		Agreement dated 14 August 1563
			Note that all matters to do with Pelle's rental were settled by 29 September 1564
			Memorandum that £13 11s 4d remains in the box
			7 December 1564; box itself is with William Hopkins, mayor (who held office for the year beginning 2 November 1564).
	f 53	1561	'masturs ... in the Citie of Coventre Anno Dni 1561

then beyng mayor M Richard Smyth vinter'; Smith
was mayor from 2 February 1560–1. From here the
accounts are usually dated by regnal year and mayoralty.

ff 1-2* *(31 December)*

...

Allso has byn Agreed that the day of our Assemble & ffest
from this day fforwarde shyall be the last day of December ...

5

Item hyt ys A greed that euery man off the sayd ffeleshyp schall
haue In reddines a goun of sade peweke tawne other ells of
(blank) be *(blank)* of an *(blank)* & an hode the on halfe tawne
blake & the other halfe skyarlet of the sed hod for thys *(blank)*
all old tymes *(blank)* | ffurst to be *(blank)* to the *(blank)* of all   10
my *(blank)* the holl felloschyppe secund *(blank)* the master or
masturs *(blank)* so to pay at euery tyme for hys *(blank)*

Allso hyt ys A greed that the sam day a bove sayd when dyner
Is done that then the hole feleschypp after old Custum schall go   15
to gedder In a place Convenyent and ther for to chuse iiij neue
masturs whych iiij for to se good order kyeptt In the occupacion
and the prest payed his Celere the pressonn kept on Corpus
crysty daye the pageond & play well brought fforth *with* harness
off men & the watche kept at mydsomur on Seynt peters nyght   20
with order & good Customes whiche have byn usyd In old tyme
to the laude & prays of god & ye worschypp of thys Cytte

...

f 3   25

...

Alls hyt ys a greyd that ewery coprncy of mastures aftur there
yere ys Cumyn up shall bryng In there accowmpts before owr
lladye daye nextt ffollowyng and yff the do not to fforffett
[iij s iiij d]   X S   30

7-10 / *Sharp, p 164, fn p, reads* a gown of "Sad pewke, tawne, otherells off browne
blewe whych be nere of one color & an hode, the on halfe tawne or pewke & the other
halfe skarlet".

f 4* *(1534:1535)*

...

furst Receyts

...

Itm of humfrey Walker for ye old pagent howse	iiij s	5
Itm of John lonsdale for ye new pagent howse	ij s	

...

paymentes of the same Cownte

...

Itm for kepyng and skowrynge whyt harnes	v s	10
Itm for Cressy lygth on Seynt Johns & Seynt pet*ers* nyghts	v s	
Itm for ye hyre of iiij almayne Revetts	ij s	
Itm for iiij men on fare freydaye beryng harnes	viij d	
Itm for iiij men *ya*t bare whyt harnes on Seynt John and Seynt pet*ers* nyghts	ij s viij d	15
Itm for beryng almayne Revetts	xvj d	
Itm for ye Stremer berers	xvj d	
Itm for the berers of Cresetts	xvj d	
Itm for a bag and beryng of cressett lyght	v d	
...		20
Itm for ye Reherssys of the pagents	ij s viij d	

...

Itm for poynts to harnes men & to ye pleyers in ye pagent	xij d	
Itm for mendyng John lansdalls street dore	xij d	
Itm for ij new Ropys for ye pagent	xvj d	25
Itm for ordynarie Charges to ye pagents hawyng in and owt and mendyng	xxj s	

...

f 5 *(1525)*   30

...

Itm R*eseuyd* ffor howmffrey Wallker & the old pageantt house	iiij s	
Itm R*eseuyd* ffor the new pagant hous	ij s	
...		35

f 6

...

Paymennts of the Same Accommpt

...		40
Itm payd for kepynng & Skowryng harrnes	v s	

Itm payd ffor cressett lyght bothe the nyghtts   v s
Itm payd for hyre of iiij pere Allmayn ryvetts   ij s
Itm payd for iiij men on ffeyre ffreyday berynng harrenes   viij d
Itm payd to iiij men Werrynng complytt harnys bothe
nyghts   ij s viij d   5
Itm payd to iiij men Werrynng Allmayn ryvetts   xvj d
Itm payd to iiij Streymer beres   xvj d
Itm payd to iiij Cressetberers   xvj d
Itm payd ffor berynng off Creccettlyght   v d

...   10

Itm payd for Russhes in the paganntt   ij s viij d

Itm payd for poynnts to harnes men & pleyars   xij d
Itm payd for charges & ordynnce of the pagante in hauynng out
& in & for myndynng   xxiij s iiij d

...   15

Itm payd for Russes peystraw holly & Evee   ij s viij d
...

f 7   *(undated)*

...   20

          Repacyonne of a house at Gosford barres

...

Itm for repacyanns off the olde paganntt house   x d
Itm for Carryage of the Weyvers lomes and laying in the pagants
house   vj d   25

...

Reseued of houmffrey Walker for ye hoold padgond howsse   iiij s
Reseued of Rychard golldryng for ye new padgon howsse   ij s

...   30

f 16[a]
          Thes be the payments of the same kownte

...

p for holy Ive ruhssys & peystrawe   xxij d
...   35
p for kepyng & koloryng of owre whyt harnes   v s
p for kressett lyght on saynt Johns nyght & saynt peters
nyght   v s vj d
p for ye hyre of iiij payre off allman rryvetts   ij s viij d
p for iiij men on fayre frydey to beyre hernes   viij d   40

9 / Creccettlyght *odd reading; no difference in Daffern's* e's *and* c's

p for iiij men yat bayre harnes on both nyghts ij s viij d
p to iiij men yat bayre allman reyvetts for both nyghts xvj d
p to hym yat bayre ye podyngs for both nyghts vj d

f 8   *(1524)*   5

...

Reseiued of Howmffrey Walker for the olde pageant house iiij s
Reseiued of John Lannesdale ffor the new pagant house ij s

...

                                                                               10
f 9

...

                          Paymentts done by vs

...

Itm payd for holly Ivee pestrawe & Russhes xx d 15

...

Itm payd for kepynng & Skouryng harnes v s
Itm payd for Cressett lyght ij nyghts v s
Itm payd for iiij pere of allmayn Ryvetts berynng ij s
Itm payd on ffeere ffreday to iiij men for Berynng harnes v d 20
Itm paid to iij men that bare Whytt harnes on Sent Johns nyght
& Petters nyght ij s viij d
Itm payd for iiij pere of allmayn Ryvett & hyrynng & bering xvj d
Itm payd bering of Streymars xvj d
Itm paid for bering of Cressett lyght xx d 25
Itm payd for mynding of the pagannte howse Dore & ffor a kaye
to the same dore v d

...

Itm spente att Reheyrsys of the pagante ij s viij d
Itm payd ffor ordynere chargs having In and out of & myndng of 30
the pagennte xx s xj d

...

Itm payd for poynntts for harnes men and Playerss in the
Pagannte xij d
Itm payd for ij Judas Torches ij s ij d 35

...

ff 10-11   *(1537)* *(Receipts)*

...

Itm of Humfrey Walker for the olde pagent howse iiij s 40
Itm of Richard Golderyng for the newe pagent howse ij s

...

The Payments

...

Itm for holy & Ive Rysshes & pese strawe   xx d

...

It for kepyng & Scowryng our white harnes   v s   5
Itm for Cresset lyght on Saynt Johanys & Saynt Petur nyghts   v s |
Itm for the hyre of iiij payre of Almayne Ryvetts   ij s
Itm to iiij men on fayre freday for beryng harnes   viij d
It to iiij men that bare white harnes on Saynt Johns nyght &
Saynt Petur   ij s viij d   10
Itm to iiij men that bare Almayne Ryvetts on both nyghts   xvj d
Itm to the berers of the Stremers   xvj d
Itm to the berers of the Cresseth lyght   iiij d
Itm to the berers of the Cressetts   xvj d
...   15
Itm Spent at Rehersys of the playe   ij s viij d

...

Itm for the Ordynarye charges of the pagent   xxj s ij d

...

It for poyntes to harnes men and for the players   xvj d   20

...

Itm for mendyng the demones heeds   vj d
It for mendyng the white & the blake soules cots   viij d
...

                                                                                                               25

f 12 *(1538)* *(Receipts)*

...

Itm of david for the newe pagent howse   iij s viij d
It of Humfrey walker for the olde pagent howse   iiij s
...   30

f 13 *(Payments)*

...

It for holy Ive rysshes & pese strawe   xxij d
...   35
Itm for kepyng & the scowrynge of our white harnes   v s
Itm for Cresset lyght on Saynt John & Saynt petur nyghts   vj s
Itm for the hyre of iiij payre of Almayne Ryvetts   ij s viij d
Itm to iiij men that bare harnes on fayre freday   viij d
Itm to iiij men that bare [harnes] white harnes on both   40
nyghts   ij s viij d

Itm to iiij men that bare almayne Ryvetts on both nyghts   xvj d
Itm to the beyrers of stremers both nyghts   xvj d
Itm to the beyrers of the cressetts for both nyghts   xvj d
Itm for the beryng of the lyghts to the *(blank)*   iiij d
...   5
Itm spent at the Reherses of our pagent   ij s viij d
Itm for the ordynary charges of the of the pagent   xxj s j d
Itm for mendyng of our Lady orgaynes   vj s viij d
Itm for poynts for the harness men and players at all tymes xiiij d
Itm for v eluys of Canvas for shyrts & hose for the blakke Soules   10
at v d the elue   ij s j d
Itm for Coloryng & makyng the same cots   jx d
Itm for mendyng iiij Cressetts   vij d
Itm for makyng & mendynge of the blakke of Soules Coats
hose   vj d   15
Itm for a payre of newe hose & mendyng of olde for the white
soules   xviij d
Itm for makyng of the Crosse & coloryng yt   ij d
Itm for ij Clampes of Iron to the pagent whele & nayles for all
the pagent   ix d   20
Itm spent at the settyng owt of the pagent   vj d
Itm for a pownde of sope   j d ob
Itm for payntyng & makyng newe hell hede   xij d
...
                                                                          25

f 14 *(1539)* *(Receipts)*
...
Itm for the Newe pagent howse   ij s
Itm of Humfrey walker for the olde pagent howse   iij s iiij d
...   30

ff 15-16 *(Payments)*
...
Itm for holy & Ivye Russhes & peystrawe   xxij d
...   35
Itm for iiij newe torches weyng vj pownds   iij s iiij d
...
                  The Charges & payments for the pagent
In pmis for the Rehersys of the pagent   ij s viij d
Itm for mendyng a Rope to the pagent thre ffedom longe   v d   40

7 / of the of the *MS dittography*   10 / eluys *for* elnys
11 / elue *for* elne

Itm for makyng an Angels scytte	xij d	
Itm for burdes to the pagent	vj d	
Itm for nayles & teynter hokes	ij d	
Itm for mendyng of hell hede	vj d	
Itm for mendyng the Trumpetts	vij d	5
Itm for sope to the pagent	ij d	
Itm for pakke thrydde to the pagent	ob	
Itm payd vnto hym that playeth goddes parte	iij s iiij d	
Itm payd to iiij Angeles	xvj d	
Itm to iij patriarches	xij d	10
Itm to iij white [Souels] Soules	xviij d	
Itm to iij blakke Soules	ij s	
Itm to iij Demones	iij s	
Itm for kepyng hell hed	vj d	
Itm for kepynge the Wynde	vj d	15
Itm to Dyxson for Ropes to the Wyndoes	ij d	
Itm for Settyng furth & bryngynge yn the pagent	xij d	
Itm to the Players for theyr supper	ij s j d	
Itm for theyr brekefaste at the settyng yn the pagent	xij d	
Itm to hym that drove the pagent	ij d	20
Itm for Ale to the pagent	vj d	
Summa xxiiij s j d ob		

...

The Charge & payments ffor the Watche at Mydsom.

In pmis to old beyle for cresset lyght	vj s	25
Itm for harnes beryng on both nyghts	iiij s	
Itm for beryng of the Stremers	xvj d	
Itm for lyght beryng & the cressetts	xx d	
Itm to Willm lynes for kepyng & scowrynge the white harnes	v s	30
Itm for hyrynge of iiij payre of alman ryvetts	ij s	
Itm for poynts	xij d	
Itm for iiij harnesse men fayre ffreday	viij d	
Summa xxj s viij d		
		35

f [15a]

p to ye beyrers of the kressett lyght for both nyghts	xvj d
p to ye streymar beyreers for both nights	xvj d

...

13 / iij Demones *probably for* ij Demones *(cf all other accounts)*

Spent at the reyheresys of owre padgeone   ij s viij d

...

p for ordenarye chargs of owre padgeone   xxj s j d

...

p for pownts for ye hernys men at all tymes & for the pleyers   5
of ye padgone   xvj d
p for mendyng of whyt Soells ketts & blake   xij d
p for mendyng with ye takyng fourth of owre padgeond
whelle   xv d
p for a torch yat wodhowsse had for ye Juddasys   xvj d   10

...

        Thes be the repraschuns of the same kownt

...

p for ye mendyng of owre padgeon howse wyndo with ye
settyng   ij s vj d   15

...

f 17 *(1540) (Receipts)*

...

Itm for the new pagent howse   ij s viij d   20
Itm for the old pagynt howse   iij s iiij d

...

f 18   *(Payments)*

...   25
Itm for holy Evy Rusches & pestraw   ij s j d
It for the ordynary Chargs of ye pagent   xxv s vij d

...

It for mending the iiij cressetts with iiij hopes of Iron & peynting
the polls   xx d   30

...

It for keping the white harnes   v s
It for skowring iij saletts and iij peire of splentts   xij d
It for hyring of iiij peire of Almayne Ryvetts   ij s
It for bering of cressetts   xvj d   35
It for bering of stremers   xvj d
It for bering of cressett lyght   iiij d
It for cressett light making   v s v d
It for iiij men bering harnes on feire fryday   viij d
It iiij men bering white harnes   ij s viij d   40
It iij men bering Almayne Ryvetts   xvj d

It for a lode of cley lathe & neyls and workemanchype to ye
new pagent howse   viij d

...

It for poyntes for the pleyers and for the harnes men   xij d

...   5

It for meeting the locke *with* a new key and a stapull to ye new
pagent howse   iiij d

It for peynting & making new iiij peire of Angells wyngs *with*
ij demens heds   ij s ij d

It to the smythe for Iron bonds and neyls to the pagent   iiij d   10

It to John bern for a lase & me*n*ding the bawling yn the toppe
of the pagent   viij d

It for pesyng the wynde rappe   ij d

...   15

f 19 *(1541:1543) (Receipts)*

...

it for ye newe pagant howse   ij s viij d

...

it for the wolde pagant howse   iij s iiij d   20

...

f 20 *(Payments)*

...

It for holly & yve Rosshys & pestrawe   ij s j d   25

It for ye iij Reyhersys   ij s viij d

It for ordynary Chargys to ye pagant   xxij s

...

It for kepyng whyte harnes   v s

It for hyere off iiij perre off almeyn Ryffetts   ij s   30

It for beyryng off Cressetts   xvj d

It for beyryng streymers   xvj d

it for beyryng Cressyt lyght   iiij d

it for makyng Cressett lyght   vj s

it for iiij men beyryng alme*n* Ryffytts on bothe nyghts & on   35
ferre frydaye   ij s

11 / bawling *for* bateling

it for iiij men beyryng whytt harnes   ij s viij d
it for poyntes for harnes men & for pleyers   xij d

...

it for mendyng ye pagant & a newe Rope   xv d
it for makyng helle hede   viij s ij d   5

...

it for wyllyam yonges gowne   xiiij s
it for ye pagant that was gyven to m*aiste*r merre on mydsomer
nyght off ye Crafte   xxxvj s viij d

...   10

f 21 *(1542:1544)*

...

It ffor holy & Ive ruchssys & pestrawe   ij s iiij d

...   15

f 22 *(1543:1545)*

...

It p ffor iij reyhersys   ij s viij d
It ffor haweyng ffourth off the padgeon & for the mendyng of   20
hyt to lewys   xxij d
It payd ffor hassppeys stapulls for the pageond howsse
wyndosse   vij d
It payd to dyxun elleatt & wryght ffor ther labor at y*at*
tyme   vj d   25
It p ffor ordynrry chargs of the padgeond   xxij s iij d
It p ffor a new roppe ffor the wynd   xviij d
It p ffor the mendyng of the whytt Sollskotts xvj d *with* the
ij skyns y*at* went to yem
It p ffor the kepyng of the whyt harnes   v s   30
It p ffor the hyre of iiij payre of allman reyvytts   ij s
It p ffor kressett lyght to holld beyle   vj s
It p ffor beyryng of streymers   xvj d
It p ffor beyryng of kressetts   xvj d
It p ffor beyryng of kressett lyght   iiij d   35
It p iiij men beyryng whyt harnes   ij s viij d
It iiij men allman revetts ffor both nyghts and on ffaire
ffrydey   ij s
It ffor powynts ffor harnes men & ffor pleyars   xij d

...   40

It p to m*aiste*r portter ffor hys kownsell ffor the padgand
howse   v s
...

f 23   5
...

It for the ordenary chargys of owre pageant   xxij s ij d
...

It for neylys & a wryght to mend the pageant   vij d
It to iiij harnesyd men on freyr frydey   viij d   10
It to harnesyd me*n* on ye sumar nyght sent petars nyght for
cressyt beyrars & streymar beyrars   vij s
It for cressyt lyght   vj s
It to wyll hays for kepyng owre harnes all the yere   v s
It for hyryng of iiij payre of allmayne Ryvyts   ij s   15
...

It for holy & yve Russhys & pestraw   ij s
...

It for iiij Torchys   iiij s viij d
It for whyt papar & whyt threde   j d   20
It for poynts for harnesyd men & for the pageant   xiiij d
It for a pownd of Sope for ye corporas clothys   ij d
...

It to Wyll young for warnyng the ocupacyon & beyryng hys
torchys   iij s   25
...

f 24 *(1546)*

...

iiij hernest men on ffer ffreydaye   viij d   30
ffor medssomer neyght & sen petteres neyghtt and for beryng of
stremeres cressett & cressett lyght   vij s
To Wellm balley for leyght   viij s
payd to Wellm lynes for Scweryng and keppyng ower hernes ye
yer   v s   35
payd for iiij payer of allmay Revetts heyer   ij s
...

f 25
for holle eve & rosses & pes straye   ij s   40
...

for powents   xij d

...

ff 26-7* *(1535)*   5

...

It payd for torche lyght at the Saluees   ij s
It payd for the ordenary chargs of the pagdn   xxij s vj d
It payd for [ha] the iiij harnes men on the fere fryday   viij d
It payd for harnes men on both the wach nyts & lyte   xiij s |
It payd for pynts all the yere   xvj d   10
It payd for Rysshys all the yere   xvj d
It for beryng forth of the organs   iij d

...

f 27 *(1536)*   15

...

It payd for the ordenary Chargys of the pagan   xxij s viij d
It payd for harnes & stremurs & cresets on mydsomur
nyght   iij s vj d
It payd for poynts all the yere   xij d   20
It payd for creset lyght   iiij s
It payd to lyne for kyppyng the harnes al ye yere   vj s viij d

...

It payd for Rysshys & pesstraw   xxij d

...   25

f 28 *(1537:1550)*

...

It payd for the ordenary charges of the paggan   xxij s vj d
...   30
It payd for beryng of harnes on fere fryday   viij d
It payd for beryng of harnes & stremors & cresets on mydsomere
nyght   iij s vj d
It payd for creset lyght   iiij s
It payd for pynts all the yere   xiiij d 35

...

It payd for Rycsshes   xix d
It payd for a Roppe for the pagan   ij s iiij d

...

It payd to wyllya lyne for kyppyng the harnes   vj s viij d 40
It payd for ij new cresets & mendyng of the old   viij s viij d

...

f 29 *(1551)*

...

Itm payd for berynge of harnys on mydSomer nyght & fere fryday	iiij s ij d
Itm payd for poynntts	xiiij d
Itm payd for cressyt lyght	iiij s viij d
Itm payd to Wyllyam lynnys for kepyng the harnys	vj s viij d
Itm payd for Reherssyng	ij s viij d
Itm payd for Russys & pestrawe	ij s ij d

...

f 32 *(1565)*

...

Itm payd for the ordynare chargys of the pagande	xxij s viij d
Itm payd for beryng of harnys on fare fryday	viij d
Itm payd for beryng of harnys of mydsomer nyght	iij s vj d
Itm payd for cresset lyght	iij s
Itm payd to Wyllyam lynnys for kepyng the harnys	vj s viij d
Itm payd for poynttys all the yeer	xvj d
Itm payd for Repracyons of the pagende	ij s j d
Itm payd for a dossyne of Skyns for the sollys cottys	iiij s vj d
Itm payd for makyng the Sollys cottays	iij s

...

f 33 *(1566)*

...

Itm payd for the ordynarye chargys of pagande	xxij s viij d
Itm payd for the paynting hell hede newe	xx d
Itm payd for beryng harnys of fere frydaye	viij d
Itm payd for beryng harnys of mydssomer nyght *with* stremers & cressytts	iij s vj d
Itm payd for cressytt lyght	iij s v d
Itm payd for poyntts all the yere	xiij d
Itm payd to Wyllyam lynnys for keepyng the harnys all the yere	vj s viij d

...

f 34*

...

Itm payd for the ordynare chargys of the pagande	xxiij s

...

Itm payd for beryng harnys on fere fryday	viij d

Itm payd for beryng harnys & cressytts & stremarys at mydsomer
nyght   iij s vj d
Itm payd for cressytt lyght   iiij s viij d
Itm payd to wyllyam lynnys for kepyng the harnys all the
yere   vj s viij d   5
...
Itm payd for poyntts all the yere   xij d
...
memorandum that we hawe payd for owr occupacyon the xxxi
day of Januarye when the duke of Suffolk was takyn   10
Itm payd for warkynge to the harnys men for vij days & viij
nyghtts   lviij s vj d
Itm payd for a sheffe of Aroys   ij s viij d
Itm payd for the fetheryng of xvj Aroys & vij newe Aroys &
mendyng the cassys of them   xviij d   15
Itm payd for iij dossyn of poyntts   vj d
Itm payd iij Swordr gyrdyllys   xviij d
Itm payd for ij gyrdyllys for Sheffe Aroys   iiij d
Itm payd for bostryngys & a brassar   iij d
                                          Summa iij li v s ij d   20
for the chargys of mydsomyr nyght when master norton was
mere
Itm payd to xviij gonnarys   ij s iiij d
Itm payd for xij li of gonepother   xij s vj d
Itm payd for playnge wyght the stage   vj s viij d   25
Itm payd for the hyryng of the stage   viij d
Itm payd for ij Dromys   iij s
Itm payd for paynttyng of a Drome   xij d
                                          Summa iiij li ij s ij d
                                                                                     30

f 35* (1567)
                         for prenttyssys
...
Resseyvyd at the dyner & for the playe   xx s iiij d
...   35
                         Paymentts
...
Itm payd for berynge of harnys of farye fryday   viij d
Itm payd to viij men for berynge harnys on mydsomer nyght   ij s
Itm payd for beryng of stremerys & cryssytts & lyght   ij s iiij d   40

25, 26 / stage: *Sharp (p 198) reads* slage

Itm payd for xiiij stone of cressytt lyght   x s iiij d
Itm payd for iiij newe cressytts   xij s
Itm payd to wyllyam lymes for a xj menys harnys kepyng all the
yere   vj s viij d
Itm payd for poyntts for mydsomer nyght & the pagande   ij s   5
...

Itm payd for beryng the orgyns from master nethurmylls   iiij d
...

ff 36-7*   10
                        for mydsomer nyght
Itm payd to xiiij gonnars & a layte   lix s
Itm payd for xij ti of gonne powther   xiiij s
Itm payd to thomas shawe for the flage & playng   xx s
Itm payd to [thomas] hewe hopkyns for playnge upon the   15
drome & to slye & messett   iiij s
Itm payd to Robart crowe for makyng of the gyanes   xx d
Itm payd to ij men for berynge of the gyones   xxij d
                                        Summa v li xiij s x d
                        chargys for the pagande   20
Itm payd for canvas for the sollys cottys
xix ellys   xxiiij s iij d
Itm payd for iiij elys of lynyne cloth for the playars
gownys   iij s viij d
Itm payd for ix elys of canvas yallow   xij d   25
Itm payd for x elys of canvas made blake   x d
Itm payd for iiij pare of angyllys wyngys   ij s viij d
Itm payd for makyng of iij worldys to crowe   ij s
Itm payd for iij chefferellys & a berde of hree   iij s xd
Itm payde for iiij dyadynnes   ij s viij d 30
Itm payd for vj goldyn skynnes   v s
Itm payd for vij skynnes for godys cott & the baryll for the
yerthe quake   iij s
Itm payd ^ 'for' the pyllar for the wordys & the baryll   iij s iiij d
Itm payd for ij pessys of yallow bekaram   vij s vj d   35
Itm payd for iiij yardes of Rede bekuram   ij s viij d
Itm payd for a demonys face   ij s
Itm payd to franssys tayller for makyng the Sollys cotts   vj s viij d
Itm payd for makyng of iij gownys & a cotte   vj s
Itm payd for iij Reherssys of the pagande   vij s iiij d 40
Itm payd to God   iij s iiij d
Itm payd to ij demen   iij s

Itm payd to iij whytt sollys   v s
Itm payd to iij blake sollys   v s
Itm payd to ij Spryttys   xvj d
Itm payd for the prolouge   viij d
Itm payd to iiij angellys   ij s   5
Itm payd to iij pattryarkys   xviij d
Itm payd to ij clarkys for Syngyng   ij s
Itm payd for ther Supare   iiij s
Itm payd for Settyng owt of the pagande   vj d
Itm payd for a ponde of Sope   ij d   10
Itm payd for nayllys Russys & Rossyn   vj d
Itm payd for cleynyng of the pagande & kepyng hell hede &
the Wynd   iiij s viij d
Itm payd to the trompyttar   iij s iiij d
Itm payd for drynke to the pagande   xij d   15
Itm payd to Raffe Aman for playng on the ryggellys   vj d
Itm payd for payntyng of the Worldys & the pyllur   iij s iiij d
Itm payd for blakyng the Sollys fassys kepyng fyre & the
baryll   xij d
                              Summa v li xvij s vij d | 20
                 Charges of owre dener

...

Itm payde to the players   v s

...

Resevyd at the dener & for the playe   xix s iiij d   25

...

f 38   (1568) (Receipts)

...

Resevythe for the hour of the gonnes vysse at medsumer ij s iiij d   30

...

                    paymenttes

...

payd for beryng of iiij mens harnes at the fayre   viij d
...   35
payd for pwenttes for fayre fryday & medsomur neght   x d
payd for Rwsses for the pangen & the churche & pestray ij s viij d
payd for vij stone of cressett lyghte for medsomar nyght   vij s
payd for berryng of harnes & of stremer & cressets cresset
lyghte   iij s vij d   40
payd to wyllyam lynes for kepyng of the harnes all the
yer.   vj s viij d

payd to Robart crowe for makyng of the boke for the
paggen   xx s
...

f 39*   5
                 paymenttes for the pagges
payd for thre Rehersses   v s
payd for a ponde of sovpe   ij d
payd for facheng of a pere of hovrgens at hamton & the carrege
of them whovme   ij s   10
payd for settyng fovrthe of the paggen   vj d
payd for a pere of glowes for crowe   ij d
payd to the truppetur   iij s iiij d
payd to the plears when the fyrste paggen was pleyed to
drynke   ij s   15
payd for tentur hovckes & packthryd   v d
payd for aylle for the plears at thre tymes   xiiij d
payd to god   iij s vj d
payd to threy patryharkes   xviij d
payd for the fyer   ix d   20
payd towe to dewelles   iij s iiij d
payd for pwenttes   v d
payd for the prolouge   viij d
payd to threy whyte sowlles   v s vj d
payd to threy blake sowlles   v s vj d   25
payd for berreng of the orgens   vj d
payd for the blackyng of the sowlles faysses   vj d
payd to ij spryttes   xviij d
payd for iiij hangells   ij s
payd to the clarkes for sengyng   ij s   30
payde for kepng of the wynd   viij d
payd for kepeng of hells mouth   viij d
payd for a lauther   iiij d
payd for dryvng of the paggen   xv d
payd for ij whourlles   iij s viij d 35
payd to hym that kepe the fyer   iij d
payd for settyng out of the paggen & svpper & makyng   viij d
                                  sum xlvij s iiij d

...

22 / *Daffern glosses* pwenttes *as* points   35 / *Daffern glosses* whourlles *as* worlds

f 40 *(1558)* *(Dinner Charges)*

...

payd to the plears   v s

...

5

f 41*

...

payd for holly & evey   viij d

...

payd for harnes beryng one fere fryday   ij s   10
payd for poyntes   viij d
payd to men that bare harnes of mydsomer nyght   ij s
payd for poynes for them   viij d

...

payd for resshes for the paggand & ye churche &   15
pestrawe   ij s viij d
payd for viij stone of cressett lyght   viij s
payd for carryng of viij cressett [lyght] & stremeres & beryng of
lyght   ij s vj d
payd for mendyng of a cressett   xij d   20
payd for payntyng of the gyenans wyffe   ij s iiij d
payd for the beryng of the gyans wyffe   xxiij d
payd for struett & drome   ij s iiij d
payd for a long corde & the scutyng & skoryng   xij d
payd for a wysseler   xij d   25
payd for xx gonnes & a slagberd & ij lockes   iiij l xvj s iiij d
payd for xvij l of gonpover   xxj s iiij d
payd wen the harnes was fachede a waye from lynnes   iiij d
payd to lynes for kepynges of ye harnes all the yere   vj s viij d

...   30

payd for amas for to lyne the gorgettes to lynes   ij d

...

f 42
payd for iiij sodyer cottes makyng & the red crosses   ij s iiij d   35

...

paymentes for pagane

payd for iij Rehersses   v s
payd for a ponde of sope   ij d

---

26 / xx gonnes...lockes: *M.D. Harris*, Drapers' Company, *27*, *reads* 15 guns and a
flagbearer and 2 'lakes'

payd for settyng ovt of ye pagand & settyng yn	xiiij d
payd for a pere of gloves for god	ij d
payd to the plears to dryncke	ij s
payd to the trvmpyter	iij s iiij d
payd to Jhon to synge the basse	iiij d 5
payd for a corde to the pagande wyndes	iiij d
payd for borde & nele to the pagande & woorkemansshepe	ij s ij d
payd for Rosen & Rosshes	v d
payd for alle for dryuers of the pagane	xiiij d
payd to god	iij s vj d 10
payd to iij patryarkes	xviij d
payd for settyng the worlde of fyer	v d
payd for tyntyng the yorthe quake	iiij d
payd to ij devells	iij s iiij d
payd for poyntes	xij d 15
payd for the proloug	viij d
payd for iij blake soles	v s vj d
payd for iij wytte soles	v s vj d
payd for blakyng of ye solles faces	vj d
payd for ij sprets	xviij d 20
payd for iiij angells	ij s
payd to the clarkes for syngyng & playng	ij s vj d
payd for kepyng of ye wynde	viij d
payd for kepyng of hell movthe	viij d
payd for dryvyng the pagente	xx d 25
payd for iij worldes	iij s viij d
payd for kepyng of fyer at hell mothe	iiij d

Som lj s vj d
charges for the dyner

...   30

payd ye mynstrell	xij d

ff 44-5* *(1560)*

...

Reseyvyd of m browell & mr smalwod to pare the gonnes	iij li vj s viij d 35
Reseyvyd more of edward pelle to paye gonners	xiij s iiij d

...

paymetes for the pagen

payd for iij reherses	v s viij d 40
payd to blower wen he to hamton	viij d
payd for settynge forth of the pagene	vj d

payd for a corde to tye the pagone dore   j d
payd to the plears when the fruste pagene was plear   ij s
payd to the trupetere   iij s iiij d
payd for neles   ij d
payd for russes   ij d   5
payd for pakthred   ij d
payd for rossen   ij d
payd for sope   j d ob
payd for settynge yn the pagene   vj d
payd to ij develes for playnge   iij s iiij d   10
payd to iij whyt soles   v s
payd to iij blake soles   v s
payd to ij sprytes   xvj d
payd to iiij angeles   ij s
payd to the clarkes for syngyns   ij s   15
payd to the pleares for ther sopers   iiij s |
payd for ponttes   vj d
payd to iij petteryyes   xij d
payd for penttyng of the blake soles faces   vj d
payd for penttyng of the croste   ij d   20
payd for a ponnes of candeles   j d ob
payd for a torg   xij d
payd for the proloug   viij d
paid for [dryvng] dryvyng of the pagenes & kepyng hell mothe
& kepyng the wynde   iij s ix d   25
payd for the eartquake & settyng the warde afyer   viij d
payd for mendyng of the pagen   ij d
payd for hangeng the pagen   iiij d
payd for hangyng of the wyndowes   iiij d
payd for iiij ganes of hall   xij d   30
payd to as for pleayng god   iij s iiij d
payd to hym for makynge the waddes   iij s viij d
payd [to] hym for mendyng the devels cottes   xx d
sum ys liiij s ix d
payments of myssomer nyght   35
payd to James of the sward for playng of the slag   vj s ij d
payd to thomas sawton the capten   vj s viij d
payd to ij lakes   v s
payd to xj gonners v s a pesse   lv s
payd for pleyng of the drume before the gonners   ij s   40

22 / torg *for* torch?

payd to the wyssthold	xij d
payd for xj dossen ponttes	xj d
payd for sckowyng the harnes	viij s
payd to the harnes men that beare harnes	iij s vj d
payd for viij stone of lyght	v s iiij d 5
payd for the pentyng of the gyans wyffes	ij s vj d
payd to eades for the waxe	v s
payd for iiij harnes men at the feare fryday	viij d
payd for caryng iiij stremers & viij cressets	ij s
payd for beryng the pewdeges	ij d 10

                                sum ys v l iij s xj d

...

ff 48-9 *(1560)*

...   15

payd for berynge harnes on the ferye fryday	viij d

...

payd for skwrynge of harrynes	viij s

...

                  the charges of the pageante   20

pd for iij Reherses	vj s
pd to the trumpetter	iij s iiij d
pd to the players to drynke	ij s
pd for ale to the dryvers	x d
pd to god	iij s iiij d 25
pd to ij devyll	iij s iiij d
pd for the prologue	viij d
pd to iij whyte sowles	v s
pd to iij blake sowles	v s
pd to ij sprytes	xvj d 30
pd to iiij anngells	ij s |
pd to the syngers	ij s
pd for kepynge the wynde	viij d
pd for kepynge hell mowthe	viij d
pd for iij worldes	iij s viij d 35
pd to hym *y*at kepte the [fryer] fyre	iiij d
pd for settynge owte the pagen	vj d
pd for settynge yt yn	vj d
pd for apentynge & shuttynge	iiij d
pd for blackynge the facys	vj d 40
pd to x men for dryvynge yt	ij s vj d
pd for dressynge of yt	iiij d

pd for iij patryarkes   xviij d
pd for the players supper   iiij s
pd for playnge of the Rygells   xij d
                                                          sum lj s iiij d

               the charges of the watche   5
pd for x stone cressytte lyght   viij s iiij d
pd for j peande Resen   j d
pd for pacthrydde   ij d
pd for sope   ij d
pd for Rossen   ij d   10
pd for nayles   j d
pd to iiij men for bearynge harnes   xvj d
pd for iiij men harnes   viij d
pd to iij streamers   viij d
pd to iiij cressytt bearers   viij d   15
pd to ij lyght bearers   iiij d
pd for the gyanes   xx d
pd for candulls   j d
                              sum xiiij s iiij d
...   20

f 50
...
pd for the seconde paymente as yt dothe playnlye
appeare   xxiiij s viij d   25
pd for the charges of the pageante as yt appeare   lj s iiij d
pd for the charges of the watche as yt appeare   xiiij s iiij d
...

Undated Records

Petition of Mary Marston CRO: W 83*

To the worshipfull ffeoffees of Certayne Lands Sumtyme Parcell
of the Late desolued Priory of our Lady in the City of Coventry

                    5

The Humble Pettition of Mary Marston widdow
Showeth
That wheras it Pleased your worshipps in Consideration yat you
hadd bestowed Hir Estate in the Priory Orchard Garden be
Croste with the Housinge vpon your officer Mr. Phillip Adams, &   10
a Lease beinge Granted unto him for the Terme of 21 years
under the Cittys Seale was not to bee made voyde But your
Goodnes Sayed you would in Lew Therof doe your Pettitioner
Good if she Could fynd wherin you might doe it. Now your
Petitioner rather Chusinge one Shillinge with your Love & Favour   15
then one Pound by any other waye
    Humbly Prayeth a Lease of 26 years in reversion after the
Expiration of that Lease immediatly to begin & she shall sease to
Troble your worships But never sease to Praye for your euerlasting
Hapines. /   20

A *'A rentall of certaine landes & tenements belongyinge to the
Corporation of the cyety of Coventre'*
Warwickshire Antiquarian Magazine, 1 (1859-77)
p 481   25

                Rents of assyse

...

The mersers A rent out of the pagen house   vij s
...   30

p 482
Heylane
James Huwet A tenement ther   xiij s iiij d
...
    5

p 488
Smythford strete
Wyll'm Styffe A ten*ement*   x s
...
    10

p 493
...
Myllane
A quit rent out of the Smyth pagen house   v s
                              Som pat*et*   15
...

p 502
...
Other payments   20
...
Payd to ye iiij waytts   iiij £
...

AC   *Waits' Regulations*   BL: Add MS 43645   25
     f 166v
ffor the Waites
The vsuall manner for the playing of the Waites in this Cytie was
thus *videlicet* to play on half of everie quarter throughout the
yere   30
The first quarter they begann the first weeke in Cleane Lent, and
continued till Easter
They divided the Cytie into foure parts, and playd foure severall
mornings beginning at two of aclock⟨.⟩
The daies the played on were Munday, twesday, wednesday, and   35
Thursday.
The next quarter they begann the first day of May and conti*n*ued
till Middsummer
The third quarter they begann at Lammas and continue'd' till
Michaelmas, these two quarters were playd in the same manner   40
as the first were.

The fourth and last quarter begann at Allhollantide and continued
till Christmas.
They were to play all this quarter for five daies in every weeke
throughout the towne, that is on Mondaies Twesdaies wednesdaies,
ffridaies, and Saturdaies.   5
They vsually begann at twelue of the Clocke at middnight, and
continued till foure in the morning.

A   *Smiths' Accounts* CRO: Acc 251
     p 145   10
     ...

                          Allso what *person* [of the] or *person* of the sayd Crafts that
A penialtie for   wyll not goo yn the Watchys on myds*u*mr nyght Sent peters
them yt wyll   nyght or breake the Wache wythe owt annye lawfull cawse to
not go yn ye   forfyt for mydsum*er*.nyght iij s iiij d yn the name of A payne   15
wache   And for [them] Sent petars nyght xx d wythe owt ysua
                          ...

AC   *Tilers' Ordinances* BL: Harley 6466
     f 1   20

     Out of an old Manuscript belonging to the Company of Tilers &
     kept at St. Nicholas's Hall
     N.B. that I spel every word as it is written in ye said MS °Harl
     6466°   25
     In the name of God Amen These benne the poyntys & the
     ordynanns of the Tylers Craft of Coventre ...
     Also whatte men that benne chosen Masterus as for the here thei
     schullen bye an honest lyuerye tha⟨.⟩ the Crafte may be honestly
     clothed ynne agenest Corpus chr*ist*i daye In worshcippe of god &   30
     owre mayr & the Cite
     ...

     f 3
                                                                      35
     Also hit is ordeynede that eu*ery* man that is of the lyverey schall
     come on corp*us* chr*ist*i daye And honestlych to goo wyth the
     procession and serve her torches eu*ery* man up the peyne of a
     pound of waxe wythoute he haue a resonaball excusation
     ...   40

f 5*

...

Also yt ys ordeynyd bye a general Counsel of all the Crafte &
Craftes; and also that the Wryghts Crafte of Coventre schall paye
to the Pageant 10s uppon Whytsonday or else by Corpus christi   5
daye uppon the payne of 20s hallfe to the mayor & hallfe to the
Crafte & bycause they haue no more to doo wythe the Pageant
but payeyng there 10s &c

...

                                                                       10
ff 7-8

Also hyt is ordeynd and a gred by the wholl body of the Craft of
the Cottyers & ffletchers of the Citie of Coventre in this behalfe
and by ther on Wull that what stranger that is mad Brother with   15
them after ther ordinaunce a forseid that 6s 8d of his Brotherhede
to remayn to the Cost & reparacion of the pagent of the pynners
Tyllers & Coupers of Couentre In payne of 20s halfe to the Maire
& half to the Crafte |
Also hit is ordeynde and a grede by the woll body of the Craft of   20
the Tylmakers of Stoke by ther one will that what stranger that
is made Brother with them after ther ordinance that 6s 8d of his
Brotherhode to remayn to the Cost and reperacion of the Payant
of the Pynners & Tyllers & Coupers of Coventre on payne of 20s
halfe to the Major & halfe to the Crafte   25

14 / cottyers *for* bowyers

APPENDIX 4
Inventories

All the inventories printed here are connected with the pageantry of guild, city, church, and individual in Coventry. The full inventory from the Cardmakers and Saddlers' Indentured Conveyance is given to provide some notion of the splendour of a guild chapel. These records will, it is hoped, show the quantity and quality of guild worship and entertainment beyond the production of the Corpus Christi play. The inventory, as well as being unique in Coventry, touches upon a feature of religious worship little recorded elsewhere in the city's documents. The list of relics found in St Mary's Cathedral also suggests a quality of worship that contributed to the city's daily life.

In sixteenth century England, not only did dress proclaim a man's estate, and frequently his civic office, but governments, both national and local, legislated what items of dress might or must be worn by certain ranks of people. A man's wardrobe, especially if he is a citizen of wealth and importance, can tell us much. Edmund Brownell, a wealthy draper — his will mentions fourteen houses that he owned besides the one in Bayley Lane in which he lived, and reckons his sum worth to be £339 6s — was the mayor who welcomed Elizabeth to Coventry in 1566.

1537
Cardmakers and Saddlers' Indentured Conveyance CRO: Box I
sheet 2 *(8 January)*

Here After ensue the *particu*lers & certentie of the ornament*es*   5
Iuell*es* goodes & Implement*es* app*er*teynyng to the Chappell
mencioned in thyndentures hereunto Annexed
ffurste a Masse Booke & A Chalese / Item a vestement of Rede
velvett w*ith* Steeres of Golde It*em* an Albe w*ith* an Ammyse A
Stole & a phanon of the same / It*em* a Corp*or*as & a Case of grene   10
borde Alysander w*ith* a Crose of siluer & ou*er* gilt compased w*ith*
perle & pre*c*iouse Stones And sett in siluer & gilt & enameled /
It*em* a vestement of Rede damaske w*ith* albe Ammyse Stole &

phanon of the same with a Corporas & a Case of Rede velvett
with iij lyons Cowchaunt / Item a vestement of blake silke with
white Columbynes with albe amyse Stole & phanon of the same
& case of Rede silke / Item a vestement of white fustiane Steyned
for lenton with albe amyse Stole & phanon of the same / Item ij   5
Auter Clothes of the passion for lenton And a frontell of the
Auter / Item ij Auter Clothes Counterfett Cloyth of golde with
Compase in a Sheilde Item oon Auter Cloith of blewe silke
steyned with liberdes hedes of golde rased / Item a frontlett of
blake damaske with R & I & Sterres of golde / Item iiij pelowes   10
of yalow silke with lyons of Rede Item a pelow of purple velvett /
Item ij lynyne Auter Clothes / Item a Towell / Item an Auter
Cloithe steyned with an Image of seynt Thomas / Item a pax
with a Crucifix of Marie & Iohn / Item a table of the Mounte of
Synay / Item iiij Candlestickes of mastelen to sett vpon the Auter   15
for tapers / And ij for Talough Candelles / Item a smale pax with
a Crosse of Iverey / Item a pax of Ihesus of Marie of petie / Item
ij pagiont Clothes of the passion / Item a frontelett of blewe
velvett / Item a vestement of blewe ⟨...⟩ed with R & I of gold Item
ij great standerdes of Candelstickes of latten / Item a peire of   20
Auter Clothes of Cristmas Item Cloithe of the liff of seynt
Thomas / Item v pencelles of blewe with Cuppes of golde / Item
a vestement of blewe satten of the gift of Sir Roger Cou⟨.⟩he with
albe & Amyse of the same / Item a Rede vestement of Satten of
the gift of Sir Iohn Elligge with albe Amyse & Stole of the same /   25
Item a Corporas of blake velvett of the gift of my ladie Marler /
Item ij Auter Clothes of diaper / Item a pece of Cloith of golde in
a box / Item a frontelett of silke & golde with pecockes

St Mary's Cathedral: Inventory BL: Egerton 2603 no. 17   30
ff 26-7

The Inventorie of All maner of Reliqes conteynyd | in the
Cathedrall Churche of Coventrie //
ffirst A shryne of Saynt Osborne of Copper and gylte   35
Saynt Osbornes hedde Closyd in Copper and gylt
A parte of the hollye Crosse in Syluer and gylt
A Reliqe of [Saynt] Thomas of Canterburie / parte syluer &
parte Copper
A pece of Owre ladyes Tombe / Closyd in Copper   40
A Relyquie of Saynt Ciscilies foote / parte syluer and parte
Copper

A Crosse with A Relyquie of Saynte Iames / Syluer & gylt & set
with stones
An Image of Saynt [Iorge] George with a bone of his in his
shelde Syluer
An Arme of Saynt Iustyne in Syluer   5
An Arme of Saynt Ierome in Syluer
An Arme of Saynt Augustyne in Syluer
A Reliquie of Saynt Androwe in Copper and gylt
A Ribbe of Saynt lawrence in Syluer
An arme of Saynt Sylvyne in Syluer   10
A Image of on of the chylderne of Israell of Syluer
A smale shryne of the Appostells of Copper and gylt
A Reliquie of Saynt kateryn / in Copper
A barrell of Reliqes of Confessors / of Copper
A Reliqe of the thre kynges of Colleyne of Copper   15
iiij lyttell Crosses of Copper
ij Bagges of Reliquies
Owre ladies mylke in Syluer and gylt

  °And among thees reliqies your lordeshipp shall fynde a   20
  peece of the most holy iawe bone of the asse that kyllyd
  Abell with dyuers like |
  (endorsed)
  Reliquies in the Priorye of Coventre
  notatu dignum °   25
  °Inuentarum Reliquarum ecclesie monachorum Coventrie°

1573
Inventory of Edmund Brownell Lichfield Joint Record Office: B/C/11
(6 April probated)   30
  ...

In Apparrell

In primis, one skarlet gowne, with a velvet typpett	vij li.	
Item, ij gownes faced with foynes, edged with velvet	vj li.	
Item, one gowne faced with damaske, edged with velvet	iij li.	35
Item, one workday gowne, & a nyght gowne	xxx s.	
Item, one velvett coate withe sleves, & la(.)ed on wythe		
double-lace	vj li.	
Item, one sleveles coate of velvett	xl s.	
Item, one damas cassock, garded with velvet, one		40
kassocke of grograyne chamlett, edged with frynge,	iiij li.	
one kassock of worsted edged with velvett		

Item, one damask coate *with* chamlett sleves   xxvj s viij d
Item ij cloth coat*es* layd on *with* lace, & one fryse coate   xxx s
Item iij Cloakes, ij dublett*es* sleved *with* satten   v li.
Itt*em*, iiij payre of hose, vj shyrtes, ij cappes, ij hatt*es*, ij velvet
nyghtcaps, & one satten nyghtcapp.   iij li. x s   5
...

Holy Trinity Churchwardens' Accounts

The earliest surviving records of this church — a miscellaneous collection of memoranda, parts of accounts, excerpts from deeds, etc (the earliest of which is dated 1463) — are kept with the later records of the church in Coventry. The present incumbent, the Reverend N.D.B. Abbott, has arranged for a microfilm of the book to be held at the Warwick County Record Office (DR 302). The earliest complete churchwardens' accounts are kept in the same office and comprise accounts for 1559-61, 1565-6, 1570-7, 1580-4, not in exact chronological order and on unnumbered folios. The volume also contains the accounts for 1638 and some random notes of expenses for 1553 (DR 581/45). As these volumes are all that remain of the record books of either Holy Trinity or St Michael's churches, the two parish churches of Coventry, a few extracts concerned with liturgical processional have been transcribed, as well as those illustrating the activities of the waits and the sale of vestments after the Reformation — both of the latter having possible connections with the playing of the pageants.

Waits

Three of the city waits were also clerks at Holy Trinity. In 1573, a marginal note concerning 'Clarkes wages' names '⟨.⟩ Sadler vj li. Thomas nycholas vj li. Stiffe iiij li.' (Warwick County Record Office: DR 581/45, f 42). These are all familiar names from other civic and guild records (see pp 243, 251). In 1577, they are entered in more regularly (f 91v):

> Clarkes wages
> Payd to Richard Sadler ffor a yeare   vj li
> Payd to Thomas Nycolas ffor a yeare   vj li
> Payd to Goodman styffe ffor a yeare   iiij li vj s viij d
> ...

In 1581, Richard Sadler died and his place was taken by Antony Stiff who had been a city wait since at least 1573: 'Anthony Stiffe to haue by yere iiij li. & Enteringe att migellmus anno 1581' (f 101).

The first of two undated fragments in DR 302 (f 32v) records annual payments of
£5 to Richard Stiff and £4 to Antony Stiff. If Antony's appearance dates this as
post 1581, there remains the puzzle of Richard not having been heard of since payment as a wait in 1568 (p 243). He may well be a 'new' Richard, and one more of
this musical family led by 'goodman' Stiff. A second undated extract from an account
shows the clerks being paid by instalments of twenty shillings each at Easter, Midsummer, Michaelmas, and one later unnamed time. William heads this list of quarterage payments with an extra one of twenty shillings made on 3 February (f 33v).

Among the payments of the Trinity guild to Bablake College in 1545 are eight for
'Two Clerks for singing there 4l. each' and 'Two Boys singing 20s, each per annum'
(Sharp, *Illustrative Papers*, 135). A payment for what are probably similar services is
recorded by the pittancer of St Mary's Cathedral and Priory in his accounts for 1505-6:
'Item *pro* ministrilis *pro termi*nis ix li ij s' (BRL: 168235).

Church Vestments and Furnishings

The following is a list of vestments and decorations sold by the church in 1547
(Warwick County Record Office: TD 74/22, f 13):

Sold they vj day of Ieneuere

v cops of red teyssew to Mr raghers now mayre Mr semand parkar		
Mr Ihon tallane Mr Ihon harford Mr Thomas Whettley pryes of		
ye sayd v copes	x li.	
Item to Mr Damport & Ihon West ij other copes of red		5
tessew	iij li. vj s viij d	
Mr Ieyner a cope of red velvet	xxxiij s iiij d	
Mr schewyll a grene velvet cope	xxx s	
to bawde dosseld on cope of red velvet	v li.	
Mr smythe ventener iiij cops of Whyt damaske pry*ces*	v li. x s	10
Thomas kyrven ij olde copes pry*ces*	xxxiij s iiij d	
Ihon snayde & Thomas sandars ij blew copes pry*ces*	xxxvj s iiij d	
symon cowten a Whyt cope	x s	
bawden doseld ij olde copes	x s	
Mr 'Iamys' roghers on banar clothe	v s	15
Thomas owrre on banarclothe	ij s	
Mr harford one banarcloth	xvj d	
Rychard nonde on streme*r*	xx d	

The Smiths, in 1544, bought a 'bysschops taberd of scarlet ... in the trenete church'
(see p 170). After the brief resurgence of Roman Catholicism, the church once more
had to sell its ornaments and change its furniture. Sharp's untraceable MS annal puts
the matter thus: 'This year Mass was put down, all Images and Popish reliques beaten

down and burnt in open streets; the Gospel preached freely' (*Illustrative Papers*, 120). The churchwardens' accounts handed down in 1560 and covering the year beginning at Easter 1559 include the following items (DR 581/45):

f 8v

...

R*e*seyv*y*d for iij pyllar*es* & þe crosse þ*at* þe rode was on	ij s
R*e*seyv*y*d for þe vayle	v s
R*e*seyv*y*d for þe thyng þ*at* þe sacrament was in over þe awter	xij d
R*e*seyv*y*d for a pese of wode	iij d
R*e*seyv*y*d for a heyre þ*at* vppon þe awter	v d
R*e*seyv*y*d for wod sold at holbrokes	iij li.
R*e*seyv*y*d of M*a*ste*r* meyr for a bell Rope	viij d
R*e*seyv*y*d of Wyll*i*am Ioyner for bell Rope	viij d
R*e*seyv*y*d of Wyll*i*am ko[w]k for yerd of bellrop	iiij d

5

10

...

f 10   15

...

Ite*m* payd for beryng of þe Crose & banner*es* of pawmsonday   vj d

...

Ite*m* payd for beryng þe Crosse & banner & stremer*es* vppon
saynt markes day & saynt gorges day   viij d   20

...

Ite*m* payd for beryng þe Crose & banners in Crose wyke   viij d

...

Ite*m* payd for beryng þe Crose banner*es* & stremer*es* on holy
thorsday & wyt sonday   x d   25

...

f 10v

...

Ite*m* payd for a pro clamacion & a pro cession boke   iiij d   30
Ite*m* payd for takyng down þe rode & marie & Ihon   iiij s iiij d

...

Ite*m* payd to Rychard lynse þe organpleer for his Ernst   j d

...

35

f 11

...

Ite*m* spent at Mr smythes at þe selle of þe gere of Iesus

chappell   iij s vj d

...

Item payd to thomas wotton for pryckyng songes for þe
churche   viij d

...   5

Item payd to lynse for mendyng of þe organes   ij s iiij d

...

f 11v

...   10

Item payd for carriyng in þe organes in to Iesus chapell   iiij d

...

Item spent at Mr smythes at þe sellyng of þe plate & cappe &
vest mentes   xij s xj d

...   15

It is worth remarking that in 1563 the Dyers paid five shillings to 'lynsey for the
hartte' (p 225); it is not an uncommon name, but where so few occur such a conjunction is interesting.

Two final notes mark the two sides of cheerful entertainment associated with the
church. The seventh charge in directions 'To the curate and Churchewardens of the
trynytie parishe in Coventre' is 'Item chardge to be gyven to the curate and churche
wardens that in the tyme of Dyvyne service no dawnsinge singinge playinge nor
pastaunce be kepte' (Warwick County Record Office: TD 74/22 f 4). Also, at the end
of three pages of the most detailed accounting for bell-ringing that I have seen in
Coventry's records, for the year 1620, is entered 'ffor. iiij. peales rong on pleasure
the vij[th] of Aprill in the mornig vpon Wagers (blank)' (Warwick County Record
Office: DR 581/46).

APPENDIX 6
Thomas Massey

It is no surprise that the name of Thomas Massey, as a master upholsterer from his admittance into the Mercers' company on 6 December 1576 until he drops out of sight in 1624, appears frequently in guild (and civic) records.* From what is known of his father, Robert Massey, it is no more surprising that many of these appearances are because of fines for non-attendance at guild meetings, his refusal over the years to pay rents, and his battle in the cause of civic religious drama.

He was born c 1556, the eldest of four sons and seven daughters. His father was a prosperous, if cantankerous, upholsterer: the inventory of his household goods, taken 22 May 1576, valued them at £66 13s (his will is at the Staffordshire County Record Office, Lichfield). The Mercers' Account Book (CRO: Acc 15) records that Robert Massey was one of twelve men 'Apoynted to take order in all Suche matteres that belongeth to owr company ffor this yere to the natyvite of ower Lord god Anno 1563' (f 4 col a). Nonetheless, on 14 November 1562 an order 'ffor the Appesing of all controversy And stryfe betwixt Robard massy and Randall ffolled his sarvand' was made: each was fined one shilling and, if the strife broke out again, each was to be fined twenty shillings, no matter who started the argument. A year later, on 16 November 1563, 'Controversies & varyans' broke out again and the two men 'vsed themselues to their reproche & molestacion of all the holle Company' (f 6). Massey was fined ten shillings, Randall Lloyd twenty shillings. Thomas carried on in this mode but was more successful in evading fines: 'Received of thomas massie for A fyne he beinge fyned at xx s for Contempt to the maister xvj d beinge by peticion to the Companye Release the Rest' (f 57, 1592).

Thomas Massey's skill was never in question; he worked for his own guild in 1605-6 (Mercers' Account Book, f 96) and 1607-8 (f 99v), for the Drapers in 1588 (Drapers' Accounts, CRO: Acc 154, f 112), and several times for the council between 1589 (Chamberlains' and Wardens' Account Book II CRO: A 7 (b), p 181) and 1617 (p 611). Perhaps a little more frequently than most, he missed company meetings; nonetheless, he rose slowly through the ranks of his powerful guild. In 1592-3, he was fourth master (f 40), in 1598-9 third master (f 78v), and in 1605-6 second master (f 95). More significantly, despite his seniority, age, and undoubted skill, he never became master of his company.

Native argumentativeness did not help his cause. On 3 September 1603, although 'contryverses' between himself and Thomas Saunders were concluded in his favour, at the same time 'A fetherbed of thomas Masseyes taken for A distres which vppon his submyssion was deliuered him agayne' (Mercers' Minute Book (1602-1760), CRO: A 100, f 28v). On the death of his father, Massey inherited property called Whaberley's ground on which twelve years rent was owing (Cheylesmore Manor Account Book, CRO: A 9, p 92). Massey maintained his father's intransigence; in 1599 the bailiff is still marking the rent as uncollected. In 1593, Massey added to the bailiff's misery: among 'Rentes not Receivid' is 'ij s for a Cheiffe rent out of a tenement in hey lane which Thomas massie shold paye & Refuseth to paye it' (p 174).* The rent is still being sought vainly in 1599 (p 208).

Massey's contentious obstinacy seems to have been translated into a more single-minded forcefulness where dramatic art was concerned. Clearly he had a passion for the theatre and found there a perfect outlet for his energies. The only record of his participation in civic drama before 1579 is his provision of 'a trwse for Judas' for the Smiths in 1578 (p 289). The Mercers' Account Book, however, begins in 1579 with only a summary account of pageant expenses, but it is unlikely that so 'theatrical' a man as Massey did not have a hand in his own guild's pageant. His interest in props carried over into 1584 when the Mercers gave him 16d for unspecified purposes (p 306), while he continued to aid the Smiths and received three shillings for 'the Temple and for his beardes' (p 309).

By the time of the 1591 plays, however, Massey had obviously consolidated his position as the man to manage civic drama. The Cappers (p 333), Drapers (p 335), and Mercers (p 333) handed him their levies toward the production of the play. The Weavers (p 334) and the Smiths (p 335) gave theirs directly to the mayor. There is no explanation given for this division. The Wardens made a separate contribution of twenty shillings 'To Thomas massie & his parteners' (p 332). The wording of this, when compared with that of similar awards of twenty shillings made in 1593 (p 338), 1594 (p 341), and 1596 (p 346) for Massey and William Showell to arrange the celebrations of the Queen's holiday, suggests that its purpose was the same. This event may have been celebrated more frequently, such is the tolerant manner in which civic events are sometimes recorded, and Massey may have devised more entertainments than we know.

It was Massey's misfortune that he was born just too late and that there were not enough civic pageants and plays with which to occupy himself. His bold solution was to make up his own plays and cast royalty, the nobility, and the leaders of Coventry government in leading roles. Civic drama itself was to be a play within this play. To this end, he proposed to use the excuse of the king's holiday, to be associated in the citizens' minds, presumably, with the celebrations he had directed for Queen Elizabeth's day. The ensuing entanglement was fought out for over seven years. The city's case is presented in the following document (BL: Add MS 43645 ff 88-8v*):

...

In March 1603 Thomas Massie intimated to the Maior and his
brethren then in Councell, that his intent was to make a Shew
vppon the King*es* Daie, and to that purpose Craued allowance,
who receiued answere thence, that such toyes (as he would sett   5
abroch) deserued noe Contribucion. But seconding his request,
and makeing offerr to perform yt vppon his own Charges (so that
[m] there might be onely approbac*i*on of the House) his Proiect
and Speaches were referred to the view of two Preachers; who
mislyking many thing*es* both in Subiect and forme, there was an   10
order prescribed for his proceeding, and he confined in his
Shews. After wh*i*ch tyme of limitac*i*on we heard nothing of his
determinac*i*on to goe forward vntill there was notice giuen by the
sayd Massie that he had beene w*i*th Lord Harrington to make his
L*ordship* acquainted w*i*th his Deuises, & by his L*ordships*   15
mediac*i*on to entreat the Lady Elizabeth her grace together w*i*th
her Traine to Come to Couentry to see them w*i*thin two daies
after. Wh*i*ch sudden and vnexpected report of the presence of so
great personages Could not but yeeld great Discontent to the
said Maior and his brethren, then vnprouided to giue such   20
entertainment as was fitting such estat*es*. Whereuppon the said
Maior and his brethren sent to the Lord Harrington to know if
there were anie such resolution, and receiued answere that
there was noe such intenc*i*on [at all] , his L*ordship* not hauing so
much as heard of any such matter, nor had any Conference w*i*th   25
Massie at all. So that vppon Massie his vntrue report, ⌈a⌉
Commaund was giuen him, that he should not make any further
progresse till he heard from them: after wh*i*ch tyme he Came noe
more to them. But afterward*es* abusing the Preachers for Censuring
his Deuises, and beeing vppon their iust Complaint Conuented   30
before the Maior and his brethren for the same, he returned
ansuere that yf it were for any such matter wh*i*ch did Concern
the Preachers, he would not Come, but rather haue it heard where
he might haue iustice. But beeing sent for the second tyme he
Came, and beeing Demaunded the reason of his abuse toward*es*   35
the Preachers, said he would not tell them the Cause, they replying
and asking, whether he thought he should not be heard
indifferently there, answeared, noe, and that he looked for noe
iustice at their hand*es*, but affirmed that he would haue his Causes
heard where he should haue iustice, and where he should stand   40
w*i*th his hatt on his head, and they stand by him bareheaded.

Which Mr Clark and Mr Touy then present and hearing said, lett him Complaine, when he will, Shame shall be his reward, Massie presently answearing, Shame on their faces, telling Mr Clark also at the same tyme, that he was a better man then Mr Clark out of Couentry, spitefully and falsly obiecting to him, that he was but   5
a Milners Sonn, and that his Pedigree Came out of the Tole-dish. At which tyme a Magistrate standing by & distasting these speaches sayd, that his Comparison was odious, the said Massie replying, that there was noe more Comparison between Mr Clark and him, then between a Custard and a Dunghill. ffurther at that tyme after   10
Mr Touy had shewed Massie his abuses towardes him, and hauing ended his speach was by the Maior wished to putt on his hatt, and sytt down, Massie hereat discontent, bidd Mr Touy Come stand by him with his hatt in his hand. ffor he would hereafter be heard, where Mr Touy should stand bare and he him self be | 15
Couered. Moreouer Massie beeing then taxed for wrong done to other Magistrats said that their Mayraltys finished, they were noe more Magistrates but Commoners as him self, and that his Ancestors kept as good men for their dogg-keepers as they were. ffor these before inserted and such other lawlesse and vnreuerent   20
speaches to the Maior, Iustices, and other their brethren of the Councell of the Cytie, the said Massie was by a generall and vniform Consent Committed to warde with this tender of fauour nothwithstanding to be presently deliuered putting in security for his good behauiour, who Denyed absolutely so to doe, but   25
some of his frendes earnestly labouring to haue him released, the Maior answeared them, that yf Massie would come to him and Confesse his fault and liue in peace, he should be released, and so his frendes vndertakeing so much in his Cause, he was deliuerd vppon promise to Come in againe, but after by this means he   30
once got loose he refused euer after to return to the Maior, but kept his house continually.

Besydes all this the said Massie in Conference with one William Tunckes a Gold-smith in Couentry (who hath subscribed yt)   35
spake these or the like wordes ensuing, *videlicet* that after he had finished his Suite then in hand, meaning by the Circumstance of his wordes then vsed those which he had with Mr Clark and Mr Page, he would Commence a new suite against Dick Page, for his promise of Charges Concerning his Paieant.   40

Massie beeing before the Councell the twentyth of october

1610 beeing denyed to haue a Coppie of these his misdeameanors, said there was never such oppression offred to any man.

In his reply (BL: Add MS 43645 f 86*), Massey craves pardon lest he is tedious. His vigour prevents tedium but it also rushes him out of immediate clarity at times. He speaks with angry familiarity of matters that cannot now be easily understood. However, it is the voice of an individual, of a tempestuous character in his own large play. He addresses himself 'To the right Worshipfull Master Maior and the rest of his Bretheren':

...

In all humblenes sheweth and beseecheth you and the rest of this
Worshipfull assembly. That whereas your poore supplyant
Thomas Massei. When Mr Page was Maior: At Coventrie first
ffayre, your supplyant was sent for to the Parlour where he   5
∧ 'was' caviled wthall by Mr: Roger Clarke before Master Maior
and vj others and for that he spake the truthe to Mr: Clarke, he
was comytted to prison for xv: dayes amongst them that had the
Plague, & must not come out, vnles he would be bound to the
Good behauiour, or yeild hymself in a faulte, or saye, he was   10
sorry he offended, or wryte .2. or .3. wordes of Submission, or
send neighbors, & frendes to intreate for hym, or send to some of
them that consented to his imprisonement. And whereas he was
thus imprisoned for speaking the truthe. Mr: Clarke said, Massei
should be punisht, and punisht. then your Supplyant said to Mr: 15
Clarke, Out of Coventrie he was a better man then he for he was
a braunche of the Baronry, and knighthood of Masseyes Dunham
in Chesire, and Mr: Clarke was a braunche of the Toledishe of
Darlyson, in Shropshire: saith one, Comparisons be odious. True,
said I, to compare a Custard and a Dunghill togeather. This was   20
the cause of xv. daies imprisonement. But Mr: Clarke that sett
the Cyttie on an Vproare when he was Maior, had nothing said,
nor don vnto hym. ffor said Mr: Page, if I lett hym out, wthout
yeelding vs some of these matters, Massei might bring his Accion
of faulse inprisonement against me: being nothing yeilded vnto,   25
at the xv: dayes end I was thrust out of prison by violence of the
Gaolers. Wherevppon by advyse of Councell: I put Mr: Page (and
those .vj. that consented to my faulse inprisonement) in suite;
where some of them, in the name of the rest, submitted themselves
to the Censure of the reverend Iudg Warbarton: who vndertooke   30

to order me. They had informed the Iudg of what they list, to
obscure the right of my cause, from Iudiciall hearing in locall
place, made so light matter of so waighty a cause. That he awarded
I should haue vj li. xiij s iiij d towardes my charges to surcease
following my vij. Accions in suite: and the monney I had of the   5
reverend Iudge to end all those vij. matters in question. The
monney was the Comon stocke monney. Mr: Thomas Prichard
had better then .xx. Markes for one dayes Imprisonement by Mr:
christofer Davenport. I did never tell the Iudge. how Mr. Page
Maior did threaten to clapp me by the heeles, yf I did showe any   10
thing for the honour of the Kinges Maiestie: Neither told I the
Iudge; how this Mr: Page Maior, did buffit me wth both his clutch
ffists, manny blowes; and spitt filthily in my face, for telling hym,
I heard saye. The Lady Elizabeths grace, was desyrous to see
Coventrie. About .2. or .3. yeares after, It pleased the reverend   15
Iudg to wryte his frendly lettere from Nottingham dated the ffirst
of August. 1612 to meete hym at his howse at Grafton, wch was
accomplished. where the good Iudg over ruled me: to forbeare a
tyme, and not to sue Mr. Clarke, for publishing manny slaunders
against me, and could proove nothing. Where I toulde hym, what   20
I did for the honour of the Kinges Maiestie, by the consent of Mr
Page Maior, and his Bretheren. I then willed hym not to over rule
me in that nor no such matters, wch he promysed me, he would
not, but would do me any good. and did send his frendly letteres
to Mr: Hopkins Maior, and one to Mr: Breres. That I might haue   25
a competent Summ towards my charges. Mr: Willington, had .2.
or .3. bills of the same. whereas some say, The Iudg ended the
matters he never heard of. I agreed to the vij Accions in question,
and no more. Nor will I not sell threatening to be clapt by the
heeles, yf I did any thing in showe, for the honour of the Kinges   30
Maiestie. Nor sell buffetting about the Eares, for telling the Maior,
I heard saye The Ladie Elizabeths grace, was desyrous to see
Coventrie: Nor I did sell vij Accions of faulse Imprisonement,
Lx li. an Accion Neither did I sell xxij li. charges I was at for the
honour of the Kings Maiestie: I did not sell, All these things for   35
vj li. xiij s iiij d of the Comon stockemonney. I cannot, neither
will afforde any such Large pennyworthes, besides manny
Iniuryes don me, one in anothers necke (to be seene at Large). In
the tyme of this faulse inprisonement. Paul Emmarson was
suffered to arrest me for iiij li. of Mr: Haddons monneye. the said   40
Emarson was but suretie for . wth many other Iniuryes putt
vppon me, most vnchristianly and vnneighbourly. In Love, I

comytt this vnto you, rather then els where, to haue yt shewed
to men of Estate. I desyre to be paid my charg*es* I was at for the
hono*u*r of the King*es* Ma*i*estie by the consent of the Maior and
his Bretheren, and for forbearing of the same. The charge came
neere to xxij li. I haue borne it long, and haue ben kepte from yt;   5
and I hope I shall not Loose yt. And whereas Mr Henry Sewall
saith, the reverend Iudge Warbarton ended all matters. | the simple
know, an vnlikly thing. That he would take from me aboue v .C.
li. was in suite, and most likly to be recovered, and neere xxij li.
borne long he never heard of till afterward*es*, nor other wrong*es*   10
don me faulsly, as aforesaid. It was not his meaning that for vj li.
xiij s iiij d of the Comon stocke monney, to leaue me in yo*u*r
debte: He agreed not, neither haue I consented thereto, nor will.
I think the good reverend Iudg his true meaning was not to haue
 ⌃ ⌈me⌉ Iniured any waye. But if all matters be ended, Lett me   15
haue my Bond vp for the .x.li. of the .3. yeares monney, and my
bond of iiij li. I am suertie for, for Leonard Browne. I am but
suerty for it, and the monney I paied for suertishipp, those
Bonds vp, (all but a poore satisfac*c*ion to me) that it maye be
found All matters are ended. And for the xx. li. I paid twyce, (or   20
my monney for for bearing of the same so lonng) I had but .x.li.
of yt for iiij*or*. yeares: the rest was stopt, for Iohn Showells debte:
but yf the Truthe might haue ben suffered to appeare, It would
haue ben founde. whether I had faulse imprisonement, &
extor*c*ion, & Iniustice, & periurye exacted vppon me: or not, and   25
other wise wronged, and gaulled & wronged. If I had tryall, or
my cause heard Iudicially, or otherwise, I should haue ben better
righted, and satisfied, wth good content for other matters given
me wth love yet I do expecte to be well dealt wthal, and good
content. and all disgrace you could impose vppon mee to   30
discreddit me you haue given me, to be seene. Thus craving p*ar*don,
yf I be tedious vnto you.

There is no account of the final outcome of this matter, but Massey's opponents
were powerful. Their consternation at learning of the imminent arrival of Princess
Elizabeth, her guardian Lord Harington, and her retinue, with or without the prospect of some grandiose pageantry welcome, is easily understood. It would be very
interesting to know the extent of Massey's preparations. He claimed the generous
sum of £22 for the preparations that he put in suit: Judge Warburton was sufficiently

21 / b *of* bearing *written over* f

impressed to award him £6 13s 4d, more in damages perhaps than as an indication of the actual outlay of £22 by Massey on the proposed entertainment. Certainly the entertainment was sufficiently far forward for it to be examined by 'two Preachers' who condemned it; one is reminded of Captain Cox's complaint about 'Preacherz ... sumwhat too sour in preaching awey theyr pastime' (p 273).

What is just as surprising is that some forms of civic play-making might have continued during this fracas. Inevitably, Massey again figured largely; so did the Weavers who had kept their pageant costumes. Massey hired them in 1606 for what play, show, or purpose is not revealed. The occasional payment to him for some guild or civic purpose akin to the royal celebration days still occurred: in 1602, the Mercers grant him twenty shillings 'at the comandment of the companie' (f 90); the Weavers turned to him again on 'fayre day', 1612 (f 108v). The last payment to him made by the Mercers might be to do with such matters: five shillings 'which he leiyd out for the good of the Company' (f 125v). This is a formula which often takes its meaning from its context and the man to whom it is paid. Cushions or drama are Massey's first contexts, although this might not always have been his own order of precedence.

He last appears in the city's records in 1624 when, in his late sixties, his name is written, without any mark against it, in a 'Book of loans and Charity moneys &c' (CRO: A 12) in connection with Haddon's loan money, £20 of which he had contracted to repay in instalments of four each Michaelmas from 1617 on (Miscellaneous Papers, Book of Debts, Rentals, &c, vol I: CRO: A 8, f 38v). If Massey survived to the accession of Charles I (27 March 1625), he would have been a Caroline producer of that drama which we call 'medieval'.

APPENDIX 7

Feasts

Guild and civic accounts contain many lists of detailed costs for grand dinners. Two are given here by way of example. That of the Drapers is for their annual guild dinner of 1560; the costs of the individual items, as well as of the whole dinner, give one measure of comparison against which the expenses of the Corpus Christi play may be set. The second is that given when Princess Elizabeth came to Coventry, on the visit which Thomas Massey took such pains to celebrate with some kind of dramatic entertainment.

    1560

A   *Drapers' Accounts* CRO: Acc 154
    ff 45-6

    ...

paymentes for dyner		5
payd for iij g q d of coles	iij s vj d	
payd for a lod wod	ij s iiij d	
payd for iij stryk wheat	vj s	
payd for gryndyng & bultyng the wheat	vj d ob	
payd for swanes	xvj s	10
payd for a sester of all	iiij s vj d	
payd for a sester of beare	iiij s	
payd for a sester of ij shyllyng all	xij d	
payd for iij wod cakes	xviij d	
payd for xvj cepell cones	x s	15
payd for meat for the ketchen folk	xij d	
payd for eages	xxij d ob	
payd for butter vj quartes	iiij s	
payd for creme	iiij s ij d	
payd for ges	xj s	20

    6 / g *an error*; q *for* quarter, d *for* dimidium

payd for capones	viij s iij d
payd for gyntys of byffe	xij s iiij d
payd for iij leges of weale	ij s ij d
payd for more flower	v d
payd for salt	ij d ob 5
payd for hotmell	ob
payd for water	vj d
payd for vynnyger	iij d
payd for swthe	ij s viij d
payd for systs for the supper	x d 10
payd for holy & yue	j d
payd for the gyantes wyffe standyng	ij d
payd for a powne hall candles	vj d
payd for to thrwstons	xij d
payd to reaner	viij d 15
payd to thomas hewes	vj d
payd to roo	vj d
payd to Iohn fasson	iiij d
payd to alls	vj d
payd myllnar the coke	v s 20
payd to hym for a strener	iij d
payd to hym for conyskynes	xij d
payd for the hall vesell	viij d
payd to poll	xviij d
payd to stomfore for iij ganes quartt wyn	iiij s iiij d 25
payd for a sesand	xvj d
payd for a partreg	xij d
payd for v dossen [potts] of brede	v s
payd for hyer ij dossen potts	iiij d
payd for hyer of ij dossen vessell	xvij d 30
payd to blower	xx s
payd for swypyng drapry	ij s viij d
payd for washyng alter cloths	xij d
payd for spysse for the dyner	xxix s ix d
sum of thys ys viij l xviij s iij d	35

...

26 / sesand *for* fesand?

1604
Chamberlains' and Wardens' Account Book II CRO: A 7(b)
pp 379-81
...

The Charges of the dynner at the Coming   5
of the princes Elizabeth the kinges dowghter

Paid for egges   viij s vij d
paid for Butter   xxviij s iiij d
paid for Capons & hennes   xl s j d
paid for Rushes   xx d   10
paid for iiij Duckes   ij s
paid for salt   xviij d
paid for pigeons   xvj s vj d
paid for Chickens   xxv s ij d ob.
paid for iij Salmons   xxxvj s   15
paid for a turbut ij skates & j stores   xvj s x d
paid for Sweping the hall & washing it   iij s viij d
paid for onyons   x d
paid for viij pigges   x s viij d
paid for washing the parlors & paynting the Chymney & freshing   20
the picktures   iij s viij d
paid for washing & paynting the nether parlor   v s
paid for making the Casement in the parlor   v s vj d
paid for flower & wheat   xv s
paid for wyne to Richard Dafforne   v li. xviij s   25
paid to william Showell for Apottell of Renyshe wyne   ij s |
Paid for xij quarters of Charcoles   xvij s
paid for xxxjᵗⁱ bittes of water   iij s viij d
paid for ale & beare   xxv s xj d
paid for grocerie ware   vj li. xiij s ob.   30
paid to the Ioyner for mending the wyndowes in the parlor ij s
paid for orrenges   iij s [⟨.⟩] iij d
paid maistris asheborne for wood   vij s
paid for Butcherie meat   vij li. iiij s j d
paid for apples   iiij s xj d   35
paid for Creame   viij s viij d
paid for ling & haberdyne to Edward walker   x s
paid for Rabittes   viij s vj d
paid for herbes & flowers   vij s iij d
paid for Rose water & perfumes   vj s ix d   40
paid for wyne viniger & other vineger   iiij s xj d
paid for bread   xxxj s

paid for wardens & Quynces   iiij s viij d
paid for Candles panchens & mustard   iiij s vij d
paid for neyles Rosen & otemell   iij d ob.
paid for hier of Roughe vessell & for vessell that was lost xv s j d
given to william muston for his paynes   ij s   5
paid to Thomas harryson for gylding and for goold   v s iiij d
paid to Iohn hawkes for workmanship   xviij d
                       To the Cookes
paid to mr hasselwood   xx s
paid to Edward Cartwright   x s   10
paid to phillipp Coke   xx s
paid to william Gibbes   x s
paid to Robert Cooper   x s
paid to Iohn lawnder   iij s iiij d
paid to harvie   v s   15
paid to Iohn hall   ij s
paid to ffoxe   ij s iiij d
paid to Iohn Chaundler   ij s
paid to hoaues for keping the ovens   xviij d
paid to Davie   ij s   20
paid to two women   ij s iiij d |
paid to heming   viij d
paid to ij women for skowring the peweter   iij s vij d
paid to foote for keping the dore   vj d
paid to ix turnespittes   ij s iiij d 25
paid to lavrance for vj dayes worke   ij s
                   Summa totall of
                              xliiij li. xij s.
                   this Charge
       ...   30

The Berkeleys and Caludon Castle

Caludon Castle was largely built and rebuilt from a surviving twelfth century manor house during the fourteenth century. Mowbray is reckoned to have prepared himself at Caludon for his aborted joust with Bolingbroke on Gosford Green in 1398. After the death of the last Mowbray, duke of Norfolk, the lords Berkeley inherited the castle through the descendants of Isabel, daughter of the first duke, who had married James, first Lord Berkeley, in 1424. After that the Berkeley name occasionally appears in Coventry's records.* Sharp (*Illustrative Papers,* 121) mentions, concerning Holy Trinity: '1583, Paid to William Randle's doughter for strawing herbs, to strawe the seate when my lord Barkley came to Mr. Maior's seat, to his Chaplen's sermon, ij d'.

Several members of the family were buried at Coventry. The Carpenters' Accounts for 1516 include: 'Item payd ffor the beryng off torchees ffor my lady barkeley ij d' (CRO: Acc 3/2, f 66v). Excerpts from the description of this funeral are included below (taken from Bliss Burbidge's *Old Coventry* where it is wrongly dated 1506). The Dyers' Accounts for 1528 mention: 'It resevyd at the beryng of my Ladye Barceley, v s.' (Bodl: MS Top. Warwickshire c.7, f 116). John Smyth of Nibley, for over forty years clerk and confidant to the family, provides the description of the grandiose funeral of Lady Berkeley in 1596. It is taken from *The Lives of the Berkeleys Lords of the Honour, Castle and Manor of Berkeley In the County of Gloucester From 1066 to 1618 ...,* Sir John Maclean (ed), vol 2 (Gloucester, 1883). I have included it as an exhibition of civic processional at a time when occasions for such display were rare, and as an example of solemn processional pageantry amid the many celebratory pageants in this collection.

> **1516**
> AC   *Lady Isabel Berkeley's Funeral* Burbidge: *Old Coventry*
>   pp 178-9
>
>   ... A curious MS. of one Thomas Try, described as "a special   5
>   officer and servant" of the Berkeleys, gives a highly interesting

account of the funeral of Isabel, Lady Berkeley, who died at
Coventry in 1506, at the age of seventy. Our worthy Thomas
addresses his narrative to Lady Berkeley's son, and I give it in his
own words.

"This bill bee delivered to his right worshipfull and special   5
maister, Sir Maurice Berkeley, knight; pleseth your good
mastership, the ordering at the interment of my Lady your
mother hereafter followeth:

(1) First, when I perceived she bygan to draw from this liff, I
caused certen priests to say divers orisions, and also to shewe hir   10
of the passion of Crist and of the merits of the same, wherunto
she gave merveluous goodly words, for after hir aneyling (extreme
unction) she came to good and perfect remembrance.

(2) Item, after she was departed I caused David Sawter (Psalms
of David) to bee said continually untill the day of her burying,   15
for as soon as oon company had seid, on other company of prests
bygan, and so she was watched with prayer continually fro
Wensday untill Monday.

(3) Item, ryngyng dayly with all the bells continually, that is
to say, at St. Mighells xxxiij peles, at Tryntye xxxiij peles, at St.   20
John's xxxiij peles, at Babylake because hit was so nygh hyr, lvij
peles, and in the Mother Church, the priorye, xxx peles and every
pele xijd.

(4) Item, upon sonnday when her horse letyr (litter) was
appeled, and wax and all other things redy, she was set forwards   25
after this maner.

(5) First, xxxti women of her levery in blake gownes and
kerechews upon their heds, of oon ele every kyrchew, which was
not furveled nether hemmed bycause they might be knowen lately
cut out of new cloth, and every woman beryng a tapyr of wax of   30
a LB wyght and a half.

(6) Item, after theym fowlowed xxxiij crafts with their lights
to the number of CC torches.

(7) Item, about hir horseleter was hir owne servants and others,
berynge torches of cleyne wax, to nomber of xxx in blake gownes.   35

(8) Item, the orders of freers wyght and gray, with their crosses,
next after the lyghts of the crafts.

(9) Item, prests to the nomber of oon C and more which went
with their crosses next before the hersse.

(10) Item, after the horseleter V gentylwomen morners.   40

(11) Item, after them *Master* Recorder and I, Mr. Bonde, and
my cozen Porter, ynstede of the xecutors and supervysors.

(12) Item, then *Master* Maire, the *Master* of the Yeld (Guild), Aldermans, Shreffs, Chamberlyns, and Wardens.

(13) And soe she was conveyed to the Mother Churche, the Priorye, wher she rested yn the quore byfore the high altar all that nyght, and had a solemn derege, and the Maire and his   5
Brethren went to St. Mighell, ther as was derege in like maner; and after the derege the Maire and his Brethren went into St. Mary hall, wher as a drynkyng was made for them; first cakys, comfetts, and ale; the second course marmelet, Snoket, redd wyne and claret; and the 3rd course wafers and Blanch powder   10
with romney and muskadele; and I thank God that noe plate ne spoones was lost, yet ther was xxti dozen spoones.

(14) Upon Monday she sate forward after Mase with the said lyghts and crafts, the seyd V morners rydyng in sedsaddells and ther horses traped with blake, *Master* Recorder and I, Mr. Bonde   15
and Porter rydyng after theym, and then *Master* Maire, Aldermen, Sherifis, Wardens, and Chamberlyns rydyng in like order as they were; and at Binley Brygge met my Lord the Abbot of Combe with his mitre sensyng the herse, and in his company Mr. Broune, Mr. Bowghton, and many other ye may be sure, to the nomber of   20
V or VI thosand pepull: I am of a suerty ther was at every syttyng above xixx or xijxx messes, and the bordes was divers times sett, and Thomas Berkeleis prest say the orderyng of all. Wyrten at Caloughdon the xvj day of Aprle. Your servant, Thomas Try."

...   25

1596
AC *Funeral of Lady Katharine Berkeley*
John Smyth: *The Lives of the Berkeleys*, vol 2
pp 388-91   30
...

A Declaration of the funerall of the lady Katharine Berkeley, as it was performed on Thursday the 20th. of May, 1596. being Ascension day.

Her Corps having continued at Callowdon in the Chamber   35
where shee dyed, honored with all accustomed Ceremonies aswell by night as by day, from wednesday the 7th. of Aprill before, on which day shee dyed, untill the second evening before the funerall, when the Coffin with her whole body inclosed was privately by persons of good quallity conveyed by night to Coventry to the   40
house of Sampson Hopkins in the end of Earles Street; where honored with like ceremonies, it continued untill the funerall

houre, which was in manner following.

The wholl traine being, as travellers from Callowdon and other
places, assembled by ten of the clock in the forenoon, were by
Garter king at Armes and Chester herauld, set in order and
directed thus to proceed from the said house to the Church of St.   5
Michaell, in this manner.

ffirst went six of your principall yeomen called the conductors
of the traine, in longe black clokes, with black staves in their
hands, directed to conduct the traine all the length of that street,
to the Barre yates, and thence to crosse cheeping, and soe through   10
the north side of Trinity churchyard, to the great west doore of
St. Michaells church: Both sides of which passage neare a quarter
of a mile longe, was impaled by many thousands of people
assembled to behold the honor therof; Next after those six
conductors, in mourning gownes and Holland kercheefes, came   15
70 poore weomen; Then came thirty gentlemens servants in black
coats, Then followed the servants of gentlemen and Esquires in
black clokes; Next them the servants of knights in black clokes
also; Then came your Lordships yeomen, And after them your
gentlemen (all two by two) with some of the lady Stranges   20
gentlemen interplaced with them, yours being 74. whereof my
self went as one of her secretaries; Then the officers of your
houshold, as Clark of the kitchen, gentlemen of the horse,
Auditor, and Steward, in their gowns and hoods, your Steward
bearing a white rod in his hand: Next behind the Steward came   25
Mr. Henry Beamont bearing the great banner of honnor; After
him followed the Esquires and cheefe gentlemen of the Country,
as Mr. Clement ffisher, Mr. William Cotton, Mr. Elmes, Mr. ffulke
Butteris, |young Mr. Beamont, &c. Then came your Lordships
Chaplins, And after them, and next before the Coffin, went   30
Chester herald assisted by Mr. Walter Denis as a necessary marshall
to the better direction of the traine. The Coffin was borne by
eight of your cheife gentlemen and yeomen, and supported by
fower other gentlemen of most note; vizt. Mr. Edward Deveroux,
Sir John Spencer, Sir Thomas Leigh, and Mr. George Shirley your   35
son in law.

Neere to the fower corners whereof, went fower Esquirs vizt.,
Mr. Robert Spencer son and heire of the said Sir John, Mr. Basell
ffeilding of Newnham, Mr. Samuell Marrowe, and Mr. William
Norwood, each of them bearing a Baneroll, with her Armes and   40
your Lordships quartered.

Next behind the Coffin came Mr. Richard White as her

gentleman usher, with a small white rod in his hand, accompanied
with the gentleman usher of the lady Strange, both of them
bareheaded, between whom went Garter in his kingly Coate of
Armes.

Next after them came the lady Strange, eldest daughter to the   5
late Earle of Derby, and for this day principall mourneresse, in
her gown, mantle, trayne, hood, and tippet of blacke, and in her
parys head, tippet, wimple, vaile, and barbe of fine lawne; on
whose right hand went your son Sir Thomas Berkeley, and on her
left hand your brother in law Sir George Carey, supporting her   10
by the Armes, called the two principall assistants, who were
apparelled in their gowns, hoods and tippetts of finest black:
Then came Mrs. Audeley Denis bearing the trayne of the principall
mourneresse, apparalled as an Esquiresse in her gowne and lyned
hood of black, with a pleated kercheefe and barbe of lawne.   15

Then came Mrs. Elizabeth Berkeley your daughter in lawe, and
the lady Carey, side by side, apparelled as Baronesses, and in all
points sutable to the principall Mourneresse, save that their traines
were tucked up and not borne.

Then followed in semblable order Mrs. Deveroux and lady   20
Leigh, apparelled as knights wives, in their black gownes, hoods,
and tippetts, and in their round parys heads, boungrace, and
barbes of fine lawnes.

In answerable order, next came Mrs. Beomont and Mrs. Spencer
apparelled as knights wives like the former; which seaven were   25
called the seaven principall mourneresses and estates of the
funeralls. |

Next after whom in like correspondency, two by two, came
fower Esquiresses, vizt, Mrs. ffeilding, Mrs. ffisher, and her
daughter, and Mrs. Dilkes, apparelled as the trainbearer, save that   30
they wanted hoods.

Then followed your late ladys gentlemen, the principall
mourneresses two gentlewomen, knights and Esquires wives
gentlewomen, all like apparelled in black gownes, kercheefes, and
barbes of lawn, to the number of fourteen; And next after these   35
came eight Chambermaids, servants to the estates and ladies
aforesaid, in gowns and kercheifs of lawne only, All which were
furnished at the only charges of your Lordship.

After all these and last of all came Mr. Maior of Coventry, the
Sherriffs, Aldermen and Comons in great number, & great   40
proporcion.

In this order passed this traine with slow steps and frequent pauses to the church aforesaid, In the first Isle whereof stood the foresaid 70. poore weomen paling the passage on either side, through whom passed the whole action up to the east end of the church, where the pulpit was purposly placed, and also the hearse.

The 7. principall mourneresses were placed by Mr. Garter king   5
at Armes within the inward raile of the hearse with their faces towards the same; And the rest of the Gentlemen, ministers to the funerall, were placed in the utter railes about two yards distant from the Pall of the Coffin; All others in seats adjoyning.

The company thus placed, And the psalme ended, (which had   10
received the corse at the entrance into the Church,) your Chaplyn Edward Cowper ascended the pulpit, And towards the end of his learned sermon tooke a fit occation to speak of her learned and virtuous life, (a lady never known to dissemble or heard to swere, which speech (modestly carryed,) sealed also with the knowledge   15
of many hundreds there present,) wrought such effect, That seldom hath been beheld a more sorrowfull assembly at a subjects funerall, nor teares more droping down.

The sermon ended another psalme was begun, during which all such mourners as before are said to weare heads of lawne,   20
togeather with two assistants, walked in procession wise about the hearse: In which procession the waiting gentlewomen and chamber maids were severed from the rest, and aptly seated on one side of the Isle extending to the offertory, where they continued till all ceremonies were ended: I But all the rest by   25
their circuler walk were seated in their former places; which done, the offertory began, first by the principall mourneresse, and after by the other six each conducted by Mr. Garter. Then were the banners offered up by such as formerly I have noted to beare them; which finished, Mr. Berkeley your eldest son, was by Mr.   30
Garter led to the offertory and there by him invested with the honor of his deceased mother, by delivery and acceptance of the banners and other ceremonies; which done, and hee solemly conducted back to his former place, Then were next brought before the herse the two principall officers of the houshold, the   35
steward and gentleman usher, who after many obeysances and humble reverences, brake their rods, commending them to the custody of the corps and herse: which ceremony ended, the whole company arose, And in the order they came returned to Mr. Hopkins house aforesaid, and thence to Callowdon, where   40
your Lordship for them and many hundreds more had soe plentifully provided, That the excesse herein appeared, when

with suche dishes as for most part passed untouched at former
tables, more then one thousand poore people were plentifully
fed the same afternoone: And thus have you performed that part
of your late *lett*re to her brother the lord Henry Howard, That as
her life was honorable, soe you intended her funerall should bee.   5
Finis. Thus the paper I delivered to this lord.

   Her body was after interred in a vault in the northeast corner
of that Church neare the drapers Chappell there; And I think it
hardly possible to have all things better performed then were at
this funerall, and after at the feast, wherein noe error was by any   10
observed to bee committed, soe carefull were the servants of this
lord in their severall offices and charge committed to them; who
also for more comlines had attired themselves, the gentlemen in
black sattin suites and black silk stockings with gold chaynes
folded in black scarfes, And the yeomen in silk sashes, grograns,   15
and taffetyes, of black colours.
            Reliquit nomen, narrantur laudes.
            God graunt us all such race to runne,
            To end in Christ, as shee hath done.

APPENDIX 9
Jonson's *Masque of Owls*

Ben Jonson's *Masque of Owls* was performed before Prince Charles on 19 August 1624. It was 'Presented by the Ghost of Captaine *Coxe* mounted in his Hoby-horse.' Jonson sketches the historical setting for Cox's previous performance at Kenilworth and his connections with Coventry but, for a full appreciation of the masque, the prince and his court would have needed to know more of the occasion in 1575 than Jonson tells them (see pp 272-5).

Just over half of the masque's 180 lines are directly concerned with Cox, Coventry, Kenilworth, and 1575. The mechanism of the masque was the presentation of six owls, probably impersonated by 'rustic actors who danced out as Captain Cox sprung them one by one upon the company.... A second version of the description of the third Owl is given at the end, 166-79. Evidently Ben's satire on the "pure native Bird" and the Puritanism of Coventry (116-35) had to be suppressed for the performance, and he substituted the "Crop-eard Scrivener", characteristically restoring the original text in the manuscript left behind him for the printer' (C.H. Herford & Percy and Evelyn Smith [eds], *Ben Jonson*, vol 10 [Oxford, 1925-52], 700). The text below is quoted from *The Workes of Benjamin Jonson. The second Volume* (London: Richard Meighen, 1640), STC 14754.

pp 125-6*

THE MASQUE
OF
OWLES
AT
KENELWORTH.

Presented by the Ghost of Captaine *Coxe*
mounted in his Hoby-horse.
1626.

title / 1626 for 1624

CAP. COXE.

Roome, roome, for my Horse will wince,
If he come within so many yards of a Prinee,
And though he have not on his wings,
He will doe strange things.   5
He is the *Pegasus* that uses
To waite on *Warwick* Muses;
And on gaudy-dayes he paces
Before the *Coventrie* Graces;
For to tell you true, and in rime,   10
He was foald in Q. *Elizabeths* time,
When the great Earle of *Lester*
In this Castle did feast her.
   Now, I am not so stupid
To thinke, you thinke me a *Cupid*;   15
Or a *Mercurie*, that sit him:
Though these Cocks here would fit him.
But a spirit very civill,
Neither Poets God, nor Devill,
An old *Kenelworth* Fox,   20
The Ghost of Captaine *Cox*,
For which I am the bolder,
To weare a Cock on each shoulder.
   This Captaine *Cox*, by St. *Mary*,
Was at *Bullen* with King *Hary*;   25
And (if some doe not vary)
Had a goodly library,
By which he was discerned
To be one of the learned |
To entertaine the Queene here,   30
When last she was seene here.
And for the Towne of *Coventrie*
To act to her soveraigntie.
But so his lot fell out,
That serving then afoot,   35
And being a little man;
When the skirmish began

3 / Prinee *for* Prince

'Twixt the *Saxon*, and the *Dane*,
(For thence the storie was tane)
Hee was not so well seene   40
As he would have beene o' the Queene.
Though this sword were twice so long
As any mans else in the throng
And for his sake, the Play
Was call'd for the second day.   45
But he made a vow
(And he performes it now)
That were he alive, or dead,
Hereafter, it should never be sed
But *Cap. Cox* would serve on horse   50
For better or for worse,
If any Prince came hither.
     And his horse should have a feather
Nay, such a Prince it might be
Perhaps he should have three.   55
     Now, Sir (in your approach
The rumbling of your Coach
Awaking me, his Ghost)
I come to play your Host;
And feast your eyes and eares,   60
Neither with Dogs, nor Beares,
Though that have beene a fit
Of our maine-shire wit,
In times heretofore,
But now, we have got a little more.   65
     These then that we present
With a most loyall intent
And (as the Author saith)
No ill meaning to the Catholique faith,
Are not so much beasts, as Fowles,   70
But a very Nest of Owles,
And naturall, so thrive I,
I found them in the Ivy,
A thing, that though I blundred at,
It may in time be wondred at,   75
If the place but affords
Any store of lucky birds,
As I make 'em to flush
Each Owle out of his bush. |

pp 127-8

...

Hey, Owle third.

A pure native Bird
This, and though his hue
Be not *Coventrie*-blue,
Yet is he undone   120
By the thred he has spunne,
For since the wise towne
Has let the sports downe
Of May-games, and Morris,
For which he right sorry is: 125
Where their Maides,and their Makes,
At dancings, and Wakes,
Had their Napkins, and poses,
And the wipers for their noses. |
And their smocks all-be-wrought   130
With his thred which they bought,
It now lies on his hands,
And having neither wit, nor lands,
Is ready to hang, or choke him,
In a skeyne of that, that broke him.   135

...

The Troughton Drawings

Dr Nathaniel Troughton (1794-1868) left over a thousand drawings of Coventry. It was his habit to rise very early and walk about the city sketching what he saw. Much of the city was little changed from Tudor times when he did this in the middle of the nineteenth century, and thus he gives a very fair impression of Tudor Coventry. His chief imaginative drawings are of the supposed appearance of St Mary's Priory and Cathedral. One of these has been included in order to give an impression both of the style and dominating size of St Mary's, as well as of the impressive clerical heart of Coventry.

In present day Coventry, a museum of such ancient houses as have survived the years and the wars has been set up in Spon Street. In that street, some fifteenth century shops and other old buildings have been cleared of their later coverings and restored to their original condition. Other Tudor and Elizabethan houses of the few remaining in Coventry have been dismantled and re-erected there.

Jordan Well (west)

Greyfriars Lane

Little Park Street (north)

Cross Cheaping

Cathedral with Holy Trinity and St Michael's

Much Park Street (south)

Translations

The Latin documents have been translated as literally as possible in order to help the reader understand what the documents say. The arrangement of the translations parallels that of the text for the Records. Place names and Christian names have been normalized but not surnames. Capitalization and punctuation are in accordance with modern practice. As in the text, diamond brackets indicate obliterations and square brackets cancellations. Round brackets enclose words not in Latin but needed for grammatical sense in English.

1392

AC *St Mary's Priory: Cartulary* Sharp: *Dissertation*
p 8 fn m*

... "between the holding of the prior and convent on one side and the pageant house of the Drapers of Coventry on the other."

1407
Quitclaim I CRO: 184*
(3 February)

May all know by these present that I, John, the son and heir of Richard Clerk, merchant of Coventry, have remitted, released, and, for myself and my heirs in perpetuity, entirely quitclaimed to William Attilburgh, Richard Southam, senior, John Wymondeswold, John Onley, John Preston, and John Happesford all my right and claim which I had, have, or could have in some way in the future after the death of the aforesaid Richard my father, in all those messuages, lands, tenements, rents, reversions, and services, with all their appurtenances, which were Thomas Graunpe's in Much Park Street, in Coventry, and Biggen. Also, that I have remitted and quitclaimed for myself and my heirs to

the aforesaid William, Richard Southam ... John Happesford all
my right and claim which I had, have, or could have in some way
in the future after the death of the aforesaid Richard, my father,
in one grange with a garden adjoining, one cottage, two other
cottages, one pageant house in Hill Street which the masters of
the Whittawerscraft occupy, and two other cottages in the same
street of Hill Street which Thomas Penkeston occupies, one curtilage in the same street adjoined to the land of Richard Bykenhull,
one big field called Muryholt, another field called Chilternfeld,
another field called Chilternhull, and another field called Wyndennilnfeld, with appurtenances in Coventry. (And that) all the
aforesaid messuages, lands, tenements, rents, reversions, and
services with all their appurtenances, and also the aforesaid grange
with a garden adjoining, the cottages, curtilage, and fields with
(their) appurtenances are to be had and held by the aforesaid
William, Richard Southam, ... John Happesford, their heirs and
assigns, freely, quietly, well, and in peace, of the lords in chief of
that fee, by the service owed from it and customary according to
law in perpetuity, such that neither I, the aforesaid John, the son
and heir of the aforesaid Richard Clerk, nor my heirs, nor any
one else on my behalf nor in my name nor ours, can require or
claim in any way from now on any right or claim in all the aforesaid messuages, lands, tenements, rents, reversions, and services
with all their appurtenances and also in the aforesaid grange with
a garden adjoining, cottages, curtilage, and fields with appurtenances nor in any part of the same, but we are hereby excluded
in perpetuity by these present from every action of right or claim.
And I indeed, the aforesaid John, the son and heir of the aforesaid
Richard Clerk, and my heirs shall guarantee and defend in perpetuity by these present all the aforesaid messuages, lands, tenements, rents, reversions, and services with all their appurtenances,
and also the aforesaid grange with a garden adjoining, cottages,
curtilage, and fields with appurtenances to the aforesaid William,
Richard Southam, ... John Happesford, their heirs and assigns
against all people. In testimony of which I have put my seal to
this writing in three copies with these witnesses: John Botone,
then mayor of the city of Coventry; Robert Broddesworth and
Laurence Waldegrane, then bailiffs of the same city; John de
Barwe, John Scardeburgh, Nicholas Dudley, and others. Given at
Coventry on the Thursday next after the feast of the Purification
of the blessed Virgin Mary, in the eighth year of the reign of King
Henry the fourth after the Conquest.

1410-11
St Mary's Priory: Pittancer's Roll PRO: E 164/21
f 27*
...

Little Park Street in Coventry

The same John Preston holds by charter one tenement or four
cottages on the east side of Little Park Street, by the gift of
Thomas Marschall, mercer, until the end of his life. Their reversion
belongs to the office of the pittancer after the death of the said
John by the grant of the aforesaid Thomas. These cottages are in
fact worth 40s a year, as is set forth by the charter of the said
tenant, and they are to be held in mortmain by the king's licence
by William Suwet and Richard Blaby on behalf of the chantry of
the said Thomas and it (the tenement) is located between the
holding of the prior and convent which John Goate holds, belonging to the chantry of Sir Thomas Poley on the one side and the
pageant house of the Drapers of Coventry on the other, in breadth
and length according to the boundaries, etc.
...

1424
Leet Book I CRO: A 3(a)
f 27 *(24 October)*

For the Weavers

... Item, they have decided and ordered that the said journeymen
and each of them will pay to the said masters yearly in the future
4d for the benefit of the pageant of those same men and that the
journeymen themselves shall have drink or food with their masters
as they have been accustomed to do before ...

1434
Leet Book I CRO: A 3(a)
f 73* *(12 June)* *(Visit of King Henry VI)*

Memorandum ... that the men of Coventry shall ride to meet the
king in green robes and red caps ...

Weavers' Deeds CRO: 100/37/1

This indenture bears witness that Richard Molle, Richard Semer,
Thomas Darnewell of Coventry, Thomas Donton, and Thomas

Whitton of Sheldon gave over, granted, and ⟨...⟩ to ⟨John⟩
Plymmer, John Perkyn, Robert Thomas, Robert Styff, John
Bordale, Robert Glowcestre, Nicholas Gryve, and Thomas Lerdyf
of Coventry, one plot of land in the Mill Lane in Coventry flanked
by the land called the tailor pageant (house) on one side and the
land of the aforesaid Richard ... Thomas on the other, and (running) lengthwise on the royal highway there as far as the land of
the aforesaid Richard ... Thomas — and the aforesaid plot of land
contains thirteen and a half feet in breadth along the road and
seventeen and a half feet in length. The aforesaid plot of land is
to be had and held by the aforesaid John ... Thomas and their
assigns from the feast of St Michael the archangel in the thirteenth
year of the reign of King Henry the sixth after the conquest until
the end of a term of the next eighty years, following year by year
thereafter, and fully completed by paying thereupon every year
to the same Richard ... Thomas and their assigns 3s 8d sterling on
the feast of St Michael the archangel. And the aforesaid John ...
Thomas will build from the start a house called a pageant house
within the aforesaid term well and ably, and when it has been
built in this way, they will keep up, repair, and maintain that
house with its own costs and expenses during the aforesaid term.
And should it occur that the aforesaid rent be in arrears for one
month after any feast upon which it is due, the aforesaid Richard
... Thomas, their heirs, and assigns may thereupon properly enter
upon the aforesaid plot of land and distrain (it), and retain the
distraints thus taken for their own use until they be fully satisfied
of the aforesaid rent. And should it happen that the aforesaid
rent be partly or wholly in arrears for a year after any feast upon
which it is due, the aforesaid Richard ... Thomas may thereupon
properly enter upon the aforesaid plot of land and return it to its
original state, this lease notwithstanding. And the aforesaid
Thomas Whitton warrants the aforesaid plot of land with its
appurtenances to the aforesaid John ... Thomas and their assigns
against all (persons) by these present for the duration of the
aforesaid term. In testimony of which matter, the (parties) being
present, that is, the aforesaid Richard ... Thomas, as well as the
aforesaid John ... Thomas, affixed their seals one after another.
Witnesses: John Michell, mayor of the city of Coventry; Robert
Southam, one bailiff of the aforesaid city; Richard Sharp; John
Waraunt; William Swanne; and many others. Given at Coventry
on the feast and in the year aforesaid.

1439
Weavers' Deeds CRO: 100/37/2

This indenture bears witness that Richard Molle of Coventry,
weaver; Richard Somer of the same, weaver; Thomas Dernwell of
the same, wiredrawer; and Thomas Dunton of Sheldon, husband-
man, granted, gave over, and let to William Gale and William
Flowter, wardens of the Cardmakers' craft of Coventry; Richard
Twig, warden of the Saddlers' craft; John Warde, warden of the
Painters' craft; Henry Stevons and (Henry) Cl(e)rk, wardens of
the Freemasons' craft; and their successors, one vacant plot of
land lying in the Mill Lane in Coventry flanked by the land of
Thomas Wutton, weaver, which the masters of the Weavers' craft
hold, and the land of the guild of the Holy Trinity of Coventry
and (running) lengthwise along the royal highway as far as the
land ⟨...⟩ of the parish of St Michael of Coventry according to the
boundaries and divisions made there; the aforesaid vacant plot of
land to be had and held by the aforesaid William Gale ... Henry
Clerk and their successors from the next feast of the nativity of
St John the Baptist after the present date until (the term) of the
⟨...⟩ and one years following year by year hereafter and fully
completed by paying a rent of 4s sterling upon it yearly during
the lifetime of the aforesaid Thomas Wutton, weaver, in equal
portion on the quarter-days, viz, on the feasts of St Michael, (of
Christmas), of the Annunciation of the blessed Virgin Mary, and
of the nativity of St John the Baptist to the aforesaid Richard
Molle ... or their assigns and by paying a rent of 2s to the aforesaid
Richard Molle ... Thomas Dernwell ⟨...⟩ or their assigns on the
aforesaid feasts after the death of the same Thomas Wutton. And
moreover, the aforesaid William ... Henry will well and ably keep
up, repair, and maintain the aforesaid vacant plot of land after
construction done there in their own costs ⟨...⟩ and expenses during the entire aforesaid term. And the aforesaid Richard Molle ...
Thomas, their heirs, and assigns warrant and defend by these
present against all persons the aforesaid vacant plot of land to the
aforesaid William ... Henry and their successors until the end of
the aforesaid term in the matter and form stated. In testimony of
which matter, the aforesaid parties have affixed their seals in turn
to these indentures. Given at Coventry on the twelfth day of the
month of May in the seventeenth year of the reign of King Henry
the sixth after the conquest.

1441
Leet Book I CRO: A 3(a)
f 102v* *(22 April)*
...
It was ordered that Robert Eme and all others who perform on
the feast of Corpus Christi shall perform well and reliably so that
no hindrance may occur in any play, on pain of 20s from each
offender to be levied for the use of the town wall by the mayor
and chamberlains, etc.
Item, they order that the mayor and bailiffs on their own behalf
and that of the other good men of the town of Coventry shall
ride once before the next feast of St Michael the archangel to
view the limits and bounds of the franchise of Coventry, etc.
...

Weavers' Deeds CRO: 100/37/3

Know all ye present and future that we, Richard Molle, Richard
Somer, Thomas Dernwell, of Coventry, and Thomas Donton of
Sheldon, gave, granted, and by this our present charter have confirmed to Richard Cokkes, John Tebbe, William Pace, Thomas
Dycons, Richard Glover, and John Egull, weavers of Coventry,
one plot of land having a building upon it called the Weavers'
pageant house, on the lane called Mill Lane in Coventry, fourteen
feet wide and flanked by the land of the aforesaid Richard Molle
... Thomas Donton, which the masters of the Scissormakers' craft
hold and the land which the masters of the Cardmakers' craft
hold and (running) lengthwise from the royal highway there as
far as the land belonging to the altar of St Mary in the church of
St Michael of Coventry according to the boundaries and divisions
made there; the aforesaid plot of land having a building upon it
to be had and held by the aforesaid Richard Cokkes ... John
Egull, their heirs and assigns freely, quietly, well, and in (peace)
in perpetuity, by paying a rent upon it annually of 1d at the feast
of St Michael the archangel to Thomas Wutton of Coventry,
weaver, during his whole life, if it (the rent) be sought, and after
the death of this Thomas Wutton, by their paying the aforesaid
rent upon it annually to the master, brothers, and sisters of the
hospital of St John the Baptist of Coventry, and their successors
in perpetuity, in place of all other secular services and claims.
And we, the aforesaid Richard Molle ... Thomas Donton, and our
heirs warrant, acquit, and in perpetuity defend by these present

the aforesaid plot of land having a building upon it called the Weavers' pageant house to the aforesaid Richard Cokkes ... John Egull, their heirs, and assigns, in the aforesaid lease against all men. In testimony of which matter, we have affixed our seals to this present charter. Witnesses: John Warant, then mayor of the city of Coventry; John Lee and John Lynne, then bailiffs of the same city; Richard Osbarn; John Grynder; John Maydeford; Thomas Maydeford; and others. Given at Coventry on the sixth day of October in the twentieth year of the reign of King Henry the sixth after the conquest.

Weavers' Deeds CRO: 100/37/4

Know all ye present and future that we, Richard Cokkes, John Tebbe, William Pace, Thomas Dycons, Richard Glover, and John Egull, weavers of Coventry, gave, granted, and by this our present indenture have confirmed to Thomas Wutton of Coventry, weaver, for his whole life an annual rent of 4s from a plot of land having a building upon it called the Weavers' pageant house in the lane called Mill Lane in Coventry, containing fourteen feet in breadth and flanked by the land of Richard Molle ... Thomas Donton which the masters of the Scissormakers' craft hold and the land which the masters of the Cardmakers' craft hold, and (running) length-wise from the royal highway there as far as the land belonging to the altar of St Mary in the church of St Michael of Coventry according to the boundaries and divisions made there; the said annual rent to be held and received by the said Thomas Wutton and his assigns every year for his entire life, to be paid in equal parts, viz, on the feasts of Christmas, the Annunciation of the blessed Virgin Mary, the nativity of St John the Baptist, and St Michael the archangel. And should it happen that the said rent of 4s be partly or wholly in arrears for one month after any of the said quarter-days during the life of the same Thomas Wutton, if it be sought, then the said Thomas Wutton and his assigns may properly distrain (property) in the said plot of land and lead away, and keep for their own use the distraints thus seized until they be fully satisfied and paid for the said rent with all arrears on it which there may be. And we, the aforesaid Richard Cokkes ... John Egull, and our heirs warrant, acquit, and defend by these present the aforesaid annual rent of 4s to the said Thomas Wutton and his assigns for his whole life, as is said above, against all men. In testimony of which matter we have affixed our seals to this our present indenture. Witnesses: John Warant, then mayor of the city of Coventry; John Lee and John Lynne, then bailiffs of the same city; Richard Osbarn; John Grynder; John Maydeford; Thomas Maydeford; and others. Given on the tenth day of October in the twentieth year of the reign of King Henry the sixth after the conquest.

1442
Leet Book I CRO: A 3(a)
f 103v *(25 January) (Waits)*
...
They wish that they should have their livery as this billet requires, and on the condition that they would get a trumpet as mention is made below, etc, and they will have badges upon the finding of security, and viz: they shall have one dozen (lengths) of cloth for livery, and owed them by the wardens, costing 20s, and against the feast of Corpus Christi ...

1447
Leet Book I CRO: A 3(a)
f 131v *(15 April)*
...
And that the riding on the feast of Corpus Christi is to take place as it was accustomed to from old times, etc
...

1448
Leet Book I CRO: A 3(a)
f 133v* *(30 March)*
...
They desire and order ... that from henceforth no one shall break the pavement (ie, sidewalk) to put branches on it on the eve of the nativity of St John Baptist nor on St Peter's Eve ...

1449
Carpenters' Account Book I CRO: Acc 3/1
f 4*
...
Item paid to the Pinners for the pageant   10s
...
Item paid on the feast of Corpus Christi for torchbearers   4d

Item paid for fetching of torches   ½d

...

1450
Leet Book I CRO: A 3(a)
f 149v *(18 April)*

...

They have ordered that forty decent men of a good and honest
manner of life, and physically strong to work and be on guard,
will guard and watch the town every night from the ninth hour
until the ringing of the bell called 'Daybell', during which time
they will guard this town well and fully according to the usual
oath, etc. On any given night, these men shall be well and fully
equipped with jacks, sallets, pole-axes, or glaives,[1] and other similar (weapons), etc. And beyond the time of the watch, they leave
to the discretion of the mayor and council how these forty men
shall be ruled, if, etc

...

1453
Carpenters' Account Book I CRO: Acc 3/1
f 58

...

Robert Crudworth, harper, and Alice, his wife, made an agreement for 4s and for the light, 6d.

...

1459
AC   *Holy Trinity Guild Accounts* Sharp: *Dissertation*
p 160

...

Expenses incurred on the feast of Corpus Christi, viz, for four
torchbearers to carry four torches during the time of the procession
about the wagon in which the body of the Lord is contained.   12d

...

1 / *see English Glossary under* Iak, salet, polax, *and* gleave

1470
Leet Book I CRO: A 3(a)
f 209 *(12 April)*

...

Memorandum, that on the twelfth day of April in the tenth year of King Edward IV (Richard Braytoft Jr and Richard Alen being wardens), Richard Wode, grocer, delivered a silver badge with a collar of silver that had been ordered for one of the waits of the town of Coventry.

1482
Leet Book I CRO: A 3(a)
f 249v* *(19 August)* *(Bond against William Bristowe)*

... the mayor and commonalty of the town of Coventry, on their own behalf and on behalf of the holders of each and every holding and of the residents in the aforesaid Coventry, demand ... to hold and exercise in the same plots of land all their kinds of amusements and games every year, daily and whenever it pleases them, viz, archery, wrestling, racing with men and horses, and dancing, and also hawking ...

1486

A   *Holy Trinity Guild Accounts* Templeman: *Records*
p 78*

...

Allowed from two holdings for two waits at 26s 8d by
the year   26s 8d

...

1488
Corpus Christi Guild Account Book CRO: A 6
f 6v

...

Item received yearly for one building in the same place which
John Bluet holds   24s

...

f 8

...

Item he seeks allowance for expenses incurred on the memorial days, at burials, on the feast of Corpus Christi, (and) of St

Nicholas, for the lords in chief, for the poor, and for other payments and (for payments) concerning the livery of clothes as is
set out by the book of expenses, etc   £30 10s 1½d
...

1489
Corpus Christi Guild Account Book CRO: A 6
f 17v
...
Item received yearly for one holding in the same place which
John Bluet holds   24s
...

f 19
...
Item he seeks allowance for payments for the obits, for the lords
in chief, for the poor, for beggars, for various payments, and for
the distribution of clothes   £22 11s 3d
...

1490
Corpus Christi Guild Account Book CRO: A 6
f 27v *(Guild Fees)*
...
Item he seeks allowance for distributions of clothes as is
set out   £5 4s 2d
...

1491
Corpus Christi Guild Account Book CRO: A 6
f 34v *(Guild Rentals)*
...
Item received yearly for one holding in the same place which
John Bluet recently held   24s
...
Item for one holding in the same place which John Bluet now
holds   20s
...

f 36

...

Item he seeks allowance for the distribution of clothes,
etc   £5 4s 2d

...

1528

Proof of Majority of Walter Smythe PRO: C 142/46/45
(11 January)

... And the aforesaid John Hyll, sixty years of age and more,
when he was examined alone about the age of the aforesaid Walter
Smythe, said on oath that the aforesaid Walter was twenty-one
years of age and more, because he saw when the said Walter was
carried to the aforesaid church to be baptized, and when he came
back from the aforesaid church, baptized, with a large company,
in the manner and forms which the aforesaid Thomas Forman
said. And he (John Hyll) further said that he remembered (this)
well, because at the next Pentecost after the said baptism, in the
aforesaid twenty-first year (of the reign of Henry the seventh), a
great play called 'Saint Christian's Play' was held and put on in a
field near the aforesaid city of Coventry called Little Park, in the
time of John Dudsburye, then mayor of the aforesaid city....
William Bredon, fifty years of age, when he had been examined
alone about the age of the aforesaid Walter Smythe, said on his
oath that the aforesaid Walter Smythe was baptized on the day
and year and in the place, just as the aforesaid sworn witnesses
alleged and said upon their aforesaid oath, as he well remembers,
because he saw the aforesaid Walter carried to the aforesaid
church to be baptized, with two torches which were never lit,
and with the other aforesaid appurtenances. And he also saw him
carried back from the aforesaid church baptized, with the aforesaid torches, which were lit at that time, one of which torches
Robert Store, a capper, carried. And on the next feast of Pentecost following the aforesaid baptism, a great play, called 'Saint
Christian's Play' was held and put on in a field near the aforesaid city, called Little Park, in the time of John Dudsburye, then
mayor of the aforesaid city. This play, as he remembers well, was
put on at the aforesaid feast of Pentecost in the twenty-first year
of the aforesaid King Henry the seventh ...

1590
Shearmen and Tailors' Deed of Conveyance CRO: 100/37*

To all the faithful in Christ to whom this present charter may
come, John Messem of the city of Coventry in the county of the
same, shearman; John Rychardson of the same, shearman; Richard
S⟨...⟩t of the same, shearman; Thomas Tymson of the same, tailor;
William Nebee of the same, shearman; Richard Yates of the same,
tailor; Thomas Barrwes of the same, shearman; Thomas Robynson
of the same, shearman; Francis Farmer of the same, tailor; John
Robyns of the same, shearman; John Rowley of the same, yeoman; John Barret of the same, tailor; and Maurice Reve of the
same, tailor, (wish) eternal salvation in the Lord. Know ye that
we, the aforesaid John Messem ... Maurice Reve, for a certain reasonable and suitable sum of good and legal English money, well
and faithfully paid on hand to us, the aforesaid John Messem ...
Maurice Reve by John Wylkes of the city of Oxford, clerk; where-
fore, we, the aforesaid John Messem ... Maurice Reve state that
we have been fully paid, satisfied, and contented, (and) secondly,
that by these present, John Wylkes, his heirs, executors, and
administrators, and any one of them is hereby quit and discharged
of debt in perpetuity. We have alienated, enfeoffed, bartered,
sold, and given, conceded, and by this, our present charter, we
have confirmed to the aforesaid John Wylkes one building with
all their (its) appurtenances recently called the Tailors' and Shearmen's pageant house situated, lying, and being in the aforesaid
city of Coventry on a street called Mill Lane (running along) the
west side of the same (building); ⟨having the building⟩ recently
belonging to Christopher Waryn, recently a dyer of the aforesaid city of Coventry, now dead, called the Tilers' and Coopers'
pageant house on the south side; and the lands belonging to the
Weavers' craft recently called the Weavers' pageant house on the
north side as its limits in width and extending in length from the
aforesaid street as far as the garden now or recently in the tenure
or occupation of a certain *(blank)* Morgan, a tailor of the aforesaid city of Coventry, as is more fully clear and apparent according to the boundaries and divisions made in the same place.

   (We further confirm that) the aforesaid building with all their
(its) appurtenances is to be had and held by the aforesaid John
Wylkes, his heirs, and assigns, to the sole and proper use and benefit of the same John Wilkes, his heirs, and assigns in perpetuity,

to be held of the lords in chief of that fee by the services previously owed by it and customary according to law. And we indeed, the aforesaid John Messem ... Maurice Reve, and our heirs,
shall wholly warrant and defend in perpetuity by these present
the aforesaid building with all their (its) appurtenances to the
aforesaid John Wylkes, his heirs, and assigns, to the aforesaid use
and benefit against ourselves and our heirs and our successors.

Moreover, know ye that we, the aforesaid John Messem ...
Maurice Reve have made, ordered, and put and established in our
place by these present our beloved in Christ, Robert Lawton, a
tanner of the aforesaid city of Coventry, as the legitimate attorney
for our affairs to enter for ourselves (and) in our place and names
⟨into⟩ the aforesaid building with their (its) appurtenances, and to
take possession and seisin for ourselves (and) in our place and
names and, after this possession and seisin has been thus taken
thereof and by possession (of it), to deliver for ourselves (and) in
our place and names to the said John Wilkes or his attorney in
this matter full and peaceful possession thereof, according to the
approved tenor, force, form, and effect of this, our present
charter. They have and shall have all and ⟨...⟩ our attorney may
make for ourselves (and) in our place and names in the foregoing
matters by these present. In testimony of which thing, we, the
aforesaid John Messem ... Maurice Reve have affixed our seals to
this, our present charter, as a sign. Given the first day of September in the thirty-second year of the reign of our lady Elizabeth,
queen by the grace of God of England, France, and Ireland,
defender of the faith, etc, 1590.

(signed with 6 other signatures done by personal marks)
IM Richard Sharratt Thomas Robynson IR John Rowlye IB
Maurice Reve

Appendix 1

Cappers' Records SC: Account Book I
f 3v
...
Memorandum: David *(blank)*, the organ player in St Michael's
(and his wife) was received in the aforesaid fraternity and 6s 8d
must be paid in fines.

Appendix 4

St Mary's Cathedral: Inventory BL: Egerton 2603 no.17
f 27

...
(endorsed)
°A note-worthy inventory of relics of the minster church of
Coventry °

Endnotes

3 *Dissertation* p 8 fn m
This remains the earliest reference to civic religious drama in Coventry. The earliest surviving references in Coventry are 1403 (see below) and 1407 (see pp 5-7).

3 *Chronicles of England* vol 3 pp 494-5
A 1538 list of common land includes a field named for the site of the aborted joust: 'Item the
kynges feildes or ludlowe feildes at Gosford Grene by yeire xv s' (Leet Book I, CRO: A 3(a),
f 372v).

5 184
This quitclaim seemingly concludes a long legal wrangle about this property. Its history — which
may reveal a mention of civic religious drama in Coventry before 1392 — lies in the Close, Fines,
Parliament, and Patent Rolls of Richard II and Henry IV. At this time, only the following outline
(itself tentative) of this lately discovered litigation can be given.
    John Grauntpe (father of Thomas?) first owned the property. He enfeoffed it to his brother-in-
law, William Feriby, a royal clerk, c 1355–60 on condition of re-enfeoffment. Feriby was dead by
26 October 1400 and his estate forfeited to the king (*Calendar of Close Rolls Henry IV*, vol 1
[London, 1927], p 225). He had not re-enfeoffed Grauntpe who had, however, used the property
as his own and dowered his daughter Joan with it when she married Hugh de Meryngton. Hugh
had issue Guy and Katharine. Hugh and Guy had died by 6 August 1398 when Richard II appointed
an inquisition into the lands they held at their deaths (ibid, pp 119, 134). Guy's son, Thomas, was
dead by 6 May 1401 when Grauntpe won the property from Feriby's escheated estate (*Calendar of
Patent Rolls Henry IV*, vol 1 [London, 1903], p 517). Thomas' aunt, Katharine, and her husband,
William Wymondeswold, possessed the property at that time and successfully claimed it back on
18 December 1402 only for it to revert to the king on 10 April 1403 when a commission from the
Exchequer denied Feriby's original right to the property (ibid, vol 2 [London, 1905], p 278). The
matter then went into chancery (*Calendar of Close Rolls Henry IV*, vol 2 [London, 1929], p 290).
The property is described in the last two entries and in the same terms as those of the quitclaim.
How long the Whittawers' pageant house was part of the property before 1403 is not yet known.
    The men named in this quitclaim include nine mayors. Richard Clerk was mayor 1386-7, 1397-8;
William Attelburgh in 1406-7; Richard Southam in 1414-15; John Onley in 1396-7 and 1418-19
(father and son?); John de Barwe (sometimes known as John Smithier) in 1404-5; John Scardeburgh in 1391-2; Nicholas Dudley in 1401-2; and John Preston in 1398-9.
    The Whittawers' pageant house (p 6, l. 10) is the only one of the nine whose locations are known
to be situated on the east side of the city (the others were on the west side). There is a single

reference in the CRO: A11 MS to a property rented by the Whittawers in Hill Street that may be connected with their pageant house there: 'Item the Rent of a house chaber in babelack set to the Whittawers vj s viij d' (f 110v).

7 E 164/21 f 27

In the pittancer's roll for 1505–6 in the Birmingham Central Reference Library (168235) is this rental: 'Vicus parci minoris ... Et de viij s de thoma Raymond pro alio Cotagio ibidem iuxta pagent howse....'

7 Dissertation p 8

No civic record has been found to confirm this date. On 1 May, the Emperor Sigismund arrived for a vastly expensive and unduly prolonged visit of nearly four months. Henry V was fond of Kenilworth Castle which was only five miles from Coventry (in 1412, Mayor John Hornby supposedly arrested him while he was prince of Wales in the Priory), but it is unlikely that such a retinue as Henry and Sigismund together commanded, let alone the presence of the emperor himself, would be ignored by all but one annalist, and that he would sum up the whole company as merely 'Nobles.' Corpus Christi fell on 18 June in 1416; on 26 June, Henry set off from London for Southampton and France. This would be a tight schedule.

However, allowing that Henry and his nobles did come to see the plays, they saw long-established plays 'invented' in fresh revisions, not 'pageants' played for the first time. It has generally been assumed that the 'invention' holds true for the Hock Tuesday play. I have seen no reason offered for this, except the silent one that Sharp so thought. If, as Sharp avers, the annalist confused two kinds of civic drama and meant only to record the beginning of the Hock Tuesday play, the date would read more acceptably. Hock Tuesday fell on 28 April in 1416, a more likely time for Henry to have been in Coventry than 18 June. Whatever the explanation, it is unfortunate that no other annalist recorded this visit, whenever it was. The two entertainments are confusingly linked together once more in 1568 when a discontinuity in the performance of the Hock Tuesday play is erroneously made to apply to the pageants as well. See p 243, also p 276 Dissertation pp 11-12 and its endnote on pp 583-4.

The earliest reference to Hock Tuesday itself that Reader was able to find in Coventry is, in Nowell's words: '1316, when it is recorded that a house in Bishop Street was sold by Thomas le Peckere to John Piers, alias Hercy, a servant of the Prior, which agreement was dated on the Sabbath day next after the "Hoke-Day"' (Nowell: Reader MSS 25 February 1927, p 45). Reader, in the same place, suggests that the military entertainment at the Cross in 1614 was 'evidently founded upon' the Hock Tuesday play (Reader dates this show 1613). See endnote to MS Top. Warwickshire d.4, f 33 on page 595.

8 A 3(a) f 18

Only Matthew Ellerton, of these four men, is mentioned again in the Leet Book: he contributes one shilling eight pence to a civic loan of £100 made to Henry VI in 1435 (LB, p 176). He was then living in the Cross Cheaping Ward of the city.

9 A 3(a) f 21v

The Bull Ring was situated at the bottom of Great Butcher Row: the Priory gate also opened into this space (see VCH Warks, vol 8, pp 26, 28; Desolation of a City, p 77, n 36).

9   A 3(a) f 45v

John Goot was mayor in the year beginning 2 February 1420. The leet records, however, begin at
Michaelmas in his year and do not mention the Smiths being discharged of the Cutlers' pageant.
Giles Allesley's request of the Smiths is not mentioned in the leet records of his mayoralty. Both
events predate the earliest accounts of the Smiths' company.

10   A 3(a) f 73

Green and scarlet (l. 13) were, and are, the civic colours. The men of Coventry carried with them,
as a gift for the king, a silver-gilt cup that cost £7 2s and £100 to fill it. No other details of the
king's visit are known. Earlier in the year the city had presented the duke and duchess of Bedford
with fifty marks each, fishes, and wine (in addition the duchess received a silver-gilt cup, value five
marks). These were formally presented at Fulbrook, just outside Burford, in Oxfordshire.

11   A 3(a) f 82v

The Carpenters' Accounts begin in 1449; until the cessation of the performance of the Corpus
Christi cycle, the Carpenters regularly paid ten shillings each year toward the Pinners and Tilers'
pageant. Sharp (pp 78-9) quotes from a copy of the Rules and Orders of the Company of 'Pynners
& Nedelers.' dated 1414, that the subject of the pageant was 'the takyng down of god fro þe cros.'
I have not been able to find this document.

12   A 3(a) f 99

The leader of the waits was paid no more than his fellows. In an outdoor group of instrumentalists
(which is primarily what the waits were), it was natural that the trumpet, the loudest instrument,
should be the leader of the group. When Hewet and Goldston led the waits in the latter part of the
sixteenth century and the beginning of the seventeenth, the frequency of their names in the records
suggests that they made something more than an honorary post out of being leader. The trumpeter
in the Drapers' *Doomsday* pageant, it may be noted, was always extremely highly paid; sometimes
he was the most highly paid performer in the pageant.
     Sharp (p 208) dates this entry 1438, a year for which the Leet Book contains no entries.

13   A 3(a) f 102v

Robert Eme's name appears thirty-four times in the Leet Book between 1434 and 1465. He appears
first as 'Robertus Eme cardmaker,' heading those living in the Much Park Street Ward who contributed to the present given to Henry VI on his visit to the city. This, his third appearance, is as an
actor who had, apparently, been lax in his performances in a pageant: at this time the Cardmakers,
in association with the Saddlers, Masons, and Painters, maintained their own pageant (see pp 15-16).
In 1444, he became a councillor; he moved to Jordan Well and gradually became a senior member
of the council and took various leading roles in collections of monies from his ward. In 1453, he
was one of the chamberlains and, in 1456, one of the bailiffs and sheriffs. He last appears in January
1465, as one of the electors of the civic officials for that year.

16   A 3(a) f 122v

In this list the first are last. Fluctuations in the prosperity of the guilds are reflected in the changes
that are seen in guild partnerships supporting individual plays in the Corpus Christi cycle. For another survey of the city's commercial enterprises, see the endnote to A 3(a) f 143, page 544.

17   A 3(a) f 133v

Such old traditions were not to be put down by a single order of leet; many of their orders were clearly evaded or ignored as the reiteration of them proves. In 1480, the prior presented a long list of complaints to the mayor. One was that 'þe people of þe Cite yerely in somur throwen down & beren away þe vnderwode of the seid priour as Birches, holyes, Oke, hauthorn & other' (Leet Book I, f 237). The mayor agreed that this was reprehensible. At the behest of himself and his brethren, the masters of the city's guilds annually repeated the ordinance against taking boughs: 'and yf eny vndisposed creature offend to the Contrarie ayeynst their will no defalt þerin oweth to be ascryued in them remembryng þat the people of euery gret Cite as london & other Citeez yerely in somur doon harme to diuers lordes & gentyles hauyng wodes & Groves nygh to such Citees be takyng of boughes & treez, and ȝit the lordes & gentils suffren sych dedes ofte tymes of theire goode will And ofte tymes þe offenders can not be knowen wherthorough punysshement myght be don &c' (f 239). In his replication, the prior dropped this matter.

Sharp (pp 174-206) collects many Coventry references, together with others from such places as Warwick and London, to do with celebrations of the Watch kept on Midsummer and St Peter's Eves; decorations with branches, especially birch boughs, he deals with on pages 179-80.

17   Acc 3/1 f 4

The date for this entry is fixed by a given date on folio 5. The general ordering of entries in this book is chronological, of course, but with the widest variety of dates in the late pages; also some items are inserted well before or long after the year being written up. The scribal hand is usually of little help in reordering the entries.

The Carpenters' association with the Pinners and Tilers was arranged by an order of leet dated 1435 (see p 11).

17   A 3(a) f 143

The execution of this command was delegated to the guilds who were told to bring in 'the [what] names of euery parsone that is abull to make hym stuff & to aray hym after the seide ordenaunse' (f 143v). The returns of the guilds are entered in no regular order. They do not follow the order laid down in 1445 for the Corpus Christi procession; the scribe treats separately guilds which were joined together in that procession. They are not ranged by size. The distinctions made between what is expected of different classes of citizens allows a ranking of 'civic power' among the guilds, but the scribe does not follow this either. These matters are of interest because they tell us some of the differences that existed between the guilds who were charged with the support of one of the ten pageants.

The following list of the number subscribing in each guild and the order of the guilds follows the Leet Book sequence. The number in brackets after each guild gives its place in order of numerical superiority. Where guilds include mayors, bailiffs, chamberlains, or wardens in their membership, this is noted and the bracketed number following such a list gives the place in order of 'civic power.' Those guilds which produced plays are marked by an asterisk.

38 Mercers (7)*
    2 mayors, 6 bailiffs, 5 chamberlains or wardens (2)

59 Drapers (2)*
   7 mayors, 6 bailiffs, 4 chamberlains or wardens (1)
37 Dyers (8)
   1 mayor, 2 bailiffs, 4 chamberlains or wardens (3)
22 Girdlers (11)*
   2 chamberlains or wardens (6)
57 Weavers (3)*
   1 bailiff, 1 chamberlain or warden (5)
64 Tailors and Shearmen (1)*
27 Walkers (9)
40 Wiredrawers (5)
   1 bailiff, 1 chamberlain or warden (5)
   8 journeymen are also listed: the only guild to have such able to contribute (adding these would
   not alter the Wiredrawers' numerical position)
39 Corvisers (6)
49 Smiths (4)*
13 Fishmongers (15)
20 Whittawers (12)*
   1 mayor, 1 bailiff (4)
23 Butchers (10)
 7 Saddlers (19)*
 7 Cardmakers (19)*
 7 Masons (19)*
 9 Skinners (17)
10 Pinners and Tilers (16)*
   1 chamberlain or warden (7)
19 Bakers (13)
15 Barbers (14)
20 Wrights (12)*
 8 Barkers (18)*
 5 Cooks (20)

For a discussion of the earlier spread of crafts in the city see: 'Crafts and Industries: Medieval Industry and Trade,' Joan C. Lancaster, VCH *Warks*, vol 8, pp 151-7.

19   Acc 3/1 f 56
Twenty wrights (as they are called in the roll) contributed to the 'Provision of Armour' called on 15 January (see pp 17-18). Presumably the craft took the chance to have an extra jacket made for their own processional use at this time.

19   MS Top. Warwickshire c.7 f 83
'The Accounts of this Company commence in 1449' writes Sharp (p 13) and both he and Reader (the latter extensively) quote from the first account in this book. Halliwell-Phillipps (*Illustrations*, p 52) quotes some items from this account which duplicate those of Reader dating them 1450. As

his dating has been accepted for this company (see Introduction pp lvii-lviii), all of Sharp's and Reader's entries for 1449 have been updated by one year.

The pageant wagons gathered at the top of Gosford Street between Gosford Bars and Gosford Gate before moving off to follow the year's processional route. William Haddon (l. 39) was a smith who lived in Gosford Street (*LB*, p 250). For a leet order concerning 'þe standyng for paiant*es* in Gosford street,' see page 79.

20 *Dissertation* p 15 fn t

Halliwell-Phillipps knew Sharp's *Dissertation* well and did not hesitate to correct it, but in writing 'The Smiths' Company in 1440 paid three shillings and sixpence halfpenny for "cloth to lap abowt the pajent" ' (*Illustrations*, p 54); he seems to have followed Sharp into error. Despite his transcription in footnote t on page 15: '1449. — "It*em* pro cloth to lap abowt pajent payntyng & all — iij s vj d ob.," ' Sharp slightly alters his transcription and date on page 19. There he notes 'in 1440 the following entry: "item pro cloth to lap abowt þe pajent, payntyng & all iij s vj d ob. " ' This collection of conflicting evidence nicely encapsulates the problems facing the editor of Coventry's antiquarians.

21 A 3(a) ff 156-6v

M.D. Harris pragmatically notes: 'The political position of Coventry, its prominence among the Lancastrian strongholds of the kingdom, possible divisions among its citizens as followers of York or Lancaster, the frequent visits of the Court involving a constant drain of money to provide presents and pageants for the queen and courtiers, all tended to throw the municipal finances into confusion' (*Life in an Old English Town*, p 120). The Red Rose (later the Rose) and the White Rose (or Roebuck) were ınns which catered to the two contending parties of Lancaster and York.

23 Acc 3/1 f 12v

The reference (l. 23) to an armed man is the only one in this account book. Presumably he paraded for the Carpenters in one of the summer processions, perhaps in the first flush of their having, seemingly, retained for themselves from the recent military requirements for the king, 'a Iak ... j salet ... j bowe' (ff 56-6v).

23 Scrapbook Wb 137 p 100

Midsummer Day and Corpus Christi fell on the same day in 1451, but Halliwell-Phillipps heads this extract in his original transcription, '1450 29 H VI.' This regnal year ran from 1 September 1450 to 31 August 1451. The day and the year would match if the accounts were handed down before 31 August, a remarkably quick time for the accounts to be drawn up. Halliwell-Phillipps elsewhere does not make this error (an error, that is, only in the light of the other regnal years and years of accountability that he gives in his transcriptions published and unpublished). In Scrapbook Wb 191 p 108, he slightly corrects two entries of Sharp's for 1451 (p 31), at the same time adding the regnal year, '30 H.6.' The correction to page 31 consists of the addition of 'that went thereto': this matches the phraseology of Sharp's item on page 33, no doubt reflecting the original scribe's wording as much as Sharp's tendency to abbreviate items. The unpriced item (p 24, l. 13) 'glovys to the players' is also dated 1451. Sharp (p 186) says that payment to 'cressetberrers' (p 24, l. 1) is the first mention of cressets in any company's books. The best discussion of cressets is found in

Randall Monier-Williams, *The Tallow Chandlers of London, Ebb and Flow*, vol 4 (London, 1977), 102-17, 240-2, 291-3.

25 *Dissertation* p 206
Sharp (p 206) lists four spear-bearers in his Midsummer Watch expenses of 1451, whereas Halliwell-Phillipps in his, which marks the conjunction of Midsummer and Corpus Christi, lists three. Such nice distinctions in chronology's aid are, unhappily, rare.

25 Acc 3/1 ff 19-19v
The lower part, especially the right hand edge, of folio 19 is badly faded.

The Carpenters commonly met at least once a year for a guild dinner and the taking of quarter-age at the White Friars (l. 39) where they maintained a priest.

Robert Crudworth (p 26, ll. 8, 14), who appears by name in the 1450 accounts (p 19, l. 28), is here officially made a brother of the craft. His name appears only once more as paying his 'fynes' or dues in 1454 (p 28, ll. 33-4). In 1451, he is presumably the single minstrel paid (p 23, l. 18); in succeeding years the guild veers between paying a single minstrel and a vague 'minstrels.' From 1454, William Banbroke (Barnbroke) was available also as a minstrel and, from 1461, William Metcalf was also associated with the guild as a minstrel. Both Banbroke's and Metcalf's names appear regularly in the quarterage lists, so one must assume that Crudworth died or left the guild shortly after he was made a member (for Metcalf and Banbroke, see endnote to Acc 3/1 f 95, p 552).

With reference to naming a man by his profession (as 'Robert harper'), it should be mentioned that the St Mary's Hall quarterage of 1451, in addition to a payment of 6d to minstrels, lists: 'Item payd to Thomas loot iiij d' (f 13). He does not appear again in the St Mary's documents, but is mentioned once in the Leet Book as one of the poorer residents of Bayley Lane in the accounts for the loan to Henry VI in 1444. It is possible that he was a lute-player. The Smiths paid a luter at their Midsummer celebrations in 1452/3.

26 34/1 f 2v, f 5, ff 5v-6
The ordinances are dated only by the regnal year, 31 Henry VI. The Weavers elected on 25 July and delivered their accounts on 23 January following the end of the accountable year. Both meetings in 31 Henry VI took place in 1453.

The journeymen (p 26, l. 42) are never paid the agreed 6s 8d. The most they receive is 5s 4d in 1525. Between 1541 and 1555, their reward varies between 4s and 4s 4d, but from 1556 it stays steady at 5s.

This (p 27, l. 12) is one of the very rare references to special gathering of money for pageant expenses (see also Smiths' Accounts, p 192; Cappers' Accounts, p 220; and City Annals, p 426). The Weavers' rentgatherers paid annual sums to the masters of the craft on Trinity Sunday that may have been associated with their pageant (see endnote to Acc 100/18/1 f 48, p 569). On a single occasion, the Carpenters' annual ten shilling donation toward the costs of the Pinners and Tilers' pageant is accounted for by detailed levy (see endnote to Acc 3/1 f 55, p 550).

27 *Dissertation* p 190
Sharp makes it clear that the 'xij pencells for torches' were part of a list of craft goods which were handed to the 'ensuing' master in 1453. He refers to a similar list of the goods in 1468 in which occur the following items: 'xij newe pencells for the torches & iiij newe torches & iiij judasses &

the bolles & iiij surplis & iiij stre hatts.' However, the list of items, of a very similar nature, which he then prints, is also dated 1468 (see p 46).

27 *Dissertation* p 15
In the partial extracts from the accounts of 1449 and 1451, Colclow was paid 43s 4d to manage the play. Whether this represents part fulfilment of an earlier contract to 'have þe Rewle of þe pajaunt' for a certain number of years cannot be told. It is clear that the Smiths favoured such arrangements; in 1473, John Yale held this post (Sharp, p 193, fn x) and, in 1481, another management contract was made with Sewall and Rengold (Sharp, p 15, fn s). A John Yale was a pewterer (and hence allied to the Smiths' guild) of good standing in the city. He was better off than Colclow, judging by differing contributions they made to such levies as are recorded (*LB*, pp 236 [1449], 318 [1461], 365, and 368 [1471]). In 1475, he was one of the city's chamberlains (*LB*, p 416); after this his name does not appear in the city records again. A 'John Ryngold' was the gaoler in 1481 (*LB*, p 496) and it was possibly this Rengold/Ryngold whose man Thomas 'playtt pylatts wyff' in 1495 (see also Corpus Christi Guild Accounts, p 82). Colclow's twelve years were up in 1464 and, if a similar twelve year contract was made with Yale, it would have run from 1465 until 1477. However, the contract with Rengold was made in 1481. It is always dangerous to seek neatly repeating patterns in these records, but Sharp's notes inevitably raise speculations about the nature and timing of these 'similar' agreements. It is at such moments that our dependence upon Sharp's (and Halliwell-Phillipps' and Reader's) extracts from the accounts of a guild whose concern with, and management of, their pageant was different from that of the other guilds we know about is most tantalizing. The Smiths add to the mystery by not itemizing the details of the ruler's costs.

28 MS Top. Warwickshire c.7 f 84
Sharp quotes only the payment to the 'waytez,' with the comment that 'This was at the annual Dinner on St. Loy's Day, & they had a luter also' (p 212). When the Smiths' ordinances were approved at the Michaelmas leet of 1540 (*LB*, p 743), it was agreed that the three keepers of the guild should be chosen on this day. Cheney (*Handbook of Dates for Students of English History* [London, 1970], 50) gives 25 June for St Loy's (Eligius') Day. M.D. Harris, however, dates the festival 1 December (which is the date given in *The Oxford Dictionary of the Christian Church*, F.L. Cross [ed] [London, 1966], 445). Reader dates it 1 May in an editorial note to an item for 1553: 'payd for seyeng masse on Seynt Leoy's day 4d' (Bodl: MS Top. Warwickshire c.7, f 83). The authority of Cheney and the pattern of guild elections favours 25 June. This would call for three feast days in one week in 1453; however, St Loy's Day and Midsummer could as easily be combined as were Corpus Christi and Midsummer in 1451.

29 A 3(a) f 170
The sixth pageant of King Arthur (p 33) was apparently presented by the Smiths; Sharp quotes the following item from their accounts, dating both it and the visit 1455: 'Item to have owght the pagent at the comyng of the quene that ys the parell to þe pagent and harneste men and þe harnes to [harnes] hem wyth and a cote armyr for arture & a crest *with* iij grevyvyes ... xvij s xj d ob' (p 149, fn p).
    The Leicester civic records are unfortunately sparse for this period and no mention of John Wedurby (p 34, l. 28) can be found. Following the payment to Wedurby, there are listed various costly presents to the royal family. The marginal gloss for these reads: 'A present to the Queen.'

This is transcribed by M.D. Harris (*LB*, p 292) as 'A pagent to the Queen' and placed at the head of a list of extra payments, including that made to Wedurby.

34   Acc 3/1 f 18v
Amid the confusions for this year in the Carpenters' Accounts, there are two payments to the Pinners and Tilers of ten shillings. Presumably one was for the regular play in the Corpus Christi cycle and the other was for whichever part of the welcome to the queen the Pinners and Tilers were responsible.

35   Acc 3/1 ff 26, 28
These items are from an account that duplicates one already written up on folios 16v–18v. The regnal year is given here as 34 Henry VI, whereas in the earlier account it was given as 33 Henry VI. The items on folio 26 have been let stand but those on folio 28 have been crossed out by the scribe. The first two entries on folio 28 refer to 1450 and have also been crossed out. Such confusions are common in this first book of the Carpenters' Accounts.

35   *Dissertation* p 149 fn p
Sharp dates the visit and this entry 1455.

35   A 3(a) f 173
The special relationship between the queen and the city is noticed in this ceremonial departure: 'Hitherto this ceremony in its completeness had only been observed when the king was in question' (*Life in an Old English Town*, p 165).

37   A 3(a) f 173v
M.D. Harris (p 300) dates this entry, in the margin, 'May 31.' Corpus Christi Day was 16 June in 1457; the queen thus came to Coventry in the evening of the fifteenth.

It was the Drapers' pageant that was not played (l. 5). M.D. Harris adds that 'Domesday is the subject of one of the miserere seats in the drapers' chapel in S. Michael's' (p 300, fn 3). Richard Wode (l. 7) lived in Earl Street, a continuation of Gosford Street at the further end of which the pageant wagons gathered before beginning the procession and performance of the plays. His house was at, or very close to, the traditional first acting place of the plays, I believe. In 1471, the players drank ale at Wode's door (see Smiths' Accounts, p 50).

38   *Illustrative Papers* p 134
Sharp's note: 'Sometimes this item is "ad lez mynstrels Civitatis." '

40   Acc 3/1 f 38v
These two entries are in a different (lighter) ink than the other five in the set but are in the same hand. The seven items make up the skimpy records of this account.

40   MS Top. Warwickshire c.7 f 84
The Leet Book for this year contains much information about Coventry's strong financial support of the Yorkist cause: £100 'was gedered for the men that went with the Erle of Marche vp to London' after the battle of St Albans (*LB*, p 313); another £80 was collected to support 'oure

sou*e*rayn liege lord kyng Edward the iiij^the to the felde yn the north' — Towton Moor (*LB*, p 315); and yet another £100 and a cup to welcome him back from that victory which ensured his throne. There is no mention of civic entertainment with pageants on either of Edward's visits — not as earl of March in February on his way to London, nor as king on his triumphant return in June. Indeed, the visit in February is only obliquely referred to. A welcome with pageantry when the strife was over seems more likely, but the pageant of Samson the man of strength who overcame his enemies could as well have encouraged the earl as welcomed the king. That the Smiths chose to welcome neither earl nor king, but 'pryns' typifies the tantalizing refusal of so many of these records to indulge in 'the naming of parts' in the way the modern mind likes. That the Leet Book ignores the pageantry opens the door to speculation as to what other such shows may have been left unnoticed in official records.

Reader (and Sharp) date the visit and pageant 1460.

40   Acc 3/1   f 55
This account lacks a date but is in the same hand as the scribe who entered the accounts for 1461 and 1463; the list of names entered matches those of the 1461 and 1463 fellowship precisely, and the use of 'hys ffellow' (p 40, l. 39) and 'his felay' (p 41, l. 21) rather than the customary 'masters' also links the entries.

This isolated entry is the only one indicating that a special levy was made to gather the ten shillings given each year to the Pinners and Tilers toward their pageant. The money collected is less than ten shillings and the list of those contributing is less than half of the fellowship during the time of Thomas a Woode's first mastership.

42   MS Top. Warwickshire c.7   f 83
Sharp quotes, at some length, Stowe's description of the marching Watch of London in which the cresset-bearers 'every one had a strawen hat, with a badge painted' (p 177). In further explanation, he adds a footnote drawn from BL: Harley 3741, 'a Booke conteyning the Manner and Order of Watche ... upon the even at Night of Sainct John Baptist and Sainct Peeter.' This book is dated 1585 and says that cresset-bearers must have 'a broade strawne hatt according to th'olde order' (p 177, fn g).

42   Acc 3/1   f 82v
This memorandum is placed in the early portion of the accounts of Nicholas Harison and Robert Clerk who were masters from 28 October 1465 until 13 October 1466. However, it clearly refers to the two consecutive years when Thomas a Wode and Harison were masters (1461-2, 1462-3). Harison's claims cover half the torch-bearing costs, all the St Peter's Watch costs, and one third of the minstrels' costs (see p 41). The ten shillings to Wode is added, in a different and fainter ink, in a convenient half line at the end of the claims for first year payments. It may have some connection with the regular payment to the Pinners and Tilers (and possibly with the curious list on folio 55). The second year claims cover half the Corpus Christi Day torch-bearing, all the St Peter's Watch costs (for bread and ale), and one third of the clerk's wages. No other master is so meticulous about what he has contributed.

42   MS Top. Warwickshire c.7   f 115
Reader notes that in 1497 (17 July), two members agree that on their death each of them will give

to the guild a suit of 'whyt harnes' which at present is hired only.

43 *Dissertation* p 212
Sharp notes here that 'The general charge varies from 9s. to 15s. for Pageant, Procession, &c.' It would have been helpful to have examples, especially of the higher payments; as it is, the immediate example he gives is for 8s 8d.

43 Acc 3/1 f 72v
Westeley (l. 11) was not a carpenter but the Carpenters occasionally conducted business at his house (inn?). The last three items of the dinner charges from folio 76, which include that for the minstrel, are repeated at the head of folio 76v but crossed out.

44 Acc 3/1 f 77v
Cooks and their assistants and minstrels are usually listed separately and each of them receives more than this extraordinarily low joint sum of five pence.
    In the upper left hand corner of the folio a hand, emerging from a wrist band, points a finger at the heading: 'In the secund yer*e* of Iohn hall & Rathebant.' A similar hand is found at the beginning of other accounts on folio 81 (1465), folio 87v (1466), and folio 92v (1469).

44 *Illustrations* p 52
The Smiths are the only guild to mention washing the pageant wagon; they are also the only guild whose accounts mention preparations to the pageant on the evening before the day of performance. It is not clear whether the reference is to the individual parts of the wagon and some of its accoutrements or to the fully prepared wagon. If the latter, it presumably was left out overnight? See also entries for 1471 (see p 50) and 1480 (p 63) and endnote to *Outlines I*, p 339 on page 555.

44 *Dissertation* p 21
Only in the Smiths' accounts is mention made of rehearsing in the park. Presumably the Little Park is meant where the play of St Katherine was acted in 1491 and that of St Christian in 1505.

45 A 3(a) f 207v
This provision allowed the waits to visit the monastic houses at Combe, Kenilworth, Knowle, Maxstoke, Stoneleigh, and Warwick.

45 Acc 3/1 f 90v
The expenses in the two year mastership of Harry Daulby and John Sturdy are enumerated very scantily: there are only feast and burial expenses entered for 1467.

46 *Dissertation* p 194
Sharp adds: 'Midsummer Night, Bread, Ale, Spices, Wine, Armour and bearing the same, costs 25s. 8d.' He also distinguishes between '*staining* ... the term usually applied when cloth or silk is painted, but *painting* to wood or iron' (p 194, fn a).
    The items for bells (ll. 11, 23) are explained by Sharp: 'a small bell was suspended from the spear head, and underneath a pencel or little banner of buckram, painted and fringed' (*Dissertation*,

p. 195). He also enters, on page 194, this item from the Dyers' 1477 accounts: 'Item paid for a bell to the sper iij d.'

47 Acc 3/1 f 95
This is the first mention (l. 24) of William Metcalf and William Banbroke (Barnbroke) as minstrels; both are long members of the fellowship. Metcalf first appears in the quarterage lists of 1461 (ff 64v, 66) but is only admitted to full membership in 1463: 'William metcalf & iohanna his wyf is made brodur & sistur þat day [14 August] he to pay for fynys xx s. & for wax viij d & þat is to say iij s iiij d to the newe masters Iohn hall & Rathebant & euery ȝere aftur to his power for wax vj d' (f 68). Between 1463 and 1470 he pays quarterage regularly. Only on his last appearance in these lists is he again referred to as a minstrel (f 98v).

William Banbroke presents a different case. His participation in Carpenters' affairs dates back to 1454 when he is named as one of those made a brother in the time of Harry Daulby and John Toppe: 'William Barnebroke ys receyvid as broder in to the sed crafte the the [dittography] yere aforseid & he to pay for his fynes xx s. receyvid for Wax syluer vj d & also to pay of his seid fynes on the tyme of those maisters. iij s iiij d receyvid for the clerke for the sompnour ij d' (f 25). He then appears in the accounts until 1475; his payments of quarterage are not smoothly regular, but scarcely any member's are. From 1471, Banbroke's house (tavern?) becomes one of those at which the Carpenters liked to do business or to gather for food and drink after business. He is not heard of between 1473 and 1475 when 'barnbrokes wyffe' pays the dues (f 121). The last mention of him occurs in the entertainments held at his (his widow's?) house in 1476 (f 125).

The copious references to Metcalf and Banbroke stand in sharp contrast to the few made to the Carpenters' other minstrel, Robert Crudworth (see endnote to Acc 3/1, ff 19-19v, p 547).

48 Dissertation p 21
Sharp's comment on this item is as follows: 'As this is the only item that has been discovered of a similar payment, it must be left to conjecture whether these men were employed in the Pageant as a guard to Herod or Pilate, or attending the Crucifixion (subordinate to the Knights) or whether as the words "about the pagent" seem to imply, they were stationed in the street around it, to prevent any improper intrusion from the spectators. No such charge occurs in the other Companies' Accounts; but the necessity of some such regulations is sufficiently obvious, and a charge in the same Accounts of this Company, in 1564, of 6d. "pd for chassyng stafhed," seems to strengthen the conjecture.'

49 MS Top. Warwickshire c.7 f 33
'The Smiths ... in 1470, for five men, 13 d.' (Nowell: Reader MSS 22 April 1927, p 49 col a).

50 Acc 3/1 f 103
The date for this entry has been awkwardly altered from 'lxj' to 'lxxij' in a smudgy manner that might be mistaken for a change from 'lxj' to 'lxiiij.'

52 MS Top. Warwickshire c.7 f 83
Nicholas Brome lived in Broadgate; he appears in the Leet Book as collector and contributor and signatory of civic agreements between 1469 and 1481. His last appearance is as one of the mayor's twenty-four advisors.

The order (ll. 26-9) presumably reflects an unwillingness in some of the Smiths' company to turn out regularly on such occasions; the Smiths were always called on to bring out their pageant on royal visits, no matter how few guilds were called on to do so.

The mayor was most anxious that every display of loyalty to Edward IV should be made. Coventry had traditionally been a Lancastrian stronghold – Henry VI and Margaret were very fond of it: 'the queen's secret harbour' was one name for the city. What falling off there may have been in the city's loyalty to her was completed by the savagery of her behaviour in 1460 and early 1461. Coventry became Edward IV's city. The Earl of Aylesford's Roll dates from 1461 and is primarily an assertion of Edward's right to the English throne by descent from Brutus, Cadwallader, Ethelbert of Kent, and William I, and to the French throne through his great-grandfather, Peter of Castile. The civic annal on the dorso of the Roll ends in 1461, but its final years are extremely detailed surveys of events in England and Coventry. It is, in essence, a propaganda piece in the Yorkist cause. Coventry kept this loyalty until 1469 when Warwick rose against his king, captured him in late July, and held him prisoner until 9 August in Coventry. He had only just left when his queen's father and brother, the lords Rivers and Woodville, having been taken by Warwick, were brought to Coventry and executed there on Gosford Green (also known as the 'King's Field' where the joust was held: *LB*, p 732; see pp 3-5). In March 1471, Edward returned from exile and marched on Coventry where he was twice denied entry (29 March, 5 April). After the second, he proceeded to Barnet and his great victory. Margaret and her son, Edward, landed two days after that battle: Prince Edward at once wrote seeking aid from Coventry but the letter and its bearer were sent to Edward IV at Abingdon. This show of loyalty did not appease Edward's wrath. He paused at Coventry in mid-May only to collect Margaret, deprive Coventry of its rights, the mayor of his sword, and levy a fine of 500 marks.

Eventually, the special pleading of Clarence (who had owed the city 300 marks for over two years, loaned against plate, jewels, and a crown which the city still held) won a pardon from Edward. Clarence was remitted some of his debt and his valuables were returned to him. Edward's pardon was dated 20 June 1472. The ordinary citizen's reaction to this time of confusion is reflected in the dating of the Carpenters' account for 1473: '*Memorandum* þat on seynt lewke day þe ȝere off kyng [henry þ] Edward þe [v^te] iiij^te ...' (CRO: Acc 3/1, f 111).

Some local remembrances of Edward and his rule and his connection with the city, not apparent today, must explain why the topic of 'the historie of K E the 4' was one of three plays agreed upon by the mayor and council in 1591 (see p 332).

52   *Dissertation* p 193

In this year John Yale was ruler of the pageant (see endnote to *Dissertation*, p 15 on p 548).

53   A 3(a) ff 221-1v

M.D. Harris (p 855) believes that the 'Childer of Issarell' (p 54, l. 20) were the Holy Innocents from the *Shearmen and Tailors' Play*. This accords with the following pageant which calls for the 'iij kynges of Colen' (p 54, ll. 23-4); as Hardin Craig suggests (*Two Coventry Corpus Christi Plays*, p 115, fn 4), the company would have the necessary costumes. The only other company known to have set forth their pageant for this visit is the Smiths: '*Expenses* for bryngyng furth the pagent a ȝenst the comyng of the Quene & the prince vij d' (p 56). This is remarkably cheap, especially when compared with the 'xvij s xj d ob' they spent when Queen Margaret visited Coventry in 1456 (see p 35, l. 17).

55 A 3(a) f 219
The scribe consistently omits a brevigraph in the MS 'Coiens' (l. 15) for 'commons.'

55 Acc 2/E f 13
There is an ambiguity about dates here. According to the Leet Book (f 221), 'the xxviij[th] day of the Moneth of Aprill cam oure lorde prince Edward out of Walys so by Warrewik to Couentre ...' and was welcomed by a series of six shows. The decision to give him one hundred marks and a cup was taken at a meeting held on the twenty-fourth of April. There is no mention of Henry's being in the city. BRL: 115915 assigns the matter to Robert Onley's mayoralty in the next year, adding that afterward Henry kept 'his Christmas heere at Chellesmore house.' The other annals assign the matter to Braytoft's year. Easter Day fell on 10 April in 1474. The mayor and his brethren took an oath of allegiance to Prince Edward on 3 May, presumably at Cheylesmore, the royal manor, but possibly in the Priory. On 4 September, the queen ordered her gamekeeper at Feckenham to send a dozen bucks to the mayor and mayoress of Coventry, marking the letter as from Coventry. By 30 November she is at Ludlow Castle, from whence she writes to the mayor apologizing for the unruly behaviour of one of her courtiers and thanking the city again for its kindness to herself and her children. Edward's family, it seems, spent some time in the city, and he made one of his visits before the prince arrived.

56 *Dissertation* p 164
This is the first mention of expenses for horses in any records. Sharp assumes that it is linked with payment in 1476 for the horse upon which Herod rode in the Corpus Christi procession (see p 58). Herod was the only character from any pageant to ride in the procession according to existing records. Why more than one horse is not known unless an attendant rode with Herod, or the Smiths used horses to pull their pageant (see pp 88, 91, and 254 and endnote to *Dissertation*, p 20 on p 559). For Herod's costume in the procession see page 71.

57 Acc 3/1 f 118v
The edges of this folio have been badly torn but there is no doubt about the lost words and letters.

60 *Dissertation* p 29
'The items anno 1477 follow each other in the Account Book, and from similar entries in the Cappers' Accounts, are undoubtedly connected; they consequently relate to the ornamenting of *Crests*, of which most likely Herod's was one: indeed no other instances of *Crests* occur in the Smiths' Pageant Accounts; two therefore probably belong to the Knights, who would be clad in armour, of which the Company had three suits. It might have been expected that Herod would have been dressed with a crown, but the contrary is evident from the extracts given above, though a conjecture may arise as to the crest, whether it did not represent a crown, and the materials certainly are suitable to such a purpose; though after all, perhaps a splendid and gay effect in the crest was all that was aimed at. It will be remarked that a sattin gown (probably blue) was provided for this character,whereas in other instances a painted dress sufficed' (Sharp's note, pp 29-30). The conclusion is probably sound but the premise uncertain; sequences of items in accounts do not necessarily mean that they refer to a single ceremony.

60 *Dissertation* p 30
Sharp suggests 'sleeves' for 'Shevys' (fn v). In his annotated copy (BL: 43645), he offers 'shoes' as a better solution.

61 Scrapbook Wb 155 p 29
Halliwell-Phillipps notes that the Smiths delivered their accounts on St Clement's Day, 23 November, in this period, but adds that by the middle of the sixteenth century they were delivered on 8 January of the year following that for which they accounted.

62 Acc 3/2 f 10 col b
This is fairly regular payment, but rarely are we told that the young friars were paid for singing.

63 *Dissertation* p 214
Sharp adds: 'This last item is not very intelligible, since nothing similar has been found in the Accounts of the other Companies; and this is the only entry of the kind in those of the Dyers. The most plausible solution is, that some Journeymen of the Craft were occasional Minstrels, and employed by the Company at their dinner, in preference to other performers.'

63 *Outlines* I p 339
This entry is a stronger indication than the 1465 entry that pageant wagons were 'got out' the day before Corpus Christi for last minute checking before the day of performance. There would be no time on the morning of the performance for such examination and repair; indeed, the scope of some repair activities suggests that the wagon was looked to well in advance of Wednesday before Corpus Christi Day. The payments may have been associated with one or more of the rehearsals, but these were usually held indoors (the Smiths, for example, rehearsed in the old Bishop's Palace). 'The Wedonsday' (l. 38) suggests the very day before Corpus Christi, when the wheels (already found to be needed and ready at hand?) were fixed and the carpenter did his work.

The Smiths' pageant house sat on a plot of ground twelve feet square; if it were at least as high or higher inside, the wagon could be stored without being taken apart, in which case it could be wheeled out and attended to the day before the plays were performed and returned after repairing. However, there must always have been much to do on Corpus Christi Day in order to explain the regular expenses for setting out and setting in (for this and all guilds). If the wagon had to be assembled and taken apart again on Wednesday, the procedure would have to be repeated the following day.

64 Acc 3/2 f 15 col b
In a short discussion of the procession by the mayor, other civic officials, and company representatives which officially opened the Trinity Fair, Reader offers this item as an early example of the Carpenters' contribution (Bodl: MS Top. Warwickshire c.7, ff 33-4). It seems more likely, however, that it had to do with the Watch; it is one of three similar items scattered throughout the first fifteen years of the second book of Carpenters' Accounts (1476-91). The other two are: 'It*em* so payd for ij men to þe may(.) to kepe þe cete viij d' (1477, f 10, col b); and 'It*em* to the meyres Sergeant for going abowt þe Cite ij d' (1491, f 28v col a). It is not until 1569 that the accounts begin to show payments for men in company armour for this procession. The only other reference

to an armed man is earlier in 1451 (see endnote to Acc 3/1, f 12v on p 546).

64   Dissertation p 213
The Smiths used more music — or paid more handsomely for what music they regularly required — than any other company. The Weavers made their minstrel a brother in 1533 (see p 137).

64   A 3(a) f 249v
An important result of this relaxation was to enable the citizens to maintain their fitness and skills necessary to military service. Each guild was required to maintain its own butts where members could practise. One of the prior's complaints in 1480 was that the townsfolk ruined his warrens with their hunting and hawking: 'and also the people maken the same seuerall grounde & Sportyng place with schotyng & oþer games, and hurten his grasse / And when they ben chalenged by his seruantes they gyven hem schort langage saying that they will haue hit their sportyngplace' (f 237). Thus to sport and game illegally was the prior's affair and he should sue the wrongdoers said the mayor in reply. In 1534, the mayor ordered certain common grounds, ploughed because of a dearth of corn now gone by, to be made common again, because keeping them in farmers' hands was of 'greate hurte preiudice & nocument of all other the Citizens ... puttyng theme frome ther recreacions & walkes in Shotyng & other laudable & honest pastymes' (f 363v). Two street names remain to memorialize these places, Barker Butts Lane and The Butts.

66   Dissertation p 199
Sharp says that these items appear only in the Dyers' Accounts, and that this is the first occurrence. He adds: 'These entries immediately follow the usual charges for bearing armour, torches, &c. on the two nights; and it must be recollected that the Dyers had no Pageant.'

66   273978
There is no mention of either visit in the Leet Book. Corpus Christi Day was 2 June. Henry VII slept at the mayor's house. The accounts for Henry's gift and the entertainment offered to him are entered in the first leet of the next mayor. In the same leet, the accounts for the provisions sent to Bosworth Field for Richard are also entered (LB, pp 529-32).

67   Records p 78
These houses are probably those entered in the 1486 rental: 'De ij^obus tenementis de xiij s iiij d per annum xxvj s viij d' (Records, p 59). Templeman notes: 'The two waytes or waits were the city trumpeters and they were provided with a cottage rent free by the Trinity Guild ...' (p 78, n 2).

67   273978
Corpus Christi fell on 14 June in this year, so it would seem that a special performance of the cycle was presented on 29 June for the victorious king. The very few available extracts from the Smiths' Accounts for this year do not indicate such a special performance. It is possible that the gathering of the king's council in the days before Corpus Christi and the times of emergency made it necessary to postpone the playing of the cycle. The king and his advisers could hardly have watched a performance on the fourteenth and reached Newark, some sixty miles northeast, for the battle on the sixteenth. St Peter's Day fell on Sunday this year; the execution of Harrington at one of the central playing-places in the city, watched by many who had three days earlier watched the

Corpus Christi plays there, marks an unusually sharp juxtaposition of the religious and the secular.

69 *Dissertation* p 28
Halliwell-Phillipps dates the first and third of these items 1488; Sharp's Corpus Christi costs have, therefore, been adjusted from his date of 1487 to 1488. After the entry on line 10, Sharp adds 'Many similar entries occur in subsequent years.' He at once quotes a specially interesting one from 1495 (misdated 1494).

69 Scrapbook Wb 191 p 110
After the first quoted entry from page 110, Halliwell-Phillipps scribbles a note showing his mind at work: 'I believe, rehearsals. not sure.' He then scores out 'not' and writes above it, 'all but.' Then he takes the last step and adds: 'In short, quite sure.'

70 *Dissertation* p 199
Sharp notes this plus a similar entry in 1509 as items occurring only in the Dyers' Accounts.

71 *Outlines* II p 290
Sharp dates these extracts 1489; in his original notes in the Folger, so does Halliwell-Phillipps (5 Henry VII) but he published only those concerning Herod's garments, etc, and dated them 1490.
     Sharp notes that Herod's garment was that which he wore when he rode in the Corpus Christi Day procession (*Dissertation*, p 28 fn q). For entries on Herod's horse see pp 56, 58, and endnote to *Dissertation*, p 164 on p 554.

72 *Dissertation* pp 15-17
Sharp relies heavily upon this list, quoting items from it throughout the *Dissertation*. The repetitions are not always exact, eg, 'Item ij Cheverels gyld for Jhe & petur' (p 17); 'Item a cheverel gyld for Ihesu,' 'Item a cheverel gyld for Petur' (p 32).

74 273978
St Katherine's guild was formed in 1343 and worshipped at its patroness's chapel in the church of St John's Hospital. In 1393, it was formally recognized as part of the newly solemnized guild of Holy Trinity, St Mary, St John the Baptist, and St Katherine of Coventry. There was also a chantry or chapel dedicated to St Katherine in St Michael's Church.
     The Wigston's were a powerful trading family both in Coventry and Leicester (see endnote to *Dissertation*, p 36 on p 579).

75 *Dissertation* p 36 fn e
It cannot be said whether this refers to a new copy of the old and worn playbook or to a newly revised version of their play. See also pages 85, 101-2, 225.

76 *Dissertation* p 213
Sharp marks these as payments on two occasions, his argument being that the musicians are called waits in their official capacity as city musicians, and minstrels when performing privately (cf contract of Smiths and waits, p 64; Carpenters' Accounts, p 62). 'It may be remarked,' he adds, 'that soon after 1570, the term "musicians" prevails over their ancient appellation' (p 213).

Without commenting upon Sharp's major point, it can be added that the emergence of 'musicians' as a general term covering what was once dealt with under the terms 'waits' and 'minstrels' is general in the guild accounts in the later years of the sixteenth century and thereafter.

77   A 3(a) f 271
At the Easter leet, held on 18 April of this year, the Tallowchandlers had been united with the Smiths 'accordyng as it hath be ordeyned be lete afore tyme' (f 270v). At the Michaelmas leet of 1473, the mayor had taken over the running of the Chandlers' affairs.

77   *Antiquities of Warwickshire* p 149 col a
This entry led to the belief that the Grey Friars acted the Coventry plays or possibly even wrote them. William Dugdale so understood the force of 'by,' saying that the plays were 'acted with mighty state and reverence by the Friers of this House, had Theaters for the severall Scenes, very large and high, placed upon wheels, and drawn to all the eminent parts of the City, for the better advantage of Spectators: And contain'd the story of the [Old and] New Testament, composed into old English Rithme, as appeareth by an antient MS. intituled *Ludus Corporis Christi*, or *Ludus Coventriae*. I have been told by some old people, who in their younger years were eye witnesses of these *Pageants* so acted, that the yearly confluence of people to see that shew was extraordinary great, and yeilded no small advantage to this City' (p 183). As in the 1416 annal entry, this appears to be a mingling of facts and suppositions. Sharp (p 5) accepts the whole on the grounds of Dugdale's 'known correctness,' his boyhood education in Coventry, his sister's marrying into an old Coventry family, and the availability of 'oral information' to him. In addition, the records of the Grey Friars were lost at the Dissolution. However, leet and guild records disprove the Grey Friars' command of the plays at this time: the description of the 'Theaters' is close to that of David Rogers' description of the Chester 'pagiantes or carige' (*Chester*, Lawrence M. Clopper [ed], Records of Early English Drama [Toronto, 1979], 239); the title, *Ludus Coventriae* was to mislead long after Dugdale's day; 'so acted' can only refer to the playing on wagons drawn about the streets as Dugdale's eye-witnesses, were they questioned in his Coventry boyhood, could only have witnessed the closing years of the plays' performances. Sharp discusses the matter at some length (pp 5-8). The force of Dugdale's words is not yet fully abated, however. Roy Palmer, in *The Folklore of Warwickshire* (London, 1976) writes: 'The Grey Friars, part of whose church still remains, were celebrated for their performances of the Corpus Christi cycle, named after the day on which it was given. The subject was announced in a prologue by the Vexillator, who carried a flag with the subject painted on it' (pp 102-3).

79   A 3(a) f 273v
The pageant procession gathered in Gosford Street before setting off to perform; see Smiths' Accounts, pages 23 and 41.

82   A 6 f 60
For information on Rengold, see endnote to *Dissertation*, p 15 on page 548.

82   A 3(a) ff 275-5v
There was considerable disturbance about lammas lands in the city at this time, chiefly fomented by Laurence Saunders (his father had been mayor in 1469). This action by the mayor (p 83, ll. 38

following) added more fuel to the fire and within eight days after Lammas 'some evell disposed person vnknowen' pinned a harsh piece of doggerel on the north door of St Michael's which included among its seven couplets:

> And nowe a noþer rule ye do make
> þat non shall ryde at lammas but they þat ȝe take.

85   *Dissertation* p 29
In Halliwell-Phillipps (*Outlines* II, p 290), the first and second items are dated 1495; Sharp's entries for 1494 (those entered here) have been redated.

87   Acc 241 pp 3-4
Page references are to the typescript of the lost MS whose foliation is that given in the subheading. See also pages 103 and 192-3.

88   *Dissertation* p 20 fn f
The Smiths have entries for 'horssyng of the padgeant,' in 1497, 1498, and 1570 when they pay 'laburrars for horssyng the padgang' (see p 254). The last entry could suggest an extension of the verb from horses to men: it was customary for pageant wagons in Coventry to be pulled by men, usually the journeymen, with one overseer who was called the driver. However, a team of horses would also need a driver and, possibly, assistants. Herod, from their play, rode in the Corpus Christi procession (putting one horse at their disposal). The entry for 1474 (see p 56) shows that they had more than one; by their profession they were closely linked with horses; finally, they are unique once more in being the only guild to provide armoured men on horseback for the Midsummer Watch (see pp 212 and 214, where, in accordance with the accounts' willingness to provide puzzles, only two or possibly three horses are called for).

   The Drapers pay for 'horssyng the pagen' in 1591 (p 335), perhaps in itself an enigmatic comment on whatever performance was given that year. This is the only record outside the Smiths' Accounts of the pageant wagons being hauled in this way.

89   A 3(a) f 281v
Both Sharp (pp 155-7) and Craig (pp 116-18) print transcriptions of this reception for Prince Arthur.

91   MS Top. Warwickshire c.7 f 33
To attend on the mayor's procession which opened the fair. Nowell adds in shorthand form from Reader's extracts from the Dyers' records: '1528, six men; 1549, two men' (Nowell: Reader MSS, 22 April 1927, p 49 col a).

93   *Dissertation* p 35
Sharp, who dates this and the other entries for this year 1498, writes: '... it is evident that those characters which were not played in maskes or vizors, as was the case with Herod and the Devil, were represented with the faces of the performers painted. Indeed many other similar entries occur' (p 35). Sharp's reasoning does not follow necessarily upon the entry he quotes, but see page 181.

95 MS Top. Warwickshire d.4 f 14
There are no Trinity guild records for this period. The account book of the Corpus Christi guild
does not mention Henry's membership at this time. However, CRO: A 28 and CRO: Acc 2/D
record that the king and queen were made brother and sister only of the Holy Trinity guild. Bodl:
MS Top. Warwickshire d.4 agrees with BRL: 273978 in stating that they joined both guilds.

96 *Dissertation* p 196
Sharp follows the entry with this note: '1546, and subsequently, four Bearers receive 8d.'

100 Acc 2/F f 18
See Proof of Majority of Walter Smyth (pp 127-8) where the impact made by this play is such
that it springs readily to mind, twenty-three years later, as an event by which to measure time
past.

103 Acc 241 pp 4-5
The Leet Book contains no record of this confirmation.

103 Harley 6388 f 27v
The Bakers had been ordered to make this payment by an order of leet passed on 20 April 1507.
This entry indicates that in 1508, the mayor had to make the Bakers obey the order or had confirmed it (see p 102). The entry itself is undated, but it is part of an orderly chronological sequence
of entries for each year, so the date can be calculated from other dated entries. Richard Smith was
mayor in 1508. The same entry is found in BL: MS 11364 under 1508.

104 A 3(a) f 305v
Richard Smith was mayor in 1508; this official order of leet apparently makes Smith's order public and legally binding.

105 A 6 f 171v
St Nicholas Hall was in West Orchard (see map) and was the meeting place for members of the parish of Holy Trinity (*LB*, p 110) as well as for the Corpus Christi guild, whose name the hall sometimes bore (*LB*, p 66). In 1584, the Smiths rehearsed there (see p 309).
    The church of St Nicholas seems to have been just outside the city walls, beyond the Bishop
Street Gate. Both its location and early history are vague. It was closely connected with the Corpus Christi guild, however, which was known from 1488 until its dissolution as the guild of Corpus
Christi and St Nicholas. Although the guild met and worshipped there, even by 1535 the fabric of
the church was decayed and, by Dugdale's time in the city (as a schoolboy between 1615 and
1620), the church had vanished. For full details see Sharp, *Illustrative Papers*, pp 127-9 and VCH
Warks, vol 8, pp 6, 31, 318, 330-1.

106 A 7(a) p 38
There were other payments for work on this gate — 4d for 'clensyng' it, another 5d for further
work on it, 2½d for putting 'sparres' and 'nailles' to it, and 1s 8d for two labourers dealing with
rubbish there and at other places. However, such work about the various city gates was a regular
yearly business and can hardly be charged to special efforts to welcome Henry VIII.

107   Acc 2/E f 16

The distinction between pageants and plays is unusual. CRO: Acc 2/E follows CRO: Acc 2/F in wording as does Bodl: MS Top. Warwickshire d.4. CRO: Acc 2/D and Hearne mention three pageants but give only the place for the third; BRL: 273978 gives places for the three pageants but nothing else (all annals giving places agree on them). BRL: 115915 mentions no places but says that there were '2 Paggenes and A Stage play' (mb 6). The only other entry akin to this is in CRO: A 48 for 1526: 'The Princess Mary came to Coventry ... and see the Merc∧'ers' [⟨.....⟩] Pagent play being finely drest in the Cross Cheeping ...' This suggests that 'a goodly Stage Play' was a play from the Corpus Christi cycle; the other two pageants may simply have been *tableaux vivants* or pageants wherein emblematic figures made formal speeches such as were presented to Prince Arthur in 1498, although the Broadgate pageant with its 'divers beautifull Damsells' gives little clue as to content. See also City Annals entry for 1576 (see p 276) 'the Pageants or Hox tuesday.'

107   A 6 f 183

John Rastell was a member of a well-known Coventry family. Templeman suggests that John, who was coroner in 1507–8, and Thomas, who was coroner in 1505–6, may have been connected with the legal profession (Templeman, *Records*, vol 2, pp 14 and 172). John married Thomas More's sister Elizabeth. M.D. Harris, noting the printing of the *Hundred Merry Tales*, his possible writing of *The Four Elements*, and his printing of works by Anthony Fitzherbert, wondered 'Is it possible that Rastell had anything to do with the play of *S. Christian* performed in the Little Park in 1505, or with the "interlude" at the Priory 1505–6?' (see Appendix 5, p 492; for Fitzherbert, see Templeman, *Records*, vol 2, pp 170-1, fn 10).

111   Acc 3/2 f 69 col b

This is one of the rare years in which no record of a payment of 10 shillings to the Pinners and Tilers occurs.

112   A 6 f 221v

From a lost register of the Holy Trinity guild, Sharp notes that in 1516 'Iohanni mores Organplayer' was, or became (the note is not clear but the latter is probably meant), a member of the guild (Annotated *Illustrative Papers*, BL: 44932, f 62).

112   A 7(a) p 53

The sergeant (and mace-bearer) is William Alen: the two gowns are for him. The red and green gown is probably what is always later called 'a jacket' which he wears in the riding at Lammas. The gowns were regular perquisites of his office, and repeated occurrence is not listed. Neither are similar entries for 'bedell*es* Coitt*es*' (CRO: A 7(a), p 233).

112   PROB 11/19 f 67v

Pisford is first mentioned in Leet Book I in 1481; thereafter he rose quickly in civic standing and in prosperity. He was mayor in 1501–2.

114   Acc 2/F f 19v

Only BRL: 273978 records the open house during the twelve days of Christmas; it does not mention a lord of misrule.

114   *Dissertation* pp 11, 132

Sharp does not identify the source for the first of these quotations. The second is from 'MS. Annals of Coventry, written in 1588 (Butler's Roll).' 'In 1820, Sharp and Reader met William Staunton at Kenilworth, where, under the direction of the steward (named Butler), they excavated to a depth of seventeen feet to find out if there had ever been a subterranean room in Caesar's Tower ...' (Nowell: Reader MSS, 19 February 1926). Could this steward be the owner of the 'Butler's Roll'?

Despite the curious belief that it always rains in England, that the cycle should actually have to be performed on a wet day is rarely taken into account in discussions of production and performance problems. CRO: Acc 2/E notes of 1347 that, 'This year was much rain for it rained from Chri⟨..⟩mass to Midsomer so that there was not a day but it rained so⟨..⟩what' (f 6v). In the next year, the same annal reports: 'in this yeare it rained from March till ye end of July' (f 6v). The weather being inclement, it was unfortunate that 'new playes' were introduced at Corpus Christi-tide. Neither item is corroborated in an extant annal; Sharp himself offers both 1519 and 1520 as dates for these plays and in a footnote adds that no surviving guild record offers support for the claim in the annals. Elsewhere, Sharp mentions that in 1520 the Trinity guild sold the Drapers timber 'to make their Pageant' for which they were paid 7s 7d (p 66). Considerable renovations if not rebuilding of a pageant might be done with such an amount of timber. Possibly the Drapers' work on their pageant is connected with the new plays.

114   Acc 3/2 f 74v

'The first mention of Cressets in these Accounts, occurs in 1519, when the Company purchased four, previous to which time Torches were used' (*Dissertation*, pp 185-6). Sharp also notes the earliest appearance of cressets in the Smiths' Accounts (1451) and the Cappers' Accounts (1518).

115   Scrapbook Wb 173 p 2

This isolated payment to players is the first such one in these records.

116   Account Book I f 25v col b

Robert Crow, who was made brother in 1510, was master this year. His relationship to the 'Robart Crow' who was made brother this year (l. 13) and to the reviser of the Shearmen and Tailors' and the Weavers' plays in 1534 is a matter of conjecture.

120   A 6 f 257v

In this year wax money was received from the organist of Holy Trinity Church: 'De Iohn osgathorpe organpleyer of þe trinite xiiij d' (f 256v). He was likely related to William, son of William Osga-thorpe the weaver, who is listed as paying his yearly dues in 1522 and 1523 (ff 254v, 259v).

121   Acc 100/17/1 f 3

Only the Weavers list actors whose services in the pageant are confirmed by their being made members of the company (see pp 124, 127, 168, 183, 186, and 188). The leet order dated 25 January 1444 requiring the mayor's permission for persons to act in pageants other than those of their own craft suggests that there was sometimes competition for actors. That there were always far fewer pageants than there were companies to produce them would exacerbate this problem. John Careles, the weaver who was released on the strength of his own character to 'play in the Pageant about the City,' appears nowhere in the Weavers' records and probably acted for some other guild (see endnote to *Acts and Monuments*, p 569). Some of the actors named by the Weavers were themselves weavers; Harry Bowater and Christopher Dale who played Simeon's clerk and Jesus in 1550, 1551, and probably 1549 were weavers, and Bowater was master in 1558. Other actors were not of the trade: 'rychard ye capp*er* borsleys man that playth ane' (p 168) and Hugh Heyns who played Anne (pp 183, 186, and 188). The Borsley and Heyns families were important members of the Cappers' guild. Nicholas Heynes was mayor in 1525 (see endnote to Account Book I f 36 below) and John of the family was master of the company in 1574; John Borsley was second master in 1534 and master in 1539. Brethren outside the trade were not sought only to provide actors; the Weavers received into their brotherhood, among others, a baker, a barber, a butcher, a draper, a hostler, a painter, the prior of Coventry, a shoemaker, a tanner, and a whittawer.

122   Acc 100/17/1 f 3v

These actors' names occur only once more, when brotherhood is granted them in 1527 (on that occasion Sogdyn's name is omitted).

123   Account Book I f 36 col a

The occasion of this celebration was the election of Nicholas Heynes, a capper, to the mayoralty. His term was marred by a rising of the commons on Lammas Day when 'the gates & hedges of the grounds inclosed, & they that were in the Citty, shutt New gate against the Chamberlaines & their Company & the said Major allmost smothered in the thronge, he held with the Co*mm*oners for which meanes the Major was carried as Prisoner to London & the said Major was put forth his Office & Mr John Humfrey served out his yeare' (CRO: Acc 2/E f 17v).

The gravity of this insurrection, for such it was, and the firm mingling of severity and clemency with which Henry VIII handled it are clearly set down by Phythian-Adams (*Desolation of a City*, pp 254-7).

124   Acc 100/17/1 f 5v

This year's accounts are incomplete. I believe one leaf is missing, on the recto of which the account is completed and on the verso of which the account for 1526 begins. Sharp avers that 'Four leaves are here wanting' (*Presentation in the Temple*, p 20), but this is too many for the pattern of the detailed accounts offered in 1525 or for the summary accounts presented for 1523-4, 1526–40. Sharp's handling of the accounts of the Weavers is wayward in these early years. His statement that there are no Corpus Christi Day payments in 1534-6 is wrong; there are regular payments except in 1534, a year for which there are no accounts entered at all (there are accounts for 1534 in the first Rentgatherers' Book).

The receipt of 16s 4d 'for pagynt money' is unique in these accounts. The Rentgatherers' Books give no help at this time, but in 1555, the first of a series of payments to the masters that may be 'pagynt money' occurs (see endnote to Acc 100/18/1 f 48 on p 569). See also Smiths' Accounts 1552 (p 192) and endnote to *Dissertation*, p 22 on page 569.

124   MS Top. Warwickshire c.4 f 57v

Reader has misdated this item: Mary Tudor did not visit Coventry until 1526.

125   A 3(a) f 344v

This is the only mention of a pageant belonging to the Painters. The first reference to them concerned with a pageant is in 1435 when an order of leet made them and the Saddlers contribu-tory to the Cardmakers' pageant (see p 11). The Masons made a fourth in this pageant-producing team. A dispute among the four in 1444 was settled by the mayor and council who commanded that they maintain their joint pageant as heretofore (see pp 15-16). The four crafts rode together in the Corpus Christi procession (see p 16). The association of the Carvers with the Painters is reaf-firmed in an order of leet passed on 11 May 1528 (*LB*, p 695), and yet again 14 September 1530 (*LB*, p 702). At what time the Painters lost their pageant cannot be told, but the order of leet passed on 14 May 1532 reveals that they had been for some time contributory to the Girdlers' pageant (see p 134).

125   A 7(a) pp 85, 86

The cleaning of the city gates and streets was much more thorough than usual this year 'ageinst my ladie princessis commyng' (Mary Tudor). The goriest spectacles presented at the city gates were the heads and quarters of criminals. In 1523, for example, 'Pratt & Slouth were Exeuted for Treason, there designe was to have Killd the Mayor of Cov*entry* & his Brethren to have Robbed St Mary Hall & taken Killingworth Castle, they were Had to London for Iudgment & Executed att Coventry Being drawn on A Sledd to the Gallows & y*er* hanged & Quartered, ye head of Slouth was sett on Newgate with a Leg & shoulder, & the Rest of him Bestowed on Bishopgate, & the Head of pratt was sett on Babelake with A Head & Shoulder & the Rest of him was Bestowed one Grayfryers Gate ...' (BRL: 273978).

125   273978

The badge of the Mercers' guild showed Mary rising among clouds with the motto, 'Honor Deo.' The Assumption group of plays may well have been their part of the cycle; this would make the choice of their pageant to welcome Princess Mary a proper compliment to royalty (see Hardin Craig, *Two Coventry Corpus Christi Plays*, pp xvi-xvii). Only one annal disagrees about the chosen pageant: the Bodley annal (MS Top. Warwickshire d.4) says that 'The Maiors Padgen was gallantly trimd, & stood in the Crosse cheeping' (f 17).

Mayor Henry Wall (l. 34) was a weaver; the Weavers' play of the Purification and the Doctors in the Temple could also have been a Marian compliment to the princess.

127   A 7(a) p 97

These two men are more usually known as beadles and the city allowed for two jackets for them annually. Their job is best described in an entry for 1642: 'keeping out of [the] strong beggars & disorderly people from wandring vp & downe the streets idely' (CRO: A 7(c), p 98). They were especially called upon at market times.

128   A 3(a) f 350v, f 351v

There is no memorial in either the Weavers' or the Cappers' accounts of this business. Phythian-Adams, marking the decline in the Weavers' company strength in the 1520s, comments on the 'dif-ficulty experienced by the fellowship in maintaining its Corpus Christi pageant. In 1529, indeed, the play, props and wagon were temporarily conveyed lock, stock and barrel to the wealthy Cap-pers' fellowship, the Weavers being left responsible only for an annual subvention of 6s 8d. Two years later, however, even if the play was then back in the hands of the Craft, its performance was now being subsidised by contributions from two other fellowships' (*Desolation of a City*, p 212).

Until 1528, the pageant cost the Weavers on an average 24s 3d a year; from 1529, when they received contributions toward its production, their annual burden was reduced to an average of 17s 1d. For more detailed comment on the Weavers' economics generally, see Phythian-Adams (Index, *s.v.* 'Craft fellowships — weavers'') and, on the economics of their pageant production, R.W. Ingram, 'Pleyng geire accustumed belongyng & necessarie,' pp 64-74. The Weavers' and Cappers' ignoring of this order of leet demonstrates that such orders were not automatically carried out. The Walkers' payment (p 129, l. 5) is first recorded by the Weavers in their 1530 accounts (see p 130).

129 *Dissertation* p 186
Sharp's note to this entry is, 'four Surplices occur in Inventories of the Companies' Goods, classed with Armour, Pencels, &c' (p 186, fn t).

130 Acc 100/17/1 f 11
This payment satisfies an order of leet passed 12 October 1529 (see p 129).

131 A 3(a) f 358
The order concerning the Barbers and Girdlers (p 133) was rescinded in 1552 (see p 190). These payments ordered from the Walkers and Skinners (p 133) are first recorded by the Weavers in their 1532 accounts (see p 135).

134 MS Top. Warwickshire c.7 f 33
Reader dates this item '1531 & 1532': this may be meant to imply a single item 1531/2 (as is his usual case in dealing with occasional recognition of old and new dating, cf 1503-4 in these accounts). Reader's own note remarks that apart from the years 1517, 1520, and 1528, the company provided four men for the Fair Day procession until 1549. After that 'and subsequently for many years, only 2 were provided.'

135 Acc 100/17/1 f 14
The receipts (ll. 27-8) satisfy an order of leet passed in 1531 (see p 133).

136 MS Top. Warwickshire c.7 f 33
See note to MS Top. Warwickshire c.7, f 33 above.

136 Account Book I f 45v col b
This is the first mention (in the Cappers' Accounts) of a giant being borne in the Midsummer Watch; the six preceding accounts give only the sum of the expenses with no details, so it is possible that the giant was carried earlier. Not until the Drapers' Accounts in the mid-1550s is such a figure mentioned again (see p 474).

137 Acc 100/17/1 f 14[a]
The Weavers ensure the services of their minstrel, William Blakbowrn (his name is given in the account for 1535), as they did those of their actors, by making him a brother of the guild. The Smiths had tried to solve the problem of being sure of musicians for celebrations by making a contract with city waits in 1481 (see p 64).

138   *Records* p 156
According to Templeman (p 152), these entries, contained in a rental book for 1532, were probably a rough draft of the accounts.

140   Reader MSS 25-6 March 1927 p 47
Nowell, in discussing the part taken by the Smiths in keeping the Midsummer and St Peter's Watches, says: 'References to the watch — principally for payments of such things as the hire of suits of armour, buying cloth for banners, etc., occur in the years 1449, 1450, 1452, 1468, and 1546 ... Four "Judases" were bought in the year 1544 ...'

141   Acc 100/17/1 f 15v
This account is dated MlvCxxx[iiij] 'ty'v.

142   Acc 100/17/1 f 16
At the end of the MS of the Weavers' play is written: 'Tys matter nevly translate be Robart Croo in the yere of owre lord god M¹ vCxxxiiij^te then beyng·meyre Mastur palmar beddar and Rychard smythe an *(blank)* Pyxley masturs of the weywars thys boke yendide the seycond day of Marche in yere above seyde' (f 17). There follow two songs: 'Rejoyce Rejoyce all that here be' which is headed by the name Thomas Mawdycke in a hand distinct from all others in the MS (17th century?). At the end of the song is written the name 'Rychard,' in the same hand as the song and the same hand in which two marginalia occur in the body of the play (f 5v and f 11). On folio 5v is written 'Richard' in what may be the hand of Richard Pyxley who was a member of the company by 1591 when he paid for his man's indentures. Among the MS scribblings on the endpapers are: 'Allin pyxley the day of Aprill' (he was master of the company in 1567 and in 1570) and 'Rychard pyxlye is my nam.' He may later have written the song down. However, two of the waits named in 1566 are Richard Stiff and Richard Sadler. It would be more natural for either of them to have written down the song, especially as the other song, 'beholde [h] now hit ys come to pase,' is signed 'Iamis hewyt,' leader of the waits for many years, who is named as player of the regals in the Weavers' play from 1561-73.

144   A 7(a) p 156
The pageant wagons gathered at Gosford Street Gate before beginning their processional performance through the city. The 'pale' and the 'gild barne' may refer to some place associated with the wagons' starting place. This is the only reference to such a place.

144   Box I sheet 2
The full text of this indentured conveyance is given in Appendix 4 (pp 486-7) as it is the only document in Coventry surviving which describes the extent and character of a guild's possessions.

148   SP/1/142 ff 66-6v
The suppression of the monasteries hit Coventry particularly hard. Earlier appeals by Coton and his brethren (20 September 1538) had had no effect. Coton's letter speaks of the pressures of this difficult time (see VCH *Warks*, vol 2, pp 22-31; for the general decay of trade dating from the 1520s, see VCH *Warks*, vol 8, pp 4, 210-11 and *Desolation of a City, passim*). In 1556, the day

when the mayor assumed office was changed from 2 February to 1 November; thus it chanced that Robert Colman, the Roman Catholic mayor who had been forced upon the city by Queen Mary, held office for only nine months in 1556. One annal notes the change of 'All sayntes day for Allholland day at which day ye new maior makes agreat feast in St Mary hall, & bidds abundance of people to make merry with him there, such as he shall like of best either in towne or country, or in both, either rich or poore, or both' (Bodl: MS Top. Warwickshire c.7, f 20). The force of this tradition is attested to by two Jacobean entries in BRL: 273978: 'In ye year 1622 ... Allholland Dinner Kept att the Mayors House ...' and 'In ye year 1623 ... the Mayors Feast Kept att St Mary Hall, which Much please ye Cityzen(.) ...'

It remains unclear what financial support the city gave to the production of the Corpus Christi plays. Surviving guild records suggest that the guilds alone found the money for their own plays. What incidental costs were met by income from certain lammas lands is not known, nor what that income amounted to (see City Annals, p 426, and endnote pp 597-8). Pride may well have driven some men, masters as well as tradesmen, to contribute past their ability to the support of the plays. Generally, however, Coton appears to be pitching his appeal in the most telling way that he can: urgent appeals must be made to sound very desperate. The city's charges at this time were largely a private concern of the city; the Crown did not coerce the citizens into performing plays or having celebratory feasts. Coton may have been seeking another way to stress the plight of Coventry to Cromwell or to secure strong backing for whatever economic cutbacks he wanted to introduce. Whatever his reasons, whatever Cromwell's reply (it has not survived), the inaugural feast, the Corpus Christi Day celebrations, and the parade of the Watch continued. The mayor's brethren and probably many of the citizens were stubborn that the old ways should continue.

152   Account Book I f 52v col b
Accounting for the minstrel money is puzzling: in this year of 70 brethren listed, 53 pay 1d, 15 pay nothing, 2 are lost due to tight MS binding. There seems no link between iij s ij d and these figures.

156   Acc 100/17/1 ff 25-5v
Expenses for food and drink will no longer be given for these celebrations.

167   Account Book I f 63 col a
The payment for 'ye spade' (l. 40) is the first mention of the appearance of Adam (by inference) in this pageant — a silent character (see the Cappers' inventories, pp 240-1 and 334).

168   Acc 100/17/1 f 30
A little above the receipts from the players (ll. 34-6) on the same leaf is: 'Resseyvyd of Iohan heynnys capere ye [ly] laste of hys brodere hed xx d.' He had started paying his dues three years before. He was presumably a member of the notable family of Cappers, one of whom, Nicholas, was mayor in 1525 but did not serve his entire term. The Weavers did not restrict membership to members of their own trade (see endnote to Acc 100/17/1 f 3 on pp 562-3).

170   *Dissertation* p 28
See Appendix 5 for large scale disposal of vestments by Trinity Church and the possibility of their becoming players' costumes.

170   Account Book I f 64v col a
The Cappers do not record performance costs for 1545 and 1546. The Weavers enter no such costs for 1546 and 1547 (see Introduction, p lvi). Other craft records offer very little help in resolving this discrepancy: the Smiths played in 1547 but whether they did in 1545 and 1546 cannot be told; there are no Carpenters' Accounts for 1544-6, but they made their customary payment of ten shillings to the Coopers and Pinners in 1547. The Drapers' records are in especial disarray at this time, but in two years in the mid-forties they did not play their pageant; the Corpus Christi Day procession and pageant took place, for the last two times, in 1545 and 1546. The one year when no crafts played their pageants, so far as can be told, was 1546. However, in this year Corpus Christi Day and Midsummer Day fell on the same day; the Corpus Christi procession was held and the Weavers entered expenses for Midsummer celebrations.

It is likely that an outbreak of plague troubled Coventry at this period. The Cappers' Accounts for 1547 list an unexpectedly large number of deaths: Phythian-Adams notes that this list is 'significantly inflated by suspiciously unusual numbers of deaths within the same families' (*Desolation of a City*, pp 236-7, n 27). In 1546, the number of deaths they recorded had also been more than usual – sixteen. The larger concern occasioned to the city is reflected in the order of leet (18 October 1547) for a census 'with particulars concerning houses, landlordage, length of residence, marriage, family, and capacity for work,' plus a careful survey of employers and their needs and the current workforce employed (*LB*, pp 783-6).

174   *Dissertation* p 182
Sharp dates this item by one of his rare references to the regnal year – 'Account Book, 38th Henry VIII.' The regnal year 38 Henry VIII ran from 22 April 1546 to his death 28 January 1547. Whether the Smiths rendered their account on 23 November or 8 January, this entry is fixed as 1546.

177   Acc 100/17/1 f 34v
This inventory has not survived. See endnote to Cappers' inventory, Add MS 43645, f 57v on page 591.

177   Account Book I f 71v col a
This is the only entry of this nature in any craft accounts. The Whittawers had their own pageant and probably would have their own pageant wagon and equipment.

181   A 3(a) f 408
The pageantry of these occasions included the giants which the Cappers and the Drapers carried in parade. What other companies may have done in such kind is not known, although on at least one occasion, some kind of tableau or staged show was presented before the mayor by the Drapers (see p 469). For a suggestion about the civic expenses incurred, see the endnote to *Dissertation*, p 12 on page 597. (See also Sharp, pp 174-206, and *Desolation of a City*, pp 141, 176, 263-5.)

181   A 7(a) p 215
This is the first mention of the waits in these accounts. The Leet Book contains no mention of the institution, or reinstitution, of the waits at this time. The Council Book, wherein notice of their appearance and instruments might be looked for, begins in 1555. See Chamberlains' Accounts

(p 205) for this entry being a livery payment. Their official salary of £4 a year is paid by the wardens, whose account book does not begin until 1574.

190 A 3(a) f 418
This order cancels that one made in 1531 (see p 133).

192 *Dissertation* p 22
Sharp dates this item only by a regnal year – '6 Ed*ward* IV.' His comment runs: 'It also appears that an annual collection was made in the Company, called *"Pagent pence."* This varied from 2s. 2d. to 3s. 4d. and sometimes more' (p 22). The only other record of this payment is for 1561 when it is 3s (see p 218).

193 A 7(a) p 232
From 1553, these accounts include the rentals and costs arising from the manor of Cheylesmore. The procession way in Bayley Lane would lead, in one direction, to the west front of St Michael's Church and so to Broadgate; in the other, it would lead to Jordan Well and Gosford Street.

196 Acc 15 f 1v
Fair Friday parade officially opened the Trinity Fair; the Mercers dressed six men to march in it. See pages 450-1 for a full guild armoury and also pages 17-18 for citizens' armour.

204 Acc 100/18/1 f 48
These payments are not accorded any specific purpose. It is probable, I think, that they were intended to help defray annual expenses which would include Corpus Christi Day activities. However, they are not regularly included on the receipts portion of the accounts in the years when they are given and, not being a regular payment (the most regular is the 8s on Trinity Sunday), they are included here but not elsewhere in this collection.

207 *Acts and Monuments of Martyrs*, vol 2 pp 1920 col b–1921 col a
In the *Acts of the Privy Council*, John Roche Dasent (ed), ns vol 4 (A.D. 1552–1554) (London, 1892), 368, is an order concerning 'Misdemeanours at Coventry,' dated 20 November 1553. 'This daie were sent to the Lordes by the Maiour of Coventree Baldwyn Clerc, wever, John Careles, weavour, Thomas Wylcockes, fishemonger, and Richard Astelyn, haberdassher, for thier lewde and sediciouse behaviour on All Hallowe Daye last passed; whereupon, and for other thier noughtie demeanour, the said Careles and Wylcockes are committed to the Gatehouse, and the said Clerke and Astelyn to the Marshallsie, there to remayn till further order be taken with them.' Foxe says that he was imprisoned for two years, 'first being in Coventry Jayl' (p 1920, col b), then was removed to London, where he died 1 July 1556. The details of the religious excitement which seized Coventry in the early 1550s can be found in VCH *Warks*, vol 2, pp 33-4.

John Careles's name does not appear in any of the surviving Weavers' documents. Clarke's does, for the first time in 1542, when in the list 'Reyss*eyvyd* of brethern of the craft In my yere' is found 'Reyss*eyvyd* of bavden clarke weyver iij s iiij d' (CRO: Acc 100/17/1, f 26v). Foxe quotes several of Careles's letters to fellow prisoners, all of which are marked by a bright sense of the joy of martyrdom, usually worked out in imagery of song and dance. The impossibility of nicely distinguishing religious currents in Coventry at this time is illustrated by Careles. In one letter, he refers to 'owre late good kinges dayes' (p 1929, col a). In a time when the plays were presumably accepted as proper shows for a Catholic city, Careles was released to act, and was willing to act in them. The good esteem in which the jailer and others held him hardly holds with the mean-spirited letter that 'certayne backe friendes' wrote to the council in London.

209   A 14(a) p 14
Ralph a Man is named as a musician again when he plays the regals in the Drapers' pageant in the 1550s (see p 475). The Drapers do not name the regals player again until 1563 when James Hewet, the city wait, is their man. The only other mention of 'Ralph a man' occurs in the Holy Trinity Churchwardens' Accounts for 1559/60 and 1560/61 (Warwick County Record Office: DR 581/45):

Accounts delivered 11 August 1560
f 7
...

R*esevyd* of Raffe a man in well stret   [iij s] xvj s
...

f 7v *(Trinity land)*
...

R*esevyd* of Raffe a man at allesley   xx s
...

f 8 *(Burials)*
R*esevyd* for [ryffe] raffe a manes wyffe grave & hys own grave in þe
voett   iij s
...

Accounts delivered 3 August 1561
f 1v *(Rents of our Lady land)*
...

R*eseved* of Raffe a man in þe well stret a yeres rent   xvj s
...

He is last mentioned as a recipient of Sir Thomas White's alms money in 1564 when he is called 'the weit' (see p 225).

212   Acc 100/18/1 f 53
This item is tucked in at the bottom right hand corner of the account; the corner itself has been torn off but what may be a minim of the pence total is visible.

212 *Dissertation* p 193
'... the four men harnessed who *rode*, were those wearing complete or bright armour, and the *footmen* Almayn Rivets, a description of persons specifically enumerated by Stowe as composing part of the Marching Watch' (Sharp, pp 198-9). Stowe thought that the riding and the marching watches in London were distinct bodies. Sharp is arguing here that no such division occurred in Coventry.

   In discussing the Watch, he also comments on the Smiths' proclivity for music as an accompaniment to their ceremonies and the consequent oddity of occasional items in their accounts:

ie, '... in 1559 and 1562, there are items of payment by this Company to the Waits on Midsummer Night, when the attendance of the City Band upon the Mayor would be indispensible' (Sharp, p 212). St Peter's Watch ceased in 1549 and the Midsummer Watch ended in 1563.

214 *Dissertation* p 193
Sharp assumes that the expenses for horses are for the Midsummer Watch (see entries pp 56, 58, 71, 88, 91, and endnotes pp 554, 559).

215 *Dissertation* p 11
Sharp's quotation from a lost annal is supported by Reader: 'Hox Tuesday Play put down. MS Annals' (Bodl: MS Top. Warwickshire c.7, f 18). On the same leaf, after referring to Laneham's account, he has 'see [MS Annals page 76].' No other annal mentions the play but BRL: 273978, f 7v notes that 'one Moor Faining himselfe to be Christ was whiped.' CRO: A 28, f 36 has a similar note. It is not clear whether the 'faining' was done in Coventry. Although the Drapers' Accounts begin with income from certain properties (notably the old and the new pageant houses) whose rentals vary in size, this is the only detailed list of all the property owned by the company. The current pageant house and its garden are mentioned but not the old one in Little Park Street mentioned in the St Mary's Cartulary of 1392 (see p 3) and in the Pittancer's accounts 1505–6 (see endnote to E 164/21 on p 542).

217 Acc 154 f 54
'Bro' may be Daffern's error for 'Cro'; Robert Crow made the worlds (and the Midsummer giants) at this time (see pp 224, 237, 474). However, there was a Bro(ugh) family then in Coventry.

218 Scrapbook Wb 191 p 110
See page 192 and endnote to *Dissertation* p 22 on p 569.

218 A 7(a) p 254
I can find no reason why Hewet is the only wait granted the customary livery allowance this year. That he appears as the second of three items under the heading of 'Reparaciones,' the other two of which do refer to repairs, suggests that this payment had been overlooked when the earlier part of the account was being drawn up.
    James Hewet, the leader of the waits until 1584, frequently appears in the Weavers' Accounts (1554–73) as player of the regals in their play. He also supplied the same instrument to the Drapers for their play. See endnote to A 7(a) p 262 on page 573 for fuller details of his career.'

219 MS Top. Warwickshire c.7 f 34
'Sometimes this Company furnished 10 armed men at the Fair, but a gradual reduction commencing about 1590, brings the number in 1640 to 4....' In 1601, they bought a new harness and a 'poll-axe' for 6s 8d according to an extract from Reader (Nowell: Reader MSS 22 April 1927, p 49).

220 *Dissertation* p 81 fn s
Sharp adds that 'This payment was regularly made, with the exception of the years 1566, 1580, 1581, 1582, and 1583, until 1584, when they paid 20s.' 1566 is possibly an error for 1564 when plague prevented performance of the plays.

220 *Outlines* I p 339
This is one of the rare indications that members of the guild gathered to 'approve' the wagon and actors before the first performance (a similar instance occurs in the Smiths' records for 1471, p 50). The entry may mean that a group of Cappers met to decide what needed to be done to the wagon and costumes, etc, in preparation for the year's production. The sum of money is quite large and suggests something that might, sadly, be called 'a pageant committee.'

223 MS Top. Warwickshire c.7 f 159
This entry most likely refers to legal or business 'wryttynges' but may possibly cover work on the play which was in the midst of a period of revisions. Grene was a regular scribe for his company and received five shillings for 'makynge the booke' of their 1584 part in 'The Destruction of Jerusalem' (see p 307). He was an actor for the Cappers (1566) and was master of the company in 1568.

225 *Dissertation* p 36
For arguments whether this was the same man who revised the Weavers' play and that of the Shearmen and Tailors in 1534, and contributed in many ways to civic religious drama in Coventry for over forty years, see R.W. Ingram, ' "To find the players and all that longeth therto": Notes on the Production of Medieval Drama in Coventry,' *The Elizabethan Theatre* v, G.R. Hibbard (ed) (Toronto, 1975), 17-44.

225 Acc 2/F f 27
Although there were rehearsals, the Corpus Christi cycle was not performed this year, undoubtedly because of this plague.

227 *Dissertation* p 21
Sharp (p 21) suggests that the 'stafhed' might have been used by guards to keep the public away from the spectacle during performances, but Pilate's son or the Knights could have used it.

231 Scrapbook Wb 177 p 21
Halliwell-Phillipps took more than the usual care with the dating of the accounts of 1565-7. In Scrapbook Wb 177, p 21, he notes: 'A.D. 1565 in body of MS. 1566 at commencement of MS,' adding that these accounts were delivered on 8 January 1566 and cover 1565. As a confirmation he adds, presumably from the MS, 'Bromyll mayor'; Brownell was mayor for the year beginning 1 November 1565 (see pp 488-9 for inventory of his will).
    From the same page come the 1566 accounts he transcribes: 'A.D. 1566 in body of MS. 1567 at commencement of MS.' Again the mayor, Smalwood, is given; his year began 1 November 1566. The brief 1567 items come from a torn half sheet of transcription in box 2 of Safe Box E. It is headed 'AD 1567 in body of ms. 1568 at big 9 of vol Kryvyne mayor.' Kirvin followed Smalwood as mayor, but what the 'big 9 of vol' is I do not know. Reader dates the first two of these entries 1568 (Bodl: MS Top. Warwickshire c.7, f 84).
    On page 29 of the same scrapbook, in a list of theatrical appliances of another trading company which he does not identify, for 1565, Halliwell-Phillipps mentions the inclusion of 'three paynted clothes to hang abowte the pageant.' It is difficult to name this company; according to *Illustrations* (p 54), the company is another than the Cappers. It is not the Weavers or the Drapers as far as

existing records reveal. If it is the Smiths, then neither Halliwell-Phillipps nor any other antiquarian has left any record of such 'clothes' belonging to that company. It is curious for Halliwell-Phillipps to be precise about the quotation but so vague about 'another trading company.' Halliwell-Phillipps writes 'I find that there were frequently three rehearsals in Eliz.'s time, as in 1565.1566' (Scrapbook Wb 148, p 57).

231 A 7(a) p 262
James Hewet is first mentioned in 1559 as a recipient of Sir Thomas White's money: he is called an 'organpleier' (see p 211). He played the regals in the Weavers' play between 1554 and 1573 (possibly longer, the name of the musician is not always given). Between 1563 and 1568, he is also named as regals player by the Drapers. It is just possible that he could have played for both plays by dint of careful planning. The fact that he seems to have done it for only a very few years suggests that the arrangement did not work satisfactorily. Hewet was paid for his services to *The Destruction of Jerusalem* in 1584 (see p 308). Thomas Nicholas is almost certainly the Thomas 'Nycles' who set the song for the Drapers in 1566 (see p 237) and the Thomas 'Nyclys' who was paid for 'prikinge' the songs in the Cappers' play in 1569 (see p 249). It is probable that all the waits aided the performances of individual Corpus Christi plays in one way or another. The plays called for singers as well as instrumentalists and the extremely scanty surviving clerical records of sixteenth century Coventry reveal that some of the waits were also paid as singing clerks in Holy Trinity Church (see Appendix 5, pp 490-4).

The 'charges in pavyng ageynst the quenes comyng' (pp 262-4) were extraordinarily extensive; the fact but not the details are here noted.

231 A 17 p 13
William Hopkins was the mayor. The considerable sum suggests that all the guilds contributed 'ageynst the quenes comyng,' not only those four (Drapers, Tanners, Smiths, Weavers) whose pageants welcomed the queen. However, there is scarcely anything in surviving guild accounts suggesting such unusual expense. There are no Carpenters' Accounts for 1563-5; that for 1566 records a double payment (20s instead of 10s) to the Pinners and Tilers which may have some connection with the visit's levy. The Drapers do not mark a second showing of their pageant, but much repair of the wagon, sets, and costumes is listed for 1565. The Smiths similarly painted and gilded 'many Pageant articles on the above occasion' (Sharp, p 158, fn d; errata p 226). See also Receipt Book entry for 1575, page 270.

233 MS Top. Warwickshire d.4 ff 24-4v
The disagreement about whether there were four pageants or three displayed cannot now be resolved; there are no account books for the Tanners' guild surviving for this period. Sharp's source, CRO: Acc 2/F, CRO: A 26, and Hearne all agree that there were four; BRL: 273978 agrees with Bodl: MS Top. Warwickshire d.4. Elizabeth's progress from Leicester by way of Wolvey would make the Bishop Street Gate her natural entry to the city. However, when Princess Mary came to Coventry in 1604, she 'ridd alonge out at the Bishopp gate to the Sponn end & so alonge downe the Sponnstreete' (see p 365); this meant she left by the Bishop Street Gate and re-entered the city by the Spon Gate, a clumsy procedure according to what maps we have but presumably not an uncommon one. It might help if the location of the 'Swann dore' could be fixed; a mid-eighteenth century rental mentions a Swan in Smithford Street; this is the earliest reference to a tavern of

that name. It was a known halting place for pageant performers — the Drapers' players take ale there in 1570 and 1573, for instance (see pp 253, 264).

234   Acc 3/2 f 188 col b
This extra payment is unlikely to have been intended to cover any expenses incurred by Queen Elizabeth's visit, as the Pinners' pageant was not shown. It is more likely to have been for 1565 and 1566 as there are no Carpenters' Accounts for 1563-5 and the Corpus Christi cycle was not performed in 1564 because of plague.

235   Add MS 43645 f 57
It is not at once clear whether these men are agreeable that the Cappers' pageant should be made available to entertain the queen or whether they themselves were willing to be actors if required. However, the latter seems to be the meaning as these members of the Cappers' guild — although they were very representative of the company membership — were by no means the body of senior men who would formally decide whether the pageant should or should not be made available. That decision presumably antedated this announcement of willingness to act and was not recorded. The men on this list range in age from Jobber, who became a brother in 1526-7 and was master in 1541-2, to Newman, who became a brother in 1553-4. Assuming that a capper was about twenty or twenty-one years old when his apprenticeship of seven to nine years came to an end and full brotherhood began, Jobber might be reckoned to be in his sixties, the next oldest was in his early fifties, five were in the mid-forties, eight were in their thirties, and nine (whose brotherhood dates cannot be found because they were presumably recorded in the lost book) were in their twenties. In his early forties a man was considered old and past his best; the whole age range of the guild was thus engaged in the pageant affairs of the company. (See *Desolation of a City*, pp 81-93 for a full commentary on life cycles at this time in Coventry.) Cappers of the best families, of all ages, and of all ranks within the company found it congenial to have an interest in the pageant; for instance, Grene, Heyns, Jobber, Pytmann, and Walden had been or would become masters. It was not something left to the younger men to manage as a sport. However, their zeal was not called upon by the city on this occasion, as three (or four) other companies were chosen (see City Annals p 234).

Sharp dates the entry 1565; if the council collected guild money against the visit in September 1565, it is possible that other preparations were similarly made far in advance. However, as Halliwell-Phillipps dates the list 1566, his date has been chosen. Their transcriptions differ only in Halliwell-Phillipps' reading 'agreyd' instead of 'agrayd.' He copied out only the heading, as his interest at that time was in the possibility of women acting and his only comment on the list, not given, is 'all men' (Folger: Scrapbook Wb 206, p 63).

240   MS Top. Warwickshire c.7 f 100
This was a frequent and necessary cost for cleaning Butchery Row. It was a steeply raked street that was only pulled down in 1935 to make way for a new road. Reader also quotes the following items:

1575	pd ffor xv bytts of water by Mr Meyres apyentment,	x d
1585	Item payde for ij byttes of water for the strete agaynst Conventre fayre	ij d
1587	Itm payde for iiij byttes of water to skowre the butcherye	iij d

240   Add MS 43645 f 57
This is one of two surviving inventories of the Cappers' company. The other is dated 3 January 1591 (see pp 334-5). This first one comes from the period covered by the 'smale black boke' of accounts used by the Cappers between 1556 and 1571, and that there is no trace of it now is unexceptional. However, the 1591 inventory cannot be traced in the existing account book. Presumably both were transcribed from loose papers once in Sharp's possession before passing into the Staunton collection. It may have been customary so to draw up inventories because that taken by the Weavers in 1547 (see p 177) is unknown save for the cost of celebrating its achievement. On the 13 June 1569, however, the Cappers agreed 'that the Kepers for their yere beynge shall not from hence feorthe dese⟨...⟩ to give up their account on ye same day [ie 25 January] at the ferthest. and allso to delyver up in wrytynge all their accounte to the fellowshipp with an Inventory of all soche gooddes and Implementes as pertayne to ye fellowship vpon payne for neglectynge of this order The maysters to paye the some of iij li ...' (f 95v). If the rule concerning the inventory was followed by having one newly made annually, all but one of the required lists have been lost. It is, however, far more likely that annual inventories were never made, as suggested by the postscript (ll. 10-12). See Sharp (plate 9 facing p 51) for illustration of the 'Club or Mall' (p 240, l. 32).

241   Acc 154 ff 70-1
The payment to 'plears for Syngyng' (p 242, l. 21) is the only occasion when musicians (singers?) are called players.

243   Safe E3 No 2
Sharp dates the Hock Tuesday reference 1568 (*Dissertation*, p 126). For details of Halliwell-Phillipps' dating, see endnote to Scrapbook Wb 177, p 29 on pages 572-3.

   Only in Smiths' Accounts is mention made of extra costs incurred by displaying a company pageant before a royal visitor (see pp 35, 40, 56).

243   MS Top. Warwickshire d.4 f 24v
BL: Harley 6388 mentions both the visit and the plays: '... ye *Queen* came to Kenilworth castle unlooked for. the Pageants & Hocke Tewsday played' (f 36). No other annal mentions both events. BRL: 273978 mentions only the visit: 'the *Queen* Came vnexpected to Killingworth Castle' (f 8). The Dugdale-Thomas annal's single item seems to be part of the same visit: 'Paid for a yoke of fat Oxen and 20 fat Weathers given to my Lord of Leicester 20l. 0 0. Paid more for a yoke of fate Oxen and 20 fat Weathers for him, 23l 7s. 0' (p 150, col a). Nichols reports progresses in this year only from 4 July. In August(?), Elizabeth was at Easton Neston and Grafton Regis in Northamptonshire and may have travelled to Kenilworth on this part of her progress. That there is no other record of this visit is not unusual; the Coventry accounts of her 1566 visit are the only evidence of her being at the city then. That the visit was 'unlooked for' (an especially unnerving business when Elizabeth was the surprise guest) may explain the lack of other information as it does the urgent need of meat.

   The linking of the pageants and Hock Tuesday with the visit suggests that Elizabeth saw performances of them. The pageants were performed regularly during her reign except for two years when plague outbreaks caused them to be cancelled — 1564 and 1575. The regularity of the Hock Tuesday play performance is a less certain affair (see endnote to MS Top. Warwickshire d.4, f 24v on pages 573-4). Corpus Christi fell on 21 June in 1576. If she saw the plays on this day (and for royal visitors they could be performed at other times — on St Peter's Day for Henry VII, see p 68), there would be little time for other entertainment. What seems most likely is that three or four pageants were dressed to welcome her, as was usual, and the Hock Tuesday play was performed because it had been boasted of to her two years earlier (see p 233).

246   Acc 154 ff 73-4
Sharp (p 216) transcribes the payment to Pyninge (p 247, l. 10) as 'v d' not 'v s' — so low a sum as to make Daffern's reading almost certainly correct. Sharp adds that 'most assuredly it is for making a fair copy of *the Play*, as Pynyng was an excellent penman.' It is still possible that the payment was for composition as much as for copying. Francis Pyninge was paid by the Cappers for copying their account in the first decade of the reign of James I. His brother Hugh also copied for them (SC: Account Book I, f 137, col a, 1598). His will, dated 22 July 1606 (and naming him as a capper) is deposited at the Lichfield Joint Record Office.

247   *Illustrative Papers* p 50
The essays edited by Felicity Heal and Rosemary O'Day in *Church and Society in England, Henry VIII to James I* (London, 1977) provide background for such radical deeds. Coventry's religious fervour had always been strong. It was early and late a seat of Lollardy (see John A.F. Thomson, *The Later Lollards, 1414-1520* [Oxford, 1965]). In 1404, Henry IV called a parliament at Coventry: 'In the same Parlement, the archbischop [Arundel], as he went in the strete, happed to mete the prest beryng the Sacrament to a seke man; for there was grete pestilens in the town at that tyme. The archbischop and othir many ded reverens to the Sacrament as it was her deute. Many of the puple in the strete turned her bakkes, and avaled not her hodes, ne ded nor maner reverens. This was told onto the Kyng, and he ded in this matter dew correccion, for many of hem were of his hous' (John Capgrave, *The Chronicle of England*, Rev. F.C. Hingesten [ed], Rolls Series, vol 1 [London, 1858], 288). The Aylesford Annal for 1413 reads: 'That 3ere was iiij. lollardys were hanged and draw and quartred at Couentre.' In 1519, seven men and women were burned 'because they had the lordes praier, ye Creed, & ye tenn Commandementes in English' (Bodl: 31431, f 16a: the reasons given are wrong as this had long been common practice in England). Popular Protestantism in the city had its roots in Lollardy; no less than forty-five members of the group were tried by Bishop Blythe in 1511-12. Their adherents ran from ordinary citizens to some of the leading families in the city — the Cokes, Pisfords, and Wigstons (Richard Coke was mayor in 1486 and 1503, John Wigston in 1491, and William Pisford in 1501). Imogen Luxton discusses these matters in her essay in the above collection, 'The Reformation and Popular Culture' (pp 57-77), and the 1511-12 trial in 'The Lichfield Court Book: a Postscript,' *BIHR* 44 (1971), 120-5. The mood of Coventry much of this time is described in a letter to Henry Bullinger by Thomas Lever, who returned from exile in Switzerland after Mary's death to hold a radical lectureship in Coventry: 'a city ... in which there have always been, since the revival of the gospel, great numbers zealous for evangelical truth; so that in that last persecution under Mary, some were burnt [at the stake], others went into banishment together with myself; the remainder, long tossed about in great difficulty and distress, have at last, on the restoration of pure religion, invited other preachers, and myself in particular, to proclaim the gospel to them at Coventry. After I had discovered, by the experience of some weeks, that vast numbers in this place were in the habit of frequenting the public preaching of the gospel, I consented to their request, that I should settle my wife and family among them; and thus, now for nearly a whole year, I have preached to them without any

hindrance, and they have liberally maintained me and my family in this city. For we are not bound to each other, neither I to the townsmen, nor they to me, by any law or engagement, but only by free kindness and love' (*The Zurich Letters ...*, Rev. Hastings Robinson [ed], Parker Society Publication 43 [Cambridge, 1842], 86-7). It was upon such a city that Queen Mary had to force 'sum Catholike and grave man to be chosen thier Maiour for this yere comyng' at the beginning of 1555 and presented a short list of three candidates (*Acts of the Privy Council*, John Roche Dasent [ed], ns, vol 5 [A.D. 1554–1556] [London, 1892], 218). W.J. Shields' essay in Heal and O'Day's collection, 'Religion in Provincial Towns: Innovation and Tradition' (pp 156-76) is also useful for sensing the religious atmosphere in which Coventry existed.

Not to be blamed upon the citizens, though they may have been willingly gullible, was the work perpetrated in St Michael's Church. This is reported by Sir John Harington (a cousin of Lord Harington, see pp 364-5) in *A Briefe View of the State of the Church of England ... To the Yeere 1608* (London, 1653), 85, where he tells how 'The pavement of *Coventry* Church is almost all Tombstones, and some very ancient; but there came in a zealous fellow with a counterfeit commission, that for avoyding of superstition, hath not left one penny-worth, nor one penny-bredth of brasse upon the Tombes, of all the inscriptions, which had been many and costly.' In 1609, in a purely local demonstration of a zealous council, the statue of Christ was taken down from the city cross and replaced, albeit briefly, with that of a naked Godiva. Soon thereafter she was replaced by the more neutral plaque of the king's coat of arms (Hearne, p 1463; Bodl: MS Top. Warwickshire d.4; BRL: 273978).

251 A 17 p 21
Civic payments to players, musicians, etc, do not receive notice by the chamberlains until 1574. Whatever earlier account book such cancelled payments as these went into is now lost.

Murray gathers several references to a company (companies?) connected with Coventry which puzzle him. He posits a 'Sir Francis Smith's Company' suggesting that 'A comparison of dates seems to indicate that this company may have been the one which played in Leicester and Coventry from 1564 to 1571-2, under the title of 'The Players of Coventry.'

1568-9.	Sept. 7, '69,	Nottingham.	('Ser Fraunces Smyth's' players).
	Sept. 11, '69,	Leicester.	('Mr. Smiths' players).
1569-70.	Aug. 7, '70,	Leicester.	('Mr Smythes' players).
1570,		Abingdon.	('Mr. Smythes Players of Coventrie').'

(*English Dramatic Companies, 1558-1642*, vol 2 [London, 1910], 94-5). Murray's own list of performances by the 'Players of Coventry' in his section dealing with 'Town Companies' (vol 2, p 113) lists only performances at Leicester during the period 1563-72:

1563-4.	Jan 6, '64,	Leicester.
1566-7.	Jan. 31, '67,	Leicester.
1568-9.	Jan. 12, '69,	Leicester
1571-2,		Leicester

Their only appearance at Coventry is nearly twenty years later when an item refers to 40s 'given to Coventrie players' entered in the accounts for the period beginning 26 November 1589 and ending

30 November 1590 (see p 328). Murray, in a footnote (vol 2, p 113, fn 2), suggests that the 'Players of Coventry' and Sir Francis' men may be the same troupe, but the twenty year gap in their history weakens the suggestion.

To his list may be added, from Sharp: '1569 [May 13]. – to the players of Coventre v s' (p 209, fn u). He gives his source as 'In the ancient MS. Accounts of a Noble Family, are the ensuing items of expenditure in the course of a Journey to the Metropolis, in June, 1565, under the head "Gifts and rewards."' The payment to the players is presumably from elsewhere in the same MS. Halliwell-Phillipps includes: '... "Item, paid to the players of Coventrie by the commaundement of Mr. Mayer and thaldremen, x.s.," Bristol Corporation MSS., December, 1570. They were at Abingdon in the same year and at Leicester in 1569 and 1571, but there is no record of the nature of their performances. Those at Coventry were no doubt of a more impressive character, the players there having the advantage of elaborate appliances. "Item paide at the commaundiment of master mayor unto Mr. Smythes players of Coventree, iij. s." Abingdon Corporation MSS., 1570. There can be little doubt that "Mr." in this last extract is an error for "the"' (Outlines II, p 296). What relation, if any, there is between these players and those Captain Cox took to Kenilworth in 1575 is not known (see Robert Laneham's Letter, pp 272-5). If Halliwell-Phillipps is right, there arises the prospect of a trade guild's actors travelling with their pageant or play, but the word is incontrovertibly 'Mr.' There is no reason why it should be an error for 'the.'

253 Acc 154 f 81
'The swanne dore' (l. 35) cannot be placed: see endnote to MS Top. Warwickshire d.4, ff 24-4v on pages 573-4.

254 Outlines I p 339
See entries on pp 88, 91 (Smiths), 335 (Drapers), and endnote to Dissertation p 20, fn f on page 559.

260 Illustrations p 55
These items do not appear to be out of the ordinary; however, the seeming clarity is deceptive. Halliwell-Phillipps (Outlines I, p 340) announces the introduction of a 'new play' and, oddly enough, given the cast list both Halliwell-Phillipps and Sharp cite for the following years, neither is clear whether the new play ran 'in conjunction with' the old one or whether it was performed after the old play. If it was a revised and extended version of the old with new characters, and even new situations, would not the addition of the new characters to the old list be obvious? Halliwell-Phillipps continues to call it a 'new play' but offers little, if anything, from the accounts as support. Thus, he writes: 'In 1577 the old mystery and the "new pley" were again performed by the Smiths' Company.... The expenses of the old pageant are stated as follows ...' (Outlines I, pp 340-1). The expenses for 1577 (see p 285) seem remarkably like those of the 'new pley' to a modern reader.

Sharp and Halliwell-Phillipps agree on the dating of this year's entries. The latter dates the Smiths' 'new pley' from this year: here it seems that the 'too damsselles' were first required. Halliwell-Phillipps notes this: 'This entry occurs amongst the other payments to other actors, but qy. were 2 women introduced into the Smiths' Pag. Yes. This entry refers to the "New Play", 1572.' (Scrapbook Wb 206, p 63). However, Sharp (p 36), for once describing the appearance of the MS he is transcribing, makes it clear that the Smiths are now producing two plays; having mingled the payments for the two in the preceding year when they introduced the novelty, they now distinguish between them. No other Coventry company is known to have produced two plays in the pageant, unless the parts of the Shearmen's and Weavers' plays are so counted. Sharp introduces his cast list: 'In 1573, after the usual entry of payments to performers and other expences of the Pageant as heretofore, a short break occurs, and in the margin is written "New play," after which follow these items' (p 36). This has the ring of authenticity. The matching of his and Halliwell-Phillipps' transcripts of the costs of this play would seem to confirm 1573 as the right date for the introduction of a new play, and of a play that seems to be intended to follow upon the regular one. In the absence of any extracts from the costs of the old play, one can only assume that it continued in performance. A cessation would surely have been marked by its historians. The old play, however, seemingly had been undergoing that alteration which was common enough in the Coventry plays. Judas and Peter had always been in the cast but the 'too damsselles' that Halliwell-Phillipps mentions in the 1572 production presage the new play where they regularly appear. How long had they been listed in the old play? The fragmentary extracts tease out no answer; it would surely be stretching the meaning of the word to let it stand for Pilate's wife and any attendant or friend she might have acquired during the years in which the play was acted? Halliwell-Phillipps is interested in the question of women acting on the stage and thus takes just the single item he requires for his supposition. But he does mention 'other actors' and the fact that the 'damsselles' were introduced, presumably for the first time, into the Smiths' play. If the 'new pley' proper did not begin until 1573, was it an outgrowth of an experiment in 1572?

260   Account Book I f 106
It is not surprising that Pilate's club (p 262, l. 2) should demand repair, whatever comically melodramatic use he may have made of it. It is unexpected, however, that one should be hired for their star performer when he had presumably used the company's own for so long. Sharp found the last one in a company chest in 1790; it is illustrated facing page 51 in his *Dissertation*.

264   *Dissertation* p 36
Sharp comments on 'gowne' (p 265, l. 7): 'This was a gown belonging to Sir William Wigston, as appears in other entries, and was frequently borrowed by the Smiths for their Pageant. The charge of 8d. is for wine given in return for the use of the gown, which was worn by Herod' (p 36, fn f). The Wigstons had long been a powerful mercantile family in Coventry and in Leicester, where the leading grammar school was named for them (see *Desolation of a City* for the power of this family). John Wigston, a keen Lollard, was mayor in 1491; Roger was recorder 1527–40; a later John was a chantry priest at St Michael's in 1534 (Sharp, *Illustrative Papers*, p 38). The family had a house at Wolston Priory, some four miles east of Coventry, where two of the Martin Marprelate tracts were printed in 1589 (Donald J. McGinn, *John Penry and the Marprelate Controversy* [Rutgers, N.J., 1966], 101-16, 133, 154-5).

265   A 7(b) p 2
Details of the history of these companies of actors can be found in E.K. Chambers, *The Elizabethan Stage*, vol 2 (Oxford, 1923, rpt with corrections 1951) and Gerald Eades Bentley, *The Jacobean and Caroline Stage Dramatic Companies and Players*, vols 1 & 2 (Oxford, 1941).

266   unnumbered
The following earlier notices of rent payment for the Girdlers' pageant house come from a collection

of rentals bound together as CRO: 8 Rentals, and are additional to those for 1574 (see p 266), 1597 (p 349), and 1639 (p 443):

> 1545?
> f 185 (*Cheylesmore rental*)
>
> ...
>
> It*em* the Girdelers for ther pagyaunt house   iiij d
>
> ...
>
> 15?? (*1565?*)
> f 218 (*Cheylesmore rental*)
>
> ...
>
> The Girdilers for ther pagyaunt house   iiij d
>
> ...

In an undated rental roll (CRO: unnumbered) that is marked as 'before 1639,' this pageant house rental recurs: 'Of the Company of Girdlers iij d.' The rental continues under this description until 1658.

269   A 7(b) p 7
The accounts for this year clearly show some of the extra costs incurred by the city because of Queen Elizabeth's visit to Kenilworth Castle. She arrived at the castle on 9 July (for full details of the visit see Nichols' *The Progresses and Public Processions of Queen Elizabeth*, vol 1, pp 485-523; a fine evocation of the visit occurs in Sir Walter Scott's *Kenilworth*, chapters 30 and 31).

  The clerk of the market saw to the housing and feeding of the queen's retinue and pleasing the queen's taste: 'If the ale of the country will not please the queen, then it must come from London, or else a brewer to brew the same in the towns near' (MSS of the Pepys Library, MS 178, as abstracted in Historical Manuscripts Commission's *Report on the Pepys MSS* [1911], 179). Oxford and Coventry were to serve as providers of extra bread if need be. Letters were sent 'to know how the Queen may be served of beeves, muttons, veales and lambs, herons, shovelards, bittors, and any kind of fowl or fresh-water fish, rabbits &c, and what may be served by the day at Woodstock, Coventry, Warwick and Killingworth and price set for the same for the time of her abode there' (*ibid*, p 179). This extra work probably explains an odd item among the payments to entertainers: 'Item p*ai*d for returnynge of the Statut for Artificers & laborers iij s viij d' (CRO: A 7(b), p 8). The payment for meat-cattle noted in the Payments Out Book (pp 270-1) was also doubtless connected with the visit.

  So far in advance of the queen's visit preparations were laid, and so much was Coventry, a large city only five miles from Kenilworth, engaged in them. Cox had plenty of time to prepare his Hock Tuesday show.

271   MS Top. Warwickshire d.4 f 25v
BRL: 273978, f 8v says that thirty people died in the Bablake ward alone. The outbreak of the plague caused the Corpus Christi plays to be postponed this year.

272   Acc 100/17/1 f 67
Only the Drapers record a similar payment this year (the plays were cancelled because of plague);

both companies paid rather less than half what they usually spent on the production of their plays. The 1564 cancellations led to no such payments.

272   Acc 154 f 91

Daffern misdates these entries 1775 for 1575(?).

272   15191 pp 32-8

For a preliminary discussion of this letter and the Coventry Hock Tuesday play, see Introduction, pp xix-xx and notes 15, 16, pp lxiii-lxiv. Laneham travelled with Elizabeth's court to Kenilworth in his position of 'Clark of the Councel chamber door,' which position Leicester had obtained for him. In his 'Letter' he refers to himself as both Laneham and Langham, but he is always Langham in the court payments accounts; for this primary identification I follow R.J.P. Kuin, 'Robert Langham and his "Letter,"' *Notes and Queries*, ns, 25, no 5 (October, 1978), 426-7. The letter is dated at its close, 20 August 1575: it is addressed to a friend in London, Humfrey Martin, who was, like Laneham, a member of the Mercers' company of that city. In 'Leicester's Men at Kenilworth, Laneham's Letter,' *The Rise of the Common Player: a Study of Actor and Society in Shakespeare's England* (London, 1962), 141-61, the most recent study of this *Letter* in terms of theatrical history, Muriel Bradbrook, apparently unaware of the court accounts that Kuin used, dismisses the identification of Laneham with the mercer Langham and calls the description of his office 'imaginary — at least it finds no support in the queen's household accounts' (p 146). Miss Bradbrook argues 'that this document was written by a member of the Earl of Leicester's Men, John Laneham, and that it represents the common player's point of view' of the 1575 entertainments (p 143).

Elizabeth, missing most of the play on 9 July, had it acted again on the Tuesday following, 11 July (p 275, ll. 21-2 and p 45 of Laneham's letter). I have found no reference to Captain Cox (p 273, l. 27) in the city's records. The library of popular stories, books, plays, and songs he had 'at his fingers endz' may as well have been part of his patter as proof of his familiarity with them.

The four plays referred to on page 274 (ll. 10-11) are moral interludes. 'Nugize' or 'New Custom' is hardly 'auncient' as the limits for dating its writing are 1570?-1573 (Alfred Harbage, S. Schoenbaum [rev], *Annals of English Drama 975-1700* [London, 1964], 42). For the 'Hundred Mery talez' (p 274, ll. 7-8), see Introduction, note 8, page lxii.

The 'Alecu*n*ner' (p 274, l. 28) was chosen by the bailiff and summoned by each brewer to test his new beer: for each fault detected he received a gallon of the best ale (*Life in an Old English Town*, p 295).

Henry Goldingham (p 274, ll. 33-4) was a minor poet, writer, and actor in pageants. One of the masques of welcome to Elizabeth on her visit to Norwich in 1578 was his work. For her visit to Kenilworth he joined with George Ferrers and William Hunnis, master of the Children of Chapel Royal, poet and playwright, in writing a nightpiece based on an adventure of the Lady of the Lake.

The Coventry men were 'dignified' and 'beatified' (p 275, ll. 29-30) in ways they did not dream of fifty years later when, at Kenilworth on 19 August 1624, Ben Jonson's *Masque of Owls* was performed before Prince Charles (see Appendix 9).

276   A 16 p 31

This is the only indication that the Mercers had more than one pageant house. Sharp adds this note: 'Their Pageante House was situated in Gosford streete and was charged with a chief rente of 7s per ann: which upon the dissolution of the Gilds and Chantries came to the Crown — was granted inter alia 6 Edw VI to the Corporation and redeemed by the Mercers Compa*n*y 1660 at which time it was a dwelling House' (BL: 43645, f 89v). Sharp quotes also from Trinity Guild accounts (now lost): 'for 1473, 13th Edward IV ... *Recepti* Joh*anne* Thrumpton & Thoma Colyns custodib*us* de m*er*cers p*ro* reddit*u* de pagent house lij s vj d and a like payment occurs so late as 1516' (*Dissertation*, p 77). John Thrumpton was mayor in 1472.

The payment of the chief rent for the Gosford Street property is recorded in four pre-dissolution accounts edited by Geoffrey Templeman in the second volume of the records of the Trinity Guild.

Property rental for 1485–6 (here the rental is not entered as a 'chief rent': see Templeman's note 2 on p 69 for a comment on 'chief rent' and see endnote to 184, on p 541):

p 53

...

De magistro de le mercers   per annum vij s

...

Property rental for 1532–3:
p 119

...

Item the master of the Mercers for cheif of a tenement ther   vij s

...

First part of a property rental dated October 1534:
p 137

...

Item the Master of the Mercers for cheif   vij s

...

Four surviving rentals of properties transferred at the dissolution (CRO: A 11) mention the Mercers' single pageant house:

Undated
f 64v (*Trinity guild properties*)

...

It*em* the M*ai*ste*r* of the Marcers for a like Rent goyng owt of a ten*ement* ther   vij s

...

['Ther' is Gosford Street, clarified by the entry following in that rental.]

1559
f 196v (*Trinity guild properties*)

...

The M*ai*ste*r* of the Mercers for a like rent goyng owt of a ten*ement* ther pagynte howse   vij s

...

1564

f 104v *(Trinity guild properties)*

...

The Mercers for a Rent owt of ther pagiaunt house ther   vij s

...

1566

f 224 *(29 September) (Guild and chantry lands)*

...

It*em* the Mercers for a rent owt of ther pagyaunt house ther   vij s

...

There is a further notice of this rent in an undated (pre-1584) 'rentall of certaine landes & tenements belongyinge to the Corporation of the cyety of Coventre' (*Warwickshire Antiquarian Magazine*, 1 [1859–77], 481):

Rents of assyse

...

The mersers A rent out of the pagen house   vij s

...

In a lease dated 1 June 1602, 44 Elizabeth, the masters of the company let 'a messuage or tenement "lately being a pagent house" in Gosford "Street" to Richard Bankes, "yoman," his executors and assigns, at a yearly rent of twenty-seven shillings' (John Cordy Jeaffreson, 'The Manuscripts of the Corporation of Coventry (Second Report),' p 150). This is the 'howse in gosford Street, Late the Pageone howse' of which Banks' tenancy begins to be recorded in the Mercers' Accounts for 1602 (see p 361). The rent of twenty-seven shillings remains unchanged until 1642, and the Banks family hold tenure of it until 1657. It is referred to as a pageant house in the rental roll until 1607. Thereafter it is so called only twice more, in 1633 and 1634 (see pp 435, 436).

No other record, however, explains the plural 'padgyn howse*s*.' The leasing of the 'garden at the pagant howse' to Richard Fearman, the company clerk, in 1592 (see p 336 and its endnote p 591) refers to one pageant house. The amount spent suggests extensive enough repairs to cover more than one house. In the absence of the Mercer guild records before 1579, the question of house or houses cannot be resolved. To spend so freely on pageant affairs only three years before performances ceased posits strong confidence that the plays would continue.

276 *Dissertation* pp 11-12

Sharp (p 12) identifies the source of the first of these quotations as 'MS. Annals, Codex Dugd.' He does not specify one for the second. As Reader comments in a long note headed 'Hox Tuesday Play': 'There is an error in confounding the pageants with the Hox Tuesday Play, perhaps [⟨.⟩] ⸢an⸣ error in transcribing the original writing has converted *of* into *or* ...' (Bodl: MS Top. Warwickshire c.7, f 18). A similar error might explain the 1416 confusion of the two plays (see p 7). This entry concludes the gap-toothed history of the Hock Tuesday play which, although it delighted both Henry V and Elizabeth, frequently displeased the city fathers. Whether it was performed without a break from its first mention in 1416 (see p 7) cannot be said; it was put down in 1561 (see p 215), possibly as a token recognition of the Proclamation of 1559 (see E.K. Chambers, *The Elizabethan Stage*, vol 4 [Oxford, 1923], 263-4). The play seems to have been revived, at least in the year of Queen Elizabeth's visit, in 1566, if only to enable the city recorder to boast, with impermanent truth, that the show was performed 'in this Citty yearely' (see p 233). It seems to have been revived purely for her visit; the puzzling notice in the annal for 1568 of the play's being performed (see p 243 and endnote to MS Top. Warwickshire d.4, f 24v on pp 575-6) would scarcely have been needed unless the Hock Tuesday play had been put down again after Elizabeth's 1566 visit. Clearly, confirmation of the suppression comes in Cox's appeal to Elizabeth that he and his men and fellow citizens might 'haue theyr playz vp agayn' because they had been 'of late laid dooun' (see p 273). Her pleasure allowed the appeal and so, after a space of eight years — since the 1568 performance in fact — the play was seen again (see p 276). It is heard of no more; the laying down of the pageants only is noted by the 1580 annalists (see p 294).

279   Acc 15 f 12v
This is the first mention of Thomas Massey, who was to take a leading role in the Mercers', and the city's, drama and public entertainments for the next thirty-eight years. His name occurs regularly in these accounts — as a payer of quarterage, master of apprentices, occasional delinquent in atten-dance, upholsterer for his guild's chapel, and thrice when he was one of the assistant masters of the guild (1593, 1599, and 1605); however, only those entries directly concerned with his dramatic activities are entered hereafter. The narrative history of his dramatic struggles is gathered in Ap-pendix 6.

280   Acc 99/6/1 f 1
This ordinance was taken from a small, thirty-two leaf, unbound, badly stained notebook that appears to be late seventeenth century (there is a torn frontispiece of a gentleman in late seven-teenth century dress). The book is in good reading condition except for the bottom right hand corners of the first four leaves; on the fourth is the extract cited. Much of this corner is now crumbled into dust. Approximately 35 mm of line 11 is lost and 25 mm of line 12.

The street (l. 43) is Gosford Street. The two adjoining houses are listed as being in the tenant-ship of Edmund Donycliff and of 'the widdowe Dowley.' Neither of these two names appears in the Drapers' lists of rentpayers for this year or for those before and after it.

286   A 7(b) p 26
This is the only occasion on which the celebrations of the queen's holiday specifically mention plays (ll. 19-20). The payments made in 1593 and 1594 (see pp 338 and 341) were for unspecified 'paynes,' but generous enough to cover a play or plays (when compared with what touring acting troupes received). In 1596, 'singers' are mentioned for the only time (see p 346).

293   A 7(b) p 45
Although the same general heading ('Laid out at *maister* maior his Comaundem*ent*') is kept, a fresh method of grouping the accounts was started this year so that payments to troupes of actors are entered in one block.

293 *Dissertation* p 37
Sharp's note: 'This also was a gown borrowed or hired of the Sheremen and Taylors' Company,
who put forth a Pageant as well as the Smiths. Whether they had at this time discontinued exhibit-
ing cannot be ascertained, as the ancient Accounts of that Company are lost or destroyed' (p 37,
fn h). All the surviving company records notice a performance this year so that there would seem
to be no reason to believe the Shearmen and Tailors had ceased to produce their play. The gown
may have been borrowed for the character who usually wore the one loaned by Sir William Wigston (see endnote to *Dissertation* p 36 on p 579).

294 MS Top Warwickshire d.4 f 26ᵥ
Lest one think that the ending of the performances is ominously connected with the natural terrors
and dire illnesses of the year, it should be added that the annals frequently mention incredible natural
phenomena. In 1383 'yer was so great an Earthquake yat men did think ye last day came' (CRO:
Acc 2/E, f 8); CRO: Acc 2/D reports an earthquake which was universal in 1426 (p 49). If an omen be
sought, in 1578 'a great blazing starre' was seen (Bodl: MS Top. Warwickshire d.4, f 26); a portent
more dire appeared on 26 August 1581 — 'a commet or blazing starre, & a great smoake seene in the
aire whereout did come great flashing flames of fire' (Bodl: MS Top. Warwickshire d.4, f 26v).

294 *Dissertation* p 39
The quotation is from a lost annal; the 'again' is puzzling unless the non-performance in 1575 is
counted.
    Extant guild records show no sign that the plays would not be seen after 1579. Mayor Saunders'
leets would have been held in 1580: this suggests that the order to put down the plays probably
came at the Easter leet (Easter fell in the first week in April in 1580).

296 A 24 p 8
Sharp (BL: 43645, p 40) adds a note: 'A lease dated 12 July 1674 describes a tenement on the
eastside of Mill Lane as being "sometimes the place where the Smythes pagean house stood containing by the said street side 4½ Yards and so is square of that measure. It did sometime belong to
the Monastery of Rowley."' Sharp's further note, keyed to 'house,' reads: 'The House belongs
now (and did in 1671) to the Corporation of Coventry.'
    Four payments of rent for the Smiths' pageant house are recorded in the assorted rentals col-
lected in CRO: A 11:

	Undated	
	f 166v *(Rental of lands once belonging to the monastery of Rowley)*	
	...	
Millne	It*em* to a Ret of v goyg owt of the smythes paygont house in mylnelae	v s
	...	
	[This entry is very roughly scrawled.]	
	1564	
	f 121v	
	The Land*es* of the Lait Monasterie off Rowley	
	...	

Milne Lane		
	A rent owt of the smythes pagyaunt house ther	v s
	...	
	Undated	
	f 219v	
	...	
(.)ilne	It*em* a Rent goyng owt of the smythes pagiaunt house ther	v s
	...	
	1566	
	f 225v	
	...	
Mylne Lane	It*em* a quyt rent owt of the smythes pagyant house	v s

A further rental of this pageant house occurs in an undated (pre-1584) 'rentall of certaine landes & tenements belongyinge to the Corporation of the cyety of Coventre' (*Warwickshire Antiquarian Magazine*, 1 [1859–77], 493):

	Myllane	
	A quit rent out of the Smyth pagen house	v s
	...	

297   A 7(b) pp 64, 68

For some reason only three waits were paid this year. In 1570, the waits were named as James Hewet, Richard Sadler, William Styff, and Thomas Nichols. In 1583, they are named as John Thomas, James Hewet, Old Styff, and Anthony Styff.

300   Acc 468/D 11/Box 5 no. 429

As can be seen from the map, Jordan Well is a continuation of Gosford Street leading into Earl Street.

The Drapers' accounts mention both an old and a new pageant house; the old one is presumably that mentioned in 1392 as being in Little Park Street (see p 3). The Mercers' pageant house (or pageant houses according to the 1576 entry in the Payments Out Book, see p 276) was also in Gosford Street. The 'pagient Howses' may, therefore, refer to those of the Drapers and the Mercers. It is also possible that this is a reference to the Tanners' pageant house whose whereabouts is nowhere mentioned in existing records.

The commercial power of the Drapers may be gauged from the fact that, of those drawing up this indenture, Thomas Nicolas was mayor in 1570–1, Richard Barker was mayor in 1571–2, Ralph Joynour was mayor in 1576–7, Robert Letherbarowe was mayor in 1577–8, John Riley was mayor in 1591–2, Michael Joyner was sheriff in 1579–80, and Henry Sewall was mayor in 1587–8.

302   A 9 p 127

The Cheylesmore leets were held on the days following the city leets and their costs were met by the bailiff. Goldston became the leader of the city waits at about this time. The unexpectedly high reward of 10s may be the musicians' reward for playing at both leet dinners.

303   A 16 p 51
This is extremely generous reward for Mr Smith's pains. It has been inferred that his pains consisted
in taking the play from the vice-chancellor of his university, Thomas Legge, just as the latter had
'at last refined it to the *purity* of the *Publique Standard*' (Thomas Fuller, *A History of the Worthies
of England* [London, 1662] , *s.v.* 'Norwich,' 276). Chambers quotes Fuller merely to wonder if there
is a connection between the taking of the one play and the appearance of Smith's of the same
name at Coventry (*Elizabethan Stage*, vol 3, pp 408-9). W.W. Greg ('Lost Plays,' *A Bibliography of
the English Printed Drama to the Restoration*, vol 2 [London, 1951] , 997) adds some details of
drama history but essentially leaves Fuller's report of 'some Plageary' beside the Coventry record.
Further than this one cannot go without more evidence; so bold and public a theft one hopes unlikely, if only for Smith's and Coventry's reputations. Until proved guilty, Smith must stand inno-
cent. Sharp's biographical footnote (p 40, fn o) tells us that Smith was 'a native of Warwickshire,
[who] was in 1577, at the age of 14, elected a Scholar at St. John's College, Oxford, being one of
the earliest students sent from the Free School in Coventry, upon Sir Thomas White's foundation
in that College.... Wood says he was greatly esteemed in the University for his piety and learning,
and that after filling the situation of Lecturer in St. Paul's Cathedral, London, with much credit to
himself for some time, he was in 1592 appointed Vicar of Clavering, in Essex, where he died in
1616.'
    The size of the city's payment to Smith is matched by what we know of the expenses lavished on
this production. The plot, so far as can be gathered, seems to be based on Josephus' *Jewish War*.
All 1584 references to the play suggest that it was performed only once; if it was the play elected
to be performed in 1591, the council allowed it to be acted both upon Midsummer Day and St
Peter's Day.

303   MS Top. Warwickshire d.4   f 26v
It is disappointing to the dramatic historian that what was so obviously a spectacular final produc-
tion of civic religious drama in England should attract only the passing attention of one annalist.
The 1591 play(s) are mentioned by none.

305   Acc 3/2   f 208   col b
Certainly the expenses for playing *The Destruction of Jerusalem* this year were between two and
three times what was spent to play the cycle in its last years, but this is still a curious entry. There
are no Carpenters' Accounts for 1578-83 so that the 'iij yeres' might be 1578, 1579, and 1584.

307   *Illustrations* pp 56-7
Sharp (p 37) writes 'no less than six rehearsals took place previous to the public exhibition of this
new Pageant.' Sharp (p 37, fn k) identifies John Deane (p 308, l. 5) as the company's summoner.

310   A 7(b) pp 118, 119, 122
Four waits are paid but only three named — James Hewet's name is missing. He had for many
years been their leader. The payment to Goldston (l. 31) marks the first appearance of the man
who was to take Hewet's place as leader of the waits and first musician in the city. He had earlier
played at a civic dinner (see Cheylesmore Manor Account Book, p 302). He is called 'leader' in
1590 (see Wardens' Accounts, p 327) but may have been so in 1587 when he is paid for sounding

the trumpet (see p 317). An undated note, scribbled at the top of an empty page in the MS (p 65, col a) in the midst of a long alphabetical list of recipients of Sir Thomas White's alms money, notes: 'Delyveed to goldstone the sylver collers weinge xxxj once.' This entry is in the same hand that inserts in this same list, beginning on page 67, an inventory of city armoury dated 21 May 1589 (see pp 324-5). The delivery of the official badges of the waits to Goldston in 1589 would sort well with his being named as leader of the waits in 1590.

'Old Styffe' (p 310, l. 5), head of a musical family and a favourite in the city (he was well-pensioned, see p 311), makes his last appearance this year. John Wallans (Walland) (p 310, l. 16) was Lord Compton's bearward (see also 320, l. 36).

311   A 14(a)   p 185

John Marston was a distinguished member of the Middle Temple and his name is often found in civic and guild records until his death in 1599. He was the father of John Marston, the dramatist, who was raised and educated in Coventry (though surviving grammar school records do not mention him). The dramatist inherited property in Coventry when his mother died in 1621, but the only mention of it occurs in a letter written by his widow(?) seeking reversion of title to all, or some, of that property (see p 482). This property is presumably that which was leased to Phillip Adams (for many years the city's mace-bearer) at the council meeting held on 2 August 1637.

311   Acc 3/2   f 210v

The payment for minstrels and singers (l. 35) revives an old custom of the Carpenters (see Introduction, p xxi and p 62). Such extravagant rewards are given the musicians only in this year (possibly because they were the waits or other professional men?). Thereafter the music is that of the boys of Bablake.

315   Acc 3/2   f 212v

The Carpenters had a traditional fondness for music at their guild feasts. The boys of Bablake (choristers of St John's) undoubtedly came to sing; they were often accompanied by their music master, John Launder (see p 326).

318   Acc 100/18/2   f 7v

The last appearance of the rebuilt pageant house occurs in the Rentgatherers' Accounts for 1594, Book II, f 23: 'Item in prymis payd for setting of to cressetes on the tope of the Chimney at the house in myllane vj d.'

319   Acc 100/18/2   ff 8, 8v

The paintings presumably decorated the cloths that hung about the pageant wagon. The scribe decided that no details were needed of the subject matter. The entry on folio 8v refers to what must have been the last meeting before work on taking down the pageant house was begun.

321   Acc 15   f 45v

One might expect to find Thomas Massey's name among those buying 'pagant stufe'; however, those who bought were much more powerful figures in the company than he. Henry Kirvin was the master in 1588, as he had been in 1579 and 1583; Roger had been master in 1582; yet another Kirvin, John, was an undermaster in 1582 and 1589, and the family supplied mayors of Coventry in 1535, 1559, 1567, and 1632. The Diglens were another ruling civic and guild family. Gilbert, who buys here, had been mayor in 1582, and master of the company in 1585 and 1589. John Whitehead was undermaster in 1585 and 1587, the master's fellow in 1589, master in 1592, and died in office while mayor in 1596. Edward Walker was the master's fellow in 1588. Thomas Darlinge was an undermaster in 1583 and 1586. Massey was not chosen as an undermaster until 1593.

323   A 7(b) p 182
The payment to Goldston (l. 35) is presumably for services in the singing school. The two previous entries are: 'given to mr holland at the scoole xx s' and 'given to mr hamon the vsher x s.' Holland is Philemon Holland (1552–1637) the distinguished classical scholar. He was connected with the grammar school from at least 1588 when, on 18 December, he received a payment as an usher, but he was not appointed headmaster until 1628, a promotion made as much out of charity as anything else. His fame is as a translator of Camden, Suetonius, and other classical writers. In *The Dunciad* (1729) one finds: 'the groaning shelves Philemon bends' (Bk I, l. 134); Winstanley commented on this line as follows: '*he* translated *so many books*, that a man would think he had done *nothing else*, insomuch that he might be call'd *Translator General of his age*. The books alone of his turning into English, are sufficient to make a *Country Gentleman a compleat Library*.' His name occurs frequently in civic and parish records. The city treated him kindly in his old age with a pension, continued to his widow. A full survey of his career, especially in Coventry, can be found in Sharp's *Illustrative Papers*, pp 178-84.

324   A 14(a) p 67 col b
This is the first full description of the contents of the city armoury. It shows what could be drawn upon for occasions of display and, if necessary, defence.

326   Acc 3/2 f 218v
John Launder later became the music master at the grammar school. See endnote to A 7(b) p 379 on page 593.

327   MS Top. Warwickshire c.7 ff 83v, 84
The queen's holiday was Elizabeth's coronation day, 17 November (see also p 338). The Smiths were breaking up their pageant at this time. Sharp (p 15) says 'Velvet Hose were sold in 1590' as part of this business.

328   A 7(b) p 198
For 'The Players of Coventry' see endnote to A 17 p 21 on page 577-8.

328   100/37
The Wilkes family achieved some prominence in the sixteenth century in Coventry. John Wilkes was chamberlain in 1513–14 and one of the council of twenty-four in the next year; a William was a sheriff in 1566 and mayor in 1581 (he was a tailor). John, the Oxford clerk, seems clearly to have been a member of this family for the ex-pageant house of the Tailors and Shearmen, deeded to him here, was sold by 'William Wilkes of the cittie of Coventre Skynner' (see p 376). One further distinguished member of the family (by name, if not of close blood relationship) was also an important property-holder in the city and a man connected with drama in an indirect way. Dr William

Wilkes, a favourite preacher of James I and father-in-law of John Marston the dramatist, rented a house very close to where Marston grew up. In an entry dealing with the Priory dye-house occurs: 'The site and ground of the saied pryorie late purchased by the Cytie containeth iiij Acres of ground and better within which Cyrcuyte Mr. Denton holdeth A garden and A Crofte by lease ...' (1581 Survey, CRO: A 24, p 44). In another list of city properties taken in 1613 (CRO: A 29) is: 'Mr. Doctor Wilkes for the Rent of his garden there beinge parcell of the Scite of the Priory there xxviij s.' In the Council Book (p 278), Wilkes' lease of his garden, the Priory, is remade, dated 44 Elizabeth, 7 November 1601 – 16 November 1602. In the same list, in the section recording 'guilds and chantries lands' in Cross Cheaping is this entry concerning Wilkes: 'Mr. Doctor Wilkes a rent Charge out of his house there xl s.' This is likely the property Denton held there in 1581: 'There is A Tenemente and a garden which Mr. Denton holdeth wherein he dwelleth in Fee Farm paieing to the Cittie xl s by yeare' (p 54). Wilkes also held valuable property — the Moathouse Farm estate — just beyond the city walls to the northwest. 'A lettere to the Maior of Couentree for a lease in reuercion of the whole farme of Coundon to be made to Dr. Wilkes, one of his Maiesties ordynarie Chaplens, And a Tennant of the same farme, for xli^{tie} yeares to begynne after thexpiracion of his lease in being, for the Rentes now payable out of the same, without fyne, in as aumple maner as the Late Prior graunted the lease yet in possession. procured by the Lord Henry Howard' (dated 5 January 1604, PRO: S.P. 38 Doquets 7, p 49). The lease in Coundon is declared void and the city takes over the property on 17 March 1620 (Council Book, pp 455-6). John Marston married Dr Wilkes' daughter, Mary, circa 1605, her father at that time being incumbent of Barford, Wiltshire. Perhaps they first met in Coventry.

John Richardson (l. 41) was mayor in 1586. Thomas Barrowes (p 329, l. 2) may have been the man insulted by one of the Lady Elizabeth's players (see pp 393-4). A Christopher Waren (p 329, l. 31), probably the dyer's son, bought this property in 1609 (see pp 376-7); he was mayor in 1611.

332   A 7(b)   p 213
At this time Thomas Massey (p 332, l. 9) was in charge of the city's celebrations of the queen's holiday; in such matters his partner was generally William Showell (see pp 338, 341). Here the 'parteners' may be the singers mentioned for that celebration in 1596 (see p 346). However, this year the last of the great civic plays was produced, seemingly under Massey's direction, and this payment may be connected with that show.

332   A 14(a)   p 216
The choice offered deliberately (?) excludes the possible revival of all or part of the Corpus Christi cycle ('& non other playes'). Corpus Christi Day fell on 3 June, thereby removing the performance days from possible association with the old religion. The extravagance of The Destruction of Jerusalem was probably beyond the city's purse. The Conquest of the Danes revives memories of the Hock Tuesday play; history plays were the popular mode of the time. The council took as they gave — this is the last mention of maypoles in the city records.

333   Acc 3/2   f 222v
This reduction in the traditional pageant payments matches the generally stringent financing of the play this year.

334   MS Top. Warwickshire c.7 f 100v
Whelar was presumably the master of the Whittawers or the man who managed their contribution
to the 1591 performance.

334   Add MS 43645 f 57v
The date should read 'the thirde daye of Januari 1590 in the xxxiiith' (l. 23) and one assumes that
Sharp misread two not very clear final minims. However, the third of January in the xxxixth of
Elizabeth would fall in what would then have been dated 1596. A confusion of 0 and 6 is equally
likely. However, whether or not Sharp noticed the discrepancy, I have elected to follow 'the thirde
daye of Januari 1590' and date the inventory 1591. See endnote to previous Cappers' inventory,
Add MS 43645, f 57 on page 574.

336   Acc 15 f 3v
The arrangement with Fearman resembles a pension. Fearman had been clerk of the company since at
least 1579, and in 1592 Michael Sandbrook was paid 3s 4d for his first year's wages and the same
amount for drawing up the account. Thereafter, until 1598, both Fearman and Sandbrook received
13s 4d a year; Fearman's was called his 'fee,' Sandbrook's, his 'wages' as clerk. From 1599, only
Sandbrook's name appears, and as clerk he received 26s 8d.
     The brief rental rolls of the company (thirteen tenements, nine of them leased jointly) make no
mention of either a pageant house or its garden, nor is there any mention of the garden after this
1592 agreement. Fifteens (a property tax) are paid on the pageant house from 1595 until 1600
(see Payments Out Book 1576, p 276 and its endnote on pp 581-3).

339   Acc 15 f 60
Is it possible that the 'Wheeles' entry represents the last 'pagant stufe' disposed of? The Cappers
used such 'little wheels' for the scaffold of their pageant.

341   A 16 p 70
This entry, dated 26 March, was also entered in the Council Book (CRO: A 14(a), p 230) where it
is crossed out:

                    ...
          [paid more the same tyme to maister maior for william showell & massie for
          their paynes on the queenes holliday last xiij s iiij d]
          ...

353   A 7(b) pp 317, 318
Thomas Goldston was the son(?) of the leader of the city's waits. Sir John Harington's college was
King's College, Cambridge. His family seat was at Combe Abbey, just outside Coventry. (For the
extensive land he held see VCH *Warks*, vol 8, p 105.) He was recorder for Coventry at this time; on
his death in 1613, he was succeeded very briefly by his son who died in 1614 and was followed in
this office by Sir Edward Coke. At the coronation of James I he was created Baron Harington of
Exton and shortly thereafter appointed guardian of James' daughter, Princess Elizabeth. For the

latter part of his life and connections with Coventry, see endnote to MS Top. Warwickshire d.4 on page 593.

The earl of Essex (p 353, ll. 25-7) is the only earl mentioned in this section of the accounts, Mr Wheat receiving 21s 4d for a purse given to the earl. Mr Hancock was also paid 7s 6d 'for Changing gold that the Earle of Essex had 17 of aprill 99' (p 317). The earl also was expensively entertained (40s) at the Bull on 29 March (p 320).

355   A 7(b)   p 331

The 'fyle of Record' (l. 40) cannot be found and no mention of the matter occurs elsewhere in extant civic records.

A previous trouble with players at Coventry worried Sir Henry Bedingfield, Princess Elizabeth's rigorous gaoler, when she was in his keeping. On the 30 July 1554, in one of his reports 'to the Councell,' he wrote: 'Theare hathe Com to my knowledge synce my last wrighting vnto your lordships, ij severall matters tending to notable sedicion; The holle circumstances whereof appering by divers letteres my sayd brother hathe to deliver vnto your lordships. In which cases, or the lyke hereafter to insue, I shall beseche you to put order for the ponyshement of the offenders. Sir William Reynsford hathe taken great payne in Ryding to Coventry for the taking of one of the offenders.' As his next letter makes clear, the 'offenders' were players at Coventry. Their offence is not revealed and nothing in the extant Coventry records brings any light to the matter or to Sir William's earnest visit. In his next report, dated 16 August, Sir Henry reverts to the matter: 'At my laste sendyng to your lordshipps by my brother Anthonie, I advertised yow off certayn players, and off oon heywoode, which wrote a sedicious letter at Coventrie, and there remayneth In prison. Yff yt myght plese your lordshipp to determyn your order to the comissioners and other officers towching the same, yt sholde be moche comforte to them In their service, and terrour to the lyke offendours.' It is not clear whether Heywood is one of the offending players or an individual unconnected with them. John Heywood, the playwright, who married into the Coventry family of Rastell, was an adherent of Mary's — he left England for good on Elizabeth's accession — and was hardly likely to be writing seditious letters against her or her policies.

This brief commentary throws a little more light on the mood of Coventry at the time when John Careles was being released to play his pageant part (see pp 207-8).

The letters are quoted from: 'State Papers Relating to the Custody of the Princess Elizabeth at Woodstock, in 1554 ... Communicated by the Rev. C.R. Manning,' *Norfolk Archaeology*, 4 (1855), 133-231. The two quotations used above come from pages 201-2 and 205-6.

356   A 7(b)   pp 332, 333

Goldston has presumably become music master at the grammar school as well as leader of the waits. In 1600, the usual salaries are paid to the masters: Tovy receives 20s, Arnold 10s, Cawdrey 6s 8d, and Goldston 5s. It is not known where 'the angell' (l. 18) was situated. In 1459, the duke of Buckingham lodged there when he came to see why the city was laggard in answering a commission of Henry VI (*LB*, p 308). In 1626, the Carpenters held a guild dinner there (CRO: Acc 3/2, f 315v). In the nineteenth century, a favourite departure station for carriers was the Angel in Cook Street. Some inn names persist over the centuries; if the Angel is one, its situation can be marked.

357   Acc 100/17/1   f 93v

The Weavers still had their pageant costumes at this time (they were hiring them in 1604; see p 366). This puzzling item is probably for a gown hired out for some unknown purpose.

358   A 7(b) pp 345, 346
I have been unable to discover whether widow Massam lived in Coventry where her husband made
virginals or whether she was being helped to Basingstoke where her husband's trade had been plied.
In the undated wardens' rental (pre-1584, quoted in 'A rentall of certaine landes & tenements
belongyinge to the Corporation of the cyety of Coventre,' *Warwickshire Antiquarian Magazine*, 1
[1859–77] , 485), John Massam occupies a tenement in Little Park Street. Judging by the marginal
note 'a chen & A bucket,' it had a well. The rent was high: 23s 4d. In the accounts of guild and
chantry lands (CRO: A 21(a), p 3) made on 14 December 1573, an item of repair reads: 'Vppon
Iohn Massams howsse in lyttle parke strete vj s viij d.'
      The payment to Goldston (l. 34) was made at the viewing of the grammar school.

361   Acc 15 f 88
In his *Calendar of the Books, Charters, Letters Patent, Deeds &c*, Jeaffreson abstracts a deed dated
21 June, 44 Elizabeth, of a lease for sixty-one years by the masters and wardens of the Mercers'
company 'of a messuage or tenement "lately being a pagent house" in Gosford Streete of the said
city, to Richard Bankes of the same city yoman, his executors and assigns, at a yearly rent of
twenty-seven shillings' (p 72). Richard Banks continues to pay the same annual rent for this
house until 1642 (it remains in his or his family's hands until 1657); this regular rent is not noted
here after 1603. It is last referred to as the pageant house in the annual rental rolls in 1607 (Acc
15, f 97). In the lists of the Chief Rents, it is so called twice more, in 1633 and 1634 (see pp 435
and 436). See also endnote to A 16, p 31 on pages 581-3.

364   A 7(b) p 379
John Launder is mentioned regularly in these accounts between 1588 and 1641. The singing school
master was apparently the son of one of the longest lived servants of the city; they are later occasionally differentiated as 'the younger' and 'the elder.' The elder began as a labourer on the conduits in1588, work which he eventually oversaw; he also helped in the kitchen at grand mayoral
feasts, achieved a post (never explained) which brought him twenty shillings annually, and accumu-
lated a variety of jobs at Bablake — looking to the leads, sweeping the church, attending to its bells
and chimes and clock. By 1617, the city found it convenient to pay him 'xij d the weeke' (p 605).
In 1637, a 'tenement and grarden in Gosford street late in the occupacion of old Iohn Launder
now deceased' (CRO: A 7(c), p 22) date his death. John Launder the younger was a teacher in the
grammar school from 1605 until our records cease in 1642. The granting to him of a school house
is recorded in the Council Book, 19 September 1593.

364   MS Top. Warwickshire d.4 ff 30v-1
It was for this visit that Thomas Massey went to such lengths to have some dramatic show made by
the city. As an example of what the city did do, the money it did spend, and the extent of a grand
civic banquet, the accounts for the banquet made for the Lady Elizabeth are given in Appendix 7.
      Lord Harington, guardian of Princess Elizabeth (see endnote to A 7(b), p 317 on p 591), ap-
pointed John Tovy (l. 40), headmaster of the free school in Coventry, as his chaplain and as tutor
to Elizabeth, who was almost eight years of age on her visit to Coventry. A few months later, to
guard her against a plot to kidnap her, proclaim her queen, and bring her up a Roman Catholic,

Harington hurried her to Coventry on 6 November where she stayed with Mayor Hopkins. In a letter to Mr Secretary Barlow describing the 'wild riot, excess, and devastation of time and temperance' at James's court, Sir John Harington added: 'My cosin, Lord Harington of Exton, doth much fatigue himself with the royal charge of the princess Elizabeth; and, midst all the foolery of these times, hath much labour to preserve his own wisdom and sobriety' (*Nugae Antiquae: Being a Miscellaneous Collection of Original Papers in Prose and Verse* ..., vol 1 [London, 1804], 353). The extravagance of Elizabeth did not allow him to preserve his own fortune. In 1613, he, Lady Harington, and Tovy accompanied Elizabeth and her husband, the elector palatine, abroad. Harington died at Worms, in August 1613, on his way home. Catholic hatred of him led to speculation of foul play. Tovy, who had the reputation of being an uncompromising Protestant, did return home but died the next year; his death was attributed to poison at the hands of the Jesuits (J. Tom Burgess, *Historic Warwickshire* [London, 1893], 137-46, and Sharp, *Illustrative Papers,* pp 176-7).

374   A 7(b) pp 442, 444
Assuming, as is very likely, that the entry: 'Paid to the lorde Comptons men xl s' (l. 8) is a payment to a troupe of actors forgotten when the main list of such payments was drawn up, this is the first time that such a troupe is given a 'present' of a small entertainment (ll. 13-15). Such 'presents' were normally reserved for distinguished visitors and were far more costly. In this same year, for instance, 28s 6d was spent on the prince of Germany at the Bull, and a further 20s on a 'bankett at m*aiste*r maiors howse'; 14s on the countess of Derby at the Bull; to the lord treasurer at the Bull and at Mr Breres' house, £11.12.9., an exceptional amount (CRO: A 7(b), p 443). The second time a company is given a small entertainment occurs in 1616 when the prince's men are offered sack at the mayor's parlour (see p 396).

375   A 7(b) p 455
This is the only time when a performance on this day is mentioned. Probably the traditional leet dinner and the troupe's visit happily coincided.

376   100/37
For details of the Wilkes family, see endnote to 100/37 on page 589. Edmund Brownell (Brownhyll) was mayor at the time of Elizabeth's visit, was elected MP for Coventry in 1571 and 1572, and died in February 1573; he was a draper of great wealth. The inventory of his properties was taken on 31 March 1573 and its worth amounted to £339 6s (see pp 486, 488). Fourteen houses and tenements are listed in his possession; one of these is in 'the mylne lane one the west syde' (Will and Inventory in Lichfield Joint Record Office). Samuel (p 377, l. 18) was his son. Christopher Waren (l. 32) was mayor in 1611–12.

381   A 7(b) p 487
In a period when 5s is the least sum given to a company of players, and the average over the previous three years is 11s, 2s 6d divided between four companies is ludicrously small. This was no year of special economy in the city; indeed, the civic officials seemed to have received extra clothing allowances this year (such an allowance was a regular part of their salaries).

383   Acc 100/18/2 f 56
The accounts for 1609 are followed by those for 1611 and 1612. Each of the latter two records

rents for a whole year plus one extra quarter. This may explain why the account following 1612 is skimpily introduced only by the names of the rentgatherers rather than the fuller formula of names, company, date, and occasionally regnal year, and why it only collects half a year's rent and presumably covers part of 1610 which is otherwise missing from the sequence of accounts. After this oddity (further marked by the paginator [Sharp?] having chosen here to omit a leaf in his numbering), the regular series of accounts takes up again. The accounts for 1614 are dated at the head 1615, but this mistake, repeated at the end of the accounts, is there corrected.

384   A 16   p 105
There is no sure definition for 'vauters' in this context. The term may mean vaulters, in the sense of tumblers or acrobats, or it may possibly be a local form of 'vewters,' keepers of greyhounds come to the city to show off their dogs.

390   MS Top. Warwickshire d.4   f 33
This 'statagem' is entered in a hand different from any other found in the annal. The large-scale mock battle may have some roots in the burlesque fight which was the central action of the Hock Tuesday play (see endnote to *Dissertation*, p 8 on p 542). When Queen Anne visited Bristol, a mock sea-battle was performed for her entertainment on 4 July 1613 (see Revd. Samuel Seyer, *Memoirs Historical and Topographical of Bristol and its Neighbourhood, from the Earliest Period down to the Present Time*, vol 2 [Bristol, 1823], 266-7).

393   A 14(a)   p 394
The increase of the number of waits from four to five and their salary from £4 to £7 a year may be connected with the reassertion of the duties and size of the Watch which is entered in the Council Book at the council held on 2 July 1614 (CRO: A 14(a), pp 382-3):

Watch

At this day it is agreed that there shall be warned for the Watch everie night fyfteen, of whom the Conestable shall be allowed one man for warning them, and that eleven persons shall watch besyds one of the officers, to whom shall be allowed the other three men for his pains, and that they shall watch from the first of Aprill vntill the first of September from nyne a clocke of the night vntill three in the morning, and from the first of Septembre to the first of Aprill from nyne to [three] fore and yf any of M*aiste*r Maiors officers shall not duly obserue these howers or some other sufficient man for him, to see the watch truly kept, then vppon iust proof / made by any of the Conestables of his negligenc⟨.⟩ herein, he shall loose his night*es* wages, and the conest⟨....⟩ that so fyndeth out his fault shall have the wage⟨.⟩ for that night in recompence of his pains therin.

There was no fixed number of waits in England; four to six was usual.

Although it was the duty of the waits to play at such 'solom ffeast*es*' as the mayor shall command, it was usual for them to receive an extra payment for this (see 'allholland dynner' this year, p 392, ll. 35-6).

393   A 16 p 119
The matter 'Concerning the Players' may well have been their playing against the wishes of the
mayor. Possibly the sum covered an award given to players at Warwick. There is nothing elsewhere
to explain the payment; the pertinent Warwick records were destroyed by the fire which swept the
town in 1694.

393   Misc 4   1946/9
Barrowes' letter is dated 28 March, as is Coke's (pp 394-5), but Coke's cannot be an instant reply
to it. The company was being troublesome, as a lost letter from the mayor to Sir Edward Coke
must have proved. In such a contentious time, one of the actors may well have insulted Barrowes,
whose indignation took him to the mayor. In 1615, the 28 March fell on the Tuesday between
Passion and Palm Sunday.
       The player, Robert Fintche (p 394, l. 16), does not appear in Bentley's *The Jacobean and
Caroline Stage*.

394   A 79 p 113
Sir Edward Coke, recorder of the city at this time (elected 7 March 1613, see Council Book,
p 379), was 'an official always unfriendly to players' (Bentley, *The Jacobean and Caroline Stage*,
vol 6, p 81). Clearly, the Lady Elizabeth's players wished to perform on a Sunday, contrary to the
mayor's wish; Coke's powerful words were intended to settle the matter, and presumably did for
in the upshot, the company did not play at all. Their name does not occur in the wardens' list of
payments to players.

396   A 7(b) p 591
See endnote to A 7(b), p 444 on page 594.

400   A 7(b) p 611
James Cranford was elected headmaster of the grammar school on 25 March 1611, a post he held
until January 1628 (see Sharp, *Illustrative Papers*, p 178).

400   A 16 p 139
The payment to Burley the tailor (ll. 33-4) was presumably to replace apparel lost in travel or by
accident at Coventry during the royal visit.

401   MS Top Warwickshire d.4 ff 33v-4
Fuller details of this visit are given by Nichols (*The Progresses of James I*, vol 3, pp 422-31), some
from documents no longer extant. Excerpts from these follow in the text (see pp 403-5).

404   *Progresses of James I* vol 3 pp 430-1
These figures were sent to Nichols by Sharp; Nichols acknowledges this aid in footnote 4, page 422.

407   Account Book I f 156
Henry Owyn (l. 19) had been a member of the guild since 1604 and was a master in 1613 and
1617; what he had done or failed to do in 'Pageon street' I do not know. The Cappers' pageant
house was in Mill Lane, as were those of the Weavers, Shearmen, Whittawers, Pinners, and Smiths.

414 A 16 p 193
Full information about Daniell, a provincial player, can be found in Bentley, *The Jacobean and Caroline Stage*, vol 2, pp 420-1. This visit is not recorded by Bentley.

416 Acc 154 f 188
Two new fairs were granted in 1621; 21-3 April and 16-18 August. These were in addition to the great Corpus Christi fair and the 21-3 October fair instituted in 1552 (see VCH *Warks*, vol 8, p 165).

421 A 7(b) p 748
These staves were probably black (or blackened) in recognition of the death of James I on 27 March.

422 A 7(b) p 758
The year is the accounting one: in the next year's accounts the king's players are rewarded for a visit made on 16 November 1626. Visiting troupes are few and far between in these years, however.

423 A 7(b) p 776
In 1615 (see p 393), five waits were named rather than the city's usual four. There seems to have been some effort to set the waits on a new footing this year as new instruments were bought for two of them, one being Edward Man, who was the leader in 1615.

426 *Dissertation* p 12
There is no other mention of the city helping defray the pageant expenses. The city controlled the organization of the cycle but, so far as is known, did little to help carry the financial burden it imposed — rather the contrary according to Mayor Coton's letter to Cromwell in 1539 (pp 148-9). His awareness of general money problems for his citizens had been shown earlier in his mayoralty. In 1538, he and his brethren called fifty 'discreit & credible *persones*' to debate with them how best to make sure that the city as a whole benefited from the use of the lammas lands rather than the few. 'And thereupon for the good gou*er*naunce, rule & conse*r*uacion of the said Com*i*naltie & commoners and for the vniu*er*sall profit & commoditie of the same' (*LB*, p 730), it was decided to rent certain named pieces of land taken from the common lands, thereby winning hard financial 'profite, ease & comoditie of the said Com*i*naltie in manou*r* & fourme folowyng, That is to say, ffor the gen*er*all & com*en* paymen*tes* which hereafter shal-be & ought to be payed by the Com*i*naltie of the said Citie as fivetenes & suche other com*m*on charges' (*ibid*, p 734). Fines for infractions of usage were similarly to be 'put in a Com*en* box to the vse & behove of the said Com*i*naltie' (*ibid*, p 733). One of the thirty-nine named pieces was: 'Barnes-feild*es* by yeir ... xxiij s iiij d.' (*ibid*, p 732). Only three rents were higher than this; twenty-four rents were 10s a year or less.

Perhaps from this 'Com*en* box' some of the expenses incurred in the wider civic celebrations of Corpus Christi Day and the Midsummer Watch were met (see p 181). However, Coton may have overstated his case to Cromwell of the burdens thrust upon Coventrians, from highest to lowest, by the demands of these celebrations upon the purse; it is clear that guild accounts do not cover every guildsman's out-of-pocket expenses for those days.

In turning to the lammas lands for support the city authorities were attempting to use a very fractious element in civic life. The lammas lands were incessantly troublesome: they are first mentioned in a dispute of 1384 (Leet Book, pp 2-6), and not until 1860 was a considerable part of the controversy about them settled. M.D. Harris succinctly describes the issues involved: 'Perhaps the townsmen were more sensitive with regard to the Lammas lands than on any other point. From time immemorial they possessed certain rights over the common and Lammas pastures which surrounded the city. On the former there was pasture for their cattle the whole year through, while on the other hand, they merely shared with the various freeholders the use of the Lammas ground, driving their cattle upon it at certain seasons of the year, namely, from Lammas to Candlemas (August 1 to February 2); during the remaining months the fields were in private hands. The extent of the common pastures was well known, but the peculiar tenure of the Lammas lands made it a more difficult matter to determine the exact area of pasture, held six months "in commonalty," and six "in severalty"' (*Life in an Old English Town*, pp 107-8).

The determinations of individual landholders and the citizens were frequently at odds. As has been noted (see endnote to Account Book I, f 36, col a, p 563), one such difference cost Nicholas Heynes his mayor's office in 1525. In an earlier fierce dispute between the city and the Bristowe family: 'the mayor and divers citizens — such is the account of the affair Bristowe gave in his petition to Edward IV. in the following year — "stered and provokyd and comaundyd mony and dyuers rotys personys ... to the number of vc (500) personys and more ... [who] in manere of warre arrayed, that is for to say [with] byllys, launcegayes, jakkys, salettys, bowes, arrowes, and with mottokys and spadeys, sholles and axes," with evil intent came to Bristowe's fields.' There they ripped up hedges, cut down trees, and were only stayed from destroying the mills by Bristowe's servants' literally buying them off. What was salt to Bristowe's wounds was the fact that: 'William Pere, oon of the aldermen of the same cite, by the commaundment of the seid late mayre and Richard Braytoft, browght with hym the wayteys of the same cite to the seid riotours in reresyng of their seid rioteys, and like as the[y] hade doon a grete conquest or victori, ... made theym pype and synge before the said riotours all the weye ... to the seid cite, which ys by space of a myle largele or more' (*Life in an Old English Town*, pp 210-11, quoting an untraced document, Corp. MS. F.3.).

Bristowe's enclosures were southwest of the city at Whitley, which is where 'Barnes close' (usually called Baron's field) is situated. The control of the lammas lands was in the hands of the city chamberlains, but nothing in their accounts gives any suggestion of support for the pageants.

Reader's note on this riot by the 'poore Commoners,' as quoted by Nowell, is: 'A considerable number of Lammas fields had been enclosed and let by the Corporation to pay the expenses of the Midsummer Night's watch, but in 1628, in consequence of a riot, they were reopened' (Nowell: Reader MSS 25 February 1927, p 47 col a). How far this statement is based upon the facts already discussed in this note, and how far it rests upon information now no longer available, cannot be said. One of the earliest, best documented, and most lively disputes over lammas lands involves Laurence Saunders (see endnote to A 3(a), ff 275-5v on pp 558-9). An excellent recital of this narrative, which gives a not-often-found insight into purely local affairs, is written by Paul Murray Kendall in 'Rebel against the Mayor,' *The Yorkist Age: Daily Life During the Wars of the Roses* (London, 1962), 117-33.

429   A 14(a) p 579

Sharp dates this settlement 1629 (Charles I's regnal years lend themselves easily to misreading, running as they do from 27 March). He notes that his information is taken from the St Michael's Church Account Book. 'In 1628, a controversy having arisen betwixt the Parish of St. Michael and the Cappers' Company concerning this Chapel [St Thomas' or the Cappers' chapel], it was agreed that the Parish should pay £15 to the Cappers, on their surrendering the Chapel (with their pageant house), reserving to the Company six convenient seats, for which they were to pay 4d. each. Accordingly, on 24th March, 1629, the Company received £15, and executed a deed of surrender' (*Illustrative Papers*, p 31).

The 'controversie' may have some connection with a testy libel case in 1626 between William Pywell and William Burton, masters of the Cappers, and Richard Mastergent, Richard Austen, Joseph Mayer (or Meyer), and Robert Crow, who persisted in occupying seats, in the Cappers' chapel in St Michael, which had been assigned to them by the mayor. The full papers of this case are lodged in the Lichfield Joint Record Office.

433   A 7(b) p 859
The first payment is to the only unidentified company in these accounts; why the accountant was unable to fill in the space I do not know. The date is oddly close to 6 May 1633 when the mayor and justices of Banbury wrote to the privy council concerning the suspicious patent that a company of players had shown up with in their town. The six players rested in gaol until advice from the council. The patent was forged, but in quite what way the contradictory evidence of the players does not make clear; G.E. Bentley probably comes as close as is possible to unravelling the affair in his discussion of Edward Whiting, one of the leaders of the troupe (*The Jacobean and Caroline Stage*, vol 2, pp 617-18). One of the players maintained that Edward Whiting, possibly the original securer of the patent, lived in Coventry. It was clear that the troupe had been playing within twenty miles of Coventry at several places prior to their arrest. Two of the players, Bartholomew Jones and Richard Collewell, said that they had had a reward at Coventry even though they had not played. The wardens' accounts do not bear this out. The matter is dealt with by Murray in detail (*English Dramatic Companies*, Appendix C, vol 2, pp 163-7).

446   A 7(c) p 88
This is the first indication that the five city waits, having been disbanded in 1635 for being 'verie troublesome' (see p 437), had been reinstituted.

Appendix 2

460   Acc 154 ff 1-2
An occasional word defeats Daffern but this is the only time that a passage is beyond his ability. Sharp, in a discussion of companies' livery for the Corpus Christi procession, transcribes this passage without any direct reference to the account book: 'The Drapers Livery was a gown of "Sad pewke, tawne, otherells off browne blewe whych be nere of one color & an hode, the on halfe tawne or pewke & the other halfe skarlet"'' (p 164, fn p).

461   Acc 154 f 4
The 'old pagent howse' (ll. 5, 32-3) was in Little Park Street (see p 3), 'the new pageant howse' (ll. 6, 34) in Gosford Street (see p 280).

471   Acc 154 ff 26-7
The 'beryng forth of the organs' (l. 12) is explained by two later items (see p 474, l. 5 and p 476,

ll. 9-10). They were kept at 'master nethurmylls' at Hamton, probably Hampton-in-Arden, a village some six miles west of Coventry. The Nethermills were a powerful Draper family; the elder Julinus was mayor in 1523, John in 1557.

472   Acc 154 f 34
The duke of Suffolk (p 473, l. 10) was father of Lady Jane Grey.

The very large discrepancy between the (complete) costs listed (p 473, ll. 21-9) and the total given is removed if, instead of 'ij s iiij d' for the 'gonnarys,' one follows Sharp (p 193) and reads 'lxij s iiij d.' The other costs are confirmed by Sharp (p 198) where he reads 'slage' (fn e, 'A kind of Kettle-Drum') for 'stage.' These figures accepted, the total is undercast by four shillings and one penny.

473   Acc 154 f 35
The receipt may have been a special levy to help meet the unusual costs entailed in remaking the pageant; however, it becomes an annually repeated item, its purpose not always specified.

See also endnote to ff 26-7 above for 'master nethurmylls' (p 474, l. 5).

474   Acc 154 ff 36-7
Sharp (p 201) reads 'xx s' for 'xx d' (p 474, l. 15), a more reasonable amount for this rather large job than 'xx d.' Accepting Sharp's figure brings the costs to £5 18s 10d, leaving the given total undercast by five shillings. A large part of this account is given over to the considerable costs of remaking the pageant. The charges of the dinner were even more extravagant — £10 5s 6½d. The cost for 'the players' (p 475, l. 23) is the last item on the dinner account before the 'summa' for that feast. Then follows the xx s iiij d (together with other regular contributory items toward the dinner expected from the four masters for swans) which I take to be a repetition of the item on folio 35 (see p 473) with an error of a shilling; such repetitions, with or without errors, are not unknown in guild accounts.

476   Acc 154 f 39
The Drapers several times mention the fetching and carrying of their portable organs (see pp 471, 474, and endnote to ff 26-7 above). 'Whovme' is still current dialect in Coventry for 'home' (see Drapers' Accounts, p 259).

477   Acc 154 f 41
Sharp (p 202) reads 'xviij' for 'xxiij' (l. 22), probably correctly, since 'xxiij' is an unusual fiscal number.

478-80   Acc 154 ff 44-5
Sharp gives these payments as one of some 'Specimens of the entire entries in several of the Companies' Books, for the charges of Midsummer Night' (pp 205-6). He omits from this entire entry, presumably on the grounds that it has nothing to do with Midsummer celebrations, the payment to harness men on Fair Friday. He differs from Daffern in various transcriptions. 'James of the sward' (l. 36) becomes 'James of the Swan': actors in, and drivers of, the pageant took refreshment at the unplaceable Swan (see endnote to MS Top. Warwickshire d.4, ff 24-24v on pp 573-4 and pp 140, 223, 233-4, 253, 264, and 284). 'Sawton' (l. 37) becomes 'fawton' and Daffern's 'viij s'

for scouring the harness (p 480, l. 3) is altered to 'viij d': in this instance Daffern is certainly right because the sum of the costs is correct with Daffern's reading (£5 3s 11d). The provider of wax, 'eades' (p 480, l. 7), changes to 'endes.' Sharp reads 'iij stremers,' and 'pewdenges' rather than 'pewdeges' (p 480, ll. 9-10).

Appendix 3

482   W 83

Mary Marston could be either the playwright Marston's mother or his widow. If she is his widow (which the writing suggests), the property she seeks may be the garden her father held (see endnote to 100/37 on pp 589-90). This appears to have been the same land granted by the city to Phillip Adams and his wife, on Adams' retirement from the post of great mace-bearer 'by reason of his age & infirmities' (Council Book, 7 October 1640, p 714).

485   Harley 6466   f 5

This is the third of some additional ordinances: the first of these is dated as being passed by John Swift when Richard Wode was mayor at the latter's Easter leet, 1432. However, Wode was mayor in 1454 and 1467, and in none of his leets is such an ordinance mentioned.

Appendix 6

495

Massey's admission to the Mercers' company (l. 2) is noted in CRO: Acc 15, f 12v as follows:

> Item the vj^th day of the moneth of Decembr Anno domini 157ʳ2'6 [3]
> Thomas Massy vpholstre is admytted into the ffeloeship & company &
> hathe promysed [y] to the mastr & is consented to gyve for his ffreedom
> ˄ 'theefor' the Somme of xxx s Lawfull moneye. In consyderacon of a
> yeres service & more vnserved of his aprentyship as by his Indentures then
> showed dyd apeare & hathe promysed to paye xx s therof on St Ihons daye
> next ffolloyng & the other x s at mydsomer next comyng, promising then
> to occupy his onlye Trade of Vpholstrye.
> > > > > > > > > > (signed) by me Thomas masse

496

The tenement referred to (ll. 9-10) was not, apparently, where Massey lived. The family house was in Earl Street (allowing Massey, as he grew up, an excellent vantage point for watching the play procession). In the 1581 survey occurs: 'There ys A Rente Charge of viij s going out of a Tennement in the holding of Iane Masseye Wyddowe lyeing 0 in the Earlstreetwarde on the North syde of the same streete' (CRO: A 24, p 28). Massey, his wife, and a maid are listed as living there in 1613.

497

For the actual visit of Princess Elizabeth (ll. 16-17), see pages 364-5.

498

William Toncks' name (ll. 34-5) appears frequently in the city's books as he was clearly the city's leading goldsmith and looked after the civic regalia. It is interesting to note that Massey referred to his project as a 'Paieant.'

Richard Page (l. 39) was mayor in 1603–4; it was in March 1604 that Massey approached the mayor and his council. 'The King*es* Daie' was the day of accession of James I, 24 March. Massey was given barely three weeks' notice at best.

499

The 'first ffayre' (ll. 4-5) was that of Corpus Christi which fell on 7 June in 1604. The annals make no mention of an 'Vproare' (l. 22) in Clerk's mayoralty. Sir Peter Warburton (1540?–1621) (l. 30) was a Cheshire man; thus, he may have known Massey through the Dunham stock with which Massey claimed kinship. He had much connection with that county during his legal career (for a summary of which see *DNB*), and maintained his home there. The seven actions (p 500, l. 5) were presumably taken against '*Master* Maior and vj others.'

500

Christopher Davenport (l. 9) was mayor in 1602–3.

Judge Warburton (ll. 15-17) spent the last years of his life at his house in Grafton, a village some seven miles south of Chester. Massey's handling of dates is confusing here. Sampson Hopkins (l. 5) was mayor for the year beginning November 1609. If, as seems Massey's point, Warburton wrote to Mayor Hopkins, it could not have been a result of talking with Massey consequent to the latter's being invited to Grafton in August 1612. Mr Breres (l. 25) was the son (?) of Henry Breres who died in August 1597 during his year of mayoralty.

Haddon's money (l. 40) was an annual loan made 'at the feast of St Andrewe the Apostle': 'Walter Haddons money delivered out amongst the co*m*moners the same day and yere afore specified, iiij li. a man, so farr forth as. lxxxxv li. . reachethe' (CRO: A 28, f 27v). This was one of several loan funds available to citizens, generally of the richer sort. Massey regularly availed himself of it but he failed to meet his due date because he was in gaol. However, the mayor was able to reach him by a stern application of the loan return rule. The punctuation does not help as much as it could, especially as Massey's explanations of his financial predicament and the city's seeming to take advantage of it tumble out hurriedly.

501

'Iohn Showell' (l. 22), for whom Massey seems to have stood surety was probably a close kinsman to William Showell with whom Massey organized the queen's holiday shows in 1593 (see p 338) and 1594 (p 341).

Appendix 8

507   ll. 6-7

Only once are the mayor and his brethren recorded as dining with Lord Berkeley at Caludon — in 1612 when the wardens had to meet the fees given to his lordship's men. It is not clear whether this was his acting troupe who performed for the guests or his retainers in general. See page 384.

Appendix 9

515
I do not know whether the claim (l. 25) that Cox was with Henry VIII when he took Boulogne in 1544 is a romantic decoration of Jonson's or a genuine event in Cox's life which Jonson had found out. Cox was obviously a remembered man to merit his role as presenter of the masque.

515
Cox may have come unofficially to entertain the queen on a previous occasion (l. 30), but he was set down as having been Coventry's official representative in 1575.

516
The vow (ll. 46-52) was likely one that Cox did indeed vauntingly make after the success of his 1575 show, and one not forgotten in the area.

Glossaries: Introduction

Words are included in the Latin glossary if they are not to be found in Lewis and Short, *A Latin Dictionary*, the standard reference work for classical Latin. Words listed in Lewis and Short which have had a change or restriction of meaning in medieval Latin are also cited. Many words in these documents are common classical Latin words using medieval spellings. Such variations have not been considered significant, ie, as producing new words. They are:

> ML *c* for CL *t* before *i*
> ML *cc* for CL *ct* before *i*
> ML *d* for CL *t* in a final position
> ML *e* for CL *ae* or *oe*
> ML *ff* for CL *f*, especially in an initial position
> ML addition of *h*
> ML omission of CL *h*
> ML *n* for CL *m* before *m* or *n*
> intrusion of ML *p* in the CL consonant cluster *mn* or *ms*
> ML doubling of CL single consonants and singling of CL double consonants

In addition, medieval Latin words can vary in spelling by alternation between *i* and *e* before another vowel. Scribal practice has been followed in such cases, as well as with *i/j* and *u/v* variants. Headwords are given in the standard form: ie, nouns are listed by nominative, genitive, and gender; adjectives by the terminations in the nominative singular; verbs by their principal parts. Where the same word occurs in spellings which differ according to the list above, the most common spelling is designated as standard and used for the headword. Anomalous inflectional forms are dealt with in one of two ways: they are listed separately and cross-referenced to the main entry or, if they follow the headword alphabetically, they are listed under that headword and set apart by bold-face type.

The English glossary lists, for the most part, words which have not survived in modern English and words which, in the records, bear meanings which do not survive in modern use. All variant spellings of such words are listed. Forms of English words interesting from a purely phonological or morphological point of view have generally not been included in the glossary, but some unusual spellings of words which might not be easily identified (and which are spelled recognizably else-where) are glossed. Words that look unusual because of the absence of an abbreviation mark (eg, *pte* for *parte*, *goyg* for *goyng*) have not been glossed. It is assumed that the reader is familiar with such common spelling alternations as *d/th*, *c/s*, *þ/y*, *y/ʒ*, *i/e*, *ye/e*, *ea*, *y*, or *e* for *ai* and *ay*, and *i* or *y* for *oi* and *oy*. Article-noun combinations (eg, *ton* for 'the one,' *thappostles* for 'the apostles') have generally not been listed. Where variant spellings of the same form occur, the first spelling in alphabetical order has normally been chosen as headword. However, where this would result in an odd or rare spelling becoming a headword, a more common spelling has been given precedence. Spellings separated from their main entries by more than two intervening ones have been cross-referenced.

Words which appear in records quoted in the appendixes and endnotes are also listed in the glossary, according to the principles outlined above.

Manuscript capitalization has been ignored. Only the first three occurrences of each word are given with page and line number separated by an oblique stroke. If the word occurs in marginalia, this is indicated by a lower-case *m* following the page and line reference.

Works consulted

Du Cange, Charles du Fresne. *Glossarium Mediae et Infimae Latinitatis*. 6 vols (Paris, 1733).
Kurath, Hans and Sherman M. Kuhn. *Middle English Dictionary*. Fascicules A.1–N.3 (Ann Arbor, 1952–79).
Latham, R.E. *Dictionary of Medieval Latin from British Sources*. Fascicule 1, A–B (London, 1975).
– *Revised Medieval Latin Word-List from British and Irish Sources* (London, 1965).
Lewis, Charlton T. and Charles Short. *A Latin Dictionary* (Oxford, 1879).
The Compact Edition of the Oxford English Dictionary. 2 vols (New York, 1971).

Abbreviations

adj	adjective		pa	past tense
adv	adverb		phr	phrase
art	article		pl	plural
CL	Classical Latin		poss	possessive
comm	common		pp	past participle
comp	comparative		pr	present
conj	conjunction		prep	preposition
f	feminine		pron	pronoun
imper	imperative		prp	present participle
indecl	indeclinable		refl	reflexive
inf	infinitive		sg	singular
intr	intransitive		subj	subjunctive
m	masculine		tr	transitive
ML	Medieval Latin		v	verb
n	noun		vb	verbal
nt	neuter			

Latin Glossary

aceciam *conj* and also 6/19, 6/29, 6/37

acquieto, -are, -avi, -atum *v tr* make quit of (as an obligation) 14/17, 15/17, 329/23

adiacens, -entis *adj* adjacent, located nearby 6/10, 6/20, 6/30, etc

administrator, -oris *n m* administrator, representative of the estate of one who leaves no will 329/23

advincula *prep phr (the name of a feast) see* festum

alieno, -are, -avi, -atum *v tr* alienate, *ie,* transfer (by sale, gift, or subinfeudation) a holding, usually of land 329/24

alloco, -are, -avi, -atum *v tr* allot (*ie,* funds); allow, make allowance for (*ie,* expenses) 67/26, 70/10, 72/16, etc

alternatim *adv* one after another, in turn 11/21, 13/8

annuatim *adv* yearly, every year 9/12, 10/35, 12/30, etc

annunciacio, -onis *n f* announcement; the Annunciation 12/34, 15/2

aretro *adv* in arrears 11/4, 11/10, 15/6

arreragium, -i *n nt* arrears, arrearage 15/11

ars, artis *n f* trade, craft; craft guild 12/16, 12/17, 12/18, etc

assignatus, -i *n m* assign, *ie,* a person to whom some right or property is legally transferred 6/23, 6/41, 10/31, etc

attornatus, -i *n m* private attorney 330/20, 330/26, 330/29

ballivus, -i *n m* bailiff 7/3, 11/23, 13/20, etc

barganizo, -are, -avi, -atum *v tr* barter, sell 329/25

beatus, -a, -um *adj* blessed; *as a title* Saint 7/6, 12/24, 13/40, etc

billa, -e *n f* billet 15/30

bunda, -e *n f* bound, boundary 13/23

camerarius, -i *n m* chamberlain, *ie,* a member of the town council 13/19, 84/2m

cantaria, -e *n f* chantry, an endowment for maintaining priests to say masses for the souls of their patron, *or* a chapel or church supported by such an endowment 7/21, 7/22

capicium, -i *n nt* headgear, cap 10/13

capitalis, -e *adj see* dominus

cappitalis, -e *adj form of* capitalis 330/3

carta, -e *n f* charter; legal instrument 7/14, 7/19, 13/30, etc; — indentata indenture, *ie,* a deed, agreement, or contract originally executed in several copies all having matching indentations at the top 14/31, 15/18

cissor, -oris *n m* scissormaker 13/37, 14/37

citra *prep* before (*only of time*) 13/21

civitas, -tatis *n f* city 7/2, 7/4, 11/22, etc

clameum, -i *n nt* claim 5/42, 6/7, 6/27, etc

clamo, -are, -avi, -atum *v tr* claim; *see* quietus

clericus, -i *n m* clerk, *ie,* one in minor orders 329/16

colerium, -i *n nt* collar 48/18

collatis, -onis *n f* food; meal 9/15

comitatus, -us *n m* county 328/40

communitas, -atis *n f* commonalty, commonwealth, community 64/36 competens, -entis *adj* suitable 329/11

concedo, -ere, -cessi, -cessum *v tr* grant, give 10/19, 12/15, 13/30, etc

concessio, -onis *n f* grant 7/18

conquestum, -i *n nt* conquest, *ie,* the Norman Conquest 7/7, 10/33, 13/9, etc

consuetus, -a, -um *adj* usual, customary 6/24, 19/7, 330/4

contentatus, -a, -um *adj* contented 329/21

conventus, -us *n m* convent, religious house 3/7, 7/22

conversatio, -onis *n f* way of life, manner of living; *in idiom* bona et honesta conversatio, a good and honest manner of life 19/4

corpus, -oris *n nt* body; *in phr* Corpus Christi (*the name of a feast*) *see* festum; *in phr* corpus domini the consecrated Host 39/35

cotagium, -i *n nt* cottage 6/10, 6/12, 6/20, etc

curro, -ere, cucurri, cursum *v intr* race, hold races 64/41

curtilagium, -i *n nt* curtilage, *ie,* a court or garden attached to a house property and considered part of it 6/13, 6/20, 6/30, etc

custos, -odis *n m* warden, officer of a craft guild 12/16, 12/17, 12/18

data, -e *n f* date 12/28

decetero *adv* henceforth, from now on 6/31, 17/19

deficiens, -entis *n comm* delinquent, offender 13/18

delibero, -are, -avi, -atum *v tr* deliver, give to 48/16, 330/26, 377/14

demandum, -i *n nt* claim, demand 14/11

denarius, -i *n m* penny 9/13, 10/37, 14/7

dies, diei *n m* day; — Iouis Thursday 7/5; — generales yearly memorial days for dead members of a guild or confraternity; anniversary of the deaths of the same; *probably synonymous with* obitus 70/10

dimissio, -onis *n f* lease 11/13

dimitto, -ere, -misi, -missum *v tr* let, lease 12/15

discrescio, -onis *n f* discretion, judgement 19/11

distribucio, -onis *n f* distribution, livery, (*especially of clothes*) 72/17, 74/33, 76/16

districtio, -onis *n f* distraint, *ie,* seizure of certain goods or property for the repayment of debt 11/7, 15/9

distringo, -ere, -trinxi, -trinctum *v tr* distrain, *ie,* seize goods or property for repayment of debt 11/7, 15/9

divisa, -e *n f* division 12/24, 14/1, 14/41

domina, -e *n f* lady (*especially as a title*) 330/36

dominus, -i *n m* lord (*title of a peer, knight, bishop, Benedictine choir monk, or priest*) 7/23; the Lord 15/2, 39/35, 329/6; — capitalis *n phr* lord in chief 6/23, 70/11, 72/16, etc

erga *prep* against (*of time*) 15/34

executor, -oris *n m* executor, *ie,* representative of the estate of one having a will 329/22

extunc *adv* thereafter 10/34, 11/5, 11/11, etc

feodum, -i *n nt* fee, *ie,* inheritable and derivative tenure of land by a tenant, *and* the land so held 6/24, 330/3

feofo, -are, -avi, -atum *v tr* enfeoff, grant to someone a holding in fee (*see* feodum) 329/25

festum, -i *n nt* feast day, holy day; — advincula sancti petri feast of St Peter in chains, Lammas Eve (1 August) 84/5-6m; — annunciacionis beate Marie virginis Lady Day (25 March) 12/34, 15/2; — Corporis Christi Corpus Christi (the first Thursday after Trinity Sunday) 13/17, 15/34, 17/11, etc; — natalem domini Christmas (25 December) 15/2; — nativitatis sancti Iohannis Baptiste nativity of St John the Baptist (24 June) 12/27, 12/35, 15/2-3; — Penticoste Whitsunday (fifty days after Easter) 128/6, 128/22, 128/26; — purificationis beate Marie virginis Candlemas (2 February) 7/6; — sancti Michaelis St Michael's Day (29 September) 10/31-2, 10/37, 12/33-4, etc; — sancti nicholai St Nicholas' Day (6 December) 70/11

finis, -is *n m* end 10/33, 13/5

finis, -is *n m* fine, a sum of money set either as penalty or as dues or fees by the Crown, a court, or a corporate organization 26/14, 451/22

franchisa, -e *n f* franchise, liberty of a town, *ie,* its privileged area 13/23

frater, -tris *n m* fellow member (male) of a guild, confraternity, or religious order 14/9

fraternitas, -tatis *n f* guild 451/21

gardianus, -i *n m see* guardianus

gardinum, -i *n nt* garden 6/9, 6/19, 6/30, etc

generalis, -e *adj see* dies

grangia, -e *n f* grange, *ie,* farmhouse and its out-buildings, *especially* an outlying one 6/9, 6/19, 6/30, etc

gratus, -a, -um *adj see* ratus

guardianus, -i *n m* warden, officer of the town 48/18; **gardianus, -i** 15/33

histrio, -onis *n m* minstrel, wait (?) 38/22

hospitalis, -is *n nt* hospital, hospice, a place for the reception of guests, travellers, and strangers or for the care of the sick or indigent 14/9

huiusmodi *indecl adj* such, of this sort 330/23

imperpetuum *adv* in perpetuity 5/39, 6/25, 6/33, etc

indentatus, -a, -um *adj see* carta

indentura, -e *n f* indenture, *ie,* deed, agreement or contract, originally executed in several copies all having matching indentations at the top 10/17, 12/12, 13/7

infuturo *adv* in the future 5/42, 6/8

insolutus, -a, -um *adj* unpaid; — aretro be in arrears 11/4, 11/10, 15/7

inventarum, -i *n nt* inventory 488/26

iocum, -i *n nt* play, game 13/18, 64/39

ius, iuris *n nt* right; law 5/41, 6/7, 6/24, etc

levo, -are, -avi, -atum *v tr* levy, assess 13/19

liberata, -e *n f* livery 70/12

licentia, -e *n f* licence, permission 7/20

ludo, -ere, -i, lusum *v intr* play, perform (in a play) 13/16, 13/17

ludum, -i *n nt* play 128/8

ludus, -i *n m* play 128/23, 128/26

lurciatrium, -i *n nt* hawking (?) 64/42

lusus, -i *n m* game 64/39

magister, -tri *n m* master (of a craft or guild) 6/11, 9/12, 9/14, etc

maior, -oris *n m* mayor 7/2, 11/22, 13/19, etc

manus, -us *n f* hand; per manus by the hand of, by the good offices of *(with genitive)* 81/25; pre manibus on hand 329/16

manuteneo, -ere, -ui, -tum *v tr* maintain 11/2, 12/42

mendyauns, -ntis *n comm* beggar 72/17

mercator, -oris *n m* merchant 5/38

mercerus, -i *n m* mercer, *ie,* shopkeeper 7/16

mesuagium, -i *n nt* messuage; land which is the site of a dwelling and its appurtenances 6/2, 6/17, 6/28, etc

monachus, -i *n m* monk; ecclesia monachorum minster church 488/26

moneta, -e *n f* money 329/12

mortifico, -are, -avi, -atum *v tr* place a holding in mortmain, *ie,* dispose it by will to be held inalienably by an ecclesiastical body of some kind for religious or charitable purposes 7/19

obitus, -us *n m* anniversary service for the dead 72/16

occupatio, -onis *n f* occupation, physical possession of a holding; *perhaps* residence upon a holding 329/37

occupo, -are, -avi, -atum *v tr* be in physical possession of a holding; *perhaps* reside in a holding 6/11, 6/13

opus, -eris *n nt* work, labour; ad — for the use or benefit of *(with genitive)* 9/13, 330/2, 330/11

ordino, -are, -avi, -atum *v tr* order, ordain 9/11, 13/16, 13/20, etc

pannarius, -i *n m* draper 3/7, 7/24

pannus, -i *n m* cloth; *pl* clothes 15/33, 70/12, 72/18, etc

parcella, -e *n f* piece, part, parcel *(usually of land)* 6/31, 10/22, 10/27, etc

parcus, -i *n m* park 6/4, 7/13, 7/16

parochia, -e *n f* parish 12/23

pavimentum, -i *n nt* pavement 17/19

pertinentia, -e *n f* appurtenance, belonging 6/3, 6/16, 6/19, etc

pitanciarius, -i *n m* officer of a religious house responsible for the distribution of small allowances, pittancer 7/17

placea, -e *n f* plot, parcel (of land) 12/19, 12/25, 12/40, etc

plenarie *adv* fully 10/35, 11/8, 12/30, etc

prior, -oris *n m* prior (of a religious house) 3/6, 7/21

probus, -a, -um *adj* honest, respectable 13/20

processionalis, -is *n m* procession 39/34

pulsacio, -onis *n f* ringing, striking (of a bell) 19/6

quiete *adv* quietly 6/23, 14/5

quietus, -a, -um *adj* quit (*as of a rent or other payment*) 81/25m, 110/17; **quietum clamo** quit claim, *ie,* renounce a claim upon a thing or right 5/39, 6/5

ratus et gratus *adj phr* approved 330/28

redditus, -us *n m* rent 6/2, 6/18, 6/28, etc

relaxo, -are, -avi, -atum *v tr* release (a claim) 5/38

reliqua, -e *n f* relic (of a saint, etc) 488/26

remitto, -ere, -misi, -missum *v tr* remit 5/38, 6/4

reversio, -onis *n f* reversion, *ie,* return to an original owner or his heirs of property upon the expiry of a grant for whatever cause 6/2, 6/18, 6/28, etc

rubius, -a, -um *adj* red 10/13

seisina, -e *n f* possession (of property) 330/22, 330/24

servicium, -i *n nt* service, *especially* that service in virtue of which land is held 6/3, 6/18, 6/24, etc

sigillatus, -a, -um *adj* sealed 377/14

signium, -i *n nt* seal 330/34

societas, -tatis *n f* company 128/4

solidus, -i *n m* shilling 10/36, 12/33, 12/38, etc

soror, -oris *n f* fellow member (female) of a guild or confraternity 14/9

sterlingus, -i *n m* sterling 10/37, 12/33, 12/38

strata, -e *n f* street 6/12, 6/13

superedifico, -are, -avi, -atum *v tr* build over 13/33, 14/2, 14/14, etc

tenementum, -i *n nt* building; holding, tenement, *ie,* a generic term for any tenure 6/2, 6/18, 6/28, etc

tenens, -ntis *n m* tenant 7/19, 64/36

tenura, -e *n f* tenure 329/37

terminum, -i *n nt* term, *ie,* specific period of time of a contract or agreement, etc 7/14, 10/40, 11/3, etc; **quatuor termina** four quarters into which the year was divided by the quarter-days: Lady Day (25 March), Midsummer (24 June), Michaelmas (29 September), and Christmas (25 December) 12/33

testatio, -onis *n f* witness 10/17

tortex, -icis *n m* torch 39/34

trepidiendum *gerund* dancing 64/41

venella, -e *n f* lane 13/34, 14/34

veredictum, -i *n nt* sworn oath 128/15

vestura, -e *n f* clothing, livery 15/30, 15/33

video, videre, vidi, visum *v tr* see; view (bounds, etc) 13/22, 128/2, 128/16, etc

vigilacio, -onis *n f* watch, ward 19/10

vigilia, -e *n f* vigil, eve (*especially* of a holy day); — **nativitatis sancti Iohannis Baptiste** St John's Eve (23 June) 17/20; — **sancti Petri** St Peter's Eve (31 July) 17/20-1

vigilo, -are, -avi, -atum *v tr* be on watch; keep watch 19/4, 19/5

villa, -e *n f* town 13/21, 19/5, 19/7, etc

warantizo, -are, -avi, -atum *v tr* warrant, guarantee 6/41, 11/17, 13/6, etc

English Glossary

abes *see* albe

abey *v inf* make obedient 32/18

abey *v pr 2 pl subj* obey 22/41

abothsidez *adv* on both sides 274/40

abroch *adv in phr* sett abroch set afoot, publish 497/5-6

acolacion *see* colacion

acordid *pp* caused to agree 27/29

adjoyn *v inf* unite 79/22; adioyned *pp* 80/3

aicompt *n* account, reckoning 232/7

albe *n* full length vestment of white cloth 486/9, 486/13, 487/3, etc; abes *pl* 236/22, 249/18; albes 163/30, 170/20, 170/35, etc; allbas 230/12; allbes 185/2; alles 162/23; awbes 335/1; awbus 98/34

alecunner *n* inspector of ales 274/28

alen *v pr 3 sg subj* give or lend 18/24

alete *see* leet

allbas, allbes *see* albe

allder poll *n phr* staff made of alder 274/38

alleged *pp* pleaded 130/23

alles *see* albe

allholland *adj (genitive pl in origin)* of All Saints' Day, 1 November 392/35

allhollantide *n* season of All Saints 484/1

allman revetts *n phr pl* kind of light armour made of plates sliding on rivets 469/37; allman reyvetts 463/2; allman reyvytts 469/31; allman rryvetts 462/39; allmay revetts 470/36; allmayn ryvett 463/23; allmayn ryvetts *pl* 462/2, 462/6, 463/19; allmayne ryvyts 470/15; alman ryvetts 466/31; almayne revettes 334/30; almayne

revetts 461/12, 461/16; almayne ryvets 205/27; almayne ryvettes 196/8, 311/22; almayne ryvetts 200/14, 464/7, 464/11, etc; almayne ryvittes 311/20; almen revitts 134/23, 136/4; almen ryffytts 468/35; almeyn ryffetts 468/30; almon reyvettes 197/9; awmon ryvets 240/16

alls *adv* also 460/27

almon corslet *n phr* piece of body armour of German origin 324/30, 324/31, 324/33; almon corslettes *pl* 324/26

almon reyvettes *see* allman revetts

alysander *see* borde alysander

amas *n* fur or furred cloth used as lining (?) 477/31

amyse *n* oblong piece of linen put around the head and shoulders, worn with the alb 487/3, 487/5, 487/24, etc; ames 165/41; ammyse 486/9, 486/13; amys 156/31; amesses *pl* 162/24, 174/23; amessus 98/34

amyte *n* friendly relations 79/3

aneyling *vb n* extreme unction 508/12

ap *adv* up 62/11

apagent *see* pachand

apen *see* pen

apentynge *vb n* appointing, arranging 480/39

appareld *pp* adorned, decorated 89/33

apparelles *n pl* apparatus 131/20

appeled *pp* called for 508/25

appellant *n* one who challenges another to combat 4/35

apperteyning *prp* belonging 301/4; apperteynyng 145/11, 486/6 appurtenances *n pl* appendages belonging to more important property 145/9, 145/22, 301/5; **appurtenaunces** 131/20, 132/6, 376/39

aray *n* behaviour 8/16

aray *n* formal order 29/21m, 36/25; **araye** 88/36; **arraie** 3/17

aray *v inf* adorn, decorate 31/18; **arayed** *pp* 21/14, 31/2; **arayede** 22/9; **arraied** 54/24; **arrayed** 53/14

aray *v inf* furnish with weapons and armour 544/28

arayed *pp* furnished 29/11

arerage *n* debt 110/12

aresdyke *n* arsedine, ornamental metallic material of gold colour 85/9; *see also* **assaden**

arraie *see* aray

arraied, arrayed *see* aray

arrerages *n pl* items overdue 78/41, 125/12

assaden *n* arsedine, ornamental metallic material of gold colour 61/27; **assady** 51/12, 51/14; **assadyn** 60/4; **assyden** 241/21; *see also* **aresdyke**

assignes *n pl* persons appointed to act for others 376/32, 376/33, 376/40, etc

assises *n pl* sessions of a court of civil actions 328/4; **assisses** 317/15

associat *adj* allied, united in fellowship 125/6, 125/9m, 132/1, etc; **associate** 11/40

associate *v inf* join, unite 136/21m

assyden *see* assaden

assyse *n in phr* **rents of assyse** fixed rents 482/27

astaplee *see* staple

astroke *see* streke

auncient *n* ensign, banner 408/34; **awncyente** 308/37

aungsels *n pl* angels 172/9

awbes, awbus *see* albe

awmon ryvets *see* allman revetts

awncyente *see* auncient

axeltre *n* bar around which wheels of wagon revolve 261/6, 261/17; **axeltrie** 261/4; **axetre** 235/26; **axyll tree** 91/40; **exaltre** 245/6, 253/11; **extre** 252/35

ay *adv* always 91/23

backe friendes *n phr pl* insincere friends 208/11m

balet *n* ballad, song 91/3; **ballets** *pl* 274/12

balles *n pl* balls for some purpose (?), bowls (?) 163/36

banar *n in phr* **banar clothe** fabric part of a banner carried in church processions 492/15; *see also* **banarcloth**

banarcloth *n* fabric part of a banner carried in church processions 492/17; **banarclothe** 492/16

bandeleeres *n pl* belts worn across the breast 448/13; **bandeleers** 438/18; **bandelers** 395/36; **bandeliers** 324/42; **bandileres** 438/10, 443/38

baneroll *n* square banner borne at funerals and placed over the tomb 510/40

bangz *n pl* loud thumping noises 275/1

barbe *n* piece of white linen passed over the chin and down to the waist, as part of a woman's headdress 511/8, 511/15; **barbes** *pl* 511/23, 511/35

barber *n* one who cuts hair, shaves beards, and lets blood 304/21; **barbars** *pl* 133/14, 133/18m; **barbors** 118/12, 190/18, 190/19m; **barbours** 83/2, 83/5

barded *pp* protected by leather or metal covering 4/8, 4/39

barkers *n pl* tanners of hides 16/35, 89/33

barrier *n* stockade 3/28

barriers *n pl* fences used to enclose the tournament area 4/6, 4/10

base pyppe *n phr* woodwind instrument with low pitch 270/26

bauier *n* lower portion of face-guard 6/12

bawling *n error for* 'bateling,' battlements 468/11

baxsters *n pl* bakers 16/30

bayes *n* baize, a fabric of fine, light material 423/35, 446/40

bayes *n pl* leaves of the bay tree 304/33

bayly *n* elected town official 18/4, 18/15, 18/16; **bayles** *n pl* 9/24, 21/27; **baylies**

22/35; *see also* **baylyffe**

baylyffe *n* agent of lord of the manor 316/33; **bayliffes** elected town official 8/22; **baylyffes** 8/19; **beilleffes** 143/43, 144/30, 145/31; *see also* **bayly**

bayrwarde *see* **bearward**

bays *n pl* dams or embankments 281/2

bays *n pl* wall recesses 105/28

baytyd *pp* set upon with dogs 9/6

beadles *n pl* heralds 431/40

beadles *see* **bedull**

bearward *n* keeper of bears for baiting 265/41, 269/35, 269/37, etc; **bayrwarde** 300/1; **beareward** 286/24, 286/26, 290/11, etc; **bearewarde** 265/32, 265/34; **bearwarde** 265/36, 270/12, 276/5; **bereward** 282/3; **berward** 324/2, 445/11; **bearewardes** *pl* 338/15, 346/9m, 353/2, etc; **bearwardes** 320/28, 320/35m, 323/39m, etc

beatified *pp* made very happy 275/30

bedeman *n* one who prays for another 30/38, 149/26

bedull *n* porter or messenger 59/27, 73/29, 73/30, etc; **bedell** 93/12; **bedyll** 61/17, 71/24; **bydull** 63/28

behove *n* use 132/19

bek *n* bow 274/15

bekaram, bekuram *see* **bokeram**

belfrey *n* bell tower 36/15

belle *n* the best 32/36; **balle** 32/6

bendes *n pl* ornamental strips of cloth 29/27, 29/29, 29/32

berars *n pl* metal support bars 289/22

bereg *n* transport, carriage (*or* 'bearing'?) 301/38

bereward, berward *see* **bearward**

berne *n* baron 90/30

berrage *n* beverage 308/3

berras *n pl* bearers 159/11, 186/40; **beyras** 58/10; **beyrres** 86/34

bettyng *n* material used for kindling 115/17; **bettinges** *pl* 127/26; **bettings** 118/21; **bettynges** 129/24; **bettyngs** 115/18, 118/18, 119/42; *see also* **betyng**

betyng *prp* kindling 61/37; *see also* **bettyng**

bid *v inf* offer 32/22

bill *n* memorandum 7/41, 8/26, 83/26, etc; **billes** *pl* 436/1; **bills** 425/18, 427/13, 428/36, etc

bills *see* **byll**

bittes *n pl* leather bottles or flasks 505/28

bittors *n pl* bitterns 580/30

blakbokrem *n* black buckram (*see* **bokeram**) 86/12; **blakebuccram** 20/14

blanchpowder *n* powdered white sugar and ginger 157/11; **blanch powder** 590/10

blank *adj probably error for* 'blauk' (*ie,* 'black') 217/26

blankyng *vb n* making pale (*or error for* 'black-ing'?) 217/36

blowe bokeram *n phr* blue buckram (*see* **bokeram**) 97/4

bochere *n* slaughterhouse with meat stall 156/30, 161/23, 165/38, etc; **bocchere** 204/9; **boccherre** 169/12; **bocherre** 186/35; **bochery** 207/1, 210/25, 212/7, etc; **bocherye** 209/8, 219/15, 222/33, etc; **bucherey** 268/24; **butcherie** 505/34

bokeram *n* fabric of fine linen or cotton, or of coarse linen cloth stiffened with paste (?) 71/41, 73/21, 73/25, etc; **bekaram** 474/33; **bekuram** 474/34; **bockram** 236/15; **bokaryn** 28/8; **bokern** 170/18; **bokram** 175/1, 454/35; **buckeram** 238/2, 256/24; **bukram** 46/9, 66/3, 230/39; **bukrame** 46/12; **bvckram** 277/30

boklar *n* small round shield 451/6

bolle *n* bowl used as a receptacle in a torch 58/39; **bolles** *pl* 46/25, 548/1

bony *adj* beautiful 274/14, 274/15

booe *n* (archery) bow 248/4

booget *n literally*, a leather bag 274/7

borde alysander *n phr* expensive silk cloth 486/11

bordes *n pl* Lord's tables or tables for celebra-tion of the Eucharist 509/22

bordur *n* ornamental edge 92/39

bote *n in phr* to bote in addition 205/5

bott *prep* only 119/4

bottlemen *n pl* carriers of wine 405/14

bottomyng *vb n* hollowing out 168/18

boundeth *v pr 3 sg in phr* boundeth vppon adjoins 296/27; bounding *prp* 281/4; boundynge 301/10

boungrace *n* shade worn as part of the head-dress to protect the face from the sun 511/22

bowyers *n pl* maker and/or seller of archery bows 136/21

braband *n* kind of linen 84/42

brassar *n* armour for the upper arm 473/19

brekethe *v pr 3 sg* terminates 152/29

brekyn irons *see* brygantyrens

brether *n pl* brothers, members 101/29

breue *adj* brief 91/21

breuiary *n* short account 274/11

brideale *n* wedding feast 275/20

brigandines *n pl* suits of body armour 112/4; brygerdyns 99/12; *see also* brygantyrens

briges satten *n phr* satin of Bruges, made of a warp of silk and woof of thread 170/17; *see also* saten of brygees

broad cloth *n phr* fine black cloth 423/34; brode cloith 138/36

brodoryd *pp* embroidered, decorated with needlework 98/19; brodurd 81/12, 81/14

brugeses *n pl* freemen of the town 174/19; brygeses 170/28; burgese 173/5; burgeses 152/19, 155/5, 162/20

brygantyrens *n pl* type of light body armour consisting of front and back halves 451/14; brekyn irons 453/18; brygantyrones 450/8; bryggnyrns 85/43; *see also* brigandines

brygees *see* saten of brygees

brygerdyns *see* brigandines

bryggnyrns *see* brygantyrens

bryne *v inf* burn 155/1, 157/28, 166/22

bucherey *see* bochere

buck *n* book 260/5; buke 20/20

buckeram, bukram, bukrame, bvckram *see* bokeram

bucklemaker *n* maker of buckle clasps 77/17

buke *see* buck

bulk *n* stall 403/39; bulks *pl* 403/25

bull *n* bill 9/38

bullett moulde *n phr* hollow form for making

bullet balls 443/39

bullryng *n* area for baiting bulls 9/5

bultyng *vb n* sifting 503/9

bunche *n* a specified quantity 257/18

burgese, burgeses *see* brugeses

burings *vb n* buryings 87/34

burlettis *n pl* hoods 73/31

butcherie *see* bochere

butting *prp* bounding 281/5

bydull *see* bedull

byll *n* a kind of halberd 325/27; bills *pl* 314/18, 325/16, 367/38, etc; bylles 196/9, 196/11, 250/38, etc

bynke *n* bench 221/31

cace *n* condition 34/21

callivers *n pl* light muskets 325/30

cambes *n pl* claws (?), *n sg* canvas (?) 246/19

canape *n* covering for the shrine 162/20, 170/29; canapy 99/1, 108/37, 108/41; canope 81/12; canopy 98/37

candelmase *n* feast of the Purification of the Virgin 123/12, 123/26; candelmasse 149/2; candlemas 374/31, 415/25, 426/24

cankered *pp* rusted 368/24

canns *n pl* drinking vessels 407/3

cap *n* hat or headdress 36/22, 274/33; cappe 44/24, 279/39, 288/38, etc; capes *pl* 423/38; capps 94/35; cappus 44/23, 71/15

capones *n pl* castrated cocks 504/1; capons 37/11, 505/9

capper *n* maker of caps 128/21, 168/34, 188/41; cappers *pl* 79/19, 83/27, 128/34, etc

cardmaker *n* maker of wool cards 543/33; cardemakers *pl* 11/33, 11/33, 12/16, etc

carlde *adj* made of carde, a kind of fabric 357/11

cart nayle *n* nail used for the wheels of a cart 241/36; carte nayles *pl* 226/19, 230/36, 235/23, etc; cart nales 185/39

cartwright *n* maker of carts and wagons 83/24

carver *n* woodcarver 125/7; caruers *pl* 132/21; carvers 125/5, 125/8m, 125/10

caryar *n* transporter 205/5

cassock *n* long, loose coat or gown 488/40,

kassock 488/42; kassocke 488/41

caue *n* injunction or rule 146/10

caviled *pp* found fault with 499/6

cedule *n* piece of paper or parchment 145/12

celere *n* reward, honorarium 460/18

cepell cones *n phr pl* braces or couples of rabbits (conies) 503/15

cester *n* liquid measure of ale, beer and wine 20/16, 152/12, 152/13; sester 503/11, 503/12, 503/13

chaber *n error for* 'chamber' 542/2

chafts *n pl* shafts 46/12, 46/34

chalese *n* cup used for administering wine in the Eucharist 486/8; chalys 98/1

chamburlen *n* city receiver 18/7, 18/8, 18/16, etc; chamberlayne 379/3; chamberleyn 84/3; chaimbrleyns *pl* 55/16; chamberlayns 55/15m; chamberleyns 83/41, 84/1; chamberlyns 509/2; chamburlayns 9/5; chamburlens 11/35; chaummburlens 55/22

chamlet *n* expensive fabric from the Near East 119/4; chamlett 488/41, 489/1

change *n* alteration 438/37

chantries *n pl* endowments for the maintenance of a priest or priests to sing masses for the souls of the founders, etc; chapels or parts of a church so endowed 296/22m

chape *n* metal plate for point of sheath 299/38, 368/20

chapeletts *n pl* crowns or garlands 70/40; schapletes 105/17

chapman *n* merchant 274/9

chassyng *prp* for hunting 227/4

chaummburlens *see* chamburlen

chaundeler *n* maker of candles 78/39; chaundelers *pl* 77/11, 78/36, 78/36m; chaundlers 77/11m

chefferellys *see* cheverel

cheif rent *n phr* rent paid for a fief held in chief from a lord 582/20, 582/25; cheiff rent 349/12; cheiffe rentes *pl* 349/12m

chelde *n* child 216/7

cheverel *n* wig 93/24; chefferellys *pl* 474/27; cheverels 74/3, 227/8

chewssynge daye *n phr* election day 290/32;

chowsimge daye 326/16; chusynge daye 236/36

childer *n pl* children 54/20, 166/22, 174/19; childers 173/5

choyse daye *n phr* election day 307/5, 315/7, 318/19, etc; chossday 312/27; chosse day 312/29; choyce daie 427/4, 430/40

chusynge daye *see* chewssynge daye

citacons *n pl* summonses 453/39

clamp *n* brace 261/17; clampe 78/1, 309/14, 309/15; clampes *pl* 168/3, 179/11, 190/42, etc; clampys 49/4, 95/14

clapp *v inf* arrest or put in irons 500/10; clapt *pp* 500/29

clarcke *n* scribe 219/7, 228/2, 248/27, etc; clark 124/21, 172/7, 199/25, etc; clarke 121/11, 126/5, etc; clerk 42/32, 81/1; cllarke 239/24; clarkes *pl* 304/15

claret *n* wine of a light red or yellowish colour 509/10

clark *n* officer who keeps records and accounts 510/23; clarke 97/31; clerke 21/36

clarkes *n pl* men ordained to the ministry or service of the church 476/30, 478/22, 479/15, etc; clarkys 475/7; clerkes 22/9, 170/35

claspe *n* metal fastener 92/38; claspes *pl* 92/38, 249/13, 249/15, etc

cleane lent *n phr* the period of Lent 483/31

cler *adj* free of liability 110/17

clerk *see* clarcke

clerke *see* clark

clerkes *see* clarkes

cllarke *see* clarcke

closet *n* private chapel 21/36; closette 21/37, 22/8, 22/15

closyd *pp* put into a surrounding material 487/36, 487/40

cloutenayle *n* flat-headed nail 52/35; cloutnayle 50/6

cloutt *n* metal shield for an axletree 241/17; clowte 235/26, 252/36, 267/12; clowtt 259/7; clowtes *pl* 261/6; clowtts 259/9

cloyes *n pl* cloths 27/34

clype *n* metal device for holding things tightly

together 218/7; **clyppes** *pl* 162/37, 278/2, 283/20, etc; **clyppis** 52/36; **clypps** 241/36

cofer *n* chest or trunk 334/33; **cofor** 20/19; **coofer** 226/38; **cofferes** *pl* 240/37; **coffers** 334/33

cofyns *n pl* baskets 37/13

cognizances *n pl* badges 380/11; **cunisons** 413/31

colacion *n* a money collection 43/11

coller *n* armour for neck 324/30, 324/31; **collers** *pl* 324/26, 324/28; **collors** 324/25

columbynes *n pl* ornaments in the shape of columbine flowers 487/3

comfettes *n pl* sweetmeats made of fruits preserved in sugar 157/10; **comfetts** 509/9; **counfetys** 37/14

cominalte *n* citizenry 21/15, 22/27, 36/37, etc; **cominaltie** 144/1, 144/30, 145/3, etc; **cominalteez** *pl* communities 79/4

committed *pp* consigned to custody 498/23

commytte *pp* consigned to confinement 83/10; **comitted** 355/37; **comytted** 499/8

comoditie *n* benefit 276/29

comon *v pa 3 pl* came 22/29

comorions *n pl* type of helmet 325/10; **comorrians** 324/35

compas *v inf* encircle, surround 163/12; **compased** *pp* 486/11

compase *n* circle (?) 487/8

compromytted *v pa 3 pl refl* bound themselves 16/11

comyn *pp and prep* come in 54/10

comytt *v pr 1 sg* entrust 501/1

conabull *adj* suitable 31/41

conand *n* agreement, bargain 19/35

condite *n* water conduit 53/28, 53/29, 54/36, etc; **conduite** 68/3; **cundit** 31/1, 31/32, 34/5; **cundyt** 90/15; **conduits** *pl* 404/9

conductors *n pl* leaders 510/7, 510/15

conseyue *v inf* perceive 31/16

contentacion *n* satisfaction 233/32

controler *n* checker of expenditures 282/7

conuented *pp* brought together 497/30

conuenticuls *n pl* gatherings 22/38

conyskynes *n pl* rabbit skins 504/22

coofer *see* **cofer**

copars, copers *see* **coupers**

cope *n* silk vestment like a cloak 98/32, 492/7, 492/8, etc; **copes** *pl* 22/10, 492/4, 492/5, etc; **cops** 492/2, 492/10; **copus** 81/14

coprncy *n* co-operancy, working together 460/27

corne pouder *n phr* granulated gunpowder 322/19; **corne powder** 391/22

corporas *n* linen cloth on which the consecrated elements are placed during Mass 470/22, 486/10, 487/1, etc

corpusday *n* feast of Corpus Christi 164/42

corpustyd *n* feast of Corpus Christi 171/38

correspondency *n* arrangement 511/28

cors *n* band of silk used as a belt 81/7, 81/9, 98/4, etc

corslet *n* piece of body armour 367/40, 367/43, 368/1; **corselete** 240/15; **corslett** 367/41; **corslettes** *pl* 324/24, 324/28, 367/39, etc

cortenns *n pl* curtains 240/29

corueseres *n pl* shoemakers 102/27; **coruesers** 104/29; **coruisers** 16/36, 79/19; **corvisers** 103/15, 192/39

cotelers *see* **cutler**

coterellis *n pl* pins or bolts 92/39

cottays *n pl* coats 472/22

cotter *n* pin or bolt 308/3

cottyers *n pl transcriber's error for* 'bowyers' (?) 485/14

counfetys *see* **comfettes**

count *n* account, reckoning or presentation of accounts 414/3, 424/33; **cownte** 347/6, 461/8; **kownt** 467/12; **kownte** 462/32

counterfett *adj* imitation 487/7

coupers *n pl* makers of barrels 141/23, 199/5, 203/24, etc; **copars** 148/3; **copers** 176/35, 179/24; **cowpars** 183/10, 211/20, 218/28; **cowpers** 110/24, 129/16, 143/4; **cowperys** 143/14, 146/31; **cvipers** 158/25m

cowchaunt *adj* lying with the body resting on the ground, but the head up 487/2

cownte *see* **count**

cowntters *n pl* imitation coins 260/15

cowpars, cowpers, cowperys *see* **coupers**

cowpe *n* wagon 39/34

coyffe *n* close-fitting cap 334/37; **coyffes** *pl* 241/1

crassett *see* **cresset**

crast *see* **crest**

creccettlyght *n* light provided by iron vessels containing burning material and hung from poles 462/9

cresset *n* iron vessel used for holding material burned for light and hung on a pole 20/13, 20/18, 25/27, etc; **crassett** 140/27; **creset** 173/42, 204/15, 471/21; **cresett** 212/15, 212/16, 214/9; **cressete** 143/9; **cresseth** 464/13; **cressett** 121/41, 122/6, 123/31, etc; **cressit** 211/10; **cressy** 461/11; **cressyt** 164/25, 164/32, 168/18, etc; **cressytt** 171/16, 171/17, 198/27, etc; **cressytte** 481/6; **cresyt** 217/14; **cryset** 169/33; **crysset** 180/32, 180/33, 192/10, etc; **cryssyt** 135/4, 135/6, 135/13, etc; **kressett** 462/37, 466/37, 469/32, etc; **cresetes** *pl* 143/11; **cresets** 471/18, 471/32, 471/41; **cresettes** 151/4, 212/14; **cresetts** 461/18; **cresittes** 213/12; **cressetes** 115/38, 115/39, 116/9, etc; **cressets** 169/31, 200/7, 207/24, etc; **cressettees** 214/8, 216/19, 216/20, etc; **cressettes** 114/39, 116/20, 116/21, etc; **cressetts** 115/11, 115/16, 115/17, etc; **cressites** 334/35; **cressittes** 211/12, 215/18; **cressytes** 164/33, 171/23, 176/9, etc; **cressyttes** 168/12, 171/13, 178/15, etc; **cressytts** 472/31, 473/1, 474/2; **cryssetts** 180/34; **cryssytts** 473/40; **kressetts** 469/34

cressetberers *n pl* carriers of iron vessels containing material burned for light 462/8; **cressetberrers** 24/1

crest *n* device borne above the shield and helmet in a coat of arms 242/1

crest *n* plume, tuft, or other ornament fixed on top of a helmet or head-dress; the helmet or head-dress itself 35/16, 85/8, 95/27; **crast** 69/10; **creste** 71/15, 73/32, 85/10; **crestes** *pl* 324/35; **crestis** 52/42; **crests** 51/12, 51/14, 51/16, etc

crestes *n pl* ceremonial regalia worn, hanging

from ribbons around the neck, by the city waits 423/25, 423/26; **crests** 434/38

crochons *n pl* staffs of some kind (?), pots or vessels of some kind (?) 117/40

crosear *n* pastoral staff or crook of a bishop or abbot 81/6; **crosyar** 98/10

crosstaffe *n* staff with cross attached; a processional cross 98/1

croste *n error for* 'croft' (?) 482/10

crowne *n* head-dress or garland worn by piper (?) 20/6

cryset, crysset, cryssetts, cryssyt, cryssytts *see* **cresset**

cullern *vb n* colouring or painting 242/23

cundit, cundyt *see* **condite**

cunisons *see* **cognizances**

cure *n* care 91/8

curius *adj* expert (*or error for* 'curagious'?) 32/7

curriors *n pl* a kind of fire-arm 325/29

curtalls *n pl* a kind of bassoon 338/24; *see also* **double curtall**

cutler *n* maker of knives and other cutting instruments 314/12, 324/22; **cuttler** 438/37; **kuttler** 196/4; **cotelers** 9/26

cvipers *see* **coupers**

cytyng *vb n* summoning to appear before a court 453/41

damaske *n* expensive silk fabric 5/4, 73/23, 98/24, etc; **damas** 488/40; **damask** 489/1

dawber *n* plasterer 257/16

dawbing *vb n* plastering 319/3; **dawbyng** 263/40

daybell *n* morning bell 19/6

deadym *n* crown or crowning ornament 97/35

deepe *adj* wide 429/27

deliberatlie *adv* with careful consideration 5/19

demene *n* control 22/33, 29/39

deputy marshall *n phr* assistant to the knight marshall *see* **knight marshall** 404/41

derege *n* song sung at burial 509/5, 509/6, 509/7

deuer *n* duty 31/26

deuised *pp* considered 5/20

deuises *n pl* plans 497/15, 497/30

deuoir *n* best effort 4/35

deuysen *v pr 3 pl* assign, give 301/1; **deuysed** *pp* 300/41

deyntez *n pl* honour, esteem 32/26

deys *n* raised platform 105/30

deysters *n pl* dyers of cloth 17/3, 65/42

diamond *n* demon 69/25; **dyamond** 71/26; **dymons** *poss* 240/29

diaper *n* silk fabric woven over with gold thread 487/27

dimised *pp* transferred 145/2; **dymysed** 144/2

disseuer *v inf* separate 31/25

distaffe *n* staff for winding flax or wool 334/41; **dystaff** 240/33

distasting *prp* having an aversion to 498/7

distrayne *v inf* oppress 90/39

distresse *n* seizure of goods 133/19, 379/9

diuers *adj* various 364/27, 365/3; **diuerse** 31/29; **divers** 66/23, 107/7, 390/12, etc; **dyvers** 300/40, 376/30

diuers *n* indefinite number of individuals 53/7, 54/24

dobbe *v inf* smear 110/29; **dobbyng** *vb n* 110/32

dobell ffifteene *n phr* tax amounting to twice the value of a fifteenth of the property 354/23; **doobell 15** 351/40; *see also* **ffifteene**

doblet *n* close-fitting body garment for men 182/1; **dooblet** 182/2; **dooblitt** 181/42; **dublettes** 119/3, 489/3; **dublit** 334/36; **dublyt** 240/23; **dwblettes** 118/39

double curtall *n phr* musical instrument an octave lower than a curtal 424/4; *see* **curtalls**

dowsemeris *n pl* dulcimers, stringed musical instruments 53/30

draper *n* maker and/or seller of cloth 91/28, 95/4, 225/37, etc; **drapers** *pl* 17/4, 217/22, 234/21, etc

draught *n* pulling 92/35

drevyng, dreyvyng *see* **dryvyng**

drivers *see* **dryvers**

driving, drivinge, drivynge *see* **dryvyng**

dryve *v inf* draw, propel 27/2; **dryved** *v pa 3 pl* 191/20

dryvers *n pl* those who draw or propel the pageant wagon 140/4, 194/29, 197/39, etc; **drivers** 236/24; **dryuers** 159/33, 478/9; **dryveres** 163/38; **drywares** 153/13

dryvyng *vb n* drawing, propelling 124/26, 140/12, 478/25, etc; **drevyng** 180/39; **dreyvyng** 183/35, 186/31; **driving** 268/20; **drivinge** 303/39, 306/19, 306/32; **drivynge** 236/26; **dryuyng** 169/14, 217/35, 221/3, etc; **dryveeng** 215/40; **dryveng** 161/21, 213/29; **dryving** 222/20; **dryvinge** 245/31; **dryvng** 242/11, 264/20, 476/34; **dryvynge** 210/9, 211/36, 223/24, etc; **dryweng** 150/10

duble gilt *adj phr* covered with two layers of gold 365/17

dublettes, dublit, dublyt *see* **doblet**

dwblettes *see* **doblet**

dyadem *n* crown 175/13; **dyadynnes** *pl* 474/28

dyamond *see* **diamond**

dycke *n* truncheon or pike 250/39

dyer *n* one who dyes cloth 329/32, 376/33; **dyers** *pl* 79/18

dyet *n* provision of food 401/15

dyghtyng *vb n* preparing 39/4, 39/14, 65/17; **dyttyng** 69/36

dymons *see* **diamond**

dymysed *see* **dimised**

dyne *adj* divine 90/20

dysse *n* dice 73/22

dystaff *see* **distaffe**

dysworschipp *n* dishonour 188/21

dyttyng *see* **dyghtyng**

dyvers *see* **diuers**

eftesones *adv* afterward 83/22; **eftsones** 83/12, 84/9

egall *adj* equal 89/19

ell *n* length measure equal to forty-five inches 28/7, 236/15; **ele** 508/28; **ellen** 86/11 86/12; **ellne** 97/11; **elne** 170/19; **elue** (*see footnote*) 465/11; **ellys** *pl* 474/20; **eluys** (*see footnote*) 465/10; **elys** 474/21, 474/23, 474/24; **blues** (*see footnote*) 241/33

empeyrede *pp* harmed, damaged 18/32

encreyng *vb n error for* 'entreyng,' entering in
  writing (?) 453/42

endosed *pp* confirmed 9/39

ensignes *n pl* standard bearers 390/13

enterlud *n* light or humorous play 265/27

enterprise *v inf* make attempt 4/31

eschewed *pp* avoided 36/6; eschewyng *vb n*
  8/13, 8/15

escutcheons *see* schochyn

esquires *n pl* members of the gentry, ranking
  below knights 510/17, 510/27; esquirs
  510/37; esquires *poss* 511/33

esquiresse *n* female esquire (*see* esquires)
  511/14; esquiresses *pl* 511/29

eve, evee, evey, evy *see* ive

exacted *pp in phr* exacted vppon inflicted on
  501/25

exaltre *see* axeltre

excedent *prp* surpassing 54/29

excusation *n* excuse 484/39

exemble *v inf* assemble 26/31

expende *pp* spent 41/38

extollence *n* uplifting of dignity 91/16

extre *see* axeltre

eyde *n* assistance 131/24

faced *pp* turned up with another kind of
  material 488/34, 488/35

fachede, facheng, fachynge *see* fet

faculteez *n pl* abilities 79/8

facultie *n* trade, occupation 144/33, 144/35,
  144/36, etc; faculties *pl* 144/42, 146/18

fanes *n pl* banners 50/6; faynes 241/6; ffannes
  241/3

fanons *n pl* embroidered bands attached to the
  left wrist of celebrant at Mass; maniples
  98/35; *sg* phanon 486/10, 487/1, 487/3

fareeres *n pl* those who shoe horses 180/5

farryshe *adj* made of fur (?) *or* of a Pharisee (?)
  259/36

farye *n in phr* farye fryday the Friday on which
  the fair is held 473/38; fayrer fryday
  248/36; feare fryday 480/8; ferye fryday
  480/16; ffeere ffreday 463/20; freyr frydey
  470/10

fatched *see* fet

fatheryng *vb n* feathering 453/17

fauchon *n* curved broad sword; falchion 59/36;
  fawchon 73/33, 95/27; fawchyne 231/4;
  faychon 200/40

fayn *adj* glad 32/17, 91/16

faynes *see* fanes

fee farme *n phr* holding of land for fixed rent,
  without services required 296/25; ffee
  farme 296/25m; *see also* ferme

fens *n* art of fencing 273/28

fensmaster *n* teacher of fencing 274/35

ferme *n in phr* to ferme letten *v pr 3 pl* give over
  for fixed rent 301/1; to ferme lett *pp*
  300/41; *see also* fee farme

ferye *see* farye

fet *v pa 3 pl* fetched 22/16; fachede *pp* 477/28;
  facheng *vb n* 476/9; fachynge 17/31;
  fochyng 49/23; fatched *pp in phr* fatched
  vpp with supplied with 394/2, 394/5-6

ffaggotts *n pl* bundles of sticks for burning; *in
  phr* bare ffaggotts were burned at the stake
  107/10-11

ffalle *n* type of collar 450/9, 451/4

ffannes *see* fanes

ffarfatur *n* forfeiture 119/10

ffedom *n* fathom, length between outstretched
  arms 465/40

ffee farme *see* fee farme

ffeoffees *n pl* persons who hold land by a fee,
  on condition of service to a lord 482/3

ffeore *n* fur 119/2; fforre 118/39; fforrees *pl*
  119/3

ffifteene *n* tax amounting to a fifteenth of the
  value of the property 356/37; ffiftine
  352/25, 355/6; ffivetene 345/3; fivtene
  347/13; ffysteenes *pl* 420/4; fifteens
  349/39; fivetenes 597/33; *see also* dobell
  ffifteene

ffletchers *n pl* makers of arrows 485/14;
  flechers 136/21

ffor asmoch as *see* foralsomyche as

fforre, fforrees *see* ffeore

ffoynees *n pl* beech martens 118/39; *see also*
  foynes

ffreedom *n* right to participate in the privileges of a company 279/10

ffremasons *n pl* itinerant stone workers 12/18

ffreres, ffrerys *see* **freres**

ffyns *see* **finis**

ffysshemongers *n pl* dealers in fish 79/18; **fishemongers** 136/21

ffysteenes *see* **ffifteene**

fifteens *see* **ffifteene**

finis *n pl* fees paid on entry into the brotherhood of a guild 64/18, 64/22, 64/22; **ffyns** 452/40; **fynees** 122/27; **fynnys** 186/13; **fyns** 116/14, 186/15, 186/16; **fynys** 42/27, 142/1

fishemongers *see* **ffysshemongers**

fivetenes, fivtene *see* **ffifteene**

flage *n error for* 'slag,' type of kettle drum 474/12; *see also* **slag**

flechers *see* **ffletchers**

fochyng *see* **fet**

foll all *phr* quite all (?) *or* nonsense refrain fa-la (?) 91/18

folles *n pl poss* fools' 240/30

foote clothes *n phr pl* ornamented cloths hung over the backs of horses 232/26-7

foralsomyche as *conj phr* seeing that 29/29; **ffor asmoche as** 79/3; **for asmoch as** 131/28; **forassmuch as** 193/7-8

forbeng *vb n* polishing 29/21

forde *adj* furred 142/20

foreners *n pl* non-members of the guild 43/12

forepart *n* front 324/32; **foreparte** 162/40

foreward *n* vanguard 274/35

forseyng *prp* taking care (that) 79/5

fostyan *n* a kind of cloth 453/19; **fustiane** 487/4

foynes *n pl* furs of beech martens 488/34; *see also* **ffoynees**

fraie *n* conflict 4/26

frankynsence *n* gum resin used for burning as incense 156/32, 208/42

fraternitie *n* guild 144/36, 145/25, 145/27, etc; **fraternities** *pl* 146/3; **fraternyties** 144/41

fraunchice *n* area over which the privileges of the corporation extend 35/29, 35/37, 37/23

freat *n* ornament 250/18; **fretts** *pl* 230/35, 230/38

freres *n pl* convent of an order of friars 25/39

freres *n pl* friars; members of a type of religious order distinguished from monks, canons, etc 62/15, 65/33, 67/3, etc; **ffreres** 70/28; **ffrerys** 58/15

freshe *adv* anew 46/34

freshing *vb n* renewing, repairing 505/20

freyr *see* **farye**

frindging *vb n* putting on a border 395/38

frontelett *n* cloth used to cover the upper part of the cloth covering the front of the altar 487/18, 487/28; **frontell** 487/6; **frontlett** 487/9

fruste *adj* first 479/2

fryse *n* kind of coarse woollen cloth 489/2

fryst *adv* first 147/18

fullers *n pl* those who beat cloth for cleaning and thickening 83/27

furniture *n* armour and accessories 354/7

furreers *n pl* dealers in furs 203/32

furveled *pp* with edges decorated by frills 508/29

fustiane *see* **fostyan**

fynding *vb n* support 112/38

fyne *n* fee paid as part of an adjustment in conditions of tenancy 400/19

fynees, fynnys, fyns, fynys *see* **finis**

gallance *n pl* gallons 238/28

galleyes *n pl* gallows 308/7

ganes *n pl* gallons 479/30, 504/25; **gawnes** 229/18

garded *pp* trimmed 488/40

gassetts *n pl* pieces of flexible material used to fill up space between plates at the joints of armour 86/7; **gosetes** 450/9

gauen *see* **gone**

gaulled *pp* harassed 501/26

gawnes *see* **ganes**

generall dayes *n phr pl* days on which all members of a guild meet 152/11m, 154/40-1m, 162/13-14m, etc; **generall days** 130/9, 170/22-3m

gentilwomen *n pl* term used to describe women of a certain rank within the guild 166/17

gentleman shewers *n phr pl* those in charge of seating at table and the serving of the meal 405/9

gentleman ushers *n phr pl* gentlemen acting as ushers to nobles 405/10

gentlemen harbingers *n phr pl* those who are sent ahead to provide lodgings 405/17

gentlewomen *n pl* women attendant on a noble lady 511/33, 511/34, 512/22, etc

gerdylars, gerdyllars *see* girdelers

giandes, giant *see* gyant

gifters *n pl* giftures, gifts 365/33

girdle *n* belt 334/28; girdull 81/7, 81/9; gordell 450/11, 451/3; gyrdull 98/4, 98/6; gyrdyll 23/37, 231/11; girdelles *pl* 158/37; girdles 314/16; gyrdyllys 473/17, 473/18

girdelers *n pl* makers of belts 83/27, 83/28m, 83/29, etc; gerdylars 454/12; gerdyllars 454/6; girdlers 305/12, 305/30, 349/12, etc; gorddelors 115/42; gordelares 451/26, 452/20, 452/25, etc; gordelarus 451/31, 452/6, 452/30, etc; gordelers 117/25, 117/33, 454/34, etc; gordellares 452/13; gordilares 452/1; gordlers 119/17; gordleyrs 454/27; gudelers 123/21; gurdelars 452/35, 453/1, 453/6, etc; gurdelers 17/1, 129/4, 133/15, etc; gurdelres 453/27; gyrdelers 120/25, 121/39, 190/20, etc; gyrdlers 266/10

glaciars *n pl* glazers of windows 332/36

gladdid *pp* made glad 30/8

gladsum *adj* filled with joy 272/39

gleave *n* lance, bill, or sword 367/42; gleves *pl* 325/14; gleyves 19/9

glouers *n pl* makers or sellers of gloves 16/32

glowos *n pl* gloves 150/33

gom *n* gum 110/31

gone *n* gown, robe 97/5, 97/17, 357/11; gauen 71/14

gonies *n pl* guns 340/11

gorddelors, gordelares, gordelarus, gordelers, gordellares, gordilares, gordlers, gordleyrs *see* girdelers

gordell *see* girdle

gorgett *n* armour covering the throat 195/36, 410/38; gorgettes *pl* 196/9, 477/31; gorgetys 86/7; gorgyts 240/18

gosetes *see* gassetts

goven *pp* given 65/33

gouernaince *n* government 89/18; gouernanse 8/13; gouernauns 8/15, 273/22; *see also* gouernance

gouernance *n* control 8/17; gouernaunce 9/30, 131/15, 132/2; *see also* gouernaince

grarden *n* garden 593/33

gravyn *pp* engraved 98/1

grece *n* grease 159/40, 229/21

gret *n* grit, soil 94/35

grevyvyes *n pl* pieces of leg armour 35/17

grisly *adv* savagely 275/7

grocer *n* wholesale seller or retailer of spices, sugar, etc 37/8, 48/16

grocerie ware *n phr* grocery merchandise 505/30

groged *v pa 3 pl* complained 36/3

grograns *n pl* clothes made of grogram 513/15; *see* grograyne

grograyne *n* grogram, coarse fabric of silk and/or wool and mohair 488/41

grondsyll *v inf* lay foundation 263/30; grondsyllyng *vb n* 263/31

grooms *n pl* male attendants 405/8

grounder *n* establisher 53/37

gudelers, gurdelars, gurdelers, gurdelres *see* girdelers

gyant *n* giant 136/31, 139/22, 139/23, etc; giant 160/14; gyand 188/3, 188/9; gyeand 188/10, 191/39; gyeande 178/14, 178/17; gyeant 176/13, 176/15; ioyand 182/5, 195/3, 195/9, etc; giandes *poss* 334/40; gyans 477/22, 480/6; gyantes 504/12; gyenans 477/21; gyanes *pl* 474/15, 481/17; gyantysse 217/15; gyones 474/16

gybbyt *n* gibbet, gallows 281/28

gyntys *n pl* joints, portions of a carcass 504/2

gyrdelers, gyrdlers *see* girdelers

gyrdull, gyrdyll, gyrdyllys *see* girdle

haberdyne *n* kind of cod, usually served salted 505/37

haburion *n* coat or jacket of mail or scale armour 18/12; **haburions** *pl* 18/2, 18/5, 18/9; **habyrgyns** 86/6

hach *n* half-door (?) 264/1

hait lath *n phr* type of narrow strip of wood 264/5

halberdes *n pl* weapon combining spear and battle-axe 368/7; **holbeardes** 325/13; **holbertes** 438/8; **holberts** 390/14

hale *n* temporary shelter 71/27

hall *n* ale 479/30

hall vesell *n phr* gold or silver container stamped with a hall-mark, indicating a standard of quality 504/23

haloyng *vb n* consecration 108/42

hangells *n pl* angels 476/29

hanyng *see* have

harbinger *see* knight harbinger

harbingers *see* gentlemen harbingers, yeoman harbingers

harneis *n* body armour 383/14, 391/32, 399/17, etc; **harn⟨...⟩** 49/23; **harnees** 430/39; **harnenes** 216/17; **harnes** 20/12, 20/18, 35/15, etc; **harnese** 363/13; **harness** 95/35, 312/24, 388/30, etc; **harnesse** 20/11, 140/5, 182/30, etc; **harneys** 372/21, 388/10, 395/23, etc; **harnies** 434/10, 435/35; **harnis** 231/18, 243/7, 251/19, etc; **harnise** 363/15; **harnish** 355/4, 367/4; **harnisse** 428/4; **harny** 359/4; **harnys** 46/31, 88/12, 147/19, etc; **harnyse** 224/37; **harnysh** 345/25; **harrenes** 462/3; **harrnes** 461/41; **harrynes** 480/18; **hernes** 23/39, 186/40, 462/40, etc; **hernis** 137/40; **hernys** 467/5; **hernyse** 118/12; **horenes** 385/33; **hornenes** 426/17; **hornes** 301/24, 301/25, 369/6, etc; **hornese** 366/21, 366/23; **hornies** 418/39; **hornis** 372/27; **hornish** 385/25, 385/26; **harneses** *pl* 220/11, 223/27, 236/28; **harnessees** 212/12, 214/6; **harnesses** 196/10, 207/6, 209/13, etc; **harnises** 267/7, 277/6; **harnisses** 266/34, 277/13, 278/10, etc; **harnyses** 283/22; **harnysses** 252/1, 262/10, 262/11, etc; **harnyssis** 279/1

harnesbearrers *n pl* carriers of harness armour 315/14

harnesmen *n pl* men dressed in harness armour 299/6, 451/13; **harneysmen** 174/1; **harnysmen** 173/40; **hernystmen** 184/3; *see* harneis

harnessyng *vb n* equipping in harness armour 200/13, 200/14, 219/40, etc; **harneshynge** 345/23; **harnessing** 216/30, 219/35, 352/20; **harnessinge** 363/33; **harnishinge** 350/18; **harnyshyng** 256/9; **harnysshng** 250/31; **harnyssyng** 264/32; **harnessed** *pp* 68/39, 381/14; **harnesst** 357/30; **harnest** 169/30, 254/18, 296/43, etc; **harneste** 35/15, 336/42; **harnesyd** 470/10, 470/11, 470/21; **harnissde** 386/10; **harnste** 180/31; **harnysed** 238/10; **harnyste** 344/18; **harnysyd** 224/35, 230/10; **harrnyst** 192/13; **hernest** 470/30; **hornist** 298/34; *see also* harneis

harnest *pp* ornamented 81/7, 81/9, 98/6; **harnesyd** 98/4

harper *n* harp player 19/21, 20/13, 21/3, etc

harrenes, harrnes, harrynes *see* harneis

hart *n* male deer 205/14, 205/15; **hartt** 200/20, 205/11, 205/13, etc; **hartte** 225/4; **hartts** *poss* 200/18, 205/10

haspes *n pl* metal clasps used with staples to fasten doors 163/11, 163/13; **hassppeys** 469/22

haut grece *n phr in phr* of haut grece well-fattened 37/12

have *v inf* move from one place to another 35/14, 41/41, 44/14; **haue** 27/1; **havyng** *vb n* 20/4, 24/6, 40/38, etc; **hanyng** (*see footnote*) 217/33, 223/40; **hauvyng** 175/15, 175/16, 229/37; **hauyng** 221/2; **hauynng** 462/13; **having** 463/30; **havinge** 72/32; **havynge** 95/16, 229/10, 309/10; **haweng** 153/17; **haweyng** 469/20; **hawyng** 92/1, 461/26

headded *pp* tipped 325/20, 325/21

heasre *n* hair (?) 247/6

hed pens *n phr pl* pegs or bolts with wide heads 297/24

hell hede *n phr* head representing the mouth of hell 465/23, 466/4, 472/28, etc; **hell hed**

466/14; **helle hede** 469/5

helver *n* handle 325/27

hendly *adv* courteously 32/9

hernes, hernis, hernys, hernyse *see* **harneis**

hernest *see* **harnessyng**

hernystmen *see* **harnesmen**

hether *adj* nearer 426/6

hewkus *n pl* hooded cloaks 64/28

heyre *n* hair-cloth 493/8

high sherriffes *n poss* of the sheriff of the shire, appointed by royal patent 425/25

hoc tuesday *n phr* second Tuesday after Easter 276/26-7, 276/30; **hocke tuesday** 243/41; **hockes tewesday** 279/41-2; **hockes tuesday** 271/10; **hockestewysday** 244/39; **hocks tewysdaye** 280/22; **hocks tuesday** 114/32-3; **hocks twesday** 251/19; **hoc-tewsdaye** 246/5; **hoge tuesday** 243/7; **hogh tuysday** 47/31; **hok tuisday** 272/34m; **hoktwsday** 171/3; **hox tuesday** 7/32, 215/11, 276/34; **oxe tewsday** 277/13

hocus pocus *n phr* magician 442/14

holbeardes, holbertes, holberts *see* **halberdes**

holbert diers *n phr pl* soldiers armed with halberds, halberdiers 390/14; *see* **halberdes**

hold *n* tenure 96/17

holland *n* type of linen fabric made in Holland 510/15

homage *n* formal acknowledgement of allegiance 89/27

hopes *n pl* hoops 467/29; **hopps** 20/1

horenes, hornenes, hornes, hornese, hornies, hornis, hornish *see* **harneis**

horne flaskes *n phr pl* vessels for liquids in shape of horn 325/5

hornist *see* **harnessyng**

horsbred *n* bread used as food for horses 56/26; **horsebred** 214/40

horseleter *n* litter hung on poles, which are borne by two horses 508/34, 508/40; **horse letyr** 508/24

hotmell *see* **otemell**

hovrgens *n pl* organs 476/9

howe *n error for* home 20/4

hox tuesday *see* **hoc twesday**

hree *n* hair 474/27

husbondman *n* farmer 12/14

hyngyng *n* drapery hanging 105/30

iak *n* stuffed or quilted tunic used as body protection 19/22; **iakke** 18/12, 18/33; **iakkes** *pl* 18/2, 18/5, 18/9, etc; **jackes** 240/17; **jacks** 334/31; **jakks** 45/4; **jakkus** 52/12

iaket *n* kind of body armour 114/19, 451/10; **jaket** 63/28; **iackettes** *pl* 138/37; **iakettees** 119/3; **iakettes** 127/12; **jaketes** 97/10; **jakkets** 97/11; **jakketts** 73/21, 73/26

iakked *adj* wearing a jack (*see* **iak**) 29/11; **jaked** 48/9; **jakked** 48/35, 71/4; **jakkud** 47/4

ierkyns *n pl* close-fitting jackets or jerseys 118/40

iern *n* iron 255/32; **iorn** 162/37, 179/14; **iorne** 168/3, 182/41, 190/42; **iourne** 318/36

ierneymen, iernneymen *see* **iorney man**

iesse *n* tree representing genealogy of Christ 30/1

ihesus day *n phr* festival of the name of Jesus, 7 August 173/29; **ihesus daye** 178/3

ihit *conj* yet 33/11, 33/21

imbrodered *pp* ornamented 4/4, 4/8, 4/40

impaled *pp* surrounded enclosed 510/13

implementes *n pl* equipment 128/36, 132/6, 145/9, etc; **implements** 241/12; **implments** 334/22

imployed *pp* bestowed 270/33

importabl *adj* unbearable 273/3

inacted *pp* ordained by legislative authority 118/37

inclosed *pp* fenced in and taken out of the Common ground 426/7, 426/12

inclyne *v inf* bow 32/17

incoll *n* kind of linen tape 167/24, 187/28

incontinentlie *adv* straightaway 4/14

indented *pp* cut into copies with a zig-zag line 144/1, 144/10, 324/20

indenture *n* deed between parties, with copies cut away with a zig-zag edge 144/27, 300/29; **indentures** *pl* 144/40, 145/12, 146/13, etc; **indenturs** 354/29

indeuor *n in phr* **doo mine indeuor** exert myself to the uttermost 4/12 indued *pp* invested 207/39

inholder *n* keeper of an inn 274/24

inquest *n* body of men conducting legal inquiry
103/13, 103/22

insuperable *adj* unconquerable 90/21

interment *n* burial 508/7

interplaced *pp* placed among 510/21

interred *pp* buried 513/7

iocunder *adj comp* merrier 275/24

iodas torchees *n phr* Paschal candlesticks
113/21; iodas torchys 142/17; judas torches
463/35; *see also* judas

iorn, iorne *see* iern

iornettes *n pl* short outer garments for men
163/20

iorney man *n phr* worker who has passed
apprenticeship and earns wages 26/26;
iorneyman 27/5; iorneymann 26/23;
ierneymen *pl* 183/35, 183/37; iernneymen
180/39, 186/31; ioorneymen 453/37;
iornemen 189/11; iorneymen 26/42,
156/36, 165/33, etc; iornneymen 169/14;
iornnymen 180/22; iurnemen 268/20;
iurneymen 121/16, 172/1; jernamen
100/12; jorneymen 43/38, 95/15, 95/35;
jurneymen 49/11, 63/11

iourne *see* iern

ioy *v inf* rejoice (in) 30/9, 30/10; ioye 30/18

ioyand *see* gyant

ioynars, ioyners *see* joyner

irysshe mantylles *n phr pl* blankets used as
clothing in the rustic parts of Ireland
307/36

isle *n* aisle 512/1, 512/24

italian motion *n phr* puppet show 434/27,
442/12-13, 444/28; italiann motion 433/6-7;
see also motion

iuelles *n pl* expensive ornaments 131/18, 145/9,
486/6; iuels 80/42, 97/30

iure *n* Jewry, the Jewish people 32/36

iurnemen, iurneymen *see* iorney man

ive *n* ivy 462/34, 464/3, 464/35, etc; eve
470/40; evee 462/16; evey 477/8; evy
467/26; ivee 463/15; ivye 465/34; yue
504/11; yve 468/25, 470/17

jackes, jacks, jakks, jakkus *see* iak

jaked, jakked, jakkud *see* iakked

jaket, jaketes, jakkets, jakketts *see* iaket

jeȝie *n error for* 'Judas' (?) 281/28

jernamen *see* iorney man

jorneymen *see* iorney man

joyner *n* maker of wooden objects 50/10;
ioynars *pl* 332/36; ioyners 266/20, 271/22,
277/1, etc

judas *n* Paschal candlestick 58/39; judaces *pl*
115/9, 116/36; judasses 46/3, 46/24, 69/31,
etc; judasys 47/11; juddasys 467/10; *see
also* iodas torchees

judas torches *see* iodas torchees

jurneymen *see* iorney man

kassock, kassocke *see* cassock

kaye *n* key 163/32, 463/26

kechyn *n* cooking 62/29, 72/32, 72/37, etc

keper *n* warden or custodian 27/33; kepers *pl*
27/33, 27/36, 41/22, etc; keprs 82/33

kercheefe *n* piece of cloth used to cover the
head 511/15; kercheife 125/37; kerchyff
53/12; kercheefes *pl* 510/15, 511/34;
kerchiefs 511/37

kertell *n* woman's gown 240/23

kerver *n* carver of wood 83/23, 84/16

ketts *n pl* coats 467/7

keveryng *vb n* covering 230/32

knight harbinger *n phr* officer of the royal
household, whose function was to provide
lodgings in advance of the monarch 405/12

knight marshall *n phr* officer of the royal household who has jurisdiction over transgressions
within twelve miles of the palace 405/5

kownsell *n* advice 470/1

kownt, kownte *see* count

kressett, kressetts *see* cresset

ku *n* frame of mind 272/35

kuttler *see* cutler

kyppyng *vb n* keeping 471/22, 471/40; kypyng
257/2

lace *n* cord 163/12; lase 468/11; lasys *pl*
259/13

lachet *n* loop of cord, leather, etc, used as fastener 48/4

laeth *see* lathe nayle

lacke *n* latch (?) 253/33

lackies *n pl* footmen, followers 304/31; lakes 479/38

lamas *n* 1 August 55/17m, 317/9, 400/25, etc; lammas 286/5, 289/38, 293/38, etc; lammasse 83/40, 84/1, 84/3; lammes 114/19

lap *v inf* wrap 20/25; lapt *pp* 273/38

lase *n* noose 260/15, 285/40; *see also* lace

lasys *see* lace

lath *see* hait lath

lathe *n* long, thin piece of wood 93/6, 257/18, 319/19; *see also* hait lath, lathe nayle, sappe lath

lathe nayle *n phr* small nails for fastening laths 263/32; laeth nayles *pl* 277/42; *see also* hait lath, lathe, sappe lath

laton *n* yellow metal, like brass 46/23; latten 487/20

laude *n* praise 460/22

launcegayes *n pl* lances of a certain kind 598/17

launsknights *n pl* mercenaries 274/37

lauther *n* ladder (*or* maker of laths?) 476/33

lawne *n* kind of fine linen, like cambric 511/8, 511/15, 511/37, etc; lawn 511/35; lawnes *pl* 511/23

layd downe *pp phr* discontinued 294/15-16m, 294/18

laydto *pp phr* set to work (on) 235/35

layte *n* light (?) *or* lighter (?) 474/10

leddur *n* leather 60/18; leddur 93/25; letter 454/40

ledge *n* traverse bar of wood attached to door, furniture, etc 214/26, 245/28, 285/7, etc; leadg 250/22; leddgys *pl* 224/9; ledges 245/29; ledgis 277/27; ledgs 256/26; ledgys 237/34, 263/34; legges 49/5

leet *n* local court empowered to adjudicate lesser offences and legislate in certain jurisdictions 103/10, 139/3, 139/6, etc; alete 9/26; leete 55/20, 56/38, 103/20, etc; lete 7/41, 8/3, 9/21, etc; leetes *pl* sessions of court leet 321/15m; letes 78/36, 321/16

lege *adj* entitled to feudal service 32/30

legeman *n* vassal sworn to the service of a lord 29/9

legerdemaine *n* sleight of hand 429/4; legerdemeane 447/39

legges *see* ledge

lene *v pr 3 sg subj* conceal 18/24

lenton *n* Lent 487/5, 487/6

leoff *n in phr* leoff bred bread made in loaf form 152/11; lovebred *n* 157/26

lese *v inf* lose 78/40, 79/40, 80/24, etc; lesyng *vb n* 149/18

lete, letes *see* leet

lethering *vb n* covering with leather 195/37

lett, letten *see* ferme

letter *see* ledder

letteres patentes *n phr* document conferring rights or privileges 434/28-9, 434/30-1; letters patentes 392/23; *see also* patent

leverey *n* distinctive suit of clothing worn by an official or servant 85/35, 87/14, 88/22, etc; levery 82/11, 120/8; liuerey 138/35, 151/41, 158/1; liuery 364/29, 365/23; livery 232/20, 364/33, 365/11; liuerye 424/11; lyuerey 11/41, 155/13, 155/14; lyuerye 484/29; lyverey 484/36; lyvery 25/42; leueris *pl* 134/30; levereys 130/12; liueres 269/29; liuereyes 138/38, 210/42; liueries 141/6; liveryes 379/32; lyuereyes 22/39, 138/41, 190/27, etc; lyuerez 78/28; lyueries 265/20; lyvereyes 205/34, 208/18; lyvereys 138/32

leysur *n in phr* by goodly leysur with deliberation, in course of time 16/7

liberdes *n pl poss* leopards' 487/9

liberties *n pl* district extending beyond city boundaries which is under control of civic authority 232/21, 233/41

like *adv* likely 131/25; lyke 16/4

like *v pr 3 sg subj* please 233/5; lyke 8/12, 8/14; liked *pa 3 sg* 36/30

linages *n pl* families 3/18

linckes *see* lyncke

ling *n* type of long gadoid fish 505/37

list *v pa 3 pl* desired 500/1

listes *n pl* fences enclosing combat area 3/19, 4/3, 4/7; lists 3/27, 4/19, 4/20, etc

littermen *n pl* those who carry a litter or couch shut in with curtains 405/3

liueres, liuerey, liuereyes, liueries, liuery, liverye, liveryes *see* leverey

loccar *n* chest with lock 214/28; locker 249/17; lockers *pl* 202/19

longen *v pr 3 pl* belong 27/40, 188/17; longes 108/3; longeth 27/33, 80/42; longith 200/20; longth 147/18; longythe 98/11; longeng *pp* 18/4, 18/6, 18/10, etc; longyng 16/1, 16/15, 46/22, etc

look *n* lock 172/28

loot *n* lute player (?) 547/23

lord high chamberlaine *see* lorde chamberlain

lorde chamberlain *n phr* head of the officers of the king's chamber 266/1; lord high chamberlaine 403/30; lord chamberlayns *poss* 270/21, 298/13, 310/11, etc; lord chamberlens 323/38; lord chamberlyns 282/10

lorde privey seall *n phr* keeper of the privy seal, which was affixed to a certain class of documents 149/30

losse *n* defeat 428/42

lottes *n pl* prizes in a lottery 407/8

loute *v pr 1 sg* bow 33/40

lovebred *see* leoff

lowe brethern *n pl* 'love-brothers,' good friends of the guild 137/22

lowlely *adv* humbly 33/40; lowly 31/39

luter *n* lute player 28/15

lyke *see* like

lyly pennes *n pl* pegs or bolts with lily-shaped heads (?) 241/2

lymyt *pp* assigned 79/38; lymyted 131/32

lyncke *n* torch made of tow and pitch 242/28; lynke 224/13, 230/33; linckes *pl* 447/10; lynkes 356/15

lyne *n* line of ancestry and descent 53/35, 54/10

lyuerey, lyuereyes, lyuerez, lyueries, lyuerye, lyverey, lyvereyes, lyvereys, lyvery *see* leverey

mace *n* ceremonial sceptre 232/39, 233/34, 233/42, etc; mase 21/21, 21/22, 21/23, etc; masse 73/42; maces *pl* 201/14, 201/14m; mases 21/28, 36/2; massus (?) 97/18

magnificens *n* title of honour 30/6, 33/22; magnyficence 90/27

maine-shire *adj* inland shire (?) 516/63

major drummer *n phr* drum major, officer in charge of drummers 425/26

male *n* metal rings used for making chain armour 196/9, 334/31; mayle 86/6, 86/7 (2); mayll 98/18, 450/9

mall *n* heavy staff or club, maul, mace; bag (?) 167/40, 167/42, 256/1; malle 153/25, 182/42, 187/30, etc; mawlle 240/32

mantle *n* sleeveless cloak 511/7; mantels *pl* 36/27; *see also* irysshe mantylles

mantylles *see* irysshe mantylles

marke *n* monetary unit equal to two thirds of a pound sterling 275/25; markes *pl* 118/42, 233/2, 424/11, etc; marks 233/1m

marking iorn *n phr* branding iron 438/36

marshall *n* lord marshal, high officer of state 4/1, 4/10, 4/31, etc

marshall *n* one who organizes and arranges ceremonies 274/26, 510/31

marshall *see* knight marshall

martially *adv* in a warlike manner 274/38

marturnes *n pl* European marten 118/39

marturn sabull *n phr* European sable 22/13

mase, mases, masse, massus *see* mace

mason *n* worker or builder in stone 16/40, 273/27; masones *pl* 319/2; masons 15/40, 16/3m

mastelen *n* a light-coloured copper alloy 487/15

mawlle *see* mall

mayle, mayll *see* male

measne *n* means 79/25, 79/28, 82/24

medsomer *n* 24 June 100/12, 180/29, 184/1, etc; medsomar 475/38; medsomere 186/38; medsommar 133/33; medsomur 475/36; medssomer 470/31; medssomere 192/8; medsumer 475/30; middsummer 483/38; midsomar 26/8; midsomer 16/28, 19/28, 28/25, etc; midsumer 158/13;

midsummer 120/3, 426/9; missemer 106/7;
missomer 25/23; missomore 20/10;
missomour 23/34; mydsom 466/24;
mydsomer 8/7, 41/25, 42/38, etc;
mydsomere 471/32; mydsommer 168/9;
mydsommor 173/35; mydsomor 133/37;
mydsomur 67/5, 70/22, 460/20; mydsomyr
473/21; mydssomer 472/30; myssomer
39/13, 39/25, 43/21, etc; myssommor
126/13; myssomor 143/27; myssomur
115/37, 117/22; myssymar 150/40;
myssymor 153/38, 153/39, 153/41;
medssomers *poss* 169/28
meeting *vb n* fitting (?) 468/6
mellyflue *adj* mellifluous 30/19
mendefaunces *n pl* friars of the begging or men-
dicant orders 130/10
menestrell *n* professional entertainer using
music, singing, story-telling, juggling, etc
451/33, 451/35, 451/40, etc; mensterell
150/4, 153/12; mensterll 151/3; menstrel
187/6; menstrell 39/25, 62/15, 111/11, etc;
menstryll 209/18; menstyrell 149/39;
menstyrll 150/42; minstrell 38/4;
mynestrell 140/25; mynstele 146/33;
mynsterll 141/31; mynstrall 23/18;
mynstrel 55/41, 147/28, 184/8; mynstrele
76/23; mynstrell 19/37, 20/2, 20/4, etc;
mynstrelle 41/32, 42/29; mynstryll 198/1,
209/4, 210/29, etc; menestrells *pl* 80/36;
mensterelles 111/41; mensterlles 153/39;
menstrelles 148/16, 152/37, 153/41, etc;
menstrells 190/10; menstyrlles 150/25;
minstrells 158/17; minstrels 38/33,
263/10; minstrilles 297/9; mynstralles
58/10; mynstrallus 66/12; mynstreles
245/13, 280/11, 298/41, etc; mynstrelles
10/5, 10/6, 42/17, etc; mynstrellez 24/39;
mynstrells 8/34, 24/25, 25/16, etc;
mynstrellyes 143/12; mynstrellys 156/2;
mynstrels 28/25, 38/16, 70/22, etc;
mynstrilles 44/36; mynstryles 312/21,
312/27, 316/4; mynstrylles 106/5; mynstryls
211/13; mynstylles 198/28
menstrys *n pl* minsters, monasteries (?) *or error*

for menstrylls, minstrels (?) 135/7
mercer *n* dealer in small wares or textiles 107/4,
243/39; mercers *pl* 17/5, 125/35, 276/20,
etc; mersers 482/29
messe *n* course of food 365/13
messes *n pl* masses, celebrations of the Eucharist
509/22
messuage *n* house site with or without house
and appurtenances 387/31; mesuages *pl*
301/2, 301/3
met *adj* suitable 451/14
michaelmas *n* feast of St Michael, 29 September
21/36, 21/38, 321/17, etc; myȝhelmas
23/26; myhelmas 204/31
middsummer, midsomar, midsomer, midsumer,
midsummer *see* medsomer
milners *n poss* miller's 498/6; milners *pl* 16/30
ministracion *n* administration 79/5
minstrell, minstrells, minstrels, minstrilles *see*
menestrell
misdemeanor *n* class of offences less serious
than a felony 394/30; misdeameanors *pl*
499/1
missemer, missomer, missomore, missomour
see medsomer
mitre *n* tall, arch-shaped cap, worn by bishops
and some abbots 509/19; mytor 161/33,
177/20; mytter 98/1, 98/10; myters *pl*
73/36, 245/39, 278/4, etc; mytters 240/26;
myttyrs 95/21
moiter *n* mortar; lime and sand mixture for
joining stones or bricks 319/6
moo *adj* more 36/23, 36/27, 37/19, etc
moought *see* mowe
morels *n poss* of a dusky-coloured horse
273/38
morrians *n pl* type of helmet with no vizor
324/37; morrions 324/36
motion *n* puppet show 442/2; motions *pl*
419/25; *see also* italian motion
moulde *n* pattern for making bullets 443/39;
mouldes *pl* 395/37
mourneresse *n* female mourner 511/6, 511/14,
511/18, etc; mourneresses *pl* 511/26, 512/5;
mourneresses *poss* 511/33

mowe *v pr 3 sg* may 31/18; mowe *pr 3 sg subj*
33/23; mowe *pr 3 pl* 53/22; moought *pr 3
sg subj* 273/11; moought *pr 3 pl subj*
272/42, 275/27
mukk *n* cattle manure 125/26
muskadele *n* sweet wine made from muscatel
grapes 509/11
musket *n* hand gun used by infantry 341/19,
402/25, 438/34, etc; muskett 341/30,
345/26, 368/17, etc; muskit 418/42,
438/35; mvskit 326/10; muskitte 334/28;
musketes *pl* 399/10, 448/11; muskets
359/40; muskettes 339/32, 344/41, 395/36,
etc; musketts 399/12; mvsketes 361/29;
mvskets 331/30; mvskites 322/18
muster *n* expected attendance 275/20
muster *n* assembly of soldiers 282/27, 443/40;
musters *pl* 274/26
musturdevylers *n* type of gray woollen cloth,
originally from Montivilliers 29/24
mvssiones *n pl* musicians 337/11
mydsom, mydsomer, mydsomere, mydsommer,
mydsommor, mydsomor, mydsomur,
mydsomyr, mydssomer *see* medsomer
myȝhelmas, myhelmas *see* michaelmas
mynding *vb n* mending, repairing 463/26;
myndng 463/30; myndyng 169/13;
myndynng 462/14
mynestrell, mynstele, mynsterll, mynstrall,
mynstralles, mynstrallus, mynstrel,
mynstrele, mynstreles, mynstrell, mynstrelle,
mynstrelles, mynstrellez, mynstrells,
mynstrellyes, mynstrellys, mynstrels,
mynstrilles, mynstryles, mynstryll,
mynstrylles, mynstryls, mynstylles *see*
menestrell
mynstralcy *n* performing of music 53/30, 54/6,
55/1; mynstrallcy 53/15; mynstralsy 54/25
mynstrelship *n* performing functions of
minstrels 50/22; *see also* menestrell
myrth *n* object of joy 34/11
myschaunce *n* ill luck 90/35
myssomer, myssommor, myssomor,
myssomur, myssymar, myssymor *see*
medsomer
mysterye *n* trade guild 82/18

myters, mytor, mytter, mytters, myttyrs *see*
mitre

nail *n* measure of length for cloth, equal to 2¼
inches 404/24
ne *conj* nor 18/24, 18/25, 18/26, etc
neckloopes *n pl* loop-shaped ornaments for the
neck of a garment (?), scarves (?) 447/2
nedeth *v pr 3 sg* is necessary 149/5
neene *adj* nine 391/20, 391/24
nells *n pl* nails 256/23, 297/26, 297/27
nether *adj* lower 145/17, 505/22
nippitate *n* high quality ale or other liquor
274/30
nott *n* cup shaped like a nut 98/12
nowne *adj* own 90/9
noysed *pp* rumoured about 188/20
nuez *n pl* news 273/39

obett *n* ceremony or office in commemoration
of soul of deceased 138/16; obetes *pl*
130/9
obeysaunse *n* act expressing submission 21/20,
21/35, 22/5; obeysances *pl* 512/36
obles *n pl* wafers 54/20
oder to oder *pron phr* one to the other 9/28
offertory *n* part of the service in which offerings
are made 512/27
offertory *n* a particular place in the Church of
St Michael, Coventry 512/24, 512/31
oft *n* 20/20; *see* offertory, *first definition*
ole *n* oil 179/42
olyvaunte *n* elephant 382/15
omberty *n* abundance 274/3
oplase *see* plase
ordenance *n* authoritative decree 55/25, 82/19,
84/7; ordenaunce 27/6; ordinaunce 485/16;
ordynance 16/11; ordynanns 484/27;
ordynnce 462/13; ordenances *pl* 55/25;
ordynancez 7/42
ordeynede *v pa 3 sg* furnished, equipped 18/23
originall *n* original copy 27/39; orygynall 85/3,
102/1
orisions *n pl* prayers 508/10
os *n* house (?) 119/36

otemell *n* oatmeal 506/3; hotmell 504/6

ouer hande *n phr* superior position 133/7, 133/9

ouercharged *pp* overburdened 79/23, 82/25

ouerpluse *n* surplus 132/31

ouersight *n* knowledge 273/29

over end *n phr* far end 281/3

oversight *n* supervision 283/15

owe *v pr 3 sg* ought 36/5; oweth 544/8; owethe 29/9; owed *pa 3 sg* 36/4

oxe tewsday *see* hoc twesday

oysteridge *n* ostrich 382/16

pachand *n* wagon used as a stage; *or,* a play performed on such a wagon 9/26, 9/30, 9/32, etc; padgand 214/26, 231/6, 231/7, etc; padgande 221/40; padgane 214/25; padgang 254/24; padgange 289/28; padgant 318/35, 318/36; padgeant 88/8; padgeantt 91/40, 92/1; padgen 242/2, 315/36; padgent 319/26; padgeon 430/7, 467/14, 469/20; padgeond 467/8, 469/22; padgeone 467/1, 467/3; padgin 215/23; padgon 355/6, 355/8, 462/28; padgond 462/27; padgone 467/6; padgyn 257/15, 276/20; padiant 87/24, 192/38, 192/40, etc; padyent 27/12; pagan 264/17, 471/17, 471/38; pagand 216/28, 220/4, 243/8, etc; pagande 218/5, 472/14, 472/27, etc; pagane 477/37, 478/9; pagannte 463/26, 463/34; paganntt 462/11, 462/23; pagant 26/23, 39/20, 40/5, etc; pagante 40/14, 292/14, 292/20, etc; pagantte 73/2; pagaunte 92/40, 240/21; pagaynt 167/2, 167/17, 167/20; pagdn 471/7; pagean 421/34; pageand 19/18, 185/39, 229/10, etc; pageande 177/30, 182/38, 182/40, etc; pageant 42/12, 44/13, 44/16, etc; pageante 480/20, 481/26; pageantt 461/32; pageantte 237/4; pageaunt 87/42, 119/36, 121/1, etc; pagen 191/19, 191/24, 241/29, etc; pagend 17/27, 176/21, 266/10; pagende 472/20; pagene 337/3, 339/27, 351/40, etc; pagennte 463/30; pagent 7/23, 9/13, 9/27m, etc; pagente 95/13, 95/15, 95/16, etc; pagentt 215/29, 215/38, 215/40, etc; pageon 301/26, 407/19; pageond 112/39, 460/19, 469/22; pageone 342/18, 345/3, 347/13, etc; paggan 218/4, 471/29; paggand 477/15; paggane 186/26; paggant 169/13, 169/15, 169/23; paggen 436/33, 476/11, 476/14, etc; paggent 26/25, 27/2, 27/4, etc; paggente 318/39; paggon 337/38; paggyn 214/23, 402/17; pagiand 229/11, 229/18, 236/26, etc; pagiande 236/20; pagiant 136/20, 159/20, 159/33, etc; pagiaunt 125/8, 128/35, 128/36, etc; pagient 301/11, 370/25; pagiente 41/40; pagin 283/9, 283/38, 284/1, etc; pagion 296/22, 306/28, 306/32, etc; pagiont 54/5, 146/24, 487/18, etc; pagon 172/1; pagone 315/26, 479/1; pagont 171/43; pagyand 220/10, 220/12, 220/14, etc; pagyande 228/21; pagyant 133/16, 133/22, 160/9; pagyante 253/12, 306/40, pagyaunt 132/5, 144/4, 174/33; pagyaunte 279/24, 280/1; pagyent 115/3, 234/42, 248/21, etc; pagyente 244/22, 248/40, 252/18, etc; pagyn 239/4, 244/4, 246/18, etc; pagyne 318/10; pagynt 124/13, 467/21; pagyon 190/32, 191/20, 191/26, etc; paiant 24/37, 82/32, 82/33, etc; paiaunt 23/12; paidint 75/21; paieant 498/40; paient 19/36, 19/39, 20/1, etc; paiet 20/4; paionde 113/3, 113/5; paiont 10/23, 10/39, 11/32; pajant 27/34, 27/35, 27/41; pajaunt 27/31; pajen 281/11; pajent 20/1, 20/25, 52/25; pangen 475/37; payant 485/23; paygant 92/37; paygaunt 92/35; paygent 206/35, 206/37, 209/5, etc; paygentt 211/36, 213/30; pagants *poss* 462/24; padgantes *pl* 334/3; padgins 233/37, 243/41, 294/18, etc; pagans 87/33; pagantes 79/12, 79/23, 198/20, etc; pageantes 79/37; pageants 7/32, 103/38, 107/6, etc; pageauntes 56/39; pageaunts 335/25; pagenes 479/24; pagens 332/25; pagentes 27/15, 31/33, 37/6, etc; pagents 461/21, 461/26; pageons 332/22m; pagiantes 234/13; pagiauntes 146/2, 146/9; pagyauntes 272/10; pagyns 333/14; pagyontes 149/8; paiantes 79/37m, 80/12

packthryd *n* stout thread or twine often used

for bundling 222/29, 239/27, 242/29, etc;
pacckthrydd 221/25; pacck thrydde
224/10, 230/6; pack thryd 209/6; packe
thrid 210/22; packe thride 278/11; packe
thryd 206/39, 237/31; packthide 291/13;
packthred 212/4, 219/10, 235/9; packthryde
228/5; pacthred 213/40, 216/8; pacthrid
268/19; pacthryd 189/16, 199/32;
pacthrydde 481/8; pakethrd 169/24; pakke
thrydde 466/7; pakthred 479/6; pakthryd
204/6; pakthyrd 172/12

padgand howse *n phr* building used as shelter for
pageant wagons 285/31; padgant howse
318/36; padgen house 315/36; padgeon
house 430/7; padgeon howse 467/14;
padon house 355/6, 355/8; padon howsse
462/28; padgond howsse 462/27; padgyn
howse 257/15; pagandhous 268/38;
pagannte howse 463/26; pagannt house
462/23; pagant hous 461/34; pagant house
333/34, 463/8; pagant housse 306/21;
pagant howse 336/37, 468/18, 468/20;
pagante housse 292/14; paganthouse
322/21; pagants house 462/24-5; page
howse 247/19; pagean howse 421/34;
pageant house 202/12, 463/7; pageant
hovse 179/9, 179/16; pageant howse
163/15, 309/17, 376/38; pageant-howse
316/25, 316/31-2, 316/34; pageante-howse
316/36; pageantt house 461/32-3; pageaunt
house 429/38; pageaunt os 119/36; pagen
house 281/11, 297/2, 340/27, etc; pagen
howse 246/13, 247/18, 253/27, etc; pagen
howsse 312/42; pagend hovse 176/21;
pagend howse 266/10; pagene howse
337/3, 339/27-8, 351/40, etc; pagent house
220/34, 220/35-6, 224/17-18, etc; pagent
hows 47/37, 93/4; pagent howse 47/38,
134/9, 147/6, etc; pagent howss 172/28,
172/29; pagente hows 93/5; pagenthous
6/10; pageon howse 301/26; pageond howsse
469/22; pageone howese 363/7; pageone
howse 342/18, 345/3, 347/13, etc; paggente
house 318/39; paggon howse 337/38;
paggyn house 402/17-18; paggyn howse

214/23; pagiand house 245/30; pagiaunt
house 132/5, 144/8-9, 145/7, etc; pagient
howse 370/25-6; pagin house 348/8,
435/27; paginhowse 341/31; pagion howse
296/22; pagyant house 586/12; pagyaunt
house 144/4, 583/10; pagyn howse 263/25,
296/33, 325/41, etc; pagyn howsse 256/23;
pagyne howse 318/10; pagynt howse
467/21; pagynte howse 582/43; pajen house
281/11; paygont house 585/38; padgyn
howses *pl* 276/20; paggen houses 436/33-4;
pagiaunt housez 146/9-10; pagient howses
301/11

pagan, pagand, pagande, pagane, pagannte,
pagannt, pagans, pagant, pagante, pagantes,
pagants, pagantte, pagaunte, pagaynt, pagdn,
pagean, pageand, pageande, pageant,
pageante, pageantes, pageants, pageantt,
pageantte, pageaunt, pageauntes, pageaunts,
pagen, pagend, pagende, pagene, pagenes,
pagennte, pagens, pagent, pagente, pagentes,
pagents, pagentt, pageon, pageond, pageone,
pageons, paggan, paggand, paggane, paggant,
paggen, paggent, paggente, paggon, paggyn,
pagiand, pagiande, pagiant, pagiantes,
pagiaunt, pagiauntes, pagient, pagiente,
pagin, pagion, pagiont, pagon, pagone,
pagont, pagyand, pagyande, pagyant,
pagyante, pagyaunt, pagyaunte, pagyauntes,
pagyent, pagyente, pagyn, pagyne, pagyns,
pagynt, pagyon, pagyontes *see* pachand
pagent pencys *n phr pl* fees levied for production of the pageant 192/22

paiant, paiantes, paiaunt, paidint, paieant,
paient, paiet, paionde, paiont, pajant,
pajaunt, pajen, pajent *see* pachand
paine *n* penalty 4/32, 4/37, 5/27, etc; payn
26/28, 152/31; payne 9/41, 18/21, 87/26,
etc; peyn 40/7, 48/41, 79/27, etc; peyne
11/34, 18/14, 18/35, etc; peynes 79/23
pain-house *n* structure built onto the wall of a
house to serve as a shelter or porch 403/39;
paint-houses *pl* 403/25
pajen house *see* padgand house
pakethrd, pakke thrydde, pakthred, pakthryd,

pakthyrd *see* packthryd

pale *n* fence 144/19

paling *prp* surrounding 512/2

pall *n* robe or cover of rich material 261/10,
512/9; palle 175/2; paule 175/4; palles *pl*
278/17; pawelles 240/20; pawles 334/34;
pawls 349/22

pallys *n* bishop's palace 309/31; palys 293/21

panchens *n pl* pancheons; large bowls used for
separating cream from milk, or for other
purposes 506/2

pane *n* penny 157/1; pene 157/1

pangen *see* pachand

panyer *n* basket 37/12, 37/13

panȝer *n* vessel in which oil was burnt for light
25/27

papuos *n pl* papers 51/15 (3), etc

parcell *n* portion, division, bunch 18/25, 377/1,
482/3; parceles *pl* 322/1; parcelles 321/42,
322/2, 322/3; parselles 130/7; parsells
196/7, 321/41

parchment *n* treated sheep skin 274/16

pare *v inf* prepare or decorate 478/35

parell *n* apparatus, equipment 35/15

parell *n* peril, danger 90/38

parselles, parsells *see* parcell

parsone *n* person 544/28

part *n in phr* of my part from me or by me
154/6

partaking *vb n* participating or taking sides
4/27

partie *n* matter, respect 78/41, 79/16, 79/27,
etc

partizant *n* type of long-handled spear 367/38,
367/39, 367/41, etc; partizantes *pl* 325/12

partletees *n pl* piece of clothing covering the
neck and upper part of the chest 118/40

party *adj* parti-coloured 73/26

party *n* region 30/22

parys head *n phr* type of head-dress made in
Paris 511/8; parys heads *pl* 511/22

pastaunce *n* pastime 494/24

patent *n* document conferring a privilege or
right 394/10, 394/14, 442/5, etc; *see also*
letteres patentes

paveor *n* one who paves or lays pavement
161/31

pax *n* osculatory, decorated tablet kissed at
Mass 487/13, 487/16, 487/17, etc

pay *v inf* please 34/23

payant, paygant, paygaunt, paygent, paygentt
see pachand

paygont house *see* padgand house

paymosts *n pl* payments, expenses 383/20

payn *v inf* pay 84/18

payn, payne *see* paine

paynemaynes *n pl* loaves of highest quality
37/11

paynym *n* pagan 33/19

peached *pp* impeached, accused 107/10

peande *n* pound 481/7

pele *n* ringing of a bell 508/23; peles *pl*
508/20 (2), 508/21, etc

pelow *n* pillow 487/11; pelowes *pl* 487/10

pen *n in phr* apen a pin, *or error for* 'apec,' a
peg (?) 242/23

pencells *n pl* long narrow flags or streamers
27/24, 46/2, 46/8, etc; pencelis 101/4;
pencelles 487/22; pencels 108/16; pensell
29/19, 29/20, 29/33; penselles 163/20;
pensells 47/12, 47/13, 240/22; pensels
88/37 (2); penselys 99/5, 99/6; pensils
334/39

pene *see* pane

peners, penneeres, penneres, penures *see* pynnar

pensell, penselles, pensells, pensels, penselys,
pensils *see* pencells

pentyse *n* structure attached to outer wall of a
building 252/37

perclois *n* screen or partition 3/29

pescodes *n pl* pea pods 37/13

pestrawe *n* parts of the pea plant used as straw
463/15, 468/25, 469/14, etc; pes straye
470/40; pese strawe 464/3, 464/34;
pesstraw 471/24; pestraw 467/26, 470/17;
pestray 475/37; peystraw 462/16;
peystrawe 462/34, 465/34

pesyng *vb n* mending by tying pieces together
468/13

petie *n* pity, *or error for* 'Petir,' Peter (?) 487/17

petteryyes *n pl* patriarchs 479/18

pewdeges *see* **podyng**

peweke *n* high quality woollen cloth used for gowns 460/7; **puke** 232/20

peyn, peyne, peynes *see* **paine**

peystraw, peystrawe *see* **pestrawe**

phanon *see* **fanons**

pike *n* weapon with a long wooden shaft and pointed metal head 367/40, 419/35, 439/19; **pikes** *pl* 367/39, 367/41, 367/42, etc; **pykes** 325/20, 325/22, 367/38

pinnares *see* **pynnar**

pipe *n* cask of definite capacity 37/11; **pypis** *pl* 54/21

pipyns *n pl* kind of apple 37/13

plarars *n pl* players 167/30

plase *n* place 22/29

plates *n pl* the thin pieces of steel or iron composing plate-armour 296/35, 387/3; **platis** 85/8

playnge *vb n* painting (?) 473/25

plear *error for pp* 'plead,' played 479/2

plesaunce *n* enjoyment 9/32

plesaunce *n* fine kind of linen or gauze 53/12

plumer *n* worker in lead 263/41; **plommer** (*error for* 'player'?) 300/16; **plymars** *pl* (*error for* 'pinnars') 133/31, 135/21

podyng *n* vessel in which oil was burned for light 129/23; **pewdeges** *pl* 480/10; **poddoyngs** 180/37; **podynges** 207/10, 209/17; **podyngs** 184/7, 184/22, 187/3, etc; **puddyngs** 218/15; **pvdyng** 168/13

poinctes, poinetes, pointes, points *see* **poynt**

polax *n* battle-axe 150/34; **poll ax** 73/40; **pollax** 196/11, 399/22; **polaxes** *pl* 19/9, 317/32; **poleaxes** 235/29, 282/23; **polleaxes** 410/19

ponard *n* dagger 196/10

ponnes *n* pound (?) 479/21

pontes, ponttes, ponytes, ponytts *see* **poynt**

pontificals *n pl* bishop's robes 22/8

poollye *n* pulley 260/14

poppittes *n pl* puppets 353/8, 396/25

portraiture *n* picture or representation 434/29; **portraitures** *pl* 429/11

postell *n* door post or gate post 170/23

pottell *n* vessel containing two quarts of liquid 308/14

pouther *n* gunpowder 369/14, 378/20

powne *n* pound 504/13

poynt *n* lace or cord of twisted material used for fastening parts of clothing 260/35; **poinctes** *pl* 279/41; **poinetes** 249/5; **pointes** 298/35, 354/19, 359/17, etc; **points** 200/16; **pontes** 139/25, 140/7; **ponttes** 23/21, 150/8, 153/22, etc; **ponytes** 315/34; **ponytts** 307/24; **powents** 471/1; **powynts** 469/39; **poynctes** 280/9, 285/4; **poynes** 477/13; **poynnts** 462/12; **poynntts** 463/32, 472/5; **poyntees** 263/13, 268/35; **poyntes** 86/34, 163/31, 167/23, etc; **poynts** 42/40, 95/35, 192/14, etc; **poynttes** 157/17, 160/3, 166/8, etc; **poyntts** 20/13, 20/17, 25/25, etc; **poynttys** 472/19; **poyntys** 40/31; **pwenttes** 475/36, 476/22; **pwyntes** 214/34, 243/7, 260/15; **pwynttes** 218/9; **pyntes** 172/18, 174/1, 179/39, etc; **pynts** 471/10, 471/35

precession *n* procession 98/20

preface *n* the actor who speaks the preface 261/31

preferment *n* advancement 148/33

prelates *n pl* churchmen of high authority 89/38

prelatt *n* some kind of garment (?); perhaps the same as a burlett (?) 140/20; *see* **burlettis**

premisses *n pl* things or matters stated before, especially land or dwellings previously described 34/29, 149/19, 376/42, etc; **premissez** 79/29, 82/26, 145/21

prenttyssys *n pl* apprentices 473/32

pressonn *n* procession 460/18; **pressyon** 111/8

prest *n* loan or advance 154/6

prickinge *vb n* writing down musical notes 397/41; **prikinge** 249/26; **prikynge** 236/21, 245/38; **pryckyng** 494/3

prickt *v pa 3 pl* rode 274/36

prime *n* six a.m. 4/6

priory *n* monastery or nunnery governed by a prior or prioress 21/30, 21/36, 88/42, etc; **priorye** 488/24 priour *n* superior officer of a religious house or order 36/18; priours *pl* 45/12

priste *n* priest 78/38, 83/30

proccur *n* procurement or proclamation 453/43

processe *n in phr* in processe in due course 90/31

profer *n* attempt 89/23

promotion *n* advancement 207/41

promulgated *pp* made public 403/18

provost *n* overseer 405/5

pryckyng *see* prickinge

puddyngs *see* podyng

puke *see* peweke

purchaz *n* seizing 275/8

pursevauntes *n pl* followers 394/6; pursivauntes 394/2

purveaunse *n* arrangements 29/17

purveyor of the skullery *n phr* person in charge of providing plates, dishes, and kitchen utensils 405/16

pvdyng *see* podyng

pwenttes, pwyntes, pwynttes *see* poynt

pwintes *n pl* points, regulations 188/17

pwynttes *n pl* pints 238/27

pykes *n pl* a kind of large, fresh-water fish 37/12

pykes *see* pike

pyne *n* suffering or punishment 32/20, 33/19

pynnar *n* maker of pins 103/43; peners *pl* 176/35, 179/24; penneeres 75/21; penneres 111/9, 113/19; penures 62/11; pinnares 143/14; plymars (*error for* 'pinnars') 133/31, 135/21; pynars 24/37, 50/37, 51/34, etc; pynears 105/3; pyneres 39/20; pynerrus 66/10; pyners 183/10; pynnarees 148/3; pynnares 146/31; pynnars 99/34, 105/38, 140/21, etc; pynneres 116/30; pynners 11/41, 16/33, 19/18, etc

pyntes, pynts *see* poynt

pypis *see* pipe

quarter *n* one fourth of a pound 198/4; quarters *pl* 505/27

quarter *n* one fourth of a yard 29/22, 29/23 (2), etc

quarterage *n* rent, wage, or fee paid four times

yearly 8/39, 61/21, 75/14, etc; quarteridg 393/13; quartrage 87/34; quartreg 136/37; quarterages *pl* 43/12; quarterayges 454/11; quartrages 62/11

quartered *pp* placed in alternate quarters 510/41

quarters *n pl* four sections into which human bodies were cut in a form of execution 125/20

quarter waiters *n phr pl* members of a lower class of gentlemen ushers, who remained in waiting for a quarter of a year 405/11

quit rent *n phr* small charge paid in lieu of services owed 483/14

quitt claymed *pp phr* given up, released 376/32

quore *n* choir, chancel 509/4

quynces *n pl* quinces (a fruit of the pear family) 506/1

quytances *n pl* releases 9/27

ranks *n pl* lines of soldiers abreast 275/3 (2)

rappe *n* rope 468/13

rattell *n* noise-maker of some sort 167/40

raygete *n* surplice-like linen vestment; rochet 69/4

ream *see* reme

rearyng *vb n* constructing, erecting 319/14

recreant *adj* unfaithful or cowardly 4/37

recreated *v pa 3 sg* refreshed 271/8

rehearse *n* rehearsal 229/6, 260/31, 260/33, etc; rehears 260/29; reheres 150/32, 153/28, 153/30; rehers 19/36, 44/42, 150/31, etc; reherse 72/25, 72/31, 77/35, etc; rehersse 24/5, 163/25, 163/26, etc; rehearces *pl* 305/35; rehearses 306/27; rehearsys 27/18, 255/3, 257/42, etc; reherces 132/6, 305/34; reherses 160/7, 267/5, 303/35, etc; reherssees 211/35, 213/29; rehersses 206/23, 208/31, 210/8, etc; reherssesees 215/39; reherssys 186/29, 192/4, 218/42, etc; rehersys 139/30, 175/14, 203/35, etc; reheyrsys 463/29; reyheresys 467/1; reyherssys 171/39, 199/19; reyhersys 156/20, 161/13, 165/25, etc

rehearz *v inf* recount or mention 274/12;

rehearz *pr 1 sg* 273/41; rehersed *pp* 21/12, 21/22, 37/34, etc; rehersede 18/22, 18/24, 29/15; rehersid 16/8

rehersall *n in phr* maketh rehersall recount(s) 53/38, 90/3

rehers, reherse, reherses, rehersse, reherssees, rehersses, reherssesees, reherssys, rehersys, reheyrsys *see* rehearse

reioyseth *v pr 3 sg* gladdens 53/21

reliqe *n* venerated object, such as part of the body or an article of clothing, associated with a particular saint 487/38, 488/15; relikes *pl* 33/20; reliqes 487/33, 488/14; *see also* reliquie

reliquie *n for definition see* reliqe 488/8, 488/13; relyquie 487/41, 488/1; reliqies *pl* 488/20; reliquies 488/17, 488/24

reme *n* realm 30/18, 30/40, 31/23, etc; ream 273/7; royme 55/5

remember *v inf* remind, recall to mind 188/17; *pp* 233/19

remove *v inf* go away, depart 22/25; remoueth *pr 3 sg* 35/38m, 37/19m; remeved *pa 3 sg* 35/24, 37/19; removed 89/13

remysed *pp* given over, surrendered 376/31

rennyng *prp* flowing or pouring 53/31, 54/21, 55/1, etc

renu *v inf* revive 272/42

renuing *vb n* restoring 70/40

renyshe wyne *n phr* wine from the Rhine region 505/26

repacyanns, repacyonne *see* reparacion

repaire *v inf* go 5/17

reparacion *n* repair 41/38, 47/37, 131/21, etc; repacyonne 462/21; reperacion 93/5, 485/23; repacyanns *pl* 462/23; reparacions 132/17, 139/29, 142/42, etc; reparacons 403/31; reparacyons 173/23, 195/9; reparasyons 176/19; reparcyons 193/40; reperacyons 247/15; repercyons 256/13; repracions 155/30; repracyons 472/20; repraschuns 467/12; reprasyons 228/32

reparellynge *vb n* repairing or restoring 73/2; reparellyd *pp* 73/20

reparrell *n* apparel 304/7

repealed *pp* recalled from exile 5/27

reperacion, reperacyons, repercyons *see* reparacion

replete *adj* filled 30/7

repracions, repracyons, repraschuns, reprasyons *see* reparacion

reresyng *vb n* raising (?) 598/23

resen *n* resin, substance secreted by trees and used as varnish and adhesive, and for kindling torches 481/7; ressyn 118/20; *see also* rossen

resshes, resshis *see* russe

ressyn *see* resen

rest *n pl* supports for fire-arms, used to steady the barrel 438/39

restyng *vb n* temporary storage (?), *error for* 'restoring' (?) 250/26

revelles *n pl* office in the royal household 437/22, 439/10, 440/26, etc; revells 423/16

reversion *n in phr* in reversion to return to the grantor 482/17

revetts, revettes, reyvettes, reyvetts, reyvytts *see* allman revetts

revitts *n pl* rivets, or a kind of light armour made of plates sliding on rivets 179/38; *see also* allman revetts

rewle *n* control 27/31, 44/22; rule 12/7, 131/15

reyggalles *see* rygalls

reyheresys, reyherssys, reyhersys *see* rehearce

rigalls, rigoldes *see* rygalls

rightwesnes *n* justice 31/5m, 31/5

roche *n* rock alum (?) 84/42

roles *n pl* pieces of rolled cloth serving as part of a head-dress 256/2, 261/13; rolles 66/3 (2), 256/1, etc

romney *n* type of sweet Greek wine 509/11

roos candells *n phr* rush-candles, candles made by dipping the pith of a rush in tallow or other grease 246/20

roots *n pl* musical instruments, perhaps of the violin class 434/31

rosches, roshes, rossches, rosshes, rosshys *see* russe

rose water *n phr* water distilled from or scented

with roses and used as a perfume 505/40

rossen *n* rosin, resin secreted by trees and used as varnish and adhesive, and for kindling torches 51/16, 94/4, 221/27, etc; **rosen** 478/8, 506/3; **rossin** 242/35; **rosson** 230/9; **rossyn** 246/22, 253/33, 475/11; **rosyn** 110/31, 237/31, 250/16, etc; *see also* **resen**

rotys *adj* riotous 598/16

roughe vessell *n phr* drinking vessel in unfinished condition (?) 506/4

royall paper *n phr* paper measuring 24 x 19 inches (for writing) and 25 x 20 inches (for printing) 429/26

royme *see* reme

rryvetts *see* allman revetts

ruchssys, ruhyssys *see* russe

rule *n* order or decree 16/11, 80/7

rule *see* rewle

russe *n* rush; type of plant found in wet ground and used for strewing on floors and for making rush-lights 213/40; **resshes** *pl* 477/15; **resshis** 19/38; **rosches** 150/5, 153/18; **roshes** 223/20; **rossches** 204/6; **rosshes** 169/24, 229/16, 249/17, etc; **rosshys** 468/25; **ruchssys** 469/14; **ruhssys** 462/34; **rusches** 467/26; **rushes** 306/30, 505/10; **russees** 212/4; **russes** 160/1, 199/32, 216/8, etc; **russhes** 27/35, 155/7, 157/34, etc; **russhess** 209/6; **russhys** 470/17; **russis** 268/19; **russys** 156/32, 161/24, 165/39, etc; **ruysshes** 50/8; **rvchys** 197/38; **rvssches** 191/27; **rwsches** 194/31; **rwschys** 202/14; **rwsses** 475/37; **rwssys** 167/21; **rycsshes** 471/37; **rysches** 44/14, 163/28, 175/24, etc; **ryses** 242/29; **ryshes** 237/30; **ryssches** 182/34; **rysschys** 51/23; **rysshes** 49/4, 140/8, 259/11, etc; **rysshys** 471/11, 471/24; **ryssys** 172/12

russet *n* reddish-brown colour 403/37

rut *n* state of sexual excitement 274/41

ruydyng *vb n* riding 17/11

ruffetts, ryffytts *see* allman revetts

ruysshes, rvchys, rvssches, rwsches, rwschys, rwsses, rwssys, rycsshes, rysches, ryses, ryshes, ryssches, rysschys, rysshes,

rysshys, ryssys *see* russe

rygalls *n pl* small portable musical organs 217/39, 224/33, 230/20, etc; **reyggalles** 199/33; **rigalls** 237/24; **rigoldes** 268/28; **rygales** 292/39; **rygalles** 221/19; **rygals** 250/2; **rygells** 481/3; **ryggellys** 475/16; **rygoles** 206/34, 212/5, 216/9, etc; **rygolles** 228/6, 235/10, 239/28, etc; **rygols** 208/41

rygenale *n* original copy of a book 75/27

ryvets, ryvett, ryvettes, ryvetts, ryvyts *see* allman revetts

sabull *see* marturn sabull

sacke *n* name of a class of Spanish white wines 396/37

sade *adj* dark or deep 460/7

sadelers *n pl* makers or sellers of saddles 11/31, 15/40, 16/40, etc; **sadlers** 16/2m, 266/27, 266/31, etc

salet *n* type of round head-armour 23/20, 546/31; **salette** 18/12; **sallet** 39/4, 39/14; **sallett** 451/7; **salettes** *pl* 18/2, 18/5, 18/9, etc; **saletts** 240/18, 467/33; **sallettes** 325/11; **sallyttes** 311/21

saletted *pp* wearing a sallet (*see* salet) 29/11

saluees *n pl* displays of fire-arm discharges 471/6

sapient *adj* wise 90/1

sappe lath *n phr* long, thin piece of sap wood 264/6; *see also* **hait lath, lathe, lathe nayle**

sarcenet *n* fine, soft silk material 317/42; **sarsnet** 98/18

sargant *n* officer of a court, whose duty was to make arrests and serve summonses 357/24, 359/30

sashes *n pl* scarves worn over the shoulder or around the waist 513/15

saten of brygees *n phr* satin of Bruges, made of a silk warp and thread woof 119/4; *see also* **briges satten**

sattyng *vb n* setting up 254/6

say *n* cloth of fine texture resembling serge 241/7; **saye** 246/29; **sea** 251/14

scabbard *n* case or sheath for a sword 400/30;

scabbarde 368/21; scabbers *pl* 399/14;
scaberdes 325/6

scaffold *n* temporary raised platform used for a
performance 3/18, 253/13; scaffolde 261/3;
scaffoll 258/26; scaffolld 249/15; scafolde
245/28; skaffold 190/37, 202/10, 238/29;
skaffolde 162/38, 163/5, 167/36, etc;
skafforde 267/14; scaffolds *pl* 444/41;
skaffoldes 303/40, 306/19

schankees *n pl* lower parts of animals' forelegs,
used as a source of trimming fur 119/2

schapletes *see* chapeletts

scheryffe *n* one of two officials chosen by the
corporation for law enforcement duties
119/2; sherriff 379/2; shyrryf 201/16;
scheryffees *pl* 118/37; schirreves 49/16;
sherefes 22/35; shereffes 181/21; sherieffes
103/13; sherieffs 103/21; sheriffs 22/33m,
511/40; sheriues 232/19; sherriffes 95/39;
sherriffs 446/5, 446/6; shireffes 118/40m,
138/31, 138/34, etc; shirrefes 55/21;
shirreffes 55/16; shirrefs 35/38; shyrryfes
201/5, 201/6, 201/12, etc

schochyn *n* the shield on a coat of arms 48/18;
escutcheons *pl* 448/11

scituate *adj* situated 301/5, 376/35

sckowyng *see* skowring

scoper *n* supper 135/16

scorges *n pl* whips 74/2

scorrynge, scoureinge, scourynge, scowaring,
scowreing, scowringe, scowryng, scowrynge
see skowring

sculls *n pl* metal skull caps 325/19

scutyng *vb n* shooting of a gun 477/24

scweryng *see* skowring

scytte *n* seat 466/1

sea *see* say

seare *n* some kind of ornament or trim (?); wax
applied to thread or fabric (?) 247/5

seargants *n pl* assistants 114/12

seargeaunt *n* lower level municipal officer
273/39; seargiant 324/11; sergeant 112/31;
seriant 21/21; seriaunt 138/32, 139/3;
serieante 382/3; sergeantes *pl* 201/14;
seriantes 382/5; seriauntes 138/35, 138/38,

138/40, etc; serjaunts 201/12m

sedsaddells *n pl* sidesaddles 509/14

seisin *n* possession 376/34

selldall *n* gown of rich silken material (?); or
seat (?) 214/24

selle *n* sale 493/38

semblable *adj* like, similar 511/20

sendall *n* rich silken material 4/4, 230/31

senssares *n pl* thuribles, vessels in which incense
is burnt 153/26

sensyng *prp* perfuming by swinging a vessel
filled with burning incense 31/29, 90/13,
509/19; seynsyng 54/19

sergeant, sergeantes, seriant, seriantes, seriaunt,
seriauntes, serieante, serjaunts *see*
seargeaunt

sergiantes *n pl* in the military, non-commissioned
officers of the rank above corporals 390/17

seriant *n* officer of the royal household, in
charge of the king's trumpeters 408/27,
412/15; serjant 439/40; *see also* serjeant
trumpeter

serieant at arms *n phr* one of a body of twenty-
four knights in direct attendance on the
king 406/22

serjeant trumpeter *n phr* officer of the royal
household, in charge of the king's trumpeters
405/7; *see also* seriant

servers *n pl* attendants 200/7, 200/16

sesand *n error for* 'fesand,' pheasant (?) 504/26

sester *see* cester

seth *conj* since, seeing that 34/15

setlis *n* chair or bench 334/26

sevennyght *n* week 129/8

severall *adj* private 426/11

seynsyng *see* sensyng

seyt *n* seat 289/22

sharman *n* shearer of woollen cloth 316/35,
328/41 (2), etc; sherman 17/2; sharmen *pl*
212/22, 304/14; sheremen 293/26;
shermans *poss* 316/38

shavyng *vb n* paring or cutting down 72/4

sheares *n pl error for* 'sheaths' (?) *in phr* dagger
sheares 399/14-15

sheff *n* bundle of twenty-four 18/2, 18/6,

18/9, etc; sheaf 250/35; sheaffe 248/5; sheffe 18/12, 473/13, 473/18; sheiffe 325/19; sheffs *pl* 240/19; sheas 250/36

sherefes, shereffes, sherieffes, sherieffs, sheriffs, sheriues, sherriff, sherriffes, sherriffs *see* scheryffe

sheremen, sherman, shermans *see* sharman

sherriffes *see* high sherriffes

shevys *see* wyff shevys

shewers *see* gentlemen shewers

shewting *vb n* shooting 287/26

shireffes, shirrefes, shirreffes, shirrefs *see* scheryffe

shoare *n* drainage ditch or sewer 281/2

sholles *n pl* shovels 598/18

shope *n* soap 92/36

shovelards *n pl* spoonbills 580/30

showt in *v inf phr* shoot with 359/40; shute in 344/41; shott in *pa 3 sg* 368/34; shot in *pa 3 pl* 339/32

shute *n* suit of clothes 406/32

shute in *see* showt in

shyrryf, shyrryfes *see* scheryffe

silvering *vb n* covering with silver 410/19

sithen *conj* since 90/4, 91/9

skaffold, skaffolde, skaffoldes, skafforde *see* scaffold

skates *n pl* type of large, flat fish 505/16

skeane *n* quantity of thread measured by turns on a reel 278/15, 278/17; skene 170/18, 175/3; skaynes *pl* 261/10

skecons *n pl* badges 15/32

skeners *see* skynner

skermidg *n* skirmish 390/15

skinners *see* skynner

skoryng *see* skowring

skorte *n* lower part of a coat or gown 176/15

skower *n* wad or sponge for cleaning the bore of a gun 359/21, 443/39

skowring *vb n* polishing or cleaning by hard rubbing 23/20, 402/25, 476/33, etc; sckowyng 480/3; scorrynge 228/34; scoureinge 391/14; scourynge 340/11; scowaring 418/40; scowreing 440/4;

scowringe 236/28, 366/8, 374/21; scowryng 395/13, 395/16, 464/5; scowrynge 464/36, 466/29; scweryng 470/34; skoryng 179/33; skouring 195/36; skouryng 463/17; skoweringe 326/23; skowringe 277/6; skowryng 86/6, 154/26, 183/2, etc; skowrynge 262/10, 271/31, 290/34, etc; skwrynge 480/18

skullery *see* purveyor of the skullery

skynner *n* one who prepares animal skins for commercial purposes 27/31, 271/21, 376/28; skeners *pl* 169/5, 183/19, 206/19, etc; skinners 443/32; skyners 187/10, 210/2, 211/29; skynnares 213/23, 215/34; skynnars 332/35, 353/33; skynneres 196/19, 218/37, 222/14, etc; skynners 16/34, 79/18, 83/2, etc

slag *n* type of kettle drum 479/36; stage (*error for* 'slage'?) 473/25, 473/26

slagberd *n* board for mounting the slag (*see* slag) 477/26

slop *n* loose outer garment 63/22

smalethryd *n* fine thread 258/9, 262/39

snoket *n* candied fruit 509/9

socour *v inf* help, assist 34/18

socoure *n* help, assistance 55/4, 55/10

sodyer *n* soldier 477/35; sodyars *pl* 451/15

sollskotts *n pl* souls' coats 469/28

solyng *vb n* putting covering on the bottom of 226/22

somner *n* guild officer responsible for assembling those involved in a procession or performance, as well as other duties 26/35, 126/6, 203/17, etc; sumner 241/11; summers *pl* 304/15

sonde *n* messenger 54/15

sope *n* soap 41/41, 51/23, 150/6, etc; soop 177/15; soope 165/39; soppe 279/37; soupe 237/30, 253/29; sovpe 476/8

sororz *n pl* sorrows 274/8

soteltes *n pl* ornamental constructions made of sugar 123/29; soteltys 123/12; sutteltes 123/27

souerayn *adj* holding the position of king or queen 29/40, 32/11, 33/1, etc; soueraign

82/28, 90/20; **souereigne** 144/28; **soueren** 21/12 (2), 21/17, etc; **souerenne** 29/12; **soveraign** 280/37; **soveraigne** 300/30, 334/24, 377/10

souerayne *n* one who surpasses all others in his class 33/27

soupe, sovpe *see* **sope**

soveraign, soveraigne *see* **souerayn**

spare *n* long, moderately thick piece of timber 77/40; **spares** *pl* 319/11; **sparis** 257/16; **sparres** 305/32; **sparrys** 93/5, 263/33

spitlhouse *n* charitable foundation for the sick or needy 274/6

splent *n* one of the overlapping plates of metal of which certain parts of armour, especially elbow coverings, were composed 177/41; **splentes** *pl* 334/30, 450/10, 453/20, etc; **splenttes** 196/9; **splentts** 240/17, 467/33

spoke *n* one of the rods extending from the hub of a wheel to the rim 218/7, 231/7; **spokes** *pl* 251/8

spret *n* spirit 159/23, 175/10, 175/31, etc; **sprete** 182/21; **sprett** 139/36, 164/6; **sprit** 150/15, 153/3; **spryt** 167/7, 178/30, 191/8, etc; **spryte** 185/23, 261/33; **sprytt** 228/26; **spyryt** 240/27; **spryryts** *poss* 240/28, 240/31; **sprets** *pl* 478/20; **sprytes** 479/13, 480/30; **spryttes** 476/28; **spryttys** 475/3

spring *n* dawn 3/24

spykynges *n pl* large nails 52/36

squadron *n* small body of soldiers 390/10

squadrons *n pl* soldiers arranged in square formation 275/4

stable packe *n phr* expenses for stabling horses or stablemen 404/33

stafhed *n* metal point on a spear or lance 227/4

stage *n* location at which a play is performed 220/41, 241/19, 242/10, etc; **stages** *pl* 220/12, 223/22, 229/14, etc; **stagys** 194/29

stage *see* **slag**

standard *n* upright bar 263/35

standarts *n poss* of a banner 71/41, 72/4; **standarts** *pl* 75/31; **standerdes** 172/20, 427/40

standerdes *n pl* candlesticks 487/20; **standers**

178/6, 179/17

staple *n* bent piece of metal driven into a surface at both ends to serve as a hold 179/10, 182/41, 194/34; **staplee** 319/10; **stapull** 468/6; **stapelles** *pl* 163/11, 163/13; **stapulls** 469/22

staves *n pl* spears or lances 282/23, 314/18, 325/21, etc

steeres *n pl* stars 486/9; **sterres** 487/10

stener *n* painter or one who ornaments cloth 72/1

stenyng *vb n* colouring or ornamenting with designs 71/12; **steyning** 66/3; **steynyng** 28/8, 46/10, 108/2

stevenn *n* stone (?), *ie*, the stone used to close the mouth of the sepulchre 240/36

steward *n* civic officer 321/9; **stward** 321/16

steward *n* officer appointed to transact legal and financial business for the lord of the manor 510/24 (2), 510/25, etc

stewardes *n pl* guild officers below the aldermen 134/30, 136/11

steyles *n pl* sticks 241/6

steyned *pp* ornamented with pictures 487/4, 487/9, 487/13, etc

steyning, steynyng *see* **stenyng**

stinges *n pl* staffs, or pike- or spear-shafts 439/1

stocke monney *n phr* fund set aside for certain expenses 500/7, 501/12; **stockemonney** 500/36

stodes *n pl* props, supports 319/11

stof *n* material for making clothing 24/18, 25/11; **stufe** 259/42; **stuffe** 18/34, 44/23

stole *n* narrow strip of silk or linen hung over the shoulders of a priest or deacon 486/10, 486/13, 487/3; **stolus** *pl* 98/35

ston *n* measure of weight equal to fourteen pounds 119/42, 139/20, 154/2, etc; **stone** 141/30, 169/33, 187/4, etc; **stonne** 213/11, 215/7; **stoon** 118/21, 198/41

stondare *n* suit of armour 450/9; **stondares** *pl* 451/4

stores *n* sturgeon 505/16

storiall *adj* historical 272/42

strameres *see* **stremer**

strange *adj* from another town 26/23, 427/20; **straunge** 433/11

stranger *n* one from another town 485/15, 485/21; **strangers** *pl* 188/21; **straungers** 149/4

stratagem *n* skilfully devised spectacle 390/9, 390/11m

straunge *see* **strange**

straungers *see* **stranger**

straymers *see* **stremer**

stre *adj* made of straw 548/1; **stree** 42/5

streamer, streamers *see* **stremer**

streke *n* curved piece of iron used for rimming a cart wheel 259/19; **stroke** 235/25

stremer *n* long, narrow pointed flag 200/15, 309/17, 317/36, etc; **streamer** 390/18; **stremere** 184/4, 192/15; **stremmer** 189/32, 197/6, 199/40; **streymar** 466/38, 470/12; **streymer** 462/7; **strameres** *pl* 198/29; **straymers** 157/15; **streamers** 178/16, 334/35, 481/14; **stremares** 164/34, 171/24, 182/8, etc; **stremars** 168/14, 171/14, 176/29, etc; **stremarys** 473/1; **stremas** 26/1; **stremeres** 176/11, 207/8, 207/17, etc; **stremers** 86/26, 86/34, 147/20, etc; **stremerus** 96/5; **stremerys** 473/40; **stremmers** 162/3, 166/5; **stremors** 471/32; **stremurs** 471/18; **streymars** 173/40, 463/24; **streymers** 112/10, 468/33, 469/33

strener *n* strainer, sieve 504/21

stroke *see* **streke**

struett *n* musical instrument of some kind (?), *error for* 'flute' (?) 477/23

strycke *n* unit of dry measure, usually equal to a bushel 247/19, 263/29; **stryk** 503/8

studdyng *vb n* supplying with upright support posts 264/4

stufe, stuffe *see* **stof**

stward *see* **steward**

sudere *n* sudary; a napkin or handkerchief used to wipe sweat or tears from the face 96/38

sueng *see* **suyth**

suerte *n* bond, security 83/12, 84/9; **suertee** 83/21

suertie *n* person who takes on liability for

another 501/17; **suerty** 501/18; **suretie** 500/41

suertishipp *n* security, bond 501/18

suerty *n* certainty 509/21

sumner, sumners *see* **somner**

supplyant *n* humble petitioner 499/2, 499/5, 499/15

supportacion *n* maintenance 26/32

surcease *v inf* be discontinued 500/4

surcotes *n pl* rich outer garments 36/27

surplesse *n* loose church vestment of white linen 260/4; **surplis** 46/25, 129/42, 261/12, etc; **surplys** 130/1; **svrplyse** 184/42; **surplesses** *pl* 174/23, 259/41; **surplisses** 267/23; **svrplisses** 278/13, 283/18

surveyors of the ways *n phr pl* those who supervise construction of roads 404/43

sutteltes *see* **soteltes**

suttyng *vb n* shutting 242/13, 246/26

suyth *v pr 3 sg* follows 37/10; **sueng** *prp* 22/25; **suyng** 35/34, 36/11, 37/3, etc

svrplisses, svrplyse *see* **surplesse**

svruitars *n pl* attendants 353/34

swrede *n sg* sword 450/10

swthe *n* sweets (?) 504/9

swyers *n pl* squires 22/40

swypyng *vb n* sweeping 504/32

syd *adj* positioned at the side 150/18; **syde** 139/41, 175/34, 182/23; **syed** 178/32

sygh *v pa 3 sg* saw 37/6

sylle *n* strong horizontal timber used as a foundation 93/5

syngyns *vb n* singing 479/15

synnapers *adj* bright red, vermilion 51/15

systs *n pl* large vessels for holding water or drink 504/10

tabarde *n* loose, sleeveless garment covering the upper body 67/18; **taberd** 170/4

taces *n pl* series of overlapping plates forming a kind of kilt for protecting the lower body and thighs 324/24, 324/27, 324/28

taffata *n* glossy silk material 317/42, 429/23, 429/24; **taffetyes** *pl* 513/16

talough *n* hard animal fat used in candles, soap,

etc 487/16; **talowe** 50/7

tanner *n* one who converts hides into leather
253/36, 330/19; **tanners** *poss* 102/27m; *pl*
102/28, 103/15, etc

taper *n* candle 152/3, 155/1, 157/28, etc;
tapares *pl* 206/33, 210/19; **tapars** 208/42;
tapers 157/32, 166/23, 487/16

target *n* light shield 274/43

tarturne *n* rich fabric, perhaps of silk 29/19

tassell *n* pendant consisting of fringe of threads
hanging from a knob 29/20; **taselles** *pl*
184/41

tawne *adj* colour composed of brown and
yellow or orange 460/7, 460/8

taynter howkes *see* **tenter hock**

temporall *adj* secular 67/34

tenauntes *n pl* holders of land from a lord
53/25

tender *n* offer 498/23

tender *v inf* regard favourably 149/19

tending *vb n* taking care of or causing to work
437/43; **tendyng** 191/21, 194/28, 198/19;
tentyng 194/24, 198/18, 202/40; **tyntyng**
478/13

tendurnes *n* care 29/8

tenement *n* land or property held of another
3/5, 78/23, 82/4, etc; **tenemente** 301/8;
tenementes *pl* 96/17, 132/18, 158/3m, etc;
tenements 280/35

tenour *n* meaning 29/5, 144/9

tenter hock *n phr* metal hook used for hanging
articles 259/11; **taynter howkes** *pl* 277/42,
287/29; **tenter hockes** 210/22; **tenter hocks**
250/17; **tenter hookes** 230/5, 261/14;
tenterhookes 191/1, 202/17, 255/13, etc;
tentorhokys 150/28; **tentr hocks** 256/32,
264/7; **tentur hookes** 224/6; **tentur hovckes**
476/16; **teter hocks** 242/29; **teynter hokes**
466/3; **teynter howkes** 291/2-3;
teynturhokes 52/35

tentyng *see* **tending**

tenure *n* holding, legal possession 301/9

tepettes *see* **tippet**

terran *n* inventory of lands 280/34

tessew *n* a kind of rich cloth, sometimes

interwoven with gold and silver 108/38,
108/42, 492/6; **teyssew** 492/2; **tussu** 22/13;
tyssew 98/26

teter hocks *see* **tenter hock**

tewke *n* canvas 108/39

teylres *see* **tyler**

teynter hokes, teynter howkes, teynturhokes
see **tenter hock**

teyssew *see* **tessew**

thatthng *vb n* covering a house with straw
263/40

theale *n* board or plank 238/29; **thele** 267/11;
theyll 156/38

thridd *n* thread 385/25

thynkyth *v pr 3 sg in phr* vs **thynkyth** it seems
to us 8/14; **thynkyuth** 8/12

tide *see* **tyde**

tileres, tilers, tilleres *see* **tyler**

tiling *vb n* applying tiles 319/3; **tyllyng**
258/39

tipped staffe *n phr* staff with a metal tip 4/5

tippet *n* narrow slip of cloth, attached to the
hood or sleeve, or loose 511/7, 511/8;
typpet 201/11; **typpett** 488/33; **tepettes** *pl*
81/14; **tippets** 201/9m; **tippetts** 446/10,
511/12, 511/22

towe *prep* to 476/21

tochboxes *n pl* containers for gunpowder used
in igniting a fire-arm 324/40; **towch boxes**
314/16-17; **tuchboxes** 325/31

tole-dish *n* bowl of specified size for measuring
toll or amount of grain due to miller 498/6;
toledishe 499/18

tonswoord *n* kind of sword 274/34; **tonsword**
273/29

torg *n* torch (?) 479/22

towch boxes *see* **tochboxes**

trainbearer *n* person carrying the trailing end of
a long gown 511/30

traine *n* company of followers and attendants
365/32, 384/39, 497/17, etc

traine *n* the part of a long gown which trails
behind on the ground 365/2; **trayne** 511/13;
traines *pl* 511/18; **treyne** 36/21, 36/26

translacion *n* death, removal from earth to

heaven (*of saints, etc; used in names of feast days*) 132/13

translating *vb n* transforming or renovating 418/34

traped *pp* adorned with trappings, covered with cloth over the saddle 509/16

trauerses *n pl* barriers 5/7

trayne *see* traine

tre hopps *n phr pl* wooden hoops 20/1

trendell *n* hoop or wheel 253/13; trendyll 258/26

tressylles, tresteles, trestles *see* trostyll

treyne *see* traine

trist *v imper in phr* trist to have confidence in 34/23

troly lo *interjection phr* song refrain expressing joy 274/14

trostyll *n* wooden support consisting of a horizontal beam with pairs of legs at the ends 221/30; tressylles *pl* 193/35; tresteles 245/22; trestles 245/15

troubloous *adj* confused, sorrowful 273/1

trulles *n pl* small wheels 231/10; tr[u] 'e' lles 231/9

trunchions *n pl* staffs 410/20

trupetere *n* trumpet player 479/3; truppetur 476/13

trwse *n* framework of timber or iron 289/20

tuchboxes *see* tochboxes

turbut *n* type of large flat fish 505/16

turkey purse *n phr* purse made in Turkey or of Turkish fabric 404/24

turnebroche *n* man or boy employed to turn a roasting spit 44/5

turnespittes *n pl* people employed to turn roasting spits 506/25

tussu *see* tessew

twelly *adj* made with twilled cloth 98/25

tyde *n* time, season 19/35, 23/10, 34/36, etc; tide 77/20, 138/37, 149/6

tyler *n* one who covers roofs with tiles 247/17, 263/38; teylres *pl* 39/4; tileres 11/40; tilers 11/42m, 35/3, 109/36, etc; tilleres 62/5, 62/11; tylars 66/35, 66/36, 70/20, etc; tyleres 75/21; tylerrus 66/10; tylers 16/33, 23/11, 64/5, etc; tyllars 50/37, 57/8, 57/40, etc; tyllers 38/12, 39/20, 100/32, etc; tyllores 141/23

tyllyng *see* tiling

tynaculles *n pl* church vestments resembling tunics 98/33

tyntyng *see* tending

typpet *see* tippet

tyringe *vb n* equipping 409/30

tyrrys *n pl* curved pieces of iron used for rimming cart wheels 20/7

tyssew *see* tessew

tytle *n* legal right to possession of property 376/34, 376/42, 377/2, etc

usher *n* officer whose duty is to walk before a dignitary in procession 511/1, 511/2, 512/36

usher *see* gentleman ushers, yeoman usher

uttermasse *n* utmost 87/33

vake *adj* empty, vacant 193/24

vakes *n pl* vacancies 158/2m

valure *n* value, worth 119/5

vambraces *n pl* pieces of armour covering the arm 324/24, 324/27, 324/28

vane *n* weather vane or metal flag 219/29

vaunted *v pa 3 pl* boasted 275/29

vauters *n pl* vaulters (?) 384/27 (*see endnote p 595*)

ventener *see* vintiner

vestueres *n pl* apparel, clothing, equipment 240/21; vestures 287/25

vigill *n* eve of a festival or holy day 82/35, 83/5, 83/28, etc

vintiner *n* wine seller 114/11; ventener 492/10; vintner 406/38

virginall *n* keyed musical instrument set in a box without legs 358/28

visor *n* movable front part of a helmet 4/18

vnderwode *n* brushwood growing beneath higher trees 544/5

vndisposed *adj* ill-disposed 544/8

vnheadded *pp* without tips 325/23

vnprouided *pp* not equipped 497/20

vnright *n* unfairness, injustice 32/22

vnye *v inf* unite, join 80/15; vnyed *pp* 80/3

voett *n* vault 570/25

vsed *pp* accustomed 79/38, 132/8, 146/2

vsher *n* assistant to a schoolmaster 360/28, 372/7

vtmast *adj* farthest from the centre 37/23

vysse *n* use (?) 475/30

wache *n* revel held on the eve of a festival 88/2, 106/16, 188/26, etc; wach 471/9; watch 152/28m, 192/30, 426/9, etc; watche 16/28, 27/12, 152/30, etc; watches *pl* 132/29, 133/5, 152/29; watchis 174/7

waddes *n pl* worlds (?); wads for some purpose (?) 479/32

waightes, waitees, waites, waits *see* wayt

waite-players *n pl* musicians employed by the civic government 379/1, 437/13; waite playars 428/35; waite players 379/5, 427/30-1, 429/13; waitplayers 434/18; wayte-players 379/2m, 414/15, 435/43; wayte players 412/5, 412/8, 412/18, etc; wayt players 423/33; waytplayers 422/40; weight-players 414/17; weightplayers 414/20; *see also* wayt

wales *n pl* walls 319/12

walkeres *n pl* workers whose occupation is to clean and thicken cloth by beating 206/18, 211/28, 213/22, etc; walkers 17/2, 129/5, 129/7, etc; waukeres 215/33

ward *n* administrative division of a city 8/15, 8/16 (2), etc; warde 8/22; wards *pl* 421/21; wardys 8/20

warde *n* custody 498/23

warde *n* world 479/26

warden *n* one of two officers appointed annually for the collection of rents 18/7, 18/8, 18/16, etc; wardens *pl* 29/33, 34/26, 44/22, etc

wardens *n pl* officials appointed for security on midsummer and St Peter's nights 8/17, 8/22

wardens *n pl* type of baking pear 506/1

warder *n* baton or staff used to signal the commencement or cessation of battle or a tournament 5/15

ware *see* grocerie ware

warning *vb n* notifying (someone or of something) 389/33; warninge 305/34, 366/14; warnyng 470/24; warned *pp* 389/31

warrant *n* document conveying legal authority or permission 351/5, 395/2, 396/24, etc

warrante *v inf* guarantee the security of 377/8

wast *n* consumption (of candles, torches, etc) 206/33, 208/42; waste 210/19

watch *n* keeping guard and order in the streets at night 389/31, 389/40

watch *v inf* keep guard 389/33, 389/35

watch, watche, watches, watchis *see* wache

watched *pp* attended with a vigil for devotional purposes 508/17

wates, wattes *see* wayt

watyng of *prp phr* attending on 86/19

waukeres *see* walkeres

wax silver *n phr* money paid toward the purchase of wax for candles 64/23; wax sylver 452/42

waxt *v pa 3 sg* became gradually 274/39

wayt *n* musician employed by the civic government 64/16, 64/17, 64/18, etc; weit 225/24, 225/25, 225/30, etc; weyt 158/3; weytt 151/33, 298/28; waightes *pl* 400/24, 428/28, 432/33; waitees 312/5, 446/20; waites 138/11, 243/26, 269/24, etc; waits 393/12m, 431/15, 434/21, etc; wates 38/41; wattes 62/16; waytes 38/40, 45/11, 48/19, etc; waytez 28/15; wayts 60/24, 64/15, 74/10, etc; waytts 172/35, 483/22; weightes 269/29, 414/29, 417/4, etc; weites 155/9, 193/19, 213/5, etc; weytes 45/19, 85/16, 158/11, etc; weyts 64/19; weyttes 173/7, 197/17, 208/18, etc; weytts 76/23; whaytes 12/8; weites *poss* 210/42; *see also* waite-players

wayte-players, wayte players, wayt players, waytplayers *see* waite-players

weale *n* veal 504/3

weene *v pr 1 sg* believe, think 274/19

weightes, weit, weites *see* wayt

weighting *vb n* waiting 409/24

weight-players *see* waite-players

weket *n* small opening or grill 48/3

weemen *n pl* women 275/12

wele *n* welfare 30/31

welke *n* welkin, firmament, vault of heaven (?) 224/24

welyard *n* yard in which a well is located 36/14

wenkyll *n* periwinkle; perhaps the colour (?) 153/23

wesontyde *see* whitsontide

weyt, weytes, weyts, weytt, weyttes, weytts, whaytes *see* wayt

whelewright *n* maker of wheels 83/24, 83/25; whyllwryght 156/40

whinny *n* whin or furze bush, or group of such bushes (?) 274/14

whipcord *n* type of thin, tough cord, usually used for whiplashes 274/17

whissone tyde *see* whitsontide

whitleder *n* whitleather; soft, pliant leather of a white colour 25/4

whitsonday *n* seventh Sunday after Easter 36/11, 151/39, 332/28; whitsunday 36/21m; whytsonday 485/5

whitsontide *n* seventh Sunday after Easter and the days immediately following 77/19, 138/39; wesontyde 75/14; whissone tyde 129/14; whitsontyde 142/31

whitsun weeke *n phr* week beginning seventh Sunday after Easter 114/30; whyssonwoke 40/40; whytson wycck 309/7; whyttsonweke 72/31; wytson weke 62/26; wytsone weke 77/37; wytsonweke 25/41; wytson-weke 27/35

whittawerescraft *n* guild of those who make whitleather 6/11; *see also* whitleder

whittawers *n pl* makers of whitleather 16/32, 82/24m, 82/25, etc; whyttawers 177/29; whyttawyers 230/12, 307/13; *see also* whitleder

whod *n* hood 167/35

whon *adv* home 259/2; whovme 476/10

whourlles *n pl* small wheels or pulleys 476/35

whyllwryght *see* whelewright

whylom *adv* once upon a time 273/1

whyssonwoke, whytson wycck, whyttsonweke

see whitsun weeke

whytsonday *see* whitsonday

whyttawers, whyttawyers *see* whittawers

will *v inf* desire 394/38; will *pr 1 pl* 22/35; willed *pa 1 sg* 500/22; willed *pa 3 sg* 36/36

wimple *n* woman's garment worn around the head, chin, sides of the face and neck 511/8

wind *see* wynd

wirdrawer *n* one who draws metal out into wire 12/14; wirdrawers *pl* 16/39

wod cakes *n phr pl* woodcocks 503/14

wold *adj* old 122/27; wolde 468/20

wolsted *n* worsted, type of woollen fabric in which the fibres are combed to make them parallel 119/4; worsted 488/42

wordys *n pl* worlds 474/32

worme *n* screw on the end of a rod, used for withdrawing the charge from a muzzle-loading gun 443/39

worship *n* honour or good name 33/3, 33/32, 33/38, etc; worschip 8/2; worschypp 460/22; worshcippe 484/30; worshipp 145/30; worshippe 149/24; worsshipe 87/42

worsted *see* wolsted

wrethes *n pl* metal rings 162/39

wreyth *n* wreath (?) 115/39

wryght *n* woodworker, carpenter 153/15, 157/4, 161/35, etc; wright 83/23 (2); wrightes *pl* 83/16, 83/18; wryghtes 16/33, 83/14, 167/38, etc; wryghts *poss* 485/4

wurche *v imper pl* work 8/26

wurschipfull *adj* honourable 7/40

wyend *see* wynd

wyff shevys *n phr pl* white sleeves (?), wife's sleeves (?); *(see endnote p 555)* 60/12

wyke *n* wick 94/4

wynd *n* windlass 469/27, 475/13, 476/31, etc; wind 249/17; wyend 150/35; wynde 185/30, 466/15, 468/13, etc; wyndes 478/6; *see also* wynles

wyndor *n* wind-door, ie window 241/29, 295/21

wynles *n* windlass 240/36; *see also* wynd

wysseler *n* piper (*or* money-changer?) 477/25
wyssthold *n* piper (?) 480/1
wystyllyng *vb n* piping 20/6
wyteyle *n* victuals, food 77/36
wytson weke, wytsone weke, wytsonweke,
    wytson-weke *see* whitsun weeke

yaff *v pa 3 sg* gave 37/32; yeven *pp* 138/41,
    271/1; yevyn 453/37; yevyng *prp* 53/11
yare *n* yard 246/29
yate *n* gate 21/30, 30/1, 30/12, etc; yates *pl*
    125/21
yeildes *n pl* payments 296/22m
yeld *n* guild, religious association 97/30,
    97/32, 109/2, etc; yelde 80/42, 81/2
yeoman of the mouth *n phr pl* attendants
    responsible for providing the king's food
    405/13
yeoman porters *n phr pl* attendants whose

function is to transport articles 404/40
yeoman usher *n phr* doorkeeper 404/36,
    404/39
yeomen *n pl* high ranking servants of the house-
    hold of a noble 510/7, 510/19, 510/33, etc
yeomen harbingers *n phr pl* attendants sent
    ahead to arrange lodgings 404/34
yernewerk *n* ironwork 45/43
yeven *n* eve, day before 37/3
yeven, yevyn, yevyng *see* yaff
yhit *conj* yet 33/40
yoman *n* small landowner, ranking below a
    gentleman 329/5
yomen *n pl* assistants to an official 201/15
yomen *n pl* bodyguards of the king 22/20
yorthe *n* earth 478/13
yue, yve *see* ive

ȝorne *n* yarn, spun fibre 163/12

Index

The Index combines subject headings with places and names for ease of reference. Where the same word occurs in two or more categories, the order of headings is people, places, subjects, and book or play titles (eg, Norwich, Edward of precedes Norwich, Norf).

Place names, titles, and given names appear in their modern form where this is ascertainable; surnames are normally cited in the most common form used in the text and are capitalized ('ff' is therefore rendered 'F' in the headword; 'I' is sometimes converted to 'J' in accordance with modern usage). The headword spelling of Coventry mayors' names conforms to the list in the official municipal handbook. Both places and surnames are followed by their variant spellings in parentheses. Names of saints are indexed under 'St' and the precise dates of their feast days added in parentheses where appropriate from C.R. Cheney (ed), *Handbook of Dates for Students of English History*, rev ed (London, 1970). The following major sources for identification of peers and ecclesiastical officials were used: *The Dictionary of National Biography;* G[eorge] E[dward] C[okayne], *The Complete Peerage of England ...*; F. Maurice Powicke, and E.B. Fryde (eds), *The Handbook of British Chronology*. Where a family name is known for these dignitaries, it has been chosen as the main headword, with a cross reference from the official's title (eg, Hunsdon, lord *see* Carey).

The format for names and titles has been largely taken from R.F. Hunnisett, *Indexing for Editors* (Leicester, 1972). Thus family relationships, where known, have been used rather than succession numbers to distinguish members of noble families. Where no given name is known, the occupation has been supplied or, that lacking, ellipsis marks. A question mark following a name signifies insufficient information. A reasonable attempt has been made to distinguish different individuals with identical names, but no absolute claim is made for the identity of a single person across a range of pages. Mayors are identified as such and their dates of mayoralty supplied in parentheses according to the municipal handbook; when two dates for a mayor are given and the interval between them is large, a question mark immediately follows the date less likely for the man in question. The number of occurrences of a place or name on a page in the records text is given in parentheses after the page number (eg, Goldston, Mr 323 (2)).

Modern subject headings are provided with some complex groupings, such as costumes (individual) and instruments, musical, to aid research. Individual pageants in the Coventry cycle are listed under Corpus Christi play by name of the guild or guilds responsible for their production. The title of *The Destruction of Jerusalem*, the play performed in 1584, has generally been abbreviated as *Destruction*. Where names of monarchs fall within subject headings, they are given in chronological order; peers are listed according to their rank in the kingdom (eg, under minstrels (travelling), lord chamberlain precedes earl of Essex).

RECORDS OF EARLY ENGLISH DRAMA

York edited by Alexandra F. Johnston and Margaret Rogerson. 2 volumes. 1979.

Chester edited by Lawrence M. Clopper. 1979.

Coventry edited by R.W. Ingram. 1981.

Newcastle-upon-Tyne edited by J.J. Anderson. 1982.